About the Cover Images

Craftsmen at Work, Egyptian Funerary Chapel, Fresco, ca. 1350 B.C.E. This lively composition of skilled artisans at work was created for the funerary chapel of a prominent man, Nebamun, who lived in Egypt during the fourteenth century B.C.E. Nebamun was a craftsman, so his tomb's decoration highlighted the activities, such as writing on pottery or carving a sphinx, that he likely oversaw as part of his professional life. The painting also expressed his hopes for continuing that life in the hereafter. The chapel located above his tomb provided a place where family and friends could visit to remember him. Other funerary chapels often showed the deceased with their families or participating in local festivals. Tomb of Nebamun and Ipuky, ca.1390–49 B.C.E. (fresco), Egyptian 18th Dynasty (ca. 1567–1320 B.C.E.). Facsimile by Norman de Garis Davies (1865–1941)/Metropolitan Museum of Art, New York, USA/Photo © Zev Radovan/Bridgeman Images

Detail, Porcelain Plate with Blue and White Decoration, China, 14th century Chinese porcelain like that depicted here had long been sought after by consumers across the Afro-Eurasian world. The trade in Chinese porcelain prospered during the Ming Dynasty (1368–1644), and its popularity was reflected in the efforts of craftsmen in other regions to copy the intricate decorative patterns, delicate designs, and distinctive blue and white color scheme. Charger with blue and white decoration, 1325–1355 (porcelain)/Chinese School (14th century)/ THE WILSON (CHELTENHAM ART GALLERY AND MUSEUM)/ The Cheltenham Trust and Cheltenham Borough Council/ Bridgeman Images

D0141478

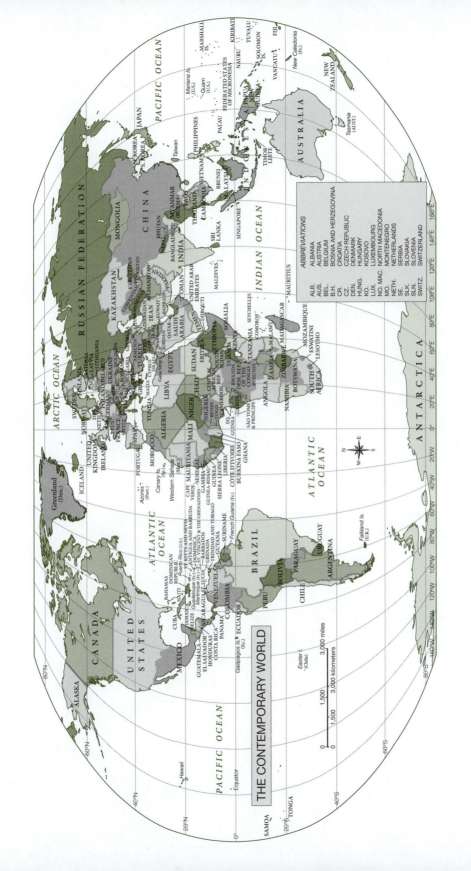

THE CONTEMPORARY WORLD

ALASKA
CANADA
UNITED STATES
MEXICO
GUATEMALA
BELIZE
EL SALVADOR
HONDURAS
NICARAGUA
COSTA RICA
PANAMA
CUBA
BAHAMAS
HAITI
JAMAICA
DOMINICAN REPUBLIC
Puerto Rico (U.S.)
ST. KITTS AND NEVIS
ANTIGUA AND BARBUDA
Guadeloupe (Fr.)
DOMINICA
Martinique (Fr.)
ST. LUCIA
ST. VINCENT & THE GRENADINES
BARBADOS
GRENADA
TRINIDAD AND TOBAGO
COLOMBIA
ECUADOR
Galápagos Is. (Ec.)
PERU
VENEZUELA
GUYANA
SURINAME
French Guiana (Fr.)
BRAZIL
BOLIVIA
PARAGUAY
CHILE
ARGENTINA
URUGUAY
Falkland Is. (U.K.)
Easter I. (Chile)

Greenland (Den.)
ICELAND
UNITED KINGDOM
IRELAND
Azores (Port.)
Canary Is. (Sp.)
Western Sahara (Mor.)
CAPE VERDE
MAURITANIA
MALI
SENEGAL
THE GAMBIA
GUINEA-BISSAU
GUINEA
SIERRA LEONE
LIBERIA
CÔTE D'IVOIRE
BURKINA FASO
GHANA
TOGO
BENIN
NIGERIA
EQ. GUINEA
SÃO TOMÉ & PRÍNCIPE
GABON
CONGO
DEM. REP. OF THE CONGO
ANGOLA
NAMIBIA
BOTSWANA
SOUTH AFRICA
LESOTHO
ESWATINI
MOZAMBIQUE
MADAGASCAR
ZIMBABWE
ZAMBIA
MALAWI
TANZANIA
COMOROS
SEYCHELLES
MAURITIUS
MOROCCO
ALGERIA
TUNISIA
LIBYA
NIGER
CHAD
CENTRAL AFRICAN REP.
CAMEROON
SUDAN
SOUTH SUDAN
ETHIOPIA
ERITREA
DJIBOUTI
SOMALIA
KENYA
UGANDA
RWANDA
BURUNDI
EGYPT

PORTUGAL
SPAIN
FRANCE
NORWAY
SWEDEN
FINLAND
DENMARK
NETH.
BEL.
LUX.
GERMANY
SWITZ.
ITALY
MALTA
AUS.
CZ.
SLK.
SLN.
CR.
B.H.
SE.
KO.
ALB.
NO. MAC.
GREECE
HUNG.
POLAND
ESTONIA
LATVIA
LITHUANIA
BELARUS
UKRAINE
MOLDOVA
ROMANIA
BULGARIA
TURKEY
CYPRUS
GEORGIA
ARMENIA
AZERBAIJAN
SYRIA
LEBANON
ISRAEL
Gaza Strip
JORDAN
IRAQ
IRAN
KUWAIT
BAHRAIN
QATAR
SAUDI ARABIA
UNITED ARAB EMIRATES
OMAN
YEMEN

RUSSIAN FEDERATION
KAZAKHSTAN
UZBEKISTAN
TURKMENISTAN
TAJIKISTAN
KYRGYZSTAN
AFGHANISTAN
PAKISTAN
MONGOLIA
CHINA
NEPAL
BHUTAN
BANGLADESH
INDIA
MYANMAR (BURMA)
LAOS
THAILAND
CAMBODIA
VIETNAM
MALDIVES
SRI LANKA
SINGAPORE
BRUNEI
MALAYSIA
PHILIPPINES
JAPAN
KOREA
S. KOREA
D.P.R. KOREA
Taiwan
PALAU
INDONESIA
TIMOR-LESTE
PAPUA NEW GUINEA
FEDERATED STATES OF MICRONESIA
Guam (U.S.)
Mariana Is. (U.S.)
MARSHALL IS.
NAURU
KIRIBATI
TUVALU
FIJI
SOLOMON IS.
VANUATU
New Caledonia (Fr.)
AUSTRALIA
Tasmania (AUST.)
NEW ZEALAND
TONGA
SAMOA
Hawaii

ARCTIC OCEAN
PACIFIC OCEAN
ATLANTIC OCEAN
INDIAN OCEAN
ANTARCTICA

Equator

ABBREVIATIONS
ALB.   ALBANIA
AUS.   AUSTRIA
BEL.   BELGIUM
B.H.   BOSNIA AND HERZEGOVINA
CR.   CROATIA
CZ.   CZECH REPUBLIC
DEN.   DENMARK
HUNG.   HUNGARY
KO.   KOSOVO
LUX.   LUXEMBOURG
NO. MAC. NORTH MACEDONIA
MO.   MONTENEGRO
NETH.   NETHERLANDS
SE.   SERBIA
SLK.   SLOVAKIA
SLN.   SLOVENIA
SWITZ. SWITZERLAND

0   1,500   3,000 miles
0   1,500   3,000 kilometers

80°N 60°N 40°N 20°N 0° 20°S 40°S 60°S

160°W 140°W 120°W 100°W 80°W 60°W 40°W 20°W 0° 20°E 40°E 60°E 80°E 100°E 120°E 140°E 160°E

N E W S

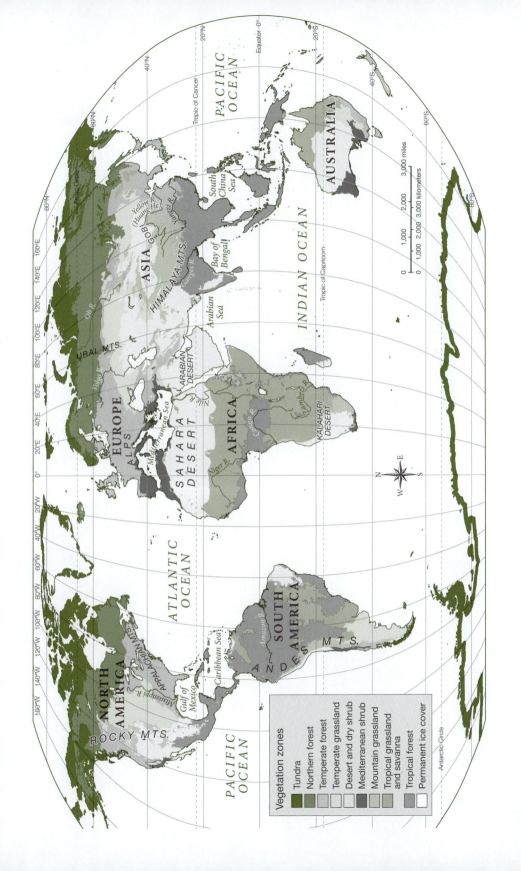

Ways of the World

VALUE EDITION

VALUE EDITION

Ways of the World
A Brief Global History

Fifth Edition

Volume 1: Through the Fifteenth Century

Robert W. Strayer
The College at Brockport:
State University of New York

Eric W. Nelson
Missouri State University

bedford/st.martin's
Macmillan Learning

Boston | New York

For Evelyn Rhiannon with love

Vice President: Leasa Burton
Senior Program Director: Erika Gutierrez
Senior Executive Program Manager: William J. Lombardo
Director of Content Development: Jane Knetzger
Senior Development Editor: Heidi Hood
Associate Development Editor: Stephanie Sosa
Assistant Editor: Carly Lewis
Director of Media Editorial: Adam Whitehurst
Media Editor: Mollie Chandler
Senior Marketing Manager: Melissa Rodriguez
Senior Director, Content Management Enhancement: Tracey Kuehn
Senior Managing Editor: Michael Granger
Executive Content Project Manager: Christina M. Horn
Senior Workflow Project Manager: Lisa McDowell
Production Supervisor: Robin Besofsky / Lawrence Guerra
Director of Design, Content Management: Diana Blume
Interior Design: Lumina Datamatics, Inc.
Cover Design: William Boardman
Cartographer: Mapping Specialists, Ltd.
Text Permissions Editor: Michael McCarty
Text Permissions Researcher: Elaine Kosta, Lumina Datamatics, Inc.
Executive Permissions Editor: Cecilia Varas
Photo Researchers: Bruce Carson / Cheryl Du Bois, Lumina Datamatics, Inc.
Director of Digital Production: Keri deManigold
Executive Media Project Manager: Michelle Camisa
Copyeditor: Susan Zorn
Indexer: Rebecca McCorkle
Composition: Lumina Datamatics, Inc.
Printing and Binding: LSC Communications

Copyright © 2022, 2019, 2016, 2013 by Bedford/St. Martin's. All rights reserved. No part of this book may be reproduced, stored in a retrieval system, or transmitted in any form or by any means, electronic, mechanical, photocopying, recording, or otherwise, except as may be permitted by law or expressly permitted in writing by the Publisher.

Library of Congress Control Number: 2021909456

ISBN 978-1-319-24445-3 (Combined Edition)
ISBN 978-1-319-34063-6 (Volume 1)
ISBN 978-1-319-34065-0 (Loose-leaf Edition, Volume 1)
ISBN 978-1-319-34070-4 (Volume 2)
ISBN 978-1-319-34071-1 (Loose-Leaf Edition, Volume 2)

Printed in the United States of America.
1 2 3 4 5 6   26 25 24 23 22 21

ACKNOWLEDGMENTS

Text acknowledgments and copyrights appear at the back of the book on page 374, which constitutes an extension of the copyright page. Art acknowledgments and copyrights appear on the same page as the art selections they cover.

For information, write: Bedford/St. Martin's, 75 Arlington Street, Boston, MA 02116

Preface

The Value Edition of *Ways of the World* is an intentionally brief global history of the human experience that focuses on the **big pictures of world history**, using examples selectively rather than cluttering the narrative with endless details. It repeatedly highlights major transformations in global history, makes frequent comparisons, and spotlights interactions among culturally different peoples. These elements appear in the narrative text and now for the first time in **Achieve**, Macmillan Learning's innovative new learning platform. Built with instructors and students in mind, **Achieve for *Ways of the World*** comes loaded with the full-color e-book of the comprehensive version (*Ways of the World: A Brief Global History with Sources*), with its innovative thematic sets of primary and secondary source and other special features, plus **LearningCurve**, an adaptive quizzing tool that spurs students to read the text before class. It also contains the popular companion source reader *Thinking through Sources for Ways of the World*, along with a wealth of **assessment options**, including an autograded **exercise for building and supporting a thesis statement**, **chapter summative quizzes**, robust **reporting and insight tools**, and more. All of this is built around a book that has been revised to further promote **historical thinking skills**, such as chronological reasoning, empathy, analysis and interpretation, and awareness of historical controversies.

A Distinctive Approach to World History

The main title of the book, *Ways of the World*, evokes three dimensions of its distinctive approach, all of them based on our experience as teachers and scholars. The first is **diversity** or **variation**, for the "ways of the world," or the ways of being human in the world, have been many and constantly changing. This book seeks to embrace the global experience of humankind, both in its common features and in its vast diversity, while noticing the changing location of particular centers of innovation and wider influence.

Second, the title *Ways of the World* invokes major **panoramas**, **patterns**, or **pathways** in world history rather than a highly detailed narrative, which can often overwhelm students. Thus most chapters are organized in terms of broad global or transregional themes, illustrated by a limited number of specific examples.

A third implication of the book's title lies in a certain **reflective quality** that appears in the Big Picture essays that introduce each part, in the Conclusions and Reflections section at the end of each chapter, and periodically in the narrative itself. This dimension of the book offers many opportunities for pondering larger questions about how historians operate, about the dilemmas they face in reconstructing the human journey, and about the relationship of the past to the present.

These elements of *Ways of the World* find expression repeatedly in what we call the **four Cs** of world history: context, change, comparison, and connection. The first "C," **context**, refers to the larger frameworks within which particular historical figures, events, societies, and civilizations take shape. In our telling of the human past, context is central, for in world history nothing stands alone. Like Russian nesting dolls, every story finds a place in some more inclusive narrative. European empires in the Americas, for example, take on new meaning when they are understood as part of a global process of imperial expansion that also included the growth of the Inca, Russian, Chinese, and Ottoman empires.

The second "C," large-scale **change**, both within and especially across major regions of the world, represents another prominent emphasis in *Ways of the World*. Examples include the peopling of the planet, the emergence of "civilization," the linking of Eastern and Western hemispheres in the wake of Columbus's voyages, the Industrial Revolution, and many other significant changes during the course of human history. The flip side of change, of course, is continuity, implying a focus on what persists over long periods of time. And so *Ways of the World* seeks to juxtapose these contrasting elements of human experience. While civilizations have changed dramatically over time, some of their essential features — cities, states, patriarchy, and class inequality, for example — have long endured.

A third "C" involves frequent **comparison**, bringing several regions or cultures into our field of vision at the same time. It means constantly asking "what's the difference?" Thus this book makes comparisons between the Agricultural Revolution in the Eastern and Western hemispheres; between the beginnings of Buddhism and the early history of Christianity and Islam; between the Russian and Chinese revolutions; and between feminism in the Global North and the Global South. These and many more comparisons frequently punctuate our account of the global past.

The final "C" emphasizes **connections**, networks of communication and exchange that increasingly shaped the character of the societies that participated in them. In our account of the human story, world history is less about what happened within particular civilizations or cultures than about the processes and outcomes of their meetings with one another. Cross-cultural encounters then become one of the major motors of historical transformation. Examples include the clash of the ancient Greeks and the Persians, the long-distance commercial networks that linked the Afro-Eurasian world, the numerous cross-cultural interactions spawned by the spread of Islam, the trans-hemispheric Columbian exchange of the early modern era, and the more recent growth of a thoroughly entangled global economy.

How Has the Content Changed in the Fifth Edition?

History books are always works in progress rather than finished products. The changes in this fifth edition of *Ways of the World* have been driven by two major goals. Our primary goal has been to strengthen the book's support for developing historical thinking skills, because those skills — such as chronological reasoning, empathy, analysis and interpretation, and identification of historical issues and problems — will last long after particular pieces of information have been forgotten. But since high-quality content is central to all historical study and to the development of historical thinking skills, we have also updated the book with new **scholarship** and new **points of view**.

In terms of both content and skill development, this edition — particularly when amplified through Achieve's targeted assignments and resources — addresses our students' ability to make connections between the past and their own lives in the present even as they develop analytical skills and historical empathy. Thus a new feature found in Achieve for *Ways of the World* (and in the comprehensive print text) called **Then and Now** examines a particular theme, one for each part of the book, in both historical and contemporary settings. Themes include patriarchy, slavery, science, China's role on the global stage, and more. The skill of connecting with the past is also reinforced at the beginning of each chapter through updated vignettes called **Connecting Past and Present** that illustrate the continuing relevance of the chapter's material in our world today.

For further skill development, the Working with Evidence primary source features and Historians' Voices secondary sources features available in Achieve provide rich material to engage students and hone their historical comprehension, empathy, analysis, interpretation, and research skills. These thematic collections include fruitful topics such as "Society during China's Golden Age" (Chapter 8), "Cultural Encounters in Muslim Spain" (Chapter 9), "Consumption and Culture in the Early Modern World" (Chapter 14), and "The Socialist Vision and Its Enemies" (Chapter 17). The two brief secondary sources found in the Historians' Voices features in Achieve address topics related to the primary sources in each chapter's Working with Evidence feature. These features illustrate diverse scholarly views on China's economy (Chapter 8), on religious tolerance in Muslim Spain (Chapter 9), on consumer culture in the early modern world (Chapter 14), and on the legacy of Karl Marx (Chapter 17).

Further content changes in the book have derived from new scholarship in the rapidly expanding field of world history. The **earliest history of our species** has been thoroughly updated to take into account important recent research such as new dating for the first emergence of *Homo sapiens*, new evidence of early failed migrations out of Africa and interactions with other hominid species, new thinking on migration into the Americas, and new discoveries of cave paintings in Indonesia and bone flutes in Germany. Examination of Paleolithic and Neolithic societies now includes new scholarship on the practice of slavery among gatherers and hunters in Alaska, new evidence of the fragility of many early agricultural communities, and updated population estimates for the Neolithic period. Coverage of First Civilizations has also been updated to incorporate new archeological evidence of early trade patterns and recent revisions in the dating of the Indus Valley, Chinese, Oxus, and Nubian civilizations. The revised Part 2 opening now explores the reasons that First Civilizations collapsed, with special emphasis on climate change, environmental degradation, and migrations.

We have also systematically revised our coverage of **modern science** for the fifth edition. Thus the section on the **Scientific Revolution** in Chapter 15 has been heavily reworked to incorporate recent scholarship on earlier Chinese and Islamic influences on European science and to discuss how the vast and unprecedented flow of knowledge from across the globe into Europe impacted the Scientific Revolution during the early modern period. This revision is complemented by a new Chapter 15 Then and Now feature in Achieve entitled "Science" that explores the relationship between the advances of the initial Scientific Revolution and science today. A new section entitled **"A Second Scientific Revolution"** in Chapter 22 examines how scientific breakthroughs in the twentieth century profoundly changed our understanding of the cosmos with important cultural implications and laid the groundwork for technological innovations that have transformed modern life.

Coverage of the environment and disease has provided a third focus of revision. In Chapter 11, we expand our analysis of the **long-term impact of the plague** on European society, especially the shift toward laborsaving technologies and the revival of slavery in Europe. In Chapter 13, we update our account of the **Little Ice Age** to reflect recent research, and in Chapter 17 we explore the links between the **Industrial**

Revolution and our current climate crisis. Finally, we have revised the section "Microbes in Motion" in Chapter 23 to discuss the **COVID-19 pandemic** in the context of other modern pandemics, and we incorporate a new Then and Now feature on the relationship between humankind and the natural environment today and in the past.

A further focus of revision has involved reworking and expanding our coverage of the **Indian Ocean world** in Chapters 7 and 9 to more fully discuss the spread of Islam in that region. In Chapter 7, we discuss the arrival of Islam in Southeast Asia, with expanded coverage of Melaka, among the first globalized cities in world history. In Chapter 9, we focus on Islam's establishment in southern India, especially in the Hindu Vijayanagar empire, adding another dimension to the theme of Muslim cultural encounter in India. In addition to these major revisions, we have fully updated Part 6 to take into account recent developments in the early twenty-first century.

These changes remind us that textbooks are not fixed and finished compilations of what happened in the past. Rather, such books develop as they respond to new technologies, to new historical research, and to the evolving political, social, and economic conditions of the contemporary world. As authors, we are acutely aware of how much debate and controversy lie behind many of the issues that are explored in *Ways of the World*. This book, then, is a snapshot of our current understanding of world history, shaped by the particular time (the early twenty-first century) and place (the United States) in which it was composed. Such a book written fifty years ago, or in contemporary China, Nigeria, Iran, or Brazil, or in the mid-twenty-first century, would surely be very different. Thus *Ways of the World* can and should be criticized, assessed, and argued with, not simply accepted as a definitive account of the global past.

Enhancements for Nurturing Skill Development

Obviously, the study of history requires some assimilation of information, data, or "facts." But instructors also want to enable their students to manipulate the information in their textbooks, using its ideas and data to answer questions, to make comparisons, to draw conclusions, to criticize assumptions, and to infer implications that are not explicitly disclosed in the text itself. This kind of skill development occurs most effectively as students directly and actively engage with the material in the text.

Ways of the World is designed to promote skill development in various ways. Most obviously, the source-based features found in Achieve (Working with Evidence and Historians' Voices) and those in the companion reader (*Thinking through Sources for Ways of the World*, also available in Achieve) invite students to engage actively with documents and images alike, assisted by abundant questions to guide that engagement. Updated **Connecting Past and Present chapter-opening vignettes** and **Then and Now** features in Achieve encourage students to examine the links between the past and present. **Zooming In** essays in Achieve, which call attention to particular people, places, and events, offer opportunities to develop the skill of contextualization, situating particulars in a larger framework. Appearing once in each chapter, Zooming In addresses topics such as Göbekli Tepe and monumental construction before agriculture (specially updated for this edition), Trung Trac and female-led resistance to the Chinese empire, gunpowder, the end of the Byzantine Empire, feminism and nationalism in Java, the Cuban Revolution, and many more.

The **Controversies** feature in Achieve, which appears in one chapter of each part, develops skills in identifying and analyzing historical issues through the exploration of important debates: the origins of major religious traditions, the idea of the Atlantic world, why the Industrial Revolution began in Europe, the concept of globalization, and more. These features counteract the notion of a textbook as an authoritative, encyclopedia-like tome to be assimilated, while conveying an understanding of world history as a frequently contested conversation.

Skills-based active learning also means approaching the text through questions to explore, rather than simply dutifully completing the reading. *Ways of the World* provides such questions in abundance, offering students something to look for as they read. New to this edition, each part-opening Big Picture essay includes **First Reflections** questions that set the stage for actively reading the part ahead but also can help students reflect on the part as a whole after they have read it. A **Seeking the Main Point** question at the start of each chapter helps students focus on the chapter's central theme. In Achieve, **Mapping History** exercises invite students to read maps carefully and to interpret their implications. **Skills-based questions** accompany the narrative text in Achieve, and the most important of these questions, labeled "Core Ideas," are repeated in the **"Revisiting Core Ideas"** section in the chapter review to ensure that students absorb the chapter's most important takeaways. **A Wider View** questions at the end of each chapter deal with matters not directly addressed in the text. Instead, they provide opportunities for integration, comparison, analysis, and sometimes speculation.

Skill development is also encouraged by providing frequent contextual markers. Student readers need to know where they are going and where they have been. Thus part-opening **Big Picture essays** preview what follows in the subsequent chapters, while a **chapter outline** suggests what is coming in each chapter. A **Landmarks** visual timeline, providing a chronological overview of major events and processes, appears at the beginning of each part and each chapter in Achieve. **Snapshot boxes** present succinct glimpses of particular themes, regions, or time periods, adding some trees to the forest of world history. A **list of key terms** at the end of each chapter invites students to check their grasp of the material. And in Achieve, students will enjoy a **full-color illustration and map program** with additional images from the comprehensive version that enhance the narrative.

In addition, whenever an instructor assigns the **Achieve e-book** (with the option of bundling in the print book for a small additional fee), students not only have at their disposal all the resources of the print text, including the special features and primary and secondary sources of the comprehensive edition, but they also gain access to **LearningCurve**, an online adaptive learning tool that helps students actively rehearse what they have read and achieve a deeper understanding and retention of the material. With this adaptive quizzing, students accumulate points toward a target score as they go, giving the interaction a game-like feel. Feedback for incorrect responses explains why the answer is incorrect and directs students back to the text to review before they attempt to answer the question again. The end result is a better understanding of the key elements of the text. Instructors who assign LearningCurve report that their students come to class prepared for discussion and enjoy using it. In addition, LearningCurve's reporting feature allows instructors to quickly diagnose which concepts students are struggling with so they can adjust lectures and activities accordingly.

Further opportunities for skill development are available through the special activities provided in Achieve, many of which are available for the first time with the fifth edition of *Ways of the World*. These easy-to-use assignments include new **journaling reflection activities** that invite students to reflect on what they have read in each chapter, **instructor activity guides** that instructors can use for either remote or in-person collaborative learning, **source and feature quizzes**, **research and writing tutorials**, and more. Most notably, Achieve offers six new **Building a Historical Argument** activities. Provided once per part, these autograded activities enable students to hone their skills in constructing a thesis and identifying evidence to sustain historical arguments. By offering students the opportunity to compose a conclusion to the argument they have constructed, these activities also support the development of writing skills. When required by instructors, the wrap-around pedagogy provided in Achieve virtually ensures active learning. Achieve is a rich asset for instructors who want to support students however they encounter them, whether teaching in a face-to-face, hybrid, or fully remote setting. Thus *Ways of the World* combines an engaging narrative with a rich set of digital and print features that promote the comprehension of content, active learning, and skill development. It seems to us an impressive package. (To learn more about the benefits of LearningCurve, Achieve, and the different versions to package with these digital tools, see the Versions and Supplements section on page xix.)

"It Takes a Village"

In any enterprise of significance, "it takes a village," as they say. Bringing *Ways of the World* to life in this new edition, it seems, has occupied the energies of several villages. Among the privileges and delights of writing and revising this book has been the opportunity to interact with our fellow villagers.

We are grateful to the community of fellow historians who contributed their expertise to this revision. We especially thank our colleagues Bryan Brinkman, Tonia E. Tinsley, and John F. Chuchiak IV for their translations for our primary source features. We also thank the following reviewers of this edition: Dorian Borbonus, University of Dayton; Matthew Conn, Eastern Michigan University; Adrianna L. Ernstberger, Marian University; Andrei Gandila, University of Alabama at Huntsville; MayaLisa Holzman, Oregon State University; Toby Huff, Harvard University; Jeremy LaBuff, Northern Arizona University; Susan Maneck, Jackson State University; Dean Pavlakis, Carroll College; Charles V. Reed, Elizabeth City State University; Kimberly B. Sherman, Cape Fear Community College; Ira Spar, Ramapo College of New Jersey; Bianka Rhodes Stumpf, Central Carolina Community College; Jeanne M. Vloyanetes, Brookdale Community College; Erin Warford, Hilbert College; and Tara S. Wood, Ball State University.

We also offer our gratitude to reviewers of earlier editions: Andreas Agocs, University of the Pacific; Tonio Andrade, Emory University; Maria S. Arbelaez, University of Nebraska–Omaha; Monty Armstrong, Cerritos High School; Melanie Bailey, Piedmont Virginia Community College; Djene Bajalan, Missouri State University; Veronica L. Bale, Mira Costa College; Anthony Barbieri-Low, University of California, Santa Barbara; Christopher Bellitto, Kean University; Christine Bond, Edmond Memorial High School; Monica Bord-Lamberty, Northwood High School; Mike Burns, Concordia International School, Hanoi; Stanley Burstein, California State University–Los Angeles;

Elizabeth Campbell, Daemen College; Theodore Cohen, Lindenwood University; Ralph Croizier, University of Victoria; Gregory Cushman, the University of Kansas; Edward Dandrow, University of Central Florida; Bradley Davis, Eastern Connecticut State University; Peter L. de Rosa, Bridgewater State University; Carter Findley, Ohio State University; Amy Forss, Metropolitan Community College; Denis Gainty, Georgia State University; Duane Galloway, Rowan-Cabarrus Community College; Steven A. Glazer, Graceland University; Sue Gronewald, Kean University; Andrew Hamilton, Viterbo University; J. Laurence Hare, University of Arkansas; Jay Harmon, Houston Christian High School; Michael Hinckley, Northern Kentucky University; Bram Hubbell, Friends Seminary; Ronald Huch, Eastern Kentucky University; Michael Hunt, University of North Carolina at Chapel Hill; Elizabeth Hyde, Kean University; Mark Lentz, University of Louisiana–Lafayette; Ane Lintvedt, McDonogh School; Aran MacKinnon, Georgia College and State University; Harold Marcuse, University of California, Santa Barbara; Kate McGrath, Central Connecticut State University; Merritt McKinney, Volunteer State Community College; C. Brid Nicholson, Kean University; Erin O'Donnell, East Stroudsburg University; Sarah Panzer, Missouri State University; Donna Patch, Westside High School; Charmayne Patterson, Clark Atlanta University; Dean Pavlakis, Carroll College; Chris Peek, Bellaire High School; Tracie Provost, Middle Georgia State University; Masako Racel, Kennesaw State University; Jonathan T. Reynolds, Northern Kentucky University; James Sabathne, Hononegah High School; Christopher Sleeper, Mira Costa College; Ira Spar, Ramapo College and Metropolitan Museum of Art; Kristen Strobel, Lexington High School; Eddie Supratman, Arkansas State University–Beebe; Michael Vann, Sacramento State University; Peter Winn, Tufts University; and Judith Zinsser, Miami University of Ohio.

The fine people at Bedford/St. Martin's (Macmillan Learning) have provided a second community sustaining this enterprise and the one most directly responsible for the book's fifth edition. It would be difficult for any author to imagine a more supportive and professional publishing team. Our chief point of contact with the Bedford village has been Heidi Hood, our development editor. She has coordinated the immensely complex task of assembling a new edition of the book and has done so with great professional care, with timely responses to our many queries, and with sensitivity to the needs and feelings of authors, even when she found it necessary to decline our suggestions.

Others on the team have also exhibited that lovely combination of personal kindness and professional competence that is so characteristic of the Bedford way. Vice president Leasa Burton, program director Erika Gutierrez, and program manager William Lombardo have kept an eye on the project amid many duties. Christina Horn, our content project manager, managed the process of turning a manuscript into a published book and did so with both grace and efficiency. Assistant editor Carly Lewis has efficiently and thoughtfully prepared manuscript, reviewed e-book pages, and handled countless other project details. Operating behind the scenes in the Bedford village, a series of highly competent and always supportive people have shepherded this revised edition along its way. Photo researcher Bruce Carson identified and acquired the many images that grace this new edition of *Ways of the World* and did so with a keen eye and courtesy. Copyeditor Susan Zorn polished the prose and sorted out our many inconsistent usages with a seasoned and perceptive eye. Melissa Rodriguez has overseen the marketing process, while Bedford's sales representatives have reintroduced the book to the academic world. Associate development editor Stephanie Sosa and media editor Mollie Chandler supervised the development and preparation of supplements and media products to support the book, and William Boardman ably coordinated research for the lovely covers that mark *Ways of the World*.

A final and much smaller community sustained this project and its authors. It is that most intimate of villages that we know as a marriage. Sharing that village with me (Robert Strayer) is my wife, Suzanne Sturn. It is her work to bring ideas and people to life onstage, even as I try to do so between these covers. She knows how I feel about her love and support, and no one else needs to. And across the street, I (Eric Nelson) would also like to thank two other residents of this village: my wife, Alice Victoria, and our daughter, Evelyn Rhiannon, to whom this new edition is dedicated. Without their patience and support, I could not have become part of such an interesting journey.

To all of our fellow villagers, we offer deep thanks for an immensely rewarding experience. We are grateful beyond measure.

Robert Strayer, La Selva Beach, California
Eric Nelson, Springfield, Missouri

Versions and Supplements

Adopters of *Ways of the World* and their students have access to abundant digital and print resources and tools, including documents, assessment and presentation materials, the acclaimed *Bedford Series in History and Culture* volumes, and much more. *Ways of the World* is now available for the first time in Achieve, Macmillan's new complete course platform, which provides access to the narrative as well as a wealth of primary sources and other features, along with assessments and robust insight reports at the ready, all in one affordably priced product. Achieve also includes a download-able e-book for reading offline. See the following text for more information, visit the book's catalog site at **macmillanlearning.com**, or contact your local Bedford/ St. Martin's sales representative.

Get the Right Version and Volume for Your Course — Digital, Print, and Value Options

Whether it's a digital course platform, e-book, print book, value option, or package combining digital and print products, *Ways of the World* is available in a variety of volumes and formats so you can choose what works best for your course. The **comprehensive** *Ways of the World* includes a full-color art and map program and a rich set of features and primary and secondary sources. Digital options for the comprehensive version include the full course platform of Achieve for *Ways of the World* (see below for the description of Achieve's benefits), as well as e-books. The comprehensive version is also available in print in three volume options. For great value in a streamlined product, *Ways of the World,* **Value Edition**, offers the unabridged narrative and selected two-color art and maps — without special features or primary or secondary sources — at a steep discount. The Value Edition is available in e-book format as well as print in three volume options, with loose-leaf format available for the least expensive print option. For the best value, purchase Achieve on its own or package it with the print version of your choice for a small add-on cost. *Ways of the World* is available in the following volume configurations:

- **Combined Volume** (Chapters 1–23): available in Achieve (1- and 2-term subscriptions), e-books, and print volumes for the comprehensive and Value editions
- **Volume 1: Through the Fifteenth Century** (Chapters 1–12): available in Achieve (1- and 2-term subscriptions), e-books, and print volumes for the comprehensive and Value editions, including loose-leaf format for the Value Edition
- **Volume 2: Since the Fifteenth Century** (Chapters 12–23): available in Achieve (1- and 2-term subscriptions), e-books, and print volumes for the comprehensive and Value editions, including loose-leaf format for the Value Edition

As noted below, any of these volumes can be packaged with additional titles for a discount. To get ISBNs for discount packages, visit **macmillanlearning.com** or contact your Bedford/St. Martin's representative.

Assign Achieve—A Comprehensive Course Platform with E-book, Skill-Building Assessments, and Analytics for Instructors

Affordably priced, intuitive, and easy to use, Achieve is a breakthrough solution for building students' skills and confidence in history courses. Achieve for *Ways of the World* includes the rich resources and skill-building content of the e-books for the complete comprehensive text and companion reader, *Thinking through Sources for Ways of the World*, alongside a robust set of summative and formative assessments—many autograded—that help students build confidence in their mastery of the material, reflect on their learning, and build critical, higher-level thinking skills. Achieve for *Ways of the World* includes LearningCurve adaptive quizzing that—when assigned—helps ensure that students do the reading before class; autograded exercises that teach students how to build a thesis and support an argument; quizzes that check student comprehension of primary sources and boxed features; chapter summative quizzes that test student knowledge after they've completed the reading; tutorials with quizzing that build skills such as working with primary sources and avoiding plagiarism; assignable chapter reflections questions that encourage students to engage with their learning; active reading activities that help students read actively for key concepts; class activity guides that can be used in synchronous and asynchronous courses; and iClicker polling questions that engage students during class. These features, plus additional primary source documents, map quizzes, customizable test banks, and detailed reports on student progress, make Achieve an invaluable asset for any instructor.

Achieve easily integrates with course management systems, and, with fast ways to build assignments and organize content, it lets teachers build the courses they want to teach while holding students accountable. For more information, or to arrange a demo or class test, contact us at **historymktg@macmillan.com**.

Assign LearningCurve So Your Students Come to Class Prepared

Students using Achieve receive access to LearningCurve for *Ways of the World*. Assigning LearningCurve in place of reading quizzes is easy for instructors, and the reporting features help instructors track overall class trends and spot topics that are giving students trouble so they can adjust their lectures and class activities. This online learning tool is popular with students because it was designed to help them rehearse content at their own pace in a nonthreatening, game-like environment. The feedback for wrong answers provides instructional coaching and sends students back to the book for review. Students answer as many questions as necessary to reach a target score, with repeated chances to revisit material they haven't mastered. When LearningCurve is assigned, students come to class better prepared.

iClicker, Active Learning Simplified ▷ iClicker

iClicker offers simple, flexible tools to help you give students a voice and facilitate active learning in the classroom. Students can participate with the devices they bring to class using our iClicker student app (which work with smartphones, tablets, or laptops) or iClicker remotes. We've now integrated iClicker with Macmillan's Achieve to make it easier than ever to synchronize grades and promote engagement — both in and out of class. iClicker can be used synchronously through its polling feature, or asynchronously for assignments. To learn more, talk to your Macmillan Learning representative or visit us at **www.iclicker.com**.

Take Advantage of Instructor Resources

Bedford/St. Martin's has developed a rich array of teaching resources for this book and for this course. They range from lecture and presentation materials and assessment tools to course management options. Most can be found in Achieve or can be downloaded or ordered at **macmillanlearning.com**.

Instructor's Resource Manual. The instructor's manual offers both experienced and first-time instructors tools for presenting textbook material in engaging ways. It includes content learning objectives, annotated chapter outlines, and strategies for teaching with the textbook, plus suggestions on how to get the most out of LearningCurve and a survival guide for first-time teaching assistants.

Guide to Changing Editions. Designed to facilitate an instructor's transition from the previous edition of *Ways of the World* to this new edition, this guide presents an overview of major changes across the book and of changes in each chapter.

Online Test Bank. The test bank includes a mix of fresh, carefully crafted multiple-choice, short-answer, and essay questions for each chapter. Some of the multiple-choice questions feature a map as the prompt. All questions appear in an easy-to-use test bank software that allows instructors to add, edit, re-sequence, filter by question type, and print questions and answers. Instructors can also export questions into a variety of course management systems.

The Bedford Lecture Kit: **Lecture Outlines, Maps, and Images.** Look good and save time with *The Bedford Lecture Kit.* This resource includes fully customizable multimedia presentations built around chapter outlines that are embedded with maps, figures, and images from the textbook and are supplemented by more detailed instructor notes on key points and concepts.

Print, Digital, and Custom Options for More Choice and Value

For information on free packages and discounts up to 50%, visit **macmillanlearning .com**, or contact your local Bedford/St. Martin's sales representative.

Thinking through Sources for Ways of the World, **Fourth Edition.** Designed to accompany *Ways of the World,* each chapter of this reader contains approximately five to eight written and visual primary sources organized around a particular theme, issue, or question. Each of these projects is followed by a related Historians' Voices secondary source feature that pairs two brief excerpts from historians who comment on some aspect of the topics covered in the primary sources. *Thinking through Sources for Ways of the World* provides a broad selection of over 140 primary source documents and images as well as editorial apparatus to help students understand the sources. This companion reader is an exceptional value for students and offers plenty of assignment options for instructors, and it is included in Achieve with autograded quizzes for each source. *Thinking through Sources for Ways of the World* is also available on its own as a downloadable e-book.

Bedford Document Collections. These affordable, brief document projects provide 5 to 7 primary sources, an introduction, historical background, and other pedagogical features. Each curated project—designed for use in a single class period and written by a historian about a favorite topic—poses a historical question and guides students through analysis of the sources. Examples include "The Silk Road: Travel and Trade in Pre-Modern Inner Asia," "The Spread of Christianity in the Sixteenth and Early Seventeenth Centuries," "The Singapore Mutiny of 1915: Understanding World War I from a Global Perspective," and "Living through Perestroika: The Soviet Union in Upheaval, 1985–1991." These primary source projects are available in a low-cost, easy-to-use digital format or can be combined with other course materials in Bedford Select to create an affordable, personalized print product. For more information on using Bedford Select to customize your course materials with these and other resources, visit **macmillanlearning.com/bedfordselect**.

Bedford Tutorials for History. Designed to provide resources relevant to individual courses, this collection of over a dozen brief units, each 16 pages long and loaded with examples, guides students through basic skills such as using historical evidence effectively, working with primary sources, taking effective notes, avoiding plagiarism and citing sources, and more. For more information, visit **macmillanlearning.com /historytutorials**.

The Bedford Series in History and Culture. Now also available in low-cost e-books as well as print volumes, the more than 100 titles in this highly praised series combine first-rate scholarship, historical narrative, and important primary documents for undergraduate courses. Each title is brief, inexpensive, and focused on a specific topic or period. Recent titles in the series include *The First World War: Brief History with Documents*, Second Edition, by Susan R. Grayzel; *Spartacus and the Slave Wars: A Brief History with Documents*, Second Edition, by Brent D. Shaw; *Apartheid in South Africa: A Brief History with Documents* by David M. Gordon; *Politics and Society in Japan's Meiji Restoration: A Brief History with Documents* by Anne Walthall and M. William Stele; and *The Congo Free State and the New Imperialism: A Brief History with Documents* by Kevin Grant. For a complete list of titles, visit **macmillanlearning.com**. Package discounts are available.

Trade Books. History titles published by sister companies Hill and Wang; Farrar, Straus and Giroux; Henry Holt and Company; St. Martin's Press; Picador; and Palgrave Macmillan are available at a 50% discount when packaged with Bedford/St. Martin's textbooks. For more information, visit **macmillanlearning.com/tradeup**.

A Pocket Guide to Writing in History. Available in a low-cost e-book as well as in print and updated to reflect changes made in the 2017 *Chicago Manual of Style* revision, this portable and affordable reference tool by Mary Lynn Rampolla provides reading, writing, and research advice useful to students in all history courses. Concise yet comprehensive advice on approaching typical history assignments, developing critical reading skills, writing effective history papers, conducting research, using and documenting sources, and avoiding plagiarism—enhanced with practical tips and examples throughout—has made this slim reference a best seller. Deep discounts are available when bundled with a survey textbook.

A Student's Guide to History. Available in a low-cost e-book as well as in print and updated to reflect changes made in the 2017 *Chicago Manual of Style* revision, this complete guide to success in any history course provides the practical help students need to be successful. In addition to introducing students to the nature of the discipline, author Jules Benjamin teaches a wide range of skills, from preparing for exams to approaching common writing assignments, and explains the research and documentation process with plentiful examples. Deep discounts are available when bundled with a survey textbook.

Brief Contents

Contents

CHAPTER 8

China and the World: East Asian Connections, 600–1300   218

CHAPTER 9

The Worlds of Islam: Afro-Eurasian Connections, 600–1450   246

CHAPTER 10

The Worlds of Christendom: Contraction, Expansion, and Division, 600–1450   277

CHAPTER 11

Pastoral Peoples on the Global Stage: The Mongol Moment, 1200–1450   308

Maps, Figures, and Tables

Prologue
From Cosmic History to Human History

History books in general, and world history textbooks in particular, share something in common with those Russian nested dolls in which a series of carved figures fit inside one another. In much the same fashion, all historical accounts take place within some larger context, as stories within stories unfold. Individual biographies and histories of local communities, particularly modern ones, occur within the context of one nation or another. Nations often find a place in some more encompassing civilization, such as the Islamic world or the West, or in a regional or continental context such as Southeast Asia, Latin America, or Africa. And those civilizational or regional histories in turn take on richer meaning when they are understood within the even broader story of world history, which embraces humankind as a whole.

In recent decades, some world historians have begun to situate that remarkable story of the human journey in the much larger framework of both cosmic and planetary history, an approach that has come to be called "big history." It is really the "history of everything" from the big bang to the present, and it extends over the enormous, almost unimaginable timescale of some 13.8 billion years, the current rough estimate of the age of the universe.[1]

The History of the Universe

To make this vast expanse of time even remotely comprehensible, some scholars have depicted the history of the cosmos as if it were a single calendar year (see Snapshot). On that cosmic calendar, most of the action took place in the first few milliseconds of January 1. As astronomers, physicists, and chemists tell it, the universe that we know began in an eruption of inconceivable power and heat. Out of that explosion of creation emerged matter, energy, gravity, electromagnetism, and the "strong" and "weak" forces that govern the behavior of atomic nuclei. As gravity pulled the rapidly expanding cosmic gases into increasingly dense masses, stars formed, with the first ones lighting up around 600 million years after the big bang or toward the end of January on the cosmic calendar.

Hundreds of billions of stars followed, each with its own history, though following common patterns. They emerged, flourished for a time, and then collapsed and died. In their final stages, they sometimes generated supernovae, black holes, and pulsars—phenomena at least as fantastic as the most exotic of earlier creation stories. Within the stars, enormous nuclear reactions gave rise to the elements that are reflected in the periodic table known to all students of chemistry. Over eons, these stars came together in galaxies, such as our own Milky Way, which probably emerged in March or early April, and in even larger structures called groups, clusters, and superclusters. Adding to the strangeness of our picture of the cosmos is the recent and controversial notion that perhaps 90 percent or more of the total mass of the universe is invisible to us, consisting of a mysterious and mathematically predicted substance known to scholars only as "dark matter."

SNAPSHOT	**THE HISTORY OF THE UNIVERSE AS A COSMIC CALENDAR**	
Big bang	January 1	13.8 billion years ago
Stars and galaxies begin to form	End of January	13.2? billion years ago
Milky Way galaxy forms	March / early April	10 billion years ago
Origin of the solar system and earth	September 9	4.5 billion years ago
Earliest life on earth	Late September	3.8 billion years ago
Oxygen forms on earth	December 1	1.3 billion years ago
First worms	December 16	658 million years ago
First fish, first vertebrates	December 19	534 million years ago
First reptiles, first trees	December 23	370 million years ago
Age of dinosaurs	December 24–28	66 to 240 million years ago
First human-like creatures	December 31 (late evening)	2.7 million years ago
First agriculture	December 31: 11:59:35	12,000 years ago
Birth of the Buddha / Greek civilization	December 31: 11:59:55	2,500 years ago
Birth of Jesus	December 31: 11:59:56	2,000 years ago

Source: Information from Carl Sagan, *The Dragons of Eden* (New York: Random House, 1977), 13–17; David Christian, *Origin Story: A Big History of Everything* (New York: Little, Brown, 2018), 13–14.

The contemplation of cosmic history has prompted profound religious or philosophical questions about the meaning of human life. For some, it has engendered a sense of great insignificance in the face of cosmic vastness. In disputing the earth- and human-centered view of the cosmos, long held by the Catholic Church, the eighteenth-century French thinker Voltaire wrote: "This little globe, nothing more than a point, rolls in space like so many other globes; we are lost in this immensity."[2] Nonetheless, human consciousness and our awareness of the mystery of this immeasurable universe render us unique and generate for many people feelings of awe, gratitude, and humility that are almost religious. As tiny but knowing observers of this majestic cosmos, we have found ourselves living in a grander home than ever we knew before.

The History of a Planet

For most of us, one star, our own sun, is far more important than all the others, despite its quite ordinary standing among the billions of stars in the universe and its somewhat remote location on the outer edge of the Milky Way galaxy. Circling that star is a series of planets, formed of leftover materials from the sun's birth. One of those planets, the third from the sun and the fifth largest, is home to all of us. Human history — our history — takes place not only on the earth but also as part of the planet's history.

That history began with the emergence of the entire solar system, including the earth, about two-thirds of the way through the history of the universe, some 4.5 billion years ago, or early September on the cosmic calendar. Geologists have learned a great deal about the history of the earth: the formation of its rocks and atmosphere; the movement of its continents; the collision of the tectonic plates that make up its crust;

and the constant changes of its landscape as mountains formed, volcanoes erupted, and erosion transformed the surface of the planet. All of this has been happening for more than 4 billion years and continues still.

The most remarkable feature of the earth's history—and so far as we know unrepeated elsewhere—was the emergence of life from the chemical soup of the early planet. It happened rather quickly, only about 700 million years after the earth itself took shape, or late September on the cosmic calendar. Then for some 3 billion years, life remained at the level of microscopic single-celled organisms. According to biologists, the many species of larger multicelled creatures—all of the flowers, shrubs, and trees as well as all of the animals of land, sea, and air—have evolved in an explosive proliferation of life-forms over the past 600 million years, or since mid-December on the cosmic calendar. The history of life on earth has, however, been periodically punctuated by massive die-offs, at least five of them, in which very large numbers of animal or plant species have perished. The most widespread of these "extinction events," known to scholars as the Permian mass extinction, occurred around 250 million years ago and eliminated some 90 percent of living species on the planet. That catastrophic diminution of life-forms on the earth has been associated with massive volcanic eruptions, the release of huge quantities of carbon dioxide and methane into the atmosphere, and a degree of global warming that came close to extinguishing all life on the planet. Much later, around 66 million years ago, another such extinction event decimated about 75 percent of plant and animal species, including what was left of the dinosaurs. Most scientists now believe that it was caused primarily by the impact of a huge asteroid that landed near the Yucatán Peninsula off the coast of southern Mexico, generating enormous earthquakes, tsunamis, fireballs, and a cloud of toxic dust and debris. Many scholars believe we are currently in the midst of a sixth extinction event, driven, like the others, by major climate change, but which, unlike the others, is the product of human actions.

So life on earth has been and remains both fragile and resilient. Within these conditions, every species has had a history as its members struggled to find resources, cope with changing environments, and deal with competitors. Egocentric creatures that we are, however, human beings have usually focused their history books and history courses entirely on a single species—our own, *Homo sapiens*, humankind. On the cosmic calendar, *Homo sapiens* is an upstart primate whose entire history occurred in the last few minutes of December 31. Almost all of what we normally study in history courses—agriculture, writing, civilizations, empires, industrialization—took place in the very last minute of that cosmic year. The entire history of the United States occurred in the last second.

Yet during that very brief time, humankind has had a career more remarkable and arguably more consequential for the planet than any other species. At the heart of human uniqueness lies our amazing capacity for accumulating knowledge and skills. Other animals learn, of course, but for the most part they learn the same things over and over again. Twenty-first-century chimpanzees in the wild master much the same set of skills as their ancestors did a million years ago. But the exceptional communication abilities provided by human language allow us to learn from one another, to express that learning in abstract symbols, and then to pass it on, cumulatively, to future generations. Thus we have moved from stone axes to lasers, from spears to nuclear weapons, from "talking drums" to the Internet, from grass huts to the pyramids of Egypt, the Taj Mahal of India, and the skyscrapers of modern cities.

This extraordinary ability has translated into a human impact on the earth that is unprecedented among all living species.[3] Human populations have multiplied far more extensively and have come to occupy a far greater range of environments than has any other large animal. Through our ingenious technologies, we have appropriated for ourselves, according to recent calculations, some 25 to 40 percent of the solar energy that enters the food chain. We have recently gained access to the stored solar energy of coal, gas, and oil, all of which have been many millions of years in the making, and we have the capacity to deplete these resources in a few hundred or a few thousand years. Other forms of life have felt the impact of human activity, as numerous extinct or threatened species testify. Human beings have even affected the atmosphere and the oceans as carbon dioxide and other emissions of the industrial age have warmed the climate of the planet in ways that broadly resemble the conditions that triggered earlier extinction events. Thus human history has been, and remains, of great significance, not for ourselves alone, but also for the earth itself and for the many other living creatures with which we share it.

The History of the Human Species . . . in a Single Paragraph

The history of our species has occurred during roughly the last 250,000–350,000 years, conventionally divided into three major phases, based on the kind of technology that was most widely practiced. The enormously long Paleolithic age, with its gathering and hunting way of life, accounts for 95 percent or more of the time that humans have occupied the planet. People utilizing a stone-age Paleolithic technology initially settled every major landmass on the earth and constructed the first human societies (see Chapter 1). Then beginning about 12,000 years ago with the first Agricultural Revolution, the domestication of plants and animals increasingly became the primary means of sustaining human life and societies. In giving rise to agricultural villages and chiefdoms, to pastoral communities depending on their herds of animals, and to state- and city-based civilizations, this agrarian way of life changed virtually everything and fundamentally reshaped human societies and their relationship to the natural order. Finally, around 1750 a quite sudden spurt in the rate of technological change, which we know as the Industrial Revolution, began to take hold. That vast increase in productivity, wealth, and human control over nature once again transformed almost every aspect of human life and gave rise to new kinds of societies that we call "modern."

Here then, in a single paragraph, is the history of humankind—the Paleolithic era, the agricultural era, and, most recently and briefly, the modern industrial era. Clearly this is a big picture perspective, based on the notion that the human species as a whole has a history that transcends any of its particular and distinctive cultures. That perspective—known variously as planetary, global, or world history—has become increasingly prominent among those who study the past. Why should this be so?

Why World History?

Not long ago—in the mid-twentieth century, for example—virtually all college-level history courses were organized in terms of particular civilizations or nations. In the United States, courses such as Western Civilization or some version of American History served to introduce students to the study of the past. Since then, however, a set of profound changes has pushed much of the historical profession in a different direction.

The world wars of the twentieth century, revealing as they did the horrendous consequences of unchecked nationalism, persuaded some historians that a broader view of the past might contribute to a sense of global citizenship. Economic and cultural globalization has highlighted both the interdependence of the world's peoples and their very unequal positions within that world. Moreover, we are aware as never before that our problems—whether they involve economic well-being, global warming, disease, or terrorism—respect no national boundaries. To many thoughtful people, a global present seemed to call for a global past. Furthermore, as colonial empires shrank and new nations asserted themselves on the world stage, these peoples also insisted that their histories be accorded equivalent treatment with those of Europe and North America. An explosion of new knowledge about the histories of Asia, Africa, and pre-Columbian America erupted from the research of scholars around the world. All of this has generated a "world history movement," reflected in college and high school curricula, in numerous conferences and specialized studies, and in a proliferation of textbooks, of which this is one.

This world history movement has attempted to create a global understanding of the human past that highlights broad patterns cutting across particular civilizations and countries, while acknowledging in an inclusive fashion the distinctive histories of its many peoples. This is, to put it mildly, a tall order. How is it possible to encompass within a single book or course the separate stories of the world's various peoples? Surely it must be something more than just recounting the history of one civilization or culture after another. How can we distill a common history of humankind as a whole from the distinct trajectories of particular peoples? Because no world history book or course can cover everything, what criteria should we use for deciding what to include and what to leave out? Such questions have ensured no end of controversy among students, teachers, and scholars of world history, making it one of the most exciting fields of historical inquiry.

Context, Change, Comparison, and Connection: The Four Cs of World History

Despite much debate and argument, most scholars and teachers of world history would probably agree on four major emphases of this remarkable field of study. The first lies in the observation that in world history, nothing stands alone. Every event, every historical figure, every culture, society, or civilization gains significance from its inclusion in some larger framework. This means that **context** is central to world history and that contextual thinking is the essential skill that world history teaches. And so we ask the same question about every particular occurrence: where does it fit in the larger scheme of things?

A second common theme in world history involves **change** over time. Most often, it is the "big picture" changes—those that affect large segments of humankind—that are of greatest interest. How did the transition from a gathering and hunting economy to one based on agriculture take place? How did cities, empires, and civilizations take shape in various parts of the world? What impact did the growing prominence of Europe have on the rest of the world in recent centuries? A focus on change provides an antidote to a persistent tendency of human thinking that historians call "essentialism." A more common term is "stereotyping." It refers to our inclination to define particular groups of people with an unchanging or essential set of characteristics. Women are nurturing; peasants are conservative; Americans are aggressive; Hindus are religious. Serious students of history soon become aware that every significant category of people contains endless variations and conflicts and that those human communities are constantly in flux. Peasants may often accept the status quo, except of course when they rebel, as they frequently have. Americans have experienced periods of isolationism and withdrawal from the world as well as times of aggressive engagement with it. Things change.

But some things persist, even if they also change. We should not allow an emphasis on change to blind us to the continuities of human experience. A recognizably Chinese state has operated for more than 2,000 years. Slavery and patriarchy persisted as human institutions for thousands of years until they were challenged in recent centuries, and in various forms they exist still. The teachings of Buddhism, Christianity, and Islam have endured for centuries, though with endless variations and transformations.

A third element that operates constantly in world history books and courses is that of **comparison**. Whatever else it may be, world history is a comparative discipline, seeking to identify similarities and differences in the experience of the world's peoples. What is the difference between the development of agriculture in the Middle East and in Mesoamerica? Was the experience of women largely the same in all patriarchal societies? Why did the Industrial Revolution and a modern way of life evolve first in Western Europe rather than somewhere else? What distinguished the French, Russian, and Chinese revolutions from one another? Describing and, if possible, explaining such similarities and differences are among the major tasks of world history. Comparison has proven an effective tool in efforts to counteract Eurocentrism, the notion that Europeans or people of European descent have long been the primary movers and shakers of the historical process. That notion arose in recent centuries when Europeans were in fact the major source of innovation in the world and did for a time exercise something close to world domination. But comparative world history sets this recent European prominence in a global and historical context, helping us to sort out what was distinctive about the development of Europe and what similarities it bore to other major regions of the world. Puncturing the pretensions of Eurocentrism has been high on the agenda of world history.

A fourth emphasis within world history, and in this book, involves the interactions, encounters, and **connections** among different and often distant peoples. Focusing on cross-cultural connections—whether those of conflict or more peaceful exchange—represents an effort to counteract a habit of thinking about particular peoples, states, or cultures as self-contained or isolated communities. Despite the historical emergence of many separate and distinct societies, none of them developed alone. Each was embedded in a network of relationships with both near and more distant peoples.

Moreover, these cross-cultural connections did not begin with Columbus. The Chinese, for example, interacted continuously with the nomadic peoples on their northern border; generated technologies that diffused across all of Eurasia; transmitted elements of their culture to Japan, Korea, and Vietnam; and assimilated a foreign religious tradition, Buddhism, that had originated in India. Though clearly distinctive, China was not a self-contained or isolated civilization. Thus world history remains always alert to the networks, webs, and encounters in which particular civilizations or peoples were enmeshed.

Context, change, comparison, and connection—all of them operating on a global scale—represent various ways of bringing some coherence to the multiple and complex stories of world history. They will recur repeatedly in the pages that follow.

A final observation about this account of world history: *Ways of the World,* like all other world history textbooks, is radically unbalanced in terms of coverage. Chapter 1, for example, takes on some 95 percent of the human story, well over 200,000 years of our history. By contrast, the last century alone occupies four entire chapters. In fact, the six major sections of the book deal with progressively shorter time periods, in progressively greater detail. This imbalance owes much to the relative scarcity of information about earlier periods of our history. But it also reflects a certain "present mindedness," for we look to history, always, to make sense of our current needs and circumstances. And in doing so, we often assume that more recent events have a greater significance for our own lives in the here and now than those that occurred in more distant times. Whether you agree with this assumption or not, you will have occasion to ponder it as you consider the many and various "ways of the world" that have emerged in the course of the human journey and as you contemplate their relevance for your own journey.

Ways of the World

VALUE EDITION

PART 1
First Things First:
Beginnings in History to 600 B.C.E.

The Big Picture

Turning Points in Early World History

Human beings have long been inveterate storytellers, and so too are contemporary historians. They tell stories about individuals, communities, nations, civilizations, and, in the case of world history, about humankind as a whole. All tellers of stories—ancient and modern alike—have to decide where to begin their accounts and what major turning points in those narratives to highlight. For world historians seeking to tell the story of "all under Heaven," as the Chinese put it, four major "beginnings," each of them an extended historical process, have marked the initial stages of the human journey.

The Emergence of Humankind

The first large-scale process in the human story lies in biological evolution. According to archeologists and anthropologists, the evolutionary line of descent leading to *Homo sapiens* separated from that of chimpanzees, our closest primate relatives, some 5 to 6 million years ago, and it happened in eastern and southern Africa. There, perhaps twenty or thirty different species emerged, all of them members of the Homininae (or hominid) family of human-like creatures. What they all shared was bipedalism, the ability to walk upright on two legs, facilitated by the evolution of increasingly more flexible hip joints. Over time, these hominid species changed. Their brains grew larger; they began to make and use simple stone tools; some started to eat meat, at least occasionally; eventually they learned to control fire. By 1 million years ago, some hominid species, especially *Homo erectus*, began to migrate out of Africa, and their remains have been found in various parts of Eurasia.

But all of these earlier hominid species finally died out, except one: *Homo sapiens*, ourselves. With a remarkable capacity for symbolic language that permitted the accumulation and transmission of learning, our species also appeared first in Africa and quite recently, probably no more than 260,000 to 350,000 years ago. For a long time, nearly all of the small number of *Homo sapiens* lived in Africa, and those few that ventured beyond ultimately failed to establish themselves. Then sometime after 100,000

2

years ago, a remarkable migration out of Africa began that led over tens of thousands of years to the colonization of almost every inhabitable landmass on the planet.

The Globalization of Humankind

This amazing journey represents the second major turning point in the human story. Our ancient ancestors — small in stature, not fast on foot, and armed with a very limited technology of stone tools — were able to adapt to almost every environmental setting on the planet. The phase of human history during which these initial migrations took place is known to scholars as the Paleolithic era. The word "Paleolithic" literally means the "old stone age," but it refers more generally to a gathering, hunting, and fishing way of life, before agriculture allowed people to grow crops or raise animals deliberately. Lasting until roughly 12,000 years ago, and in many places much longer, the Paleolithic era represents over 95 percent of the time that human beings have inhabited the earth. Although often neglected by historians and history textbooks, this long period of the human experience merits greater attention and is the focus of the initial sections of Chapter 1.

The Revolution of Farming and Herding

Then, a third process began to completely reshape the human experience. Around 12,000 years ago, human communities in parts of the Middle East, Asia, Africa, and the Americas began the laborious process of domesticating animals and selecting seeds to be planted. This momentous accomplishment, often called the Agricultural Revolution, surely marks the single most significant and enduring transformation of our history. Now our species learned to exploit and manipulate particular organisms, both plant and animal. Farming and raising animals allowed for a substantial increase in human numbers and over many centuries generated a profound transformation of the environment. Forests were felled, arid lands irrigated, meadows plowed, and mountains terraced. Increasingly, the landscape reflected human intentions and actions.

The Turning Point of Civilization

The most prominent and powerful human communities to emerge from this Agricultural Revolution were those often designated as "civilizations," more complex societies that were based in bustling cities and governed by formal states. Their emergence in Eurasia, Africa, and the Americas marked the fourth major transformation in human history. Because almost all of the world's people now live in such societies, states and cities have come to seem almost natural. In world history terms, however, their appearance is quite recent. Not until several thousand years *after* the beginning of agriculture did the first cities and states emerge, around 3500 B.C.E. Well after

1000 C.E., substantial numbers of people still lived in communities without any state or urban structures. Nonetheless, people living in state- and city-based societies or civilizations have long constituted the most powerful and innovative human communities on the planet. They have given rise to empires of increasing size, enduring cultural and religious traditions, new technologies, sharper class and gender inequalities, new conceptions of masculinity and femininity, and large-scale warfare. The earliest of these civilizations provide the focus of Chapter 2.

Time and World History

Reckoning time is central to all historical study, for history is essentially the story of change over time. Recently it has become standard in the Western world to refer to dates prior to the birth of Christ as B.C.E. (before the Common Era), replacing the earlier B.C. (before Christ) usage. This convention is an effort to become less Christian-centered and Eurocentric in our use of language, although the chronology remains linked to the birth of Jesus. Similarly, the time following the birth of Christ is referred to as C.E. (the Common Era) rather than A.D. (*Anno Domini*, Latin for "year of the Lord"). Dates in the more distant past are designated in this book as B.P. (before the present), or simply as so many "years ago." Of course, these conventions are only some of the many ways that human societies have charted time, and they reflect the global dominance of Europeans in recent centuries. But the Chinese frequently dated important events in terms of the reign of particular emperors, while Muslims created a new calendar beginning with Year 1, marking Muhammad's forced relocation from Mecca to Medina in 622 C.E. As with so much else, the ways we represent change over time reflect the cultures in which we have been born and the historical experience of our societies.

World history frequently deals with very long periods of time, often encompassing many millennia or centuries in a single paragraph or even in a single sentence. This panoramic perspective provides context, a big picture framework in which we can situate particular events, societies, and individual experiences. Doing so allows us to discern patterns and trends that may be invisible from the viewpoint of a local community, a single nation, or one civilization. In the narrative that follows, there will be plenty of particulars — events, places, people — but always embedded in some larger setting that heightens their significance.

FIRST REFLECTIONS

1. **Questioning Chronology** The timescale of this section of the book is enormous — hundreds of thousands of years of human history. What perspectives does such a timescale suggest when considering the Agricultural Revolution and the emergence of civilization?

2. **Assessing Change** In what ways might the sequence of events as outlined here suggest a view of history as "progress"? What alternatives to such a view could you suggest?

3. **Considering Origins** What significance might you attribute to the African origins of humankind?

4. **Thinking like a World Historian** How does this brief essay reflect a distinctly "world history" outlook?

1

First Peoples; First Farmers

Most of History in a Single Chapter

to 3500 B.C.E.

CONNECTING PAST AND PRESENT

"WE DO NOT WANT CATTLE, JUST WILD animals to hunt and water that we can drink."[1] That was the view of Gudo Mahiya, a prominent member of the Hadza people of northern Tanzania, when he was questioned in 1997 about his interest in a settled life of farming and cattle raising. The Hadza represent one of the very last peoples on earth to continue a way of life that was universal among humankind until 10,000 to 12,000 years ago. In 2018, only about 1,000 Hadza survived, and of these just several hundred still made a living by hunting game, collecting honey, digging up roots, and gathering berries and fruit. Almost certainly, Gudo Mahiya's way of life is doomed, as farmers, cattle herders, governments, missionaries, and now tourists push the Hadza toward extinction. The likely disappearance of the Hadza people and their culture is among the final chapters of a very long story in which gathering, hunting, and fishing peoples have been unsuccessfully on the defensive against more numerous and powerful neighbors for 10,000 years.

Nonetheless, that way of life sustained humankind for more than 95 percent of our time on the earth. During countless centuries, human beings successfully adapted to a wide variety of environments without benefit of deliberate farming or animal husbandry. Instead, our early ancestors wrested a livelihood by gathering wild foods such as berries, nuts, roots, and grain; by scavenging dead animals; by hunting live animals; and by fishing. Known to scholars as "gathering and hunting" peoples, they were foragers or food collectors rather than food producers. Because they used stone rather than metal tools, they also have been labeled Paleolithic, or Old Stone Age, peoples.

Then, between roughly 4,000 and 12,000 years ago, an enormous transformation began to unfold as a few human societies—in Eurasia, Africa, and the Americas alike—started to practice the deliberate cultivation of plants and the domestication of animals. This **Agricultural** or **Neolithic** (New Stone Age) **Revolution** marked a technological breakthrough of immense significance, with implications for every aspect of human life. This chapter, dealing with the long **Paleolithic era** and the initial transition to an agricultural way of life, represents most of human history—everything, in fact, before the advent of urban-based civilizations, which began only 5,500 years ago.

And yet history courses and history books often neglect this long phase of the human journey and instead choose to begin the story with the early civilizations of Egypt, Mesopotamia, China, and elsewhere. Some historians identify "real history" with writing and so dismiss the Paleolithic and Neolithic eras as largely unknowable because their peoples did not write. (See "Controversies: Debating the Timescales of History.") Others, impressed with the rapid pace of change in human affairs in more recent times, assume that nothing much of real significance happened during the long Paleolithic era—and that no change meant no history.

But does it make sense to ignore the first 200,000 years or more of human experience? The achievements of Paleolithic peoples—the initial settlement of the planet, the creation of the earliest human societies, the beginnings of reflection on the great questions of life and death—surely deserve our attention. And the breakthrough to agriculture arguably represents the single most profound transformation of human life in all of history. Our grasp of the human past is incomplete — massively so — if we choose to disregard the Paleolithic and Neolithic eras.

SEEKING THE MAIN POINT

What arguments does this chapter make for paying serious attention to human history before the coming of "civilization"?

Out of Africa: First Migrations

The first 200,000 years or more of human experience was an almost exclusively African story. While time and climate have erased much of the record of our earliest ancestors, evidence recovered to date indicates that *Homo sapiens* first emerged around 260,000 to 350,000 years ago, most likely in the highlands of East Africa. They had spread as far as Northwest Africa by around 300,000 years ago, if the dating of a recent discovery of human remains in modern Morocco is correct. Thus Africa, almost certainly, was the place where the "human revolution" occurred, where "culture," defined as learned or invented ways of living, became more important than biology in shaping behavior.

What kinds of uniquely human activity show up in the early African record?[2] In the first place, our ancient African ancestors began to create new technologies as stone blades and points fastened to shafts replaced the earlier hand axes; tools made from bones appeared, and so did grindstones. Settlements were planned around the seasonal movement of game and fish. Patterns of exchange over a distance of almost 200 miles indicate larger networks of human communication. The use of body ornaments, beads, and pigments as well as possible planned burials suggests the kind of social and symbolic behavior that has characterized human activity ever since. The earliest evidence for this kind of activity comes from the Blombos Cave in South Africa, where excavations in 2008 uncovered a workshop for the processing of ochre (a naturally occurring earth pigment with a red, yellow, or brown color) dating to around 100,000 years ago, well before such behavior surfaced elsewhere in the world.

The development and spread of human culture were highly uncertain and took place amid immense obstacles. Recent discoveries of human bones or footprints in Arabia, Israel, and Greece, one of which dates to as early as 210,000 years ago, have shown that humans ventured beyond Africa early in their history. But genetic evidence indicates that these "failed dispersals" died out, leaving no trace in the genes of modern humans. Then, around 70,000 years ago an enormous volcanic eruption on the island of Sumatra in present-day Indonesia resulted in a cooler and drier global climate and, scholars speculate, something close to human extinction. But human numbers recovered, growing slowly to perhaps 500,000 by 30,000 years ago and then to 6 million by 10,000 years ago.[3] As this recovery took shape, sometime between 60,000 and 100,000 years ago, human beings began a remarkable migration out of Africa that led over tens of thousands of years to the colonization of almost every inhabitable landmass on the planet (see Map 1.1). Much of this long journey occurred during a major cooling period of the last Ice Age that began about 120,000 years ago and reached its peak around 20,000 years ago. During this period, which only came to an end around 12,000 years ago, thick ice sheets covered much

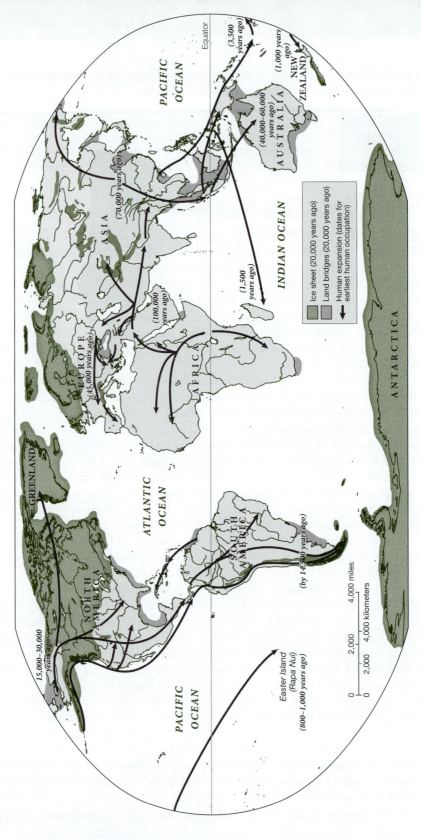

of the Northern Hemisphere. The Ice Age did give these outward-bound humans one advantage, however: the amount of water frozen in northern glaciers lowered sea levels around the planet, creating land bridges among various regions that were separated after the glaciers melted. Britain was then joined to Europe; eastern Siberia was connected to Alaska; and parts of what is now Indonesia were linked to mainland Southeast Asia.

Into Eurasia

Humans first permanently moved into the Middle East and from there to Asia sometime after 70,000 years ago and to Europe about 45,000 years ago. During this expansion they encountered and occasionally interbred with Neanderthals and Denisovans, two species of hominids that are closely related to humans. The rapid spread of some Neanderthal and Denisovan genes in the human population has led geneticists to theorize that this interbreeding was beneficial, strengthening human immune systems and making human metabolisms more adaptable to colder climates and higher altitudes.

While many aspects of early human migration remain uncertain and much debated, Paleolithic peoples left a valuable but fragile record of their world in hundreds of cave paintings. The largest concentrations so far discovered, dating from around 37,000 years ago, are located in southern France and northern Spain and were created over the course of roughly 20,000 years. But the earliest, from about 44,000 years ago, were recently discovered on the other side of Eurasia in modern Indonesia. These images frequently picture the animals that humans hunted as well as figures with both human and animal features, brilliantly portrayed in colors of red, yellow, brown, and black. Impressions of human hands and various abstract designs sometimes accompany these cave paintings.

Archeologists have also uncovered remarkable Paleolithic adaptations to Ice Age conditions. Across the vast plains of Central Europe, Ukraine, and Russia, new technologies emerged, including bone needles, multilayered clothing, weaving, nets, storage pits, baskets, and pottery. Partially underground dwellings constructed from the bones and tusks of mammoths compensated for the absence of caves and rock shelters. All of this evidence suggests that some of these people had lived in more permanent settlements, at least temporarily abandoning their nomadic journeys. Associated with these Eastern European peoples were female figurines, the oldest of which was uncovered in 2008 in Germany and is dated to at least 35,000 years ago. Carved from stone, antlers, mammoth tusks, or, occasionally, baked clay, these so-called **Venus figurines** depict the female form, often with exaggerated breasts, buttocks, hips, and stomachs. Similar figurines have been found all across Eurasia, raising any number of controversial questions. (See the image of the Willendorf Venus, page 15.) Does their widespread distribution suggest a network of human communication and

< MAP 1.1 The Global Dispersion of Humankind
After several failed forays in the more distant past, sometime between 100,000 and 60,000 years ago our species (*Homo sapiens*) began to spread from its place of origin in Africa to colonize almost every inhabitable landmass on the planet.

The Lascaux Caves Discovered by four teenage boys in 1940, the Lascaux caves in southern France contain some 2,000 images dating to perhaps 19,000 years ago. Many of them depict in quite realistic form the wild animals of the region—oxen, bulls, horses, deer, and more. (Pictures from History/Bridgeman Images)

cultural diffusion over a wide area? If so, did they move from west to east or vice versa? What do they mean in terms of women's roles and status in Paleolithic societies?

Into Australia

Early human migration to Australia, perhaps 60,000 years ago, came from Indonesia and involved another first in human affairs—the use of boats. Over time, people settled in most regions of this huge continent, though quite sparsely. Scholars estimate the population of Australia at about 300,000 in 1788, when the first Europeans arrived. Over tens of thousands of years, the peoples of Australia had developed perhaps 250 languages; learned to collect a wide variety of bulbs, tubers, roots, seeds, and cereal grasses; and become proficient hunters of large and small animals, as well as birds, fish, and other marine life. A relatively simple technology, appropriate to a gathering and hunting economy, sustained Australia's Aboriginal people into modern times.

Accompanying Aboriginals' technological simplicity and traditionalism was the development of an elaborate and complex outlook on the world, known as the **Dreamtime**. Expressed in endless stories, in extended ceremonies, and in the evocative rock art of the continent's peoples, the Dreamtime recounted the beginning of things: how ancestral beings crisscrossed the land, creating its rivers, hills, rocks, and waterholes; how various peoples came to inhabit the land; and how they related to animals and to one another. In this view of the world, everything in the natural order was a vibration, an echo, a footprint of these ancient happenings, intimately linking the current inhabitants to particular places and timeless events in the past.

The journeys of the Dreamtime's ancestral beings reflect the networks of migration, communication, and exchange that connected the continent's many Paleolithic peoples. Far from living as isolated groups, they had long exchanged particular stones, pigments, materials for ropes and baskets, wood for spears, feathers and shells for ornaments, and an addictive psychoactive drug known as *pituri* over distances of hundreds of miles. Songs, dances, stories, and rituals likewise circulated. Precisely how far back in time these networks extend is difficult to pinpoint, but it seems clear that Paleolithic Australia was both many separate worlds and, at the same time, one loosely connected world.

Into the Americas

The earliest settlement of the Western Hemisphere occurred much later than that of Australia, Asia, or Europe, for it took some time for human beings to penetrate the frigid lands of eastern Siberia, which was the jumping-off point for the move into the Americas. Experts continue to argue about precisely when the first migrations occurred (somewhere between 15,000 and 30,000 years ago), about how many separate migrations took place (by sea down the west coast of North America or by land between ice sheets across the Bering Strait), and about how long it took to penetrate to the tip of South America. But most recent scholarship points to the earliest migrants arriving by sea along a "kelp highway," named after a rich underwater ecosystem stretching down much of the Pacific coast where "forests" of kelp (a type of seaweed) supported a great variety of marine life. In turn, this marine life provided sustenance for these first human arrivals in the Western Hemisphere. They followed the coast for thousands of miles, reaching Monte Verde in South America by no later than 14,500 years ago (see Map 1.1).

Early migrants spread rapidly, adapting to many different environments, from the tropical rain forests of the Amazon to the frigid conditions of late Ice Age North America. Around 13,000 years ago some bands of hunters who had filtered into the lands east of the Rocky Mountains formed one of the first clearly defined and widespread cultural traditions in the Americas, known as **Clovis culture** because of a distinctive projectile point that is known to archeologists as a Clovis point. Scattered bands of Clovis people ranged across much of North America, camping along rivers, springs, and waterholes, where large animals congregated. Although they certainly hunted smaller animals and gathered many wild plants, Clovis bands show up in the archeological record most dramatically as hunters of very large mammals, such as mammoths and bison. The wide distribution of Clovis point technology suggests yet again a regional pattern of cultural diffusion and at least indirect communication over a large area.

Then, rather abruptly, by roughly 11,000 years ago, all trace of the Clovis culture disappeared from the archeological record at about the same time that many species of large animals, including the mammoth, also became extinct. Did the Clovis people hunt these animals to extinction and then vanish themselves as their source of food disappeared? Or did changes to the climate that came with the end of the Ice Age cause this **megafaunal extinction** (extinction of large animals)? And what impact did a final migration of people from Siberia about 8,000 years ago play in their disappearance? They seem to have largely replaced Clovis people in North America. Experts disagree, but whatever the reason for the disappearance of Clovis culture, humans continued to inhabit North America, adapting to the many different environments—woodlands, plains, deserts—that the warming climate created.

Into the Pacific

The last phase of the great human migration took place in the Pacific Ocean and was distinctive in many ways. It occurred quite recently, jumping off only about 3,500 years ago from the Bismarck and Solomon Islands near New Guinea as well as from the islands of the Philippines. It was everywhere a waterborne migration, making use of oceangoing canoes and remarkable navigational skills, and it happened very quickly and over a huge area of the planet. Speaking Austronesian languages that trace back to southern China, these oceanic voyagers had settled every habitable piece of land in the Pacific basin within about 2,500 years. And some DNA evidence suggests that they may have visited the coast of South America by around 1200 c.e. as well. Other Austronesians had sailed west from Indonesia across the Indian Ocean to settle the island of Madagascar off the coast of eastern Africa. These extraordinary **Austronesian migrations** made the Austronesian family of languages the most geographically widespread in the world and Austronesian trading networks, reaching some 5,000 miles from western Indonesia to the mid-Pacific, the most extensive. With the occupation of Aotearoa (New Zealand) and Rapa Nui (Easter Island) around 1000 to 1200 c.e., the initial human settlement of the planet was finally complete (see Map 1.2).

In contrast with all of the other initial migrations, these Pacific voyages were undertaken by agricultural people who carried domesticated plants and animals in their canoes. Both men and women made these journeys, suggesting a deliberate

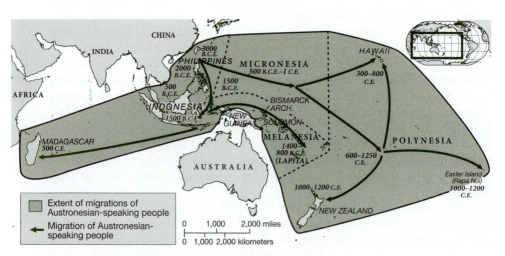

MAP 1.2   Migration of Austronesian-Speaking Peoples
People speaking Austronesian languages completed the human settlement of the earth quite recently as they settled the islands of the vast Pacific and penetrated the Indian Ocean to Madagascar, off the coast of Southeast Africa.

intention to colonize new lands. Virtually everywhere they went, two developments followed. One was the creation of highly stratified societies or chiefdoms, of which ancient Hawaiian society is a prime example. The other development was extensive deforestation and the quick extinction of many species of animals, especially large flightless birds such as the *moa* of New Zealand, which largely vanished within a century of this human intrusion into a pristine environment.

Paleolithic Lifeways

During their long journeys across the earth, Paleolithic people created a multitude of separate and distinct societies, each with its own history, culture, language, identity, stories, and rituals, but the limitations of a gathering and hunting technology using stone tools also imposed some commonalities on these ancient people. Based on the archeological record and on observations of gathering and hunting peoples that still existed in recent centuries, scholars have sketched out some of the common features of these early societies.

The First Human Societies

Above all else, these Paleolithic societies were small, consisting of bands of twenty-five to fifty people, in which all relationships were intensely personal and normally understood in terms of kinship. The available technology permitted only a very low population density and ensured an extremely slow rate of population growth. Paleolithic bands were seasonally mobile or nomadic, moving frequently and in regular patterns to exploit the wild plants and animals on which they depended. The low productivity of a gathering and hunting economy normally did not allow the production of much surplus, and because people were on the move so often, transporting an accumulation of goods was out of the question.

All of this resulted in highly egalitarian societies that lacked the many inequalities of wealth and power that came later with agricultural and urban life. With no formal chiefs, kings, bureaucrats, soldiers, nobles, or priests, Paleolithic men and women were perhaps freer of human tyranny and oppression than any later kind of human society, even if they were more constrained by the forces of nature. Without specialists, most people possessed the same set of skills, although male and female tasks often differed sharply.

Relationships between women and men usually were far more equal than in later societies. In most cases groups relied on the efforts of both men and women to secure enough food to survive, but with men most often specializing in hunting larger animals and women in gathering foods and trapping smaller prey. The balance between male and female contributions to the group's sustenance varied depending on the season and environment. This division of labor underpinned what anthropologist Richard Lee called "relative equality between the sexes with no-one having the upper hand."[4] In his 1960s study of the San, a surviving gathering and hunting society in southern Africa, he recorded that teenagers engaged quite freely in sex play, and the concept of female virginity was apparently unknown, as were rape, wife beating, and the sexual double standard. Although polygamy was permitted, most marriages were in fact monogamous because women strongly resisted sharing a husband with another wife. Frequent divorce among very young couples allowed women to leave unsatisfactory marriages easily. Lee found that longer-term marriages seemed to be generally fulfilling and stable. Both men and women expected a satisfying sexual relationship, and both occasionally took lovers, although discreetly.

When the British navigator and explorer Captain James Cook first encountered the gathering and hunting peoples of Australia in 1770, he described them, perhaps a little enviously, in this way:

> They live in a Tranquillity which is not disturb'd by the Inequality of Conditions: The Earth and sea of their own accord furnishes them with all things necessary for life, they covet not Magnificent houses, Household-stuff. . . . In short they seem'd to set no value upon any thing we gave them. . . . They think themselves provided with all the necessarys of Life.[5]

The Europeans who settled permanently among such people some twenty years later, however, found a society in which physical competition among men was expressed in frequent one-on-one combat and in formalized but bloody battles. It also meant recurrent, public, and quite brutal beatings of wives by their husbands.[6] The San in southern Africa also experienced conflict and sometimes violence around the distribution of meat, the laziness or stinginess of particular people, and rivalries among men over women. More generally, recent studies have found that in Paleolithic societies some 15 percent of deaths occurred through violence at the hands of other people, a rate far higher than in later civilizations, where violence was largely monopolized by the state.[7] Although sometimes romanticized by outsiders, the relative equality of Paleolithic societies did not always ensure a utopia of social harmony.

Like all other human cultures, Paleolithic societies had rules and structures. A gender-based division of labor usually cast men as hunters and women as gatherers. Values emphasizing reciprocal sharing of goods resulted in clearly defined rules about distributing the meat from an animal kill. Various rules about incest and adultery governed sexual behavior, while understandings about who could hunt or gather in particular territories regulated economic activity. Leaders arose as needed to organize a task such as a hunt, but permanent power was not conferred on individuals.

Economy and the Environment

For a long time, modern people viewed their gathering and hunting ancestors as primitive and impoverished, barely eking out a living from the land. In more recent decades, anthropologists studying contemporary Paleolithic societies — those that survived into the twentieth century — began to paint a different picture. They noted that gathering and hunting people frequently worked fewer hours to meet their material needs than did people in agricultural or industrial societies and so had more leisure time. One scholar referred to them as **"the original affluent society,"** not because they had so much but because they wanted or needed so little.[8] Nonetheless, life expectancy was low, probably little more than thirty-five years on average. Life in the wild was surely dangerous, and dependency on the vagaries of nature rendered it insecure as well.

But Paleolithic people also acted to alter the natural environment substantially. The use of deliberately set fires in the landscape to encourage the growth of particular plants certainly changed the environment and in Australia led to the proliferation of fire-resistant eucalyptus trees at the expense of other plant species. In many ecosystems, especially small ones like Pacific islands, the arrival of humans resulted in the rapid extinction of some native plants and animals. In Australia and North America the majority of large animals disappeared long before our ancestors learned to farm or fashion weapons from metal. Other hominid, or human-like, species (such as the Neanderthals, Denisovans, or "Flores man," discovered in 2003 in Indonesia) also perished after living side by side with *Homo sapiens* for millennia. Whether their disappearance occurred through massacre, interbreeding, peaceful competition, or something unrelated to the human presence, ultimately they did not survive the rise of humankind. Thus the biological environment inhabited by gathering and hunting peoples was not wholly natural but was shaped in part by their own hands.

The Realm of the Spirit

The religious or spiritual dimension of Paleolithic culture has been hard to pin down, because bones and stones tell us little about what people thought, art is subject to many interpretations, and the experience of contemporary gathering and hunting peoples may not reflect the distant past. The recent discovery, for instance, of a variety of bone and ivory flutes in Germany — the earliest dating to 42,000 to 43,000 years ago — has shown that our ancestors created music. Although we do not know how this music was used, we do have clear evidence for a distinctive spiritual life. The presence of rock art deep inside caves and far from living spaces suggests a "ceremonial space" separate from ordinary life. The extended rituals of contemporary Australian Aboriginals, which sometimes last for weeks, confirm this impression, as do numerous and elaborate burial sites found throughout the world. No full-time religious specialists or priests led these ceremonies, but part-time **shamans** (people believed to be especially skilled at dealing with the spirit world) emerged as the need arose. Such people sometimes entered an altered state of consciousness or a trance while performing the ceremonies, often with the aid of psychoactive drugs.

Precisely how Paleolithic people understood the nonmaterial world is hard to reconstruct, and speculation abounds. Linguistic evidence from ancient Africa

The Willendorf Venus Less than four and a half inches in height and dating to about 25,000 years ago, this female figure, which was found near the town of Willendorf in Austria, has become the most famous of the many Venus figurines. Certain features — the absence of both face and feet, the coils of hair around her head, the prominence of her breasts and sexual organs — have prompted much speculation among scholars about the significance of these intriguing carvings. (Ali Meyer/ Bridgeman Images)

suggests a variety of understandings: some Paleolithic societies were apparently monotheistic; others saw several levels of supernatural beings, including a creator deity, various territorial spirits, and the spirits of dead ancestors; still others believed in an impersonal force suffused throughout the natural order that could be accessed by shamans during a trance dance.[9] Some, but not all, scholars have identified a strongly feminine dimension to Paleolithic religious thought that may be linked to regeneration and renewal of life.[10] Many gathering and hunting peoples likely developed a cyclical view of time derived from recurring natural cycles: sunrise and sunset; changing seasons; the phases of the moon; patterns of female fertility—birth, menstruation, pregnancy, new birth—and, of course, life, death, and new life. These understandings of the cosmos, which saw endlessly repeated patterns of regeneration and disintegration, differed from later Western views, which saw time moving in a straight line toward some predetermined goal. Nor did Paleolithic people make sharp distinctions between the material and spiritual worlds, for they understood that animals, rocks, trees, mountains, and much more were animated by spirits.

Settling Down: The Great Transition

Though glacially slow by contemporary standards, changes in Paleolithic cultures occurred over time as people moved into new environments, as populations grew, as climates altered, and as different human groups interacted with one another. For example, all over the Afro-Eurasian world after 25,000 years ago, a tendency toward the miniaturization of stone tools is evident, analogous perhaps to the miniaturization of electronic components in the twentieth century. Known as micro-blades, these smaller and more refined spear points, arrowheads, knives, and scrapers were carefully struck from larger cores and often mounted in antler, bone, or wooden handles. Another important change involved the collection of wild grains, a major addition to the food supply beyond the use of roots, berries, and nuts.

But the most striking and significant change in the lives of Paleolithic peoples occurred as the last Ice Age came to an end between 10,000 and 16,000 years ago. What followed was a general global warming, though one with periodic fluctuations and cold snaps. Unlike the contemporary global warming, generated by human activity and especially the burning of fossil fuels, this ancient warming phase was a wholly natural phenomenon, part of a long cycle of repeated heating and cooling characteristic of the earth's climatic history. Plants and animals that had struggled in the Ice Age climate now flourished and increased their range, providing a much richer and more diverse environment for many human societies. Under these improved conditions, human populations grew, and some previously nomadic gathering and hunting communities, but not all of them, found it possible to settle down and live in more permanent settlements or villages. These societies were becoming both larger and more complex, and it was less possible to simply move away if trouble struck. Settlement also meant that households could store and accumulate goods to a greater degree than previously. Because some people were more energetic, more talented, or luckier than others, the thin edge of inequality gradually began to wear away the egalitarianism of Paleolithic communities.

Changes along these lines emerged in many places. Paleolithic societies in Japan, known as Jomon, settled down in villages by the sea, where they greatly expanded the number of animals, both land and marine, that they consumed. They also created some of the world's first pottery, along with dugout canoes, paddles, bows, bowls, and tool handles, all made from wood. A similar pattern of permanent settlement, a broader range of food sources, and specialized technologies occurred in parts of Scandinavia, Eastern Europe, Southeast Asia, North America, and the Middle East between 4,000 and 12,000 years ago. In Labrador, longhouses appear in the archeological record between 3,500 and 7,500 years ago, some of them accommodating 100 people. Far more elaborate burial sites in many places testify to the growing complexity of human communities and the kinship systems that bound them together. Separate cemeteries for dogs suggest that humankind's best friend was also our first domesticated animal. Some of the most stunning and unexpected achievements of such sedentary Paleolithic people come from the archeological complex of **Göbekli Tepe** (goh-BEHK-lee TEH-peh) in southeastern Turkey.

Studies of more recent gathering and hunting societies that settled permanently in particular resource-rich areas have found that these societies differed markedly from their more nomadic counterparts. Among the Chumash of southern California, for example, early Spanish settlers found peoples who had developed substantial and permanent structures accommodating up to seventy persons; hereditary political elites; elements of a market economy, including the use of money and private ownership of some property; and the beginnings of class distinctions. The Haida and Tlingit peoples of southern Alaska even practiced hereditary slavery.

This **Paleolithic settling down** — and the changes that followed from it — marked a major turn in human history, away from countless millennia of nomadic journeys by very small communities. It also provided the setting within which the next great transition would occur. Growing numbers of men and women, living in settled communities, placed a much greater demand on the environment than did small bands of people on the move. Therefore, it is perhaps not surprising that among the innovations that emerged in some of these more complex gathering and hunting societies was yet another way for increasing the food supply — agriculture.

Breakthroughs to Agriculture

The chief feature of the long Paleolithic era — and the first human process to operate on a global scale — was the initial settlement of the earth. Then, beginning around 12,000 years ago, a second global pattern began to unfold — agriculture. The terms "Neolithic (New Stone Age) Revolution" and "Agricultural Revolution" both refer to the deliberate cultivation of particular plants as well as the taming and breeding of particular animals. Thus a whole new way of life gradually replaced the earlier practices of gathering and hunting in most parts of the world. Although it took place over centuries and millennia, the coming of agriculture represented a genuinely revolutionary transformation of human life all across the planet and provided the foundation for almost everything that followed: growing populations, settled farming villages, animal-borne diseases, cities, states, empires, civilizations, writing, literature, and much more.

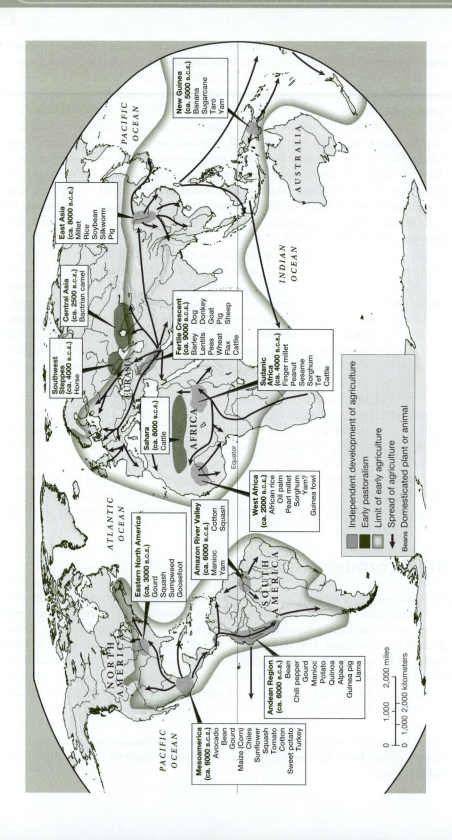

Among the most revolutionary aspects of the age of agriculture was a new relationship between humankind and other living things, for now men and women were not simply using what they found in nature but actively changing nature as well. Farmers stamped the landscape with a human imprint in the form of fields with boundaries, terraced hillsides, irrigation ditches, and canals. They also consciously "directed" the process of evolution. Farmers in the Americas, for example, transformed corn from a plant with a cob of an inch or so to one measuring about six inches by 1500. Later efforts more than doubled that length. Animals too were transformed, as selective breeding produced sheep that grew more wool, cows that gave more milk, and chickens that laid more eggs than their wild counterparts. This was "domestication"—the taming, and the changing, of nature for the benefit of humankind. In many agricultural communities, however, gathering, hunting, and fishing did not quickly disappear, but long continued to supplement agriculture and animal husbandry.

A further revolutionary aspect of the agricultural age is summed up in the term "intensification." It means getting more for less, in this case more food and resources—far more—from a much smaller area of land than was possible with a gathering and hunting technology. More food meant more people. Growing populations in turn required an even more intensive exploitation of the environment. Thus was launched the continuing effort to "fill the earth and subdue it," as the biblical story in Genesis recorded God's command to humankind.

Common Patterns

Perhaps the most extraordinary feature of the Neolithic or Agricultural Revolution was that it occurred, separately and independently, in many widely scattered parts of the world: the Fertile Crescent of Southwest Asia, several places in sub-Saharan Africa, China, New Guinea, Mesoamerica, the Andes, and eastern North America (see Map 1.3). Even more remarkably, all of this took place at roughly the same time (at least as measured by the several-hundred-thousand-year span of human history on the planet)—between 4,000 and 12,000 years ago. So why was the Agricultural Revolution so late in the history of humankind? What was unique about the period after 10,000 B.C.E. that may have triggered or facilitated this vast upheaval? In what different ways did the Agricultural Revolution take shape in its various locations? How did it spread from its several points of origin to the rest of the earth? And what impact did it have on the making of human societies?

It is surely no accident that the Agricultural Revolution coincided with the end of the last Ice Age, a process of global warming that began some 16,000 years ago. By about 11,000 years ago, the Ice Age was over, and climatic conditions were roughly similar to those of our own time. Ice ages had come and gone earlier in the earth's history, caused by minor periodic changes in the earth's orbit around the sun. The end of the last Ice Age, however, coincided with the migration of *Homo sapiens* across

< MAP 1.3 The Global Spread of Agriculture and Pastoralism
From nine or more separate points of origin, agriculture spread to adjacent areas, eventually encompassing almost all of the world's peoples.

the planet and created new conditions that made agriculture more possible in some areas, even as rising sea levels inundated other regions (see Map 1.1). Combined perhaps with active hunting by human societies, climate change in some places helped to push into extinction various species of large mammals on which Paleolithic people had depended, thus adding to the pressure to find new food sources. The warmer, wetter, and more stable conditions, particularly in the tropical and temperate regions of the earth, also permitted the flourishing of more wild plants, especially cereal grasses, which were the ancestors of many domesticated crops. What climate change took away with one hand, it apparently gave back with the other.

Over their long history, gathering and hunting peoples had already developed a deep knowledge of the natural world and, in some cases, the ability to manage it actively. They had learned to make use of a large number of plants and to hunt and eat both small and large animals, creating what archeologists call a "broad-spectrum diet." In the Middle East, people had developed sickles for cutting newly available wild grain, baskets to carry it, mortars and pestles to remove the husk, and storage pits to preserve it. In hindsight, much of this looks like a kind of unintentional preparation for agriculture. Because women in particular had long been intimately associated with collecting wild plants, they were the likely innovators who led the way to deliberate farming, with men perhaps taking the lead in domesticating animals.

Using available technologies, and benefiting from the global warming at the end of the last Ice Age, gathering and hunting peoples in various resource-rich areas were able to settle down and establish more permanent villages, abandoning their nomadic ways and more intensively exploiting the local area. In settling down, however, they found themselves now required to support growing populations. Evidence for increasing human numbers around the world during this period of global warming has persuaded some scholars that agriculture was a response to the need for additional food, perhaps even a "food crisis." Such conditions surely motivated people to experiment and to innovate in an effort to increase the food supply. Clearly, some of the breakthroughs to agriculture occurred only *after* gathering and hunting peoples had already grown substantially in numbers and had established a sedentary way of life.

These were some of the common patterns that facilitated the Agricultural Revolution. New opportunities appeared with the altered climatic conditions at the end of the Ice Age. New knowledge and technology emerged as human communities explored and exploited that changed environment. The disappearance of many large mammals, growing populations, newly settled ways of life, and fluctuations in the process of global warming—all of these represented pressures or incentives to increase food production and thus to minimize the risks of life in a new era. From some combination of these challenges, opportunities, and incentives emerged the profoundly transforming process of the Agricultural Revolution.

Variations

This new way of life initially operated everywhere with a simple technology—the digging stick or hoe. Plows were developed much later. But the several transitions to this hoe-based agriculture, commonly known as horticulture, varied considerably, depending on what plants and animals were available locally. For example, potatoes were found in the Andes region, but not in Africa or Asia; wheat and wild pigs existed in the Fertile Crescent, but not in the Americas (see Map 1.3). Furthermore, of the world's 200,000 plant species, only several hundred have been domesticated, and in more recent centuries just five of these — wheat, corn, rice, barley, and sorghum — have supplied more than half of the calories that sustain human life. Only fourteen species of large mammals have been successfully domesticated, of which sheep, pigs, goats, cattle, and horses have been the most important. Thus the kind of Agricultural Revolution that unfolded in particular places depended very much on what happened to be available locally; in short, it depended on sheer luck.

Among the most favored areas — and the first to experience a full Agricultural Revolution — was the **Fertile Crescent**, an area sometimes known as Southwest Asia, consisting of present-day Iraq, Syria, Israel/Palestine, Jordan, and southern Turkey (see Map 1.4). In this region, an extraordinary variety of wild plants and animals capable of domestication provided a rich array of species on which the now largely settled gathering and hunting people could draw. What triggered the transition to agriculture remains a much-debated question. Some have argued that a cold and dry spell between 11,000 and 9500 B.C.E., a quite rapid but temporary interruption in the general process of global warming, was the stimulus for the transition to farming. Larger settled populations, now threatened with the loss of the wild plants

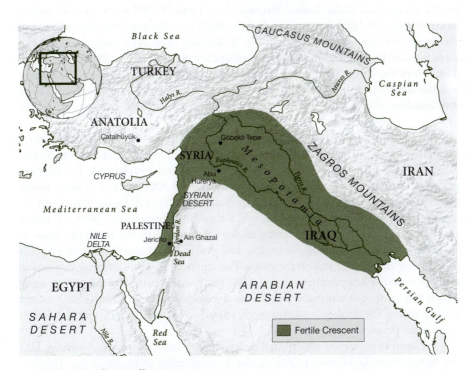

MAP 1.4   The Fertile Crescent
Located in Southwest Asia, the Fertile Crescent was the site of many significant processes in early world history, including a major breakthrough to agriculture and later the development of one of the First Civilizations.

and animals on which they had come to depend, found a solution in domestication, either during or soon after this cold and dry period passed. Figs were apparently the first cultivated crop, dating to about 9400 B.C.E. In the millennium or so that followed, wheat, barley, rye, peas, lentils, sheep, goats, pigs, and cattle all came under human control, providing the foundation for the world's first agricultural societies.

Archeological evidence suggests that the transition to a fully agricultural way of life in parts of this region took place quite quickly, within as few as 500 years. But newly agricultural communities could also collapse, particularly in less favored locations when climate change, soil degradation, or other factors made farming unsustainable. Over a thousand years or more a site could be occupied and abandoned several times, reminding us of the uncertainty that came with this new way of life. As the Agricultural Revolution took hold, signs of that transformation included large increases in the size of settlements, which now housed as many as several thousand people. In these agricultural settings, archeologists have found major innovations: the use of sun-dried mud bricks; the appearance of shrine-like buildings; displays of cattle skulls; more elaborate human burials, including the removal of the skull; and more sophisticated tools, such as new types of sickles, polished axes, and awls.

At roughly the same time, or perhaps a bit later, another process of domestication was unfolding on the African continent in the eastern part of what is now the Sahara in present-day Sudan. Between 5,000 and 10,000 years ago, this region received more rainfall than it currently does, had extensive grassland vegetation, and was "relatively hospitable to human life."[11] During these millennia, domesticated cattle appeared in the region, though whether they were tamed locally or were introduced from the Fertile Crescent is still debated. Around 6,000 years ago, the donkey was also domesticated in northeastern Africa near the Red Sea and spread from there into Southwest Asia, even as the practice of raising sheep and goats moved in the other direction.

In terms of farming, the African pattern again was somewhat different. Unlike the Fertile Crescent, where a number of plants were domesticated in a small area, sub-Saharan Africa witnessed the emergence of several widely scattered farming practices, with most crops being established by around 2000 B.C.E. Sorghum, which grows well in arid conditions, was the first grain to be "tamed" in the eastern Sahara region. In the highlands of Ethiopia, teff, a tiny, highly nutritious grain, as well as enset, a relative of the banana, came under cultivation. In the forested region of West Africa, yams, oil palm trees, okra, and the kola nut (used as a flavoring for cola drinks) emerged as important crops. The scattered location of these domestications generated a less productive agriculture than in the more favored and compact Fertile Crescent, but a number of African domesticates—sorghum, castor beans, gourds, millet, the donkey—subsequently spread to enrich the agricultural practices of Eurasian peoples.

Yet another pattern of agricultural development took shape in the Americas. Like the Agricultural Revolution in Africa, the domestication of plants in the Americas occurred separately in a number of locations—in the coastal Andean regions of western South America, in Mesoamerica, in the Mississippi River valley, and perhaps in the Amazon basin. Surely the most distinctive common feature of these regions was the relative absence of animals that could be domesticated. Of the fourteen major species of large mammals that have been brought under human control, just two, the

The Statues of Ain Ghazal Among the largest of the early agricultural settlements investigated by archeologists is that of Ain Ghazal, located in the modern state of Jordan. Inhabited from about 7200 to 5000 B.C.E., in its prime it was home to some 3,000 people, who lived in stone houses; cultivated barley, wheat, peas, beans, chickpeas, and lentils; and herded domesticated goats. These remarkable statues, between two and three feet tall and made of limestone plaster applied to a core of bundled reeds, were among the most startling finds at that site. Did they represent heroes, gods, ancestors, or ordinary people? No one really knows. (Courtesy, Department of Antiquities of Jordan [DoA]/Photo by John Tsantesi, Courtesy, Dr. Gary O. Rollefson)

llama and alpaca, existed in the Western Hemisphere, and only in the Andes region, where they proved enormously useful for food, fiber, and transportation. Without goats, sheep, pigs, cattle, or horses, the peoples of the Americas lacked sources of protein, manure (for fertilizer), and power (to draw plows or pull carts, for example) that were widely available to societies in the Afro-Eurasian world. Because they could not depend on domesticated animals for meat, many agricultural peoples in the Americas relied more on hunting and fishing than did peoples in the Eastern Hemisphere. While the Americas lacked the cereal grains that were widely available in Afro-Eurasia, they had **maize**, or corn, first domesticated in southern Mexico by 4000 to 3000 B.C.E. Unlike the cereal grains of the Fertile Crescent, which closely resemble their wild predecessors, the ancestor of corn was a mountain grass that looks nothing like what we now know as corn or maize. Thousands of years of selective adaptation were required to develop a sufficiently large cob and number of kernels to sustain a productive agriculture, an achievement that one geneticist has called "arguably man's first, and perhaps his greatest, feat of genetic engineering."[12] Beyond maize, Native American farmers domesticated squash, beans, potatoes, sunflowers, quinoa, pigweed, and goosefoot, which were harvested on a large scale.

Another difference in the unfolding of the Agricultural Revolution lay in the north/south orientation of the Americas, which required agricultural practices to move through, and adapt to, quite distinct climatic and vegetation zones if they were to spread. The east/west axis of North Africa / Eurasia meant that agricultural innovations could spread more rapidly because they were entering roughly similar environments. Thus corn, beans, and squash, which were first domesticated in Mesoamerica, took several thousand years to travel the few hundred miles from their Mexican homeland to the southwestern United States and another thousand years or more to arrive in eastern North America. The llama, guinea pig, quinoa, and potato, which were domesticated in the Andean highlands, never reached Mesoamerica.

The Globalization of Agriculture

From the various places where it originated, agriculture spread gradually to much of the rest of the earth, although for a long time it coexisted with gathering and hunting ways of life, even as it eroded and diminished those practices. Broadly speaking, this extension of farming occurred in two ways. The first, known as diffusion, refers to the gradual spread of agricultural techniques, and perhaps of the plants and animals themselves, but without the extensive movement of agricultural people. Neighboring groups exchanged ideas and products in a down-the-line pattern of communication. A second process involved the slow colonization or migration of agricultural peoples as growing populations pushed them outward.

Triumph and Resistance

Some combination of diffusion and migration underpinned the spread of agriculture to new regions, and the adoption of farming practices was at times accompanied by the spread of languages as well. For instance, between 6500 and 4000 B.C.E. the agricultural package (crops, domesticated animals, technologies) of Southwest Asia spread into Europe, Central Asia, Egypt, and North Africa. In the case of Europe, the adoption of agriculture was accompanied by the spread into the region of Indo-European languages, which had originated further east in Anatolia or, as some scholars suggest, in the area north of the Black and Caspian seas. Within Africa, the development of agricultural societies in the southern half of the continent is associated with the **Bantu migrations**, the movement of peoples speaking one or another of the some 400 Bantu languages. Beginning from what is now southern Nigeria or Cameroon around 3000 B.C.E., Bantu-speaking people moved east and south over the next several millennia, taking with them their agricultural, cattle-raising, and, later, ironworking skills, as well as their languages. They generally absorbed, killed, or drove away the indigenous Paleolithic peoples or exposed them to animal-borne diseases to which they had no immunities. A similar process brought agricultural Austronesian-speaking people, who originated in southern China, to the Philippine and Indonesian islands, with similar consequences for their earlier inhabitants (see Map 1.2).

The globalization of agriculture was a prolonged process, lasting 10,000 years or more after its first emergence in the Fertile Crescent, but it did not take hold everywhere. The Agricultural Revolution in highland New Guinea, for example, generated domesticated plants such as yams, taro, bananas, and sugarcane. But while these spread to parts of Island Southeast Asia, they did not pass to the nearby peoples of Australia, who remained steadfastly committed to gathering and hunting ways of life. The people of the west coast of North America, arctic regions, and southwestern Africa also maintained their gathering and hunting economies into the modern era.

Some of those who resisted the swelling tide of agriculture lived in areas unsuitable for farming, such as harsh desert or arctic environments; others lived in regions of particular natural abundance, so they felt little need for agriculture. Such societies found it easier to resist agriculture if they were not in the direct line of advancing, more powerful farming people. Many of the remaining gathering and hunting peoples knew about agricultural practices from nearby neighbors, suggesting that they quite deliberately chose to resist it in favor of the freer life of their Paleolithic ancestors. Nonetheless, by the beginning of the Common Era (see "Time and World History" in Part 1), the global spread of agriculture had reduced gathering and hunting peoples to a small and dwindling minority of humankind.

The Culture of Agriculture

In many accounts, the Agricultural Revolution is presented as "progress"—a great leap forward—for humankind. If evolutionary success or an increase in numbers is a measure of progress, then the Agricultural Revolution certainly fits that description, for it led to a substantial increase in human population, as the greater productivity of agriculture was able to support many more people. By 8000 B.C.E. an early agricultural settlement uncovered near Jericho in the West Bank probably had 2,000 to 3,000 people, a vast increase in the size of human communities compared to much smaller Paleolithic bands. On a global level, many scholars believe that between 12,000 years ago, when the Agricultural Revolution began, and the beginning of the Common Era the human population had grown from fewer than 10 million to as many as 150 to 300 million, an unprecedented number. Here was the real beginning of the human dominance over other forms of life on the planet.

That dominance was reflected in major environmental transformations. In a growing number of places, forests and grasslands became cultivated fields and grazing lands. Human selection modified the genetic composition of numerous plants and animals. In parts of the Middle East, within a thousand years after the beginning of settled agricultural life, some villages were abandoned when soil erosion and deforestation led to declining crop yields, which could not support mounting populations. Human life too changed dramatically in farming communities, for agriculture usually required a settled, village-based way of life. An example of such an early agricultural settlement, now called **Banpo**, has been uncovered in northern China, dating to around 6,000 years ago. Millet, pigs, and dogs had been domesticated, but diets were supplemented with wild plants, animals, and fish. Some forty-five houses covered with thatch laid over wooden beams provided homes to perhaps 500 people. More than 200 storage pits permitted the accumulation of grain, and six kilns and pottery wheels enabled the production of various pots, vases, and dishes, many decorated with geometric designs and human and animal images. A large central space suggests an area for public religious or political activity, and a trench surrounding the village indicates some common effort to defend the community.

But beyond growing populations, did such villages represent "progress," so often associated with the Agricultural Revolution? Farming involved hard work and more of it than in many earlier gathering and hunting societies. The remains of early agricultural people show some deterioration in health — more tooth decay, malnutrition, anemia, slipped disks, arthritis, and hernias; a shorter physical stature; and diminished life expectancy. Living close to animals subjected humans to new diseases — smallpox, flu, measles, chicken pox, malaria, tuberculosis, rabies — while living in larger communities generated epidemics for the first time in human history. Furthermore, since farming peoples often relied heavily on a single plant (rice, wheat, or potatoes), they were vulnerable to famine in case of crop failure, drought, or other catastrophes, while their foraging ancestors had drawn on a much wider range of food resources. The advent of agriculture bore costs as well as benefits.

Agricultural villages, however, also generated an explosion of technological innovation. Mobile Paleolithic peoples had little use for pots, but such vessels were essential for settled societies, and their creation and elaboration accompanied agriculture everywhere. So too did the weaving of textiles, made possible by collecting the fibers of domesticated plants (cotton and flax, for example) and raising animals such as sheep. Evidence for the invention of looms of several kinds dates back to 7,000 years ago, and textiles, some elaborately decorated, show up in Peru, Switzerland, China, and Egypt. Like agriculture itself, weaving was a technology in which women were probably the primary innovators, as it was a task compatible with their childbearing and child-rearing responsibilities. Another technology associated with the Agricultural Revolution was metallurgy. The working of gold and copper, then bronze, and, later, iron became part of the jewelry-, tool-, and weapon-making skill set of humankind. The long "stone age" of human technological history was coming to an end, and the age of metals was beginning.

Nok Culture The agricultural and iron-using Nok culture of northern Nigeria in West Africa generated a remarkable artistic tradition of terra-cotta, or fired-clay, figures depicting animals and, especially, people. This one dates to somewhere between 500 B.C.E. and 50 C.E. Some scholars have dubbed this and many similar Nok sculptures "thinkers." Does this notion reflect a present-day sensibility, or is it an insight into the mentality of the ancient artist who created the image? (Werner Forman Archive/Bridgeman Images)

A further set of technological changes, beginning around 4000 B.C.E., has been labeled the **secondary products revolution**.[13] These technological innovations involved new uses for domesticated animals, beyond their meat and hides. Agricultural people in parts of Europe, Asia, and Africa learned to milk their animals, to harvest their wool, and to enrich the soil with their manure. Even more important, they learned to ride horses and to hitch various animals to plows and carts. Because these animals did not exist in the Americas, this revolutionary new source of power and transportation was available only in the Eastern Hemisphere.

If the Agricultural Revolution meant "progress" in certain ways, it also claimed many victims. While the farming frontier expanded relentlessly, gathering and hunting societies were almost everywhere eroded as foragers became farmers or married into farming communities; as diseases spread from agricultural neighbors; and as more powerful farming communities violently displaced Paleolithic peoples. The plaintive cry of Gudo Mahiya, recorded at the beginning of this chapter, was certainly an echo of many such laments over many centuries.

And what of the animals? Like their human counterparts, certain animals such as cattle, pigs, sheep, and chickens greatly increased their numbers as their habitats became global. But they lost, of course, the freedom of the wild as they lived under the constraint, and often the lash, of their human masters. Many suffered a much shortened life span as they were slaughtered at a young age for human consumption. Others were required to pull carts and plows or to transport humans on their backs, while some were castrated or branded. Mothers and their offspring were frequently separated shortly after birth. No wonder one scholar has called the Agricultural Revolution a "terrible catastrophe" for the majority of domesticated animals.[14] For humans and animals alike, reproductive success for the species often translated into great suffering for many individuals.

Social Variation in the Age of Agriculture

The resources generated by the Agricultural Revolution opened up vast new possibilities for the construction of human societies, but they led to no single or common outcome. Differences in the natural environment, the encounter with strangers, and, sometimes, deliberate choices gave rise to several distinct kinds of societies early on in the age of agriculture, all of which have endured into modern times.

Pastoral Societies

One variation of great significance grew out of the difference between the domestication of plants and the domestication of animals. Many societies made use of both, but in regions where farming was difficult or impossible — arctic tundra, certain grasslands, and deserts — some people came to depend far more extensively on their animals, such as sheep, goats, cattle, horses, camels, or reindeer. Animal husbandry was a "distinct form of food-producing economy," relying on the products of animals.[15] Those animals could turn grass or waste products into meat, fiber, hides, and milk; they were useful for transport and warfare; and they could walk to market. Known as herders, pastoralists, or nomads, peoples largely dependent on their domesticated animals emerged most prominently in Central Asia, the Arabian Peninsula, the Sahara, and parts of eastern and southern Africa. What they had in common was mobility, for they moved seasonally as they followed the changing patterns of the vegetation necessary as pasture for their animals. Some of these **pastoral societies** lived a nomadic existence of constant seasonal movement, but for others it was possible to live permanently in lowland areas and move animals to more mountainous pasturelands in the summer.

The particular animals central to pastoral economies differed from region to region. The domestication of horses by 4000 B.C.E. and the mastery of horseback-riding skills several thousand years later enabled the growth of pastoral peoples all across the steppes of Central Asia by the first millennium B.C.E. Although organized primarily in kinship-based clans or tribes, these nomads periodically created powerful military confederations that played a major role in the history of Eurasia for thousands of years. In the Inner Asian, Arabian, and Saharan deserts, domesticated camels enabled humans to live in forbidding environments. The grasslands south of the Sahara and in parts of eastern Africa supported cattle-raising pastoralists. In the Americas, llamas and alpacas were tremendously important in the economy of Andean civilizations, but only in a few pockets in the Andes did human communities rely as heavily on their domesticated animals as did the pastoral peoples of the Afro-Eurasian world.

The relationship between nomadic herders and their farming neighbors has been one of the enduring themes of Afro-Eurasian history. Frequently, it was a relationship

The Domestication of Animals Although farming often gets top billing in discussions of the Agricultural Revolution, the raising of animals was equally important, for they provided meat, pulling power, transportation (in the case of horses and camels), and manure. Animal husbandry also made possible pastoral societies, which were largely dependent on their domesticated animals. This rock art painting from the Sahara (now southeastern Algeria) dates to somewhere around 4000 B.C.E. and depicts an early pastoral community. The white ovals represent a group of huts or perhaps enclosures for animals. (Musée de l'Homme, Paris, France/Erich Lessing/Art Resource, NY)

of conflict, as pastoral peoples, unable to produce their own agricultural products, were attracted to the wealth and sophistication of agrarian societies and sought access to their richer grazing lands as well as their food crops and manufactured products. The biblical story of the deadly rivalry between two brothers — Cain, a "tiller of the ground," and Abel, a "keeper of sheep" — reflects this ancient conflict, which persisted well into modern times. But not all was conflict between pastoral and agricultural peoples. The more peaceful exchange of technologies, ideas, products, and people across the ecological frontier of pastoral and agricultural societies also served to enrich and to change both sides.

Within pastoral societies, the relative equality of men and women, characteristic of most Paleolithic societies, persisted, perhaps because women's work was so essential. Women were centrally involved in milking animals, in processing that milk, and in producing textiles such as felt, which was widely used in Central Asia for tents, beds, rugs, and clothing. Among the Saka pastoralists in what is now Azerbaijan, women rode horses and participated in battles along with men. A number of archeological sites around the Black Sea have revealed high-status women buried with armor, swords, daggers, and arrows. In the Xinjiang region of western China, still other women were buried with the apparatus of healers and shamans, strongly suggesting an important female role in religious life.

Agricultural Village Societies

For thousands of years, people practiced agriculture using digging sticks or hoes, rather than plows, and even after plows came into use, many societies continued with hoe-based or horticultural farming. Most such hoe-based agricultural peoples lived in settled villages such as Banpo or Jericho, but to varying degrees they continued to augment their agricultural livelihood with gathering, hunting, and fishing. They also retained much of the social and gender equality of gathering and hunting communities, as they continued to do without kings, chiefs, bureaucrats, or aristocracies.

An example of an agricultural village society can be found at **Çatalhüyük** (cha-TAHL-hoo-YOOK), a very early settlement in southern Turkey that flourished between 7400 and 6000 B.C.E. A careful excavation of the site revealed a population of several thousand people who buried their dead under their houses and then filled the houses with dirt and built new ones on top, layer upon layer. No streets divided the houses, which were constructed adjacent to one another. People moved about the village on adjoining rooftops, from which they entered their homes. Despite the presence of many specialized crafts, few signs of inherited social inequality have surfaced. Nor is there any indication of male or female dominance, although men were more closely associated with hunting wild animals and women with plants and agriculture. "Both men and women," concludes one scholar, "could carry out a series of roles and enjoy a range of positions, from making tools to grinding grain and baking to heading a household."[16]

In many horticultural villages, women's critical role as farmers as well as their work in the spinning and weaving of textiles no doubt contributed to a social position of relative equality with men. Some such societies traced their descent through the female line and practiced marriage patterns in which men left their homes to live with their wives' families. Archeologist Marija Gimbutas has highlighted the prevalence of female imagery in the art of early agricultural societies in Europe and Anatolia, which has suggested to her a widespread cult of the Goddess, focused on "the mystery of birth, death and the renewal of life."[17] But early agriculture did not produce identical gender systems everywhere. Some societies practiced patrilineal descent and required a woman to live in the household of her husband. Grave sites in early Eastern European farming communities reveal fewer adult females than males, indicating perhaps the practice of female infanticide. Some early written evidence from China suggests a long-term preference for male children. These variations in practice suggest that gender roles were likely determined more by cultural preference than by any biological need for a sexual division of labor and power.

In all of their diversity, many village-based agricultural societies flourished well into the modern era, usually organizing themselves in terms of kinship groups or lineages that incorporated large numbers of people well beyond the immediate or extended family. Such a system provided the framework within which large numbers of people could make and enforce rules, maintain order, and settle disputes without going to war. In short, the lineage system performed the functions of government but without the formal apparatus of government, and thus did not require kings or queens, chiefs, or permanent officials associated with a state organization. Despite their democratic qualities and the absence of centralized authority, village-based lineage societies sometimes developed modest social and economic inequalities. Elders could exploit the labor of junior members of the community and sought particularly to control women's reproductive powers, which were essential for the growth of the lineage. People with special knowledge, skills, or experience could achieve higher status and greater influence. Among the Igbo of southern Nigeria well into the twentieth century, "title societies" enabled men and women of wealth and character to earn a series of increasingly prestigious "titles" that set them apart from other members of their community, although these honors could not be inherited. Lineages also sought to expand their numbers, and hence their prestige and power, by incorporating war captives or migrants in subordinate positions, sometimes as enslaved people.

Given the frequent oppressiveness of organized political power in human history, agricultural village societies represent an intriguing alternative to the states, kingdoms, and empires so often highlighted in the historical record. They pioneered the human settlement of vast areas; adapted to a variety of environments; maintained a substantial degree of social and gender equality; created numerous cultural, artistic, and religious traditions; and interacted continuously with their neighbors.

Chiefdoms

In other places, agricultural village societies came to be organized politically as **chiefdoms**, in which inherited positions of power and privilege introduced a more distinct element of inequality, but unlike later kings, chiefs could seldom use force to compel the obedience of their subjects. Instead, chiefs relied on their generosity or gift giving, their ritual status, or their personal charisma to persuade their followers.

While little is known about the earliest chiefdoms, they became a prominent feature of agricultural societies in many parts of the world. For example, chiefdoms emerged everywhere in the Pacific islands that had been colonized by agricultural Polynesian peoples. Chiefs usually derived from a senior lineage, tracing their descent to the first son of an imagined ancestor. With both religious and secular functions, chiefs led important rituals and ceremonies, organized the community for warfare, directed its economic life, and sought to resolve internal conflicts. They collected tribute from commoners in the form of food, manufactured goods, and raw materials. These items in turn were redistributed to warriors, craftsmen, religious specialists, and other subordinates, while chiefs kept enough to maintain their prestigious positions and imposing lifestyle. In North America as well, a remarkable series of chiefdoms emerged in the eastern woodlands, where an extensive array of large earthen mounds testify to the organizational capacity of these early societies. The largest of them, known as Cahokia, flourished around 1100 C.E. (See "North America: Ancestral Pueblo and Mound Builders" in Chapter 6.)

Thus the Agricultural Revolution radically transformed both the trajectory of the human journey and the evolution of life on the planet. This epic process granted to one species, *Homo sapiens*, a growing power over many other species of plants and animals and made possible an increase in human numbers far beyond what a gathering and hunting economy could support.

But if agriculture provided humankind with the power to dominate nature, it also, increasingly, enabled some people to dominate others. This was not immediately apparent, and for several thousand years, and much longer in some places, agricultural villages and pastoral communities retained elements of the social equality that had characterized much of Paleolithic life. Slowly, though, many of the resources released by the Agricultural Revolution accumulated in the hands of a few. Rich and poor, chiefs and commoners, landowners and dependent peasants, rulers and subjects, dominant men and subordinate women, enslaved and free people — these distinctions, so common in the record of world history, took shape most extensively in highly productive agricultural settings, which generated a substantial economic surplus. There the endless elaboration of such differences, for better or worse, became a major feature of those distinctive agricultural societies known to us as "civilizations."

Controversies: Debating the Timescales of History

So when does history begin? And does it matter?

If "history" refers to the story of humankind, professional historians until recently were largely in agreement that history began with writing, for as one book published in 1898 put it, "No documents, no history."[18] While humans clearly existed before writing — for hundreds of thousands of years, in fact — historians viewed their pasts as almost completely unrecoverable from the few physical remains that survived. They described these earlier peoples as prehistoric or "before history" and left their study to archeology and what was later called paleoanthropology. But writing emerged only about 5,500 years ago, and even then was limited to a few places. Furthermore, until the last several centuries writing was confined largely to elites, who wrote primarily about "the wars they fought, the literature they wrote, and the gods they worshipped."[19] Thus an understanding of the human journey based only on written records was massively skewed and incomplete.

From the mid-twentieth century onward, increasingly accurate and affordable scientific techniques—including radio-carbon dating, DNA testing, and advances in linguistics and archeology—allowed scholars to date artifacts and the movements of human populations that occurred tens or even hundreds of thousands of years ago. A much clearer understanding of early human history emerged as scholars were able to trace chronologically such crucial developments as the spread of our species across the planet and the dissemination of bronze-working technologies. The world before writing no longer seemed so unrecoverable, and many scholars—historians, archeologists, and others—broadened the definition of "history" to incorporate peoples of the distant past who had left no written record. While large gaps in our knowledge persisted, the new techniques opened up windows into the past that had been mostly shut before.

Even as historians debated the extent to which the "prehistory" of our species should or could be incorporated into historical accounts, a related question emerged about how—or whether—to locate all of human history within some greater context. Over the past several decades, some historians have begun to integrate the human story into the much larger frameworks of planetary and cosmic evolution, an approach that has come to be called "big history." Remarkable advances in the natural sciences—astronomy, geology, and evolutionary biology—suggest that the cosmos as a whole has a history, as do the stars, the solar system, the planets, including the earth, and life itself. They have a history because they have changed over time, for change is the fundamental feature of all historical accounts.

Such understandings have caused some to conclude that human history can be fully understood only if contextualized in the changing patterns of the cosmos. As the historian William McNeill has written, "Human beings, it appears, do indeed belong to the universe and share its unstable, evolving character . . . what happens among human beings and what happens among the stars looks to be part of a grand, evolving story."[20] Supporters of this view assert that big history "offers a powerful way of understanding the place of our own species, *Homo sapiens*, within the universe. By doing so it helps us to understand better what human history is all about."[21]

But not all historians agree with this perspective. Some critics of "big history" argue that its almost unimaginable timescales, measured in billions or many millions of years, leave too little room for the human story, reducing it to insignificance. The types of problems or questions that have long occupied professional historians, such as the legacies of the Chinese warring states period or the Great Depression of the 1930s, are worthy of little more than a mention in big history timescales. Others complain that the careful reading and analysis of documents have been replaced by scientific forms of inquiry. Is "big history," they ask, really history at all?

Whatever one may think of these debates, big history represents the latest chapter in a remarkable rethinking of when world history begins. At the turn of the twentieth century few historians could conceive of history beginning more than 6,000 years ago, but by the early twenty-first century some argue that the human story finds its most appropriate place in a process that began over thirteen billion years earlier.

Clearly the timescales of human history matter, because they shape the questions we ask and the techniques of inquiry that we employ. If we seek to understand the ups and downs of civilizations over the past five millennia, written records are essential. Without them, we would know little about the evolution of Buddhism, the rise and fall of empires, the Industrial Revolution, and much more. But if we want to know something of the process by which humans came to occupy almost every environmental niche on the earth, then written records are of little help, because almost all of that process took place long before writing was invented anywhere. So we must rely on DNA analysis, carbon dating, and linguistics.

Finally, when historians turn to the cosmic or "big history" timescale, they are motivated by still other concerns. For David Christian, one of the leading practitioners of "big history," that grand scale of things offers a "creation myth" for our times, a coherent and scientifically informed explanation of the origins and evolution of our universe and the place of humankind within it.[22] For those more philosophically or spiritually inclined, the "big history" outlook raises profound questions about the relationship of human history to the larger narrative of cosmic and planetary evolution. Does the human experiment represent the story of just one more species thrown up by the ceaseless transformations of the web of life on this planet? Or is human consciousness distinctive, representing perhaps the cosmos becoming aware of itself? In these perspectives the human story is solidly anchored within the unfolding of the universe, the geological transformations of the planet, and the evolution of life on the earth.

Conclusions and Reflections: History before Civilization

This initial chapter deals with over 250,000 years of the human story, in fact everything that occurred before the early civilizations and written languages of Mesopotamia, Egypt, China, India, and elsewhere began to emerge only some 5,500 years ago. Until quite recently, most accounts of human history have dismissed this enormous time period prior to the emergence of civilizations as "prehistory," unknowable or irrelevant. We disagree . . . strongly! There is much that scholars have uncovered about this early experience of humankind, and it is profoundly significant, even essential, in mapping the long arc of the human journey.

After millions of years of biological evolution, our species, *Homo sapiens*, appeared first in Africa some 260,000 to 350,000 years ago. Then sometime after 100,000 years ago, our ancestors began a remarkable migration out of Africa that took them to every inhabitable landmass on the planet. At the same time, they created "cultures," patterns of learned behavior, belief, and belonging that enabled the making of human societies. In doing so they used their complex brains, their capacity for symbolic language, and their ability to accumulate knowledge and pass it on. The economic foundation of these cultures consisted everywhere in the gathering of wild plants and the hunting or fishing of wild animals, using an increasingly sophisticated array of stone, bone, and wood tools and weapons. This was the Paleolithic era, comprising over 95 percent of the time that humans have lived on the earth.

Agriculture, the ability to domesticate both plants and animals, marked the end of the Paleolithic age and the beginning of the most profound transformation of human life in our entire history. Beginning only 12,000 years ago, the Agricultural Revolution utterly transformed human life. It required permanently settled village life; it enabled substantial population growth; its cultivated fields and grazing lands dramatically altered local ecosystems; it stimulated widespread technological innovation; it spread animal-borne diseases and epidemics; and it gave rise to farming villages, to pastoral societies that depended on their herds of animals, and in some places to chiefdoms. These were among the major changes of the Neolithic era, all of which occurred well before the cities, states, and written languages of the earliest civilizations.

Beyond its significance in offering a panoramic understanding of human experience, the world before civilization also merits our attention because it provides a lens through which more recent societies have evaluated themselves. For example, modern people were long inclined to view their Paleolithic or gathering and hunting ancestors as primitive or superstitious, unable to exercise control over nature, and ignorant of its workings. The seventeenth-century English philosopher Thomas Hobbes famously declared that human life in a "state of nature" — before civilization, organized governments, and laws — was inevitably "solitary, poore, nasty, brutish, and short."[23] Such a view was, of course, a kind of self-congratulation, designed to highlight the "progress" of modern humankind. It was a way of saying, "Look how far we have come."

In more recent decades, however, growing numbers of people, disillusioned with modernity, have looked to the Paleolithic era for material with which to criticize, rather than celebrate, contemporary life. Feminists have found in gathering and hunting peoples a much more gender-equal society and religious thinking that featured the divine feminine. Environmentalists have sometimes identified peoples in the distant past who were uniquely in tune with the natural environment rather than seeking to dominate and exploit it. Some nutritionists have advocated a "Paleolithic diet" of wild plants and animals as best suited to our physiology. Critics of modern materialism and competitive capitalism have been delighted to discover societies in which values of sharing and equality predominated over those of accumulation and hierarchy. Still others have asked, in light of the long Paleolithic era, whether the explosive population and economic growth of recent centuries should be considered normal or natural. Perhaps they are better seen as extraordinary, even pathological, as they threaten to destroy the fragile web of life on which everyone depends. All of these uses of the Paleolithic have been a way of asking, "What have we lost in the mad rush to modernity, and how can we recover it?"

Both those who look with disdain on Paleolithic "backwardness" and those who praise, often quite romantically, its simplicity and equality seek to use these ancient people for their own purposes. Nor is this surprising, for while history is about the past, it reflects always the concerns and outlook of those who study it in the present. Despite its remoteness from us in time and manner of living, the world before civilization resonates still in the twenty-first century, reminding us of our kinship with these distant people and enabling us to grasp a panoramic view of human story.

Revisiting Chapter 1

REVISITING SPECIFICS

REVISITING CORE IDEAS

1. **Describing Change** What was the sequence of human migration across the planet?
2. **Analyzing Change** In what ways did a gathering and hunting economy shape other aspects of Paleolithic societies?
3. **Explaining Change** What accounts for the emergence of agriculture after countless millennia of human life without it? Why did it occur so late in the story of humankind?
4. **Comparing Agricultural Revolutions** In what different ways did the Agricultural Revolution take shape in various parts of the world?
5. **Comparing Agricultural Societies** What different kinds of societies emerged out of the Agricultural Revolution?
6. **Assessing Change** What was revolutionary about the Agricultural Revolution?

A WIDER VIEW

1. In what different ways did human beings relate to the natural world during the early and long phases of our history explored in the chapter?
2. How do you understand the significance of the long Paleolithic era in the larger context of world history?
3. Was the Agricultural Revolution inevitable? Why did it occur so late in the story of humankind?
4. **Looking Back** What perspectives on human history emerge for you as you place it in the larger context of cosmic and planetary history as described briefly in the Prologue?

CHRONOLOGY

350,000–260,000	• Earliest *Homo sapiens*
120,000–12,000	• Ice Age glacial period
100,000	• Earliest evidence of human ritual activity: South Africa
100,000–60,000	• Permanent migration out of Africa into Eurasia
70,000	• Human entry into East Asia
60,000–40,000	• Human entry into Australia (first use of boats)
45,000	• Human entry into Europe
44,000	• Earliest surviving cave art in Indonesia
37,000	• Earliest surviving cave art in Europe
30,000	• Extinction of many large mammals in Australia
30,000–15,000	• Human entry into the Americas
13,000–11,000	• Clovis culture in North America
12,000–10,000	• Agricultural Revolution in the Fertile Crescent
12,000–4,000	• Earliest agricultural revolutions
11,000	• Extinction of many large mammals in North America
10,000	• Human population of 6 million
8,000	• Domestication of the donkey
6,000–5,000	• Domestication of horses
6,000–5,000	• Beginning of domestication of corn in southern Mexico
5,500	• Emergence of urban civilization
4,000–3,000	• Domestication of sorghum
4,000–3,000	• Domestication of potatoes in Andes region
3,500–1,000	• Austronesian migration to Pacific islands (and Madagascar)
1,000–800	• Human entry into New Zealand (last major region to receive human settlers)

Note: All dates are B.P. or Before the Present, and all dates are approximate.

2

First Civilizations

Cities, States, and Unequal Societies

3500 B.C.E.–600 B.C.E.

CONNECTING PAST AND PRESENT

"SOMETIMES THE WEIGHT OF CIVILIZATION can be overwhelming. The fast pace . . . the burdens of relationships . . . the political strife . . . the technological complexity—it's enough to make you dream of escaping to a simpler life more in touch with nature."[1] Found on the website of an organization called Mother Nature Network, this expression of discontent with modernity, written in 2010, reflects the perspectives of the back-to-the-land movement that began in the mid-1960s as an alternative to the pervasive materialism of modern life. Growing numbers of urban dwellers, perhaps as many as a million in North America, exchanged their busy city lives for a few acres of rural land and a very different way of living.

This urge to "escape from civilization" has long been a central feature in modern life. It found expression in Henry David Thoreau's musings on his sojourn at Walden Pond. It is a large part of the "cowboy" image in American culture, and it permeates environmentalist efforts to protect the remaining wilderness areas of the country. Nor has this impulse been limited to modern societies and the Western world. The ancient Chinese teachers of Daoism likewise urged their followers to abandon the structured and demanding world of urban and civilized life and to immerse themselves in the eternal patterns of the natural order. It is a strange paradox that we count the creation of civilizations among the major achievements of humankind and yet people within them have often sought to escape the constraints, artificiality, hierarchies, and other discontents of civilized living.

So what exactly are these civilizations that have generated such ambivalent responses among their inhabitants? When, where, and how did they first arise in human history? What changes did they bring to the people who lived within them? Why might some people criticize or seek to escape from them?

As historians commonly use the term, "civilization" represents a new and particular type of human society, made possible by the immense productivity of the Agricultural Revolution. Such societies encompassed far larger populations than any earlier form of human community and for the first time concentrated some of those people in sizable cities. Both within and beyond these cities, people were organized and controlled by states whose leaders could use force to compel obedience. Profound differences in economic function, skill, wealth, and status sharply divided the people of civilizations, making them far less equal and subject to much greater oppression than had been the case in earlier Paleolithic communities, agricultural villages, pastoral societies, or chiefdoms. Pyramids, temples, palaces, elaborate sculptures, written literature, and complex calendars, as well as more elaborate class and gender hierarchies, slavery, and large-scale warfare—all of these have been among the prominent features of civilization. Some of them had antecedents in earlier societies, and they emerged gradually as civilizations developed. But in the long view of world history, the emergence of civilizations marked a decisive and revolutionary transformation of human life.

| SEEKING THE MAIN POINT | What distinguished "civilizations" from earlier Paleolithic and Neolithic societies? And in what ways did these "civilizations" differ from one another? |

Something New: The Emergence of Civilizations

Like agriculture, civilization was a global phenomenon, showing up independently in seven major locations scattered around the world during the several millennia after 3500 B.C.E. and in a number of other smaller expressions as well (see Map 2.1). In the long run of human history, these civilizations—small breakthroughs to new city- and state-based societies—gradually absorbed, overran, or displaced people practicing other ways of living. Over the next 5,000 years, civilization, as a unique kind of human community, gradually encompassed ever-larger numbers of people and extended over ever-larger territories, even as particular civilizations rose, fell, revived, and changed.

Introducing the First Civilizations

The earliest of these civilizations emerged around 3500 B.C.E. to 3000 B.C.E. in three places. One was the "cradle" of Middle Eastern civilization, expressed in the many and competing city-states of **Sumer**. Sumer was located in the southern reaches of Mesopotamia, a term referring to the region between the Tigris and Euphrates rivers, mostly in present-day Iraq. Much studied by archeologists and historians, Sumerian civilization likely gave rise to the world's earliest written language, which was used initially by temple officials for record keeping. Later, Sumerian cities were absorbed by conquest into the larger empires of Akkad and Babylon, which encompassed much of Mesopotamia. Almost simultaneously, the Nile River valley in northeastern Africa witnessed the emergence of the civilization of **Egypt**, famous for its pharaohs and pyramids, as well as a separate civilization known as **Nubia**, farther south along the Nile. Unlike the city-states of Sumer, Egyptian civilization viewed itself as a uni- fied territorial state and sometimes came close to achieving this aspiration. Later in this chapter, we will compare these two First Civilizations in greater detail.

Less well known and only recently investigated by scholars was a third early civi- lization that was developing along the central coast of Peru from roughly 3000 B.C.E. to 1800 B.C.E., at about the same time as the civilizations of Egypt and Sumer. This desert region received very little rainfall, but it was punctuated by dozens of rivers that brought the snowmelt of the adjacent Andes Mountains to the Pacific Ocean. Along a thirty-mile stretch of that coast and in the nearby interior, a series of some twenty-five urban centers emerged in an area known as **Norte Chico**, the largest of which was **Caral**, in the Supe River valley.

Norte Chico was a distinctive civilization in many ways. Its cities were smaller than those of Sumer and show less evidence of economic specialization. The econ- omy was based to an unusual degree on an extremely rich fishing industry in ancho- vies and sardines along the coast. These items apparently were exchanged for cotton, essential for fishing nets, as well as food crops such as squash, beans, and guava, all of which were grown by inland people in the river valleys using irrigation agriculture. Unlike Egyptian and Sumerian societies, this Peruvian civilization did not rest on grain-based farming; its people did not develop pottery or writing; and few sculp- tures, carvings, or drawings have been uncovered so far. Furthermore, the cities of Norte Chico lacked defensive walls, and archeologists have discovered little evidence of warfare, such as burned buildings and mutilated corpses. Norte Chico apparently "lighted a cultural fire" in the Andes and established a pattern for the many Andean civilizations that followed—Chavín, Moche, Wari, Tiwanaku, and Inca.[2]

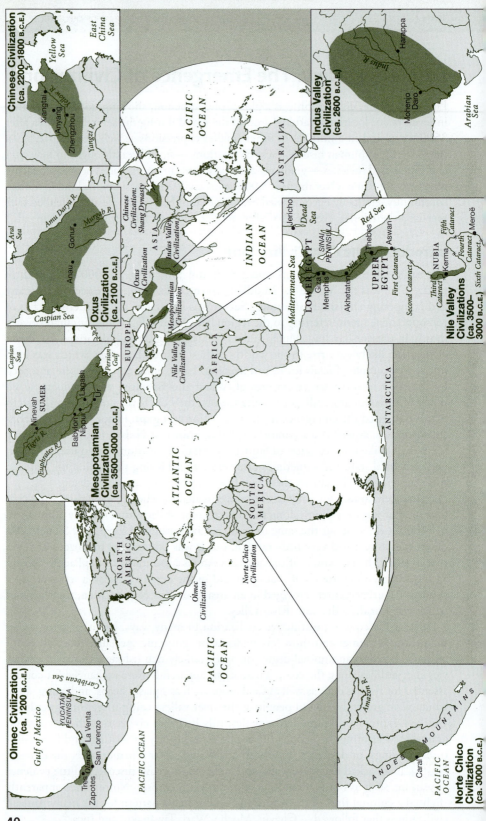

Chinese Civilization
(ca. 2200–1800 B.C.E.)

East China Sea

Yellow Sea

Yellow R.

Xiangtai
Anyang
Zhengzhou

Yangzi R.

Indus Valley Civilization
(ca. 2600 B.C.E.)

Indus R.

Harappa

Mohenjo Daro

Arabian Sea

PACIFIC OCEAN

ASIA

AUSTRALIA

Oxus Civilization
(ca. 2100 B.C.E.)

Aral Sea

Amu Darya R.

Murgab R.

Gonur

Anau

Caspian Sea

Chinese Civilization: Shang Dynasty

Oxus Civilization

Indus Valley Civilization

Mesopotamian Civilization

Nile Valley Civilizations

INDIAN OCEAN

EUROPE

AFRICA

Nile Valley Civilizations
(ca. 3500–3000 B.C.E.)

Jericho
Dead Sea
Mediterranean Sea
Red Sea

LOWER EGYPT
SINAI PENINSULA
Giza
Memphis
Akhetaten
Nile R.
Thebes
Aswan
UPPER EGYPT
First Cataract
Second Cataract
Third Cataract
NUBIA
Kerma
Fourth Cataract
Fifth Cataract
Meroë
Sixth Cataract

Mesopotamian Civilization
(ca. 3500–3000 B.C.E.)

Caspian Sea

SUMER
Nineveh
Tigris R.
Ur
Lagash
Nippur
Babylon
Euphrates R.
Persian Gulf

ATLANTIC OCEAN

NORTH AMERICA

SOUTH AMERICA

ANTARCTICA

Olmec Civilization

Norte Chico Civilization

PACIFIC OCEAN

Olmec Civilization
(ca. 1200 B.C.E.)

Caribbean Sea

YUCATÁN PENINSULA

Gulf of Mexico

La Venta
San Lorenzo
Tres Zapotes
Olmec

PACIFIC OCEAN

Norte Chico Civilization
(ca. 3000 B.C.E.)

Amazon R.

ANDES MOUNTAINS

Caral

PACIFIC OCEAN

40

Somewhat later, at least four additional First Civilizations made their appearance. In the Indus and Saraswati river valleys of what is now Pakistan, a remarkable civilization arose during the third millennium B.C.E. By 2000 B.C.E., it embraced a far larger area than Sumer, Egypt, or coastal Peru and was expressed primarily in its elaborately planned cities. All across this huge area, common patterns prevailed: standardized weights, measures, even the size of bricks. As elsewhere, irrigated agriculture provided the economic foundation for the civilization, and a written language, thus far undeciphered, provides evidence of a literate culture.

Unlike its Middle Eastern counterparts, the **Indus Valley civilization** apparently generated no palaces, temples, elaborate graves, kings, or warrior classes. In short, the archeological evidence provides little indication of a political hierarchy or centralized state. This absence of evidence has sent scholars scrambling to provide an explanation for the obvious specialization, coordination, and complexity that the Indus Valley civilization exhibited. A series of small republics or kingdoms, rule by merchant elites or priests, an early form of the caste system—all of these have been suggested as alternative mechanisms of integration in this first South Asian civilization. Although no one knows for sure, the possibility that the Indus Valley may have housed a sophisticated civilization without a corresponding state has excited the imagination of scholars.

Whatever its organization, the local environmental impact of the Indus Valley civilization, as of many others, was heavy and eventually undermined its ecological foundations. Crop yields were negatively impacted by the shifting courses of rivers, changes in climate and weather patterns, and intensive irrigation techniques that increased the amount of salt in the soil. The making of mud bricks, dried in ovens, required an enormous amount of wood for fuel, generating large-scale deforestation and soil erosion. Thus environmental degradation contributed significantly to the abandonment of these magnificent cities by about 1700 B.C.E. Nonetheless, many features of this early civilization—ceremonial bathing, burning of incense, ritual fire altars, yoga positions, styles of clothing and jewelry—continued to nourish the later civilization of the Indian subcontinent.[3]

The early Chinese civilization that emerged between 2200 B.C.E. and 1800 B.C.E. was very different from that of the Indus Valley. The ideal—if not always the reality—of a centralized state was evident from the days of the Xia (shyah) dynasty (2070–1600 B.C.E.), whose legendary monarch Wu organized flood control projects that "mastered the waters and made them to flow in great channels." Subsequent dynasties—the Shang (1600–1046 B.C.E.) and the Zhou (joh) (1046–771 B.C.E.)—substantially enlarged the Chinese state, erected lavish tombs for their rulers, and buried thousands of human sacrificial victims to accompany them in the next world. By the Zhou dynasty, a distinctive Chinese political ideology had emerged, featuring a ruler, known as the Son of Heaven. This monarch served as an intermediary between Heaven and Earth and ruled by the Mandate of Heaven only so long as he governed with benevolence and maintained social

< MAP 2.1 First Civilizations
Seven First Civilizations emerged independently in locations scattered across the planet, all within a few thousand years, from 3500 to 1200 B.C.E.

harmony among his people. This civilization also had writing; an early form of written Chinese has been discovered on numerous oracle bones, which were intended to predict the future and to assist China's rulers in the task of governing. Like Egypt, China has experienced an impressive continuity of identity as a distinct civilization from its earliest expression into modern times.

Central Asia was the site of yet another First Civilization. In the Oxus or Amu Darya River valley and nearby desert oases (what is now northern Afghanistan and southern Turkmenistan), a quite distinctive and separate civilization developed and flourished between 2100 and 1800 B.C.E. Within two centuries, a number of substantial fortified centers had emerged, containing residential compounds, artisan workshops, and temples, all surrounded by impressive walls and gates. Economically based on irrigation agriculture and stock raising, this **Central Asian or Oxus civilization** had a distinctive cultural style, expressed in its architecture, ceramics, burial techniques, seals, and more, though it did not develop a literate culture. Evidence for an aristocratic social hierarchy comes from depictions of gods and men in widely differing dress performing various functions, from eating

An Oxus Valley Axe Head Dating to around 2000 B.C.E., this exquisitely wrought axe head derives from the Oxus Valley civilization. It features in the center a heroic human figure with a bird's head and talons fighting with a wild boar on the upper right and a winged dragon on the lower left. (agefotostock Art Collection/AGE Fotostock)

at a banquet to driving chariots to carrying heavy burdens. Visitors to this civilization would have found occasional goods from China, India, and Mesopotamia, as well as products from pastoral nomads of the steppe land and the forest dwellers of Siberia. According to a leading historian, this Central Asian civilization was the focal point of a "Eurasian-wide system of intellectual and commercial exchange."[4] Compared to Egyptian and Mesopotamian civilizations, however, it had a relatively brief history, for by 1700 B.C.E., it had faded away as a civilization, at about the same time as a similar fate befell its Indus Valley counterpart. Its cities were abandoned and apparently forgotten until their resurrection by archeologists in the twentieth century. And yet its influence persisted, as elements of this civilization's cultural style show up much later in Iran, India, and the eastern Mediterranean world.

A final First Civilization, known as the Olmec, took shape around 1200 B.C.E. along the coast of the Gulf of Mexico near present-day Veracruz in southern Mexico. Based on an agricultural economy of maize, beans, and squash, Olmec cities arose from a series of competing chiefdoms and became ceremonial centers filled with elaborately decorated temples, altars, pyramids, and tombs of rulers. The most famous artistic legacy of the Olmecs lay in some seventeen colossal basalt heads, weighing twenty tons or more (see the Olmec head image, page 54). Recent discoveries suggest that the Olmecs may well have created the first written language in the Americas by about 900 B.C.E. Sometimes regarded as the "mother civilization" of Mesoamerica, **Olmec civilization** generated cultural patterns — mound building, artistic styles, urban planning, a game played with a rubber ball, ritual sacrifice, and bloodletting by rulers — that spread widely throughout the region and influenced subsequent civilizations, such as the Maya and Teotihuacán.

Beyond these seven First Civilizations, other smaller civilizations also flourished. Lying south of Egypt in the Nile Valley, an early Nubian civilization known as Ta-Seti (3200–3000 B.C.E.) was clearly distinctive and independent of its northern neighbor, although Nubia was later involved in a long and often contentious relationship with Egypt. Likewise in China, a large city known as Sanxingdui, rich in bronze sculptures and much else, arose separately but at the same time as the more well-known Shang dynasty. As a new form of human society, civilization was beginning its long march toward encompassing almost all of humankind by the twentieth century. At the time, however, these breakthroughs to new forms of culture and society were small islands of innovation in a sea of people living in much older ways.

The Question of Origins

Scholars of all kinds — archeologists, anthropologists, sociologists, and historians — have been arguing about the origins of civilization for a very long time, with no end in sight. Amid all the controversy, one thing seems reasonably clear: civilizations had their roots in the Agricultural Revolution. That is the reason they appeared so late in the human story, for only an agricultural technology permitted human communities to produce sufficient surplus to support large populations and the specialized or elite minorities who did not themselves produce food. But not all agricultural societies or chiefdoms developed into civilizations, so something else must have been involved. It is the search for this "something else" that has provoked such great debate among scholars.

Growing populations, the desire to protect favored groups, the stimulus of trade, the demands of warfare—all of these have figured in the debate about the origins of civilization. Geography surely played a role as well, for civilizations often took shape in biologically rich and productive environments such as wetlands, estuaries, and river basins. Anthropologist Robert Carneiro combined several of these factors in a thoughtful approach to the question. He argued that a growing density of population, producing more congested and competitive societies, was a fundamental motor of change, especially in areas where rich agricultural land was limited, either by geography (oceans, deserts, mountains) or by powerful neighboring societies. Such settings provided incentives for innovations, such as irrigation or plows that could produce more food, because opportunities for territorial expansion were not readily available. But circumscribed environments with dense populations also generated intense competition among rival groups, which led to repeated warfare. A strong and highly organized state was a decided advantage in such competition. Because losers could not easily flee to new lands, they were absorbed into the winner's society as a lower class. Successful leaders of the winning side emerged as elites with an enlarged base of land, a class of subordinated workers, and a powerful state at their disposal—in short, a civilization.[5]

Although such a process was relatively rapid by world history standards, it took many generations, centuries, or perhaps millennia to evolve. It was, of course, an unconscious undertaking in which the participants had little sense of the long-term outcome as they coped with the practical problems of life on a day-to-day basis. What is surprising, though, is the rough similarity of the outcome in many widely separated places from about 3500 B.C.E. to the beginning of the Common Era.

However they got started (and much about this is still guesswork), the First Civilizations, once established, represented a very different kind of human society than anything that came before. All of them were based on highly productive agricultural economies. Various forms of irrigation, drainage, terracing, and flood control enabled these early civilizations to tap the food-producing potential of their regions more intensively. All across the Afro-Eurasian hemisphere, though not in the Americas, animal-drawn plows and metalworking greatly enhanced the productivity of farming. Ritual sacrifice accompanied the growth of civilization, and the new rulers normally served as high priests, their right to rule legitimated by association with the sacred.

An Urban Revolution

It was the resources from agriculture that made possible one of the most distinctive features of the First Civilizations—cities. What would an agricultural villager have made of **Uruk**, ancient Mesopotamia's largest city? Uruk had walls more than twenty feet tall and a population around 50,000 in the third millennium B.C.E. At the city's center, visible for miles around, was a stepped pyramid, or ziggurat, topped with a temple. Inside the city, this village visitor would have found other temples as well, serving as centers of ritual performance. Numerous craftspeople labored as masons, copper workers, and weavers and in many other specialties, while bureaucrats helped administer the city. It was, surely, a "vibrant, noisy, smelly, sometimes bewildering and dangerous, but also exciting place."[6] Or in the words of the *Epic of Gilgamesh*, Mesopotamia's ancient epic poem dating to around 2000 B.C.E., cities were places where the hustle and bustle of urban life meant that "even the great gods are kept from sleeping at night."[7]

Equally impressive to a village visitor would have been the city of **Mohenjo Daro** (moe-hen-joe DAHR-oh), which flourished along the banks of the Indus River around 2000 B.C.E. With a population of perhaps 40,000, Mohenjo Daro and its sister city of **Harappa** featured large, richly built houses of two or three stories, complete with indoor plumbing, luxurious bathrooms, and private wells. Streets were laid out in a grid-like pattern, and beneath the streets ran a complex sewage system. Workers lived in row upon row of standardized two-room houses. Grand public buildings, including what seems to be a huge public bath, graced the city, while an enormous citadel was surrounded by a brick wall some forty-five feet high.

Even larger, though considerably later, was the Mesoamerican city of Teotihuacán (tay-uh-tee-wah-KAHN), located in the central valley of Mexico. It housed perhaps 150,000 people in the middle of the first millennium C.E. Broad avenues, dozens of temples, two huge pyramids, endless stone carvings and many bright frescoes, small apartments for the ordinary, palatial homes for the wealthy — all of this must have seemed another world for a new visitor from a distant village. In shopping for obsidian blades, how was she to decide among the 350 workshops in the city? In seeking relatives, how could she find her way among many different compounds, each surrounded by a wall and housing a different lineage? And what would she make of a neighborhood composed entirely of Maya merchants from the distant coastal lowlands?

Cities, then, were central to most of the First Civilizations, though to varying degrees. They were political and administrative capitals; they functioned as centers for the production of culture, including art, architecture, literature, ritual, and ceremony; they served as marketplaces for both local and long-distance exchange; and they housed most manufacturing activity. Everywhere they generated a unique kind of society, compared to earlier agricultural villages or Paleolithic camps. Urban society was impersonal, for it was no longer possible to know everyone. Relationships of class and occupation emerged alongside those of kinship and village loyalty. Most notably, the degree of specialization and inequality far surpassed that of all preceding human communities.

The Erosion of Equality

Among the most novel features of early urban life, at least to our imaginary village visitor, was the amazing specialization of work outside of agriculture — scholars, officials, merchants, priests, and artisans of all kinds. In ancient Sumer, even scribes were subdivided into many categories: junior and senior scribes, temple scribes and royal scribes, scribes for particular administrative or official functions, freelance scribes. None of these people, of course, grew their own food; they were supported by the highly productive agriculture of farmers and herders, some of whom also performed specialized tasks.

Hierarchies of Class

Alongside the occupational specialization of the First Civilizations lay their vast inequalities — in wealth, status, and power. As ingenuity and technology created more productive economies, the greater wealth now available was everywhere piled up rather than spread out. Early signs of this erosion of equality were evident in the more settled and complex gathering and hunting societies and in agricultural chiefdoms, but the advent of urban-based civilizations multiplied and magnified these inequalities many times over, as the more egalitarian values of earlier cultures were everywhere displaced. This transition represents one of the major turning points in the social history of humankind.

As the First Civilizations took shape, inequality and hierarchy soon came to be regarded as normal and natural. Upper classes everywhere enjoyed great wealth in land or salaries, were able to avoid physical labor, had the finest of everything, and occupied the top positions in political, military, and religious life. Frequently, they were distinguished by the clothing they wore, the houses they lived in, and the manner of their burial. Early Chinese monarchs bestowed special robes, banners, chariots, weapons, and ornaments on their regional officials, and all of these items were graded according to the officials' precise location in the hierarchy. In the Babylonian Empire the punishments prescribed in the famous **Code of Hammurabi** (hahm-moo-RAH-bee) (ca. 1775 B.C.E.) depended on social status. A free-born commoner who struck a person of equal rank had to pay a small fine, but if he struck "a man who is his superior, he [would] receive 60 strokes with an oxtail whip in public." Clearly, class had consequences.

In all of the First Civilizations, free commoners represented the vast majority of the population and included artisans of all kinds, lower-level officials, soldiers and police, servants, and, most numerous of all, farmers. It was their surplus production — appropriated through a variety of taxes, rents, required labor, and tribute payments — that supported the upper classes. At least some of these people were aware of, and resented, these forced extractions and their position in the social hierarchy. Most Chinese peasants, for example, owned little land of their own and worked on plots granted to them by royal or aristocratic landowners. An ancient poem compared the exploiting landlords to rats and expressed the farmers' vision of a better life:

> Large rats! Large rats! / Do not eat our spring grain!
> Three years have we had to do with you. / And you have not been willing to think of our toil.
> We will leave you, / And go to those happy borders.
> Happy borders, happy borders! / Who will there make us always to groan?[8]

At the bottom of social hierarchies everywhere were enslaved people. Evidence for slavery dates to well before the emergence of civilization, and it was clearly present in some gathering and hunting societies and early agricultural communities. But the practice of "people owning people" flourished on a larger scale in urban- and state-based civilizations. Enslaved women and girls, captured in the many wars among rival Mesopotamian cities, were put to work in large-scale semi-industrial weaving

Assyrian Attack in Egypt This stone relief from an Assyrian palace dates from about 645 B.C.E. and depicts an assault on an Egyptian city at the top, with prisoners at the bottom being led away with their hands bound behind their backs. Prisoners taken in war were a major source of enslaved people in the ancient world. (Werner Forman/Getty Images)

enterprises, while males helped to maintain irrigation canals and construct ziggurats. Others worked as domestic servants in the households of their owners. In all of the First Civilizations, enslaved people—derived from prisoners of war, criminals, and debtors—were available for sale; for work in the fields, mines, homes, and shops of their owners; or on occasion for sacrifice. From the days of the earliest civilizations until the nineteenth century, slavery was everywhere an enduring feature of these more complex societies.

Its practice in ancient times, however, varied considerably from place to place. Egypt and the Indus Valley civilizations initially had far fewer enslaved people than did Mesopotamia, which was highly militarized. Later, the Greeks of Athens and the Romans employed enslaved people far more extensively than did the Chinese or Indians (see "The Making of Roman Slavery" in Chapter 5). Furthermore, most ancient slavery differed from the type of slavery practiced in the Americas during recent centuries: in the early civilizations, enslaved people were not a primary agricultural labor force; many children of enslaved persons could become free people; and slavery was not associated primarily with "blackness" or with Africa.

Hierarchies of Gender

No divisions of human society have held greater significance for the lives of individuals than those of sex and gender. Sex describes the obvious biological differences between males and females. More important to historians, however, has been gender, which refers to the many and varied ways that cultures have assigned meaning to those sexual differences. To be gendered as masculine or feminine defines the roles and behavior considered appropriate for men and women in every human community. At least since the emergence of the First Civilizations, and in some cases even earlier, gender systems have supported **patriarchy**, which refers to a social system in which women have been made markedly subordinate to men in the family and in society generally. The inequalities of gender, like those of class, decisively shaped the character of the First Civilizations and of those that followed.

The patriarchal ideal regarded men as superior to women and sons preferable to daughters. Men had legal and property rights unknown to most women. Public life in general was associated with masculinity, which defined men as rulers, warriors, scholars, and heads of households. Women's roles—both productive and reproductive—took place in the home, mostly within a heterosexual family, where women were defined largely by their relationship to a man: as a daughter, wife, mother, or widow. Frequently men could marry more than one woman and claim the right to regulate the social and sexual lives of the wives, daughters, and sisters in their families. Widely seen as weak but feared as potentially disruptive, women required both the protection and control by men.

For men and women alike, gender and class intersected to shape the lives of individuals. Most men, of course, were far from prominent and exercised little power, except perhaps over the women and children of their own families. Upper-class women often experienced a privileged but highly restricted life, for they were largely limited to the home and the management of servants. By contrast, the vast majority of women always had to be out in public, working in the fields, tending livestock, buying and selling in the streets, or serving in the homes of their social superiors. A few women also operated in roles defined as masculine, acting as rulers, priests, and scholars, while others pushed against the limits and restrictions assigned to women. But most women no doubt accepted their assigned roles, unable to imagine anything approaching gender equality, even as most men genuinely believed that they were protecting and providing for their women.

The big question for historians lies in trying to explain the origins of this kind of pervasive patriarchy. Clearly it was neither natural nor of long standing. For millennia beyond measure, gathering and hunting societies had developed gender systems without the sharp restrictions and vast inequalities that characterized civilizations. Early farming societies, those using a hoe or digging stick for cultivation, continued the relative gender equality that had characterized Paleolithic peoples. What was it, then, about civilization that seemed to generate a more explicit and restrictive patriarchy?

One approach to answering this question highlights the role of a new and more intensive form of agriculture, involving the use of animal-drawn plows and the keeping and milking of large herds of animals. Unlike earlier farming practices that relied on a hoe or digging stick, plow-based agriculture meant heavier work, which men were better able to perform. Taking place at a distance from the village, this new form of agriculture was perhaps less compatible with women's primary responsibility for child rearing and food preparation. Furthermore, the growing population of civilizations meant that women were more often pregnant and thus more deeply involved in child care than before. Hence, in plow-based communities, men took over most of the farming work, and the status of women declined correspondingly, even though their other productive activities—weaving and food preparation, for example—continued. "As women were increasingly relegated to secondary tasks," writes archeologist Margaret Ehrenberg, "they had fewer personal resources with which to assert their status."[9] But in much of Africa, all of the agricultural areas of the Americas, and parts of Southeast Asia, hoe-based farming persisted and with it, arguably, less restrictive lives for women.

Women have long been identified not only with the home but also with nature, for they are central to the primordial natural process of reproduction. But civilization seemed to highlight culture, or the human mastery of nature, through agriculture, monumental art and architecture, and the creation of large-scale cities and states. Did this mean, as some scholars have suggested, that women were now associated with an inferior dimension of human life (nature), while men assumed responsibility for the higher order of culture?[10]

Warfare and professionally led armies, central to many of the First Civilizations, surely contributed to patriarchy. With military service largely restricted to men, its growing prominence in the affairs of civilizations enhanced the values, power, and prestige of a male warrior class and cemented the association of masculinity with organized violence and with the protection of society, especially its women.

Private property and commerce, also prominent among the First Civilizations, may have helped to shape early patriarchies. Without sharp restrictions on women's sexual activity, how could a father be certain that family property would be inherited by his offspring? In addition, the buying and selling associated with commerce were soon applied to male rights over women, as wives, concubines, and enslaved women were exchanged among men.

Patriarchy in Practice

Whatever the precise origins of patriarchy, women's subordination permeated the First Civilizations, marking a gradual change from the more equal relationships of men and women within agricultural villages or Paleolithic bands. By the second millennium B.C.E. in Mesopotamia, various written laws codified and sought to enforce a patriarchal family life that offered women a measure of paternalistic protection while insisting on their submission to the unquestioned authority of men. Central to these laws was the regulation of female sexuality. A wife caught sleeping with another man might be drowned at her husband's discretion, whereas he was permitted to enjoy sexual relations with his female servants, though not with another man's wife. Divorce was far easier for the husband than for the wife. Rape was a serious offense, but the injured party was primarily the father or the husband of the victim, rather than the violated woman herself. While wealthy women might own and operate their own businesses or act on behalf of their powerful husbands, they too saw themselves as dependent. "Let all be well with [my husband]," prayed one such wife, "that I may prosper under his protection."[11]

Furthermore, women in Mesopotamian civilization were sometimes divided into two sharply distinguished categories. Under an Assyrian law code that was in effect between the fifteenth and eleventh centuries B.C.E., respectable women, those under the protection and sexual control of one man, were required to be veiled when outside the home, whereas nonrespectable women, such as enslaved women and prostitutes, were forbidden to wear veils and were subject to severe punishment if they presumed to cover their heads.

Finally, in some places, the powerful goddesses of earlier times were gradually relegated to the home and hearth. They were replaced in the public arena by dominant male deities, who now were credited with the power of creation and fertility and viewed as the patrons of wisdom and learning. This "demotion of the goddess," argued historian Gerda Lerner, found expression in the Hebrew Scriptures, in which a single male deity, Yahweh (YAH-way), alone undertakes the act of creation without any participation of a female counterpart. Yet this demotion did not occur always or everywhere; in Mesopotamia, for example, the prominent goddess Inanna, or Ishtar, long held her own against male gods and was regarded as a goddess of love and sexuality as well as a war deity.

But expressions of patriarchy varied among the First Civilizations. Egypt, while clearly patriarchal, afforded its women greater opportunities than did most other First Civilizations. In Egypt, women were recognized as legal equals to men: able to own property, to administer and sell land, to make their own wills, to sign their own marriage contracts, and to initiate divorce. Moreover, married women in Egypt were not veiled as they were at times in Mesopotamia. Royal women occasionally exercised significant political power, acting as regents for their young sons or, more rarely, as queens in their own right. Clearly, though, this was seen as abnormal, for Egypt's most important queen, Hatshepsut (r. 1472–1457 B.C.E.), was sometimes portrayed in statues as a man, dressed in male clothing and sporting the traditional false beard of the pharaoh.

The Rise of the State

What, we might reasonably ask, held ancient civilizations together despite the many tensions and complexities of urban living and the vast inequalities of civilized societies? The answer, in large part, lay in yet another distinctive feature of the First Civilizations — states. Organized around particular cities or larger territories, early states were headed almost everywhere by kings, who employed a variety of ranked officials, exercised a measure of control over society, and defended against external enemies. The state is a quite recent invention in human history, replacing, or at least supplementing, kinship as the basic organizing principle of society and exercising far greater power than earlier chiefdoms. But the power of central states in the First Civilizations was limited and certainly not "totalitarian" in the modern sense of that term. The temple and the private economy rivaled and checked the power of rulers, and most authority was local rather than directed from the capital.

Coercion and Consent

Early states in Mesopotamia, Egypt, China, Mesoamerica, and elsewhere drew their power from various sources, all of which helped to integrate their societies. One basis of authority lay in the recognition that the complexity of life in cities or densely populated territories required some authority to coordinate and regulate the community. Someone had to organize the irrigation systems of river valley civilizations. Someone had to direct efforts to defend the city or territory against aggressive outsiders. Someone had to adjudicate conflicts among the many different peoples, unrelated to one another, who rubbed elbows in the streets of early cities. The state, in short, solved certain widely shared problems and therefore had a measure of voluntary support among the population. For many people, it was surely useful.

The state, however, was more useful for some people than for others, for it also served to protect the privileges of the upper classes, to require farmers to give up a portion of their product to support city-dwellers, and to demand work on large public projects such as pyramids and fortifications. If necessary, state authorities had the ability, and the willingness, to use force to compel obedience. As recorded in the Jewish scriptures of the Old Testament, the prophet Samuel warned the ancient people of Israel about the "ways of the king":

> He will take your sons and make them serve with his chariots and horses. . . .
> Some he will assign to be commanders . . . and others to plow his ground and
> reap his harvest, and still others to make weapons of war and equipment for his
> chariots. He will take your daughters to be perfumers and cooks and bakers. He
> will take the best of your fields and vineyards and olive groves and give them to
> his attendants. He will take a tenth of your grain and of your vintage and give it
> to his officials and attendants. Your male and female servants and the best of your
> cattle and donkeys he will take for his own use. He will take a tenth of your flocks,
> and you yourselves will become his slaves.[12]

Such was the power of the state, as rulers accumulated the resources to pay for officials, soldiers, police, and attendants. This capacity for violence and coercion marked off the states of the First Civilizations from earlier chiefdoms, whose leaders had only persuasion, prestige, and gifts to back up their authority. But as states increasingly monopolized the legitimate right to use violence, rates of death from interpersonal violence declined as compared to earlier nonstate communities.[13]

Force, however, was not always necessary, for the First Civilizations soon generated ideas suggesting that state authority as well as class and gender inequalities were normal, natural, and ordained by the gods. Rulers in many places were thought to be morally responsible for the care of their subjects, especially in times of crisis or catastrophe. Kingship everywhere was associated with the sacred. Ancient Chinese kings were known as the Son of Heaven, and only they or their authorized priests could perform the rituals and sacrifices necessary to keep the cosmos in balance, thus preventing war, pestilence, and natural disaster. Egyptians, most of all, invested their pharaohs with divine qualities. Rulers claimed to embody all the major gods of Egypt, and their supernatural power ensured the regular flooding of the Nile and the defeat of the country's enemies.

But if religion served most often to justify unequal power and privilege, it might also on occasion be used to restrain, or even undermine, the established order. Hammurabi claimed that his law code was inspired by Marduk, the chief god of Babylon, and was intended to "bring about the rule of righteousness in the land, to destroy the wicked and the evil-doers; so that the strong should not harm the weak."[14] Another Mesopotamian monarch, Urukagina from the city of Lagash, claimed authority from the city's patron god for reforms aimed at ending the corruption and tyranny of a previous ruler. In China during the Western Zhou dynasty (1046–771 B.C.E.), emperors ruled by the Mandate of Heaven, but their bad behavior could result in the removal of that mandate and their overthrow.

Writing and Accounting

A further support for state authority lay in the remarkable invention of writing. It was a powerful and transforming innovation, regarded almost everywhere as a gift from the gods, while people without writing often saw it as something magical or supernatural. Distinctive forms of writing emerged in most of the First Civilizations (see Snapshot: Writing in Ancient Civilizations, page 53), sustaining them and their successors in many ways. Literacy defined elite status and conveyed enormous prestige to those who possessed it. For Egyptians, a scribe earned a kind of immortality through his writing, for it persisted long after his death. Because it can be learned, writing also provided a means for some commoners to join the charmed circle of the literate. Writing as propaganda, celebrating the great deeds of the kings, was prominent, especially among the Egyptians and later among the Maya. A hymn to the pharaoh, dating to about 1850 B.C.E., extravagantly praised the Egyptian ruler for bringing peace and prosperity to his realm: "He hath banished its suffering; he has caused the throat of the subjects to breathe."[15]

In Mesopotamia and elsewhere, writing served an accounting function, recording who had paid their taxes, who owed what to the temple, and how much workers had earned. Thus it immensely strengthened bureaucracy. Complex calendars indicated precisely when certain rituals should be performed. Writing also gave weight and specificity to orders, regulations, and laws. Hammurabi's famous law code, while correcting certain abuses, made crystal clear that fundamental distinctions divided men and women and separated enslaved people, commoners, and people of higher rank.

Once it had been developed, writing, like religion, proved hard to control and operated as a wild card in human affairs. It gave rise to literature and philosophy, to astronomy and mathematics, and, in some places, to history, often recording what had long been oral traditions. On occasion, the written word proved threatening, rather than supportive, to rulers. China's so-called First Emperor, Qin Shihuangdi (r. 221–210 B.C.E.), allegedly buried alive some 460 scholars and burned their books when they challenged his brutal efforts to unify China's many warring states, or so his later critics claimed (see "China: From Warring States to Empire," Chapter 3). Thus writing became a major arena for social and political conflict, and rulers have always sought to control it.

SNAPSHOT　　　**WRITING IN ANCIENT CIVILIZATIONS**

Most of the early writing systems were logophonetic, using symbols to designate both whole words and particular sounds or syllables. Chinese characters, which indicated only words, were an exception. The Phoenician script was the first writing system to employ an alphabet.

Location	Type	Initial Use	Example	Comment
Sumer	Cuneiform: wedge-shaped symbols on clay tablets representing objects, abstract ideas, sounds, and syllables	Records of economic transactions, such as temple payments and taxes	bird	Regarded as the world's first written language; other languages such as Babylonian and Assyrian were written with Sumerian script
Egypt	Hieroglyphs: a series of signs that denote words and consonants (but not vowels or syllables)	Business and administration, religious inscriptions, stories, poetry, hymns, mathematics	rain, dew, storm	Cursive writing systems were developed for everyday use
Andes	Quipu: a complex system of knotted cords that conveyed mostly numerical meaning	Various accounting functions; perhaps also used to express words	numerical data, words, and ideas	Widely used in the Inca Empire; recent discoveries place quipus in Caral some 4,600 years ago
Indus River Valley	Some 400 pictographic symbols representing sounds and words	Found on thousands of clay seals and pottery; probably used to mark merchandise	6 fish	As yet undeciphered
China	Oracle bone script: pictographs (stylized drawings) with no phonetic meaning	Inscribed on turtle shells or animal bones; used by Shang dynasty rulers for predicting the future	horse	Direct ancestor of contemporary Chinese characters
Olmec	Signs that represent sounds (syllables) and words; numbering system using bars and dots	Used to record the names and deeds of rulers and shamans, as well as battles and astronomical data	jaguar	Structurally similar to later Mayan script; Olmec calendars were highly accurate and the basis for later Mesoamerican calendars
Eastern Mediterranean	Phoenician: initially 22 letters, all consonants; later alphabets incorporated vowels	First used by merchants to record trade but later for many other functions; quickly spread along Mediterranean trade routes	teth (T) / kaph (K)	Use in trade and ease of adaptation to different spoken languages spurred its spread; the most widely used lettering system in the world today

Olmec Head This colossal statue, some eight feet high and weighing twenty-four tons, is one of seventeen such carvings, dating to the first millennium B.C.E., that were discovered in the territory of the ancient Olmec civilization. Thought to represent individual rulers, each of the statues has a distinct and realistically portrayed face. (Danny Lehman/Corbis/VCG/Getty Images)

The Grandeur of Kings

Yet another source of state authority derived from the lavish lifestyle of elites, the impressive rituals they arranged, and the imposing structures they created. Everywhere, kings, high officials, and their families lived in luxurious palaces or homes, dressed in splendid clothing, bedecked themselves with the loveliest jewelry, and were attended by endless servants. Their deaths triggered elaborate burials, of which the pyramids of the Egyptian pharaohs were perhaps the most ostentatious. Monumental palaces, temples, ziggurats, pyramids, and statues conveyed the imposing power of the state and its elite rulers. The Olmec civilization of Mesoamerica (1200–400 B.C.E.) erected enormous human heads, some more than ten feet tall and weighing at least twenty tons, carved from blocks of basalt and probably representing particular rulers. Somewhat later, the Maya Temple of the Great Jaguar, 154 feet tall, was the most impressive among many temples, pyramids, and palaces that graced the city of Tikal. All of this must have seemed overwhelming to common people in the cities and villages of the First Civilizations.

Comparing Mesopotamia and Egypt

A productive agricultural technology, city living, distinct class and gender inequalities, the emerging power of states—all of these were common features of First Civilizations across the world and also of those that followed. Still, these civilizations were not everywhere the same, for differences in political organization, religious beliefs and practices, the role of women, and much more gave rise to distinctive traditions. Nor were they static. Like all human communities, they changed over the centuries. Finally, these civilizations did not exist in complete isolation, for they participated in networks of interactions with near and sometimes more distant neighbors. In looking more closely at two of these First Civilizations—Mesopotamia and Egypt—we can catch a glimpse of the differences, changes, and connections that characterized early civilizations.

Environment and Culture

The civilizations of both Mesopotamia and Egypt grew up in river valleys and depended on their rivers to sustain a productive agriculture in otherwise arid lands. Those rivers, however, were radically different. At the heart of Egyptian life was the Nile, "that green gash of teeming life," which rose predictably every year to bring the soil and water that nurtured a rich Egyptian agriculture. The Tigris and Euphrates rivers, which gave life to Mesopotamian civilization, also rose annually, but "unpredictably and fitfully, breaking man's dikes and submerging his crops"[16] (see Map 2.2). Furthermore, an open environment without serious obstacles to travel made Mesopotamia far more vulnerable to invasion than the much more protected space of Egypt, which was surrounded by deserts, mountains, seas, and to its south by unnavigable stretches of the Nile. For long periods of its history, Egypt enjoyed a kind of "free security" from external attack that Mesopotamians clearly lacked.

But does the physical environment shape the human cultures that develop within it? Most historians are reluctant to endorse a "geography is destiny" outlook, but in the case of Mesopotamia and Egypt, it is hard to deny some relationship

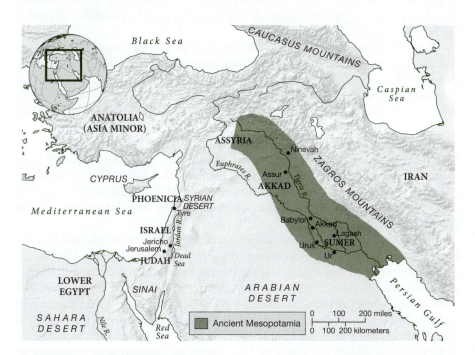

MAP 2.2 Mesopotamia

After about 1,000 years of independent and competitive existence, the city-states of Sumer were incorporated into a number of larger imperial states based in Akkad, Babylon, and then Assyria.

between the physical setting and culture. Mesopotamia's location within a precarious, unpredictable, and often violent environment arguably contributed to an outlook suggesting that humankind was caught in an inherently disorderly world, was subject to the whims of capricious and quarreling gods, and had to face death without much hope of a blessed life beyond. A Mesopotamian poet complained: "I have prayed to the gods and sacrificed, but who can understand the gods in heaven? Who knows what they plan for us? Who has ever been able to understand a god's conduct?"[17]

By contrast, elite literate culture in Egypt, developing in a more stable, predictable, and beneficent environment, produced a rather more cheerful and hopeful outlook on the world. The rebirth of the sun every day and of the river every year seemed to assure Egyptians that life would prevail over death. The amazing pyramids, constructed during Egypt's Old Kingdom (2663–2195 B.C.E.), reflected the firm belief that at least the pharaohs and other high-ranking people could successfully make the journey to eternal life in the Land of the West. Incantations for the dead describe an afterlife of abundance and tranquility that Mesopotamians could only have envied. Over time, larger groups of people, beyond the pharaoh and his entourage, came to believe that they too could gain access to the afterlife if they followed proper procedures and lived a morally upright life. Thus Egyptian civilization not only affirmed the possibility of eternal life but also expanded access to it.

If the different environments of Mesopotamia and Egypt shaped their societies and cultures, those civilizations, with their mounting populations and growing demand for resources, likewise had an impact on the environment.[18] The *Epic of Gilgamesh* inscribed in mythology the deforestation of Mesopotamia. When the ruler Gilgamesh sought to make for himself "a name that endures" by building walls, ramparts, and temples, he required much timber. But to acquire it, he had first to kill Humbaba, appointed by the gods to guard the forests. The epic describes what happened next: "Then there followed confusion. . . . Now the mountains were moved and all the hills, for the guardian of the forest was killed. They attacked the cedars. . . . So they pressed on into the forest . . . and while Gilgamesh felled the first of the trees of the forest, Enkidu [the friend of Gilgamesh] cleared their roots as far as the banks of Euphrates."[19]

In Sumer (southern Mesopotamia), such deforestation and the soil erosion that followed from it sharply decreased crop yields between 2400 and 1700 B.C.E. Also contributing to this disaster was the increasing salinization of the soil, a long-term outcome of intensive irrigation. By 2000 B.C.E., there were reports that "the earth turned white" as salt accumulated in the soil. As a result, wheat was largely replaced by barley, which is far more tolerant of salty conditions. This ecological deterioration clearly weakened Sumerian city-states, facilitated their conquest by foreigners, and shifted the center of Mesopotamian civilization permanently to the north.

Egypt, by contrast, created a more sustainable agricultural system that lasted for thousands of years and contributed to the remarkable continuity of its civilization. Whereas Sumerian irrigation involved a complex and artificial network of canals and dikes that led to the salinization of the soil, its Egyptian counterpart was much less intrusive, simply regulating the natural flow of the Nile. Such a system avoided the problem of salty soils, allowing Egyptian agriculture to emphasize wheat production, but it depended on the general regularity and relative gentleness of the Nile's annual flooding. On occasion, that pattern was interrupted, with serious consequences for Egyptian society. An extended period of low floods between 2250 and 1950 B.C.E. led to sharply reduced agricultural output, large-scale starvation, the loss of livestock, and, consequently, social upheaval and political disruption. Nonetheless, Egypt's ability to work *with* its more favorable natural environment enabled a degree of stability and continuity that proved impossible in Sumer, where human action intruded more heavily into a less benevolent natural setting.

Cities and States

Politically as well as culturally and environmentally, Mesopotamian and Egyptian civilizations differed sharply. For its first thousand years (3200–2350 B.C.E.), Mesopotamian civilization, located in the southern Tigris-Euphrates region known as Sumer, was organized in a dozen or more separate and independent city-states. Each city-state was ruled by a king, who claimed to represent the city's patron deity and who controlled the affairs of the walled city and surrounding rural area. Quite remarkably, some 80 percent of the population of Sumer lived in one or another of these city-states, making Mesopotamia the most thoroughly urbanized society of ancient times. The chief reason for this massive urbanization, however, lay in the great flaw of this system, for frequent warfare among these Sumerian city-states caused people living in rural areas to flee to the walled cities for protection. With no overarching authority, rivalry over land and water often led to violent conflict.

These conflicts, together with environmental devastation, eventually left Sumerian cities vulnerable to outside forces, and after about 2350 B.C.E., stronger peoples from northern Mesopotamia conquered Sumer's warring cities, bringing an end to the Sumerian phase of Mesopotamian civilization. First the Akkadians (2350–2000 B.C.E.), and later the Babylonians (1900–1500 B.C.E.) and the Assyrians (900–612 B.C.E.), created larger territorial states or bureaucratic empires that encompassed all or most of Mesopotamia. Periods of political unity now descended upon this First Civilization, but it was unity imposed from outside.

By contrast, already around 3100 B.C.E. Egyptian civilization had produced a unified territory that stretched some 1,000 miles along the Nile and brought together several earlier states or chiefdoms. For an amazing 3,000 years, the Egypt of the pharaohs maintained its unity and independence, though with occasional interruptions. A combination of wind patterns that made it easy to sail south along the Nile and a current flowing north facilitated communication, exchange, unity, and stability within the Nile Valley. Here was a record of political longevity and continuity that the Mesopotamians and many other ancient peoples could not replicate. An Egyptian territorial state and cultural identity persist still in northeastern Africa.

Cities in Egypt were less important than in Mesopotamia, although political capitals, market centers, and major burial sites gave Egypt an urban presence as well. Most people lived in agricultural villages along the river rather than in urban centers, perhaps because Egypt's greater security made it less necessary for people to gather in fortified towns. The focus of the Egyptian state resided in the pharaoh, believed to be a god in human form. He alone ensured the daily rising of the sun and the annual flooding of the Nile. All of the country's many officials served at his pleasure, and access to the afterlife lay in proximity to him and burial in or near his towering pyramids.

This image of the pharaoh and his role as an enduring symbol of a unified Egyptian civilization persisted over the course of three millennia, but the realities of Egyptian political life did not always match these ideals. By 2400 B.C.E., the power of the pharaoh had diminished, as local officials and nobles assumed greater authority. Having been awarded their own land, they were able to pass their positions on to their sons. When changes in the climate resulted in the Nile's repeated failure to flood properly around 2200 B.C.E., the authority of the pharaoh was severely discredited, and Egypt dissolved for several centuries into a series of local principalities.

Even when centralized rule was restored around 2000 B.C.E., the pharaohs never regained their old power and prestige. Kings were now warned that they too would have to account for their actions at the Day of Judgment. Nobles no longer sought to be buried near the pharaoh's pyramid but instead created their own more modest tombs in their own areas. Osiris, the god of the dead, became increasingly prominent, and all worthy men, not only those who had been close to the pharaoh in life, could aspire to immortality in his realm.

Interaction and Exchange

Although Mesopotamia and Egypt represented separate and distinct civilizations, they interacted frequently with each other and with both near and more distant neighbors. Even in these ancient times, the First Civilizations were embedded in larger networks of commerce, culture, and power. None of them stood alone.

Egypt's early agriculture, for example, drew upon wheat and barley, which likely reached Egypt from Mesopotamia, as well as gourds, watermelon, domesticated donkeys, and cattle, which came from the Sudan to the south. The practice of "divine kingship" probably derived from the central or eastern Sudan, where small-scale agricultural communities had long viewed their rulers as sacred and buried them with various servants and officials. From this complex of influences, the Egyptians created something distinct and unique, but that civilization had roots in both Africa and Southwest Asia.

Furthermore, once they were established, both Mesopotamia and Egypt carried on long-distance trade, mostly in luxury goods destined for the elite. Sumerian merchants had established seaborne contact with the Indus Valley civilization as early as 2300 B.C.E., while Indus Valley traders and their interpreters had taken up residence in Mesopotamia. Other trade routes connected Mesopotamia to Anatolia (present-day Turkey), Egypt, Iran, and Afghanistan. During Akkadian rule over Mesopotamia, a Sumerian poet described its capital of Agade:

> In those days the dwellings of Agade were filled with gold, / its bright-shining houses were filled with silver,
> into its granaries were brought copper, tin, slabs of lapis lazuli [a blue gemstone],
> its silos bulged at the sides . . . / its quay where the boats docked were all bustle.[20]

All of this and more came from far away.

Egyptian trade likewise extended far afield. In addition to being involved with the Mediterranean and the Middle East, Egyptian trading journeys extended deep into Africa, including Nubia, south of Egypt in the Nile Valley, and Punt, along the East African coast of Ethiopia and Somalia. One Egyptian official described his return from an expedition to Nubia: "I came down with three hundred donkeys laden with incense, ebony, . . . panther skins, elephant tusks, throw sticks, and all sorts of good products."[21]

The remarkable Uluburun shipwreck dating from around 1330 B.C.E. offers a window into the cosmopolitan networks of the Mediterranean that drew in goods from distant regions. Discovered off the coast of modern Turkey, the ship carried a remarkably diverse cargo composed of raw materials—copper, tin, and glass—and luxury items crafted out of ivory, amber, ostrich eggshells, gold, and more. All told the cargo included products from at least eleven ancient cultures stretching from the Baltic Sea in northern Europe to equatorial Africa. Along with trade goods went cultural influence from the civilizations of Mesopotamia and Egypt. Among the smaller societies of the region to feel this influence were the Hebrews. Their sacred writings, recorded in the Old Testament, showed the influence of Mesopotamia in the "eye for an eye" principle of their legal system and in the story of a flood that destroyed the world. The Phoenicians, who were commercially active in the Mediterranean basin from their homeland in present-day Lebanon, also were influenced by Mesopotamian civilization. They venerated Astarte, a local form of the Mesopotamian fertility goddess Ishtar. They also adapted the Sumerian cuneiform method of writing to a much easier alphabetic system, which later became the basis for Greek and Latin writing. Various Indo-European peoples, dispersing probably from north-central Anatolia, also incorporated Sumerian deities into their own religions as well as bronze metallurgy and the wheel into their economies. When their widespread migrations carried them across much of Eurasia, they took these Sumerian cultural artifacts with them.

Egyptian cultural influence likewise spread in several directions. Nubia, located to the south of Egypt in the Nile Valley, not only traded with its more powerful neighbor but also was subject to periodic military intervention and political control from Egypt. Skilled Nubian archers were actively recruited for service as mercenaries in Egyptian armies. They often married Egyptian women and were buried in Egyptian style. All of this led to the diffusion of Egyptian culture in Nubia, expressed in building Egyptian-style pyramids, worshipping Egyptian gods and goddesses, and making use of Egyptian hieroglyphic writing. Despite this cultural borrowing, Nubia remained a distinct civilization, developing its own alphabetic script, retaining many of its own gods, developing a major ironworking industry by 500 B.C.E.,

Egypt and Nubia This wall painting from the tomb of an Egyptian court official, dating to the fifteenth century B.C.E., shows Nubians bringing animals as tribute to Egyptian authorities. (akg-images)

and asserting its political independence whenever possible. The Nubian kingdom of Kush, in fact, invaded Egypt in 760 B.C.E. and ruled it for about 100 years.

In the Mediterranean basin, clear Egyptian influence is visible in the art of the Minoan civilization, which emerged on the island of Crete about 2500 B.C.E. More controversial has been the claim by some scholars that ancient Greek culture—its art, religion, philosophy, and language—drew heavily upon Egyptian as well as Mesopotamian precedents. Influence was not a one-way street, however, as Egypt and Mesopotamia likewise felt the impact of neighboring peoples. Pastoral peoples, speaking Indo-European languages and living in what is now southern Russia, had domesticated the horse by perhaps 4000 B.C.E. and later learned to tie that powerful animal to wheeled carts and chariots. This new technology provided a fearsome military potential that enabled various chariot-driving peoples, such as the Hittites, to threaten ancient civilizations. Based in Anatolia, the Hittites sacked the city of Babylon in 1595 B.C.E. Several centuries later, conflict between the Hittites and Egypt over control of Syria resulted in the world's first written peace treaty. But chariot technology was portable, and soon both the Egyptians and the Mesopotamians incorporated it into their own military forces. In fact, this powerful military innovation, together with the knowledge of bronze metallurgy, spread quickly and widely, reaching China by 1200 B.C.E. There it enabled the creation of a strong Chinese state ruled by the Shang dynasty. All of these developments provide evidence of at least indirect connections across parts of the Afro-Eurasian landmass in ancient times. Even then, no civilization was wholly isolated from larger patterns of interaction.

In Egypt, the centuries following 1650 B.C.E. witnessed the migration of foreigners from surrounding regions and conflict with neighboring peoples, shaking the sense of security that this Nile Valley civilization had long enjoyed. It also stimulated the normally complacent Egyptians to adopt a number of technologies pioneered earlier in Asia, including the horse-drawn chariot; new kinds of armor, bows, daggers, and swords; improved methods of spinning and weaving; new musical instruments; and olive and pomegranate trees. Absorbing these foreign innovations, Egyptians went on to create their own empire, both in Nubia and in the eastern Mediterranean regions of Syria and Palestine. By 1500 B.C.E., the previously self-contained Egypt became for several centuries an imperial state bridging Africa and Asia and ruling over substantial numbers of non-Egyptian peoples (see Map 2.3). It also became part

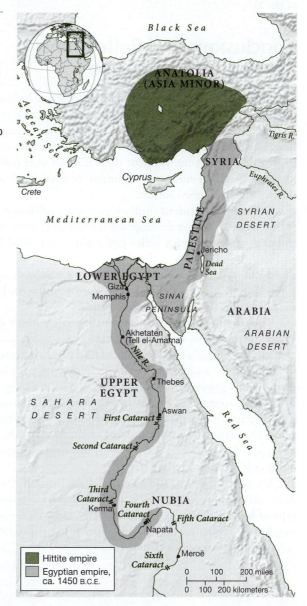

MAP 2.3 An Egyptian Empire
During the New Kingdom period after 1550 B.C.E., Egypt became for several centuries an empire, extending its political control southward into Nubia and northward into Palestine and Syria.

of an international political system that included the Babylonian and later Assyrian empires of Mesopotamia as well as many other peoples of the region. Egyptian and Babylonian rulers engaged in regular diplomatic correspondence, referred to one another as "brother," exchanged gifts, and married their daughters into one another's families. Or at least they tried to. While Babylonian rulers were willing to send their daughters to Egypt, the Egyptians were exceedingly reluctant to return the favor, claiming that "from ancient times the daughter of the king of Egypt has not been given to anyone." To this rebuff, the disappointed Babylonian monarch replied: "You are a king and you can do as pleases you. . . . Send me [any] beautiful woman as if she were your daughter. Who is to say this woman is not the daughter of the king?"[22]

Conclusions and Reflections: Pondering "Civilization"

The First Civilizations marked a radical departure in human history during the centuries between 3500 and 1000 B.C.E. All or most of them shared such common features as urban centers, state structures, specialized occupations, sharp class divisions, slavery, patriarchy and the decisive subordination of women, written languages, and large-scale architecture. None of these features were prominent in Paleolithic settlements, agricultural village communities, or pastoral societies. It was a novel and distinctive kind of human society.

Despite their evident similarities, these civilizations were hardly carbon copies of one another. China developed a unified state early in its history centered on an emperor, while the Indus Valley civilization left behind little indication of a centralized state or political hierarchy. Egypt offered its elites a more hopeful outlook on the world and its women a somewhat lighter patriarchy than its Mesopotamian counterparts. Norte Chico established a civilization in the Andes thousands of years before the Olmec did the same in Mesoamerica.

The origin of these civilizations has been much debated, but clearly a river valley environment with a temperate climate and rich agricultural possibilities facilitated their growth. So too most likely did a growing population, competition over resources, and conflict with neighboring peoples. Whatever their origins, civilizations proved to be an enduring and growing feature of human history. Their early appearance on the three major supercontinents of Eurasia, Africa, and the Americas was a global phenomenon, as was their subsequent expansion all across the planet. Thus the story of civilizations — their rise, transformation, and collapse — has become a major theme in world history, sometimes to the exclusion of other kinds of human societies.

Strangely perhaps, the concept of civilization has been highly controversial. For most world historians, it is a purely descriptive term, referring to a distinctive type of human society — one with cities and states — without implying any judgment or assessment, any sense of superiority or inferiority. But in popular usage, "civilization" suggests refined behavior, a "higher" form of society, something unreservedly positive. The opposite of "civilized" — "barbarian," "savage," or "uncivilized" — is normally understood as an insult implying inferiority. That, of course, is precisely how the inhabitants of many civilizations have viewed outsiders, particularly those neighboring peoples living without the alleged benefit of cities and states.

A further issue about using the term "civilization" derives from its implication that civilizations represent distinct and widely shared identities with clear boundaries. It is unlikely, however, that many people living in Mesopotamia or ancient China felt themselves part of a shared culture. Local identities defined by occupation, clan affiliation, village, city, or region were surely more important for most people than being of some larger civilization. Members of an educated upper class who shared a common literary tradition may have felt themselves part of some more inclusive civilization, but that left out most of the population.

Finally, modern assessments of the First Civilizations reveal a profound ambiguity about these new, larger, and more complex societies. On the one hand, these civilizations have given us inspiring art, profound reflections on the meaning of life, more productive technologies, larger populations, increased control over nature, and the art of writing — all of which have been cause for celebration. On the other hand, as anthropologist Marvin Harris noted, "human beings learned for the first time how to bow, grovel, kneel, and kowtow."[23] Massive social inequalities, state oppression, slavery, large-scale warfare, the subordination of women, epidemic disease, and environmental destruction also accompanied the rise of civilization, generating discontent, rebellion, and sometimes the urge to escape. How many people of these growing civilizations enjoyed a richer life than their Neolithic or Paleolithic ancestors? It is not an easy question to answer.

Revisiting Chapter 2

REVISITING SPECIFICS

REVISITING CORE IDEAS

1. **Describing Change** When and where did the First Civilizations emerge?
2. **Assessing Cities** What roles did cities play in early civilizations?
3. **Explaining Inequality** Why did civilizations generate such sharp inequalities of class and gender? In what ways were they expressed?
4. **Analyzing States** What were the sources of state authority in the First Civilizations?
5. **Comparing Civilizations** In what ways did Mesopotamian and Egyptian civilizations differ from each other?
6. **Identifying Interactions** In what ways were Mesopotamian and Egyptian civilizations shaped by their interactions with near and distant neighbors?

A WIDER VIEW

1. In what ways might the advent of "civilization" have marked a revolutionary change in the human condition? And in what ways did it carry on earlier patterns from the past?
2. How does historians' use of the term "civilization" differ from popular usage? How do you use it?
3. "Early civilizations were held together largely by force." Do you agree with this assessment, or were there other mechanisms of integration as well?
4. **Looking Back** To what extent did civilizations represent "progress" in comparison with earlier Paleolithic and Neolithic societies? And in what ways did they constitute a setback for humankind?

CHRONOLOGY

3500–3000	• Beginnings of Sumerian civilization
3500–3000	• Beginnings of Egyptian civilization
3200–3000	• Emergence of Nubian civilization
3000–1800	• Norte Chico civilization
ca. 3000	• Quipu in use in Norte Chico
2663–2195	• Old Kingdom; high point of pharaoh's power and pyramid building
ca. 2600	• Beginnings of civilization in Indus Valley
2200–1800	• Beginnings of Chinese civilization

2200–2000	• Beginnings of civilization in Indus Valley and Central Asia (Oxus Valley)
ca. 2100	• Emergence of Oxus civilization
2070–1600	• Xia dynasty in China
ca. 2000	• *Epic of Gilgamesh* compiled
ca. 2000	• Flourishing of the cities of Mohenjo Daro and Harappa
ca. 1775	• Code of Hammurabi
ca. 1700	• Abandonment of Indus Valley and Central Asian cities
1600–1046	• Shang dynasty in China
1550–1064	• New Kingdom in Egypt
ca. 1500	• Creation of Egyptian empire
ca. 1200	• Beginnings of Olmec civilization
1046–771	• Zhou dynasty in China
900–612	• Assyrian Empire
ca. 900	• Writing in Olmec civilization
760–660	• Kush conquest of Egypt
ca. 500	• Persian Empire established

Note: All dates are B.C.E., or Before the Common Era, and all dates are approximate.

PART 2

Continuity and Change in the Second-Wave Era 600 B.C.E.–600 C.E.

The Big Picture

The Globalization of Civilization

Studying world history has much in common with using the zoom lens of a camera. Sometimes, we pull the lens back to get a picture of the global panorama. At other times, we zoom in a bit for a middle-range shot of a particular region or civilization, or even farther for a close-up of some specific individual, event, or place. As we bid farewell to the First Civilizations, we look broadly, and briefly, at the entire age of agricultural civilizations, a period from about 3500 B.C.E., when the earliest of the First Civilizations arose, to about 1750 C.E., when the first Industrial Revolution launched a new and distinctively modern phase of world history. During these more than 5,000 years, the most prominent large-scale trend was the globalization of civilization as this new form of human community increasingly spread across the planet, encompassing more people and larger territories.

The first wave of that process, addressed in Chapter 2, was already global in scope, with expressions in Asia, Africa, and the Americas. But those First Civilizations, impressive as they were, also proved fragile. To support their growing populations, First Civilizations everywhere turned to ever more intensive methods of production that resulted in the overexploitation of natural resources. Already by around 1700 B.C.E., Norte Chico, the Indus Valley civilization, and the Oxus civilization had collapsed, due in part to environmental factors made worse by the degradation of fragile ecosystems. Then around 1200 B.C.E. a period of global cooling put the agricultural economies of many First Civilizations under great pressure and also resulted in "a great jostling of peoples" as groups abandoned their traditional lands in environmentally fragile regions, including the steppes of Central Asia.[1] These peoples on the move were attracted to the wealth and resources of civilizations, and their arrival further destabilized regions where First Civilizations had long endured. The result was the collapse of powerful states—Shang dynasty China, the Egyptian New Kingdom, and several kingdoms and empires in the eastern Mediterranean and Mesopotamia—that brought an end to the period of First Civilizations in these regions.

But there was no going back, for "civilization" as a form of social organization proved resilient despite its vulnerability. Thus, in the 1,200 years between 600 B.C.E. and 600 C.E., new or enlarged urban-centered and state-based societies emerged to replace the First Civilizations in the Mediterranean basin, the Middle East, India, China, Mesoamerica, and the Andes. In short, the development of civilization was becoming a global process.

Many of these second-wave civilizations likewise perished, as the collapse of the Roman Empire, Han dynasty China, and the Maya cities reminds us. They were followed by yet a third wave of civilizations from roughly 600 to 1500 C.E., including those of China, Western Europe, West Africa, Russia, and the Islamic world (see Part 3). Furthermore, smaller expressions of civilization began to take shape elsewhere—in Ethiopia and West Africa, in Japan, Korea, Indonesia, Vietnam, and Cambodia. Thus the globalization of civilization continued apace. So too did the interaction of civilizations with one another and with the gathering and hunting peoples, agricultural village societies, and pastoral communities who were their neighbors.

But how did these second and third waves of civilization differ from the first ones? From a panoramic perspective, the answer is "not much." States and empires rose, expanded, and collapsed, but no large-scale changes occurred amid these fluctuations. Monarchs continued to rule most of the new civilizations; women remained subordinate to men in all of them; and a sharp divide between the elite and everyone else persisted almost everywhere, as did the practice of slavery. Furthermore, no technological or economic breakthrough occurred to create new kinds of human societies as the Agricultural Revolution had done earlier or as the Industrial Revolution would do much later.

But if we zoom in a bit more closely, we can see that significant changes emerged, even if they did not result in a thorough transformation of human life. Global population, for example, grew more rapidly, though with important fluctuations, as the Snapshot illustrates. This rate of growth, though rapid in comparison with Paleolithic times, was quite slow if measured against the explosive expansion of the past century. Another change lies in the growing size of the states or empires that structured civilizations. The Roman, Persian, Indian, and Chinese empires of second-wave civilizations, as well as the Arab, Mongol, and Inca empires of the third wave, all dwarfed the city-states of Mesopotamia and the Egypt of the pharaohs.

Second- and third-wave civilizations also generated important innovations in many spheres. Cultural innovations have been perhaps the most widespread and enduring. The philosophical/religious systems of Confucianism and Daoism in China; Hinduism and Buddhism in India; Greek rationalism in the Mediterranean; and Judaism, Zoroastrianism, Christianity, and Islam in the Middle East—these traditions have provided the moral and spiritual framework within which most of the world's peoples have sought to order their lives.

Furthermore, technological innovations considerably enhanced human potential for manipulating the environment. "Chinese inventions and discoveries," wrote two prominent historians, "passed in a continuous flood from East to West for twenty centuries before the scientific revolution."[2] They included silk-handling machinery, the wheelbarrow, a better harness for draft animals, the crossbow, iron casting, gunpowder and firearms, the magnetic compass, paper, printing, porcelain, and more. India pioneered the crystallization of sugar and techniques for the manufacture of cotton textiles. Roman technological achievements were particularly apparent in construction and civil engineering—the building of roads, bridges, aqueducts, and fortifications—and in the art of glassblowing.

Nor were social hierarchies immune to change and challenge. India's caste system grew far more elaborate over time. Enslaved people in the Roman Empire and peasants in China on occasion rose in rebellion. Some Buddhist and Christian women found a measure of autonomy and opportunities for leadership and learning in the monastic communities of their traditions. Gender systems, too, fluctuated in the intensity with which women were subordinated to men.

SNAPSHOT	**WORLD POPULATION DURING THE AGE OF AGRICULTURAL CIVILIZATION**

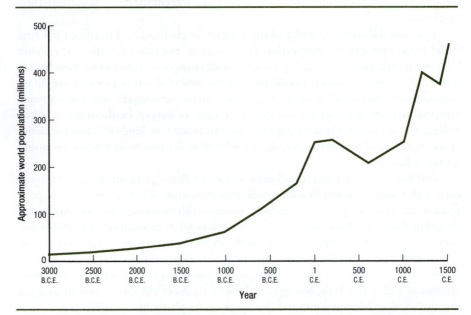

Source: Data from Stephen K. Sanderson, *Social Transformation* (Oxford: Blackwell, 1995), 103.

A further process of change following the end of the First Civilizations lay in the emergence of far more elaborate, widespread, and dense networks of communication and exchange that connected many of the world's peoples to one another. Technologies diffused widely across large areas, as did religions and diseases, often borne by long-distance trade routes, such as the Silk Roads, that traversed Eurasia. In all of these ways, the world became quite different from what it had been in the age of the First Civilizations, even though economic and social patterns had not fundamentally changed.

The first three chapters of Part 2 focus in a thematic fashion on the Eurasian/ North African civilizations of the second-wave era (600 B.C.E.–600 C.E.), which hosted the vast majority of the world's population, some 80 percent or more. Chapter 3 introduces them by examining and comparing their political frameworks and especially the empires that took shape in most of them. Far more enduring than their empires were the cultural or religious traditions that second-wave civilizations generated. These are examined, also comparatively, in Chapter 4. The social life of these civilizations, expressed in class, caste, slavery, and gender relationships, also varied considerably, as Chapter 5 spells out. In Chapter 6, the historical spotlight turns to inner Africa, the Americas, and Pacific Oceania, asking whether their histories paralleled Eurasian patterns or explored alternative possibilities.

In recalling this second-wave phase of the human journey, we will have occasion to compare the experiences of its various peoples, to note their remarkable achievements, to lament the tragedies that befell them and the suffering to which they gave rise, and to ponder their continuing power to fascinate us still.

FIRST REFLECTIONS

1. **Questioning Chronology** In this brief essay, we defined several time periods: agricultural civilizations (3500 B.C.E.–1750 C.E.), second-wave civilizations (600 B.C.E.–600 C.E.), and third-wave civilizations (600–1500 C.E.). What criteria were used to define these periods of time? Can you imagine alternative ways of dividing up this chronology, perhaps using different criteria?

2. **Assessing Continuity and Change** Are you more impressed by the continuities in civilizations over many thousands of years or the changes that occurred during the first, second, and third waves of civilization?

3. **Drawing Conclusions from Data** What conclusions might you draw from the graph of human population between 3000 B.C.E. and 1500 C.E.? And what questions does the graph suggest to you?

4. **Thinking like a World Historian** Draw your wide-angle lens out even further to include civilizations in the early twenty-first century. What continuities and changes can you identify between civilizations today and those of the first, second, and third waves?

3

State and Empire in Eurasia / North Africa

600 B.C.E.–600 C.E.

CONNECTING PAST AND PRESENT

AMERICA IS NOT ROME. IT JUST THINKS IT IS. This was the title of a 2019 article by British historian Tom Holland exploring what had become a familiar question in the early twenty-first century: "Is the United States the new Roman Empire?"[1] With the collapse of the Soviet Union by 1991, the United States emerged as the world's sole superpower, at least temporarily. Its enormous multicultural society, technological achievements, concern about foreigners penetrating its borders, determination to maintain military superiority—all of this invited comparison with the Roman Empire.

Supporters of a dominant role for the United States argued that Americans must face up to their responsibilities as "the undisputed master of the world" as the Romans did in their time. Critics warned that the

Roman Empire became overextended abroad and corrupt and dictatorial at home and then collapsed, suggesting that a similar fate may await the American empire. Either way, the point of reference was an empire that had passed into history some 1,500 years earlier, a continuing reminder of the significance of the distant past for our contemporary world. In fact, for at least several centuries, that empire has been a source of metaphors and "lessons" about personal morality, corruption, political life, military expansion, and much more.

Even in a world largely critical of empires, they still excite the imagination of historians and readers of history alike. The earliest empires show up in the era of the First Civilizations when Akkadian, Babylonian, and Assyrian empires encompassed the city-states of Mesopotamia and established an enduring imperial tradition in the Middle East. Egypt became an imperial state when it temporarily ruled Nubia and the lands of the eastern Mediterranean. Following in their wake were many more empires, whose rise and fall have been central features of world history for the past 4,000 years.

But what exactly is an empire? At one level, empires are simply states, political systems that exercise coercive power. The term, however, is normally reserved for larger and more aggressive states, those that conquer, rule, and extract resources from other states and peoples. Thus empires have generally encompassed a considerable variety of peoples and cultures within a single political system, and they have often been associated with political or cultural oppression. Frequently, empires have given political expression to a civilization or culture, as in the Chinese and Persian empires. But civilizations have also flourished without a single all-encompassing state or empire, as in the competing city-states of Mesopotamia, Greece, and the Maya peoples or the many rival states of post-Roman Europe. In such cases, civilizations were expressed in elements of a common culture rather than in a unified political system.

The major Eurasian empires of the second-wave era—those of Persia, Greece under Alexander the Great, Rome, China during the Qin (chihn) and Han dynasties, and India during the Mauryan (MORE-yuhn) and Gupta dynasties—shared a set of common problems. Would they seek to impose the culture of the imperial heartland on their varied subjects? Would they rule conquered people directly or through established local authorities? How could they extract the wealth of empire in the form of taxes, tribute, and labor while maintaining order in conquered territories? And they also shared a common destiny, as they vanished into history.

Why have these and other empires been of such lasting fascination to both ancient and modern people? Perhaps part of the reason is that they were so big, creating a looming presence in their respective regions. Their armies and their tax collectors were hard to avoid. Perhaps they fascinate also because they were so bloody. The violence of conquest easily grabs our attention, and certainly all of these empires were founded and sustained at a great cost in human life. Many people have found the collapse of these once-powerful states likewise intriguing. But empires have also commanded attention simply because they were influential. Probably the majority of humankind before the twentieth century lived out their lives in empires, where they were often governed by rulers culturally different from themselves. These imperial states brought together people of quite different traditions and religions and so stimulated the exchange of ideas, cultures, and values. Despite their violence, exploitation, and oppression, empires also imposed substantial periods of peace and security that fostered economic and artistic development, commercial exchange, and cultural mixing. In many places, empire also played an important role in defining masculinity, as conquest generated a warrior culture that gave particular prominence to the men who created and ruled those imperial states.

| SEEKING THE MAIN POINT | How might you define the role and significance of Eurasian empires in the history of the second-wave era? |

Empires and Civilizations in Collision: The Persians and the Greeks

The centuries between 600 B.C.E. and 600 C.E. witnessed the flowering of second-wave civilizations in the Mediterranean world, the Middle East, India, and China. For the most part, these distant civilizations did not directly encounter one another, as each established its own political system, cultural values, and ways of organizing society. A great exception to that rule lay in the Mediterranean world and in the Middle East, where the emerging Persian Empire and Greek civilization, physically adjacent to each other, experienced a centuries-long interaction and clash. It was one of the most consequential cultural encounters of the ancient world.

The Persian Empire

By the mid-sixth century B.C.E., the largest and most impressive of the world's empires was that of the Persians, an Indo-European people whose homeland lay on the Iranian plateau just north of the Persian Gulf. Living on the margins of the earlier Mesopotamian civilization, the Persians under the Achaemenid (ah-KEE-muh-nid) dynasty (550–330 B.C.E.) constructed an imperial system that drew on previous examples, such as the Babylonian and Assyrian empires, but far surpassed them all in both size and splendor. Under the leadership of the famous monarchs Cyrus (r. 559–530 B.C.E.) and Darius (r. 522–486 B.C.E.), Persian conquests quickly reached from Egypt to India, encompassing in a single state some 35 to 50 million people, an immensely diverse realm containing dozens of peoples, states, languages, and cultural traditions (see Map 3.1).

The **Persian Empire** centered on an elaborate cult of kingship in which the monarch, secluded in royal magnificence, could be approached only through an elaborate ritual. When the king died, sacred fires all across the land were extinguished, Persians were expected to shave their hair in mourning, and the manes of horses were cut short. Ruling by the will of the great Persian god Ahura Mazda (uh-HOORE-uh MAHZ-duh), kings were absolute monarchs, more than willing to crush rebellious regions or officials. Interrupted on one occasion while engaged with his wife, Darius

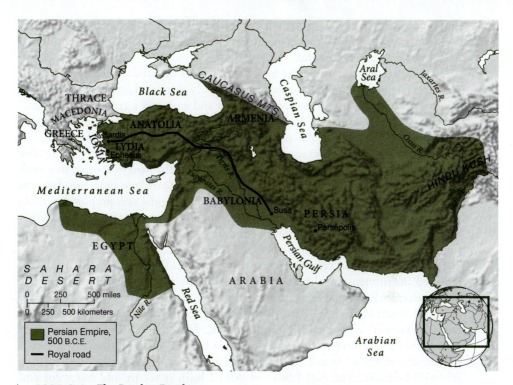

MAP 3.1 The Persian Empire
At its height, the Persian Empire was the largest in the world. It dominated the lands of the First Civilizations in the Middle East and was commercially connected to neighboring regions.

ordered the offender, a high-ranking nobleman, killed, along with his entire clan. In the eyes of many, Persian monarchs fully deserved their effusive title — "Great king, King of kings, King of countries containing all kinds of men, King in this great earth far and wide." Darius himself best expressed the authority of the Persian ruler when he observed, "What was said to them by me, night and day, it was done."[2]

But more than conquest and royal decree sustained the empire. An effective administrative system placed Persian governors, called *satraps* (SAY-traps), in each of the empire's twenty-three provinces, while lower-level officials were drawn from local authorities. A system of imperial spies, known as the "eyes and ears of the King," represented a further imperial presence in the far reaches of the empire. A general policy of respect for the empire's many non-Persian cultural traditions also cemented the state's authority. Cyrus won the gratitude of the Jews when in 539 B.C.E. he allowed those exiled in Babylon to return to their homeland and rebuild their temple in Jerusalem (see "Judaism" in Chapter 4). In Egypt and Babylon, Persian kings took care to uphold local religious cults in an effort to gain the support of their followers and officials. The Greek historian Herodotus commented that "there is no nation which so readily adopts foreign customs. They have taken the dress of the Medes and in war they wear the Egyptian breastplate. As soon as they hear of any luxury, they instantly make it their own."[3] For the next 1,000 years or more, Persian imperial bureaucracy and court life, replete with administrators, tax collectors, record keepers, and translators, provided a model for all subsequent regimes in the region, including, later, those of the Islamic world.

The infrastructure of empire included a system of standardized coinage, predictable taxes levied on each province, and a newly dug canal linking the Nile with the Red Sea that greatly expanded commerce and enriched Egypt. A "royal road," some 1,700 miles in length, facilitated communication and commerce across this vast empire. Caravans of merchants could traverse this highway in three months, but agents of the imperial courier service, using a fresh supply of horses every twenty-five to thirty miles, could carry a message from one end of the road to another in a week or two. Herodotus was impressed. "Neither snow, nor rain, nor heat, nor darkness of night," he wrote, "prevents them from accomplishing the task proposed to them with utmost speed." And an elaborate underground irrigation system sustained a rich agricultural economy in the semi-arid conditions of the Iranian plateau and spread from there throughout the Middle East and beyond.

Elaborate imperial centers, particularly Susa and Persepolis (per-SEP-uh-lis), reflected the immense wealth and power of the Persian Empire. Palaces, audience halls, quarters for the harem, monuments, and carvings made these cities into powerful symbols of imperial authority. Materials and workers alike were drawn from all corners of the empire and beyond. Inscribed in the foundation of Persepolis was Darius's commentary on what he had set in motion: "And Ahura Mazda was of such a mind, together with all the other gods, that this fortress [should] be built. And [so] I built it. And I built it secure and beautiful and adequate, just as I was intending to."[4]

Darius I This carving depicts an imperial officer paying homage to Emperor Darius I of Persia seated on his throne. It decorated the treasury, a storehouse for arms and wealth, in the Persian capital of Persepolis. (Bridgeman Images)

The Greeks

It would be hard to imagine a sharper contrast than that between the huge and centralized Persian Empire, governed by an absolute and almost unapproachable monarch, and the small competing city-states of classical Greece, which allowed varying degrees of popular participation in political life. Like the Persians, the Greeks were an Indo-European people whose early history drew on the legacy of the First Civilizations, especially Egypt. The classical Greece of historical fame emerged around 750 B.C.E. as a new civilization and flourished for about 400 years before it was incorporated into a succession of foreign empires. During that relatively short period, the civilization of Athens and Sparta, of Plato and Socrates, of Zeus and Apollo took shape and collided with its giant neighbor to the east.

Calling themselves Hellenes, the Greeks created a distinctive civilization, particularly in comparison with that of the Persians. The total population of Greece and the Aegean basin was just 2 million to 3 million, a fraction of that of the Persian Empire. Furthermore, Greek civilization took shape on a small peninsula that was deeply divided by steep mountains and valleys. Its geography certainly contributed to its political organization, which found expression, not in a Persian-style empire, but in hundreds of city-states or small settlements (see Map 3.2). Most were quite modest in size, with between 500 and 5,000 male citizens or free men. But Greek civilization, like its counterparts elsewhere, also left a decisive environmental mark on the lands it encompassed. Smelting metals such as silver, lead, copper, bronze, and iron required enormous supplies of wood, leading to deforestation and soil erosion. Plato declared that the area around Athens had become "a mere relic of the original country. . . . All the rich soil has melted away, leaving a country of skin and bone."[5]

Each of these city-states was fiercely independent and in frequent conflict with its neighbors, yet they had much in common, speaking the same language and worshipping the same gods. Every four years they temporarily suspended their continual conflicts to participate together in the Olympic Games, which began in 776 B.C.E. But this emerging sense of Greek cultural identity did little to overcome the endemic political rivalries of the larger city-states, including Athens, Sparta, Thebes, and Corinth, among many others.

Like the Persians, the Greeks were an expansive people, but their expansion took the form of settlement in distant places rather than conquest and empire. Pushed by a growing population, Greek traders in search of iron and impoverished Greek farmers in search of land undertook a remarkable emigration. Between 750 and 500 B.C.E., the Greeks established settlements all around the Mediterranean basin and the rim of the Black Sea. Settlers brought Greek culture, language, and building styles to these new lands, even as they fought, traded, and intermarried with their non-Greek neighbors.

The most distinctive feature of Greek civilization, and the greatest contrast with Persia, lay in the extent of popular participation in political life that occurred within at least some of the city-states. It was the idea of "citizenship," of free people managing the affairs of state and of equality for all citizens before the law, that was so unique. A foreign king, observing the operation of the public assembly in Athens, was amazed that male citizens as a whole actually voted on matters of policy: "I find it astonishing," he noted, "that here wise men speak on public affairs, while fools

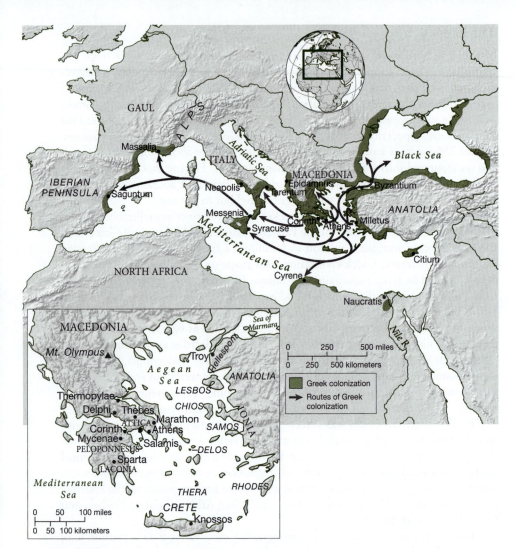

MAP 3.2   Classical Greece and Its Colonies

The classical civilization of Greece was centered on a small peninsula of southeastern Europe, but Greek settlers planted elements of that civilization along the coasts of the Mediterranean and Black seas.

decide them."[6] Compared to the rigid hierarchies, inequalities, and absolute monarchies of Persia and other ancient civilizations, the Athenian experiment was remarkable. According to one modern scholar, "the question was whether all the citizens, including the poor, might govern and whether it would be possible for them to govern as citizens, without specializing in politics. In other words, should the governed themselves actively participate in politics on a regular basis?"[7]

The extent of participation and the role of "citizens" varied considerably, both over time and from city to city. Early in Greek history, only wealthy and well-born men had the rights of full citizenship, such as speaking and voting in the assembly, holding public office, and fighting in the army. Gradually, men of the lower classes, mostly small-scale farmers, also obtained these rights as they gained the means to purchase the armor and weapons that would allow them to serve as hoplites, or infantrymen, in the armies of the city-states. In many places, strong but benevolent rulers known as tyrants emerged for a time, usually with the support of the poorer classes, to challenge the prerogatives of the wealthy. Sparta developed a distinctive political and social system, famous for its extreme military discipline and its large population of helots, conquered people who lived in slave-like conditions. Most political authority was vested in its Council of Elders, composed of twenty-eight men over the age of sixty who came from the wealthier and more influential segment of society and served for life.

It was in Athens that the Greek experiment in political participation achieved its most distinctive expression. Early steps in this direction were the product of intense class conflict, leading almost to civil war. A reforming leader named Solon emerged in 594 B.C.E. to push Athenian politics in a more democratic direction, breaking the hold of a small group of aristocratic families. Debt slavery was abolished, access to public office was opened to a wider group of men, and all citizens were allowed to take part in the Assembly. Later reformers such as Cleisthenes (KLEYE-sthuh-nees) and Pericles extended the rights of citizens even further. By 450 B.C.E., all holders of public office were chosen by lot and were paid, so that even the poorest could serve. The Assembly, where all citizens could participate, became the center of political life.

Athenian democracy was direct rather than representative, and it was distinctly limited. Women, enslaved people, and foreigners, who together constituted far more than half of the population, were wholly excluded from political participation. Nonetheless, political life in Athens was a world away from that of the Persian Empire and even from that of many other Greek cities.

Collision: The Greco-Persian Wars

In recent centuries, many writers and scholars have claimed classical Greece as the foundation of Western or European civilization. But the ancient Greeks themselves looked primarily to the East — to Egypt and the Persian Empire. In Egypt, Greek scholars found impressive mathematical and astronomical traditions on which they built. And Persia represented both an immense threat and later, under Alexander the Great, an opportunity for Greek empire building.

If ever there was an unequal conflict between civilizations, surely it was the collision of the Greeks and the Persians during a half century of intermittent military conflict known to us as the **Greco-Persian Wars** (499–449 B.C.E.). The confrontation between the small and divided Greek cities and Persia, the world's largest empire, grew out of their respective patterns of expansion. A number of Greek settlements on the Anatolian seacoast, known to the Greeks as Ionia, came under Persian control as that empire extended its domination to the west. In 499 B.C.E., some of these Ionian Greek cities revolted against Persian domination and found support from Athens on the Greek mainland. Outraged by this assault from the remote and upstart Greeks, the Persians, twice in ten years (490 and 480 B.C.E.), launched major military expeditions to punish the Greeks in general and Athens in particular.

Against all odds and all expectations, the Greeks held them off, defeating the Persians on both land and sea.

Though no doubt embarrassing, their defeat on the far western fringes of the empire had little effect on the Persians. However, it had a profound impact on Greece and especially on Athens, whose forces had led the way to victory. Beating the Persians in battle was a source of enormous pride for Greeks. In their view, this victory was the product of Greek freedoms, which had motivated men to fight with extraordinary courage for what they valued so highly. It contributed to a European construction of the world as sharply divided between East and West in which Persia represented Asia and despotism, and Greece signified Europe and freedom. The Greek victory also radicalized Athenian democracy, for it had been men of the poorer classes who had rowed their ships to victory and who were now in a position to insist on full citizenship. The fifty years or so after the Greco-Persian Wars were not only the high point of Athenian democracy but also the Golden Age of Greek culture. During this period, the Parthenon, that marvelous temple to the Greek goddess Athena, was built; Greek theater was born from the work of Aeschylus, Sophocles, and Euripides; and Socrates was beginning his career as a philosopher and an irritant in Athens.

But Athens's Golden Age was also an era of incipient empire. In the Greco-Persian Wars, Athens had led a coalition of more than thirty Greek city-states on the basis of its naval power, but Athenian leadership in the struggle against Persian aggression had spawned an imperialism of its own. After the war, Athens's efforts to solidify its dominant position among the allies led to intense resentment and finally to a bitter war (431–404 B.C.E.), with Sparta taking the lead in defending the traditional independence of Greek city-states. In this bloody conflict, known as the **Peloponnesian War**, Athens was defeated, and the Greeks exhausted themselves and magnified their distrust of one another. Thus the way was open to their eventual takeover by the growing forces of Macedonia, a frontier kingdom on the northern fringes of the Greek world. The glory days of the Greek experiment were over, but the spread of Greek culture was just beginning.

Collision: Alexander and the Hellenistic Era

By 338 B.C.E. Philip II, king of Macedonia, had politically unified Greece under his rule, bringing to an end the long-established and prized independence of its various city-states. This unification also set in motion a second round in the collision of Greece and Persia as Philip's son, known later as **Alexander the Great**, prepared to lead a massive Greek expedition against the Persian Empire. Such a project appealed to those who sought vengeance for the earlier Persian assault on Greece, but it also served to unify the fractious Greeks in a war against their common enemy.

The story of this ten-year expedition (334–323 B.C.E.), accomplished while Alexander was still in his twenties, has become the stuff of legend (see Map 3.3). Surely it was among the greatest military feats of the ancient world in that it created a Greek empire from Egypt and Anatolia in the west to Afghanistan and India in the east. In the process, the great Persian Empire was thoroughly defeated; its capital, Persepolis, was looted and burned; and Alexander was hailed as the "king of Asia." In Egypt, Alexander, then just twenty-four years old, was celebrated as a liberator from

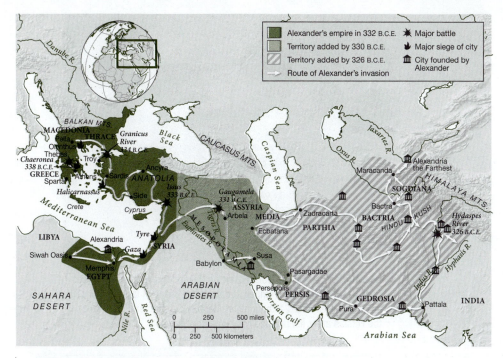

MAP 3.3 Alexander's Empire and Successor States

Alexander's conquests, though enormous, did not long remain within a single empire, for his generals divided those lands into three successor states shortly after Alexander's death. This was the Hellenistic world within which Greek culture spread.

Persian domination, was anointed as pharaoh, and was declared by Egyptian priests to be the "son of the gods." Arrian, a later Greek historian, described Alexander in this way:

> His passion was for glory only, and in that he was insatiable. . . . Noble indeed was his power of inspiring his men, of filling them with confidence, and in the moment of danger, of sweeping away their fear by the spectacle of his own fearlessness.[8]

Alexander died in 323 B.C.E., without returning to Greece, and his empire was soon divided into three kingdoms, ruled by leading Macedonian generals.

From the viewpoint of world history, the chief significance of Alexander's amazing conquests lay in the widespread dissemination of Greek culture during what historians call the **Hellenistic era** (323–30 B.C.E.). Elements of that culture, generated in a small and remote Mediterranean peninsula, now penetrated the lands of the First Civilizations—Egypt, Mesopotamia, and India—resulting in one of the great cultural encounters of the ancient world.

The major avenue for the spread of Greek culture lay in the many cities that Alexander and later Hellenistic rulers established throughout the empire. Complete with Greek monuments, sculptures, theaters, markets, councils, and assemblies, these

Alexander the Great This mosaic of Alexander on horseback comes from the Roman city of Pompeii. It depicts the Battle of Issus (333 B.C.E.), in which Greek forces, although considerably outnumbered, defeated the Persian army, led personally by Emperor Darius III. (ullstein bild/Getty Images)

cities attracted many thousands of Greek settlers serving as state officials, soldiers, or traders. **Alexandria** in Egypt—the largest of these cities, with half a million people—was an enormous cosmopolitan center where Egyptians, Greeks, Jews, Babylonians, Syrians, Persians, and many others rubbed elbows. A harbor with space for 1,200 ships facilitated long-distance commerce. Greek learning flourished thanks to a library of some 700,000 volumes and the Museum, which sponsored scholars and writers of all kinds.

From cities such as these, Greek culture spread. From the Mediterranean to India, Greek became the language of power and elite culture. The Indian monarch Ashoka published some of his decrees in Greek, while an independent Greek state was established in Bactria in what is now northern Afghanistan. The attraction of many young Jews to Greek culture prompted the Pharisees to develop their own school system, as this highly conservative Jewish sect feared for the very survival of Judaism.

Cities such as Alexandria were very different from the original city-states of Greece, both in their cultural diversity and in the absence of the independence so valued by Athens and Sparta. Now they were part of large conquest states ruled by Greeks: the Ptolemaic (TOL-uh-MAY-ik) empire in Egypt and the Seleucid empire in Persia. These were imperial states, which, in their determination to preserve order, raise taxes, and maintain the authority of the monarch, resembled the much older empires of Mesopotamia, Egypt, Assyria, and Persia. Macedonians and Greeks, representing perhaps 10 percent of the population in these Hellenistic kingdoms, were clearly the elite and sought to keep themselves separate from non-Greeks.

In Egypt, for example, different legal systems for Greeks and native Egyptians maintained this separation. An Egyptian agricultural worker complained that because he was an Egyptian, his supervisors despised him and refused to pay him.[9] Periodic rebellions expressed resentment at Greek arrogance, condescension, and exploitation. But the separation between the Greeks and native populations was by no means complete, and a fair amount of cultural interaction and blending occurred. Alexander himself had taken several Persian princesses as his wives and actively encouraged intermarriage between his troops and Asian women. In both Egypt and Mesopotamia, Greek rulers patronized the building of temples to local gods and actively supported their priests. A growing number of native peoples were able to become Greek citizens by obtaining a Greek education, speaking the language, dressing appropriately, and assuming Greek names. In India, Greeks were assimilated into the hierarchy of the caste system as members of the Kshatriya (warrior) caste, while in Bactria a substantial number of Greeks converted to Buddhism, including one of the Bactrian kings, Menander. A school of Buddhist art that emerged in the early centuries of the Common Era depicted the Buddha in human form for the first time, but in Greek-like garb with a face resembling the god Apollo. Clearly, not all was conflict between the Greeks and the peoples of the East.

In the long run, much of this Greek cultural influence faded as the Hellenistic kingdoms that had promoted it weakened and vanished by the first century B.C.E. While it lasted, however, it represented a remarkable cultural encounter, born of the collision of two empires and two second-wave civilizations. In the western part of that Hellenistic world, Greek rule was replaced by that of the Romans, whose empire, like Alexander's, also served as a vehicle for the continued spread of Greek culture and ideas.

Comparing Empires: Roman and Chinese

While the adjacent civilizations of the Greeks and the Persians collided, two other empires were taking shape — the Roman Empire on the far western side of Eurasia and China's imperial state on the far eastern end. They flourished at roughly the same time (200 B.C.E.–200 C.E.); they occupied a similar area (about 1.5 million square miles); and they encompassed populations of a similar size (50 to 60 million). They were the giant empires of their time, shaping the lives of close to half of the world's population. Unlike the Greeks and the Persians, the Romans and the Chinese were only dimly aware of each other and had almost no direct contact. Historians, however, have seen them as fascinating variations on an imperial theme and have long explored their similarities and differences.

Rome: From City-State to Empire

Like the Persian Empire, that of the Romans took shape initially on the margins of the civilized world and was an unlikely rags-to-riches story. Beginning as a small and impoverished city-state on the western side of central Italy in the eighth century B.C.E., Rome later became the center of an enormous imperial state that encompassed the Mediterranean basin and included parts of continental Europe, Britain, North Africa, and the Middle East.

Originally ruled by a king, around 509 B.C.E. Roman aristocrats threw off the monarchy and established a republic in which the men of a wealthy class, known as patricians, dominated. Executive authority was exercised by two consuls who were advised by a patrician assembly, the Senate. Deepening conflict with the poorer classes, called plebeians (plih-BEE-uhns), led to important changes in Roman political life. A written code of law offered plebeians some protection from abuse; a system of public assemblies provided an opportunity for lower classes to shape public policy; and a new office of tribune, who represented plebeians, allowed them to block unfavorable legislation. Romans took great pride in this political system, believing that they enjoyed greater freedom than did many of their more autocratic neighbors. The values of the republic—rule of law, the rights of citizens, the absence of pretension, upright moral behavior, keeping one's word—were later idealized as "the way of the ancestors."

With this political system and these values, the Romans launched their empire-building enterprise, a prolonged process that took more than 500 years (see Map 3.4). That empire began in the 490s B.C.E. with the Romans gaining control

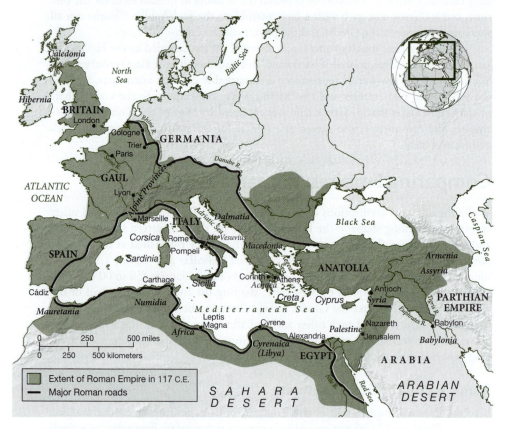

MAP 3.4 The Roman Empire

At its height in the second century C.E., the Roman Empire incorporated the entire Mediterranean basin, including the lands of the Carthaginian Empire, the less developed region of Western Europe, the heartland of Greek civilization, and the ancient civilizations of Egypt and Mesopotamia.

first over their Latin neighbors in central Italy and then, during the next several hundred years, over most of the Italian peninsula. Between 264 and 146 B.C.E., victory in the Punic Wars with Carthage, a powerful empire with its capital in North Africa, extended Roman control over the western Mediterranean, including Spain, and made Rome a naval power. Subsequent expansion in the eastern Mediterranean brought the ancient civilizations of Greece, Egypt, and Mesopotamia under Roman domination. Rome also expanded into territories in Southern and Western Europe, including present-day France and Britain. By early in the second century C.E., the Roman Empire had reached its maximum extent.

No overall design or blueprint drove the building of empire, nor were there any precedents to guide the Romans. What they created was something wholly new — an empire that encompassed the entire Mediterranean basin and beyond. It was a piecemeal process, which the Romans invariably saw as defensive. Each addition of territory created new vulnerabilities that could be relieved only by more conquests. For some, the growth of empire represented opportunity. Poor soldiers hoped for land, loot, or salaries that might lift their families out of poverty. The well-to-do or well-connected gained great estates, earned promotions, and sometimes achieved public acclaim and high political office. The wealth of long-established societies in the eastern Mediterranean (Greece and Egypt, for example) beckoned, as did the resources and food supplies of the less developed regions, such as Western Europe. There was no shortage of motivation for the creation of the Roman Empire.

Although Rome's central location in the Mediterranean basin provided a convenient launching pad for empire, it was the army, "well-trained, well-fed, and well-rewarded," that built the empire.[10] Drawing on the growing population of Italy, that army was often brutal in war. Carthage, for example, was utterly destroyed; the city was razed to the ground, and its inhabitants were either killed or sold into slavery. Nonetheless, Roman authorities could be generous to former enemies. Some were granted Roman citizenship; others were treated as allies and allowed to maintain their local rulers. As the empire grew, so too did political forces in Rome that favored its continued expansion and were willing to commit the necessary manpower and resources.

Centuries of empire building and the warfare that made it possible had an impact on Roman society and values. That vast process, for example, shaped Roman understandings of gender and the appropriate roles of men and women. Rome was becoming a warrior society in which the masculinity of upper-class male citizens was defined in part by a man's role as a soldier and a property owner. In private life, this translated into absolute control over his wife, children, and enslaved servants, including the theoretical right to kill them without interference from the state. This ability of a free man and a Roman citizen to act decisively in both public and private life lay at the heart of ideal male identity. A Roman woman could participate proudly in this warrior culture by bearing brave sons and inculcating these values in her offspring.

Strangely enough, by the early centuries of the Common Era the wealth of empire, the authority of the imperial state, and the breakdown of older Roman social patterns combined to offer women in the elite classes a less restricted life than they had known in the early centuries of the republic. Upper-class Roman women had never been as secluded in the home as were their Greek counterparts, and now the legal authority of their husbands was curtailed by the intrusion of the state into what had been private life. The head of household, or *pater familias*, lost his earlier power of life and death over his family. Furthermore, such women could now marry without transferring legal control to their husbands and were increasingly able to manage their own finances and take part in the growing commercial economy of the empire. According to one scholar, Roman women of the wealthier classes gained "almost complete liberty in matters of property and marriage."[11] At the other end of the social spectrum, Roman conquests brought many thousands of women as well as men into the empire as enslaved people, who were often brutally treated and subject to the whims of their masters (see "The Making of Roman Slavery" in Chapter 5).

The relentless expansion of empire raised yet another profound question for Rome: could republican government and values survive the acquisition of a huge empire? The wealth of empire enriched a few, enabling them to acquire large estates and many enslaved people, while pushing growing numbers of free farmers into the cities and poverty. Imperial riches also empowered a small group of military leaders—Marius, Sulla, Pompey, Julius Caesar—who recruited their troops directly from the ranks of the poor and whose fierce rivalries brought civil war to Rome during the first century B.C.E. Traditionalists lamented the apparent decline of republican values—simplicity, service, free farmers as the backbone of the army, the authority of the Senate—amid the self-seeking ambitions of the newly rich and powerful. When the dust settled from the civil war, Rome was clearly changing, for authority was now vested primarily in an emperor, the first of whom was Octavian, later granted the title of **Augustus** (r. 27 B.C.E.–14 C.E.), which implied a divine status for the ruler. The republic was history; Rome had become an empire and its ruler an emperor.

But it was an empire with an uneasy conscience, for many felt that in acquiring an empire, Rome had betrayed and abandoned its republican origins. Augustus was careful to maintain the forms of the republic—the Senate, consuls, public assemblies—and referred to himself as "first man" rather than "king" or "emperor," even as he accumulated enormous personal power. And in a bow to republican values, he spoke of the empire's conquests as reflecting the "power of the Roman people" rather than of the Roman state. Despite this rhetoric, he was emperor in practice, if not in name, for he was able to exercise sole authority, backed up by his command of a professional army. Later emperors were less reluctant to flaunt their imperial prerogatives.

During the first two centuries C.E., this empire in disguise provided security, grandeur, and relative prosperity for the Mediterranean world. This was the *pax Romana*, the Roman peace, the era of imperial Rome's greatest extent and greatest authority.

China: From Warring States to Empire

About the same time, on the other side of Eurasia, another huge imperial state was in the making—China. Here, however, the task was understood differently. It was not a matter of creating something new, as in the case of the Roman Empire, but of restoring something old. As one of the First Civilizations, a Chinese state had emerged as early as 2200 B.C.E. and under the Xia, Shang, and Zhou dynasties had grown progressively larger. By 500 B.C.E., however, this Chinese state was in shambles. Any earlier unity vanished in an "age of warring states," featuring the endless rivalries of seven competing kingdoms.

To many Chinese, this was a wholly unnatural and unacceptable condition, and rulers in various states vied to reunify China. One of them, known to history as **Qin Shihuangdi** (chihn shee-HUANG-dee) (i.e., Shihuangdi from the state of Qin), succeeded brilliantly. The state of Qin had already developed an effective bureaucracy, subordinated its aristocracy, equipped its army with iron weapons, and enjoyed rapidly rising agricultural output and a growing population. It also had adopted a political philosophy called Legalism, which advocated clear rules and harsh punishments as a means of enforcing the authority of the state. With these resources, Shihuangdi (r. 221–210 B.C.E.) launched a military campaign to reunify China and in just ten years soundly defeated the other warring states. Believing that he had created a universal and eternal empire, he grandly named himself Shihuangdi, which means the "first emperor." Unlike Augustus, he showed little ambivalence about empire. Subsequent conquests extended China's boundaries far to the south into the northern part of Vietnam, to the northeast into Korea, and to the northwest, where the Chinese pushed back the nomadic pastoral people of the steppes. Although the boundaries fluctuated over time, Shihuangdi laid the foundations for a unified Chinese state that has endured, with periodic interruptions, to the present (see Map 3.5).

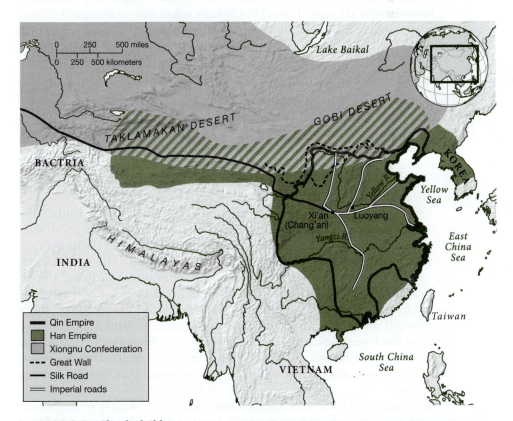

MAP 3.5   Classical China
The brief Qin dynasty brought unity to the heartland of Chinese civilization, and the much longer Han dynasty extended its territorial reach south toward Vietnam, east to Korea, and west into Central Asia. To the north lay the military confederacy of the nomadic Xiongnu.

Building on earlier precedents, the Chinese process of empire formation was far more compressed than the centuries-long Roman effort, but it was no less dependent on military force and no less brutal. Scholars who opposed Shihuangdi's policies were executed and their books burned. Aristocrats who resisted his centralizing policies were moved physically to the capital. Hundreds of thousands of laborers were recruited to construct the Great Wall of China, designed to keep out northern "barbarians," and to erect a monumental mausoleum as the emperor's final resting place. More positively, Shihuangdi imposed a uniform system of weights, measures, and currency and standardized the length of axles for carts and the written form of the Chinese language.

As in Rome, the creation of the Chinese empire had domestic repercussions, but they were brief and superficial compared to Rome's transition from republic to empire. The speed and brutality of Shihuangdi's policies ensured that his own Qin dynasty did not last long, and it collapsed unmourned in 206 B.C.E. The **Han dynasty** that followed (206 B.C.E.–220 C.E.) retained the centralized features of Shihuangdi's creation, although it moderated the harshness of his policies, adopting a milder and moralistic Confucianism in place of Legalism as the governing philosophy of the state. It was Han dynasty rulers who consolidated China's imperial state and established the political patterns that lasted into the twentieth century.

Consolidating the Roman and Chinese Empires

Once established, these two huge imperial systems shared a number of common features. Both, for example, defined themselves in universal terms. The Roman writer Polybius spoke of bringing "almost the entire world" under the control of Rome, while the Chinese state was said to encompass "all under heaven." Both of them invested heavily in public works — roads, bridges, aqueducts, canals, protective walls — all designed to integrate their respective domains militarily and commercially.

Furthermore, Roman and Chinese authorities both invoked supernatural sanctions to support their rule. By the first century C.E., Romans began to regard their deceased emperors as gods and established a religious cult to bolster the authority of living rulers. In China, a much older tradition had long linked events on Earth with the invisible realm called "Heaven." Neither a place nor a supreme being, Heaven was an impersonal moral force that regulated the universe. Emperors were called the Son of Heaven and were said to govern by the Mandate of Heaven so long as they ruled morally and with benevolence. Peasant rebellions, "barbarian" invasions, or disastrous floods were viewed as signs that the emperor had ruled badly and had thus lost the Mandate of Heaven. Among the chief duties of the emperor was the performance of various rituals thought to maintain the appropriate relationship between Heaven and Earth.

The Roman and Chinese empires also had a different relationship to the societies they governed. Rome's beginnings as a small city-state meant that Romans, and even Italians, were always a distinct minority within the empire. The Chinese empire, by contrast, grew out of a much larger cultural heartland, already ethnically Chinese. Furthermore, as the Chinese state expanded, especially to the south, it actively assimilated the non-Chinese, or "barbarian," people. In short, they became Chinese, culturally, linguistically, and through intermarriage in physical appearance as well. Many Chinese in modern times are in fact descended from people who at one point or another were not Chinese at all.

The Roman Empire offered a different kind of assimilation to its subject peoples. Gradually and somewhat reluctantly, the empire granted Roman citizenship to various individuals, families, or whole communities for their service to the empire or in recognition of their adoption of Roman culture. In 212 C.E., Roman citizenship was bestowed on almost all free men of the empire. Citizenship offered clear advantages—the right to hold public office, to serve in the Roman military units known as legions, to wear a toga, and more—but it conveyed a legal status, rather than cultural assimilation, and certainly did not erase other identities, such as being Greek, Egyptian, or a citizen of a particular city.

Various elements of Roman culture—its public buildings, its religious rituals, its Latin language, its style of city life—were attractive, especially in Western Europe, where urban civilization was something new. In the eastern half of the empire, however, things Greek retained tremendous prestige. Many elite Romans in fact regarded Greek culture—its literature, philosophy, and art—as superior to their own and proudly sent their sons to Athens for a Greek education. To some extent, the two blended into a mixed Greco-Roman tradition that the empire disseminated

A Chinese Musician This Chinese stone relief from the fifth century C.E. depicts a "celestial musician," a minor Buddhist deity, playing a *pipa*, a string instrument of Central Asian origin. (De Agostini Picture Library/G. Dagli Orti/Bridgeman Images)

throughout the realm. Other non-Roman cultural traditions — such as the cult of the Persian god Mithra or the compassionate Egyptian goddess Isis, and, most extensively, the Jewish-derived religion of Christianity — also spread throughout the empire. Nothing similar occurred in Han dynasty China, except for Buddhism, which established a modest presence, largely among foreigners. Chinese culture experienced little competition from older, venerated, or foreign traditions. It was widely recognized across much of East Asia — in Japan, Korea, and Vietnam, for example — as the model to which others should conform.

Language served these two empires in important but contrasting ways. Latin, an alphabetic language depicting sounds, gave rise to various distinct languages — Spanish, Portuguese, French, Italian, Romanian — whereas Chinese did not. Chinese characters, which represented words or ideas more than sounds, were not easily transferable to other languages. Written Chinese, however, could be understood by all literate people, no matter which spoken dialect of the language they used. Thus Chinese, more than Latin, served as an instrument of elite assimilation. For all of these reasons, the various peoples of the Roman Empire were able to maintain their separate cultural identities far more than was the case in China.

Politically, both empires established effective centralized control over vast regions and huge populations, but the Chinese, far more than the Romans, developed an elaborate bureaucracy to hold the empire together. The Han emperor Wudi (r. 141–87 B.C.E.) established an imperial academy for training officials for an emerging bureaucracy with a curriculum based on the writings of Confucius. This was the beginning of a civil service system, complete with examinations and selection by merit, that did much to integrate the Chinese empire and that lasted into the early twentieth century. Roman administration was a somewhat ramshackle affair, relying more on regional aristocratic elites and the army to provide cohesion. Unlike the Chinese, however, the Romans developed an elaborate body of law, applicable equally to all people of the realm, that dealt with matters of justice, property, commerce, and family life. Chinese and Roman political development thus generated different answers to the question of what made for good government. For those who inherited the Roman tradition, it was good laws, whereas for those in the Chinese tradition, it was good men.

Finally, both Roman and Chinese civilizations had marked effects on the environment in various ways. The Roman poet Horace complained of the noise and smoke of the city and objected to the urban sprawl that extended into the adjacent fertile lands. Rome's mining operations, the smelting of metals, its large-scale agriculture, and its growing population — all of this led to extensive deforestation and consequent soil erosion. The shortage of wood in the heartland of the empire led to the relocation of some ceramic workshops to Gaul (France), where timber was more plentiful. Lead pollution, derived from the smelting of lead ores in open furnaces and from lead water pipes and cooking pots, shows up in the bones of Roman burials and as far away as Greenland, where studies of the ice cap indicate that lead in the atmosphere increased during Roman times. Here is perhaps the earliest example of international atmospheric pollution.

Large-scale Chinese ironworking during the Han dynasty likewise contributed to substantial urban air pollution, while a rapidly growing and dense population practicing intensive agriculture stripped the north China plain of its ancient forest cover, causing sufficient soil erosion to turn the Hwang-ho River its characteristic yellow-brown color. What had been known simply as "the River" now became the Yellow River, which frequently flooded with devastating results and over many centuries dramatically changed course. In addition, as China expanded north and west into the steppe lands of the pastoral peoples, military/agricultural colonies of Chinese farmers turned pasturelands into farmlands, plowing up long-established sod. When the Chinese state subsequently grew weaker or actually collapsed, such farms were abandoned, wind erosion took hold, and deserts emerged.

The Collapse of Empires

Empires rise, and then, with some apparent regularity, they fall, and in doing so, they provide historians with one of their most intriguing questions: what causes the collapse of these once-mighty structures? In China, the Han dynasty empire came to an end in 220 C.E.; the traditional date for the final disintegration of the Roman Empire is 476 C.E., although a process of decline had been under way for several centuries. In the Roman case, however, only the western half of the empire collapsed, while the eastern part, subsequently known as the Byzantine Empire, maintained the tradition of imperial Rome for another thousand years.

Despite these differences, a number of common factors have been associated with the end of these imperial states. At one level, they both simply got too big, too overextended, and too expensive to be sustained by the available resources, and no fundamental technological breakthrough was available to enlarge these resources. Furthermore, the growth of large landowning families with huge estates and political clout enabled them to avoid paying taxes, turned free peasants into impoverished tenant farmers, and diminished the authority of the central government. In China, such conditions led to a major peasant revolt, known as the Yellow Turban Rebellion, in 184 C.E. (see "Peasants" in Chapter 5).

Rivalry among elite factions created instability in both empires and eroded imperial authority. In China, persistent tension between castrated court officials (eunuchs) loyal to the emperor and Confucian-educated scholar-bureaucrats weakened the state. In the Roman Empire between 235 and 284 C.E., some twenty-six individuals claimed the title of Roman emperor, only one of whom died of natural causes. In addition, epidemic disease ravaged both societies, though more extensively in the Roman world. The population of the Roman Empire declined by 25 percent in the two centuries following 250 C.E., a demographic disaster that meant diminished production, less revenue for the state, and fewer men available to defend the empire's long frontiers.

Historians have often linked the collapse of empires with environmental factors as well, more often with reference to Rome than to Han dynasty China. Considerable fluctuations in the climate after about 250 C.E. led to drought in the third century, cold and wet conditions in the fourth, and increased rainfall and cooler temperatures in the fifth, all of which generated substantial soil erosion and declining agricultural productivity. The North African breadbasket of the empire suffered from serious salinization and increasingly desert-like conditions. The extent to which such factors contributed to the collapse of the Roman Empire remains a point of dispute among scholars.

To these mounting internal problems was added a growing threat from nomadic or semi-agricultural peoples occupying the frontier regions of both empires. The Chinese had long developed various ways of dealing with the Xiongnu and other nomadic people to the north — building the Great Wall to keep them out, offering them trading opportunities at border markets, buying them off with lavish gifts, contracting marriage alliances with nomadic leaders, and conducting periodic military campaigns against them. But as the Han dynasty weakened in the second and third centuries C.E., such peoples more easily breached the frontier defenses and set up a succession of "barbarian states" in north China. Culturally, however, many of these foreign rulers gradually became Chinese, encouraging intermarriage, adopting Chinese dress, and setting up their courts in Chinese fashion.

A weakening Roman Empire likewise faced serious problems from Germanic-speaking peoples living on its northern frontier. Growing numbers of these people began to enter the empire in the fourth century C.E. — some as mercenaries in Roman armies and others as refugees fleeing the invasions of the ferocious Huns, who were penetrating Europe from Central Asia. Once inside the declining empire, various Germanic groups established their own kingdoms, at first controlling Roman emperors and then displacing them altogether by 476 C.E. Unlike the nomadic groups in China, who largely assimilated Chinese culture, Germanic kingdoms in Western Europe developed their own ethnic identities — Visigoths, Franks, Anglo-Saxons, and others — even as they drew on Roman law and adopted Roman Christianity. Far more than in China, the fall of the western Roman Empire produced a new culture, blending Latin and Germanic elements, that provided the foundation for the hybrid civilization that would arise in Western Europe.

The collapse of empire meant more than the disappearance of centralized government and endemic conflict. In post-Han China and post-Roman Europe, it also meant the decline of urban life, a contracting population, less area under cultivation, diminishing international trade, and vast insecurity for ordinary people. It must have seemed that civilization itself was unraveling.

The most significant difference between the collapse of empire in China and that in the western Roman Empire lay in what happened next. In China, after about 350 years of disunion, disorder, frequent warfare, and political chaos, a Chinese imperial state, similar to that of the Han dynasty, was reassembled under the Sui (581–618 C.E.), Tang (618–907), and Song (960–1279) dynasties. Once again, a single emperor ruled; a bureaucracy selected by examinations governed; and the ideas of Confucius informed the political system. Such a Chinese empire persisted into the early twentieth century.

The story line of European history following the end of the western Roman Empire was very different indeed. No large-scale, centralized, imperial authority encompassing all of Western Europe has ever been successfully reestablished there for any length of time. The memory of Roman imperial unity certainly persisted, and many subsequently tried unsuccessfully to re-create it. But most of Western Europe dissolved into highly decentralized political systems involving nobles, knights and vassals, kings with little authority, various city-states in Italy, and small territories ruled by princes, bishops, or the pope. From this point on, Europe would be a civilization without an encompassing imperial state.

Why were Europeans unable to reconstruct something of the unity of their classical empire, while the Chinese clearly did? Surely the greater cultural homogeneity of Chinese civilization made that task easier than it was amid the vast ethnic and linguistic diversity of Europe. The absence in the Roman legacy of a strong bureaucratic tradition also contributed to European difficulties, whereas in China the bureaucracy provided some stability even as dynasties came and went. The Chinese also had in Confucianism a largely secular ideology that placed great value on political matters in the here and now. The Roman Catholic Church in Europe, however, was frequently at odds with state authorities, and its "otherworldliness" did little to support the creation of large-scale empires. Finally, Chinese agriculture was much more productive than that of Europe, and for a long time its metallurgy was more advanced. These conditions gave Chinese state builders more resources to work with than were available to their European counterparts.

Intermittent Empire: The Case of India

Among the second-wave civilizations of Eurasia, empire loomed large in Persian, Mediterranean, and Chinese history, but it played a rather less prominent role in Indian history. The demise of the Indus Valley civilization by 1500 B.C.E. was followed over the next thousand years by the creation of a new civilization based farther east, along the Ganges River on India's northern plain.

By 600 B.C.E. what would become the second-wave civilization of South Asia had begun to take shape across northern India. Politically, that civilization emerged as a fragmented collection of towns and cities, some small republics governed by public assemblies, and a number of regional states ruled by kings. An astonishing range of ethnic, cultural, and linguistic diversity also characterized this civilization, as an endless variety of peoples migrated into India from Central Asia across the mountain passes in the northwest. These features of Indian civilization — political fragmentation and vast cultural diversity — have informed much of South Asian history throughout many centuries, offering a sharp contrast to the pattern of development in China. What gave Indian civilization a recognizable identity and character was neither an imperial tradition nor ethno-linguistic commonality, but rather a distinctive religious tradition, known later to outsiders as Hinduism, and a unique social organization, the caste system. These features of Indian life are explored further in Chapters 4 and 5.

Nonetheless, empires and emperors were not entirely unknown in India's long history. Northwestern India had been briefly ruled by the Persian Empire and then conquered by Alexander the Great. These Persian and Greek influences helped stimulate the first and largest of India's short experiments with a large-scale political

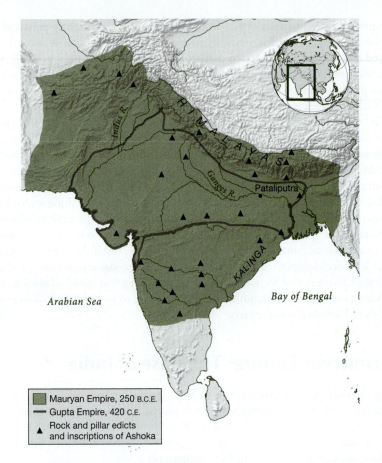

Maryan Empire, 250 B.C.E.
Gupta Empire, 420 C.E.
▲ Rock and pillar edicts
and inscriptions of Ashoka

MAP 3.6   Empire in South Asia
Large-scale empires in the Indian subcontinent were less frequent and
less enduring than those in China. Two of the largest efforts were those
of the Mauryan and Gupta dynasties.

system, the **Mauryan Empire** (321–184 B.C.E.), which encompassed all but the
southern tip of the subcontinent (see Map 3.6).

Founded by Chandragupta Maurya, of whom little is known for certain,
the Mauryan Empire was an impressive political structure, equivalent to the
Persian, Chinese, and Roman empires, though not nearly as long-lasting. With a
population of perhaps 50 million, the Mauryan Empire boasted a large military
force, a civilian bureaucracy with various ministries, and a large contingent of
spies to provide the rulers with local information. A famous treatise called the
Arthashastra (The Science of Worldly Wealth) articulated a pragmatic, even amoral,
political philosophy for Mauryan rulers. It was, according to one scholar, "a book
that frequently discloses to a king what calculating and sometimes brutal measures he must carry out to preserve the state and the common good."[12] The state
also operated many industries — spinning, weaving, mining, shipbuilding, and

The Great Stupa The Great Stupa of Sanchi, the oldest stone building in India, was commissioned by Ashoka in the third century B.C.E. to house precious relics of the Buddha. (Photo © Luca Tettoni/Bridgeman Images)

armaments. This complex apparatus was financed by taxes on trade, on herds of animals, and especially on land, from which the monarch claimed a quarter or more of the crop.

Mauryan India is perhaps best known for one of its emperors, **Ashoka** (r. 268–232 B.C.E.), who left a record of his activities and his thinking in a series of edicts carved on rocks and pillars throughout the kingdom. Ashoka's conversion to Buddhism and his moralistic approach to governance gave his reign a different tone than that of China's Shihuangdi or Greece's Alexander the Great, who, according to legend, wept because he had no more worlds to conquer. Ashoka's legacy to modern India has been that of an enlightened ruler who sought to govern in accord with the religious values and moral teachings of Hinduism and Buddhism.

Despite his good intentions, these policies did not long preserve the empire, which broke apart soon after Ashoka's death. About 600 years later, a second brief imperial experiment, known as the **Gupta Empire** (320–550 C.E.), took shape. Faxian, a Chinese Buddhist traveler in India at the time, noted a generally peaceful, tolerant, and prosperous land, commenting that the ruler "governs without decapitation or corporal punishment." Free hospitals, he reported, were available to "the destitute, crippled and diseased," but he also noticed "untouchables" carrying bells to warn upper-caste people of their polluting presence.[13] Culturally, the Gupta era witnessed a flourishing of art, literature, temple building, science, mathematics, and medicine, much of it patronized by rulers. Indian trade with China also thrived, and Indian commerce reached as far as the Roman world. When a Germanic leader named Alaric laid siege to Rome in 410 C.E., he demanded 3,000 pounds of Indian pepper to spare the city.

Thus India's political history resembled that of Western Europe after the collapse of the Roman Empire far more than that of China or Persia. Neither imperial nor regional states commanded the kind of loyalty or exercised the degree of influence that they did in other second-wave civilizations. India's unparalleled cultural diversity surely was one reason, as were invasions from Central Asia, which repeatedly smashed emerging states that might have provided the nucleus for an all-India empire. Finally, India's social structure, embodied in a caste system linked to occupational groups, made for intensely local loyalties at the expense of wider identities.

Nonetheless, a frequently vibrant economy fostered a lively internal commerce and made India the focal point of an extensive network of trade in the Indian Ocean basin. In particular, its cotton textile industry long supplied cloth throughout the Afro-Eurasian world. Strong guilds of merchants and artisans provided political leadership in major towns and cities, and their wealth supported lavish temples, public buildings, and religious festivals. Great creativity in religious matters generated Hindu and Buddhist traditions that later penetrated much of Asia. Indian mathematics and science, especially astronomy, were also impressive; Indian scientists plotted the movements of stars and planets and recognized quite early that the earth was round. Clearly, the absence of consistent imperial unity did not prevent the evolution of a lasting civilization.

Conclusions and Reflections: Enduring Legacies of Second-Wave Empires

The Eurasian empires of the second-wave era — Persian, Greek, Roman, Chinese, and Indian — played an outsized role in the history of that age. In population and territory, they were far larger than any earlier political systems. The wars of conquest by which they grew generated massive suffering among their victims, causing Ashoka of India to regret that violence. Most others, however, celebrated those wars and gloried in the subordination of subject peoples. Such empires seemed to require powerful and sometimes brutal rulers — Cyrus and Darius, Alexander the Great, Augustus, and Qin Shihuangdi. In the Roman case, the growth of empire eroded the republican values of an earlier era.

Once established, empires created a measure of stability over large areas for varying lengths of time. The Chinese ruler Qin Shihuangdi gained credibility by bringing an end to a long "era of warring states," while Romans boasted of the *pax Romana*, roughly two centuries of relative peace beginning with the reign of Augustus. Nonetheless, imperial oppression frequently generated opposition, reflected, for example, in the Vietnamese rebellion against Chinese overlords. Empires also sought on occasion to accommodate their subjects, as Persian rulers offered support for Egyptian, Babylonian, and Jewish religious organizations.

Empires everywhere fostered both economic and cultural exchange among their diverse peoples. Roman and Persian roads facilitated communication and commerce across their vast imperial domains. Alexander the Great's empire enabled the spread of Greek culture from the eastern Mediterranean to India, while the Roman Empire provided a large arena for the growth of Christianity.

While large empires easily command our attention, we might pause to notice that not all civilizations produced imperial states. Centuries of Greek civilization evolved within a system of rival city-states, and only rarely did Indian civilization generate imperial structures. Furthermore, civilizations frequently interacted with the pastoral or agricultural village societies on their borders, as illustrated by China's constant relationships with the "barbarians" north of the Great Wall.

Although these second-wave empires have long ago passed into history, their descendants have kept them alive in memory. Such ancient empires have provided inspiration for more recent imperial ventures, a basis on which later states have claimed legitimacy, and abundant warnings and cautions for those seeking to criticize contemporary empires. In bringing communism to China in the twentieth century, the Chinese leader Mao Zedong compared himself favorably to Shihuangdi, the unifier of China and the brutal founder of its Qin dynasty. Reflecting on his campaign against intellectuals in general and Confucianism in particular, Mao declared: "To the charge of being like Emperor Qin, of being a dictator, we plead guilty."[14]

In contrast, modern-day Indians, who have sought to present their country as a model of cultural tolerance and nonviolence, have been quick to link themselves to Ashoka and his policies of inclusiveness. When the country became independent from British colonial rule in 1947, India soon placed an image of Ashoka's Pillar on the new nation's currency.

In the West, it has been the Roman Empire that has provided a template for thinking about political life. Many in Great Britain celebrated their own global empire as a modern version of the Roman Empire. If the British had been civilized by Roman rule, then surely Africans and Asians would benefit from falling under the control of the "more civilized" British. Likewise, the Italian fascist dictator Benito Mussolini regarded his country's territorial expansion during the 1930s and World War II as the creation of a new Roman Empire. Most recently, the United States' dominant role in the world has prompted the question, are the Americans the new Romans?

Historians frequently cringe as politicians and students use (and perhaps misuse) historical analogies to make their case for particular points of view in the present. But we have little else to go on except history in making our way through the complexities of contemporary life, and historians themselves seldom agree on the lessons of the past. Lively debate about the continuing relevance of these ancient empires shows that although the past may be gone, it surely is not dead.

Revisiting Chapter 3

REVISITING SPECIFICS

Persian Empire, 72
Athenian democracy, 77
Greco-Persian Wars, 77
Peloponnesian War, 78
Alexander the Great, 78
Hellenistic era, 79
Alexandria, 80

Augustus, 84
pax Romana, 84
Qin Shihuangdi, 85
Han dynasty, 86
Mauryan Empire, 92
Ashoka, 93
Gupta Empire, 93

REVISITING CORE IDEAS

1. **Comparing Political Structures** How did Persian and Greek civilizations differ in their political organization and values?

2. **Assessing Cause and Effect** What were the consequences for both sides of the encounter between the Persians and the Greeks?

3. **Explaining Collapse** What do the Roman and Chinese experiences tell us about the collapse and renewal of empires?

4. **Comparing Empires** In comparing the Roman and Chinese empires, which do you find more striking—their similarities or their differences?

5. **Analyzing Differences** Why were centralized empires so much less prominent in India than in China?

A WIDER VIEW

1. What common features can you identify in the empires described in this chapter? In what ways did they differ from one another? What accounts for those differences?

2. Are you more impressed with the "greatness" of empires or with their destructive and oppressive features? Why?

3. Do you think that these second-wave empires hold "lessons" for the present, or are contemporary circumstances sufficiently unique as to render the distant past irrelevant?

4. **Looking Back** How do these empires of the second-wave civilizations differ from the political systems of the First Civilizations?

CHRONOLOGY

750–336 B.C.E.	• Era of the Greek city-states
ca. 600 B.C.E.	• Crystallization of a northern Indian civilization
550–330 B.C.E.	• Persian Empire
522–486 B.C.E.	• Reign of Darius
509 B.C.E.	• Founding of Rome
500–221 B.C.E.	• Age of warring states in China
499–449 B.C.E.	• Greco-Persian Wars
490 and 480 B.C.E.	• Greeks defeat Persia in major battles
431–404 B.C.E.	• Peloponnesian War
334–323 B.C.E.	• Conquests of Alexander the Great / beginning of Hellenistic era
331 B.C.E.	• Persia defeated at the hands of Alexander
321–184 B.C.E.	• Mauryan dynasty empire
268–232 B.C.E.	• Reign of Ashoka
221–210 B.C.E.	• Reign of Qin Shihuangdi
206 B.C.E.–200 C.E.	• Han dynasty
200 B.C.E.–200 C.E.	• High point of Roman Empire
320–550 C.E.	• Gupta dynasty empire
ca. 476 C.E.	• Collapse of western Roman Empire
581–618 C.E.	• Reunification of China under Sui dynasty

4

Culture and Religion in Eurasia / North Africa

600 B.C.E.–600 C.E.

CONNECTING PAST AND PRESENT

IN SEPTEMBER OF 2009, KONG DEJUN returned to China from her home in Great Britain. The occasion was a birthday celebration for her ancient ancestor Kong Fuzi, or Confucius, born 2,560 years earlier.

Together with some 10,000 other people—descendants, scholars, government officials, and foreign representatives—Kong Dejun attended ceremonies at the Confucian Temple in Qufu, the hometown of China's famous sage. "I was touched to see my ancestor being revered by people from different countries and nations," she said.[1] What made this celebration remarkable was that it took place in a country still ruled by the Communist Party, which had long devoted enormous efforts to discrediting Confucius and his teachings. In the view of communist China's revolutionary leader, Mao Zedong, Confucianism was associated with class inequality, patriarchy, feudalism, superstition, and all things old and backward. But the country's ancient teacher and philosopher had apparently outlasted its revolutionary hero, for now the Communist Party has claimed Confucius as a national treasure and has established over 300 Confucian Institutes to study his writings. He appears in TV shows and movies, even as many anxious parents offer prayers at Confucian temples when their children are taking the national college entrance exams.

Buddhism and Daoism (DOW-i'zm) have also experienced something of a revival in China, as thousands of temples, destroyed during the heyday of communism, have been repaired and reopened. Christianity too has grown rapidly since the death of Mao in 1976. Here are reminders, in a Chinese context, of the continuing appeal of cultural traditions forged long ago. Those traditions are among the most enduring legacies that second-wave civilizations have bequeathed to the modern world.

While the states and empires of Eurasia and North Africa transformed the political framework of the civilizations in these areas, the cultural and religious dimension of life in this huge region also changed dramatically. In China, it was the time of Confucius and Laozi (low-ZUH), whose teachings gave rise to Confucianism and Daoism, respectively. In India, a series of religious writings known as the Upanishads gave expression to the classical philosophy of what we know as Hinduism, while a religious reformer, Siddhartha Gautama (sih-DHAR-tuh GOW-tau-mah), set in motion a separate religion known later as Buddhism. In the Middle East, a distinctively monotheistic religious tradition appeared, expressed in Persian Zoroastrianism and in Judaism. Later, this Jewish religious outlook became the foundation for both Christianity and Islam. Finally, in Greece, a rational and humanistic tradition found expression in the writings of Socrates, Plato, Aristotle, and many others.

But alongside these larger and more extensive cultural systems, a multitude of locally embedded and orally transmitted religious traditions also flourished. Within the major civilizations, these "little traditions" interacted constantly with the emerging "great traditions." Thus ancient Greek gods persisted even as classical Greek philosophy took shape; older practices of Chinese ancestor veneration came to be incorporated in the emerging tradition of Confucianism; and Jews continued to be attracted to foreign deities despite the growing prominence of the one God, Yahweh. Furthermore, in societies that lay beyond the zone of civilization, such as those in

Aboriginal Australia, local traditions linked living human beings to the land, to the vegetable and animal worlds, to their ancestors, and to the gods or spirits that inhabited everything. In this chapter, however, the spotlight falls on those larger cultural or religious traditions that emerged from the civilizations of the second-wave era and that have persisted into the twenty-first century.

| SEEKING THE MAIN POINT | In what ways did the religious and cultural traditions of the second-wave era differ from one another? How did they shape the societies in which they were practiced? |

China and the Search for Order

By the eighth century B.C.E., the authority of China's Zhou dynasty had substantially weakened, and by 500 B.C.E. any unity that China had earlier enjoyed was long gone and violence grew in its wake. It was during these dreadful centuries of disorder and turmoil, known as the era of warring states (ca. 500–221 B.C.E.), that a number of Chinese thinkers began to consider how order might be restored, how the apparent tranquility of an earlier time could be realized again (see "China: From Warring States to Empire" in Chapter 3). From their reflections emerged classical cultural traditions of Chinese civilization.

The Legalist Answer

One answer to the problem of disorder—though not the first to emerge—was a hardheaded and practical philosophy known as **Legalism**. To Legalist thinkers, the solution to China's problems lay in rules or laws, clearly spelled out and strictly enforced through a system of rewards and punishments. "If rewards are high," wrote Han Fei, one of the most prominent Legalist philosophers, "then what the ruler wants will be quickly effected; if punishments are heavy, what he does not want will be swiftly prevented."[2]

Legalists generally entertained a rather pessimistic view of human nature. Most people, they believed, were stupid and shortsighted. Only the state and its rulers could act in their long-term interests. Doing so meant promoting farmers and soldiers, the only two groups in society who performed essential functions, while suppressing merchants, aristocrats, scholars, and others regarded as useless.

Legalist thinking provided inspiration and methods for the harsh reunification of China under Shihuangdi and the Qin dynasty (221–206 B.C.E.), but the brutality of that short dynasty thoroughly discredited Legalism. Although its techniques and practices played a role in subsequent Chinese statecraft, few philosophers or rulers ever again openly advocated its ideas as the sole guide for Chinese political life. The Han dynasty (206 B.C.E.–220 C.E.) and all subsequent dynasties drew instead on the teachings of China's greatest sage—Confucius.

The Confucian Answer

Born to an aristocratic family in the state of Lu in northern China, Confucius (551–479 B.C.E.) was both learned and ambitious. Believing that he had found a solution for China's problem of disorder, he spent much of his adult life seeking a political position from which he might put his ideas into action. But no such opportunity came his way. Perhaps it was just as well, for it was as a thinker and a teacher that Confucius left a profound imprint on Chinese history and culture and also on other East Asian societies, such as Korea and Japan. After his death, his students collected his teachings in a short book called the *Analects*, and later scholars elaborated and commented endlessly on his ideas, creating a body of thought known as **Confucianism**.

The Confucian answer to the problem of China's disorder was very different from that of the Legalists. Not laws and punishments, but the moral example of superiors was the Confucian key to a restored social harmony. For Confucius, human society consisted primarily of unequal relationships: the father was superior to the son; the husband to the wife; the older brother to the younger brother; and, of course, the ruler to the subject. If the superior party in each of these relationships behaved with sincerity, benevolence, and genuine concern for others, then the inferior party would be motivated to respond with deference and obedience. Harmony would then prevail. As Confucius put it, "The relation between superiors and inferiors is like that between the wind and the grass. The grass must bend when the wind blows across it." Thus, in both family life and in political life, the cultivation of *ren*—human-heartedness, benevolence, goodness—was the essential ingredient of a tranquil society.

But how were these humane virtues to be nurtured? Because people have a capacity for improvement, the key to moral progress was education, particularly an immersion in language, literature, history, philosophy, and ethics, all applied to the practical problems of government. Ritual and ceremonies were also important, for

Confucian Education This eighteenth-century image of a Korean Confucian classroom reflects the long-enduring role of Confucius in education across much of East Asia, where mastery of his teachings became an important mark of elite status and a means for social advancement. (National Museum, Seoul, Korea/Bridgeman Images)

they conveyed the rules of appropriate behavior in the many and varying circumstances of life. For the "superior person," or "gentleman" in Confucian terms, serious personal reflection and a willingness to strive continuously to perfect his moral character were essential.

Such ideas had a pervasive influence in Chinese life, and Confucianism became almost synonymous with Chinese culture. As China's bureaucracy took shape during and after the Han dynasty, Confucianism became the central element of the educational system, which prepared students for the examinations required to gain official positions. Thus generation after generation of China's male elite was steeped in the ideas and values of Confucianism.

In Confucian thinking, the family became a model for political life, a kind of miniature state. Filial piety, the honoring of one's ancestors and parents, was both valuable in itself and a training ground for the reverence due to the emperor and state officials. Such views of the family were rigidly patriarchal and set the tone for defining the lives of women and men alike. They were linked to a hierarchical and gendered understanding of the cosmos in which an inferior and receptive Earth, associated with the feminine, was in balance with the superior and creative principle of Heaven, associated with the masculine. Thus the subordinate and deferential position of women in relation to men was rooted in the structure of the cosmos itself. What this meant for women was spelled out by a somewhat later woman writer, **Ban Zhao** (bahn jow) (45–116 C.E.), in a famous work called *Lessons for Women*. "Let a woman modestly yield to others.... Always let her seem to tremble and to fear.... Then she may be said to humble herself before others."[3] Ban Zhao called for greater attention to education for young girls, not because they were equal to boys, but so that a young woman might be better prepared to serve her husband. Education for boys, on the other hand, enabled them to more effectively control their wives.

Corresponding Confucian virtues for ideal men were contained in the paired concepts of *wen* and *wu*, both limited largely to males. The superior principle of wen referred to the refined qualities of rationality, scholarship, and literary and artistic abilities, while wu focused attention on physical and martial achievements. Thus men alone, and superior men at that, were eligible for the civil service exams that led to political office and high prestige, while military men and merchants occupied a distinctly lower position in a male social hierarchy.[4]

Beyond defining gender expectations, Confucianism also placed great importance on history, for the ideal good society lay in the past. Confucian ideas were reformist, perhaps even revolutionary, but they were consistently presented as an effort to restore a past golden age. Those ideas also injected a certain democratic element into Chinese elite culture, for the great sage had emphasized that "superior men" and potential government officials were those of outstanding moral character and intellectual achievement, not simply those of aristocratic background. Usually only young men from wealthy families could afford the education necessary for passing examinations, but on occasion villagers could find the resources to sponsor one of their bright sons, potentially propelling him into the stratosphere of the Chinese elite while bringing honor and benefit to the village itself.

Confucian ideas were clearly used to legitimate the many inequalities of Chinese society, but they also established certain expectations for the superior parties in China's social hierarchy. Thus emperors should keep taxes low, administer justice, and provide for the material needs of the people. Those who failed to govern by these moral norms forfeited the Mandate of Heaven and invited upheaval and their replacement by another dynasty. Likewise, husbands should deal kindly with their wives and children, lest they invite conflict and disharmony in the family.

Finally, Confucianism marked Chinese elite culture by its secular, or nonreligious, character. Confucius did not deny the reality of gods and spirits. In fact, he advised people to participate in family and state rituals "as if the spirits were present," and he believed that the universe had a moral character with which human beings should align themselves. But the thrust of Confucian teaching was distinctly thisworldly and practical, concerned with human relationships, effective government, and social harmony. Members of the Chinese elite generally acknowledged that magic, the gods, and spirits were perhaps necessary for the lower orders of society, but educated people, they argued, would find them of little help in striving for moral improvement and in establishing a harmonious society.

The Daoist Answer

No civilization has ever painted its cultural outlook in a single color. As Confucian thinking became generally known in China, a quite different school of thought also took shape. Known as **Daoism**, it was associated with the legendary figure Laozi, who, according to tradition, was a sixth-century-B.C.E. archivist. He is said to have penned a short poetic volume, the *Daodejing* (dow-day-jihng) (*The Way and Its Power*), before vanishing in the wilderness to the west of China on his water buffalo.

In many ways, Daoist thinking ran counter to that of Confucius, who had emphasized the importance of education and earnest striving for moral improvement and good government. The Daoists ridiculed such efforts as artificial and useless, claiming that they generally made things worse. In the face of China's disorder and chaos, Daoists urged withdrawal into the world of nature and encouraged behavior that was spontaneous, individualistic, and natural. Whereas Confucius focused on the world of human relationships, the Daoists turned the spotlight on the immense realm of nature and its mysterious unfolding patterns in which the "ten thousand things" appeared, changed, and vanished. "Confucius roams within society," the Chinese have often said. "Laozi wanders beyond."

The central concept of Daoist thinking is *dao*, an elusive notion that refers to the way of nature, the underlying and unchanging principle that governs all natural phenomena. The dao "moves around and around, but does not on this account suffer," wrote Laozi in the *Daodejing*. "All life comes from it. It wraps everything with its love as in a garment, and yet it claims no honor, for it does not demand to be lord. I do not know its name and so I call it the Dao, the Way, and I rejoice in its power."[5]

Amid the world of civilization, so highly valued by Confucius, the Daoists yearned for former times, "an age of perfect virtue" that had been disrupted by Confucian striving for something better. Earlier, according to one Daoist master, "there were no paths and ramps on the mountains and no boats upon the bridges.... There were vast numbers of animals and grasses, and trees reached their natural growth. Wild animals could be taken for walks on leashes, and one could climb up to the nests of magpies and other birds." Such a vision of human harmony with nature contrasted sharply with the Confucian outlook, which gave priority to the "world of culture" while experiencing nature as hostile. To Confucians, humankind "disposes over the world of [wild] things, tames wild animals, and brings cowed vermin under his control."[6] In contrast, individual Daoists often fled to the mountains, where they might experience the dao in union with nature. Applied to human life, Daoism invited people to withdraw from the world of political and social activism, to disengage from the public life so important to Confucius, and to align themselves with the way of nature. It meant simplicity in living, small self-sufficient communities, limited government, and the abandonment of education and active efforts at self-improvement. "Give up learning," declares the *Daodejing*, "and put an end to your troubles." The flavor of the Daoist approach to life is evident in this passage from the *Daodejing*, describing a small and simple society:

> Though there were individuals with the abilities of ten or a hundred men,
> there should be no employment of them . . . ;
> Though they had boats and carriages, they should have no occasion to ride
> in them;
> There should be a neighbouring state within sight . . . ,
> but I would make the people . . . not have any intercourse with it.[7]

Like Confucianism, the Daoist perspective viewed family life as central to Chinese society, though the element of male/female hierarchy was downplayed in favor of complementarity and balance between the sexes.

Despite its various differences with the ideas of Confucianism, the Daoist perspective was widely regarded by elite Chinese as complementing rather than contradicting Confucian values. Such an outlook was facilitated by the ancient Chinese concept of *yin* and *yang*, which expressed a belief in the unity of opposites (see figure). Thus a scholar-official might pursue the Confucian project of "government by goodness" during the day, but upon returning home in the evening or following his retirement, he might well behave in a more Daoist fashion—pursuing the simple life, reading Daoist philosophy, practicing meditation or breathing exercises, retreating to mountain settings, or enjoying painting, poetry, or calligraphy.

The Yin Yang Symbol

Daoism also shaped the culture of ordinary people as it entered popular religion. This kind of Daoism sought to tap the power of the dao for practical uses and came to include magic, fortune-telling, and the search for immortality. It also on occasion provided an ideology for peasant uprisings, such as the Yellow Turban Rebellion (184–204 C.E.), which imagined a utopian society without the oppression of governments and landlords. In its many and varied forms, Daoism, like Confucianism, became an enduring element of the Chinese cultural tradition.

Cultural Traditions of Classical India

The cultural development of Indian civilization was far different from that of China. Whereas Confucianism paid little attention to the gods, spirits, and speculation about religious matters, Indian elite culture embraced the Divine and all things spiritual with enthusiasm and generated elaborate philosophical visions about the nature of ultimate reality. But the Indian religious tradition—later called Hinduism—differed from other world religions as well. Unlike Buddhism, Christianity, or Islam, Hinduism had no historical founder; rather, it grew up over many centuries along with Indian civilization. Although it later spread into Southeast Asia, Hinduism was not a missionary religion seeking converts, but was, like Judaism, associated with a particular people and territory.

In fact, "Hinduism" was never a single tradition at all, and the term itself derived from outsiders—Greeks, Muslims, and later the British—who sought to reduce the infinite variety of Indian cultural patterns into a recognizable system. From the inside, however, Hinduism dissolved into a vast diversity of gods, spirits, beliefs, practices, rituals, and philosophies. This endlessly variegated Hinduism served to incorporate into Indian civilization the many diverse peoples who migrated into or invaded the South Asian peninsula over many centuries and several millennia. Its ability to accommodate this diversity gave India's cultural development a distinctive quality.

South Asian Religion: From Ritual Sacrifice to Philosophical Speculation

Despite the fragmentation and variety of Indian cultural and religious patterns, an evolving set of widely recognized sacred texts provided some commonality. The earliest of these texts, known as the **Vedas** (VAY-duhs), were collections of poems, hymns, prayers, and rituals. Compiled by priests called Brahmins, the Vedas were for centuries transmitted orally and were reduced to writing in Sanskrit around 600 B.C.E. In the Vedas, historians have caught fleeting glimpses of Indian civilization in its formative centuries (1500–600 B.C.E.). Those sacred writings tell of small competing chiefdoms or kingdoms, of sacred sounds and fires, and of numerous gods, rising and falling in importance over the centuries. They also suggest a clearly patriarchal society, but one that afforded upper-class women somewhat greater opportunities than they later enjoyed. Vedic women participated in religious sacrifices, sometimes engaged in scholarship and religious debate, were allowed to wear the sacred thread that symbolized ritual purity in the higher castes, and could on occasion marry a man of their own choosing. The Vedas described as well the elaborate ritual sacrifices that Brahmin priests performed and for which they received substantial payments, enabling them to acquire enormous power and wealth, sometimes exceeding even that of kings and warriors.

As ritual became mechanical, formal, and expensive, criticism of Brahmins also grew. From this dissatisfaction arose another body of sacred texts, the **Upanishads** (oo-PAHN-ee-shahds). Composed by largely anonymous thinkers between 800 and 400 B.C.E., these were mystical and highly philosophical works that sought to probe the inner meaning of the rituals prescribed in the Vedas. In the Upanishads, external ritual gave way to introspective thinking, which expressed in many and varied formulations the central concepts of philosophical Hinduism that have persisted into modern times. Chief among them was the idea of Brahman, the World Soul, the final and ultimate reality. Beyond the multiplicity of material objects and individual persons and beyond even the various gods themselves lay this primal unitary energy or divine reality infusing all things, similar in some ways to the Chinese notion of the dao. This alone was real; the immense diversity of existence that human beings perceived with their senses was but an illusion.

The fundamental assertion of philosophical Hinduism was that the individual human soul, or *atman*, was in fact a part of Brahman. Beyond the quest for pleasure, wealth, power, and social position, all of which were perfectly normal and quite legitimate, lay the effort to achieve the final goal of humankind—union with Brahman, an end to our illusory perception of a separate existence. This was *moksha* (MOHK-shuh), or liberation, compared sometimes to a bubble in a glass of water breaking through the surface and becoming one with the surrounding atmosphere.

Achieving this exalted state was held to involve many lifetimes, and the notion of *samsara*, or rebirth/reincarnation, became a central feature of Hindu thinking. Human souls migrated from body to body over many lifetimes, depending on the actions of individuals. This was the law of *karma*. Pure actions, appropriate to one's station in life, resulted in rebirth in a higher social position or caste. Thus the caste system of distinct and ranked groups, each with its own duties, became a register of spiritual progress.

If Hinduism underpinned caste, it also legitimated and expressed a patriarchal relationship between women and men. Women were increasingly seen as "unclean below the navel," forbidden to learn the Vedas, and excluded from public religious rituals. The Laws of Manu, probably composed in the early centuries of the Common Era, advocated child marriage for girls to men far older than themselves and famously proclaimed: "In childhood a female must be subject to her father; in youth to her husband; when her lord [husband] is dead to her sons; a woman must never be independent."[8]

And yet some aspects of Hinduism served to empower women. Sexual pleasure was considered a legitimate goal for both men and women, and its many and varied techniques were detailed in the *Kamasutra*. Many Hindu deities were female, some life-giving and faithful and others, like Kali, fiercely destructive. Women were particularly prominent in the growing devotional cults dedicated to particular deities, where neither gender nor caste was an obstacle to spiritual fulfillment.

A further feature of Hindu religious thought lay in its provision of different paths to the ultimate goal of liberation, or moksha. Various ways to this final release, appropriate to people of different temperaments, were spelled out in Hindu teachings. Some might achieve moksha through knowledge or study; others by means of detached action in the world, doing one's ordinary work without regard to consequences; still others through passionate devotion to some deity or through extended meditation practice. Such ideas—carried by Brahmin priests and wandering ascetics or holy men, who had withdrawn from ordinary life to pursue their spiritual development—became widely known throughout India.

The Buddhist Challenge

About the same time as philosophical Hinduism was emerging, another movement took shape that soon became a distinct and separate religious tradition—Buddhism. Unlike Hinduism, this new faith had a historical founder, **Siddhartha Gautama** (ca. 566–ca. 486 B.C.E.), a prince from a small north Indian state. According to Buddhist tradition, the prince had enjoyed a sheltered and delightful youth until he

The Buddha's Enlightenment Dating from the late eighth century in Korea, this monumental and beautifully proportioned sculpture portrays the Buddha at the moment of his enlightenment, symbolized by his right hand touching the earth. Seated on a lotus pedestal, this image of the Buddha also shows the ushnisha, the round oval at the top of his head, which represents his spiritual attainment, and the dot in the center of his forehead indicating wisdom. This sculpture is located in the Seokguram Grotto or cave, where it is surrounded by numerous supernatural figures and by two Indian gods. It is widely considered a masterpiece of Buddhist art and is a Korean National Treasure. (Copyright © Cultural Heritage Administration of Korea, Courtesy of the Academy of Korean Studies, South Korea)

encountered human suffering in the form of an old man, a sick person, and a corpse. Shattered by these revelations of aging, illness, and death, Siddhartha determined to find the cause of such sufferings and a remedy for them. And so, at the age of twenty-nine, the young prince left his luxurious life as well as his wife and child, shed his royal jewels, cut off his hair, and set off on a quest for enlightenment. This act of severing his ties to the attachments of ordinary life is known in Buddhist teaching as the Great Renunciation.

What followed were six years of spiritual experimentation that finally led Siddhartha to an ancient fig tree in northern India, now known as the Bodhi (enlightenment) tree. There, Buddhist sources tell us, he began a forty-nine-day period of intensive meditation that ended with an indescribable experience of spiritual realization. Now he was the **Buddha**, the man who had awakened. For the next forty years, he taught what he had learned, setting in motion the cultural tradition of Buddhism.

"I teach but one thing," the Buddha said, "suffering and the end of suffering." To the Buddha, suffering or sorrow—experiencing life as imperfect, impermanent, and unsatisfactory—was the central and universal feature of human life. This kind of suffering derived from desire or craving for individual fulfillment, from attachment to that which inevitably changes, particularly to the notion of a core self or ego that is uniquely and solidly "me." The cure for this "dis-ease" lay in living a modest and moral life combined with meditation practice. Those who followed the Buddhist path most fully could expect to achieve enlightenment, or *nirvana*, a virtually indescribable state in which individual identity would be "extinguished" along with all greed, hatred, and delusion. With the pain of unnecessary suffering finally ended, the enlightened person would experience an overwhelming serenity, even in the midst of difficulty, as well as an immense loving-kindness, or compassion, for all beings. It was a simple message, elaborated endlessly and in various forms by those who followed the Buddha.

Much of the Buddha's teaching reflected the Hindu traditions from which it sprang. The idea that ordinary life is an illusion, the concepts of karma and rebirth, the goal of overcoming the incessant demands of the ego, the practice of meditation, the hope for final release from the cycle of rebirth — all of these Hindu elements found their way into Buddhist teaching. In this respect, Buddhism was a simplified and more accessible version of Hinduism.

Other elements of Buddhist teaching, however, sharply challenged prevailing Hindu thinking. Rejecting the religious authority of the Brahmins, the Buddha ridiculed their rituals and sacrifices as irrelevant to the hard work of dealing with one's suffering. Nor was he much interested in abstract speculation about the creation of the world or the existence of God, for such questions, he declared, "are not useful in the quest for holiness; they do not lead to peace and to the direct knowledge of *nirvana*." Individuals had to take responsibility for their own spiritual development with no help from human authorities or supernatural beings. It was a path of intense self-effort, based on personal experience. The Buddha also challenged the inequalities of a Hindu-based caste system, arguing that neither caste position nor gender was a barrier to enlightenment. The possibility of "awakening" was available to all.

But when it came to establishing a formal organization of the Buddha's most devoted followers, the prevailing patriarchy of Indian society made itself felt. Only after considerable resistance did the Buddha reluctantly allow women to join a newly created order of monks, and they could do so only in a separate order of nuns who were subjected to a series of rules that clearly subordinated them to men. Male monks, for example, could officially admonish the nuns, but the reverse was forbidden. Such policies reflected a particular strain of Buddhist thinking that viewed women as a distracting obstacle to male enlightenment.

Nonetheless, thousands of women flocked to join the Buddhist order of nuns, where they found a degree of independence unavailable elsewhere in Indian society. Buddhist nuns delighted in the relative freedom of their order, where they largely ran their own affairs, were forbidden to do household chores, and devoted themselves wholly to the search for "awakening," which many apparently achieved. A nun named Mutta declared: "I am free from the three crooked things: mortar, pestle, and my crooked husband. I am free from birth and death and all that dragged me back."[9]

Gradually, Buddhist teachings found an audience in India. Buddhism's egalitarian message appealed especially to lower-caste groups and to women. The availability of its teaching in the local language of Pali, rather than the classical Sanskrit, made it accessible. Establishing monasteries and stupas (commemorative monuments containing relics of the Buddha) on the site of neighborhood shrines to earth spirits or near a sacred tree linked the new religion to local traditions. The most dedicated followers joined monasteries, devoting their lives to religious practice and spreading the message among nearby people. State support during the reign of Ashoka (r. 268–232 B.C.E.) likewise helped the new religion gain a foothold in India as a distinct tradition separate from Hinduism.

As Buddhism spread, both within and beyond India, differences in understanding soon emerged, particularly as to how nirvana could be achieved or, in a common Buddhist metaphor, how to "cross the river" to the far shore of enlightenment. The Buddha had taught a rather austere doctrine of intense self-effort, undertaken most actively by monks and nuns who withdrew from society to devote themselves fully to the quest. This early version of the new religion, known as **Theravada Buddhism** (Teaching of the Elders), portrayed the Buddha as an immensely wise teacher and model, but certainly not divine. It was more psychological than religious, a set of practices rather than a set of beliefs. The gods, though never completely denied, played little role in assisting believers in crossing the river. Each person had to row his or her own boat. Clearly, this was not for everyone.

As the message of the Buddha gained a mass following and spread across much of Asia, some of its early features — rigorous and time-consuming meditation practice, a focus on monks and nuns withdrawn from ordinary life, the absence of accessible supernatural figures able to provide help and comfort — proved difficult for many converts. And so the religion adapted. A new form of the faith, **Mahayana Buddhism**, developed in the early centuries of the Common Era and offered greater accessibility, a spiritual path available to a much wider range of people beyond the monks and ascetics, who were the core group in early Buddhism.

In most expressions of Mahayana Buddhism, enlightenment (or becoming a Buddha) was available to everyone; it was possible within the context of ordinary life, rather than a monastery; and it might occur within a single lifetime rather than over the course of many lives. While Buddhism had originally put a premium on spiritual wisdom or insight, Mahayana expressions of the faith emphasized compassion — the ability to feel the sorrows of other people as if they were one's own. This compassionate religious ideal found expression in the notion of bodhisattvas, fully enlightened beings who postponed their own final liberation in order to assist a suffering humanity. They were spiritual beings on their way to "Buddhahood." Furthermore, the historical Buddha himself became something of a god, and both earlier and future Buddhas were available to offer help. Elaborate descriptions and artistic representations of these supernatural beings, together with various levels of Heavens and Hells, transformed Buddhism into a popular religion of salvation. Furthermore, religious merit, leading to salvation, might now be earned by acts of piety and devotion, such as contributing to the support of a monastery, and that merit might be transferred to others. This was the Great Vehicle, providing spiritual assistance and allowing far more people to make the voyage across the river. In many forms and variations, Mahayana Buddhism took root in China, Japan, Korea, Southeast Asia, and elsewhere.

Hinduism as a Religion of Duty and Devotion

Strangely enough, Buddhism as a distinct religious practice ultimately died out in the land of its birth as it was reincorporated into a broader Hindu tradition, but it spread widely and flourished, particularly in its Mahayana form, in other parts of Asia. Buddhism declined in India perhaps in part because the mounting wealth of monasteries and the economic interests of their leading figures separated them from ordinary people. Competition from Islam after 1000 C.E. also played a role. But the most important reason for the waning of Buddhism in India was the growth during the first millennium C.E. of a new kind of popular Hinduism that was more accessible than the elaborate sacrifices of the Brahmins or the philosophical speculations of intellectuals. Expressed in the widely known epic poems called the *Mahabharata* (mah-hah-BAH-rah-tah) and the *Ramayana*, this revived Hinduism indicated more clearly that action in the world and the detached performance of caste duties

Hindu Religion Widely revered by Hindus as a god of compassion and tenderness and a manifestation of the supreme god Vishnu, Krishna features prominently in Hindu art and literature. This fifth-century sculpture from northern India recounts a well-known battle between Krishna and a horse demon dispatched by his evil uncle to kill him. (The Metropolitan Museum of Art, New York /Purchase, Florence and Herbert Irving Gift, 1991/www.metmuseum.org)

(as a priest, farmer, merchant, or sweeper, for example) might also provide a path to liberation. It was perhaps a response to the challenge of Buddhism.

A much-beloved Hindu text known as the **Bhagavad Gita** (BUH-guh-vahd GEE-tuh) (compiled in its final form by 300 c.e.) conveyed the message that ordinary people, not just Brahmins, could also find spiritual fulfillment by selflessly performing the ordinary duties of their lives: "The man who, casting off all desires, lives free from attachments, who is free from egoism, and from the feeling that this or that is mine, obtains tranquility." Withdrawal from the world and asceticism were not the only ways to moksha.

Also becoming increasingly prominent was yet another religious path—the way of devotion to one or another of India's many gods and goddesses. Beginning in south India and moving northward between 600 and 1000 c.e., this *bhakti* (BAHK-tee) (worship) **movement** involved the intense adoration of and identification with a particular deity through songs, prayers, and rituals. By far the most popular deities were Vishnu, the protector and preserver of creation who was associated with mercy and goodness, and Shiva, a god representing the Divine in its destructive aspect, but many others also had their followers. This form of Hindu expression sometimes pushed against the rigid caste and gender hierarchies of Indian society by inviting all to an adoration of the Divine. Krishna, an incarnation of Vishnu as portrayed in the Bhagavad Gita, had declared that "those who take shelter in Me, though they be of lower birth—women, vaishyas [merchants] and shudras [workers]—can attain the supreme destination."

The proliferation of gods and goddesses, and of their bhakti cults, occasioned very little friction or serious religious conflict. "Hinduism," writes a leading scholar, "is essentially tolerant, and would rather assimilate than rigidly exclude."[10] This capacity for assimilation extended to an already declining Buddhism, which for many people had become yet another cult worshipping yet another god. The Buddha in fact was incorporated into the Hindu pantheon as the ninth incarnation of Vishnu. By 1000 C.E., Buddhism had largely disappeared as a separate religious tradition within India.

Thus a constantly evolving and enormously varied South Asian religious tradition had been substantially transformed. An early emphasis on ritual sacrifice had given way to that of philosophical speculation, devotional worship, and detached action in the world. In the process, that tradition had generated Buddhism, which became the first of the great universal religions of world history, and then had absorbed that new faith back into the fold of an emerging popular Hinduism.

Toward Monotheism: The Search for God in the Middle East

Paralleling the evolution of Chinese and Indian cultural traditions was the movement toward a distinctive monotheistic religious outlook in the Middle East that found expression in Persian Zoroastrianism and in Judaism. Neither of these religions themselves spread very widely, but the monotheism that they nurtured became the basis for both Christianity and Islam, which have shaped so much of world history over the past 2,000 years. Amid the proliferation of gods and spirits that had long characterized religious life throughout the ancient world, monotheism—the idea of a single supreme deity, the sole source of all life and being—was a radical cultural innovation. That conception created the possibility of a universal religion, open to all of humankind, but it could also mean an exclusive and intolerant faith.

Zoroastrianism

During the glory years of the powerful Persian Empire, a new religion arose to challenge the polytheism of earlier times. Tradition dates its Persian prophet, Zarathustra (Zoroaster to the Greeks), to the sixth or seventh century B.C.E., although some scholars place him centuries earlier. Whenever he actually lived, his ideas took hold in Persia and received a degree of state support during the Achaemenid dynasty (550–330 B.C.E.). Appalled by the endemic violence of recurring cattle raids, Zarathustra recast the traditional Persian polytheism into a vision of a single unique god, Ahura Mazda, who ruled the world and was the source of all truth, light, and goodness. This benevolent deity was engaged in a cosmic struggle with the forces of evil, embodied in an equivalent supernatural figure, Angra Mainyu. Ultimately this struggle would be decided in favor of Ahura Mazda, aided by the arrival of a final savior who would restore the world to its earlier purity and peace. At a day of judgment, those who had aligned with Ahura Mazda would be granted new resurrected bodies and rewarded with eternal life in Paradise. Those who had sided with evil and the "Lie" (which found expression as greed, anger, and envy) were condemned to everlasting punishment. **Zoroastrianism** (zohr-oh-ASS-tree-ahn-i'zm) thus placed great emphasis on the free will of humankind and the necessity for each individual to choose between good and evil.

The Zoroastrian Tradition in Persia Dating to around 500 B.C.E., this cylinder seal impression depicts the winged disk, symbolizing the power of the Zoroastrian creator god Ahura Mazda, watching over the Persian emperor Darius I during a lion hunt. The killing of a lion symbolizes the emperor's power over nature. Persian emperors were powerful patrons of the Zoroastrian faith, and Ahura Mazda was often depicted protecting or guiding their activities. (Impression of a cylinder seal depicting the Great King Darius in a chariot hunting lions/WERNER FORMAN ARCHIVE/Bridgeman Images)

The Zoroastrian faith achieved widespread support within the Persian heartland and also found adherents in other parts of the empire, such as Egypt, Mesopotamia, and Anatolia. But it never became an active missionary religion and did not spread widely beyond the region. Alexander the Great's invasion of the Persian Empire and the subsequent Greek-ruled Seleucid dynasty (330–155 B.C.E.) were disastrous for Zoroastrianism, as temples were plundered, priests slaughtered, and sacred writings burned. But the new faith managed to survive this onslaught and flourished again during the Parthian (247 B.C.E.–224 C.E.) and Sassanid (224–651 C.E.) dynasties. It was the arrival of Islam and an Arab empire that occasioned the final decline of Zoroastrianism in Persia. Like Buddhism, the Zoroastrian faith vanished from its place of origin, but unlike Buddhism, it did not spread beyond Persia in a recognizable form. Some elements of the Zoroastrian belief system, however, did become incorporated into other religious traditions. The presence of many Jews in the Persian Empire meant that they surely became aware of Zoroastrian ideas. Many of those ideas—including the conflict of God and an evil counterpart (Satan); the notion of a last judgment and resurrected bodies; and a belief in the final defeat of evil, the arrival of a savior (Messiah), and the remaking of the world at the end of time—found a place in an evolving Judaism. Some of these teachings, especially the concepts of Heaven and Hell, later became prominent in those enormously influential successors to Judaism—Christianity and Islam. Thus the Persian tradition of Zoroastrianism continued to echo well beyond its disappearance in the land of its birth.

Judaism

While Zoroastrianism emerged in the greatest empire of its time, **Judaism**, the Middle East's other ancient monotheistic tradition, was born among one of the region's smaller peoples—the Hebrews, much later known also as Jews. Their traditions, recorded in the Hebrew scriptures, tell of a dramatic history leading to the establishment around 1000 B.C.E. of a small state that soon split into two parts—a northern kingdom called Israel and a southern state called Judah.

In a region politically dominated by the large empires of Egypt, Assyria, Babylon, and Persia, these tiny Hebrew communities lived a precarious existence. Israel was conquered by Assyria in 722 B.C.E., and many of its inhabitants were deported to distant regions, where they assimilated into the local culture. In 586 B.C.E., the kingdom of Judah likewise came under Babylonian control, and its elite class was shipped off to exile. "By the rivers of Babylon," wrote one of their poets, "there we sat down, yea, we wept, when we remembered Zion [Jerusalem]." In Babylonian exile these people, now referring to themselves as Judeans, retained and renewed their cultural identity, and later a small number were able to return to their homeland. A large part of that identity lay in their unique religious ideas. It was in creating that religious tradition, rather than in building a powerful empire, that this small people cast a long shadow in world history.

From their unique historical memory of exodus from Egyptian slavery and exile in Babylon, the Hebrews evolved over many centuries a distinctive conception of God. Unlike the peoples of Mesopotamia, India, Greece, and elsewhere—all of whom populated the invisible realm with numerous gods and goddesses—Jews found in their God, whom they called Yahweh (YAH-way), a powerful, impassioned, and jealous deity who demanded their exclusive loyalty. "Thou shalt have no other gods before me"—this was the first of the Ten Commandments. It was a difficult requirement, for as the Hebrews turned from a pastoral life to agriculture, many of them were attracted by the gods of nature worshipped by neighboring peoples. Their neighbors' goddesses were also attractive, offering a kind of spiritual support that the primarily masculine Yahweh could not. Foreign deities also entered Hebrew culture through royal treaty obligations with nearby states. Thus the emerging Hebrew conception of the Divine was not quite monotheism, for the repeated demands of the Hebrew prophets to turn away from other gods show that those deities remained real for many Jews. Over time, however, the priesthood that supported the one-god theory triumphed. The Hebrew people came to understand their relationship to Yahweh as a contract or a covenant. In return for their sole devotion and obedience to God's laws, Yahweh would consider the Israelites his chosen people, favoring them in battle, causing them to grow in numbers, and bringing them prosperity and blessing.

Unlike the bickering, arbitrary, polytheistic gods of Mesopotamia or ancient Greece, who were associated with the forces of nature and behaved in quite human fashion, Yahweh was increasingly seen as a lofty, transcendent deity of utter holiness and purity. But unlike the impersonal conceptions of ultimate reality found in Daoism and Hinduism, Yahweh was encountered as a divine person with whom people could actively communicate. He also acted within the historical process, bringing the Jews out of Egypt or using foreign empires to punish them for their disobedience.

Furthermore, for some, Yahweh was transformed from a god of war, who ordered his people to "utterly destroy" the original inhabitants of the Promised Land, to a god of social justice and compassion for the poor and the marginalized, especially in the passionate pronouncements of Jewish prophets. One of them, Isaiah, describes Yahweh as rejecting the empty rituals of his chosen but disobedient people: "What to me is the multitude of your sacrifices, says the Lord. . . . Wash yourselves, make yourselves clean, . . . cease to do evil, learn to do good; seek justice; correct oppression; defend the fatherless; plead for the widow."[11]

Here was a distinctive conception of the Divine—singular, transcendent, personal, ruling over the natural order, engaged in history, and demanding social justice and moral righteousness above sacrifices and rituals. This set of ideas sustained a separate Hebrew or Jewish identity in both ancient and modern times, and it was this understanding of God that provided the foundation on which those later Abrahamic faiths of Christianity and Islam were built.

Jewish understanding of the natural world likewise informed all three religious traditions. The Jewish scriptures pronounced the original creation as real and positively valued, not simply an illusion or a distraction from spiritual concerns, as in some versions of Hindu or Buddhist thinking. The first chapter of Genesis ends with God's review of his creation: "And God saw everything that he had made, and behold it was very good." Moreover, the material world disclosed or revealed something of the overwhelming power and mystery of the Divine. The writer of the Psalms affirmed that "the heavens declare the glory of God and the firmament shows his handiwork." Finally, later Hebrew tradition gave humankind a distinct role within God's creation. They were to "have dominion . . . over all the earth," even as Adam and Eve in the Garden of Eden were instructed "to till it and keep it." In recent centuries, some have interpreted such passages as permission to exploit the world's resources and its other creatures for human purposes, while for others it has been a mandate to preserve and protect the natural order.

The Cultural Tradition of Classical Greece: The Search for a Rational Order

Unlike the Jews, the Persians, or the civilization of India, Greek thinkers generated no lasting religious tradition of world historical importance. The religion of these city-states brought together the unpredictable, quarreling, and lustful gods of Mount Olympus, secret fertility cults, oracles predicting the future, and the ecstatic worship of Dionysus, the god of wine. The distinctive feature of the classical Greek cultural tradition was the willingness of many Greek intellectuals to abandon this mythological framework, to affirm that the world was a physical reality governed by natural laws, and to assert that human rationality could both understand these laws and work out a system of moral and ethical life. In separating science and philosophy from conventional religion, the Greeks developed a way of thinking that bore some similarity to the secularism of Confucian thought in China.

The Greek Way of Knowing

The foundations of this **Greek rationalism** emerged in the three centuries between 600 and 300 B.C.E., coinciding with the flourishing of Greek city-states, especially Athens, and with the growth of its artistic, literary, and theatrical traditions. The enduring significance of Greek thinking lay not so much in the answers it provided to life's great issues, for the Greeks seldom agreed with one another, but rather in their way of asking questions. Their emphasis on argument, logic, and the relentless questioning of received wisdom; their confidence in human reason; their enthusiasm for puzzling out the world without much reference to the gods—these were the defining characteristics of the major Greek thinkers.

The great exemplar of this approach to knowledge was **Socrates** (469–399 B.C.E.), an Athenian philosopher who walked about the city engaging others in conversation about the good life. He wrote nothing, and his preferred manner of teaching was not the lecture or exposition of his own ideas but rather a constant questioning of the assumptions and logic of his students' thinking. Concerned always to puncture the pretentious, he challenged conventional ideas about the importance of wealth and power in living well, urging instead the pursuit of wisdom and virtue. He was critical of Athenian democracy and on occasion had positive things to say about Sparta, the great enemy of his own city. Such behavior brought him into conflict with city authorities, who accused him of corrupting the youth of Athens and sentenced him to death. At his trial, he defended himself as the "gadfly" of Athens, stinging its citizens into awareness. "I shall question, and examine and cross-examine him," he declared, "and if I find that he does not possess virtue, but says he does, I shall rebuke him for scorning the things that are most important and caring more for what is of less worth."[12]

The earliest of the classical Greek thinkers, many of them living on the Ionian coast of Anatolia, applied this rational and questioning way of knowing to the world of nature. For example, Thales, drawing on Babylonian astronomy, predicted an eclipse of the sun and argued that the moon simply reflected the sun's light. He was also one of the first Greeks to ask about the fundamental nature of the universe and came up with the idea that water was the basic stuff from which all else derived, for it existed as solid, liquid, and gas. Others argued in favor of air or fire or some combination. Democritus suggested that atoms, tiny "uncuttable" particles, collided in various configurations to form visible matter. Pythagoras believed that beneath the chaos and complexity of the visible world lay a simple, unchanging mathematical order. What these thinkers had in common was a commitment to a rational and nonreligious explanation for the material world.

Such thinking also served to explain the functioning of the human body and its diseases. Hippocrates and his followers came to believe that the body was composed of four fluids, or "humors," that caused various ailments when out of proper balance. He also traced the origins of epilepsy, known to the Greeks as "the sacred disease," to simple heredity, arguing that it "has a natural cause...like other afflictions."[13] A similar approach informed Greek thinking about the ways of humankind.

Herodotus, who wrote about the Greco-Persian Wars, explained his project as an effort to discover "the reason why they fought one another." This assumption that human reasons lay behind the conflict, not simply the whims of the gods, was what made Herodotus a historian in the modern sense of that word.

Ethics and government also figured importantly in Greek thinking. **Plato** (429–348 B.C.E.) famously sketched out in *The Republic* a design for a good society. It would be ruled by a class of highly educated "guardians" led by a "philosopher-king." Such people would be able to penetrate the many illusions of the material world and to grasp the "world of forms," in which ideas such as goodness, beauty, and justice lived a real and unchanging existence. Only such people, he argued, were fit to rule.

Aristotle (384–322 B.C.E.), a student of Plato and a teacher of Alexander the Great, represents the most complete expression of the Greek way of knowing, for he wrote or commented on practically everything. With an emphasis on empirical observation, he cataloged the constitutions of 158 Greek city-states, identified hundreds of species of animals, and wrote about logic, physics, astronomy, the weather, and much else besides. Famous for his reflections on ethics, he argued that "virtue" was a product of rational training and cultivated habit and could be learned. As to government, he urged a mixed system, combining the principles of monarchy, aristocracy, and democracy. (See "Controversies: Debating Religion and the Axial Age" for a discussion of controversial issues surrounding the emergence of Greek rationalism and other philosophical and religious traditions of this period.)

The Greek Legacy

The rationalism of the Greek tradition was clearly not the whole of Greek culture. The gods of Mount Olympus continued to be a reality for many people, and the ecstatic songs and dances that celebrated Dionysus, the god of wine, were anything but rational and reflective. The death of Socrates at the hands of an Athenian jury showed that philosophy could be a threat as well as an engaging pastime. Nonetheless, Greek rationalism, together with Greek art, literature, and theater, persisted long after the glory days of Athens were over. Alexander's empire and that of the Romans facilitated the spread of Greek culture within the Mediterranean basin and beyond, and many leading Roman figures sent their children to be educated in Athens at the Academy, which Plato had founded. An emerging Christian theology was expressed in terms of Greek philosophical concepts, especially those of Plato. Even after the western Roman Empire collapsed, classical Greek texts were preserved in the eastern half, known as the Byzantine Empire or Byzantium.

In the West, however, direct access to Greek texts was far more difficult in the chaotic conditions of post-Roman Europe, and for centuries Greek scholarship was neglected in favor of distinctly Christian writers. Much of that legacy was subsequently rediscovered after the twelfth century C.E. as European scholars gained access to classical Greek texts. From that point on, the Greek legacy has been viewed as a central element of an emerging "Western" civilization. It played a role in formulating an updated Christian theology, in fostering Europe's seventeenth-century Scientific Revolution, and in providing a point of departure for much of European philosophy.

Long before this European rediscovery, the Greek legacy had also entered the Islamic world. Systematic translations of Greek works of science and philosophy into

Arabic, together with Indian and Persian learning, stimulated Muslim thinkers and scientists, especially in the fields of medicine, astronomy, mathematics, geography, and chemistry. It was in fact largely from Arabic translations of Greek writers that Europeans became reacquainted with the legacy of classical Greece, especially during the twelfth and thirteenth centuries. Despite the many centuries that have passed since the flourishing of ancient Greek culture, that tradition has remained, especially in the West, an inspiration for those who celebrate the powers of the human mind to probe the mysteries of the universe and to explore the equally challenging domain of human life.

The Birth of Christianity…with Buddhist Comparisons

About 500 years after the time of Confucius, the Buddha, and Socrates, a young Jewish artisan/craftsman in the remote province of Judaea in the Roman Empire began a brief three-year career of teaching and healing before he got in trouble with local authorities and was executed. In one of history's most unlikely stories, the life and teachings of that obscure man, barely noted in the historical records of the time, became the basis of the world's second great universal religion. This man, **Jesus of Nazareth** (ca. 4 B.C.E.–29 C.E.), and the religion of Christianity that grew out of his brief career had a dramatic impact on world history, often compared with that of India's Siddhartha Gautama, the Buddha.

The Lives of the Founders

The family background of the two teachers could hardly have been more different. Gautama was born to royalty and luxury, whereas Jesus was a rural or small-town worker from a distinctly lower-class family. But both became spiritual seekers, mystics in their respective traditions, who claimed to have personally experienced another and unseen level of reality. Those powerful religious experiences provided the motivation for their life's work and the personal authenticity that attracted their growing band of followers.

Both were "wisdom teachers," challenging the conventional values of their time, urging the renunciation of wealth, and emphasizing the supreme importance of love or compassion as the basis for a moral life. Both called for the personal transformation of their followers, through "letting go" of the grasping that causes suffering, in the Buddha's teaching, or "losing one's life in order to save it," in the language of Jesus.

Despite these similarities, there were also some differences in their teachings and their life stories. Jesus inherited from his Jewish tradition an intense devotion to a single personal deity with whom he was on intimate terms, referring to him as Abba ("father"). And he gained a reputation as a miracle worker. The Buddha's original message, by contrast, largely ignored the supernatural, involved no miracles, and taught a path of intense self-effort aimed at ethical living and mindfulness as a means of ending suffering. Furthermore, Jesus' teachings had a sharper social and political edge than did those of the Buddha. Jesus spoke more clearly on behalf of the poor and the oppressed, directly criticized the hypocrisies of the powerful, and deliberately associated with lepers, adulterous women, and tax collectors, all of whom were regarded as "impure." These actions reflected his lower-class background, the Jewish tradition of social criticism, and the reality of Roman imperial rule over his people, none of which corresponded to the Buddha's experience. Finally, Jesus' public life was very brief, probably less than three years, compared to more than forty years for the Buddha. His teachings had so antagonized both Jewish and Roman authorities that he was crucified as a political rebel. The Buddha's message was apparently less threatening to the politically powerful, and he died a natural death at age eighty.

The Spread of New Religions

Neither Jesus nor the Buddha had any intention of founding a new religion; rather, they sought to revitalize the traditions from which they had come. Nonetheless, Christianity and Buddhism soon emerged as separate religions, distinct from Judaism and Hinduism, proclaiming their messages to a much wider and more inclusive audience. In the process, both teachers were transformed by their followers into gods. According to many scholars, Jesus never claimed divine status, seeing himself as a teacher or a prophet whose close relationship to God could be replicated by anyone. The Buddha likewise viewed himself as an enlightened but fully human person, an example of what was possible for all who followed the path. But in Mahayana Buddhism, the Buddha became a supernatural being who could be worshipped and prayed to and was spiritually available to his followers. Jesus also soon became divine in the eyes of his early followers, such as Saint Paul and Saint John. According to one of the first creeds of the Church, he was "the Son of God, Very God of Very God."

The transformation of Christianity from a small Jewish sect to a world religion began with **Saint Paul** (ca. 6–67 c.e.), an early convert whose missionary journeys in the eastern Roman Empire led to the founding of small Christian communities that included non-Jews. The Good News of Jesus, Paul argued, was for everyone, and Gentile (non-Jewish) converts need not follow Jewish laws or rituals such as circumcision. In one of his many letters to these new communities, later collected as part of the New Testament, Paul wrote, "There is neither Jew nor Greek . . . neither slave nor free . . . neither male nor female, for you are all one in Christ Jesus."[14] (See the Snapshot for Saint Paul's place in a long line of "wisdom teachers" during the second-wave era.)

Despite Paul's egalitarian pronouncement, early Christianity, like Buddhism, offered a mix of opportunities and restrictions for women. Jesus himself had interacted easily with a wide range of women, and they had figured prominently among his followers. One of them, Mary Magdalene, was arguably a part of his inner circle. And women played leadership roles in the "house churches" of the first century c.e. Nonetheless, some New Testament writings counseled women to "be subject to your husbands" and declared that "it is shameful for a woman to speak in church." Men were identified with the role of Christ himself, for "the husband is head of the wife as Christ is head of the Church."[15] It was not long before male spokesmen for the faith had fully assimilated older and highly negative views of women. As daughters of Eve, they were responsible for the introduction of sin and evil into the world and were the source of temptation for men.

On the other hand, Jesus' mother, Mary, soon became the focus of a devotional cult, and women were among the martyrs of the early Church. Prominent among them was **Perpetua** (181–203 c.e.), a young North African woman of Roman background who wrote a famous account of her trial and imprisonment before

SNAPSHOT   **THINKERS AND PHILOSOPHIES OF THE SECOND-WAVE ERA**

Person	Date	Location	Religion/ Philosophy	Key Ideas
Zoroaster	7th century B.C.E.(?)	Persia (present-day Iran)	Zoroastrianism	Single High God; cosmic conflict of good and evil
Hebrew prophets (such as Isaiah, Amos, Jeremiah)	9th–6th centuries B.C.E.	Eastern Mediterranean/ Palestine/Israel	Judaism	Transcendent High God; covenant with chosen people; social justice
Anonymous writers of Upanishads	800–400 B.C.E.	India	Brahmanism/ Hinduism	Brahman (the single impersonal divine reality); karma; rebirth; goal of liberation (moksha)
Confucius	6th–5th centuries B.C.E.	China	Confucianism	Social harmony through moral example; secular outlook; importance of education; family as model of the state
Mahavira	6th century B.C.E.	India	Jainism	All creatures have souls; purification through nonviolence; opposed to caste
Siddhartha Gautama	6th–5th centuries B.C.E.	India	Buddhism	Suffering caused by desire/attachment; end of suffering through modest and moral living and meditation practice
Laozi, Zhuangzi	6th–3rd centuries B.C.E.	China	Daoism	Withdrawal from the world into contemplation of nature; simple living; end of striving
Socrates, Plato, Aristotle	5th–4th centuries B.C.E.	Greece	Greek rationalism	Style of persistent questioning; secular explanation of nature and human life
Jesus	Early 1st century C.E.	Palestine/Israel	Christianity	Supreme importance of love based on intimate relationship with God; at odds with established authorities
Saint Paul	1st century C.E.	Palestine/Israel/ eastern Roman Empire	Christianity	Christianity as a religion for all; salvation through faith in Jesus Christ

she was "condemned to the beasts" for her refusal to renounce her Christian faith. Growing numbers of Christian women, like their Buddhist counterparts, found a more independent space in the monasteries, even as the official hierarchy of the Church became wholly male.

Nonetheless, the inclusive message of early Christianity was one of the attractions of the new faith as it spread very gradually within the Roman Empire during the several centuries after Jesus' death (see Map 4.1). The earliest converts were usually lower-stratum people—artisans, traders, and a considerable number of women—mostly from towns and cities, while a scattering of wealthier, more prominent, and better-educated people later joined their ranks. The spread of the faith was often accompanied by reports of miracles, healings, and the casting out of demons—all of which were impressive to people thoroughly accustomed to expecting supernatural intervention in the events of ordinary life. Christian communities also attracted converts by the way their members cared for one another. By 300 C.E., perhaps 10 percent of the Roman Empire's population (some 5 million people) identified themselves as Christians.

Although Christians in the West often think of their faith as a European-centered religion, during the first six centuries of the Christian era, most followers of Jesus lived in Southwest Asia and Africa. The first Christian communities formed along the eastern Mediterranean coast, mostly in the major towns of Syria and Anatolia. But the faith soon took root elsewhere as well. A distinctive **Church of the East** spread from Syria into Persia, where it developed a unique liturgy with strong Jewish influences and a musical tradition of chants and hymns, all in Syriac—a language

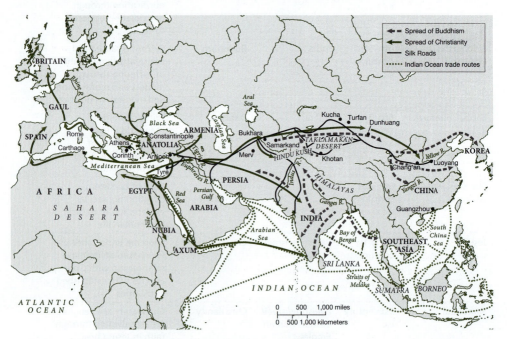

MAP 4.1 The Spread of Early Christianity and Buddhism
In the five centuries after the birth of Jesus, Christianity found converts from Spain to Northeast Africa, the Middle East, Central Asia, and India. In the Roman Empire, Axum, and Armenia, the new religion enjoyed state support as well. Subsequently, Christianity took root solidly in Europe and after 1000 C.E. in Russia. Meanwhile, Buddhism was spreading from its South Asian homeland to various parts of Asia, even as it was weakening in India itself.

closely related to the Aramaic that Jesus spoke. Its missionaries took Christianity even farther to the east. By the fourth century, and perhaps much earlier, a well-organized Church had taken root in southern India, which later gained tax privileges and special rights from local rulers. In the early seventh century, a Persian monk named Alopen initiated a small but remarkable Christian experiment in China (see "Asian Christianity" in Chapter 10). A modest Christian presence in Central Asia was also an outgrowth of this Church of the East. To the north on the slopes of the Caucasus Mountains, the Kingdom of Armenia around 310 C.E. became the first place where rulers adopted Christianity as a state religion, providing the environment for the flowering of an Armenian church. To the south, a number of Arabs had become Christian by the time of Muhammad's birth in 570, and one of them was among the first to affirm Muhammad as an authentic prophet.

In Africa, a particularly vibrant center of Christianity developed in Egypt, where priests soon translated the Bible into the Egyptian language known as Coptic and Egyptian Christians pioneered various forms of monasticism. By 400 C.E., hundreds of monasteries, cells, and caves dotted the desert, inhabited by reclusive monks dedicated to their spiritual practices. Increasingly, the language, theology, and practice of Egyptian Christianity diverged from that of Rome and Constantinople, giving expression to Egyptian resistance against Roman or Byzantine oppression. To the west of Egypt, a Church of North Africa furnished a number of the intellectuals of the early Church, including Saint Augustine, as well as many Christian martyrs to Roman persecution. Here and elsewhere, the coming of Christianity provoked not only hostility from Roman political authorities but also tensions within families. The North African Carthaginian writer Tertullian (160–220 C.E.), known as the "father of Latin Christianity," described the kind of difficulties that might arise between a Christian wife and her "pagan" husband:

> She is engaged in a fast; her husband has arranged a banquet. It is her Christian duty to visit the streets and the homes of the poor; her husband insists on family business. She celebrates the Easter Vigil throughout the night; her husband expects her in his bed.[16]

Farther south in Africa, by 350 C.E. Christianity had become the state religion of Axum, an emerging kingdom in what is now Eritrea and Ethiopia (discussed further in Chapter 6). Thus Axum adopted Christianity at about the same time that Armenia and the Roman Empire officially embraced the faith. In Axum, a distinctively African expression of Christianity took root, with open-air services, the use of drums and stringed instruments in worship, and colorful umbrellas covering priests and musicians from the elements. Linked theologically and organizationally to Coptic Christianity in Egypt, the Ethiopian Church used Ge'ez, a local Semitic language and script, for its liturgy and literature.

In the Roman world, the strangest and most offensive feature of the new faith was its exclusive monotheism and its antagonism to all other supernatural powers, particularly the cult of the emperors. Christians' denial of these other gods caused them to be tagged as "atheists" and was one reason behind the empire's intermittent persecution of Christians during the first three centuries of the Common Era. All of that ended with Emperor Constantine's conversion in the early fourth century C.E. and the proclamation of Christianity as the state religion in 380 C.E.

The First Christian Emperor Constantine Following Constantine's conversion, artists used both Roman imperial and Christian symbols to present him as a Christian emperor. In this circa fourth-century carving from what is now Croatia, Constantine is portrayed sitting on an imperial throne holding a Christian cross while a man lies prostrate before him. (DEA/A. DAGLI ORTI/Getty Images)

Roman rulers sought to use an increasingly popular Christianity as glue to hold together a very diverse population in a weakening imperial state. Constantine and his successors thus provided Christians with newfound security and opportunities. The emperor Theodosius (r. 379–395 C.E.) enforced a ban on all polytheistic ritual sacrifices and ordered the temples that practiced them closed. Christians, by contrast, received patronage for their buildings, official approval for their doctrines, suppression of their rivals, and prestige from imperial recognition. All of this set in motion a process by which the Roman Empire, and later all of Europe, became overwhelmingly Christian. At the time, however, Christianity was expanding at least as rapidly to the east and south as it was to the west. In 500, few observers could have predicted that the future of Christianity would lie primarily in Europe.

The spread of Buddhism in India was quite different from that of Christianity in the Roman Empire. Even though Ashoka's support gave Buddhism a considerable boost, it was never promoted to the exclusion of other faiths. Ashoka sought harmony among India's diverse population through religious tolerance rather than religious uniformity. The kind of monotheistic intolerance that Christianity exhibited in the Roman world was quite foreign to Indian religious practice. Whereas Buddhism later died out in India as it was absorbed into a reviving Hinduism, no renewal of Roman polytheism occurred in the West, and Christianity became an enduring element of European civilization. Finally, both of these new religions possessed strong missionary impulses and spread widely beyond their places of origin. Buddhism provided a network of cultural connections across much of Asia, while Christianity during its early centuries established an Afro-Eurasian presence.

Institutions, Controversies, and Divisions

As Christianity spread within the Roman Empire and beyond, it developed a hierar-chical organization, with patriarchs, bishops, and priests—all men—replacing the house churches of the early years, in which women played a more prominent part. At least in some places, however, women continued to exercise leadership and even priestly roles, prompting Pope Gelasius in 494 to speak out sharply against those who encouraged women "to officiate at the sacred altars, and to take part in all matters imputed to the offices of the male sex, to which they do not belong."[17] In general, though, the exclusion of women from the priesthood established a male-dominated clergy and a patriarchal church, which has lasted into the twenty-first century.

The emerging Christian movement was, however, anything but unified. Its immense geographic reach, accompanied by inevitable differences in language, culture, and political regime, ensured that a single focus for Christian belief and practice was difficult to achieve. Doctrinal differences also tore at the unity of Chris-tianity and embroiled church authorities in frequent controversy about the nature of Jesus (was he human, divine, or both?), his relationship to God (equal or infe-rior?), and the always-perplexing concept of the Trinity (God as Father, Son, and Holy Spirit). There was debate as well about what writings belonged in the official New Testament, as dozens of letters, gospels, poems, and songs circulated among the early Christian communities. A series of church councils—at Nicaea (325 C.E.), Chalcedon (451 C.E.), and Constantinople (553 C.E.), for example—sought to define an orthodox, or correct, position on these and other issues, declaring those who disagreed as *anathema* and expelling them from the Church. The Church of the East, for example, adopted Nestorianism, which emphasized the human side of Jesus' nature, an idea rejected by the Roman Catholic and Eastern Orthodox Churches.

Beyond these theological debates, political and cultural differences generated division even among the orthodox. The bishop of Rome gradually emerged as the dominant leader, or pope, of the Church in the western half of the empire, but his authority was sharply contested in the East. This division contributed to the later split between the Latin, or Roman Catholic, and the Greek, or Eastern Orthodox, branches of Christendom, a division that continues to the present. Thus the Chris-tian world of 500 C.E. was not only geographically extensive but also politically and theologically very diverse and highly fragmented.

Buddhists too clashed over various interpretations of the Buddha's teachings, and a series of councils failed to prevent the division between Theravada, Mahayana, and other approaches. A considerable proliferation of different sects, practices, teachings, and meditation techniques subsequently emerged within the Buddhist world, but these divisions generally lacked the "clear-cut distinction between 'right' and 'wrong' ideas" that characterized conflicts within the Christian world.[18] Although Buddhist states and warrior classes (such as the famous samurai of Japan) sometimes engaged in warfare, religious differences among Buddhists seldom provided the basis for the bit-terness and violence that often accompanied religious conflict within Christendom. Nor did Buddhists develop the kind of overall religious hierarchy that characterized Christianity, although communities of monks and nuns, organized in monasteries, created elaborate rules to govern their internal affairs.

Controversies: Debating Religion and the Axial Age

In 1947 a German philosopher, Karl Jaspers, coined a new term—the Axial Age. It referred to a time of particular creativity that gave rise to new cultural traditions all across Eurasia, but particularly in China, India, the Middle East, and the eastern Mediterranean region, between 800 and 200 B.C.E. Here was an "axis," a pivot, or a major turning point in human cultural history, as Buddhism, Hinduism, Judaism, Confucianism, Daoism, and Greek rationalism began to take shape.[19]

It has been a controversial idea. Why, for example, did groups or individuals willing to challenge established traditions emerge during these centuries? Historians have noted disruptions to established patterns of life that may have opened the way to new thinking, but they do not always agree on which disruptions to emphasize.[20] Were economic factors the cause—an emerging iron-age technology that generated more productive economies and more deadly warfare; greater prosperity in urban centers; or increased trade and the use of money? Or perhaps political disruptions were more important, such as the breakdown of political order during China's "age of warring states" or the endemic rivalries of Greek city-states. Social factors, such as a growing resentment against the pretensions and privileges of Brahmin priests, were likely part of the appeal of an emerging Buddhist faith. All of these disruptions, occurring in already literate societies, perhaps led thinkers to question older outlooks and to come up with new solutions to fundamental questions.

But how much did these Axial Age traditions have in common? The most enthusiastic advocates of the Axial Age idea believed they shared a great deal. All these traditions sought an alternative to an earlier polytheism, in which the activities of various gods and spirits explained what happened in this world. These gods and spirits had generally been seen as similar to human beings, though much more powerful. Through ritual and sacrifice, men and women might placate the gods or persuade them to do human bidding. In contrast, the new cultural traditions of the Axial Age sought to define a single source of order and meaning in the universe, some moral or religious realm that was sharply different from and higher than the sphere of human life.

Axial Age thinkers also shared a skepticism about the ability of human language to capture this Absolute or Ultimate Reality. Laozi in China famously declared that "the Dao that can be named is not the eternal Dao." The task of humankind, according to these new ways of thinking, was not so much to seek intellectual clarity or beseech the gods for favors as it was to transform oneself morally or spiritually by aligning with that higher order. Living morally, controlling desire, taming the ego, and developing compassion—these were the goals of Axial Age traditions.

Those traditions also meant that people might more easily question and criticize their rulers or their societies, for now there was a higher point of reference from which to judge all of human life. Thus Jewish prophets strongly denounced the injustices of their society, and the Buddha challenged India's ancient caste system. Religion was becoming more clearly ethical. And at least implicitly, the Axial Age traditions suggested the possibility of a universal spiritual outlook available to everyone.

But despite these broad similarities, many historians and other scholars have been sharply critical or entirely dismissive of the Axial Age idea. Some critics have argued that the concept of an Axial Age greatly overestimated the uniqueness of what occurred during those few centuries in the first millennium B.C.E. After all, ancient Egyptian religion had long emphasized the moral behavior of individuals and judgment after death. In addition, the fourteenth-century-B.C.E. pharaoh Akhenaten directly challenged traditional Egyptian religion as he vigorously promoted a quasi-monotheistic faith focused on worship of the sun god Aten. Furthermore, the major religious breakthroughs of both Christianity and Islam, the most prominent religions of the past 2,000 years, occurred well after the Axial Age had supposedly ended. Was it not somewhat arrogant or condescending to think that religious creativity was limited to those few centuries? Was it appropriate for Karl Jaspers, who first articulated the Axial Age idea, to declare that pre-Axial religion was "in some measure unawakened"?[21]

Furthermore, while advocates of the Axial Age concept found broad similarities among those emerging traditions, their critics noticed differences. Chinese and Greek thinkers focused more on the affairs of this world and credited human rationality with the power to understand that reality. Indian and Jewish thinkers, by contrast, explored the unseen realm of the Divine and the relationship of God or the gods to human life. While Jewish prophets located the transcendent realm in the activities of a highly personal deity actively involved in the world, Laozi, Confucius, and the Buddha largely avoided much discussion of the supernatural. This emphasis on sharp differences among cultural traditions undermined the idea of an Axial Age of common understandings.

Finally, critics of the Axial Age concept charge its proponents with "presentism," or reading the past through the lens of current values and problems. Karl Jaspers originally proposed the term in 1947, while the world was still reeling from the horrors of World War II. He, and many world historians after him, wanted desperately to find something that all of humankind might share, "a base for the unity of mankind" that was not specifically Christian or Western. And they found it in the Axial Age traditions, which, they believed, provided a foundation for moving toward a more unified and peaceful world. Critics maintain that although this may seem wonderful, in adopting the Axial Age idea as a solution for current problems, Jaspers and others gave it a solidity and coherence that it does not deserve.[22] The needs of the present do not provide a sound basis for uncovering the realities of the past.

Or do they? Would we have women's history without the demands of feminist movements? Would we have environmental history without an emerging awareness of environmental problems? Would we have world history without a growing recognition of global interdependence? Current realities always shape our understanding of the past, or at least the questions we pose about the past. Perhaps we have no choice but to conduct our historical inquiries with one eye firmly fixed on the present while the other gazes thoughtfully at the past. Navigating that tension is among the central tasks of all historical study. Both the advocates of the Axial Age idea and its critics are engaged in that enduring balancing act.

Conclusions and Reflections: Religion and Historians

Religion — or some larger cultural outlook on life — has been a constant in human affairs since the earliest times. During the 1,000 years of the second-wave era, a number of distinctive religious and cultural traditions took shape that have persisted to the present day. In studying this phenomenon, historians have asked many of the same questions that they pose to other dimensions of human life.

One of those questions involves origins. How did these religious traditions get started? The beginnings of the Chinese traditions of Confucianism and Daoism lay in the chaotic conditions of the "age of warring states." Zoroastrianism too may have arisen in response to the violence of endemic cattle raids in ancient Persia. Judaism emerged from the experience of deportation and exile in Babylon. In short, religions were rooted in the historical experiences of particular peoples.

Another question, especially prominent in world history, deals with comparison. How did these cultural traditions differ from one another? Hinduism, Judaism, and Christianity focused attention on the supernatural—God or gods—while Greek rationalism, Confucianism, and early Buddhism were more "this-worldly" in their outlook. Both Buddhism and Christianity grew out of the teachings of a particular person within established civilizations and found expression as universal faiths available to everyone. Judaism and Hinduism, by contrast, developed as part of the unfolding of their respective civilizations and expressed little of the missionary impulse of Buddhism and Christianity.

Yet another common historical issue—that of change over time—has certainly applied to these religious traditions. The Hindu tradition changed from a religion of ritual and sacrifice to one of devotion and worship. Buddhism became more conventionally religious, with an emphasis on the supernatural, as it evolved from Theravada to Mahayana forms. A male-dominated hierarchical Christian Church, with its pope, bishops, priests, and state support, was very different from the small house churches, often led by women, that characterized early Christianity. Like everything else, religions change.

Finally, historians are very interested in the relationship between religious life and the social and political dimensions of ancient societies. Confucianism, for example, became the official ideology of the Chinese empire, as did Christianity for the Roman Empire after the fourth century C.E. Earlier, however, Christianity had clearly challenged Roman authorities and was harshly persecuted for doing so. The Jewish prophets of the Old Testament and later Jesus himself were highly critical of established ways of living. Buddhism too was at odds with major elements of Hindu life and practice. Religion was a double-edged sword, both sustaining and challenging the political and social life of these ancient civilizations.

As historians seek to understand the religious dimension of human life, various tensions between scholars and believers have arisen. One of these tensions involves the question of change. Most religions present themselves as timeless revelations from the beyond, partaking of eternity or at least reflecting ancient practice. In the eyes of historians, however, the religious aspect of human life changes as much as any other. The implication—that religions are largely a human phenomenon—has been troublesome to some believers.

Historians, on the other hand, have sometimes been uncomfortable in the face of claims by believers that they have actually experienced an unseen or divine reality. Certainly, modern scholars are in no position to validate or to refute the spiritual claims of religious leaders and their many followers. Interior experience is at the heart of lived religion, but it is also the most difficult dimension for historians to grasp or verify.

Reconciling personal religious convictions with the perspectives and methods of modern historical scholarship is no easy task. At the very least, all of us can appreciate the immense human effort that has gone into the making of religious traditions, and we can acknowledge their enormous significance in the unfolding of the human story. They have shaped the meanings that billions of people over thousands of years have attached to the world they inhabit. Their ethical teachings have everywhere shaped expectations for human behavior. These religious traditions have justified the vast social inequalities and oppressive states of human civilizations, but they have also enabled human beings to endure the multiple sufferings of human life, inspired acts of compassion and fair dealing, and on occasion stimulated reform and rebellion. And the religions born in second-wave civilizations have guided much of humankind in its endless efforts to penetrate the mysteries of the world beyond—and of the world within.

Revisiting Chapter 4

REVISITING SPECIFICS

REVISITING CORE IDEAS

1. **Comparing Cultural Traditions** What different answers to the problem of disorder arose in classical China?

2. **Identifying Change** In what ways did the religious traditions of South Asia change over the centuries?

3. **Comparing Religious Traditions** What was distinctive about Zoroastrianism and Judaism in comparison to South Asian traditions, and how did these two Middle Eastern traditions differ from each other?

4. **Describing Cultural Traditions** What were the distinctive features of the Greek intellectual tradition?

5. **Describing Religious Change** In what ways was Christianity transformed in the five centuries following the death of Jesus?

6. **Explaining Religious Appeal** How might you understand the appeal of Buddhism and Christianity as opposed to that of the more rationalist approaches of Greek and Confucian philosophy?

A WIDER VIEW

1. Is a secular outlook on the world an essentially modern phenomenon, or does it have precedents in the second-wave era?

2. In what ways did religion support political authorities and social elites in the second-wave civilizations? How did it challenge them?

3. Imagine that you are a Christian traveler in the Eurasian world of 500 C.E. writing home about your encounter with other religious traditions. What similarities and differences might you notice? What might you appreciate in those traditions? And what might you find distasteful or appalling?

4. **Looking Back** What relationships can you see between the political dimensions of second-wave civilizations described in Chapter 3 and their cultural or religious aspects discussed in this chapter?

CHRONOLOGY

ca. 800–400 B.C.E.	• Upanishads compiled
ca. 7th century B.C.E.(?)	• Life of Zoroaster
ca. 600–300 B.C.E.	• Greek rationalism
586 B.C.E.	• Jewish exile in Babylon
ca. 566–486 B.C.E.	• Life of Buddha
ca. 551–479 B.C.E.	• Life of Confucius
469–399 B.C.E.	• Life of Socrates
429–348 B.C.E.	• Life of Plato
384–322 B.C.E.	• Life of Aristotle
221–206 B.C.E.	• Legalism prominent in Qin dynasty
206 B.C.E.–220 C.E.	• Confucianism prominent in Han dynasty
4 B.C.E.–29 C.E.	• Life of Jesus
ca. 45–65 C.E.	• Paul's missionary journeys in eastern Mediterranean region
ca. 100–313 C.E.	• Intermittent persecutions of Christians in Roman Empire
184–204 C.E.	• Yellow Turban Rebellion; informed by Daoist beliefs
ca. 300 C.E.	• Bhagavad Gita compiled in final form
310–380 C.E.	• Christianity becomes state religion in Armenia, Axum, and the Roman Empire
ca. 650 C.E.	• *Bhakti* forms of Hinduism emerge

5

Society and Inequality in Eurasia / North Africa

600 B.C.E.–600 C.E.

CHAPTER OUTLINE

Society and the State in China
- An Elite Class of Officials
- The Landlord Class
- Peasants
- Merchants

Class and Caste in India
- Caste as Varna
- Caste as Jati
- The Functions of Caste

Slavery: The Case of the Roman Empire
- Slavery and Civilization
- The Making of Roman Slavery

Comparing Patriarchies
- A Changing Patriarchy: The Case of China
- Contrasting Patriarchies: Athens and Sparta

Conclusions and Reflections: Pondering Inequality

CONNECTING PAST AND PRESENT

"CASTE HAS NO IMPACT ON LIFE TODAY," declared Chezi K. Ganesan in 2010.[1] Certainly, Mr. Ganesan's low-caste background as a Nadar, ranking just above the "untouchables," had little impact on the career of this prosperous high-tech businessman, who shuttled between California's Silicon Valley and the city of Chennai in southern India. Yet his grandfather could not enter Hindu temples, and until the mid-nineteenth century, the women of his caste, as a sign of their low status, were forbidden to cover their breasts in the presence of Brahmin men. Moreover, if caste has not proved to be a barrier to Mr. Ganesan, it has remained significant for many others in contemporary India. Personal ads for those seeking a marriage partner in many online services often indicate an individual's caste as well as other personal data. Affirmative action programs benefiting low-caste Indians have provoked great controversy and resentment among some upper-caste groups. The brutal murder of an entire Dalit, or "untouchable," family in 2006 sparked much soul-searching in the Indian media. So while caste has changed in modern India, it has also persisted.

The past several centuries have called into question social patterns long assumed to be natural and permanent. The French, Russian, and Chinese revolutions challenged and destroyed ancient monarchies and class hierarchies; the abolitionist movement of the nineteenth century attacked slavery, largely unquestioned for millennia; the women's movement has confronted long and deeply held patriarchal assumptions about the proper relationship between the sexes; and during and after India's struggle for independence from Great Britain in the twentieth century, some have challenged their country's ancient caste system. Nevertheless, caste, class, patriarchy, and even slavery have certainly not vanished from human society, even now. During the era of second-wave civilizations in Eurasia, such patterns of inequality prevailed widely and generated social tensions that endured well beyond that era.

As Chapter 3 pointed out, millions of individual men and women inhabiting the civilizations of Eurasia and North Africa lived within a political framework of states or empires. They also occupied a world of ideas, religions, and values that derived both from local folkways and from the teaching of the great religious or cultural traditions born in the second-wave era, as described in Chapter 4. In this chapter, the focus turns to the social arrangements of these civilizations— relationships between rich and poor, powerful and powerless, enslaved and free, and men and women. Those relationships shaped the daily lives and the life chances of everyone and provided the foundation for political authority as well as challenges to it.

Like the First Civilizations, those of the second-wave era were sharply divided along class lines, and they too were patriarchal, with women clearly subordinated to men in most domains of life. In constructing their societies, however, these second-wave civilizations differed substantially from one another. Chinese, Indian, and Mediterranean civilizations provide numerous illustrations of the many and varied ways in which these peoples organized their social lives. The assumptions, tensions, and conflicts accompanying these social patterns provided much of the distinctive character and texture that distinguished these diverse civilizations from one another.

| **SEEKING THE MAIN POINT** | In what different ways was social inequality, so characteristic of all civilizations, expressed and experienced in the Eurasian societies of the second-wave era? |

Society and the State in China

Chinese society was unique in the ancient world in the extent to which it was shaped by the actions of the state. Nowhere was this more apparent than in the political power and immense social prestige of Chinese state officials, all of them male. For more than 2,000 years, these officials, bureaucrats acting in the name of the emperor both in the capital and in the provinces, represented the cultural and social elite of Chinese civilization. This class had its origins in the efforts of early Chinese rulers to find administrators loyal to the central state rather than to their own families or regions. Philosophers such as Confucius had long advocated selecting such officials on the basis of merit and personal morality rather than birth or wealth. As the Han dynasty established its authority in China around 200 B.C.E., its rulers required each province to send men of promise to the capital, where they were examined and chosen for official positions based on their performance.

An Elite Class of Officials

Over time, this system of selecting administrators evolved into the world's first professional civil service. In 124 B.C.E., Emperor Wudi established an imperial academy where potential officials were trained as scholars and immersed in texts dealing with history, literature, art, and mathematics, with an emphasis on Confucian teachings. By the end of the Han dynasty, it enrolled some 30,000 students, who were by then subjected to a series of written examinations to select officials of various grades. Private schools in the provinces funneled still more aspiring candidates into this examination system, which persisted until the early twentieth century. In theory open to all men, this system in practice favored those whose families were wealthy enough to provide the years of education required to pass even the lower-level exams. Proximity to the capital and family connections to the imperial court also helped in gaining a position in this highest class of Chinese elites. Nonetheless, village communities or a local landowner might sponsor the education of a bright young man from a commoner family, enabling him to enter the charmed circle of officialdom. One rags-to-riches story told of a pig farmer who became an adviser to the emperor himself. Thus the examination system provided a modest measure of social mobility in an otherwise quite hierarchical society.

In later dynasties, that system grew even more elaborate and became an enduring and distinguishing feature of Chinese civilization. During the Tang dynasty, the famous poet and official Po Chu-I (772–846 C.E.) wrote a poem titled "After Passing the Examination" that shows something of the fame and fortune that awaited an accomplished student as well as the continuing loyalty to family and home that ideally marked those who succeeded:

> For ten years I never left my books, / I went up . . . and won unmerited praise.
> My high place I do not much prize; / The joy of my parents will first make me proud.
> Fellow students, six or seven men, / See me off as I leave the City gate.
> My covered coach is ready to drive away . . . / On a Spring day the road that leads to home.[2]

The Chinese Examination System The Chinese imperial government selected officials through an elaborate system of civil service exams. This Song dynasty painting shows candidates taking the highest level of these tests, known as the palace exams, at the imperial capital Kaifeng. Success opened the way to prestigious appointments at the top levels of the Chinese government. (Pictures from History/Bridgeman Images)

Those who made it into the bureaucracy entered a realm of high privilege and great prestige. Senior officials moved about in carriages and were bedecked with robes, ribbons, seals, and headdresses appropriate to their rank. Even lower officials who served in the provinces rather than the capital were distinguished by their polished speech, their cultural sophistication, and their urban manners as well as their political authority. Proud of their learning, they were the bearers, and often the makers, of Chinese culture. "Officials are the leaders of the populace," stated an imperial edict of 144 B.C.E., "and it is right and proper that the carriages they ride in and the robes that they wear should correspond to the degrees of their dignity."[3] Some of these men, particularly in times of political turmoil, experienced tension between their official duties and their personal inclination toward a more withdrawn life of reflective cultural pursuits (poetry, painting, calligraphy).

The Landlord Class

Most officials came from wealthy families, and in China wealth meant land. When the Qin dynasty unified China by 210 B.C.E., most land was held by small-scale peasant farmers. But by the first century B.C.E., the pressures of population growth, taxation, and indebtedness had generated a class of large landowners as impoverished peasants found it necessary to sell their lands to more prosperous neighbors. This accumulation of land in sizable estates was a persistent theme in Chinese history and one that was frequently, though not very successfully, opposed by state authorities. Landlords of such large estates were often able to avoid paying taxes, thus decreasing state revenues and increasing the tax burden for the remaining peasants. In some cases, they could also raise their own military forces that might challenge the authority of the emperor.

One of the most dramatic state efforts to counteract the growing power of large landowners is associated with **Wang Mang**, a high court official of the Han dynasty who usurped the emperor's throne in 8 C.E. and immediately launched a series of startling reforms. A firm believer in Confucian good government, Wang Mang saw his reforms as re-creating a golden age of long ago in which small-scale peasant farmers represented the backbone of Chinese society. Accordingly, he ordered the great private estates to be nationalized and divided up among the landless. Government loans to peasant families, limits on the amount of land a family might own, and an end to private slavery were all part of his reform program, but these measures proved impossible to enforce. Opposition from wealthy landowners, nomadic invasions, poor harvests, floods, and famines led to the collapse of Wang Mang's reforms and his assassination in 23 C.E.

Large landowning families, therefore, remained a central feature of Chinese society, although the fate of individual families rose and fell as the wheel of fortune lifted them to great prominence or plunged them into poverty and disgrace. As a class, they benefited both from the wealth that their estates generated and from the power and prestige that accompanied their education and their membership in the official elite. The term "scholar-gentry" reflected their twin sources of privilege. With homes in both urban and rural areas, members of the scholar-gentry class lived luxuriously. Multi-storied houses, the finest of silk clothing, gleaming carriages, private orchestras, high-stakes gambling—all of this was part of the life of **China's scholar-gentry class**.

Peasants

Throughout the long course of China's civilization, the vast majority of its population consisted of peasants living in small households that represented two or three generations. Some owned enough land to support their families and perhaps even sell something on the local market. Many others could barely survive. Nature, the state, and landlords combined to make the life of most peasants extremely vulnerable. Famines, floods, droughts, hail, and pests could wreak havoc without warning. State authorities required the payment of taxes, demanded about a month's labor every year on various public projects, and conscripted young men for military service. During the Han dynasty, growing numbers of impoverished and desperate peasants had to sell out to large landlords and work as tenants or sharecroppers on their estates, where rents could run as high as one-half to two-thirds of the crop. Other peasants fled, taking to a life of begging or joining gangs of bandits in remote areas.

An eighth-century-C.E. Chinese poem by Li Shen reflects poignantly on the enduring hardships of peasant life:

> The cob of corn in springtime sown / In autumn yields a hundredfold.
> No fields are seen that fallow lie: / And yet of hunger peasants die.
> As at noontide they hoe their crops, / Sweat on the grain to earth down drops.
> How many tears, how many a groan, / Each morsel on thy dish did mould![4]

Such conditions provoked periodic peasant rebellions, which have punctuated Chinese history for over 2,000 years. Toward the end of the second century c.e., wandering bands of peasants began to join together as floods along the Yellow River and resulting epidemics compounded the misery of landlessness and poverty. What emerged was a massive peasant uprising known as the **Yellow Turban Rebellion** because of the yellow scarves the peasants wore around their heads. That movement, which swelled to about 360,000 armed followers by 184 c.e., found leaders, organization, and a unifying ideology in a popular form of Daoism. Featuring supernatural healings, collective trances, and public confessions of sin, the Yellow Turban movement looked forward to the "Great Peace"—a golden age of equality, social harmony, and common ownership of property. Although the rebellion was suppressed by the military forces of the Han dynasty, the Yellow Turban and other peasant upheavals devastated the economy, weakened the state, and contributed to the overthrow of the dynasty a few decades later. Repeatedly in Chinese history, such peasant movements, often expressed in religious terms, registered the sharp class antagonisms of Chinese society and led to the collapse of more than one ruling dynasty.

Merchants

Peasants were oppressed in China and certainly exploited, but they were also honored and celebrated in the official ideology of the state. In the eyes of the scholar-gentry, peasants were the solid productive backbone of the country, and their hard work and endurance in the face of difficulties were worthy of praise. Merchants, however, did not enjoy such a favorable reputation in the eyes of China's cultural elite. They were widely viewed as unproductive, making a shameful profit from selling the work of others. Stereotyped as greedy, luxury loving, and materialistic, merchants stood in contrast to the presumed frugality, altruism, and cultured tastes of the scholar-gentry. As Confucius taught, "The gentleman is alert to what is right; the petty man [merchant] is alert to what is profitable."[5] Merchants were also seen as a social threat, as their ill-gained wealth impoverished others, deprived the state of needed revenues, and fostered resentments.

Such views lay behind periodic efforts by state authorities to rein in merchants' activity and to keep them under control. Early in the Han dynasty, merchants were forbidden to wear silk clothing, ride horses, or carry arms. Nor were they permitted to sit for civil service examinations or hold public office. State monopolies on profitable industries such as salt, iron, and alcohol limited merchant opportunities. Later dynasties sometimes forced merchants to loan large sums of money to the state. Despite this active discrimination, merchants frequently became quite wealthy. Some tried to achieve a more respectable elite status by purchasing landed estates or educating their sons for the civil service examinations. Many had backdoor relationships with state officials and landlords who found them useful and were not averse to profiting from business connections with merchants, despite their unsavory reputation.

Class and Caste in India

India's social organization shared certain broad features with that of China. In both civilizations, birth determined social status for most people; little social mobility was available for the vast majority; sharp distinctions and great inequalities characterized social life; and religious or cultural traditions defined these inequalities as natural, eternal, and ordained by the gods. Despite these similarities, the organization, flavor, and texture of ancient Indian society were distinctive compared to almost all other civilizations. These unique aspects of Indian society have long been embodied in what is now called the "caste" system, a term that comes from the Portuguese word *casta*, which means "race" or "purity of blood." That social organization emerged over thousands of years and in some respects has endured into modern times.

Caste as Varna

The origins of the caste system are at best hazy. Broadly speaking, however, the distinctive social system of India grew out of the interactions among South Asia's immensely varied cultures. Also contributing to the development of caste was the growth of economic and social differences among these peoples as the class inequalities common to "civilization" spread throughout the Ganges River valley and beyond.

Whatever the precise origins of the caste system, by around 500 B.C.E., the idea that society was forever divided into four ranked classes, or **varnas**, was deeply embedded in Indian thinking. Everyone was born into and remained within one of these classes for life. At the top of this hierarchical system were the Brahmins, priests whose rituals and sacrifices alone could ensure the proper functioning of the world. They were followed by the Kshatriya class, warriors and rulers charged with protecting and governing society. Next was the Vaisya class, originally commoners who cultivated the land. These three classes came to be regarded as possessing a distinctive nobility and purity that was conveyed by the term "Aryan." They were also called the "twice-born," for they experienced not only a physical birth but also formal initiation into their respective varnas and status as people of prestigious Aryan descent. Far below these twice-born in the hierarchy of varna groups were the Sudras, native peoples incorporated into the margins of Aryan society in very subordinate positions. Regarded as servants of their social betters, they were not allowed to hear or repeat the Vedas, an early collection of religious texts, or to take part in Aryan rituals. So little were they valued that a Brahmin who killed a Sudra was penalized as if he had killed a cat or a dog.

According to varna theory, these four classes were formed from the body of the god Purusha and were therefore eternal and changeless. Although these divisions are widely recognized in India even today, historians have noted considerable social flux in ancient Indian history. Members of the Brahmin and Kshatriya groups, for example, were frequently in conflict over which ranked highest in the varna hierarchy, and only slowly did the Brahmins emerge clearly in the top position. Although theoretically purely Aryan, both groups absorbed various tribal peoples as Indian civilization expanded. Tribal medicine men or sorcerers found a place as Brahmins, while warrior groups entered the Kshatriya varna. The Vaisya varna, originally defined as cultivators, evolved into a business class with a prominent place for merchants, while the Sudra varna became the domain of peasant farmers. Finally a whole new category, ranking lower even than the Sudras, emerged in the "untouchables," men and women who did the work considered most unclean and polluting, such as sweeping, cremating corpses, dealing with the skins of dead animals, and serving as executioners. (See Snapshot: Social Life and Duty in Classical India on page 137.)

Caste in India This 1947 photograph from *Life* magazine illustrates the "purity and pollution" thinking that has long been central to the ideology of caste. It shows a high-caste landowner carefully dropping wages wrapped in a leaf into the outstretched hands of his low-caste workers. By avoiding direct physical contact with them, he escapes the ritual pollution that would otherwise ensue. (Margaret Bourke-White/Getty Images)

Caste as Jati

As the varna system took shape in India, another set of social distinctions also arose, based largely on occupations. In India as elsewhere, urban-based civilization gave rise to specialized occupations, many organized in guilds that regulated their own affairs in a particular region. Over time, these occupationally based groups, known as *jatis*, blended with the varna system to create India's unique caste-based society.

The many thousands of jatis became the primary cells of India's social life beyond the family or household, but each of them was associated with one of the great classes (varnas). Thus Brahmins were divided into many separate jatis, or sub-castes, as were each of the other varnas as well as the untouchables. In a particular region or village, each jati was ranked in a hierarchy known to all, from the highest of the Brahmins to the lowest of the untouchables. Marriage and eating together were permitted only within an individual's own jati. Each jati was associated with a particular set of duties, rules, and obligations that defined its members' unique and separate place in the larger society. Brahmins, for example, were forbidden to eat meat, while Kshatriyas were permitted to do so. Upper-caste women covered their

| SNAPSHOT | SOCIAL LIFE AND DUTY IN CLASSICAL INDIA |

Much personal behavior in classical India, at least ideally, was regulated according to caste. Each caste was associated with a particular color, with a part of the body of the god Purusha, and with a set of duties.

Caste (Varna)	Color/Symbolism	Part of Purusha	Duties
Brahmin	white/spirituality	head	priests, teachers
Kshatriya	red/courage	shoulders	warriors, rulers
Vaisya	yellow/wealth	thighs	farmers, merchants, artisans
Sudra	black/ignorance	feet	labor
Untouchables (outside of the varna system; thus no color and not associated with Purusha)	—	—	polluted labor

Beyond caste, behavior was ideally defined in terms of four stages of life, at least for the first three varna groups. Each new stage was marked by a *samskara*, a ritual initiating the person into this new phase of life.

Stage of Life	Duties
Student	Boys live with a teacher (guru); learn Sanskrit, rituals, Vedas; practice obedience, respect, celibacy, nonviolence.
Householder	Marriage and family; men practice caste-based career/occupation; women serve as wives and mothers, perform household rituals and sacrifices, actively support children and elders.
Retirement	Both husband and wife withdraw to the forests following birth of grandchildren; diminished household duties; greater focus on spiritual practice; sex permitted once a month.
Wandering ascetic	Only for men (women return to household); total rejection of ordinary existence; life as wandering hermit without shelter or possessions; caste becomes irrelevant; focus on achieving moksha and avoiding future rebirth.

breasts, while some lower-caste women were forbidden this privilege as a sign of their subordination. "It is better to do one's own duty badly than another's well" — this frequently quoted saying summed up the underlying idea of Indian society. With its many separate, distinct, and hierarchically ranked social groups, Indian society was quite different from that of China or the Greco-Roman world.

It was also unique in the set of ideas that explained and justified that social system. Foremost among them was the notion of **ritual purity and pollution** that was applied to caste groups. Brahmins or other high-caste people who came in contact with members of lower castes, especially those who cleaned latrines, handled corpses, or butchered and skinned dead animals, were in great danger of being polluted, or made ritually unclean. Thus untouchables were forbidden to use the same wells or to enter the temples designated for higher-caste people. Sometimes they were required to wear a wooden clapper to warn others of their approach. A great body of Indian religious writing defined various forms of impurity and the ritual means of purification.

A further support for this idea of inherent inequality and permanent difference derived from emerging Hindu notions of *karma, dharma*, and rebirth. Being born into a particular caste was generally regarded as reflecting the good or bad deeds (karma) of a previous life. Thus an individual's prior actions were responsible for his or her current status. Any hope for rebirth in a higher caste rested on the faithful and selfless performance of one's present caste duties (dharma) in this life. Doing so contributed to spiritual progress by subduing the relentless demands of the ego. Such teachings, like that of permanent impurity, provided powerful sanctions for the inequalities of Indian society. So too did the threat of social ostracism, because each jati had the authority to expel members who violated its rules. No greater catastrophe could befall a person than this, for it meant the end of any recognized social life and the loss of all social support.

As caste restrictions tightened, it became increasingly difficult — virtually impossible — for individuals to raise their social status during their lifetimes. How-ever, another kind of upward mobility enabled entire jatis, over several generations, to raise their standing in the local hierarchy of caste groups. By acquiring land or wealth, by adopting the behaviors of higher-caste groups, by finding some previously overlooked "ancestor" of a higher caste, a particular jati might slowly be redefined in a higher category. India's caste system was in practice rather more fluid and changing than the theory of caste might suggest.

India's social system thus differed from that of China in several ways. It gave priority to religious status and ritual purity (the Brahmins), whereas China elevated political officials to the highest of elite positions. The caste system divided Indian society into vast numbers of distinct social groups; China had fewer, but broader, categories of society — scholar-gentry, landlords, peasants, merchants. Finally, India's caste society defined these social groups far more rigidly than in China and provided even less opportunity for social mobility.

The Functions of Caste

This caste-based social structure shaped India's emerging civilization in various ways. Because caste (jati) was a very local phenomenon, rooted in particular regions or villages, it focused the loyalties of most people on a quite restricted territory and weakened the appeal or authority of larger all-Indian states. This localization is one reason that India, unlike China, seldom experienced an empire that encompassed the entire subcontinent (see "Intermittent Empire: The Case of India" in Chapter 3). Caste, together with the shared culture of a diverse Hinduism, provided a substitute for the state as an integrative mechanism for Indian civilization. It offered a distinct and socially recognized place for almost everyone. In looking after widows, orphans, and the destitute, jatis also provided a modest measure of social security and support. Even the lowest-ranking jatis had the right to certain payments from the social supe-riors whom they served.

Furthermore, caste represented a means of accommodating the many migrat-ing or invading peoples who entered the subcontinent. The cellular, or honeycomb, structure of caste society allowed various peoples, cultures, and traditions to find a place within a larger Indian civilization while retaining something of their unique identity. The process of assimilation was quite different in China, where it meant becoming Chinese ethnically, linguistically, and culturally. Finally, India's caste system facilitated the exploitation of the poor by the wealthy and powerful. The multitude of separate groups into which it divided the impoverished and oppressed majority of the population made class consciousness and organized resistance across caste lines much more difficult to achieve.

Slavery: The Case of the Roman Empire

Beyond the inequalities of class and caste lay those of slavery, a social institution with deep roots in human history, extending into the Paleolithic era of gathering and hunting peoples but expanding greatly in agricultural civilizations. Some have suggested that the early domestication of animals provided a model for enslaving people. Certainly, slave owners have everywhere compared the enslaved to tamed animals. Aristotle, for example, observed that the ox is "the poor man's slave." War, patriarchy, and the notion of private property, all of which accompanied the First Civilizations, also contributed to the growth of slavery. Large-scale warfare generated numerous prisoners, and everywhere in the ancient world capture in war meant the possibility of enslavement. Early records suggest that women captives were the first enslaved people, usually raped and then enslaved as concubines, whereas male captives were killed. Patriarchal societies, in which men sharply controlled and perhaps even "owned" women, may have suggested the possibility of enslaving other people, men as well as women. The class inequalities of early civilizations, which were based on great differences in privately owned property, also made it possible to imagine people owning other people.

Slavery and Civilization

Whatever its precise origins, slavery generally meant ownership by a master, the possibility of being sold, working without pay, and the status of an "outsider" at the bottom of the social hierarchy. For most, it was a kind of "social death,"[6] for enslaved individuals usually lacked any rights or independent personal identity recognized by the larger society. By the time Hammurabi's law code casually referred to Mesopotamian slavery (ca. 1750 B.C.E.), it was already a long-established tradition in the region and in all the First Civilizations. Likewise, virtually all subsequent civilizations — in the Americas, Africa, and Eurasia — practiced some form of slavery.

Slave systems have varied considerably throughout history. In some times and places, such as ancient Greece and Rome, a fair number of enslaved persons might be emancipated in their own lifetimes, through their owners' generosity or religious convictions or the desire to avoid caring for them in old age, and sometimes enslaved individuals were allowed to purchase their freedom with their own funds. In some societies, the children of enslaved people inherited the status of their parents, while in others, such as the Aztec Empire, they were considered free. Enslaved people likewise varied considerably in the labor they were required to do, with some working for the state in high positions, others performing domestic duties in their owner's household, and still others toiling in fields or mines in large work gangs.

The second-wave civilizations of Eurasia differed considerably in the prominence and extent of slavery in their societies. In China, enslaved people constituted only perhaps 1 percent of the population. Among the earliest enslaved persons in Han dynasty China were convicted criminals and their families, confiscated by the government and sometimes sold to wealthy private individuals. In desperate circumstances, impoverished or indebted peasants might sell their children into slavery. In southern China, teenage boys of poor families could be purchased by the wealthy, for whom they served as status symbols. Chinese slavery, however, was never very widespread and did not become a major source of labor for agriculture or manufacturing.

In India as well, people could fall into slavery as criminals, debtors, or prisoners of war and served their masters largely in domestic settings, but religious writings and secular law offered, at least in theory, some protection for the enslaved. Owners were required to provide adequately for their enslaved servants and were forbidden to abandon them in old age. According to one ancient text, "A man may go short himself or stint his wife and children, but never his slave who does his dirty work for him."[7] Enslaved people in India could inherit and own property and earn money in their spare time. A master who raped an enslaved woman was required to set her free and pay compensation. The law encouraged owners to free their enslaved subjects and allowed the enslaved to buy their freedom. All of this suggests that Indian slavery was more restrained than that of other ancient civilizations. Nor did Indian civilization depend economically on slavery, for most work was performed by lower-caste, though free, men and women.

The Making of Roman Slavery

In sharp contrast to other second-wave civilizations, slavery played an immense role in the Mediterranean, or Western, world. Although slavery was practiced in Chinese, Indian, and Persian civilizations, **Greco-Roman slavery** was far more central to social life. By a conservative estimate, classical Athens alone was home to perhaps 60,000 enslaved persons, or about one-third of the total population. In Athens, ironically, the growth of democracy and citizenship was accompanied by the simultaneous growth of slavery on a mass scale. During the fourth century B.C.E., the greatest of the Greek philosophers, Aristotle (384–322 B.C.E.), developed the notion that some people were "slaves by nature" and should be enslaved for their own good and for that of the larger society.

"The ancient Greek attitude toward slavery was simple," writes one modern scholar. "It was a terrible thing to become a slave, but a good thing to own a slave."[8] Even poor households usually had at least one or two enslaved women who provided domestic work and sexual services for their owners. Although substantial numbers of enslaved people in Greece were granted freedom by their owners, they did not usually become citizens or gain political rights. Nor could they own land or marry citizens, and particularly in Athens they had to pay a special tax. Their status remained "halfway between slavery and freedom."[9]

Practiced on an even larger scale, slavery was a defining element of Roman society. By the time of Christ, the Italian heartland of the Roman Empire had some 2 to 3 million enslaved people, representing 33 to 40 percent of the population. Not until the modern slave societies of the Caribbean, Brazil, and the southern United States was slavery practiced again on such an enormous scale. Wealthy Romans could own many hundreds or even thousands of enslaved men and women. One woman in the fifth century C.E. freed 8,000 enslaved people when she withdrew into a life of Christian monastic practice. Even people of modest means frequently owned two or three enslaved individuals. In doing so, they confirmed their own position as free people, demonstrated their social status, and expressed their ability to exercise power. Enslaved people and former enslaved people also might practice slavery themselves. One freedman during the reign of Augustus owned 4,116 enslaved persons at the time of his death.

As the Roman Empire grew, social disruption and new wealth set loose forces that transformed it into a society in which the enslaved played a large role in the economy. In the early republic, landowning free men, who both tilled the soil and served in the army, provided the backbone of this agrarian society. But as the empire expanded through constant warfare, many ordinary Roman families found it difficult to maintain their small farms when the head of the household was away serving in the military. Meanwhile, conquest brought Rome unthinkable wealth in the form of plunder, enslaved people, and later taxes and tribute, which flowed especially to the most well connected in society. These elites bought the small holdings of impoverished Roman peasants to create large estates and employed enslaved labor, freely available from recent conquests. Displaced freemen abandoned farming and congregated in the growing cities of the empire, becoming buyers of the foodstuffs produced by these estates. Thus a combination of economic and political disruption caused by war and wealth, together with enslaved labor derived from conquest, propelled Rome down the road toward becoming a slave society.

The vast majority of enslaved persons in the Roman Empire were prisoners captured in the many wars that accompanied the empire's creation. In 146 B.C.E., following the destruction of the North African city of Carthage, some 55,000 people were enslaved en masse. Pirates also furnished enslaved people, kidnapping tens of

Roman Slavery Dating to the first century C.E., this Roman mosaic from Pompeii in Italy depicts an enslaved boy working in a kitchen. Above his head is "Iunius," Latin for the Roman month of June. The artist may have depicted an enslaved child in this image as a play on words, because in Latin *iuvenis*, a word with a similar pronunciation, means youth. (Print Collector/Getty Images)

thousands and selling them to Roman traders on the island of Delos. Roman merchants purchased still other enslaved people through networks of long-distance commerce extending to the Black Sea, the East African coast, and northwestern Europe. Enslaved people were also supplied through natural reproduction, as the children of enslaved mothers were regarded as enslaved themselves. Such "home-born" people had a certain prestige and were thought to be less troublesome than those who had known freedom earlier in their lives. Finally, abandoned or exposed children could legally become enslaved to anyone who rescued them.

Unlike American slavery of later times, Roman practice was not identified with a particular racial or ethnic group. Egyptians, Syrians, Jews, Greeks, Gauls, North Africans, and many other people found themselves enslaved. From within the empire and its adjacent regions, an enormous diversity of people were bought and sold at Roman markets.

Like owners of enslaved people everywhere, Romans regarded the enslaved as "barbarians"—lazy, unreliable, immoral, and prone to thieving—and came to think of certain peoples, such as Asiatic Greeks, Syrians, and Jews, as "natural slaves." Nor was there any serious criticism of slavery in principle, although on occasion owners were urged to treat the enslaved in a more benevolent way. Even the triumph of Christianity within the Roman Empire did little to undermine slavery, for Christian teaching held that the enslaved should be "submissive to [their] masters with all fear, not only to the good and gentle, but also to the harsh."[10] In fact, the New Testament used the metaphor of slavery to describe the relationship of believers to God, styling them as "slaves of Christ," while Saint Augustine (354–430 c.e.) described slavery as God's punishment for sin. Thus slavery was deeply embedded in the religious thinking and social outlook of elite Romans.

Similarly, slavery was entrenched throughout the Roman economy. No occupation was off-limits to the enslaved except military service, and no distinction existed between jobs for enslaved people and those for free people. Frequently they labored side by side. In rural areas, the enslaved provided much of the labor force on the huge estates, or *latifundia*, that produced grain, olive oil, and wine, mostly for export, much like the later plantations in the Americas. There they often worked chained together. In the cities, enslaved persons worked in their owners' households, but also as skilled artisans, teachers, doctors, business agents, entertainers, and actors. In the empire's many mines and quarries, enslaved people and criminals labored under brutal conditions. Enslaved individuals in the service of the emperor provided manpower for the state bureaucracy, maintained temples and shrines, and kept Rome's water supply system functioning. Trained in special schools, they also served as gladiators in the violent spectacles of Roman public life. Enslaved women usually served as domestic servants but were also put to work in brothels, served as actresses and entertainers, and could be used sexually by their male owners. Thus enslaved people were represented among the highest and most prestigious occupations and in the lowest and most degraded.

Owners in the Roman Empire were supposed to provide the necessities of life to those whom they enslaved. When this occurred, the enslaved may have had a more secure life than was available to impoverished free people, who had to fend for themselves, but the price of this security was absolute subjection to the will of the master. Beatings, sexual abuse, and sale to another owner were constant possibilities.

Lacking all rights in the law, enslaved people could not legally marry, although many contracted unofficial unions. Enslaved individuals often accumulated money or possessions, but such property legally belonged to their masters and could be seized at any time. If an enslaved person murdered his master, Roman law demanded the lives of all of the victim's enslaved people. In one case from 61 C.E., 400 enslaved people were condemned to death under this law.

For an enslaved person, the quality of life depended almost entirely on the character of the master. Brutal owners made life a living hell. Benevolent owners made life tolerable and might even grant favored enslaved individuals their freedom or permit them to buy that freedom. As in Greece, manumission was a widespread practice, but in the Roman Empire, unlike in Greece, freedom was accompanied by citizenship.

Enslaved people in the Roman Empire, like their counterparts in other societies, responded to enslavement in many ways. Most, no doubt, did what was necessary to survive, but there are recorded cases of Roman prisoners of war who chose to die by mass suicide rather than face the horrors of slavery. Others, once enslaved, resorted to the "weapons of the weak"—small-scale theft, sabotage, pretending illness, working poorly, and placing curses on their masters. Enslaved people fleeing to the anonymous crowds of the city or to remote rural areas prompted owners to post notices in public places, asking for information about their runaways, and catching runaways became an organized private business. Occasional murders of owners made masters conscious of the dangers they faced. "Every slave we own is an enemy we harbor" ran one Roman saying.[11]

On several notable occasions, the enslaved themselves rose in rebellion. The most famous uprising occurred in 73 B.C.E. when an enslaved gladiator named **Spartacus** led seventy others from a school for gladiators in a desperate bid for freedom that mushroomed into a huge uprising. Nothing on the scale of Spartacus's rebellion occurred again in the Western world of slavery until the Haitian Revolution of the 1790s. But Haitian rebels sought the creation of a new society free of slavery altogether. None of the Roman rebellions, including that of Spartacus, had any such overall plan or goal. The rebels simply wanted to escape Roman slavery. Although rebellions created a perpetual fear in the minds of owners, slavery itself was hardly affected.

Comparing Patriarchies

Social inequality was embedded not only in the structures of class, caste, and slavery, but also in the gender relationships of second-wave civilizations, as patterns of male dominance practiced in the patriarchy of the First Civilizations were replicated and elaborated in those that followed. (See "Hierarchies of Gender" in Chapter 2.) The basic idea of patriarchy, involving the sharp subordination of women to men, found expression in the Laws of Manu, an Indian compilation of prescriptions for a good society that developed around 200 to 400 C.E. It tied a woman irrevocably to the men in her life—father, husband, and son—declaring that "a woman must never be independent." Such patriarchal attitudes have been so widespread and pervasive that historians have been slow to recognize that gender systems had a history, changing over time. New agricultural technologies, the rise or decline of powerful states, the incorporation of world religions, interaction with culturally different peoples—all of these developments and more significantly changed the understandings of what was appropriate masculine and feminine behavior. Most often, patriarchies were lighter and less restrictive for women in the early years of a civilization's development and during times of upheaval, when established ways of living were disrupted.

Furthermore, women were often active agents in the histories of their societies, even while largely accepting their overall subordination. As the central figures in family life, they served as repositories and transmitters of their peoples' culture. Some were able to occupy unorthodox and occasionally prominent positions outside the home as scholars, religious functionaries, managers of property and participants in commerce, and even as rulers or military leaders. In Britain, Egypt, and Vietnam, for example, women led efforts to resist their countries' incorporation into the Roman or Chinese empires. Both Buddhist and Christian nuns carved out small domains of relative freedom from male control. In India, Buddhist nuns composed hundreds of poems that were brought together in a collection known as the *Psalms of the Sisters*, probably during the first century B.C.E. Those writings became part of the officially recognized Buddhist scriptures and represent the only early text in any of the world's major religions that was written by and about women. But these changes or challenges to male dominance occurred within a patriarchal framework, and nowhere did they evolve out of or beyond that framework. Thus a kind of "patriarchal equilibrium" ensured the long-term persistence of women's subordination despite fluctuations and various efforts to redefine gender roles or push against gendered expectations.[12]

Nor was patriarchy everywhere the same. Restrictions on women were far sharper in urban-based civilizations than in those pastoral or agricultural societies that lay beyond the reach of cities and empires. The degree and expression of patriarchy also varied from one civilization to another, as the discussion of Mesopotamia and Egypt in Chapter 2 illustrated. And within particular civilizations, elite women both enjoyed privileges and suffered the restrictions of seclusion in the home to a much greater extent than their lower-class counterparts, whose economic circumstances required them to operate in the larger social arena. China provides a fascinating example of how patriarchy changed over time, while the contrasting patriarchies of Athens and Sparta illustrate clear variations even within the much smaller world of Greek civilization.

A Changing Patriarchy: The Case of China

As Chinese civilization took shape during the Han dynasty, elite thinking about gender issues became more explicitly patriarchal, more clearly defined, and linked to an emerging Confucian ideology. Long-established patterns of thinking in terms of pairs of opposites were now described in gendered and unequal terms. The superior principle of *yang* was viewed as masculine and related to Heaven, rulers, strength, rationality, and light, whereas *yin*, the lower feminine principle, was associated with the Earth, subjects, weakness, emotion, and darkness. Thus female inferiority was seen as permanent and embedded in the workings of the universe.

What this view meant more practically was spelled out repeatedly over the centuries in various Confucian texts. Two notions in particular summarized the ideal position of women, at least in the eyes of elite male writers. The adage "Men go out, women stay in" emphasized the public and political roles of men in contrast to the domestic and private domain of women. A second idea, known as the **"three obediences,"** emphasized a woman's subordination first to her father, then to her husband, and finally to her son. "Why is it," asked one text, "that according to the rites the man takes his wife, whereas the woman leaves her house [to join her husband's family]? It is because the *yin* is lowly, and should not have the initiative; it proceeds to the *yang* in order to be completed."[13]

The Chinese woman writer and court official Ban Zhao (45–116 C.E.) observed that the ancients had practiced three customs when a baby girl was born. She was placed below the bed to show that she was "lowly and weak," required always to "humble herself before others." Then she was given a piece of broken pottery to play with, signifying that "her primary duty [was] to be industrious." Finally, her birth was announced to the ancestors with an offering to indicate that she was responsible for "the continuation of [ancestor] worship in the home."[14]

Yet such notions of passivity, inferiority, and subordination were not the whole story of women's lives in ancient China. A few women, particularly the wives, concubines, or widows of emperors, were able on occasion to exercise considerable political authority. Several others led peasant rebellions. In doing so, they provoked much antifemale hostility on the part of male officials, who understood governance as a masculine task and often blamed the collapse of a dynasty or natural disasters on the "unnatural" and "disruptive" influence of women in political affairs. Others, however, praised women of virtue as wise counselors to their fathers, husbands, and rulers and depicted them positively as active agents.

Within her husband's family, a young woman was clearly subordinate as a wife and daughter-in-law, but as a mother of sons, she was accorded considerable honor for her role in producing the next generation of male heirs to carry on her husband's lineage. When her sons married, she was able to exercise the significant authority of a mother-in-law. Furthermore, a woman, at least in the upper classes, often brought with her a considerable dowry, which was regarded as her own property and gave her some leverage within her marriage. Women's roles in the production of textiles, often used to pay taxes or to sell commercially, made a woman's labor quite valuable to the family economy. And a man's wife was sharply distinguished from his concubines, for she was legally mother to all her husband's children. Furthermore, peasant women could hardly follow the Confucian ideal of seclusion in the home, as their labor was required in the fields. Thus women's lives were more complex and varied than the prescriptions of Confucian orthodoxy might suggest.

Much changed in China following the collapse of the Han dynasty in the third century C.E. Centralized government vanished amid much political fragmentation and conflict. Confucianism, the main ideology of Han China, was discredited, while Daoism and Buddhism attracted a growing following. Pastoral and nomadic peoples invaded northern China and ruled a number of the small states that had replaced the Han government. These new conditions resulted in some loosening of the strict patriarchy of Han dynasty China over the next five or six centuries.

The cultural influence of nomadic peoples, whose women were far less restricted than those of China, was noticed, and criticized, by more Confucian-minded male observers. One of them lamented the sad deterioration of gender roles under the influence of nomadic peoples:

Ordinary Chinese Women at Work For a long time, the spinning and weaving of cloth were part of women's domestic work in China. In this detail from a Ming dynasty vase, women are shown weaving silk. (Bridgeman Images)

> In the north of the Yellow river it is usually the wife who runs the household. She will not dispense with good clothing or expensive jewelry. The husband has to settle for old horses and sickly servants. The traditional niceties between husband and wife are seldom observed, and from time to time he even has to put up with her insults.[15]

Others criticized the adoption of nomadic styles of dress, makeup, and music. By the time of the Tang dynasty (618–907), writers and artists depicted elite women as capable of handling legal and business affairs on their own and on occasion riding horses and playing polo, bareheaded and wearing men's clothing. Tang legal codes even recognized a married daughter's right to inherit property from her family of birth. Such images of women were quite different from those of Han dynasty China.

A further sign of a weakening patriarchy and the cause of great distress to advocates of Confucian orthodoxy lay in the unusual reign of **Empress Wu** (r. 690–705 C.E.), a former high-ranking concubine in the imperial court who came to power amid much palace intrigue and was the only woman ever to rule China with the title of emperor. With the support of China's growing Buddhist establishment, Empress Wu governed despotically, but she also consolidated China's civil service examination system for the selection of public officials and actively patronized scholarship and the arts. Some of her actions seem deliberately designed to elevate the position of women. She commissioned the biographies of famous women, decreed that the mourning period for mothers be made equal to that for fathers, and ordered the creation of a Chinese character for "human being" that suggested the process of birth flowing from one woman without a prominent male role. Her reign was brief and unrepeated.

The growing popularity of Daoism provided new images of the feminine and new roles for women. Daoist texts referred to the *dao* as "mother" and urged the traditionally feminine virtues of yielding and passive acceptance rather than the male-oriented striving of Confucianism. Daoist sects often featured women as priests, nuns, or reclusive meditators, able to receive cosmic truth and to use it for the benefit of others. A variety of female deities from Daoist or Buddhist traditions found a place in Chinese village religion, while growing numbers of women found an alternative to family life in Buddhist monasteries. None of this meant an end to patriarchy, but it does suggest some change in the tone and expression of that patriarchy. However, during the Song dynasty that followed, a more restrictive patriarchy reemerged.

Contrasting Patriarchies: Athens and Sparta

The patriarchies of second-wave civilizations not only fluctuated over time but also varied considerably from place to place. Nowhere is this variation more apparent than in the contrasting cases of Athens and Sparta, two of the leading city-states of Greek civilization (see Map 3.2, page 76). Even within this small area, the opportunities available to women and the restrictions imposed on them differed substantially. Although Athens has been celebrated as a major expression of democracy and rationalism, its posture toward women was far more restrictive than that of the highly militaristic and much less democratic Sparta.

In the several centuries between about 700 and 400 B.C.E., as the free male citizens of Athens moved toward unprecedented participation in political life, the city's women experienced growing limitations. They had no role whatsoever in the Assembly, the councils, or the juries of Athens, which were increasingly the focus of life for free men. In legal matters, women had to be represented by a guardian, and court proceedings did not even refer to them by name, but only as someone's wife or mother.

Greek thinkers, especially Aristotle, provided a set of ideas that justified women's exclusion from public life and their general subordination to men. According to Aristotle, "A woman is, as it were, an infertile male. She is female in fact on account of a kind of inadequacy." That inadequacy lay in her inability to generate sperm, which contained the "form" or the "soul" of a new human being. Her role in the reproductive process was passive, providing a receptacle for the vital male contribution. Compared often to children or domesticated animals, women were associated with instinct and passion and lacked the rationality to take part in public life. "It is the best for all tame animals to be ruled by human beings," wrote Aristotle. "In the same way, the relationship between the male and the female is by nature such that the male is higher, the female lower, that the male rules and the female is ruled."[16]

As in China, elite Athenian women were expected to remain inside the home, except perhaps for religious festivals or funerals. Even within the home, women's space was quite separate from that of men. Although poorer women, courtesans, and prostitutes had to leave their homes to earn money, collect water, or shop, ideal behavior for upper-class women meant assigning these tasks to enslaved servants or to men and involved a radical segregation of male and female space. "What causes women a bad reputation," declared Andromache, a female character in the Greek playwright Euripides' *The Trojan Women*, "is not remaining inside."

Within the domestic realm, Athenian women were generally married in their mid-teens to men ten to fifteen years older than themselves. Their main function was the management of domestic affairs and the production of sons who would become active citizens. These sons were expected to acquire a literate education, while their sisters were normally limited to learning spinning, weaving, and other household tasks. The Greek writer Menander exclaimed: "Teaching a woman to read and write? What a terrible thing to do! Like feeding a vile snake on more poison." Nor did women have much economic power. Although they could own personal property obtained through dowry, gifts, or inheritance, land was usually passed through male heirs. By law, women were forbidden to buy or sell land and could negotiate contracts only if the sum involved was valued at less than a bushel of barley.

There were exceptions, although rare, to the restricted lives of upper-class Athenian women, the most notable of which was **Aspasia** (ca. 470–400 B.C.E.). She was born in the Greek city of Miletus, on the western coast of Anatolia, to a wealthy family that believed in educating its daughters. As a young woman, Aspasia found

A Woman of Athens This grave stele from about 400 B.C.E. marked the final resting place of Hegeso, a wealthy Athenian woman, shown in the women's quarter of a Greek home examining her jewelry, perhaps for the last time, while attended by her slave. The domestic setting of this grave marker contrasts with that common for men, which usually showed them as warriors in a public space. (National Archeological Museum, Athens, Greece/Marie Mauzy/ Art Resource, NY)

her way to Athens, where her foreign birth gave her somewhat more freedom than was normally available to the women of that city. She soon attracted the attention of Pericles, Athens's leading political figure. The two lived together as husband and wife until Pericles' death in 429 B.C.E., although they were not officially married. Treated as an equal partner by Pericles, Aspasia proved to be a learned and witty conversationalist who moved freely in the cultured circles of Athens. Her foreign birth and her apparent influence on Pericles provoked critics to suggest that she was a *hetaera*, a professional, educated, high-class entertainer and sexual companion, similar to a Japanese geisha. Although little is known about Aspasia, a number of major Athenian writers commented about her, both positively and negatively. She was, by all accounts, a rare and remarkable woman in a city that offered little opportunity for individuality or achievement to its female population.

The evolution of Sparta differed in many ways from that of Athens. Early on, Sparta solved the problem of feeding a growing population not by creating overseas colonies as did many Greek city-states, but by conquering its immediate neighbors and reducing them to a status of permanent servitude, not far removed from slavery. Called **helots**, these dependents far outnumbered the free citizens of Sparta and represented a permanent threat of rebellion. Solving this problem shaped Spartan society decisively. Sparta's answer was a militaristic regime, constantly ready for war to keep the helots in their place. To maintain such a system, all boys were removed from their families at the age of seven to be trained by the state in military camps, where they learned the ways of war. There they remained until the age of thirty. The ideal Spartan male was a warrior, skilled in battle, able to endure hardship, and willing to die for his city. Mothers are said to have told their sons departing for battle to "come back with your shield . . . or on it." Although economic equality for men was the ideal, it was never completely realized in practice. And unlike Athens, political power was exercised primarily by a small group of wealthy men.

This militaristic and far-from-democratic system had implications for women that, strangely enough, offered them greater freedoms and fewer restrictions. As in many warrior societies, their central task was reproduction—bearing warrior sons for Sparta. To strengthen their bodies for childbearing, girls were encouraged to take part in sporting events—running, wrestling, throwing the discus and javelin, even driving chariots. At times, women and men alike competed in the nude before mixed audiences. Their education, like that of boys, was prescribed by the state, which also insisted that newly married women cut their hair short, unlike adult Greek women elsewhere. Thus Spartan women were not secluded or segregated, as were their Athenian counterparts.

Furthermore, Spartan young women, unlike those of Athens, usually married men of their own age, about eighteen years old, thus putting the new couple on a more equal basis. Marriage often began with a trial period to make sure the new couple could produce children, with divorce and remarriage readily available if they could not. Because men were so often away at war or preparing for it, women exercised much more authority in the household than was the case in Athens and actively managed family estates, some of which they controlled as their inheritance. Despite the intentions of the government, these busy women limited their fertility, sometimes through the use of various birth control practices. Over time they produced too few children to maintain the Spartan population, leading to a demographic crisis.

According to the Roman orator Cicero, they preferred the active life to "barbarous fertility," a development experienced in many other societies where women have secured greater control over their lives and activities.[17]

It is little wonder that the freedom of Spartan women appalled other Greeks, who believed that it undermined good order and state authority. Aristotle complained that the more egalitarian inheritance practices of Spartans led to their women controlling some 40 percent of landed estates. In Sparta, he declared, women "live in every sort of intemperance and luxury" and "the [male] rulers are ruled by women." Plutarch, a Greek writer during the heyday of the Roman Empire, observed critically that "the men of Sparta always obeyed their wives." Moreover, the clothing worn by Spartan women to give them greater freedom of movement seemed immodest to other Greeks. However, the freedoms of Sparta's women did not endure. After the helots permanently overthrew Spartan rule in 369 B.C.E., it seems that the Spartan government increasingly restricted the rights and status of women, bringing Sparta's gender practices more in line with those of its neighbors. Thus freedom for the helots gradually brought restrictions for Spartan women.

Sparta clearly was a patriarchy, with women serving as breeding machines for its military system and lacking any formal role in public life, but it was a less restrictive patriarchy than that of Athens. The joint efforts of men and women seemed necessary to maintain a huge class of helots in permanent subjugation at least until 369 B.C.E. Death in childbirth was considered the equivalent of death in battle, for both contributed to the defense of Sparta, and both were honored alike. In Athens, on the other hand, growing freedom and democracy were associated with the strengthening of the male-dominated, property-owning household, and within that household, the cornerstone of Athenian society, men were expected to exercise authority. Doing so required increasingly severe limitations and restrictions on the lives of women. Together, the cases of Athens and Sparta illustrate how the historical record appears in a different light when viewed through the lens of gender. Athens, so celebrated for its democracy and philosophical rationalism, offered little to its women, whereas Sparta, often condemned for its militarism and virtual enslavement of the helots, provided a somewhat wider scope for the free women of the city-state.

If Athenian and Spartan patriarchies differed substantially in the opportunities they offered to women, they were more similar in their posture toward homoerotic relationships. Ancient Greeks generally approved of such relationships, and they were fairly common for both men and women, although this did not prevent their participants from entering heterosexual marriages as well. In Athens, the ideal homosexual relationship—between an older man and a young adolescent boy—was viewed as limited in time, for it was supposed to end when the boy's beard began to grow. Spartans possessed much the same attitudes, even if their homosexual relationships were shaped by a warrior society. Plato wrote that homosexual encounters in Sparta were the result of nudity in gymnasia and the custom of men dining together, while several historians refer to specific homosexual relationships between Spartan soldiers. One modern scholar noted that "records of Sparta from the classical period seem to refer to homosexual boyfriends at least as often as to wives."[18] Unlike contemporary Western societies, where sexuality is largely seen as an identity, in ancient Greece sexual choice was viewed more casually and as a matter of taste.

Conclusions and Reflections: Pondering Inequality

Civilization and social and economic inequality have gone hand in hand since the First Civilizations emerged some 5,500 years ago. Those sharp inequalities mark civilizations as a new form of human society, quite distinct from the more egalitarian communities of the Paleolithic and Neolithic eras. In the civilizations of the second-wave era, social inequality was pervasive: class in China, caste in India, slavery in the Roman Empire, and patriarchy everywhere—these social distinctions, articulated in endless variations, sharply divided the people of these civilizations.

But inequality took shape differently across the major civilizations of the Eurasian world. Chinese and Indian civilizations alike separated their people into clearly demarcated and ranked groups, but China awarded the highest rank to political officials, while India gave priority to the Brahmin caste whose members performed religious rituals and sacrifices. Slavery was practiced in all civilizations, but it was far more prominent and widespread in the Greco-Roman world than in China or India. Patriarchy too was both universal and varied. Even in the small world of Greek civilization, the patriarchy of Athens was far more thorough and strict than in nearby Sparta.

Despite the long-term continuity of these forms of inequality, they also changed over time. While China's scholar-gentry class endured into the twentieth century, the fortunes of particular families rose and fell with regularity. At the local level, India's caste system also changed over time as particular jatis or subcastes gained or lost status in the overall caste hierarchy. China's patriarchy lightened somewhat, at least for elite women, after the collapse of the Han dynasty and the incursion of pastoral nomads. Opposition to these inequalities also surfaced, as in the Yellow Turban Rebellion of Chinese peasants and the Spartacus rebellion of enslaved Romans. And on occasion, rulers such as Ashoka in India and Wang Mang and Empress Wu in China sought to ameliorate inequalities of class or gender.

More generally, however, it is the persistence of these social inequalities in second-wave civilizations that is most impressive. How did such highly unequal societies endure over many centuries? One answer, of course, lies in the obvious power of state authorities and their capacity—and willingness—to use violence to compel obedience. Moreover, the geographical and social isolation of local communities made it very difficult to organize on a large scale to resist oppression and exploitation. And cultural or religious traditions everywhere inscribed inequality in the workings of the universe and so made them seem legitimate and inevitable. Confucianism defined most social relationships in unequal terms: father and son; husband and wife; rulers and subjects. Hindu concepts of rebirth meant that behaving in accord with one's caste duty was the only way to ensure a better birth in the next life. Christian teaching in the Roman Empire urged the enslaved to submit to their masters. For many, perhaps most, people in the second-wave civilizations, even imagining an alternative social order was next to impossible.

But this is no longer the case. In recent centuries the French, Russian, Chinese, Mexican, Cuban, and Vietnamese revolutions have challenged ancient inequalities. Socialist movements and trade unions have given voice to workers' grievances.

Abolitionist movements have ended legal slavery. Feminist movements have empowered women and put patriarchy on the defensive. All of this marks a decisive change in outlook and in the lived experience of many over the past several centuries. Few modern people feel that the social order is fixed or ordained by divine decree. Proposals for social change abound.

And yet, every society on the planet is riven by class differences. Powerful oligarchies dominate former communist states like Russia that had at one time proclaimed an end to such privileged classes; economic inequality in the United States has actually grown since the 1970s; caste persists in Indian society despite its legal abolition by the government in 1950; patriarchy thrives in many societies; and conditions similar to slavery prevail in practices such as debt bondage and human trafficking. Is substantial inequality a necessary or perhaps inevitable feature of modern life? If so, how much of it is useful or tolerable? If not, why has it been so resilient? These are questions worth pondering.

Revisiting Chapter 5

REVISITING SPECIFICS

Wang Mang, 133
China's scholar-gentry class, 133
Yellow Turban Rebellion, 134
varnas, 135
jatis, 136
ritual purity and pollution, 137

Greco-Roman slavery, 140
Spartacus, 143
"three obediences," 145
Empress Wu, 146
Aspasia, 148
helots, 149

REVISITING CORE IDEAS

1. **Describing Social Structure** How would you characterize the social hierarchy of China during the second-wave era?
2. **Analyzing the Role of Ideas** What cultural assumptions or religious ideas underpinned India's caste-based society?
3. **Comparing Social Hierarchies** How did India's caste system differ from China's class system?
4. **Comparing Systems of Slavery** How did Greco-Roman slavery differ from that of other civilizations?
5. **Identifying Change** How and why did Chinese patriarchy change over time?
6. **Comparing Patriarchies** How did the patriarchies of Athens and Sparta differ from each other?

A WIDER VIEW

1. What philosophical, religious, or cultural ideas served to legitimate the class and gender inequalities of second-wave civilizations?

2. What might an observant Chinese traveler from the Han dynasty era find surprising or offensive in India or the Greco-Roman world? What similarities might he or she notice?

3. What changes in the patterns of social life in second-wave civilizations can you identify? What accounts for these changes?

4. **Looking Back** The cultural and social patterns of civilizations seem to endure longer than the political framework of states and empires. What evidence from Chapters 3, 4, and 5 might support this statement? How might you account for this phenomenon? Is there evidence that could support a contrary position?

CHRONOLOGY

ca. 500 B.C.E.	• Varna system in place
470–400 B.C.E.	• Life of Aspasia
384–322 B.C.E.	• Life of Aristotle; proclaims slavery natural and necessary
369 B.C.E.	• Spartan helots gain their freedom
124 B.C.E.	• Imperial academy for training of officials established in China
73 B.C.E.	• Spartacus slave rebellion in Italy
ca. 50 B.C.E.	• *Psalms of the Sisters* set to writing: poetry of Buddhist nuns
8–23 C.E.	• Reforming emperor Wang Mang in power
45–116 C.E.	• Life of Ban Zhao
184 C.E.	• Yellow Turban Rebellion
ca. 200–400 C.E.	• Laws of Manu compiled in India
ca. 500–1000 C.E.	• Slavery replaced by serfdom in Europe
690–705 C.E.	• Reign of Empress Wu

6

Commonalities and Variations
Africa, the Americas, and Pacific Oceania

600 B.C.E.–1200 C.E.

CHAPTER OUTLINE

Continental Comparisons

Civilizations of Africa
- Meroë: Continuing a Nile Valley Civilization
- Axum: The Making of a Christian Kingdom
- Along the Niger River: Cities without States

Civilizations of Mesoamerica
- The Maya: Writing and Warfare
- Teotihuacán: The Americas' Greatest City

Civilizations of the Andes
- Chavín: A Pan-Andean Religious Movement
- Moche: A Civilization of the Coast
- Wari and Tiwanaku: Empires of the Interior

Alternatives to Civilization
- Bantu Africa: Cultural Encounters and Social Variation
- North America: Ancestral Pueblo and Mound Builders
- Pacific Oceania: Peoples of the Sea

Conclusions and Reflections: One History . . . or Many?

CONNECTING PAST AND PRESENT

IN EARLY 2010, BOLIVIAN PRESIDENT Evo Morales was inaugurated for his second term in office, the only Native American ever elected to that post. Before his official inauguration, Morales traveled to Tiwanaku (tee-wah-NAH-coo), the center of an impressive empire that had flourished in the Andean highlands between 400 and 1000 C.E., long before either the Incas or the Spanish ruled the area. There he sought to link himself and his administration to this ancient culture, a symbol of Bolivian nationalism and indigenous pride. On his arrival, Morales was ritually cleansed, offerings were made to traditional deities, and he was invested with symbols of both kingship and spiritual leadership, thus joining political and religious sources of authority.[1] Thus memories of this American second-wave civilization remained alive and were available for mobilizing political support and legitimating political authority in the very different circumstances of the early twenty-first century.

For many people, the second-wave era evokes most vividly the civilizations of Eurasia—the Greeks and the Romans, the Persians and the Chinese, and the Indians of South Asia—yet civilization also flourished elsewhere, both in the Americas and in sub-Saharan Africa. Furthermore, those peoples who did not organize themselves around cities or states likewise had histories of note and alternative ways of constructing their societies, although they are often neglected in favor of civilizations. This chapter explores the histories of the varied peoples of Africa, the Americas, and Pacific Oceania during this phase of world history. On occasion, those histories will extend some centuries beyond the chronological boundaries of the second-wave era in Eurasia because patterns of historical development around the world did not always coincide precisely. But the peoples described in this chapter participated in global patterns of change even as they created distinctive historical paths.

SEEKING THE MAIN POINT	To what extent did the histories of Africa, Oceania, and the Americas parallel those of Eurasia? In what ways did they forge new or different paths?

Continental Comparisons

At the broadest level, human cultures evolved in quite similar fashion around the world. All were part of that grand process of human migration that initially peopled the planet. Almost everywhere, gathering, hunting, and fishing long remained the sole basis for sustaining human life. Then, in various parts of the three supercontinents—Eurasia, Africa, and the Americas—the momentous turn of the Agricultural Revolution took place independently, as noted in Chapter 1, and subsequently generated in all three regions those more complex societies that we know as civilizations, featuring cities, states, monumental architecture, and great social inequality, as described in Chapter 2. These commonalities provide the foundation for a genuinely global history of humankind.

The world's human population was then distributed very unevenly across the three giant continents, as the Snapshot of population on page 156 indicates. Eurasia was then home to more than 85 percent of the world's people, Africa about 10 percent, the Americas around 5 percent, and Oceania less than 1 percent. That unevenness in population distribution, a pattern that has persisted to the present, is part of the reason that world historians focus more attention on Eurasia than on these other regions.

| SNAPSHOT | CONTINENTAL POPULATION IN THE SECOND-WAVE ERA AND BEYOND |

(Note: Population figures for such early times are merely estimates and are often controversial among scholars. Percentages do not always total 100 percent due to rounding.)

	Eurasia	Africa	North America	Central/ South America	Australia/ Oceania	Total World
Area (in square miles and as percentage of world total)						
	21,049,000 (41%)	11,608,000 (22%)	9,365,000 (18%)	6,880,000 (13%)	2,968,000 (6%)	51,870,000
Population (in millions and as percentage of world total)						
400 B.C.E.	127 (83%)	17 (11%)	1 (0.7%)	7 (5%)	1 (0.7%)	153
10 C.E.	213 (85%)	26 (10%)	2 (0.8%)	10 (4%)	1 (0.4%)	252
200 C.E.	215 (84%)	30 (12%)	2 (0.8%)	9 (4%)	1 (0.4%)	257
600 C.E.	167 (80%)	24 (12%)	2 (1%)	14 (7%)	1 (0.5%)	208
1000 C.E.	195 (77%)	39 (15%)	2 (0.8%)	16 (6%)	1 (0.4%)	253
1500	329 (69%)	113 (24%)	4.5 (0.9%)	53 (11%)	3 (0.6%)	477
1750	646 (83%)	104 (13%)	3 (0.4%)	15 (1.9%)	3 (0.4%)	771
2017	5,246 (69.5%)	1,256 (16.6%)	361 (4.8%)	646 (8.6%)	40 (0.5%)	7,549

Source: Population figures through 1750 from Paul Adams et al., *Experiencing World History* (New York: New York University Press, 2000), 334; 2017 figures from "World Population by Region," Worldometers, http://www.worldometers.info/world-population/#region. Accessed December 8, 2017.

Another continental difference involved the absence in the Americas of most animals capable of domestication. This meant that few pastoral societies developed in the Western Hemisphere, and only in pockets of the Andes Mountains based on the herding of llamas and alpacas. No animals were available in the Americas to pull plows or carts or to be ridden into combat. Metallurgy in the Americas was likewise far less developed than in Eurasia and Africa, where iron tools and weapons played such an important role in economic and military life. In the Americas, writing was limited to the Mesoamerican region and was most highly developed among the Maya, whereas in Africa it was confined to the northern and northeastern parts of the continent. In Eurasia, by contrast, writing emerged elaborately in many regions. Furthermore, civilizations in Africa and the Americas were fewer in number and generally smaller than those of Eurasia, and larger numbers of people in those two continents lived outside the confines of any civilization in communities that did not feature cities and states.

A final continental comparison distinguishes the history of Africa from that of the Americas and Pacific Oceania. The geological movement of the continents across the surface of the planet had placed Africa adjacent to Eurasia, while it separated the Americas and Oceania from both Africa and Eurasia. So parts of Africa were joined with Europe and Asia in a larger zone of Afro-Eurasian interaction. Early Christianity, for example, spread widely across North and Northeast Africa. Camels, probably originating in Arabia, enabled a trans-Saharan commerce that linked interior West Africa to the world of Mediterranean civilization. Bananas brought from Southeast Asia by Austronesian voyagers greatly enriched the diets of many African peoples. The Americas and Oceania, by contrast, developed almost wholly apart from this Afro-Eurasian network until that separation was bridged by the voyages of Columbus and later European explorers after 1492.

This chapter examines first the civilizations that emerged in sub-Saharan Africa and the Americas. Then our historical spotlight turns to those regions on both continents and Pacific Oceania that remained outside the zone of civilization. They remind us that the histories of many peoples unfolded without the cities, states, and empires that were so prominent within that zone.

Civilizations of Africa

When historians refer to Africa in premodern times, they are speaking generally of a geographic concept, a continental landmass, and not a cultural identity. Certainly few, if any, people living on the continent during the second-wave era thought of themselves as Africans. Like Eurasia or the Americas, Africa hosted numerous separate societies, cultures, and civilizations with vast differences among them as well as some interaction between them.

Many of these differences grew out of the continent's environmental variations. Small regions of Mediterranean climate in the northern and southern extremes, large deserts (the Sahara and the Kalahari), even larger regions of savanna grasslands, tropical rain forest in the continent's center, highlands and mountains in eastern Africa—all of these features, combined with the continent's enormous size, ensured endless variation among Africa's many peoples.

Africa did, however, have one distinctive environmental feature: bisected by the equator, it was the most tropical of the world's three supercontinents. While some regions, such as highland Ethiopia, sustained very productive agriculture, elsewhere lower crop yields and diminished soil fertility prevailed, owing to heavy but sometimes erratic rainfall, long dry seasons, and the leaching of nutrients from ancient soils. Climatic conditions also spawned numerous disease-carrying insects and parasites that have long created serious health problems in many parts of the continent. It was within these environmental constraints that African peoples made their histories. In several distinct regions of the continent—the upper Nile Valley, northern Ethiopia/Eritrea, and the Niger River valley—small civilizations flourished during the second-wave era, while others followed later. A further African civilization falling partly within this time period grew up along the East African coast in conjunction with Indian Ocean commerce. Known as Swahili civilization, it is treated in greater detail in Chapter 7.

Meroë: Continuing a Nile Valley Civilization

In the Nile Valley south of Egypt lay the lands of Nubian civilization, almost as old as Egypt itself. Over many centuries, Nubians both traded and fought with Egypt, and on one occasion, in 730 B.C.E., the Nubian Kingdom of Kush conquered Egypt and ruled it for a century. While borrowing heavily from Egypt, Nubia remained a distinct and separate civilization. As Egypt fell increasingly under foreign control, Nubian civilization came to center on the southern city of **Meroë** (MER-oh-ee), where it flourished between 300 B.C.E. and 100 C.E. (see Map 6.1).

Politically, the Kingdom of Meroë was governed by an all-powerful and sacred monarch, a position held on at least ten occasions by women, governing alone or as co-rulers. Unlike the female pharaoh Hatshepsut in Egypt, who was portrayed in male clothing, Meroë queens appeared in sculptures as women and with a prominence and

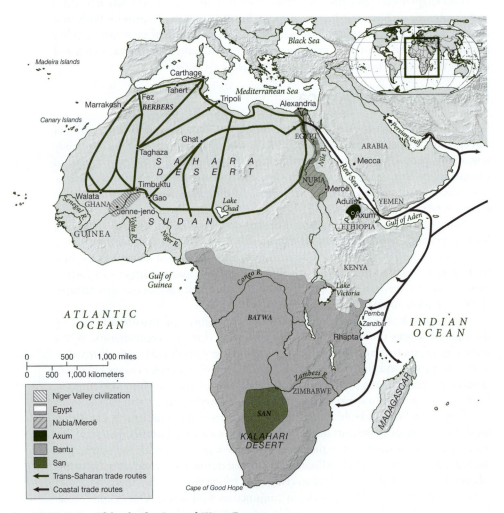

MAP 6.1   Africa in the Second-Wave Era

During the second-wave era, older African civilizations such as Egypt and Nubia persisted and changed, while new civilizations emerged in Axum and the Niger River valley. South of the equator, the process of Bantu expansion created many new societies and identities.

power equivalent to their male counterparts. In accordance with ancient traditions, such rulers were buried along with a number of human sacrificial victims.

The city of Meroë and other urban centers housed a wide variety of economic specialties—merchants, weavers, potters, and masons, as well as servants, laborers, and enslaved persons. The smelting of iron and the manufacture of iron tools and weapons were especially prominent industries. The rural areas surrounding Meroë were populated by peoples who practiced some combination of herding and farming and paid periodic tribute to the ruler. Rainfall-based agriculture was possible in Meroë, and consequently farmers were less dependent on irrigation. This meant that the rural population did not need to concentrate so heavily near the Nile as was the case in Egypt.

The wealth and military power of Meroë derived in part from extensive long-distance trading connections, to the north via the Nile and to the east and west by means of camel caravans. Its iron weapons and cotton cloth, as well as its access to gold, ivory, tortoiseshells, and ostrich feathers, gave Meroë a reputation for great riches in the world of northeastern Africa and the Mediterranean. The discovery in Meroë of a statue of the Roman emperor Augustus, probably seized during a raid on Roman Egypt, testifies to contact with the Mediterranean world. Culturally, Meroë seemed to move away from the heavy Egyptian influence of earlier times. A local lion god, Apedemek, grew more prominent than Egyptian deities such as Isis and Osiris, while the use of Egyptian-style writing declined as a new and still-undeciphered Meroitic script took its place.

In the centuries following 100 C.E., the Kingdom of Meroë declined, in part because of deforestation caused by the need for wood to make charcoal for smelting iron. Furthermore, as Egyptian trade with the African interior switched from the Nile Valley route to the Red Sea, the resources available to Meroë's rulers diminished and the state weakened. The effective end of the Meroë phase of Nubian civilization came with the kingdom's conquest in the 340s C.E. by the neighboring and rising state of Axum. In the centuries that followed, three separate Nubian states emerged, and Coptic (Egyptian) Christianity penetrated the region. For almost a thousand years, Nubia was a Christian civilization, using Greek as a liturgical language and constructing churches in Coptic or Byzantine fashion. After 1300 or so, political division, Arab immigration, and the penetration of Islam eroded this Christian civilization, and Nubia became part of the growing world of Islam.

Axum: The Making of a Christian Kingdom

If Meroë represented the continuation of an old African/Nubian civilization, **Axum** marked the emergence of a new one. Axum lay in the Horn of Africa, in what is now Eritrea and northern Ethiopia (see Map 6.1). Its economic foundation was a highly productive agriculture that used a plow-based farming system, unlike most of the rest of Africa, which relied on the hoe or digging stick. Axum's agriculture generated substantial amounts of wheat, barley, millet, and teff, a highly nutritious grain unique to that region. By 50 C.E. or so, a substantial state had emerged, stimulated by its participation in the rapidly increasing Red Sea and Indian Ocean commerce, which was itself a product of growing Roman demand for Indian products, especially pepper. At Adulis, then the largest port on the East African coast, a wide range of merchants sought the products of the African interior—animal hides, rhinoceros horn, ivory, obsidian, tortoiseshells, and enslaved people. Taxes on this trade provided a major source of revenue for the Axumite state and the complex society that grew up within it. Thus the decline of Meroë and the rise of Axum were both connected to changing patterns of long-distance commerce.

The interior capital city, also known as Axum, was a center of monumental building and royal patronage for the arts. The most famous structures were huge stone obelisks, which most likely marked royal graves. Some of them were more than 100 feet tall and at the time were the largest structures in the world hewn from a single piece of rock. The language used at court, in the towns, and for commerce was Ge'ez, written in a script derived from South Arabia. The Axumite state exercised a measure of control over the mostly Agaw-speaking people of the country through a loose administrative structure focusing on the collection of tribute payments. To the Romans, Axum was the third major empire within the world they knew, following their own and the Persian Empire.

Through its connections to Red Sea trade and the Roman world, particularly Egypt, Axum was introduced to Christianity in the fourth century C.E. Its monarch at the time, King Ezana, adopted the new religion about the same time as Constantine did in the Roman Empire. Early in his reign, the kingdom's coins featured images of gods derived from southern Arabia, while by the end, they were inscribed with the Christian cross. Supported by royal authority, Christianity took root in Axum, linking that kingdom religiously to Egypt, where a distinctive Christian Church known as Coptic was already well established. Although Egypt later became largely Islamic, reducing its Christian community to a small minority, Christianity maintained a dominant position in the mountainous terrain of highland Ethiopia and in the early twenty-first century still represents the faith of perhaps 60 percent of the country's population.

During the fourth through the sixth centuries C.E., Axum mounted a campaign of imperial expansion that took its forces into the Kingdom of Meroë and across the Red Sea into Yemen in South Arabia. By 571, the traditional date for the birth of Muhammad, an Axumite army, including a number of African war elephants, had reached the gates of Mecca, but it was a fairly short-lived imperial venture. The next several centuries were ones of decline for the Axumite state, owing partly to environmental changes, such as soil exhaustion, erosion, and deforestation, brought about by intensive farming. Equally important was the rise of Islam, which altered trade routes and diminished the revenue available to the Axumite state. Its last coins were struck in the early seventh century. When the state revived several centuries later, it was centered farther south on the Ethiopian plateau. In this new location, there emerged the Christian Church and the state that present-day Ethiopia has inherited, but the link to ancient Axum was long remembered and revered.

With their long-distance trading connections, urban centers, centralized states, complex societies, monumental architecture, written languages, and imperial ambitions, both Meroë and Axum paralleled on a smaller scale the major features of the second-wave civilizations of Eurasia. Furthermore, both were in direct contact with the world of Mediterranean civilizations. Across the continent in West Africa, a rather different civilization took shape.

Along the Niger River: Cities without States

The middle stretches of the Niger River in West Africa witnessed the emergence of a remarkable urbanization (see Map 6.1, page 158). A prolonged dry period during the five centuries after 500 B.C.E. brought growing numbers of people from the southern Sahara into the fertile floodplain of the middle Niger in search of more reliable access to water. Accompanying them were their domesticated cattle, sheep, and goats; their agricultural skills; and their ironworking technology. Over many centuries (roughly 300 B.C.E.–900 C.E.), the peoples of this region created a distinctive city-based civilization. The most fully studied of the urban clusters that grew up along the middle Niger was the city of Jenne-jeno (jihn-AY jihn-OH), which at its high point probably housed more than 40,000 people.

Among the most distinctive features of the **Niger Valley civilization** was the apparent absence of a corresponding state structure. Unlike the cities of Egypt, China, the Roman Empire, or Axum, these middle Niger urban centers were not encompassed within some larger imperial system. Nor were they like the city-states of ancient Mesopotamia, in which each city had its own centralized political structure, embodied in a monarch and his accompanying bureaucracy. According to a leading historian of the region, they were "cities without citadels," complex urban centers that apparently operated without the coercive authority of a state, for archeologists have found in their remains few signs of despotic power, widespread warfare, or deep social inequalities.[2] In this respect, these urban centers resemble the early cities of Norte Chico or the Indus Valley civilization, where likewise little archeological evidence of centralized state structures has been found.

In place of such hierarchical organization, Jenne-jeno and other cities of the region emerged as clusters of economically specialized settlements surrounding a larger central town. The earliest and most prestigious of these specialized occupations was iron smithing. Working with fire and earth (ore) to produce this highly useful metal, the smiths of the Niger Valley were both feared and revered. Archeologist Roderick McIntosh, a leading figure in the excavation of Jenne-jeno, argued that "their knowledge of the transforming arts — earth to metal, insubstantial fire to the mass of iron — was the key to a secret, occult realm of immense power and immense danger."[3]

Other specializations followed. Villages of cotton weavers, potters, leather workers, and griots (praise-singers who preserved and recited the oral traditions of their societies) grew up around the central towns. Gradually these urban artisan communities became occupational castes, whose members passed their jobs and skills to their children and could marry only within their own group. In the surrounding rural areas, as in all urban-based civilizations, farmers tilled the soil and raised their animals, but specialization also occurred in food production as various ethnic groups focused on fishing, rice cultivation, or some other agricultural pursuit. At least for a time, these middle Niger cities represented an African alternative to an oppressive state, which in many parts of the world accompanied an increasingly complex urban economy and society. A series of distinct and specialized economic groups shared authority and voluntarily used the services of one another, while maintaining their own identities through physical separation.

Terra-Cotta Statue from Jenne-jeno The artistic tradition of Niger Valley civilization includes a number of terra-cotta couples, reflecting perhaps the emphasis on the separate but complementary roles of men and women in much of African thought. This statue and others like it date to sometime after the twelfth century and may express the resistance of an indigenous tradition to the growing penetration of Islam. (Entwistle Gallery, London, UK/Werner Forman/Art Resource, NY)

Accompanying this unique urbanization, and no doubt stimulating it, was a growing network of indigenous West African commerce. The middle Niger floodplain supported a rich agriculture and contained clay for pottery, but it lacked stone, iron ore, salt, and fuel. This scarcity of resources was the basis for a long-distance commerce that operated by boat along the Niger River and overland by donkey to the north and south. Jenne-jeno itself was an important transshipment point in this commerce, in which goods were transferred from boat to donkey or vice versa. By the 500s C.E., there is evidence of an even wider commerce, and at least indirect contact, from Mauritania in the west to present-day Mali and Burkina Faso in the east.

In the second millennium C.E., new historical patterns developed in West Africa (see "Gold, Salt, and Enslaved People" in Chapter 7). A number of large-scale states or empires emerged in the region—Ghana, Mali, and Songhay, among the most well known. At least partially responsible for this development was the flourishing of a camel-borne trans-Saharan commerce, previously but a trickle across the great desert. As West Africa became more firmly connected to North Africa and the Mediterranean, Islam penetrated the region, marking a gradual but major cultural transformation. All of this awaited West Africa in later centuries, submerging, but not completely eliminating, the decentralized city life of the Niger Valley.

Civilizations of Mesoamerica

Westward across the Atlantic Ocean lay an altogether separate world, later known as the Americas, which housed two major centers of civilization — Mesoamerica and the Andes. Together, they were home to the vast majority of the population of the Americas. But unlike the Egyptians and Mesopotamians or the Persians and the Greeks, these civilizations had little if any direct contact with each other. They shared, however, a rugged mountainous terrain with an enormous range of microclimates as well as great ecological and biological diversity. Arid coastal environments, steamy lowland rain forests, cold and windy highland plateaus cut by numerous mountains and valleys — all of this was often encompassed in a relatively small area. Such conditions contributed to substantial linguistic and ethnic diversity and to the development of many distinct and competing cities, chiefdoms, and states. It also meant that states, and sometimes individual families, sought **vertical integration**, an effort to control a variety of ecological zones where a number of different crops and animals could flourish. The remarkable achievements of these early American civilizations occurred without the many large domesticated animals or ironworking technologies that were so important throughout the Eastern Hemisphere. In the Andes, an important exception to this generalization involved the domestication of the llama and alpaca, which offered food, fiber, and transport for the civilizations of that region and in a few places provided for a time the basis for largely pastoral communities.

Mesoamerican civilizations stretched from central Mexico to northern Central America. Despite its environmental and ethnic diversity, Mesoamerica was also a distinct region, bound together by elements of a common culture. Its many peoples shared an intensive agricultural technology devoted to raising maize, beans, chili peppers, and squash and based their economies on market exchange. They practiced religions featuring a similar pantheon of male and female deities, understood time as a cosmic cycle of creation and destruction, practiced human sacrifice, and constructed monumental ceremonial centers. Furthermore, they employed a common ritual calendar of 260 days and hieroglyphic writing. During the first millennium B.C.E, the various small states and chiefdoms of the region, particularly the Olmec, exchanged various luxury goods used to display social status and for ritual purposes — jade, obsidian tools, ceramic pottery, shell ornaments, stingray spines, and turtle shells. As a result, aspects of Olmec culture, such as artistic styles, temple pyramids, the calendar system, and rituals involving human sacrifice, spread widely throughout Mesoamerica and influenced many of the civilizations that followed.

The Maya: Writing and Warfare

Among Mesoamerican civilizations, none has attracted more attention than that of the Maya. Scholars have traced the beginnings of the Maya people to ceremonial centers constructed as early as 2000 B.C.E. in present-day Guatemala and the Yucatán region of Mexico (see Map 6.2). During the first millennium B.C.E., a number of substantial urban centers with concentrated populations and monumental architecture had emerged in the region. But it was during a later phase of **Maya civilization**, between 250 and 900 C.E., that their most well-known cultural achievements emerged. Intellectuals, probably priests, developed a mathematical system that included the concept of zero and place notation and was capable of complex calculations. They combined this mathematical ability with careful observation of the night skies to plot the cycles of planets, to predict eclipses of the sun and the moon, to construct elaborate calendars, and to calculate accurately the length of the solar year. The distinctive art of the Maya elite was likewise impressive to later observers.

Accompanying these intellectual and artistic achievements was the creation of the most elaborate writing system in the Americas, which used both pictographs and phonetic or syllabic elements. Carved on stone and written on bark paper or deer-skin books, Mayan writing recorded historical events, masses of astronomical data, and religious or mythological texts. Temples, pyramids, palaces, and public plazas abounded, graced with painted murals and endless stone carving.

The economic foundations for these cultural achievements were embedded in an "almost totally engineered landscape."[4] The Maya drained swamps, terraced hillsides, flattened ridgetops, and constructed elaborate water-management systems. Much of this underpinned a flourishing agriculture that supported a very rapidly growing and dense population by 750 C.E. This agriculture sustained substantial elite classes of nobles, priests, merchants, architects, and sculptors, as well as specialized artisans producing pottery, tools, and cotton textiles. And it was sufficiently productive to free a large labor force for work on the many public structures that continue to amaze contemporary visitors.

Early scholars viewed Maya civilization somewhat romantically as a peaceful society led by gentle stargazing priest-kings devoted to temple building and intellectual pursuits. This view of Maya civilization changed as scholars realized that its many achievements took place within a highly fragmented political system of city-states, local lords, and regional kingdoms with no central authority, with frequent warfare, and with the extensive capture and sacrifice of prisoners. The larger political units of Maya civilization were densely populated urban and ceremonial centers,

MAP 6.2 Civilizations of Mesoamerica
During the second-wave era, Maya civilization and the large city of Teotihuacán represented the most prominent features of Mesoamerican civilization.

ruled by powerful kings and on a few occasions queens. They were divine rulers or "state shamans" able to mediate between humankind and the supernatural.

One of these cities, Tikal (tee-KAHL), contained perhaps 50,000 people, with another 50,000 or so in the surrounding countryside, by 750 C.E. Some of these city-states had imperial ambitions, but none succeeded in creating a unified Maya empire. Various centers of Maya civilization rose and fell; fluctuating alliances among them alternated with periods of sporadic warfare; ruling families intermarried; the elite classes sought luxury goods from far away to bolster their authority and status. In its political dimensions, Maya civilization more closely resembled the competing city-states of ancient Mesopotamia or classical Greece than the imperial structures of Rome, Persia, or China.

But large parts of that imposing civilization collapsed with a completeness and finality rare in world history. Clearly, this was not a single or uniform phenomenon, as flourishing centers of Maya civilization persisted in the northern Yucatán, and many Maya survived to fight the Spanish in the sixteenth century. But in the southern regions where the collapse was most complete, its outcomes were devastating. In less than a century following the onset of a long-term drought in 840, the population of the low-lying southern heartland of the Maya dropped by 85 percent or more as famine, epidemics, and fratricidal warfare reaped a horrific toll. It was a catastrophe from which there was no recovery. Elements of Maya culture survived in scattered settlements, but the great cities were deserted, and large-scale construction and artistic work ceased. The last date inscribed in stone corresponds to 909–910 C.E. As a complex civilization, the Maya had passed into history.

Explaining this remarkable demise has long kept scholars guessing, with recent accounts focusing on ecological and political factors. Rapid population growth after 600 C.E. pushed total Maya numbers to perhaps 5 million or more and soon outstripped available resources, resulting in deforestation and the erosion of hillsides. Under such conditions, climate change in the form of prolonged droughts in the 800s may well have placed unbearable pressures on Maya society. Political disunity and endemic rivalries, long a prominent feature of Maya civilization, prevented a coordinated and effective response to the emerging catastrophe. Warfare in fact became more frequent as competition for increasingly scarce land for cultivation became sharper. Rulers dependent on ritual splendor for their legitimacy competed to mount ever more elaborate temples, palaces, and pageants, requiring more labor and taxes from their subjects and tribute from their enemies. Whatever the precise explanation, the Maya collapse, like that of the Romans and others, illustrates the fragility of civilizations, whether they are embodied in large empires or organized in a more decentralized fashion.

Teotihuacán: The Americas' Greatest City

At roughly the same time as the Maya flourished in the southern regions of Mesoamerica, the giant city of **Teotihuacán** (tay-uh-tee-wah-KAHN) was also emerging further north in the Valley of Mexico, where its control over important sources of green obsidian made it an increasingly important trading power in the region. Begun around 150 B.C.E. and apparently built to a plan rather than evolving haphazardly, the city by 550 C.E. had a population estimated at between 125,000 and 150,000.

It was by far the largest urban complex in the Americas at the time and one of the six largest in the world. Physically, the city was enormously impressive, replete with broad avenues, spacious plazas, huge marketplaces, temples, palaces, apartment complexes, slums, waterways, reservoirs, drainage systems, and colorful murals. Along the main north/south boulevard, now known as the Avenue of the Dead, were the grand homes of the elite, the headquarters of state authorities, many temples, and two giant pyramids. At the Temple of the Feathered Serpent, archeologists have found the remains of some 200 people, their hands and arms tied behind them; they were the apparently unwilling sacrificial victims meant to accompany the high-ranking persons buried there into the afterlife.

Off the main avenues of Teotihuacán in a grid-like pattern of streets lay thousands of residential apartment compounds, home to the city's commoners. In these compounds, perhaps in groups of related families or lineages, lived many of the farmers who tilled the lands outside the city, as well as thousands of Maya specialists—masons, leather workers, potters, construction laborers, merchants, and civil servants. Here also lived skilled makers of obsidian blades, who plied their trade in hundreds of separate workshops, generating products that were in great demand throughout Mesoamerica. At least two small sections of the city were reserved exclusively for foreigners.

Buildings, both public and private, were decorated with mural paintings, sculptures, and carvings. Many of these works of art display abstract geometric and stylized images.

Teotihuacán Taken from the summit of the Pyramid of the Moon, this photograph looks down the famous Avenue of the Dead to the Pyramid of the Sun in the upper left. (Alison Wright/ Science Source)

Others depict gods and goddesses, arrayed in various forms — feathered serpents, starfish, jaguars, flowers, and warriors. One set of murals shows happy people cavorting in a paradise of irrigated fields, playing games, singing, and chasing butterflies, which were thought to represent the souls of the dead. Another, however, portrays dancing warriors carrying elaborate curved knives, to which were attached bleeding human hearts.

The art of Teotihuacán, unlike that of the Maya, has revealed few images of self-glorifying rulers or individuals. Nor did the city have a tradition of written public inscriptions as the Maya did, although a number of glyphs or characters indicate at least a limited form of writing. Nonetheless, Teotihuacán cast a huge shadow over Mesoamerica, particularly from 300 to 600 C.E. A core region of perhaps 10,000 square miles was administered directly from the city itself, while tribute was no doubt exacted from other areas within its broader sphere of influence. At a greater distance, the power of Teotihuacán's armies gave it a presence in the Maya heartland more than 600 miles to the east. At least one Maya city, Kaminaljuyú in the southern highlands, was completely taken over by the Teotihuacán military and organized as a colony. In the year 378 C.E., agents of Teotihuacán apparently engineered a coup in the lowland Maya city of Tikal that placed a collaborator on the throne and turned the city for a time into an ally or a satellite. Elsewhere — in the Zapotec capital of Monte Albán, for example — murals show unarmed persons from Teotihuacán engaged in what seem to be more equal diplomatic relationships.

At least some of this political and military activity was no doubt designed to obtain, either by trade or by tribute, valued commodities from afar — food products, cacao beans, tropical bird feathers, honey, salt, and medicinal herbs. The presence in Teotihuacán of foreigners, perhaps merchants, from the Gulf Coast and Maya lowlands, as well as much pottery from those regions, provides further evidence of long-distance trade. Moreover, the sheer size and prestige of Teotihuacán surely persuaded many, all across Mesoamerica, to imitate the architectural and artistic styles of the city. Thus, according to a leading scholar, "Teotihuacán meant something of surpassing importance far beyond its core area."[5] Almost a thousand years after its still-mysterious collapse around 650 C.E., the great metropolis was dubbed Teotihuacán, the "city of the gods," by the peoples of the Aztec Empire.

Civilizations of the Andes

Yet another and quite separate center of civilization in the Americas lay in the dramatic landscape of the Andes. Bleak deserts along the coast supported human habitation only because they were cut by dozens of rivers flowing down from the mountains, offering the possibility of irrigation and cultivation. The offshore waters of the Pacific Ocean also provided an enormously rich marine environment with an endless supply of seabirds and fish. The Andes themselves, a towering mountain chain with many highland valleys, afforded numerous distinct ecological niches, depending on altitude. Andean societies generally sought access to the resources of these various environments through colonization, conquest, or trade — seafood from the coastal regions; maize and cotton from lower-altitude valleys; potatoes, quinoa, and pastureland for their llamas in the high plains; tropical fruits and coca leaves from the moist eastern slope of the Andes and the arid western slope as well (see Map 6.3).

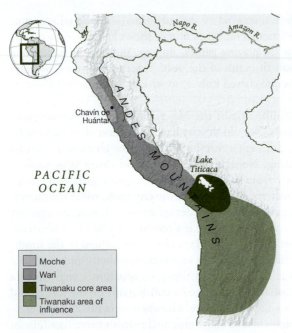

MAP 6.3   Civilizations of the Andes

No single civilization dominated the Andes region during the second-wave era. Rather, a number of religious movements, states, and empires rose and fell before the entire region was encompassed by the Inca Empire in the fifteenth century.

Moche

Wari

Tiwanaku core area

Tiwanaku area of influence

The most well known of the civilizations to take shape in this environment was that of the Incas, which encompassed practically the entire region, some 2,500 miles in length, in the fifteenth century. Yet the Incas represented only the most recent and the largest in a long history of civilizations in the area. The coastal region of central Peru had in fact generated one of the world's First Civilizations, known as Norte Chico, dating back to around 3000 B.C.E. (see "Introducing the First Civilizations" in Chapter 2). During the two millennia between roughly 1000 B.C.E. and 1000 C.E., a number of Andean civilizations rose and passed away. Because none of them had developed writing, historians are largely dependent on archeology for an understanding of these civilizations.

Chavín: A Pan-Andean Religious Movement

In both the coastal and highland regions of Peru, archeologists have uncovered numerous local ceremonial centers or temple complexes, dating between 2000 and 1000 B.C.E. Then around 900 B.C.E., one such center, situated in the Andean highlands at a village called **Chavín** (cha-BEEN) de Huántar, became the focus of a religious movement that soon swept through both coastal and highland Peru, aided by its strategic location on trade routes to both the coastal region to the west and the Amazon rain forest to the east.

By perhaps 750 B.C.E., this small center had become a town of 2,000 to 3,000 people, with clear distinctions between an elite class, who lived in stone houses, and ordinary people, with adobe dwellings. An elaborate temple complex included numerous galleries, hidden passageways, staircases, ventilation shafts, drainage canals, and distinctive carvings. Chavín artwork suggests influences from both the desert coastal region and the rain forests. Major deities were represented as jaguars, crocodiles, and snakes, all of them native to the Amazon basin. Shamans or priests likely made use of the San Pedro cactus, native to the Andes Mountains, employing its hallucinogenic properties to penetrate the supernatural world. Some of the fantastic artwork of this civilization—its jaguar-human images, for example—may well reflect the visions of these religious leaders.

Over the next several centuries, this blended religious movement proved attractive across much of Peru and beyond, as Chavín-style temple architecture, sculpture, pottery, religious images, and painted textiles were widely imitated within the region. Chavín itself became a pilgrimage site and perhaps a training center for initiates. Although some evidence suggests violence and warfare, no Chavín "empire" emerged. Instead, a widespread religious cult, erected on the back of a trading network, provided for the first time and for several centuries a measure of economic and cultural integration to much of the Peruvian Andes.

Moche: A Civilization of the Coast

By 200 B.C.E., the pan-Andes Chavín cult had faded, replaced by a number of regional civilizations. Among them, **Moche** (MOH-chee) civilization clearly stands out. Dominating a 250-mile stretch of Peru's northern coast and incorporating thirteen river valleys, the Moche people flourished between about 100 and 800 C.E. Their economy was rooted in a complex irrigation system, requiring constant maintenance, that funneled runoff from the Andes into fields of maize, beans, squash, and acres of cotton, all fertilized by rich bird droppings called guano. Moche fishermen also harvested millions of anchovies from the bountiful Pacific.

Politically, Moche was governed by warrior-priests, some of whom lived atop huge pyramids, the largest of which was constructed from 143 million sun-dried bricks. There shaman-rulers, often under the influence of hallucinogenic drugs, conducted ancient rituals that mediated between the world of humankind and that of the gods. They also presided over the ritual sacrifice of human victims, drawn from their many prisoners of war, which became central to the politico-religious life of the Moche. Images on Moche pottery show a ruler attired in a magnificent feather headdress and seated on a pyramid, while a parade of naked prisoners marches past him. Other scenes of decapitation and dismemberment indicate the fate that awaited those destined for sacrifice. For these rulers, the Moche world was apparently one of war, ceremony, and diplomacy.

The immense wealth of this warrior-priest elite and the exquisite artistry of Moche craftsmen are reflected in the elaborate burials accorded the rulers. In the absence of written texts, these artistic products are the most accessible aspect of Moche life, and much of what scholars know about the Moche world derives from the superb skill of its craftspeople, such as metalworkers, potters, weavers, and painters. Face masks, figures of animals, small earrings, and other jewelry items, many plated in gold, display amazing technical abilities and a striking artistic sensibility. Decorating Moche ceramic pottery are naturalistic portraits of noble lords and rulers and images from the life of common people, including the blind and the sick. Battle scenes show warriors confronting their enemies with raised clubs. Erotic encounters between men and women and gods making love to humans likewise represent common themes, as do grotesque images of the many Moche gods and goddesses.

Much of this, of course, reflects the culture of the Moche elite. We know much less about the daily life of the farmers, fishermen, weavers, traders, construction workers, and servants whose labor made that elite culture possible.

These cultural achievements, however, rested on fragile environmental foundations, for the region was subject to drought, earthquakes, and occasional torrential rains associated with El Niño episodes (dramatic changes in weather patterns caused by periodic warming of Pacific Ocean currents). During the sixth century C.E., some combination of these forces caused extended ecological disruption that seriously undermined Moche civilization. In these circumstances, the Moche were vulnerable to aggressive neighbors and possibly to internal social tensions as well. By the end of the eighth century C.E., that civilization had passed into history.

Wari and Tiwanaku: Empires of the Interior

Far more than the Moche and other coastal civilizations, the interior empires of **Wari** (wah-ree) **and Tiwanaku** provided a measure of political integration and cultural commonality for the entire Andean region. Growing out of ancient settlements, these two states flourished between 400 and 1000 C.E., Wari in the northern highlands and Tiwanaku to the south. Both were centered in large urban capitals, marked by monumental architecture and stratified populations numbering in the tens of thousands. Both governments collected surplus food in warehouses as an insurance against times of drought and famine.

But neither state controlled a continuous band of territory. Adapting to their vertical environment, both empires established colonies at lower elevations on the eastern and western slopes of the Andes as well as throughout the highlands, seeking access to resources such as seafood, maize, chili peppers, cocoa, hallucinogenic plants, obsidian, and feathers from tropical birds. Caravans of llamas linked distant centers, allowing the exchange and redistribution of goods, while the religious prestige and ceremonial power of the capital city provided further integration. Cultural influences from the center, such as styles of pottery and textiles, spread well beyond the regions of direct political control. Similar religious symbols and images prevailed in both places, including the ancient Andean Staff God, a deity portrayed with a staff in each hand. Versions of this image have been found in Norte Chico, Chavín, and Moche sites as well, suggesting a long-term continuity in the religious culture of the Andean region.

But Wari and Tiwanaku were hardly carbon copies of each other. Wari's agriculture employed an elaborate system of hillside terracing and irrigation, using snowmelt from the Andes. Tiwanaku's highly productive farming economy, by contrast, utilized a "raised field" system in which artificially elevated planting surfaces in swampy areas were separated by small irrigation canals. Tiwanaku, furthermore, has become famous for its elaborately fitted stone walls and buildings, while Wari's tombs and temples were built of fieldstone set in mud mortar and covered with smooth plaster. Cities in the Wari region seemed built to a common plan and linked to the capital by a network of highways, which suggests a political system more tightly controlled from the center than in Tiwanaku.[6]

Despite these differences and a 300-mile common border, little overt conflict or warfare occurred between Wari and Tiwanaku. In areas where the two peoples lived near one another, they apparently did not mingle much. They each spoke their own language, wore different clothing, furnished their homes with distinctive goods, and looked to their respective capital cities for inspiration.

In the several centuries following 1000 C.E., both civilizations collapsed, their impressive cities permanently abandoned. What followed was a series of smaller kingdoms, one of which evolved into the Inca Empire that gave to Andean civilization a final and spectacular expression before all of the Americas was swallowed up in European empires from across the sea. The Incas themselves clearly drew on the legacy of Wari and Tiwanaku, adopting aspects of their imperial models and systems of statecraft, building on the Wari highway system, and utilizing similar styles of dress and artistic expression. Such was the prestige of Tiwanaku centuries after its collapse that the Incas claimed it as their place of origin.

Alternatives to Civilization

While historians are frequently preoccupied with civilizations, other ways of organizing human communities evolved alongside those civilizations, and they too made history. Two such regions were Africa south of the equator and North America. They shared environments that featured plenty of land and relatively few people compared to the greater population densities and pressure on the land that characterized many civilizations. And a third region was Pacific Oceania, where small numbers of people navigated a sea covering about one-third of the world's surface, settled the mostly tiny specks of land that rose above the surface of that ocean, and created there a remarkable range of human communities.

Bantu Africa: Cultural Encounters and Social Variation

In the vast region of Africa south of the equator, the most significant development during the second-wave era involved the accelerating movement of Bantu-speaking peoples, cultures, and technologies into the enormous subcontinent. That process had begun many centuries earlier, probably around 3000 B.C.E., from a homeland region in what are now southeastern Nigeria and the Cameroons. Over the long run, some 400 distinct but closely related languages emerged, known collectively as Bantu. By the first century C.E., agricultural peoples speaking Bantu languages and now bearing an ironworking technology had largely occupied the forest regions of equatorial Africa, and at least a few of them had probably reached the East African coast. In the several centuries that followed, they established themselves quite rapidly in most of eastern and southern Africa (see Map 6.1, page 158), introducing immense economic and cultural changes to a huge region of the continent.

The **Bantu migrations** were not conquests or invasions such as that of Alexander the Great; nor were they massive and self-conscious migrations like the movement of Europeans to the Americas in more recent times. Rather, these migrations involved a slow movement of peoples, perhaps a few extended families at a time. And sometimes Bantu expansion was less a movement of people than the diffusion of new patterns of living involving language, root crops, grains, sheep and cattle, pottery styles, and ironworking technology. In this way, already established communities could "become Bantu" without the wholesale migration of outsiders. Taken as a whole, these processes brought to Africa south of the equator a measure of cultural and linguistic commonality, marking it as a distinct region of the continent.

These movements of individuals and cultural patterns also generated numerous interactions among culturally distinct peoples. Among those encounters, none was more significant than that between the agricultural Bantu and the gathering and hunting peoples who earlier occupied this region of Africa. Their interaction was part of a long-term global phenomenon in which farmers largely replaced foragers as the dominant people on the planet.

In these encounters, Bantu-speaking farmers had various advantages. One was numerical, as agriculture generated a more productive economy and larger populations. A second advantage was a greater immunity to animal-borne disease, acquired by prolonged exposure to both parasitic and infectious illnesses common to farming and herding societies. Foraging peoples lacked that immunity, and many quickly succumbed when they encountered the agricultural newcomers. A third advantage was iron, so useful for tools and weapons when interacting with peoples still operating with stone-age technology. Thus gathering and hunting peoples were displaced, absorbed, or largely eliminated in most parts of Africa south of the equator—but not everywhere.

In the rain forest region of Central Africa, the foraging Batwa (Pygmy) people, at least some of them, became "forest specialists" who produced honey, wild game, elephant products, animal skins, and medicinal barks and plants, all of which entered regional trading networks in exchange for the agricultural products of their Bantu neighbors. Some also adopted Bantu languages, thus becoming Bantu linguistically, while maintaining a gathering and hunting lifestyle and a separate identity.

Bantu-speaking peoples themselves also changed as they encountered different environments and peoples. In the drier climate of East Africa, the yam-based agriculture of the West African Bantu homeland was unable to support their growing numbers, so Bantu farmers increasingly adopted grains as well as domesticated sheep and cattle from the already established people of the region. They also enriched their agriculture by acquiring a variety of food crops from Southeast Asia—coconuts, sugarcane, and especially bananas—which were brought to East Africa by Indonesian Malay sailors and immigrants early in the first millennium C.E. This agricultural package and its associated ironworking technology then spread throughout the vast area of eastern and southern Africa, probably reaching present-day South Africa by 400 C.E. Some newly "Bantuized" areas incorporated musical traditions, linguistic patterns, and kinship systems derived from the earlier inhabitants. From these interactions a common set of cultural and social practices diffused widely across Bantu Africa. One prominent historian described these practices:

> [They encompassed] in religion, the centrality of ancestor observances; in philosophy, the problem of evil understood as the consequence of individual malice or of the failure to honor one's ancestors; in music, an emphasis on polyrhythmic performance with drums as the key instrument; in dance, a new form of expression in which a variety of prescribed body movements took preference over footwork; and in agriculture, the pre-eminence of women as the workers and innovators.[7]

All of this became part of the common culture of Bantu-speaking Africa.

As Bantu-derived patterns of living became established in Africa south of the equator during the thousand or so years between 500 and 1500 C.E., a wide variety of quite distinct societies and cultures took shape. Some societies—in present-day Kenya, for example—organized themselves without any formal political specialists at all. Instead, they made decisions, resolved conflicts, and maintained order by using kinship structures or lineage principles supplemented by age grades, which joined men of a particular generation together across various lineages. Elsewhere, lineage heads who acquired a measure of personal wealth, or who proved skillful at mediating between the local spirits and the people, might evolve into chiefs with a modest political authority. In several areas, such as the region around Lake Victoria or present-day Zimbabwe, larger and more substantial kingdoms evolved. Along the East African coast after 1000 C.E., dozens of rival city-states linked the African interior with the commerce of the Indian Ocean basin (see "Sea Roads as a Catalyst for Change: East Africa" in Chapter 7).

Many societies in the Bantu-speaking world developed gender systems that were markedly less patriarchal than those of established urban-based civilizations. Male ironworkers in the Congo River basin, for example, sought to appropriate the power and prestige of female reproductive capacity by decorating their furnaces with clay breasts and speaking of their bellows as impregnating the furnaces. Among the Luba people of Central Africa, male rulers operated in alliance with powerful women, particularly spirit mediums, who were thought to contain the spirit of the king. Only a woman's body was considered sufficiently strong to acquire this potent and dangerous presence. Luba art represented female ancestors as "keepers of secret royal knowledge." And across a wide area of south-central Africa, a system of "gender parallelism" associated female roles with village life (child care, farming, food preparation, making pots, baskets, and mats), while masculine identity revolved around hunting and forest life (fishing, trapping, collecting building materials and medicinal plants). It was a complementary or "separate but equal" definition of gender roles.[8]

In terms of religion, Bantu practice in general placed less emphasis on a High or Creator God who was viewed as remote and largely uninvolved in ordinary life and focused instead on ancestral or nature spirits. The power of dead ancestors might be accessed through rituals of sacrifice, especially of cattle. Supernatural power deriving from ancient heroes, ancestors, or nature spirits also resided in charms that could be activated by proper rituals and used to control the rains, defend the village, achieve success in hunting, or identify witches. Belief in witches was widespread, reflecting the idea that evil or misfortune was the work of malicious people. Diviners, skilled in penetrating the unseen world, used dreams, visions, charms, or trances to identify the source of misfortune and to prescribe remedies. Was a particular illness the product of broken taboos, a dishonored ancestor, an unhappy nature spirit, or a witch? Was a remedy to be found in a cleansing ceremony, a sacrifice to an ancestor, the activation of a charm, or the elimination of a witch?[9]

Unlike the major monotheistic religions, with their "once and for all" revelations from God through the Christian Bible or the Muslim Quran, Bantu religious practice was predicated on the notion of "continuous revelation"—the possibility of constantly receiving new messages from the world beyond through dreams, visions, or trance states. Moreover, unlike Buddhism, Christianity, or Islam, Bantu religions were geographically confined, intended to explain, predict, and control local affairs, with little missionary impulse or inclination toward universality.

North America: Ancestral Pueblo and Mound Builders

If the Americas hosted civilizations, cities, and empires in Mesoamerica and the Andes, they also housed various alternative forms of human community during the second-wave era and beyond. Arctic and subarctic cultures, the bison hunters of the Great Plains, the complex and settled communities of the Pacific coast of North America, nomadic bands living in the arid regions of southern South America — all of these represent the persistence of gathering and hunting ways of living.

Even more widespread — in the eastern woodlands of the United States, Central America, the Amazon basin, and the Caribbean islands — were societies sustained by village-based agriculture. Owing to environmental or technological limitations, it was a less intensive and productive agriculture than in Mesoamerica or the Andes and supported usually much smaller populations (see Map 6.4 and Map 12.5, page 354). These peoples too made their own histories, changing in response to their unique environments, their interactions with outsiders, and their own visions of the world. The Anasazi of the southwestern United States, now called the Ancestral Pueblo, and the mound-building cultures of the eastern woodlands provide two illustrations from North America.

The southwestern region of North America, an arid land cut by mountain ranges and large basins, first acquired maize from its place of origin in Mesoamerica during the second millennium B.C.E., but it took roughly 2,000 years for that crop, later supplemented by beans and squash, to become the basis of a settled agricultural way of living. As maize was adapted to the local environment, permanent village life gradually took hold, with people initially living in pit houses below ground level. By 900 C.E., many of these villages also included kivas, much larger pit structures used for ceremonial purposes that symbolized the widespread belief that humankind emerged into this world from another world below. Individual settlements

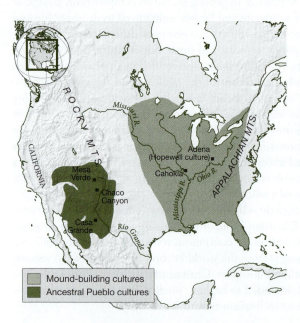

MAP 6.4 North America in the Second-Wave Era
A sparsely populated North America hosted a number of semi-sedentary agricultural societies as well as various gathering and hunting peoples rather than the "civilizations" characteristic of Mesoamerica and the Andes.

were linked to one another in local trading networks and sometimes in wider webs of exchange that brought them buffalo hides, copper, turquoise, seashells, macaw feathers, and coiled baskets from quite distant locations.

These processes of change — growing dependence on agriculture, increasing population, more intensive patterns of exchange — gave rise to larger settlements and adjacent aboveground structures known as pueblos. The most spectacular of these took shape in Chaco Canyon in what is now northwestern New Mexico. There, between 860 and 1130 C.E., five major pueblos emerged. This **Chaco Phenomenon** encompassed 25,000 square miles and linked some seventy outlying settlements to the main centers. The largest of these towns, or "great houses," Pueblo Bonito, stood five stories high and contained more than 600 rooms and many kivas. Hundreds of miles of roads, up to forty feet wide, radiated out from Chaco, prompting much debate among scholars. Without wheeled carts or large domesticated animals, such an elaborate road system seems unnecessary for ordinary trade or travel. Did the roads represent, as some scholars speculate, a ceremonial or sacred landscape leading perhaps to an entrance to the underworld?

Among the Chaco elite were highly skilled astronomers who constructed an arrangement of three large rock slabs situated so as to throw a beam of light during the summer solstice across a spiral rock carving located behind this observatory. By the eleventh century, Chaco also had become a dominant center for the production of turquoise ornaments, which became a major item of regional commerce, extending as far south as Mesoamerica. Not all was sweetness and light, however. Warfare, internal conflict, and occasional cannibalism (a matter of much controversy among scholars) apparently increased in frequency as an extended period of drought in the half century following 1130 brought this flourishing culture to a rather abrupt end. By 1200, the great houses had been abandoned and their inhabitants scattered in small communities that later became the Pueblo peoples of more recent times.

Unlike the Chaco region in the southwest, the eastern woodlands of North America and especially the Mississippi River valley generated an independent Agricultural Revolution. By 2000 B.C.E., many of its peoples had domesticated local plant species, including sumpweed, goosefoot, some gourds and squashes, and a form of artichoke. Sunflowers, originally domesticated in Mesoamerica, also found a place in diets of eastern woodland peoples. These few plants, however, were not sufficient to support a fully settled agricultural village life; rather, they supplemented diets derived from gathering and hunting without fundamentally changing that ancient way of life. Such peoples created societies distinguished by arrays of large earthen mounds, found all over the United States east of the Mississippi, prompting archeologists to dub them the **Mound Builders**. The earliest of these mounds date to around 4000 B.C.E., but the most elaborate and widespread took shape between 200 B.C.E. and 400 C.E. The builders of these mounds created what is commonly called the **Hopewell culture**, after an archeological site in Ohio.

Several features of the Hopewell culture have intrigued archeologists. Particularly significant are the striking burial mounds and geometric earthworks, sometimes covering areas equivalent to several city blocks, and the wide variety of artifacts found within them — smoking pipes, human figurines, mica mirrors, flint blades, fabrics, and jewelry of all kinds. The mounds themselves were no doubt the focus of elaborate burial rituals, but some of them were aligned with the moon with such precision as to

The Great Serpent Mound Located in Ohio, the Great Serpent mound is nearly a quarter mile long and depicts an uncoiling snake seemingly poised to consume an oval-shaped object. Scholars have established that the serpent's head aligns with the summer solstice and its tail points toward the winter solstice, but what the mound meant and how it was used by those who built it remain much debated, as does the date of its construction. (SuperStock/AGE Fotostock)

mark lunar eclipses. Developed most elaborately in the Ohio River valley, Hopewell-style earthworks, artifacts, and ceremonial pottery have also been found throughout the eastern woodlands region of North America. Hopewell centers in Ohio contained mica from the Appalachian Mountains, volcanic glass from Yellowstone, conch shells and a few sharks' teeth from the Gulf of Mexico, and copper from the Great Lakes. All of this suggests a large "Hopewell Interaction Sphere" linking this entire region in a loose network of exchange, as well as a measure of cultural borrowing of religious ideas and practices.[10]

The next and most spectacular phase in the history of these mound-building peoples took shape as corn-based agriculture, derived ultimately but indirectly from Mexico, gained ground in the Mississippi valley after 800 C.E., allowing larger populations and more complex societies to emerge. The dominant center was **Cahokia**, near present-day St. Louis, Missouri, which flourished from about 900 to 1250 C.E. Its central mound, a terraced pyramid of four levels, measured 1,000 feet long by 700 feet wide, rose more than 100 feet above the ground, and occupied fifteen acres.

It was the largest structure north of Mexico, the focal point of a community number-ing 10,000 or more people, and the center of a widespread trading network.

Evidence from burials and from later Spanish observers suggests that Cahokia and other centers of this Mississippi culture were stratified societies with a clear elite and with rulers able to mobilize the labor required to build such enormous structures. One high-status male was buried on a platform of 20,000 shell beads, accompanied by 800 arrowheads, sheets of copper and mica, and a number of sacrificed men and women nearby.[11] Well after Cahokia had declined and was abandoned, sixteenth-century Spanish and French explorers encountered another such chiefdom among the Natchez people, located in southwestern Mississippi. Paramount chiefs, known as Great Suns, dressed in knee-length fur coats and lived luxuriously in deerskin-covered homes. An elite class of "principal men" or "honored peoples" clearly occu-pied a different status from commoners, sometimes referred to as "stinkards." These sharp class distinctions were blunted by the requirement that upper-class people, including the Great Suns, had to marry "stinkards."

The military capacity of these Mississippi chiefdoms greatly impressed European observers, as this Spanish account indicates:

> The next day the cacique [paramount chief] arrived with 200 canoes filled with men, having weapons, . . . the warriors standing erect from bow to stern, holding bows and arrows. . . . [F]rom under the canopy where the chief man was, the course was directed and orders issued to the rest. . . . [W]hat with the awnings, the plumes, the shields, the pennons, and the number of people in the fleet, it appeared like a famous armada of galleys.[12]

Here then, in the eastern woodlands of North America, were peoples who inde-pendently generated a modest Agricultural Revolution, assimilated corn and beans from distant sources, developed increasingly complex chiefdoms, and created mon-umental structures, new technologies, and artistic traditions. Beyond the separate societies that emerged within this large area, scholars have noticed some similari-ties in artifacts, symbols, ceremonies, mythologies, and artistic styles, many of which seem related to marking the status of elites. A horned serpent, sometimes depicted with wings, and various animal-god representations were widely shared symbols, though the meaning of these symbols no doubt changed as they entered new cultural environments. Dubbed the Southeast Ceremonial Complex, these loose networks of connection grew outward from Cahokia for several centuries after 1200 or so. While no linguistic, cultural, or political unity emerged from these relationships, they tes-tify to a measure of exchange, borrowing, and cultural adaptation across an enor-mous region of North America.

Pacific Oceania: Peoples of the Sea

The peoples of Pacific Oceania, like those of Bantu Africa and North America, cre-ated enduring human communities without the large cities, states, and empires so prominent in civilizations. But the ecological setting for these historical journeys was distinctive, for they took place on the islands of the immense Pacific: a few larger ter-ritories, such as New Guinea and New Zealand, as well as thousands of much smaller islands, many of them specks in the sea (see Map 6.5). New Guinea had been settled

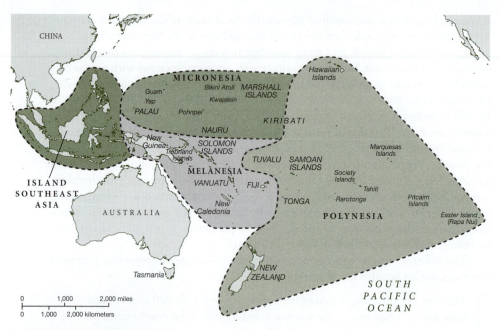

MAP 6.5   Pacific Oceania
Covering about one-third of the world's surface, the Pacific Ocean encompasses thousands of islands, which were home to many distinct societies but also constituted a cultural region that shared numerous commonalities and connections.

for perhaps 50,000 years, initially at a time when it was connected to Australia by a land bridge. But the rest of Oceania was the last part of the world to receive human settlers, who began arriving from Island Southeast Asia only about 3,500 years ago (see "Into the Pacific" in Chapter 1). By 1200 C.E., they had achieved a presence on every habitable piece of land throughout this enormous region. It was, as one historian summarized the process, "the greatest maritime expansion known to history."[13]

The settlers' arrival, however, produced an enormous and sometimes devastating environmental impact as humans entered and disrupted bountiful but fragile ecosystems, especially as their populations grew. Referring to some of the early settlers in Melanesia during the first millennium B.C.E., Pacific historian Ian Campbell wrote: "They hunted, gathered, and fished profligately, and burnt large tracts of previously undisturbed forests."[14] In New Zealand, initially settled much later, around 1200 C.E., human hunting largely eliminated the huge flightless *moa* bird within a century. Archeologists have discovered the remains of some 90,000 moa at a single butchery. A similar impact occurred in Hawaii and elsewhere as smaller birds fell victim to the rats, pigs, and dogs introduced by the settlers. Resource depletion, deforestation, and soil erosion followed, no doubt contributing to the abandonment of at least several dozen islands, as their inhabitants found themselves forced to flee or perish. Rapa Nui (Easter Island) in easternmost Polynesia had come almost to the point of ecological collapse by the time Europeans arrived in the eighteenth century, as much of its tree cover had vanished and many bird species had likewise disappeared.

Human activity had surely contributed to this outcome with overhunting, over-fishing, and the cutting down of forests. But Polynesian rats, whether introduced accidentally or intentionally by the original settlers to the island, were at least equally responsible, as their numbers exploded and they devoured the seeds of the palm trees.[15]

Growing populations also resulted in increased social complexity on some of the most densely populated islands. One example comes from the Micronesian island of **Pohnpei**, where an urban complex, constructed from stone and coral, served as the ceremonial, administrative, and burial center of a powerful Saudeleur dynasty that governed the island for several centuries after 1100 C.E. This impressive urban center, later dubbed by Europeans the "Venice of the Pacific," contained numerous seawalls and canals, over ninety small artificial islands, marketplaces, and a large tomb and funerary complex. However, local legends tell of increasingly despotic rulers whose oppressive policies triggered a revolt by lower-ranking chiefs.

The Polynesian **Tonga Islands** witnessed yet another example of growing social complexity. By the fourteenth century, powerful rulers, known as Tu'i Tonga, stood at the head of a royal court that included many wives and concubines, various relatives, ceremonial attendants, prisoners of war, and specialized craftsmen such as carvers, navigators, and fishermen. The court collected and redistributed food and various gifts to lesser chiefs, who then did the same for their followers. The widespread military and commercial influence of Tonga in the central Pacific has led some scholars to regard it as an incipient empire, while others view it as a tributary network or a system of economic interdependence.

Given the vast distances separating these island societies, considerable diversity among them is hardly surprising. And yet they also participated in the making of a single cultural region with numerous commonalities and connections. Many of their cultural and dietary similarities derive from their common origin in Island Southeast Asia and ultimately from southern China as well as from a common Pacific environment. Variations developed from the adaptation of this shared heritage to the distinctive environment of particular islands—large or small, tropical or semi-tropical, sea-level coastal terrain or mountainous interior, uninhabited or containing established societies as in New Guinea. The relative isolation of these societies, as well as periodic contact with near and more distant neighboring islands, also shaped their histories.

Linguistically, the peoples of Oceania, despite their small numbers, have spoken hundreds of different languages, over 100 on the small island chain of Melanesian Vanuatu alone. But almost all of them are members of the Austronesian family of languages, whose speakers also include those of Malaysia, Indonesia, and Madagascar. New Guinea, however, is a different story, with well over 1,000 languages, most of which are part of the Papuan language family, derived from its much earlier settlement. Similarly, Pacific islanders everywhere practiced the art of body decoration called *tatau* (which became "tattoo" in English), but particularly in Polynesia each archipelago developed distinctive designs, reflecting its unique identity.

This pattern of diversity and unity found other expression as well, both among the three major regions of Melanesia, Micronesia, and Polynesia and within them. In economic life, for example, these people of the sea drew heavily on the ocean as a major source of food, while its shells were used as currency and tools. But they were also farmers, raising pigs, dogs, and fowl, while everywhere cultivating taro, a starchy root vegetable. Other crops—yams, sweet potatoes, breadfruit, coconut palms—were also cultivated as availability and conditions allowed.

In political and social life, Oceanic societies were generally organized as chiefdoms, but with considerable variation. On small islands, chiefs and priests could hardly be distinguished from anyone else, while village councils, operating by consensus, made decisions. In parts of Melanesia, so-called "big men," or locally influential individuals, exercised authority through ceremony, feasts, and gift giving. Elsewhere, societies were more stratified and authority more centralized. In New Zealand, the Maori people distinguished among chiefly families, commoners, and enslaved people derived from prisoners of war. Frequent warfare among its chiefdoms prevented greater political unity. In Hawaii and Tonga, by contrast, elaborate social hierarchies emerged with powerful rulers who had hundreds or even thousands of warriors at their disposal.

Women everywhere in ancient Oceania were considered dangerous and polluting, especially during menstruation and childbirth, and were isolated at those times. However, gender roles differed substantially from place to place. In Melanesia, women were more actively involved in food production, but in Polynesia their labor was directed more toward the making of mats and cloth. Throughout Polynesia, women were accorded high status, and women of chiefly families could exercise considerable power through their male relatives. Melanesian women, by contrast, were more sharply subordinated to men than their counterparts in other regions of Oceania.

Religious life in Oceania was pragmatic, designed to protect against harm and to manipulate the spirits or gods in one's favor. It found expression in two pervasive concepts: *mana* **and** *tapu*. Mana was a spiritual energy or power, associated especially with chiefs and demonstrated by remarkable actions or great success. To maintain the purity of mana, ritual restriction or prohibitions known as tapu (which came into English as "taboo") served to make someone or something sacred or elevated far above the ordinary. Throughout Polynesia, only a particular official could handle the chief's food or his possessions. A Maori chief in New Zealand could not allow even his shadow to fall on food, for doing so made it forbidden to all others. Hawaiians prostrated themselves on the ground before their major chiefs. Since violating a tapu could result in death, religion provided supernatural sanctions for political authorities and social elites, as it has in so many other societies. While much of this was common across all of Pacific Oceania, the gods, ghosts, ancestors, and spirits differed considerably, as did the role of priests or shamans as well as the associated rituals and artistic expression of religious life.

Despite the distances between these island societies, they were not wholly isolated from one another. Networks of exchange and communication—both regional and at a greater distance—allowed for some interaction among the various peoples of Oceania. Between roughly 1400 and 800 B.C.E., the spread of a distinctive pottery style known as Lapita throughout Melanesia and as far as Tonga and Samoa suggests a widespread pattern of exchange involving both commercial and ceremonial elements. During this time, obsidian from the island of New Britain off the northeastern coast of New Guinea had a distribution that extended over 4,000 miles from Borneo in Island Southeast Asia to Fiji in eastern Melanesia.

In western Micronesia, another system of exchange arose in the Caroline Island chain, with a particular focus on the island of **Yap**. It involved trade in commodities

The Moai of Rapa Nui The most iconic artistic representations of Polynesian culture are these huge stone figures called moai. Carved from volcanic rock on the island of Rapa Nui sometime between 1200 and 1600, they are thought to depict sacred ancestors or clan chiefs. Around 1,000 of them were quarried and carved, and hundreds were somehow transported up to eight miles to stand on stone platforms near the coast. The largest were some thirty-three feet tall and weighed over eighty tons. (Bridgeman Images)

such as sea turtles, coconuts, and breadfruit; permission to fish near neighboring islands; and promises of refuge and shelter in times of famine. But it was also a set of tributary relationships in which the high-ranking island of Yap periodically received payments such as woven cloth, various coconut products, mats, and shells from islands of lesser rank up to 1,200 miles farther east. In return, the subordinates received gifts from Yap that exceeded the value of their tribute: wood for canoes, flint stone, food, and powdered turmeric, used as a skin paste and in coming-of-age rituals. Cast in terms of a parent-child relationship between Yap and the other islands, the whole system was supported by fears of powerful Yapese sorcery capable of generating great storms should the required tribute not be forthcoming. Such trading circuits often contained an elaborate ceremonial element in which the exchange of noneconomic items—bracelets, necklaces, feathers, or shells—served to display status, to cement bonds of mutual assistance across great distances, and to confirm relationships of dominance and submission. Small island societies were invariably vulnerable and limited in resources; such networks of exchange provided insurance for their survival.

Polynesian networks of exchange also flourished in the centuries after 1000 C.E., with Tonga at the center of a system linked by trade with Samoa and Fiji. Finely woven Samoan mats were highly valued for displaying prestige, and large logs from Fiji were prized for the huge canoes that could be carved from them for Tonga's impressive warships. From the far eastern edge of Polynesia, sailors had apparently reached the coast of South America, from which they returned with sweet potatoes and bottle gourds. Taking hold in Rapa Nui, those domesticates from the Americas then entered Polynesian voyaging networks and found their way to Hawaii, New Zealand, and elsewhere, becoming a major food source.

Linked to Asia by their distant origins and to the Americas by the slender thread of the sweet potato, the peoples of Pacific Oceania lived largely, but not entirely, in a world apart from the rest of humankind.

Conclusions and Reflections: One History . . . or Many?

Does world history consist of a single story of humankind, or is it a collection of distinct stories of particular regions or peoples? The histories of Africa, the Americas, and Pacific Oceania have often been regarded as "worlds apart," somehow separate from the "mainstream" of world history as experienced in Europe and Asia. But these regions participated fully in at least three global processes that shaped the early history of humankind: the initial migrations that populated the planet, the breakthrough to agriculture, and the development of those more complex societies that we call civilizations. In these ways, the historical trajectory of the early human journey has a certain unity across widely dispersed continental regions.

So perhaps it is not surprising that societies in Africa, the Americas, and Oceania continued to develop in ways broadly similar to Eurasian peoples during the second-wave era, even as they developed their own distinctive cultures, societies, and civilizations. Much as the civilizations of China, India, the Middle East, and the Mediterranean world differed sharply from one another, so too did the civilizations of Nubia, Axum, and the Niger Valley in Africa, those of the Maya and Teotihuacán in Mesoamerica, and Wari and Tiwanaku in South America. Each of them evolved distinct cultural traditions expressed in religious life, artistic creations, and architectural construction. Politically they developed differently too. Maya and Niger Valley civilizations, like those of classical Greece, were organized around particular cities, while Axum and Wari, for example, evolved as imperial states.

While often less densely woven than their Eurasian counterparts, the societies of Africa, the Americas, and Pacific Oceania also forged larger networks of communication and exchange. Axum took part in the trade of the Red Sea and through it was introduced to Christianity. Much earlier, the Chavín cultural complex had spread along the trade routes linking coastal and highland Peru. Elements of a common culture informed the many distinct people of the Bantu-speaking world in Africa and in a similar fashion the many separate societies of the North American Mound Builders. Both economic and cultural exchange flourished among the distant peoples of Pacific Oceania.

Despite these similarities, the historical trajectory of Africa, the Americas, and Oceania also differed from Eurasia in important ways. Most civilizations in these regions were smaller in size and population than those in Persia, India, China, or the Roman Empire. This meant that more of the population of Africa, the Americas, and Pacific Oceania lived outside of the zone of civilization, as did the peoples of northern Eurasia. The Batwa of Central Africa and the peoples of the west coast of North America continued to practice ancient gathering and hunting ways of living during the second-wave era. Likewise, Bantu farmers in Africa and the Ancestral Pueblo farmers in North America created distinctive societies and cultures without large cities or formal states. So too did the peoples of Pacific Oceania, whose stratified societies developed as chiefdoms, for example, among the Maori of New Zealand. The prominence of these stateless societies in Africa, the Americas, and Pacific Oceania reminds us that although historians have disproportionately focused their attention on civilizations, the globalization of civilization did not end other ways of living. In some regions, especially outside of Eurasia, they continued to thrive.

So the peoples of Africa, the Americas, and Oceania participated in global patterns of change and development even while constructing distinct and separate histories. In this respect, they are similar to the peoples of Eurasia. But you may have noticed that *Ways of the World* treats these vast regions in a single chapter, while devoting three chapters to Eurasia. Is this appropriate? Does it represent some kind of preference, bias, or prejudice?

Certainly such decisions reflect a common dilemma for historians: what to include and what to leave out. One standard might be duration. Perhaps long-lasting ways of living deserve the greatest attention. If so, then the Paleolithic era of gathering, hunting, and fishing societies should occupy 90 percent or more of any world history text. But if change is more important than continuity, something new — such as agriculture or civilization — merits more space than something old.

Population provides yet another principle for determining inclusion. Does the fact that Eurasia has long contained over 80 percent of the world's population represent sufficient justification for the regional imbalances of this section of the book? Furthermore, the Eurasian religions of Buddhism, Christianity, and Islam spread more widely and shaped the lives of more people than did the religions of the Maya or the Bantu-speaking peoples of Africa. Do they therefore deserve more extended treatment? Still another factor involves the availability of evidence. In this respect, Eurasia generated far more written records than either Africa or the Americas did, and therefore its history has been investigated far more thoroughly.

There is no consensus among historians about this question of inclusion. As always, the telling of the human story involves endless and controversial choices.

Revisiting Chapter 6

REVISITING SPECIFICS

REVISITING CORE IDEAS

1. **Comparing Continental Histories** What similarities and differences are noticeable in the historical development of Eurasia, Africa, and the Americas?

2. **Identifying Connections** How did the history of Meroë and Axum reflect interaction with neighboring civilizations?

3. **Assessing Significance** In what ways did Maya civilization and Teotihuacán shape the history of Mesoamerica?

4. **Assessing Significance** What was the significance of Wari and Tiwanaku in the history of Andean civilization?

5. **Applying a Concept** What features common to all civilizations can you identify in the civilizations of Africa and the Americas? What distinguishing features give each of them a distinctive identity?

6. **Comparing Societies** In what different ways did the societies of Bantu Africa, the Ancestral Pueblo and Mound Builders of North America, and Pacific Oceania represent alternatives to civilizations?

A WIDER VIEW

1. "The particular cultures and societies of Africa, the Americas, and Pacific Oceania discussed in this chapter developed largely in isolation." What evidence would support this statement, and what might challenge it?

2. How do you understand areas of the world, such as Bantu Africa, North America, and Pacific Oceania, that did not generate "civilizations"? Do you see them as "backward," as moving slowly toward civilization, or as simply different?

3. How did Africa's proximity to Eurasia shape its history? And how did America's separation from the Eastern Hemisphere affect its development?

4. **Looking Back** "The histories of Africa and the Americas during the second-wave era largely resemble those of Eurasia." Do you agree with this statement? Explain why or why not.

CHRONOLOGY

1400–800 B.C.E.	• Lapita culture
900–200 B.C.E.	• Chavín movement
730 B.C.E.	• Nubian conquest of Egypt
300 B.C.E.–100 C.E.	• Kingdom of Meroë in upper Nile Valley
300 B.C.E.–900 C.E.	• Niger Valley civilization in West Africa
200 B.C.E.–400 C.E.	• Hopewell mound-building culture
100–800 C.E.	• Moche civilization in Peru
250–900 C.E.	• Maya civilization
4th century C.E.	• Introduction of Christianity to Axum
300–650 C.E.	• Teotihuacán
ca. 400 C.E.	• Bantu-speaking peoples established in southern Africa
400–1000 C.E.	• Wari and Tiwanaku in the Andes
ca. 860–1130 C.E.	• Chaco Phenomenon
ca. 900–1250 C.E.	• Cahokia
ca. 1000 C.E.	• Tongan trading network
1100–1600 C.E.	• Saudeleur dynasty on Pohnpei
1200 C.E.	• Initial settlement of New Zealand
ca. 1200–1400 C.E.	• Southeast Ceremonial Complex

PART 3
Civilizations and Encounters during the Third-Wave Era 600–1450

The Big Picture

Patterns and Processes of the Third-Wave Era

In world history, the dates that define major periods of time are normally used symbolically rather than for denoting actual events. They point toward processes that mark major global transformations. In Part 3, the date 600 C.E. evokes the disruption, decline, or collapse of many second-wave states and civilizations between 200 and 800 C.E., including Han dynasty China, the western Roman Empire, Gupta India, Axum, Maya cities, Teotihuacán, and others. And 1450 highlights the start of European overseas expansion, which began to link the world's peoples together in new ways.

Third-Wave Civilizations

In the centuries between 600 and 1450, two large-scale processes occupied center stage in the unfolding drama of world history. First, a new phase in the continuing history of civilization took shape during these centuries. In some areas, wholly new civilizations arose where none had existed before: in Swahili city-states along the East African coast; in the West African kingdoms of Ghana, Mali, and Songhay; in Kievan Rus, located in what is now Ukraine and western Russia; in Japan, Korea, and Vietnam; in Srivijaya on the Indonesian island of Sumatra; and in the Angkor kingdom centered in present-day Cambodia. All of these represent a continuation of a long-established pattern in world history — the globalization of civilization. These newcomers to the growing number of civilizations borrowed heavily from larger or more established centers. So too did the new civilization that took shape in Western

Europe following the collapse of the Roman Empire, combining Greco-Roman and Germanic elements in a distinctive blending.

The largest, most expansive, and most widely influential of the new third-wave civilizations was surely that of Islam. It began in Arabia in the seventh century C.E., projecting the Arab peoples into a prominent role as builders of an enormous empire while offering a new, vigorous, and attractive religion. As a new civilization defined by its religion, the world of Islam came to encompass many other centers of civilization, including Egypt, Mesopotamia, Persia, India, and Byzantium.

The persistence or reconstruction of already established civilizations represented yet another historical pattern during this third-wave era. The Byzantine Empire, embracing the eastern half of the old Roman Empire, continued the patterns of Mediterranean Christian civilization and persisted until 1453, when it was overrun by the Ottoman Turks. In China, following almost four centuries of fragmentation, the Sui, Tang, and Song dynasties (581–1279) restored China's imperial unity and reasserted its Confucian tradition. Indian civilization retained its ancient patterns of caste and religion amid vast cultural diversity, even as parts of India fell under the control of Muslim rulers.

Variations on this theme of continuing or renewing older traditions took shape in the Western Hemisphere. In Mesoamerica, the Mexica or Aztec people created a powerful and impressive state in the fifteenth century, drawing on earlier patterns of civilized life in that region. About the same time, on the western rim of South America, a Quechua-speaking people, now known as the Incas, incorporated various centers of Andean civilization into a huge bureaucratic empire. Both the Aztecs and the Incas gave a new expression to much older patterns of civilized life.

The Ties That Bind: Transregional Interaction in the Third-Wave Era

A second global pattern in the third-wave era involved heightened interaction among the world's various regions, cultures, and peoples. More than before, change in human societies was the product of contact with strangers, or at least with their ideas, armies, goods, or diseases. One vehicle for the interaction of culturally different peoples was long-distance trade, which grew considerably during the third-wave era: along the Silk Roads of Eurasia, within the Indian Ocean basin, across the Sahara, and along the Mississippi and other rivers. Everywhere it acted as an agent of change for all its participants. In places where such commerce was practiced extensively, it required that more people devote their energies to producing for a distant market rather than for consumption by their own communities. Those who controlled this kind of trade often became extremely wealthy, exciting envy or outrage among those less fortunate. Such exchange among distant lands also had political consequences, as many new states or empires were constructed on the basis of resources derived from long-distance commerce.

Yet another mechanism of cross-cultural interaction lay in large empires. Not only did they incorporate many distinct cultures within a single political system, but their size and stability also provided the security that encouraged travelers and traders to journey long distances from their homelands. Empires, of course, were nothing new in world history, but those of the third-wave era were larger. The Arab Empire, which accompanied the initial spread of Islam, stretched from Spain to India. Even more extensive was the Mongol Empire of the thirteenth and fourteenth centuries. In the Western Hemisphere, the Inca Empire encompassed dozens of distinct peoples in a huge state that ran some 2,500 miles along the spine of the Andes Mountains. Furthermore, the largest of these empires were the creation of nomadic or pastoral peoples, while earlier empires in the Mediterranean basin, China, India, and Persia had been the work of settled farming societies.

Together, large-scale empires and long-distance trade gave rise to cosmopolitan urban centers such as Baghdad in what is now Iraq, Dunhuang in western China, Timbuktu in West Africa, and Melaka in Southeast Asia, where people of various backgrounds mixed and mingled. Conquest and commerce likewise facilitated the spread of ideas, technologies, food crops, and disease far beyond their points of origin. Thus Islam became an Afro-Eurasian phenomenon with an enormous reach. Chinese silk-making technology became available in Korea, Japan, the Middle East, and later in Europe. Corn gradually diffused from Mesoamerica to North America, where it stimulated population growth and the development of more complex societies. The plague, or Black Death, decimated many parts of Eurasia and North Africa as it made its deadly way from east to west in the fourteenth century.

Much of the readily visible "action" in the third-wave era, as in all earlier civilizations, featured male actors. The vast majority of rulers, traders, soldiers, religious officials, and long-distance travelers were men, as were most heads of households and families. The building of states and empires, so prominent in the third-wave era, meant war and conquest, fostering distinctly masculine warrior values and reinforcing the dominant position of men. Much of what follows in Part 3 is, frankly, men's history.

But behind all of this lay a vast realm of women's activity, long invisible to historians or simply assumed. Women sustained the family life that was the foundation of all human community; they were the repositories of language, religious ritual, group knowledge, and local history; their labor generated many of the products that entered long-distance trade routes as well as those that fed and clothed their communities. The changing roles and relationships of men and women and their understandings of gender also figure in the chapters that follow.

FIRST REFLECTIONS

1. **Questioning Chronology** How do the authors justify designating 600–1450 as a distinct period of world history? On what grounds might this choice be criticized?

2. **Assessing Continuity and Change** What was new in the third-wave era, and what continued from earlier periods of human history?

3. **Identifying Connections** In what ways did distant peoples interact with one another during this time?

4. **Thinking like a World Historian** In the final two paragraphs of this essay the authors reflect on the problem of bias in world history. Do you think that they were apologizing for writing so much "men's history"? To what extent do you think writing "men's history" is inevitable? How might it be avoided or diminished?

7

Commerce and Culture

600–1450

CONNECTING PAST AND PRESENT

EARLY IN THE TWENTY-FIRST CENTURY, Nayan Chanda, a fifty-eight-year-old journalist born and educated in India and at the time working at Yale University, was looking for a graduation gift for his son Ateesh. Deciding on an Apple iPod music player, he placed his order online. He writes: "I was astonished by what followed. I received a confirmation e-mail within minutes . . . [and learned that] the product was being shipped . . . from Shanghai, China. . . . Ateesh's personalized iPod landed on our New Haven [Connecticut] doorstep barely 40 hours after I had clicked 'Buy.'"[1] To Mr. Chanda this was an astounding transaction. Probably it was less surprising to his son. But both of them, no doubt, understood this kind of commercial exchange as something quite recent in human history.

190

And in the speed of the transaction, it surely was. But from the perspective of world history, exchange among distant peoples is not altogether new, and the roots of economic globalization lie deep in the past. In fact, several years after purchasing his son's iPod, Nayan Chanda wrote a well-received book titled *Bound Together*, describing how traders, preachers, adventurers, and warriors had long created links among peoples living in widely separated cultures and civilizations. Those early transregional interactions and their capacity for transforming human societies, for better and for worse, played an increasingly significant role in this era of third-wave civilizations.

The exchange of goods among communities occupying different ecological zones has long been a prominent feature of human history. Coastlands and highlands, steppes and farmlands, islands and mainlands, valleys and mountains, deserts and forests—each generates different products. Furthermore, some societies have been able to monopolize, at least temporarily, the production of particular goods—such as silk in China, certain spices in Southeast Asia, and incense in southern Arabia—that others have found valuable. This uneven distribution of goods and resources has long motivated exchange, not only within particular civilizations or regions but among them as well. In the world of 600 to 1450, long-distance trade became more important than ever before in linking and shaping distant societies. And so, networks of exchange and communication extending all across Afro-Eurasia, and separately in parts of the Americas as well, slowly came into being, forging or strengthening links between distinct civilizations and peoples across the world.

These commercial networks shaped the daily life of many millions partly by altering habits of consumption. For example, West Africans imported scarce salt, so necessary for seasoning and preserving food, from distant mines in the Sahara in exchange for the gold of their region. Incense grown in southern Arabia found eager consumers all across the ancient Eurasian world, where it was used for medicinal purposes, for religious ceremonies, as an antidote to the odors of unsanitary cities, and as an aphrodisiac.

Trade also affected the working lives of some people, encouraging them to specialize in producing particular products for sale in distant markets rather than for use in their own communities. Merchants often became a distinct social group, viewed with suspicion by others because of their impulse to accumulate wealth without actually producing anything themselves. In some societies, trade became a means of social mobility, as Chinese merchants, for example, were able to purchase landed estates and establish themselves within the gentry class. Long-distance trade also enabled elite groups in society to distinguish themselves from commoners by acquiring prestigious goods from a distance—silk, tortoiseshell, jade, rhinoceros horn, or particular feathers.

Trade had the capacity to transform political life. The wealth available from controlling and taxing trade motivated the creation of states in various parts of the world and sustained those states once they had been constructed. Furthermore, commerce posed a set of problems to governments everywhere. Should trade be left in private hands, as in the Aztec Empire, or should it be controlled by the state, as in the Inca Empire? How should state authorities deal with men of commerce, who were both economically useful and potentially disruptive?

Moreover, the saddlebags of camel caravans or the cargo holds of merchant vessels carried more than goods. Trade became a vehicle for the spread of religious ideas, technological innovations, disease-bearing germs, and plants and animals to regions far from their places of origin. In this fashion, Buddhism made its way from India to Central and East Asia, and Islam crossed the Sahara into West Africa. The pathogens that devastated much of Eurasia during the Black Death, as well as technologies of gunpowder, printing, and much more, also traversed the trade routes of the third-wave era.

SEEKING THE MAIN POINT	In what ways did long-distance commerce act as a motor of change in premodern world history?

Silk Roads: Exchange across Eurasia

The best known of these networks of exchange, widely known now as the **Silk Roads** after their most famous product, linked the various peoples and civilizations of the Eurasian landmass (see Map 7.1). None of this network's numerous participants knew the full extent of its reach, for it was largely a "relay trade" in

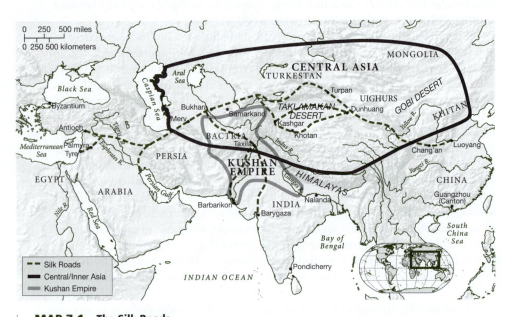

MAP 7.1   The Silk Roads
For 2,000 years, goods, ideas, technologies, and diseases made their way across Eurasia on the several routes of the Silk Roads.

which goods were passed down the line, changing hands many times before reaching their final destination.

The Growth of the Silk Roads

The beginnings of the Silk Roads lay in both geography and history. As a geographic unit, Eurasia is often divided into inner and outer zones that represent quite different environments. Outer Eurasia consists of relatively warm, well-watered areas suitable for agriculture, which provided the setting for the great civilizations of China, India, the Middle East, and the Mediterranean. Inner Eurasia—the lands of eastern Russia, Siberia, and Central Asia—lies farther north and has a harsher and drier climate, much of it not conducive to agriculture. Herding their animals from horseback, the pastoral people of this region had for centuries traded with and raided their agricultural neighbors to the south. Products of the forest and of semi-arid northern grasslands known as the steppes—such as hides, furs, livestock, wool, and amber—were exchanged for the agricultural products and manufactured goods of adjacent civilizations. The movement of pastoral peoples for thousands of years also served to diffuse Indo-European languages, bronze metallurgy, horse-based technologies, and more all across Eurasia.

The construction of the second-wave civilizations and their imperial states during the last five centuries B.C.E. clearly enhanced these ancient patterns of exchange. From the south, the Persian Empire invaded the territory of pastoral peoples in present-day Turkmenistan and Uzbekistan. From the west, Alexander the Great's empire stretched well into Central Asia. From the east, China's Han dynasty extended its authority westward, seeking to control the nomadic Xiongnu and to gain access to their horses. A distinctive Central Asian breed known to the Chinese as "heavenly horses," they had become important to Chinese military forces. By the early centuries of the Common Era, indirect trading connections, often brokered by pastoral peoples, linked these Eurasian civilizations in a network of transcontinental commerce.

Silk Road trading networks prospered most when large and powerful states provided relative security for merchants and travelers across long distances. Such conditions prevailed during the second-wave era when the Roman and Chinese empires anchored long-distance commerce at the western and eastern ends of Eurasia. Silk Road trade flourished again during the seventh and eighth centuries C.E. as the Byzantine Empire, the Muslim Abbasid (ah-BAH-sihd) dynasty, and Tang dynasty China created an almost continuous belt of strong states across Eurasia. In the thirteenth and fourteenth centuries, the Mongol Empire briefly encompassed almost the entire route of the Silk Roads in a single state, giving a renewed vitality to long-distance trade. Over many centuries, various technological innovations, such as yokes, saddles, and stirrups, made the use of camels, horses, and oxen more effective means of transportation across the vast distances of the Silk Roads.

Goods in Transit

During prosperous times especially, a vast array of goods (detailed in the Snapshot on page 194) made its way across the Silk Roads, often carried in large camel caravans

| SNAPSHOT | ECONOMIC EXCHANGE ALONG THE SILK ROADS |

Region	Products Contributed to Silk Road Commerce
China	silk, bamboo, mirrors, gunpowder, paper, rhubarb, ginger, lacquerware, chrysanthemums
Forest lands of Siberia and grasslands of Central Asia	furs, walrus tusks, amber, livestock, horses, falcons, hides, copper vessels, tents, saddles, enslaved people
India	cotton textiles, herbal medicine, precious stones, spices, pepper, pearls, ebony
Middle East	dates, nuts, dried fruit, dyes, lapis lazuli, swords
Mediterranean basin	gold coins, glassware, glazes, grapevines, jewelry, artworks, perfume, wool and linen textiles, olive oil

that traversed the harsh and dangerous steppes, deserts, and oases of Central Asia. Most were luxury products destined for an elite and wealthy market, rather than staple goods, for only readily moved commodities of great value could compensate for the high costs of transportation across such long and forbidding distances.

It was silk that came to symbolize this Eurasian network of exchange. From the time of silk's origin in China, by 3000 B.C.E. or earlier, that civilization long held a monopoly on its production. After 300 B.C.E. or so, the precious fabric increasingly found a growing market all across the linked commercial network of the Afro-Eurasian world. Although the silk trade itself was largely in the hands of men, women figured hugely in the process in terms of both supply and demand. For many centuries, Chinese women, mostly in rural areas, were responsible for every step of the ingenious and laborious enterprise of silk production. They tended the mulberry trees on whose leaves silkworms fed; they unwound the cocoons in very hot water to extract the long silk fibers; and they turned these fibers into thread and wove them into textiles. Thus Chinese homes became the primary site of textile production, with rural women as its main labor force. By the time of the Tang dynasty (618–907 C.E.), women were making a large contribution to the household economy, to technological innovation in the silk industry, and to the state, which depended heavily on peasant taxes, often paid in cloth. Nonetheless, many rural families persisted in poverty, as the thirteenth-century writer Wen-hsiang indicated:

> The silkworms have finished their third sleep and are famished. The family is poor, without cash to buy the mulberry leaves to feed them. What can they do? Hungry silkworms do not produce silk. . . . The daughter is twenty but does not have wedding clothes. Those the government sends to collect taxes are like tigers. If they have no clothes to dress their daughter, they can put the [wedding] off. If they have no silk to turn over to the government, they will go bankrupt.[2]

Elite Chinese women, and their men as well, also furnished part of the demand for these luxurious fabrics, which marked their high status. So too did Chinese officials, who required huge quantities of silk to exchange for much-needed horses and to buy off "barbarian" invaders from the north. Beyond China, women in many cultures ardently sought Chinese silk for its comfort and its value as a fashion statement.

The demand for silk, as well as for cotton textiles from India, was so great in the Roman Empire that various Roman writers were appalled at the drain of resources that it represented. They also were outraged at the moral impact of wearing revealing silk garments. "I can see clothes of silk," lamented Seneca the Younger in the first century C.E., "if materials that do not hide the body, nor even one's decency, can be called clothes. . . . Wretched flocks of maids labour so that the adulteress may be visible through her thin dress, so that her husband has no more acquaintance than any outsider or foreigner with his wife's body."[3]

By the sixth century C.E., the knowledge and technology for producing raw silk had spread beyond China. An old Chinese story attributes it to a Chinese princess who smuggled out silkworms in her turban when she was married off to a Central Asian ruler. However it happened, artisans in Korea, Japan, India, Persia, and the Byzantine Empire likewise learned how to produce this precious fabric.

As the supply of silk increased, its many varieties circulated even more extensively across Afro-Eurasian trade routes. In Central Asia, silk was used as currency and as a means of accumulating wealth. In both China and the Byzantine Empire, silk became a symbol of high status, and governments passed laws that restricted silk clothing to members of the elite. Furthermore, silk became associated with the sacred in the expanding world religions of Buddhism and Christianity. Chinese Buddhist pilgrims who made their way to India seeking religious texts and relics took with them large quantities of silk as gifts to the monasteries they visited. Buddhist monks in China received purple silk robes from Tang dynasty emperors as a sign of high honor. In the world of Christendom, silk wall hangings, altar covers, and vestments became highly prestigious signs of devotion and piety. Because no independent silk industry developed in Western Europe until the twelfth century C.E., a considerable market developed for imported silks. By the twelfth century, the West African king of Ghana was wearing silk, and that fabric circulated in Egypt, Ethiopia, and along the East African coast as well.

Compared to contemporary global commerce, the volume of trade on the Silk Roads was modest, and its focus on luxury goods limited its direct impact on most people. Nonetheless, it had important economic and social consequences. Peasants in the Yangzi River delta of southern China sometimes gave up the cultivation of food crops, choosing to focus instead on producing silk, paper, porcelain, lacquerware, or iron tools, many of which were destined for the markets of the Silk Roads. In this way, the impact of long-distance trade trickled down to affect the lives of ordinary farmers. Furthermore, merchants could benefit immensely from their involvement in long-distance trade. One such individual, a twelfth-century Persian trader named Ramisht whose ships traversed the Indian Ocean and Red Sea, made a personal fortune with which he commissioned an enormously expensive covering made of Chinese silk for the Kaaba, the central shrine of Islam in Mecca.

Cultures in Transit

More important even than the economic impact of the Silk Roads was their role as a conduit of culture. Buddhism in particular, a cultural product of Indian civilization, spread widely throughout Central and East Asia, owing much to the activities of merchants along the Silk Roads. From its beginnings in India during the sixth century B.C.E., Buddhism had appealed to merchants, who preferred its universal message to that of a Brahmin-dominated Hinduism that privileged the higher castes. Indian traders and Buddhist monks, sometimes supported by rulers such as Ashoka, brought the new religion to the trans-Eurasian trade routes. To the west, Persian Zoroastrianism largely blocked the spread of Buddhism, but in the oasis cities of Central Asia, such as Merv, Samarkand, Khotan, and Dunhuang, Buddhism quickly took hold. By the first century B.C.E., many of the inhabitants of these towns had converted to Buddhism, and foreign merchant communities soon introduced it to northern China as well.

Particularly important in this process were the Sogdians, a Central Asian people whose merchants established an enduring network of exchange with China. Two such Sogdians living in China during the second century C.E. were instrumental in translating Sanskrit Buddhist texts into Chinese. Sogdians dominated Silk Road trade for much of the first millennium C.E., and their language became a medium of communication all along that commercial network.

Conversion to Buddhism in the oasis cities was a voluntary process, without the pressure of conquest or foreign rule. Dependent on long-distance trade, the inhabitants and rulers of those sophisticated and prosperous cities found in Buddhism a link to the larger, wealthy, and prestigious civilization of India. Well-to-do Buddhist merchants could earn religious merit by building monasteries and supporting monks. The monasteries in turn provided convenient and culturally familiar places of rest and resupply for merchants making the long and arduous trek across Central Asia. Many of these cities became cosmopolitan centers of learning and commerce. Thousands of Buddhist texts, together with hundreds of cave temples lavishly decorated with murals and statues, have been discovered in the city of Dunhuang, where several branches of the Silk Roads joined to enter western China.

Outside of the oasis communities, Buddhism progressed only slowly among the pastoral peoples of Central Asia. The absence of a written language was an obstacle to the penetration of a highly literate religion, and pastoralists' nomadic ways made the founding of monasteries, so important to Buddhism, quite difficult. But as pastoralists became involved in long-distance trade or came to rule settled agricultural peoples, Buddhism seemed more attractive. The nomadic Jie people, who controlled much of northern China after the collapse of the Han dynasty, are a case in point. Their ruler in the early fourth century C.E., Shi Le, became acquainted with a Central Asian Buddhist monk called Fotudeng who had traveled widely on the Silk Roads. The monk's reputation as a miracle worker, a rainmaker, and a fortune-teller and his skills as a military strategist cemented a personal relationship with Shi Le and led to the conversions of thousands and the construction of hundreds of Buddhist temples. In China itself, Buddhism remained for many centuries a religion of foreign merchants or foreign rulers. Only slowly did it become popular among the Chinese themselves, a process examined more closely in Chapter 8.

As Buddhism spread across the Silk Roads from India to Central Asia, China, and beyond, it also changed. The original faith had shunned the material world, but Buddhist monasteries in the rich oasis towns of the Silk Roads found themselves very much involved in secular affairs. Some of them became quite prosperous, receiving gifts from well-to-do merchants, artisans, and local rulers. The begging bowls of the monks became a symbol rather than a daily activity.

Dunhuang Located in western China at a critical junction of the Silk Road trading network, Dunhuang was also a center of Buddhist learning, painting, and sculpture as that religion made its way from India to China and beyond. In some 492 caves, carved out of the rock between about 400 and 1400 c.e., a remarkable gallery of Buddhist art has been preserved. In this mixture of sculpture and painted images, the Buddha is surrounded by other enlightened beings or bodhisattvas. (Zhang Peng/Getty Images)

Sculptures and murals in the monasteries depicted musicians and acrobats, women applying makeup, and even drinking parties, all of which suggested a more wealthy and worldly style of living, far removed from traditions of Buddhist asceticism.

Doctrines changed as well. It was the more devotional Mahayana form of Buddhism (see "The Buddhist Challenge" in Chapter 4)—featuring the Buddha as a deity, numerous bodhisattvas, an emphasis on compassion, and the possibility of earning merit—that flourished on the Silk Roads, rather than the more austere psychological teachings of the historical Buddha. Moreover, Buddhism picked up elements of other cultures while in transit on the Silk Roads. In the Sogdian city of Samarkand, the use of Zoroastrian fire rituals apparently became a part of Buddhist practice. And in the area northwest of India that had been influenced by the invasions of Alexander the Great, statues of the Buddha reveal distinctly Greek and Roman influences in dress and physical features. In a similar way, the gods of many peoples along the Silk Roads were incorporated into Buddhist practice as bodhisattvas.

Diseases in Transit

Beyond goods and cultures, diseases too traveled the trade routes of Eurasia, and with devastating consequences. Each of the major population centers of the Afro-Eurasian world had developed characteristic disease patterns, mechanisms for dealing with them, and in some cases immunity to them. But when contact among previously isolated human communities occurred, people were exposed to unfamiliar diseases for which they had little immunity or few effective methods of coping. The epidemics that followed often brought suffering and death on an enormous scale to rich and poor alike. An early example involved the Greek city-state of Athens, which in 430–429 B.C.E. was suddenly afflicted by a new and still-unidentified infectious disease that had entered Greece via seaborne trade from Egypt, killing perhaps 25 percent of its army and permanently weakening the city-state.

Even more widespread diseases affected the Roman Empire and Han dynasty China as the Silk Roads promoted contact all across Eurasia, particularly from the second century C.E. on. Smallpox, measles, various forms of plague, and perhaps malaria devastated the populations of both empires, contributing to their political collapse. Paradoxically, such disasters may well have strengthened the appeal of Christianity in Europe and Buddhism in China, for both of them offered compassion in the face of immense suffering.

Again in the period between 534 and 750 C.E., intermittent outbreaks of bubonic plague ravaged the coastal areas of the Mediterranean Sea. One leading theory suggests that black rats and the infected fleas they bore carried the disease via the seaborne trade with India, Ethiopia, and Egypt. What followed was catastrophic. Constantinople, the capital city of the Byzantine Empire, reportedly lost thousands of people per day during a forty-day period in 534 C.E. The repeated recurrence of the disease over the next several centuries also weakened the ability of Christendom to resist Muslim armies from Arabia in the seventh century C.E.

The most well-known dissemination of disease was associated with the Mongol Empire, which briefly unified much of the Eurasian landmass during the thirteenth and fourteenth centuries C.E. (see "The Plague: An Afro-Eurasian Pandemic" in Chapter 11). That era of intensified interaction facilitated the spread of the bubonic plague from China to Europe. Up to half of Europe's population perished, and China and parts of the Islamic world experienced similarly terrible death tolls. In these and many other ways, disease carried by long-distance trade shaped the lives of millions and altered the historical development of entire civilizations.

In the long run of world history, the exchange of diseases gave Europeans a certain advantage when they confronted the peoples of the Western Hemisphere after 1500. Exposure over time had provided them with some degree of immunity to Eurasian diseases. In the Americas, however, the absence of domesticated animals, the less intense interaction among major centers of population, and isolation from the Eastern Hemisphere ensured that native peoples had little defense against the diseases of Europe and Africa. Thus, when their societies were suddenly confronted by Europeans and Africans from across the Atlantic, they perished in appalling numbers. Such was the long-term outcome of the very different histories of the two hemispheres.

Sea Roads: Exchange across the Indian Ocean

If the Silk Roads linked Eurasian societies by land, sea-based trade routes likewise connected distant peoples all across the Eastern Hemisphere. Since the days of the Phoenicians, Greeks, and Romans, the Mediterranean Sea had been an avenue of maritime commerce throughout the region, a pattern that continued during the third-wave era. The Italian city of Venice emerged by 1000 C.E. as a major center of that commercial network, with its ships and merchants active in the Mediterranean and Black seas as well as on the Atlantic coast. Much of its wealth derived from control of expensive and profitable goods imported from Asia, many of which came up the Red Sea through the Egyptian port of Alexandria. There Venetian merchants picked up those goods and resold them throughout the Mediterranean basin. This type of transregional exchange linked the maritime commerce of the Mediterranean Sea to the much larger and more extensive network of seaborne trade in the Indian Ocean basin.

Until the creation of a genuinely global oceanic system of trade after 1500, the Indian Ocean represented the world's largest sea-based system of communication and exchange, stretching from southern China to eastern Africa (see Map 7.2). Like the Silk Roads, these transoceanic trade routes—the **Sea Roads**—grew out of the vast environmental and cultural diversities of the region. The desire for various goods not available at home—such as porcelain from China, spices from the islands of Southeast Asia (present-day Indonesia), cotton goods and pepper from India, ivory and gold from the East African coast, incense from southern Arabia—provided incentives for Indian Ocean commerce. Transportation costs were lower on the Sea Roads than on the Silk Roads because ships could accommodate larger and heavier cargoes than camels. Thus the Sea Roads could eventually carry more bulk

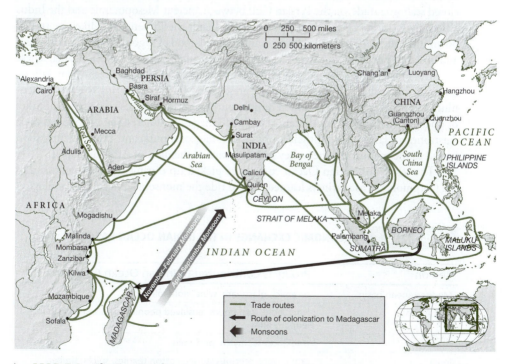

MAP 7.2   The Sea Roads
Paralleling the Silk Road trading network, a sea-based commerce in the Indian Ocean basin connected the many peoples between China and East Africa.

goods and products destined for a mass market—textiles, pepper, timber, rice, sugar, wheat—whereas the Silk Roads were limited largely to luxury goods for the few.

What made Indian Ocean commerce possible were the monsoons, alternating wind currents that blew predictably northeast during the summer months and southwest during the winter (see Map 7.2). An understanding of monsoons and a gradually accumulating technology of shipbuilding and oceanic navigation drew on the ingenuity of many peoples—Chinese, Malays, Indians, Arabs, Swahilis, and others. Collectively they made "an interlocked human world joined by the common highway of the Indian Ocean."[4]

But this world of Indian Ocean commerce did not involve exchanges between entire regions and certainly not between "countries," even though historians sometimes write about India, Indonesia, Southeast Asia, or East Africa as a matter of convenience. It operated rather across a network of towns and cities whose merchants often had more in common with one another than with the people of their own hinterlands.[5] These urban centers, strung out around the entire Indian Ocean basin, provided the nodes of this widespread commercial network.

Weaving the Web of an Indian Ocean World

The world of Indian Ocean commerce was long in the making, dating back to the time of the First Civilizations. Archeological finds in both Mesopotamia and India have disclosed seaborne trade via the Persian Gulf between ancient Mesopotamia and the Indus Valley civilization. The ancient Egyptians, and later the Phoenicians, likewise traded down the Red Sea, exchanging their manufactured goods for gold, ivory, frankincense, and enslaved people from the coasts of Ethiopia, Somalia, and southern Arabia. These ventures mostly hugged the coast and took place over short distances. Malay sailors, however, jumped off from the islands of present-day Indonesia during the first millennium B.C.E. and made their way in double-outrigger canoes across thousands of miles of open ocean to the East African island of Madagascar. There they introduced their Austronesian language and their crops—bananas, coconuts, and taro—which soon spread to the mainland, where they greatly enriched the diets of African peoples.

The tempo of Indian Ocean commerce picked up during the early centuries of the Common Era as mariners learned how to ride the monsoons. Various technological

SNAPSHOT	ECONOMIC EXCHANGE IN THE INDIAN OCEAN BASIN

Region	Products Contributed to Indian Ocean Commerce
Mediterranean basin	ceramics, glassware, wine, gold, olive oil
East Africa	ivory, gold, iron goods, enslaved people, tortoiseshells, quartz, leopard skins
Arabia	frankincense, myrrh, perfumes
India	grain, ivory, precious stones, cotton textiles, spices, timber, tortoiseshells
Southeast Asia	tin, sandalwood, cloves, nutmeg, mace
China	silks, porcelain, tea

An Arab Dhow Painted by the thirteenth-century Arab artist al-Wasiti, this image shows an oceangoing vessel of Indian or Arab origin known as a *dhow*, which was central to the commerce of the Sea Roads. In use in the Red Sea and Indian Ocean since at least the early centuries of the Common Era, dhows used triangular sails and were constructed by sewing or stitching the boards of the hull together with fibers, cords, or thongs without nails. (Pictures from History/Bridgeman Images)

innovations also facilitated Indian Ocean trade—improvements in sails, new kinds of ships such as Chinese junks and Indian or Arab dhows, new means of calculating latitude such as the astrolabe, and evolving versions of the magnetic needle or compass. Merchants from the Roman world established settlements in southern India and along the East African coast. The introduction of Christianity into both Axum and Kerala (in southern India) testifies to the long-term cultural impact of that trade. In the eastern Indian Ocean and the South China Sea, Chinese and Southeast Asian merchants likewise generated a growing commerce, and by 100 C.E. Chinese traders had reached India.

The fulcrum of this growing commercial network lay in India itself. Its ports bulged with goods from both west and east, as illustrated in the Snapshot on page 200. Its merchants were in touch with Southeast Asia by the first century C.E., and settled communities of Indian traders appeared throughout the Indian Ocean basin and as far away as Alexandria in Egypt. Indian cultural practices such as Hinduism and Buddhism, as well as South Asian political ideas, began to take root in Southeast Asia.

In the era of third-wave civilizations between 600 and 1450, two major processes changed the landscape of the Afro-Eurasian world and wove the web of Indian Ocean exchange even more densely than before. One was the economic and political revival of China, some four centuries after the collapse of the Han dynasty (see Chapter 8). Especially during the Tang and Song dynasties (618–1279), China reestablished an effective and unified state that actively encouraged maritime trade. China's population shifted southward along with many of the most productive parts of the commercial economy, which grew impressively during this period. This geographic shift led to the expansion of Chinese maritime trade as Chinese products poured out of southern port towns into the circuits of Indian Ocean commerce, even as the thriving Chinese economy attracted goods from India and Southeast Asia. Chinese technological innovations, such as larger ships and the magnetic compass, likewise added to the momentum of commercial growth.

A second transformation in the world of Indian Ocean commerce involved the sudden rise of Islam in the seventh century C.E. and its subsequent spread across much of the Afro-Eurasian world (see Chapter 9). Unlike Confucian culture, which was quite suspicious of merchants, Islam was friendly to commercial life; the Prophet Muhammad himself had been a trader. The creation of an Arab Empire, stretching from the Atlantic Ocean through the Mediterranean basin and all the way to India, brought together in a single political system an immense range of economies and cultural traditions and provided a vast arena for the energies of Muslim traders.

Those energies greatly intensified commercial activity in the Indian Ocean basin. Middle Eastern gold and silver flowed into southern India to purchase pepper, pearls, textiles, and gemstones. Muslim merchants and sailors, as well as Jews and Christians living within the Islamic world, established communities of traders from East Africa to the south China coast. Efforts to reclaim wasteland in Mesopotamia to produce sugar and dates for export stimulated a trade with East Africa that brought thousands of enslaved Africans to southern Iraq to work on plantations and in salt mines under horrendous conditions. A massive fifteen-year revolt (868–883) among these enslaved people badly disrupted the Islamic Abbasid Empire before that rebellion was brutally crushed.

Beyond these specific outcomes, the expansion of Islam gave rise to an international maritime culture by 1000, shared by individuals living in the widely separated port cities around the Indian Ocean. The immense prestige, power, and prosperity of the Islamic world stimulated widespread conversion, which in turn facilitated commercial transactions. Even those who did not convert to Islam, such as Buddhist rulers in Burma, nonetheless regarded it as commercially useful to assume Muslim names. Thus was created "a maritime Silk Road . . . a commercial and informational network of unparalleled proportions."[6] After 1000, the culture of this network was increasingly Islamic.

Sea Roads as a Catalyst for Change: Southeast Asia

Oceanic commerce transformed all of its participants in one way or another, but nowhere more so than in Southeast Asia and East Africa, at opposite ends of the Indian Ocean network. In both regions, trade stimulated political change as ambitious rulers used the wealth derived from commerce to construct larger and more centrally governed states or cities. Both areas likewise experienced cultural change as local people were attracted to foreign religious ideas from Confucian, Hindu, Buddhist, or Islamic sources. As on the Silk Roads, trade was a conduit for culture.

Located between the major civilizations of China and India, Southeast Asia was situated by geography to play an important role in the evolving world of Indian Ocean commerce. During the third-wave era, a series of cities and states or kingdoms emerged on both the islands and mainland of Southeast Asia that represented new civilizations (see Map 7.3). That process paralleled a similar development of new civilizations in East and West Africa, Japan, Russia, and Western Europe in what was an Afro-Eurasian phenomenon. In Southeast Asia, many of those new societies were stimulated and decisively shaped by their interaction with the sea-based trade of the Indian Ocean.[7]

The case of **Srivijaya** (SREE-vih-juh-yuh) illustrates the connection between commerce and state building. When Malay sailors, long active in the waters around Southeast Asia, opened an all-sea route between India and China through the Strait of Melaka around 350 C.E., the many small ports along the Malay Peninsula and the coast of Sumatra began to compete intensely to attract the growing number of traders and travelers making their way through the strait. From this competition emerged the Malay kingdom of Srivijaya, which dominated this critical choke point of Indian Ocean trade from 670 to 1025. A number of factors—Srivijaya's plentiful supply of gold; its access to the source of highly sought-after spices, such as cloves, nutmeg, and mace; and the taxes levied on passing ships—provided resources to attract supporters, to fund an embryonic bureaucracy, and to create the military and naval forces that brought some security to the area.

The inland states on the mainland of Southeast Asia, whose economies were based more on domestically produced rice than on international trade, nonetheless participated in the commerce of the region. The state of Funan, which flourished

MAP 7.3   Southeast Asia, ca. 1200 C.E.
Both mainland and island Southeast Asia were centrally involved in the commerce of the Indian Ocean basin, and both were transformed by that experience.

during the first six centuries of the Common Era in what is now southern Vietnam and eastern Cambodia, hosted merchants from both India and China. Archeologists have found Roman coins as well as trade goods from Persia, Central Asia, and Arabia in the ruins of its ancient cities. The Khmer kingdom of Angkor (flourished 800–1300) exported exotic forest products, receiving in return Chinese and Indian handicrafts, while welcoming a considerable community of Chinese merchants. Traders from Champa in what is now central and southern Vietnam operated in China, Java, and elsewhere, practicing piracy when trade dried up.

Beyond the exchange of goods, commercial connections spread elements of Indian culture across much of Southeast Asia, even as Vietnam was incorporated into the Chinese sphere of influence. (See "Vietnam and China" in Chapter 8.) Indian alphabets such as Sanskrit and Pallava were used to write a number of Southeast Asian languages. Indian artistic forms provided models for Southeast Asian sculpture and architecture, while the Indian epic *Ramayana* became widely popular across the region.

Politically, Southeast Asian rulers and elites embraced elements of Indian culture, and sometimes they employed Indians as advisers, clerks, or officials and assigned Sanskrit titles to their subordinates. While rulers continued to draw on indigenous beliefs that chiefs possessed magical powers and were responsible for the prosperity of their people, they also used imported Indian political ideas and Buddhist religious concepts to create a "higher level of magic" for themselves and to gain the prestige of association with Indian civilization.[8] Many embraced the Indian belief that leaders were god-kings, perhaps reincarnations of a Buddha or the Hindu deity Shiva.

Other elements of Indian culture also took hold in Southeast Asia. The Sailendra kingdom in central Java mounted a massive building program between the eighth and tenth centuries featuring Hindu temples and Buddhist monuments. The most famous, known as Borobudur, is an enormous mountain-shaped structure of ten levels, with a three-mile walkway and elaborate carvings illustrating the spiritual journey from ignorance and illusion to full enlightenment. The largest Buddhist monument anywhere in the world, it is nonetheless a distinctly Javanese creation, whose carved figures have Javanese features and whose scenes are clearly set in Java, not India. Its shape resonated with an ancient Southeast Asian veneration of mountains as sacred places and the abode of ancestral spirits. Borobudur represents the process of Buddhism becoming culturally grounded in a new place.

Hinduism too, though not an explicitly missionary religion, found a place in Southeast Asia. It was well established in the Champa kingdom, for example, where Shiva was worshipped, cows were honored, and phallic imagery was prominent. But the prosperous and powerful Angkor kingdom of the twelfth century C.E. hosted the most stunning architectural expression of Hinduism in the temple complex known as **Angkor Wat**. The largest religious structure in the premodern world, it sought to express a Hindu understanding of the cosmos centered on a mythical Mount Meru, the home of the gods. Later, it was used by Buddhists as well, with little sense of contradiction. To the west of Angkor, the state of Pagan likewise devoted enormous resources to shrines, temples, and libraries inspired by both Hindu and Buddhist faiths.

This extensive Indian influence in Southeast Asia has led some scholars to speak of the "Indianization" of the region, similar perhaps to the earlier spread of Greek culture within the empires of Alexander the Great and Rome. In the case of Southeast

Angkor Wat Constructed in the early twelfth century, the Angkor Wat complex was designed as a state temple dedicated to the Hindu god Vishnu and was lavishly decorated with carved bas-reliefs depicting scenes from Hindu mythology. By the late thirteenth century, it was in use by Buddhists, as it is to this day. This photo shows a small section of the temple and three Buddhist monks in their saffron robes. (Jose Fuste Raga/Getty Images)

Asia, however, no imperial control accompanied Indian cultural influence. It was a matter of voluntary borrowing by independent societies that found Indian traditions and practices useful and were free to adapt those ideas to their own needs and cultures. Traditional religious practices mixed with the imported faiths or existed alongside them with little conflict. And much that was distinctively Southeast Asian persisted despite influences from afar. In family life, for example, most Southeast Asian societies traced an individual's ancestry from both the mother's and father's line, in contrast to India and China, where patrilineal descent was practiced. Furthermore, Southeast Asian women had fewer restrictions and a greater role in public life than women in the more patriarchal civilizations of China and India. They were generally able to own property together with their husbands and to initiate divorce. A Chinese visitor to Angkor observed, "The local people who know how to trade are all women."[9] Women in Angkor also served as gladiators, warriors, members of the palace staff, poets, artists, and religious teachers.

Islam also rode the commercial currents of the Indian Ocean, drawing many Southeast Asian peoples into its wider world. By embracing the new religion, rulers of Southeast Asian states hoped to attract Muslim traders from Persia, Arabia, and India. Frequently, Islam blended easily with Hindu, Buddhist, or traditional shamanistic practices.

Melaka, located on the southeastern edge of the Malay Peninsula, illustrates the growing role of Islam in Southeast Asia, the connection of commerce and state building, and the cosmopolitan quality of the Indian Ocean network. Established in the early fourteenth century, Melaka quickly evolved from a small fishing village to a major port city that became the capital of a Malay Muslim sultanate until its conquest by the Portuguese in 1511. Its strategic location on the Strait of Melaka gave it a central role in the trade of the entire Indian Ocean basin.

By the later fifteenth century, Melaka had a population of perhaps 100,000 people, making it the largest city in Southeast Asia. Attracted by the city's stable government, low customs duties, and welcoming attitude toward traders, some 15,000 foreign merchants established themselves in Melaka, speaking dozens of languages and hailing from China, Japan, Java, Vietnam, India, the Philippine Islands, Egypt, East Africa, and elsewhere. Many of these diasporic communities had their own neighborhoods in the city, and foreign merchants helped to oversee trade and sometimes served in the sultan's government. No wonder some have called Melaka one the world's first globalized cities.

During the fifteenth century, this commercial city created a loose imperial control over neighboring regions and fostered a distinctive Malay ethnic identity, for it was during the fifteenth century that the people of the city began to refer to themselves as Malay. Melaka also became a center for Islamic learning and a springboard for the spread of an eclectic style of Islam throughout the region that demonstrated much blending with local Hindu and Buddhist traditions.

Sea Roads as a Catalyst for Change: East Africa

On the other side of the Indian Ocean, the transformative processes of long-distance trade were likewise at work, giving rise to **Swahili civilization**. Emerging in the eighth century C.E., this civilization took shape as a set of commercial city-states stretching all along the East African coast, from present-day Somalia to Mozambique.

The earlier ancestors of the Swahili lived in small farming and fishing communities, spoke Bantu languages, and traded with the Arabian, Greek, and Roman merchants who occasionally visited the coast during the second-wave era. But what stimulated the growth of Swahili cities was the far more extensive commercial life of the western Indian Ocean following the rise of Islam. As in Southeast Asia, local people and aspiring rulers found opportunity for wealth and power in the growing demand for East African products associated with an expanding Indian Ocean commerce. Gold, ivory, quartz, leopard skins, and sometimes enslaved people acquired from interior societies, as well as iron and processed timber manufactured along the coast, found a ready market in Arabia, Persia, India, and beyond. At least one East African giraffe found its way to Bengal in northeastern India, and from there it was sent on to China. In response to such commercial opportunities, an African merchant class developed, villages turned into sizable towns, and clan chiefs became kings. A new civilization was in the making.

Between 1000 and 1500, that civilization flourished along the coast, and it was a very different kind of society from the farming and pastoral cultures of the East African interior. It was thoroughly urban, centered in cities of 15,000 to 18,000 people, such as Lamu, Mombasa, Kilwa, Sofala, and many others. Like the city-states of ancient Greece, each Swahili city was politically independent, was generally governed by its own king, and was in sharp competition with other cities. No imperial system or larger territorial states unified the world of Swahili civilization. Nor did any of these city-states control a critical choke point of trade, as Srivijaya did for the Strait of Melaka. Swahili cities were commercial centers that accumulated goods from the interior and exchanged them for the products of distant civilizations, such as Chinese porcelain and silk, Persian rugs, and Indian cottons. While the transoceanic journeys occurred largely in Arab vessels, Swahili craft navigated the coastal waterways, concentrating goods for shipment abroad. This long-distance trade generated class-stratified urban societies with sharp distinctions between a mercantile elite and commoners.

Culturally as well as economically, Swahili civilization participated in the larger Indian Ocean world. Arab, Indian, and Persian merchants were welcome visitors, and some settled permanently. Many ruling families of Swahili cities claimed Arab or Persian origins as a way of bolstering their prestige, even while they dined from Chinese porcelain and dressed in Indian cottons. The Swahili language, widely spoken in East Africa today, was grammatically an African tongue within the larger Bantu family of languages, but it was written in Arabic script and contained a number of Arabic loan words. A small bronze lion found in the Swahili city of Shanga and dating to about 1100 illustrates the distinctly cosmopolitan character of Swahili culture. It depicted a clearly African lion, but it was created in a distinctly Indian artistic style and was made from melted-down Chinese copper coins.[10]

Furthermore, Swahili civilization rapidly became Islamic. Introduced by Arab traders, Islam was voluntarily and widely adopted within the Swahili world. Like Buddhism in Southeast Asia, Islam linked Swahili cities to the larger Indian Ocean world, and these East African cities were soon dotted with substantial mosques. When Ibn Battuta (IH-buhn ba-TOO-tuh), a widely traveled Arab scholar, merchant, and public official, visited the Swahili coast in the early fourteenth century, he found altogether Muslim societies in which religious leaders often spoke Arabic, and all were eager to welcome a learned Islamic visitor. But these were African Muslims, not colonies of transplanted Arabs. As a prominent historian of Ibn Battuta's travels commented, "The rulers, scholars, officials, and big merchants as well as the port workers, farmers, craftsmen, and slaves, were dark-skinned people speaking African tongues in everyday life."[11]

Islam sharply divided the Swahili cities from their African neighbors to the west, for neither the new religion nor Swahili culture penetrated much beyond the coast until the nineteenth century. Economically, however, the coastal cities acted as intermediaries between the interior producers of valued goods and the Arab merchants who carried them to distant markets. Particularly in the southern reaches of the Swahili world, this relationship extended the impact of Indian Ocean trade well into the African interior. Hundreds of miles inland, between the Zambezi and Limpopo rivers, lay rich sources of gold, much in demand on the Swahili coast. The emergence of a powerful state, known as **Great Zimbabwe**, seems clearly connected to the growing trade in gold to the coast as well as to the wealth embodied in its large herds of cattle. At its peak between 1250 and 1350, Great Zimbabwe had the resources and the labor power to construct huge stone enclosures entirely without mortar, with walls sixteen feet thick and thirty-two feet tall. "[It] must have been an astonishing sight," writes a recent historian, "for the subordinate chiefs and kings who would have come there to seek favors at court."[12] Here in the interior of southeastern Africa lay yet another example of the reach and transforming power of Indian Ocean commerce.

Sand Roads: Exchange across the Sahara

In addition to the Silk Roads and the Sea Roads, another important pattern of long-distance trade — this one across the vast reaches of the Sahara in a series of **Sand Roads** — linked North Africa and the Mediterranean world with the land and peoples of interior West Africa (see Map 7.4). Like the others, these Sand Road commercial networks had a transforming impact, stimulating and enriching West African civilization and connecting it to larger patterns of world history during the third-wave era.

Commercial Beginnings in West Africa

Trans-African trade, like the commerce of the Silk Roads and the Sea Roads, was rooted in environmental variation. The North African coastal regions, long part of Roman or later Arab empires, generated cloth, glassware, weapons, books, and other manufactured goods. The great Sahara held deposits of copper and especially salt, and its oases produced sweet and nutritious dates. While the sparse populations of the desert were largely pastoral and nomadic, farther south lived agricultural peoples who grew a variety of crops, produced their own textiles and metal products, and mined a considerable amount of gold. These agricultural regions of sub-Saharan Africa are normally divided into two ecological zones: the savanna grasslands immediately south of the Sahara, which produced grain crops such as millet and sorghum, and the forest areas farther south, where root and tree crops such as yams and kola nuts predominated. These quite varied environments provided the economic incentive for the exchange of goods.

The earliest long-distance trade within this huge region was not across the Sahara at all, but largely among the agricultural peoples themselves in the area later known to Arabs as the Sudan, or "the land of black people." On the basis of this trade, a number of independent urban clusters emerged by the early centuries of the Common Era, giving rise to the Niger Valley civilization, described in Chapter 6.

Gold, Salt, and Enslaved People: Trade and Empire in West Africa

A major turning point in African commercial life occurred with the introduction of the **Arabian camel** to North Africa and the Sahara in the early centuries of the Common Era. This remarkable animal, which could go for ten days without water, finally made possible the long trek across the Sahara. It was camel-owning dwellers of desert oases who initiated regular trans-Saharan commerce by 300 to 400 C.E. Several centuries later, North African Arabs, now bearing the new religion of Islam, also organized caravans across the desert.

What these Arab merchants sought, above all else, was gold, which was found in some abundance in the border areas straddling the grasslands and the forests of

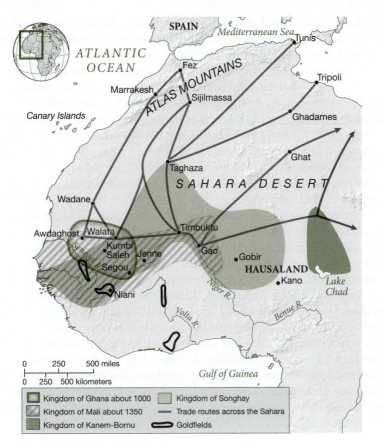

MAP 7.4   The Sand Roads
For a thousand years or more, the Sahara was an ocean of sand that linked the interior of West Africa with the world of North Africa and the Mediterranean but separated them as well.

West Africa. From its source, it was transported by donkey to transshipment points on the southern edge of the Sahara and then transferred to camels for the long journey north across the desert. African ivory, kola nuts, and enslaved people were likewise in considerable demand in the desert, the Mediterranean basin, and beyond. In return, the peoples of the Sudan received horses, cloth, dates, various manufactured goods, and especially salt from the rich deposits in the Sahara.

Thus the Sahara was no longer simply a barrier to commerce and cross-cultural interaction; for a thousand years, it was a major international trade route that fostered new relationships among distant peoples. As in Southeast Asia and East Africa, this trans-Saharan trade provided both incentives and resources for the construction of new and larger political structures. The West African peoples living in the savanna grasslands between the forests and the desert were in the best position to take advantage of these new opportunities. Between roughly 500 and 1600, a new **West African civilization** took shape in the region, stretching from the Atlantic coast to Lake Chad. It included the states of Ghana, Mali, Songhay, and Kanem-Bornu, as well as numerous towns and cities such as Kumbi Saleh, Jenne, Timbuktu, Gao, Gobir, Kano, and others (see Map 7.4).

All of these states were monarchies with elaborate court life and varying degrees of administrative complexity and military forces at their disposal. All drew on the wealth of trans-Saharan trade, taxing the merchants who conducted it. In the wider world, these states soon acquired a reputation for great riches. An Arab traveler in the tenth century c.e. described the ruler of **Ghana** as "the wealthiest king on the face of the earth because of his treasures and stocks of gold."[13] At its high point in the fourteenth century, the rulers of **Mali** monopolized the import of strategic goods such as horses and metals; levied duties on salt, copper, and other merchandise; and reserved large nuggets of gold for themselves while permitting the free export of gold dust.

This growing integration with the world of international commerce generated the social complexity and hierarchy characteristic of all civilizations. Royal families and elite classes, mercantile and artisan groups, military and religious officials, free peasants and enslaved people—all of these were represented in this emerging West African civilization. So too were gender hierarchies, although without the rigidity of more established Eurasian civilizations. Rulers, merchants, and public officials were almost always male, and by 1200 earlier matrilineal descent patterns had been largely replaced by those tracing descent through the male line. Male bards, the repositories for their communities' history, often viewed powerful women as dangerous, not to be trusted, and a seductive distraction for men. But ordinary women were central to agricultural production and weaving; royal women played important political roles in many places; and oral traditions and mythologies frequently portrayed a complementary rather than hierarchal relationship between the sexes. According to a recent scholar:

> Men [in West African civilization] derive[d] their power and authority by releasing and accumulating *nyama* [a pervasive vital power] through acts of transforming one thing into another—making a living animal dead in hunting, making a lump of metal into a fine bracelet at the smithy. Women derive[d] their power from similar acts of transformation—turning clay into pots or turning the bodily fluids of sex into a baby.[14]

Certainly, the famous Muslim traveler Ibn Battuta, visiting Mali in the mid-fourteenth century, was surprised, and appalled, at the casual intimacy of unmarried men and women, despite their evident commitment to Islam.

As in all civilizations, slavery found a place in West Africa. Early on, most enslaved people had been women, working as domestic servants and concubines. As West African civilization crystallized, however, enslaved men were put to work as state officials, porters, craftsmen, miners harvesting salt from desert deposits, and especially agricultural laborers producing for the royal granaries on large estates or plantations. Most came from non-Islamic and stateless societies farther south that were raided during the dry season by cavalry-based forces of West African states. A song in honor of one eleventh-century ruler of Kanem-Bornu boasted of his raiding achievements:

> The best you took (and sent home) as the first fruits of battle. The children crying on their mothers you snatched away from their mothers. You took the slave wife from a slave, and set them in lands far removed from one another.[15]

Most of these enslaved people were used within this emerging West African civilization, but a **trans-Saharan slave trade** also developed. Between 1100 and 1400, perhaps 5,500 enslaved individuals per year made the perilous trek across the desert, where most were put to work in the homes of the wealthy in Islamic North Africa.

The states of this West African civilization developed substantial urban and commercial centers where traders congregated and goods were exchanged. Some of these cities also became centers of manufacturing, creating finely wrought beads, iron tools, or cotton textiles, some of which entered the circuits of commerce. Visitors described them as cosmopolitan places where court officials, artisans, scholars, students, and local and foreign merchants all rubbed elbows. As in East Africa, Islam accompanied trade and became an important element in the urban culture of West Africa. Thus the growth of long-distance trade had stimulated the development of a West African civilization that was linked to the wider networks of exchange in the Eastern Hemisphere.

An American Network: Commerce and Connection in the Western Hemisphere

Before the voyages of Columbus, the world of the Americas developed quite separately from that of Afro-Eurasia. But if the Silk, Sea, and Sand Roads linked the diverse peoples of the Eastern Hemisphere, did a similar network of interaction join and transform the various societies of the Western Hemisphere?

Clearly, direct connections among the various civilizations and cultures of the Americas were less densely woven than in the Afro-Eurasian region. The llama and the potato, both domesticated in the Andes, never reached Mesoamerica; nor did the writing system of the Maya diffuse to Andean civilizations. The Aztecs and the Incas, contemporary civilizations in the fifteenth century, had little if any direct contact with each other. The limits of these interactions owed something to the absence of horses, donkeys, camels, wheeled vehicles, and large oceangoing vessels, all of which facilitated long-distance trade and travel in Afro-Eurasia.

Geographic or environmental differences added further obstacles. The narrow bottleneck of Panama, largely covered by dense rain forests, surely inhibited contact between South and North America. Furthermore, the north/south orientation of the Americas — which required agricultural practices to move through, and adapt to, quite distinct climatic and vegetation zones — slowed the spread of agricultural products. By contrast, the east/west axis of Eurasia meant that agricultural innovations could diffuse more rapidly because they were entering roughly similar environments. Thus nothing equivalent to the long-distance trade of the Silk, Sea, or Sand Roads of the Eastern Hemisphere arose in the Americas, even though local and regional commerce flourished in many places. Nor did distinct cultural traditions spread widely to integrate distant peoples, as Buddhism, Christianity, and Islam did in the Afro-Eurasian world.

Nonetheless, scholars have discerned "a loosely interactive web stretching from the North American Great Lakes and upper Mississippi south to the Andes."[16] (See Map 7.5.) Partly, it was a matter of slowly spreading cultural elements, such as the gradual diffusion of maize from its Mesoamerican place of origin to the southwestern United States and then on to eastern North America as well as to much of South America in the other direction. A game played with rubber balls on an outdoor court

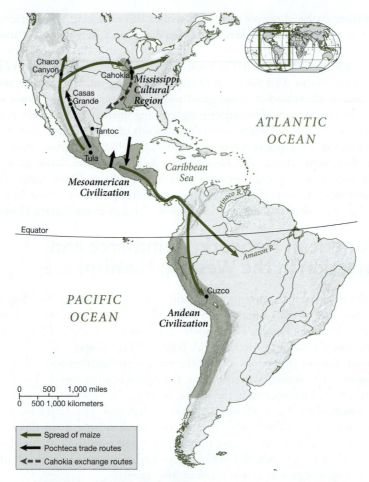

MAP 7.5   The American Web

Transcontinental interactions within the American web were more
modest than those of the Afro-Eurasian hemisphere. The most intense
areas of exchange and communication occurred within the Mississippi
valley, Mesoamerican, and Andean regions.

has left traces in the Caribbean, Mexico, and northern South America. The spread of
particular pottery styles and architectural conventions likewise suggests at least indirect contact over wide distances.

Commerce too played an important role in the making of this "**American web**."
A major North American chiefdom at Cahokia, near present-day St. Louis, lay at the
center of a widespread trading network. Those linkages brought to Cahokia shells
from the Atlantic coast, copper from the Lake Superior region, buffalo hides from
the Great Plains, obsidian from the Rocky Mountains, and mica from the southern
Appalachian Mountains. Sturdy dugout canoes plied the rivers of the eastern woodlands, loosely connecting their diverse societies.

Early European explorers and travelers along the Amazon and Orinoco rivers of South America reported active networks of exchange that may well have operated for many centuries among densely populated settlements of agricultural peoples. Caribbean peoples using large oceangoing canoes had long conducted an inter-island trade, and the Chincha people of southern coastal Peru undertook a privately organized ocean-based exchange in copper, beads, and shells along the Pacific coasts of Peru and Ecuador in large seagoing rafts. Another regional commercial network, centered in Mesoamerica, extended north to what is now the southwestern United States and south to Ecuador and Colombia. Many items from Mesoamerica — copper bells, macaw feathers, tons of shells — have been found in the Chaco region of New Mexico. Residents of Chaco also drank liquid chocolate, using jars of Maya origin and cacao beans imported from Mesoamerica, where the practice began. Turquoise, mined and worked by the people of Chaco (see "North America: Ancestral Pueblo and Mound Builders" in Chapter 6), flowed in the other direction.

But the most active and dense networks of communication and exchange in the Americas lay within, rather than between, the regions that housed the two great civilizations of the Western Hemisphere — Mesoamerica and the Andes. During the flourishing of Mesoamerican civilization (200–900 C.E.), both the Maya cities in the Yucatán area of Mexico and Guatemala and the huge city-state of Teotihuacán in central Mexico maintained commercial relationships with one another and throughout the region. In addition to this land-based trade, the Maya conducted a seaborne commerce, using large dugout canoes holding forty to fifty people, along both the Atlantic and Pacific coasts.

Although most of this trade was in luxury goods rather than basic necessities, it was critical to upholding the position and privileges of royal and noble families. Items such as cotton clothing, precious jewels, and feathers from particular birds marked the status of elite groups and served to attract followers. Controlling access to such high-prestige goods was an important motive for war among Mesoamerican states. Among the Aztecs of the fifteenth century, professional merchants known as **pochteca** (pohch-TEH-cah) undertook large-scale trading expeditions both within and well beyond the borders of their empire, sometimes as agents for the state or for members of the nobility, but more often acting on their own as private businessmen.

Unlike in the Aztec Empire, in which private traders largely handled the distribution of goods, economic exchange in the Andean Inca Empire during the fifteenth century was a state-run operation, and no merchant group similar to the Aztec pochteca emerged there. Instead, great state storehouses bulged with immense quantities of food, clothing, military supplies, blankets, construction materials, and more, all carefully recorded on *quipus* (knotted cords used primarily to record numerical data) by a highly trained class of accountants. From these state centers, goods were transported as needed by caravans of human porters and llamas across the numerous roads and bridges of the empire. Totaling some 20,000 miles, Inca roads traversed the coastal plain and the high Andes in a north/south direction, while lateral roads linked these diverse environments and extended into the eastern rain forests and plains as well. Despite the general absence of private trade, local exchange took place at highland fairs and along the borders of the empire with groups outside the Inca state.

Inca Roads Used for transporting goods by pack animal or sending messages by foot, the Inca road network included some 2,000 inns where travelers might find food and shelter. Messengers, operating in relay, could cover as many as 150 miles a day. Here contemporary hikers still make use of an old Inca trail road. (William H. Mullins/Science Source)

Conclusions and Reflections: Globalization — Ancient and Modern

"Encounters with strangers," wrote the famous world historian William McNeill, "were the main drive wheel of social change" in world history.[17] The cross-cultural commercial exchanges of the third-wave era illustrate McNeill's point. Although most people continued to focus their working lives on producing necessities for themselves or their local landlords, for some in this period, economic life changed substantially. Peasants in parts of China, for example — men and women alike — came to focus their work on producing silk and other products that entered the Silk Road trading networks, requiring them to purchase food in the growing marketplaces of an increasingly commercialized economy.

Long-distance commerce also generated social changes as mercantile elites, such as the Aztec *pochteca*, emerged as more distinct and prominent groups. An international merchant culture accompanied the growth of Indian Ocean commerce, and permanent communities of both Indian and Chinese merchants established themselves in Southeast Asia. Elite groups in many places used products from distant sources — silk, ceramics, gold, ivory, and incense, for example — to signify and reinforce their status.

Political life also changed as aspiring rulers used the resources derived from long-distance trade to create and sustain new states. The kingdom of Srivijaya in

Southeast Asia, the Swahili city-states of East Africa, and the large imperial states of West Africa illustrate this link between commerce and state building.

Among the most significant changes associated with international commerce involved the spread of cultural traditions. Commercial networks enabled the extension of Buddhism across Asia, of Hinduism into parts of Southeast Asia, of Christianity to Axum and south India, and of Islam to both East and West Africa.

These widespread networks of exchange remind us that alongside the separate histories of particular civilizations and societies, there lies another history—that of connections, interactions, and encounters across cultural boundaries—which we have recently come to call globalization. In several ways, this third-wave globalization broadly resembles that of recent centuries. In both eras, ties of commerce and culture linked distant peoples; states and their rulers drew support from the resources made available by long-distance trade; and social status was marked by the possession of prestigious goods from far away.

But the differences are surely more striking. The entangled webs of modern times—linked by networks of roads, railroads, pipelines, shipping lanes, flight patterns, fiber-optic cables, and the Internet—have created a far more densely connected world than the modest relationships generated by the Silk Roads, Sea Roads, and Sand Roads of the third-wave era. And the speed of modern commercial transactions hardly compares to the slow journeys of camel caravans and wind-driven ships.

Furthermore, most people in these earlier times still produced primarily for their own consumption rather than for the market, and a much smaller range of goods was exchanged in the marketplaces of the world. Far fewer people then sold their own labor for wages, an almost universal practice in modern economies. Because of transportation costs and technological limitations, most trade was in luxury goods rather than in necessities. In addition, the circuits of commerce were rather more limited than the truly global patterns of exchange that emerged after 1500.

Finally, the world economy of the modern era increasingly had a single center—industrialized Western European countries—that came to dominate much of the world both economically and politically during the nineteenth century. Though never completely equal, the economic relationships of earlier times occurred among much more equivalent units. For example, no one region dominated the complex pattern of Indian Ocean exchange, although India and China generally offered manufactured goods, while Southeast Asia and East Africa mostly contributed agricultural products or raw materials. And with the exception of the brief Mongol control of the Silk Roads and the Inca domination of the Andes for a century, no single power exercised political control over the major networks of world commerce.

Economic relationships among third-wave civilizations, in short, were more balanced and multicentered than those of the modern era. Although massive inequalities occurred within particular regions or societies, interaction among the major civilizations operated on a rather more equal basis than in the globalized world of the past several centuries. With the rise of China, India, Turkey, and Brazil as major players in the world economy of the twenty-first century, are we perhaps witnessing a return to that earlier pattern? Globalization, like everything else, has a history.

Revisiting Chapter 7

REVISITING SPECIFICS

Silk Roads, 192
Sea Roads, 199
Srivijaya, 203
Angkor Wat, 204
Melaka, 206
Swahili civilization, 206
Great Zimbabwe, 207
Sand Roads, 208

Arabian camel, 208
West African civilization, 209
Ghana, 210
Mali, 210
trans-Saharan slave trade, 211
American web, 212
pochteca, 213

REVISITING CORE IDEAS

1. **Assessing Outcomes** What were the major economic, social, and cultural consequences of Silk Road commerce?
2. **Analyzing Change** How did Indian Ocean commerce shape the history of Southeast Asia and East Africa during the third-wave era?
3. **Making Comparisons** To what extent did the Silk Roads and the Sea Roads operate in a similar fashion? How did they differ?
4. **Analyzing Change** What changes did trans-Saharan trade bring to West Africa?
5. **Defining Differences** How did networks of interaction among the various peoples of the Americas differ from those of the Afro-Eurasian world?

A WIDER VIEW

1. What motivated and sustained the long-distance commerce of the Silk Roads, Sea Roads, and Sand Roads?
2. "Cultural change often derived from commercial exchange in the third-wave era." What evidence from this chapter supports this observation?
3. In what ways was Afro-Eurasia a single interacting zone, and in what respects was it a vast region of separate cultures and civilizations?
4. **Looking Back** Compared to the cross-cultural interactions of earlier times, what was different about those of the third-wave era?

CHRONOLOGY

ca. 200 B.C.E.–200 C.E.	• Initial flourishing of Silk Road commerce
200 B.C.E.–300 C.E.	• Spread of Buddhism to Central Asian cities and northern China
1–300 C.E.	• Knowledge of monsoons enables Indian Ocean commerce
1–300	• Introduction of camel to North Africa/Sahara
300–400	• Beginning of trans-Saharan trade
ca. 350	• All-sea routes open between India and China
500–600	• Initial spread of silk-making technology beyond China
ca. 500–1600	• Flourishing of West African civilization (Ghana, Mali, Songhay)
610–700	• Rise and spread of Islam
670–1025	• Srivijaya kingdom
ca. 850–1250	• Chaco culture in American southwest (New Mexico) trades with Mesoamerican societies
ca. 900–1250	• Cahokia at the hub of North American commercial network
ca. 1000–1100	• Diffusion of sweet potatoes from South America to Pacific Oceania
ca. 1000–1500	• Swahili civilization flourishes along East African coast
1200–1400	• Mongol Empire revitalizes Silk Road commerce
1347	• Black Death enters Europe via transcontinental trade routes
1354	• Ibn Battuta visits West Africa
1400–1500	• Aztec and Inca empires facilitate commercial exchange

8

China and the World

East Asian Connections

600–1300

CONNECTING PAST AND PRESENT

"THERE IS ONLY ONE EARTH IN THE UNIVERSE and we mankind have only one homeland," observed the Chinese president Xi Jinping during his address before the United Nations in January 2017. "The Paris agreement is a milestone in the history of climate governance. We must ensure that this endeavor is not derailed."[1] With these words, the leader of China signaled his country's willingness to take a global leadership role in limiting climate change even as the United States was withdrawing from the Paris Accords under President Donald Trump. China's remarkable economic development since the 1980s had transformed it by the early twenty-first century into a major global power and one of the largest consumers of fossil fuels on the planet. Its decision to embrace the Paris Accords mattered to peoples and nations around the globe.

From the viewpoint of world history, China's recent prominence on the world stage was hardly something new, and its nineteenth- and twentieth-century position as a weak or "developing" country was distinctly at odds with its long history. Its leadership on climate change, even as coal fueled much of its rapidly growing industry, provided another example of China resuming in recent years a much older and more powerful role in world affairs.

In the world of third-wave civilizations, even more than in earlier times, China cast a long shadow. Its massive and powerful civilization, widely imitated by adjacent peoples, gave rise to a China-centered set of relationships encompassing Tibet, Korea, Japan, and Vietnam. China also extended its borders deep into Central Asia, while its wealthy and cosmopolitan culture attracted visitors from all over Eurasia. Far beyond its near neighbors, China's booming economy and many technological innovations had ripple effects all across the Afro-Eurasian world.

Even as China so often influenced the world, it too was changed by its many interactions with non-Chinese peoples. Northern nomads — "barbarians" to the Chinese — frequently posed a military threat and on occasion even conquered and ruled parts of China. The country's growing involvement in international trade stimulated important social, cultural, and economic changes within China itself. Buddhism, a religion of Indian origin, took root in China, and, to a much lesser extent, so did Christianity and Islam. In short, China's engagement with the wider world became a very significant element in the global interactions of the third-wave era.

SEEKING THE MAIN POINT	In what ways did China change during the third-wave era? And how was its history linked to a wider world during these centuries?

Together Again: The Reemergence of a Unified China

The collapse of the Han dynasty around 220 C.E. ushered in more than three centuries of political fragmentation in China and signaled the rise of powerful and locally entrenched aristocratic families. It also meant the incursion of northern nomads, many of whom learned Chinese, dressed like Chinese, married into Chinese families, and governed northern regions of the country in a Chinese fashion. Such conditions of disunity, unnatural in the eyes of many thoughtful Chinese, discredited Confucianism and opened the door to a greater acceptance of Buddhism and Daoism among the elite. Those centuries also witnessed substantial Chinese migration southward toward the Yangzi River valley, a movement of people that gave southern China some 60 percent of the country's population by 1000. That movement of Chinese people, accompanied by their intensive agriculture, set in motion a vast environmental transformation marked by the destruction of the old-growth forests that once covered much of the country and the retreat of the elephants that had inhabited those lands. Around 800 C.E., the Chinese official and writer Liu Zongyuan lamented what was happening:

> A tumbled confusion of lumber as flames on the hillside crackle
> Not even the last remaining shrubs are safeguarded from destruction
> Where once mountain torrents leapt—nothing but rutted gullies.[2]

A Golden Age of Chinese Achievement

While the collapse of the western Roman Empire led to permanent political fragmentation, the fall of China's Han dynasty did not, for China regained its earlier political unity under the **Sui dynasty** (581–618). Its emperors solidified that unity by vastly extending the country's canal system, which stretched some 1,200 miles in length and is described by one scholar as "an engineering feat without parallel in the world of its time."[3] Those canals linked northern and southern China economically and contributed much to the prosperity that followed. But the ruthlessness of Sui emperors and a futile military campaign to conquer Korea exhausted the state's resources, alienated many people, and prompted the overthrow of the dynasty.

This dynastic collapse, however, witnessed no prolonged disintegration of the Chinese state. The two dynasties that followed—the **Tang dynasty** (618–907) and the **Song dynasty** (960–1279)—built on the Sui foundations of renewed unity (see Map 8.1). Together they established patterns of Chinese life that endured into the twentieth century. Culturally, this era has long been regarded as a golden age of arts and literature, setting standards of excellence in poetry, landscape painting, and ceramics. Particularly during the Song dynasty, an explosion of scholarship gave rise to Neo-Confucianism, an effort to revive Confucian thinking while incorporating some of the insights of Buddhism and Daoism.

Politically, the Tang and Song dynasties built a state structure that endured for a thousand years. Six major ministries—personnel, finance, rites, army, justice, and public works—were accompanied by the Censorate, an agency that exercised surveillance over the rest of the government, checking on the character and competence of public officials. To staff this bureaucracy, the examination system was revived and made more elaborate, facilitated by the ability to print books for the first time in world history. Schools and colleges proliferated to prepare candidates for the rigorous exams, which became a central feature of upper-class life. A leading world historian has described Tang dynasty China as "the best ordered state in the world."[4]

Selecting officials on the basis of merit represented a challenge to established aristocratic families' hold on public office. Still, a substantial percentage of official positions went to the sons of the privileged, even if they had not passed the exams.

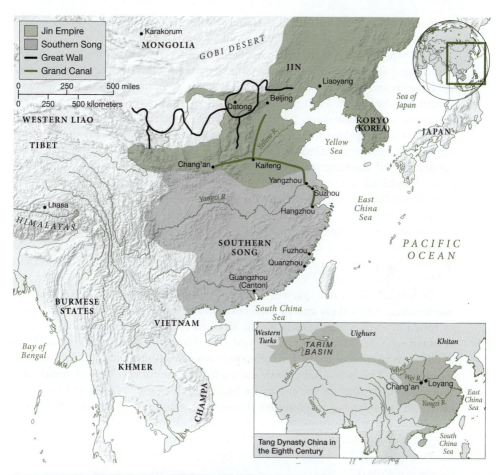

MAP 8.1 Tang and Song Dynasty China
During the third-wave era, China interacted extensively with its neighbors. The Tang dynasty extended Chinese control deep into Central Asia. Under the Song dynasty, nomadic Jurchen peoples conquered much of northern China, creating two states—the Song in the south and the Jin in the north. Both claimed to be the heirs to the Tang dynasty.

Moreover, because education and the examination system grew far more rapidly than the number of official positions, many who passed lower-level exams could not be accommodated with a bureaucratic appointment. Often, however, they were able to combine landowning and success in the examination system to maintain an immense cultural prestige and prominence in their local areas.

Underlying these cultural and political achievements was **China's economic revolution**, which made Song dynasty China "by far the richest, most skilled, and most populous country on earth."[5] The most obvious sign of China's prosperity was its rapid growth in population, which jumped from about 50 million or 60 million during the Tang dynasty to 120 million by 1200. Behind this doubling of the population were remarkable achievements in agricultural production, particularly the adoption of a fast-ripening and drought-resistant strain of rice from Vietnam.

Many people found their way to the cities, making China the most urbanized country in the world. Dozens of Chinese cities numbered over 100,000, while the Song dynasty capital of **Hangzhou** was home to more than a million people. A Chinese observer in 1235 provided a vivid description of that city.[6] Specialized markets abounded for meat, herbs, vegetables, books, rice, and much more, with troupes of actors performing for the crowds. Restaurants advertised their unique offerings, including pickled dates, juicy lungs, and pigs' feet. "Luxuriant inns," marked by red lanterns, featured prostitutes and "wine chambers equipped with beds." Specialized agencies managed elaborate dinner parties for the wealthy, complete with a Perfume and Medicine Office to "help sober up the guests." Schools for musicians offered thirteen different courses. Numerous clubs provided companionship for poets, fishermen, Buddhists, physical fitness enthusiasts, antique collectors, horse lovers, and many other groups. No wonder the Italian visitor Marco Polo described Hangzhou later in the thirteenth century as "beyond dispute the finest and noblest [city] in the world."[7]

Industrial production likewise soared. In both large-scale enterprises employing hundreds of workers and in smaller backyard furnaces, China's iron industry increased its output dramatically. By the eleventh century, it was providing the government with 32,000 suits of armor and 16 million iron arrowheads annually, in addition to supplying metal for coins, tools, construction, and bells in Buddhist monasteries. This industrial growth was fueled almost entirely by coal, which also came to provide most of the energy for heating homes and cooking and no doubt generated considerable air pollution. Technological innovation in other fields also flourished. Inventions in printing, both woodblock and movable type, generated the world's first printed books, and by 1000 relatively cheap books on religious,

Chinese Cities This detail comes from a huge watercolor scroll, titled *Upper River during Qing Ming Festival*, originally painted during the Song dynasty. It illustrates the urban sophistication of Chinese cities at that time and has been frequently imitated and copied since then. (Werner Forman/Getty Images)

agricultural, mathematical, and medical topics became widely available in China. Its navigational and shipbuilding technologies led the world. The Chinese invention of **gunpowder** created within a few centuries a revolution in military affairs that had global dimensions.

These innovations occurred within the world's most highly commercialized society, in which producing for the market, rather than for local consumption, became a very widespread phenomenon. An immense network of internal waterways stretching perhaps 30,000 miles — canals, rivers, and lakes — facilitated the cheap movement of goods, allowing peasants to grow specialized crops for sale while they purchased rice or other staples on the market. In addition, government demands for taxes paid in cash rather than in kind required peasants to sell something — their products or their labor — in order to meet their obligations. The growing use of paper money, as well as financial instruments such as letters of credit and promissory notes, further contributed to the commercialization of Chinese society. Two prominent scholars have described the outcome: "Output increased, population grew, skills multiplied, and a burst of inventiveness made Song China far wealthier than ever before — or than any of its contemporaries."[8]

Was Song dynasty China on the edge of an industrial revolution of the kind that occurred in Great Britain in the nineteenth century, as some historians have suggested? If so, it was a road not traveled, for China's remarkable economic and technological growth stalled, for reasons much debated. Prominent among those reasons were repeated and devastating invasions by nomadic peoples from the north, culminating in the Mongol conquests of the thirteenth century followed by the catastrophe of the Black Death in the fourteenth century.

Women in the Song Dynasty

The "golden age" of Song dynasty China was perhaps less than "golden" for many of its women, for that era marked yet another turning point in the history of Chinese patriarchy. Under the influence of steppe nomads, whose women led less restricted lives, elite Chinese women of the Tang dynasty era, at least in the north, had participated in social life with greater freedom than in earlier times. Paintings and statues show aristocratic women riding horses, while the Queen Mother of the West, a Daoist deity, was widely worshipped by female Daoist priests and practitioners. By the Song dynasty, however, a reviving Confucianism and rapid economic growth seemed to tighten patriarchal restrictions on women and to restore some of the earlier Han dynasty notions of female submission and passivity.

Once again, Confucian writers emphasized the subordination of women to men and the need to keep males and females separate in every domain of life. The Song dynasty historian and scholar Sima Guang (1019–1086) summed up the prevailing view: "The boy leads the girl, the girl follows the boy; the duty of husbands to be resolute and wives to be docile begins with this."[9] For men, masculinity came to be defined less in terms of horseback riding, athleticism, and the warrior values of northern nomads and more in terms of the refined pursuits of calligraphy, scholarship, painting, and poetry. Corresponding views of feminine qualities emphasized women's weakness, reticence, and delicacy. Women were also frequently viewed as a distraction to men's pursuit of a contemplative and introspective life. The remarriage of widows, though legally permissible, was increasingly condemned, for "to walk through two courtyards is a source of shame for a woman."[10]

The most compelling expression of a tightening patriarchy was **foot binding**. Apparently beginning among dancers and courtesans in the tenth or eleventh century C.E., this practice involved tightly wrapping young girls' feet, usually breaking the bones of the foot and causing intense pain. During and after the Song dynasty, foot binding found general acceptance among elite families and later became even more widespread in Chinese society. It was associated with new images of female beauty and eroticism that emphasized small size, frailty, and deference and served to keep women restricted to the "inner quarters," where Confucian tradition asserted that they belonged. Many mothers imposed this painful procedure on their daughters, perhaps to enhance their marriage prospects and to assist them in competing with concubines for the attention of their husbands.[11] For many women, it became a rite of passage, and their tiny feet and the beautiful slippers that encased them became a source of some pride, even a topic of poetry for some literate women. Foot binding also served to distinguish Chinese women from their "barbarian" counterparts and elite women from commoners and peasants.

Furthermore, a rapidly commercializing economy undermined the position of women in the textile industry. Urban workshops and state factories, run by men, increasingly took over the skilled tasks of weaving textiles, especially silk, which had previously been the work of rural women in their homes. Although these women continued to tend silkworms and spin silk thread, they had lost the more lucrative income-generating work of weaving silk fabrics. But as their economic role in textile production declined, other opportunities beckoned in an increasingly prosperous Song China. In the cities, women operated restaurants, sold fish and vegetables, and worked as maids, cooks, and dressmakers. The growing prosperity of elite families funneled increasing numbers of women into roles as concubines, entertainers, courtesans, and prostitutes. Their ready availability surely reduced the ability of wives to negotiate as equals with their husbands, setting women against one another and creating endless household jealousies.

In other ways, the Song dynasty witnessed more positive trends in the lives of women. Their property rights expanded, allowing women to control their own dowries and to inherit property from their families. "Neither in earlier nor in later periods," writes one scholar, "did as much property pass through women's hands" as during the Song dynasty.[12] Furthermore, lower-ranking but ambitious officials strongly urged the education of women, so that their wives might more effectively raise their sons and increase the family's fortune. Song dynasty China, in short, offered a mixture of tightening restrictions and new opportunities to its women.

China and the Northern Nomads: A Chinese World Order in the Making

Among China's various interactions with a larger Eurasian world, the most enduring and intense involved the many nomadic pastoral or semi-agricultural peoples of the steppes north of the Great Wall. Living in areas unable to sustain Chinese-style farming, these northern nomads had long focused their economies around the raising of livestock (sheep, cattle, goats) and the mastery of horse riding. Organized locally in small, mobile, kinship-based groups, these peoples also periodically created much larger and powerful states or confederations that could draw on the impressive horsemanship and military skills of virtually the entire male population of their societies. Such specialized pastoral societies needed grain and other agricultural products from China, and their leaders developed a taste for Chinese manufactured and luxury goods — wine and silk, for example — with which they could attract and reward followers. Thus the nomads were drawn like a magnet toward China, trading, raiding, and extorting to obtain the resources so vital to their way of life. For 2,000 years or more, pressure from the steppes and the intrusion of nomadic peoples were constant factors in China's historical development.

From the nomads' point of view, the threat often came from the Chinese, who periodically directed their own military forces deep into the steppes, built the Great Wall to keep the nomads out, and often proved unwilling to allow pastoral peoples easy access to trading opportunities within China. And yet the Chinese needed the nomads and especially their horses, which were essential for the Chinese military. Other products of the steppes and the forests beyond, such as skins, furs, hides, and amber, were also of value in China. Furthermore, pastoral nomads controlled much of the Silk Road trading network, which funneled goods from the West into China. The continuing interaction between China and the northern nomads brought together peoples occupying different environments, practicing different economies, governing themselves with different institutions, and thinking about the world in quite different ways.

The Tribute System in Theory

An enduring outcome of this cross-cultural encounter was a particular view the Chinese held of themselves and of their neighbors, fully articulated by the time of the Han dynasty (ca. 200 B.C.E.–200 C.E.) and lasting for more than two millennia. That understanding cast China as the "middle kingdom," the center of the world, infinitely superior to the "barbarian" peoples beyond its borders. With its long history, great cities, refined tastes, sophisticated intellectual and artistic achievements, bureaucratic state, literate elite, and prosperous economy, China represented "civilization." All of this, in Chinese thinking, was in sharp contrast to the rude cultures and primitive life of the northern nomads, who continually moved about "like beasts and birds," lived in tents, ate mostly meat and milk, and practically lived on their horses, while making war on everyone within reach. Educated Chinese saw their own society as self-sufficient, requiring little from the outside world, while barbarians, quite understandably, sought access to China's wealth and wisdom. Furthermore, China was willing to permit that access under controlled conditions, for its sense of superiority did not preclude the possibility that barbarians could become civilized Chinese. China was a "radiating civilization," graciously shedding its light most fully to nearby barbarians and with diminished intensity to those farther away.

That worldview also took shape as a practical system for managing China's relationship with its neighbors. Known as the **tribute system**, it was a set of practices that required non-Chinese authorities to acknowledge Chinese superiority and their own subordinate place in a Chinese-centered world order. Foreigners seeking access to China had to send a delegation to the Chinese court, where they would perform the kowtow, a series of ritual bowings and prostrations, and present their tribute—products of value from their countries—to the Chinese emperor. In return for these expressions of submission, he would grant permission for foreigners to trade in China's rich markets and would provide them with gifts or "bestowals," often worth far more than the tribute they had offered. This was the mechanism by which successive Chinese dynasties attempted to regulate their relationships with northern nomads; with neighboring states such as Korea, Vietnam, Tibet, and Japan; and, after 1500, with those European barbarians from across the sea.

   Often, this system seemed to work. Over the centuries, countless foreign delegations proved willing to present their tribute, say the required words, and perform the rituals necessary for gaining access to the material goods of China. Aspiring non-Chinese rulers also gained prestige as they basked in the reflected glory of even this subordinate association with the great Chinese civilization. The official titles, seals of office, and ceremonial robes they received from China proved useful in their local struggles for power.

The Tribute System This eighteenth-century Korean painting depicts a Korean diplomatic mission to Qing China approaching the city of Sanhaegwan on its way to offer tribute to the emperor in Beijing, 190 miles away. Such tribute missions offered opportunities for the Korean delegation to see something of China. According to diaries of Korean envoys, they categorized sites along the route to Beijing under such titles as historical, curiosity, or spectacle. (© Copyright The Korean Christian Museum at Soongsil University)

The Tribute System in Practice

But the tribute system also disguised some realities that contradicted its assumptions. On occasion, China was confronting not separate and small-scale barbarian societies, but large and powerful nomadic empires able to deal with China on at least equal terms. An early nomadic confederacy was the **Xiongnu Empire**, established about the same time as the Han dynasty (ca. 200 B.C.E.) and eventually reaching from Manchuria to Central Asia (see Map 3.5, page 85). Devastating Xiongnu raids into northern China persuaded the Chinese emperor to negotiate an arrangement that recognized the nomadic state as a political equal, promised its leader a princess in marriage, and, most important, agreed to supply him annually with large quantities of grain, wine, and silk. In return for these goods, so critical for the functioning of the nomadic state, the Xiongnu agreed to refrain from military incursions into China. The basic realities of the situation were summed up in this warning to the Han dynasty in the first century B.C.E.:

> Just make sure that the silks and grain stuffs you bring the Xiongnu are the right measure and quality, that's all. What's the need for talking? If the goods you deliver are up to measure and good quality, all right. But if there is any deficiency or the quality is no good, then when the autumn harvest comes, we will take our horses and trample all over your crops.[13]

Something similar occurred during the Tang dynasty as a series of Turkic empires arose in Mongolia. Like the Xiongnu, they too extorted large "gifts" from the Chinese. One of these peoples, the Uighurs, actually rescued the Tang dynasty from a serious internal revolt in the 750s. In return, the Uighur leader gained one of the Chinese emperor's daughters as a wife and arranged a highly favorable exchange of poor-quality horses for high-quality silk, which brought half a million rolls of the precious fabric annually into the Uighur lands. Despite the rhetoric of the tribute system, the Chinese were not always able to dictate the terms of their relationship with the northern nomads.

Steppe nomads were generally not much interested in actually conquering and ruling China. It was easier and more profitable to extort goods from a functioning Chinese state. On occasion, however, that state broke down and various nomadic groups moved in to "pick up the pieces," conquering and governing parts of China. Such a process took place following the fall of the Han dynasty and again after the collapse of the Tang dynasty, when the Khitan (kee-THAN) (907–1125) and then the Jin, or Jurchen (JER-chihn) (1115–1234), peoples established states that encompassed parts of China as well as major areas of the steppes to the north. Both of them required the Chinese Song dynasty, located farther south, to deliver annually huge quantities of silk, silver, and tea, some of which found its way into the Silk Road trading network. The practice of "bestowing gifts on barbarians," long a part of the tribute system, allowed the proud Chinese to imagine that they were still in control of the situation even as they were paying heavily for protection from nomadic incursion. Those gifts, in turn, provided vital economic resources to nomadic states.

Cultural Influence across an Ecological Frontier

When nomadic peoples actually ruled parts of China, some of them adopted Chinese ways, employing Chinese advisers, governing according to Chinese practice, and, at least for the elite, immersing themselves in Chinese culture and learning. This process of "becoming Chinese" went furthest among the Jurchen, many of whom lived in northern China and learned to speak Chinese, wore Chinese clothing, married Chinese husbands and wives, and practiced Buddhism or Daoism.

On the whole, however, Chinese culture had only a modest impact on the nomadic people of the northern steppes. Unlike the native peoples of southern China, who were gradually absorbed into Chinese culture, the pastoral societies north of the Great Wall generally retained their own cultural patterns. Few of them were incorporated, at least not for long, within a Chinese state, and most lived in areas where Chinese-style agriculture was simply impossible. Under these conditions, there were few incentives for adopting Chinese culture wholesale. But various modes of interaction—peaceful trade, military conflict, political negotiations, economic extortion, some cultural influence—continued across the ecological frontier that divided two quite distinct and separate ways of life. Each was necessary for the other.

On the Chinese side, elements of steppe culture had some influence in those parts of northern China that were periodically conquered and ruled by nomadic peoples. The founders of the Sui and Tang dynasties were in fact of mixed nomad and Chinese ancestry and came from the borderland region where a blended Chinese/Turkic culture had evolved. High-ranking members of the imperial family personally led their troops in battle in the style of Turkic warriors. Furthermore, Tang dynasty China was awash with foreign visitors from all over Asia—delegations bearing tribute, merchants carrying exotic goods, and bands of clerics or religious pilgrims bringing new religions such as Christianity, Islam, Buddhism, and Manichaeism. For a time in the Tang dynasty, almost anything associated with "Western barbarians"—Central Asians, Persians, Indians, Arabs—had great appeal among northern Chinese elites. Their music, dancing, clothing, foods, games, and artistic styles found favor among the upper classes. The more traditional southern Chinese, feeling themselves heir to the legacy of the Han dynasty, were sharply critical of their northern counterparts for allowing women too much freedom, for permitting them to use "Western makeup," for drinking yogurt rather than tea, and for listening to "Western" music, all of which they attributed to barbarian influence.

Interacting with China: Comparing Korea, Vietnam, and Japan

Also involved in tributary relationships with China were the newly emerging states and civilizations of Korea, Vietnam, and Japan. Unlike the northern nomads, these societies were thoroughly agricultural and sedentary. During the first millennium C.E., they were part of a larger process—the globalization of civilization—that produced new city- and state-based societies in various parts of the world. Proximity to their giant Chinese neighbor decisively shaped the histories of these new East Asian civilizations, for all of them borrowed major elements of Chinese culture. But unlike the native peoples of southern China, who largely became Chinese, the peoples of Korea, Vietnam, and Japan did not. They retained distinctive identities that have lasted to the present. But while resisting Chinese political domination, they also appreciated Chinese culture and sought the source of Chinese wealth and power. In so doing, Korea, Vietnam, and Japan responded to China in quite different ways.

Korea and China

Immediately adjacent to northeastern China, the Korean peninsula and its people have long lived in close proximity to their much larger neighbor (see Map 8.2). Temporary Chinese conquest of northern Korea during the Han dynasty and some colonization by Chinese settlers provided an initial channel for Chinese cultural influence, particularly in the form of Buddhism. Early Korean states emerged in the first century B.C.E. and reached their most powerful and sophisticated forms between the fourth and seventh centuries C.E.; all referred to their rulers with the Chinese term *wang* (king). Bitter rivals with one another, they also strenuously resisted Chinese political control, except when they found it advantageous to join with China against a local enemy. In the seventh century, one of these states—the **Silla** (SHEE-lah) **kingdom**—allied with Tang dynasty China to bring some political unity to the peninsula for the first time, founding what is known as the Unified Silla Kingdom. But Chinese efforts to set up puppet regimes and to assimilate Koreans to Chinese culture provoked sharp military resistance, persuading the Chinese to withdraw their military forces in 688 and to establish a tributary relationship with a largely independent Korea.

MAP 8.2 Korean Kingdoms, ca. 500 C.E.
The three early kingdoms of Korea were brought together by the seventh century in a unified state that was later governed by a series of dynastic regimes.

Under a succession of dynasties — the Unified Silla (688–900), Koryo (918–1392), and Joseon (1392–1910) — Korea generally maintained its political independence while participating in China's tribute system. Its leaders actively embraced the connection with China and, especially during the Silla dynasty, sought to turn their small state into a miniature version of Tang China.

Tribute missions to China provided legitimacy for Korean rulers and models of court life and administrative techniques, which they sought to replicate back home. A new capital city of Kumsong was modeled directly on the Chinese capital of Chang'an. Missions also enabled both official and private trade, mostly in luxury goods such as ceremonial clothing, silks, Confucian and Buddhist texts, and artwork. All of this enriched the lives of a Korean aristocracy that was becoming increasingly Chinese in culture. Thousands of Korean students were sent to China, where they studied primarily Confucianism but also the sciences and the arts. Buddhist monks visited centers of learning and pilgrimage in China and brought back popular forms of Chinese Buddhism, which quickly took root in Korea. Schools for the study of Confucianism, using texts in the Chinese language, were established in Korea (see the image on page 101). In these ways, Korea became a part of the expanding world of Chinese culture, and refugees from the peninsula's many wars carried Chinese culture to Japan as well.

These efforts to plant Confucian values and Chinese culture in Korea had what one scholar has called an "overwhelmingly negative" impact on Korean women, particularly after 1300.[14] Early Chinese observers noticed, and strongly disapproved of, free-choice marriages in Korea, as well as the practice of women singing and dancing together late at night. With the support of the Korean court, Chinese models of family life and female behavior, especially among the elite, gradually replaced the more flexible Korean patterns. Earlier, a Korean woman had generally given birth and raised her young children in her parents' home, where she was often joined by her husband. This was now strongly discouraged, for Confucian orthodoxy demanded that a married woman belonged to her husband's family. Other Korean customs — funeral rites in which a husband was buried in the sacred plot of his wife's family, the remarriage of widowed or divorced women, and female inheritance of property — also eroded under the pressure of Confucian orthodoxy. So too did the practice of plural marriages for men. In 1413, a legal distinction between primary and secondary wives required men to identify one of their wives as primary. Because she and her children now had special privileges and status, sharp new tensions emerged within families. Korean restrictions on elite women, especially widows, came to exceed even those in China itself.

Still, Korea remained Korean. After 688, the country's political independence, though periodically threatened, was largely intact. Chinese cultural influence, except for Buddhism, had little impact beyond the aristocracy and certainly did not penetrate the lives of Korea's serf-like peasants. Nor did it register among Korea's many enslaved people, who constituted about one-third of the country's population by 1100. In fact, Korean Buddhist monasteries used enslaved people to cultivate their lands. A Chinese-style examination system to recruit government officials, though encouraged by some Korean rulers, never assumed the prominence that it gained in Tang and Song dynasty China. Korea's aristocratic class was able to maintain an even stronger monopoly on bureaucratic office than its Chinese counterpart did. And in the mid-1400s, Korea moved toward greater cultural independence by developing a phonetic alphabet, known as ***hangul*** (HAHN-gool), for writing the Korean language. Although resisted by conservative male elites, who were long accustomed to using the more prestigious Chinese characters to write Korean, this new form of writing gradually took hold, especially in private correspondence, in popular fiction, and among women. Clearly part of the Chinese world order, Korea nonetheless retained a distinctive culture as well as a separate political existence.

Vietnam and China

At the southern fringe of the Chinese cultural world, the people who eventually came to be called Vietnamese had a broadly similar historical encounter with China (see Map 8.3). As in Korea, the elite culture of Vietnam borrowed heavily from China—adopting Confucianism, Daoism, Buddhism, administrative techniques, the examination system, and artistic and literary styles—even as its popular culture

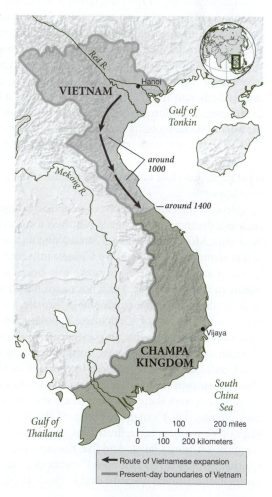

MAP 8.3 Vietnam
As Vietnam threw off Chinese control, it also expanded to the south, while remaining wary of its larger Chinese neighbor to the north.

Red R.

Hanoi

VIETNAM

Gulf of Tonkin

around 1000

—*around 1400*

Mekong R.

Vijaya

CHAMPA KINGDOM

South China Sea

Gulf of Thailand

0   100   200 miles

0   100   200 kilometers

← Route of Vietnamese expansion

— Present-day boundaries of Vietnam

remained distinctive. And, like Korea, Vietnam achieved political independence while participating fully in the tribute system as a vassal state.

Unlike Korea, however, the cultural heartland of Vietnam in the Red River valley was fully incorporated into the Chinese state for more than a thousand years (111 B.C.E.–939 C.E.). Regarded by the Chinese as "southern barbarians," the Vietnamese were ruled by Chinese officials who expected to fully assimilate this rich rice-growing region into China culturally as well as politically. To these officials, it was simply a further extension of the southward movement of Chinese civilization. Thus Chinese-style irrigated agriculture was introduced; Vietnamese elites were brought into the local bureaucracy and educated in Confucian-based schools; Chinese replaced the local language in official business; Chinese clothing and hairstyles became mandatory; and large numbers of Chinese, some fleeing internal conflicts at home, flooded into the relative security of what they referred to as "the pacified south," while often despising the local people. The heavy pressure of the Chinese presence generated not only a Vietnamese elite thoroughly schooled in Chinese culture but also periodic rebellions, on several occasions led by women.

The weakening of the Tang dynasty in the early tenth century C.E. finally enabled a particularly large rebellion to establish Vietnam as a separate state, though one that carefully maintained its tributary role, sending repeated missions to do homage at the Chinese court. Nonetheless, successive Vietnamese dynasties found the Chinese approach to government useful, styling their rulers as emperors, claiming the Mandate of Heaven, and making use of Chinese court rituals, while expanding their state steadily southward. More so than in Korea, a Chinese-based examination system in Vietnam functioned to undermine an established aristocracy, to provide some measure of social mobility for commoners, and to create a merit-based scholar-gentry class to staff the bureaucracy. Furthermore, members of the Vietnamese elite class remained deeply committed to Chinese culture, viewing their own country less as a separate nation than as a southern extension of a universal civilization, the only one they knew.

Beyond the elite, however, there remained much that was uniquely Vietnamese, such as a distinctive language, a fondness for cockfighting, and the habit of chewing betel nuts. More importantly, Vietnam long retained a greater role for women in social and economic life, despite heavy Chinese influence. In the third century C.E., a woman leader of an anti-Chinese resistance movement declared: "I want to drive away the enemy to save our people. I will not resign myself to the usual lot of women who bow their heads and become concubines." Female nature deities and a "female Buddha" continued to be part of Vietnamese popular religion, even as Confucian-based ideas took root among the elite. In the centuries following independence from China, as Vietnam expanded to the south, northern officials tried in vain to impose more orthodox Confucian gender practices in place of local customs that allowed women to choose their own husbands and married men to live in the households of their wives. So persistent were these practices that a seventeenth-century Chinese visitor opined, with disgust, that Vietnamese preferred the birth of a girl to that of a boy. These features of Vietnamese life reflected larger patterns of Southeast Asian culture that distinguished it from China. And like Koreans, the Vietnamese developed a variation of Chinese writing called **chu nom** ("southern script"), which provided the basis for an independent national literature and a vehicle for the writing of most educated women.

Vietnam after Independence This painted scroll in the Chinese style was created in Vietnam and dates from the fourteenth or fifteenth century. It depicts the triumphant return of a government official to his native village after passing his civil service exams. He rides atop an elephant, while people gather to play instruments to welcome him. Both the painting's style and its subject, the passing of civil service exams, reflect the deep influence of Chinese cultural and political traditions on Vietnamese society. (Werner Forman Archive/Bridgeman Images)

Japan and China

Unlike Korea and Vietnam, the Japanese islands were physically separated from China by 100 miles or more of ocean and were never successfully invaded or conquered by their giant mainland neighbor (see Map 8.4). Thus Japan's very extensive borrowing from Chinese civilization was wholly voluntary, rather than occurring under conditions of direct military threat or outright occupation. The high point of that borrowing took place during the seventh to the ninth centuries C.E., as the first more or less unified Japanese state began to emerge from dozens of small clan-based aristocratic chiefdoms. That state found much that was useful in Tang dynasty China and set out, deliberately and systematically, to transform Japan into a centralized bureaucratic state on the Chinese model.

The initial leader of this effort was **Shotoku Taishi** (572–622), a prominent aristocrat from one of the major clans. He launched a series of large-scale missions to China that took hundreds of Japanese monks, scholars, artists, and students to the mainland. In 604 C.E. Shotoku issued the Seventeen Article Constitution, proclaiming the Japanese ruler a Chinese-style emperor and encouraging both Buddhism and Confucianism. In good Confucian fashion, that document emphasized the moral quality of rulers as a foundation for social harmony. In the decades that followed, Japanese authorities adopted Chinese-style court rituals as well as the Chinese calendar. Later, they likewise established Chinese-based taxation systems, law codes, government ministries, and a provincial administration, at least on paper. Two capital cities, first Nara and then Heian-kyo (Kyoto), were both modeled on the Chinese capital of Chang'an.

MAP 8.4 Japan
Japan's distance from China enabled it to maintain its political independence and to draw selectively from Chinese culture.

Chinese culture, no less than its political practices, also found favor in Japan. Various schools of Chinese Buddhism took root, first among the educated and literate classes and later more broadly in Japanese society. Buddhism deeply affected Japanese art, architecture, education, medicine, views of the afterlife, and attitudes toward suffering and the impermanence of life. The Chinese writing system—and with it an interest in historical writing, calligraphy, and poetry—likewise proved attractive among the elite.

The absence of any compelling threat from China made it possible for the Japanese to be selective in their borrowing. By the tenth century, deliberate efforts to absorb additional elements of Chinese culture diminished, and formal tribute missions to China stopped, although private traders and Buddhist monks continued to make the difficult journey to the mainland. Over many centuries, the Japanese combined what they had assimilated from China with elements of their own tradition into a distinctive Japanese civilization.

In the political realm, for example, the Japanese never succeeded in creating an effective centralized and bureaucratic state to match that of China. Although the court and the emperor retained an important ceremonial and cultural role, their real political authority over the country gradually diminished in favor of competing aristocratic families, both at court and in the provinces. As political power became increasingly decentralized, local authorities developed their own military forces, the famous *samurai* warrior class of Japanese society. Bearing their exquisite curved swords, the samurai developed a distinctive set of values featuring bravery, loyalty, endurance, honor, great skill in martial arts, and a preference for death over surrender. This was ***bushido*** (boo-shee-doh), the way of the warrior. Japan's celebration of the samurai and of military virtues contrasted sharply with China's emphasis on intellectual achievements and political office holding, which were accorded higher prestige than bearing arms. "The educated men of the land," wrote a Chinese minister in the eleventh century, "regard the carrying of arms as a disgrace."[15] The Japanese, clearly, did not agree.

Religiously as well, Japan remained distinctive. Although Buddhism in many forms took hold in the country, it never completely replaced the native beliefs and practices, which focused attention on numerous *kami*, sacred spirits associated with human ancestors and various natural phenomena. Much later referred to as Shinto, this tradition provided legitimacy to the imperial family, based on claims of descent from the sun goddess. Because veneration of the kami lacked an elaborate philosophy or ritual, it conflicted very little with Buddhism. In fact, numerous kami were assimilated into Japanese Buddhism as local expressions of Buddhist deities or principles.

Japanese literary and artistic culture likewise evolved in distinctive ways, despite much borrowing from China. As in Korea and Vietnam, there emerged a unique writing system that combined Chinese characters with a series of phonetic symbols. A highly stylized Japanese poetic form, known as tanka, developed early and has remained a favored means of expression ever since. Particularly during the Heian period of Japanese history (794–1185), a highly refined aesthetic culture found expression at the imperial court, even as the court's real political authority melted away. Court aristocrats and their ladies lived in splendor, composed poems, arranged flowers, and conducted their love affairs. "What counted," wrote one scholar, "was the proper costume, the right ceremonial act, the successful turn of phrase in a poem, and the appropriate expression of refined taste."[16] Much of our knowledge of this courtly culture comes from the work of women writers, who composed their diaries and novels in the vernacular Japanese script rather than in the classical Chinese used by elite men. *The Tale of Genji*, a Japanese novel written by the woman author Murasaki Shikibu around 1000, provides an intimate picture of the intrigues and romances of court life.

At this level of society, Japan's women, unlike those in Korea, largely escaped the more oppressive features of Chinese Confucian culture, such as the prohibition of remarriage for widows and seclusion within the home. Perhaps this is because the most powerful Chinese influence on Japan occurred during the Tang dynasty, when Chinese elite women enjoyed considerable freedom. Japanese women continued to inherit property; Japanese married couples often lived apart or with the wife's family; and marriages were made and broken easily. None of this corresponded to Confucian values. When Japanese women did begin to lose status in the twelfth century and later, it had less to do with Confucian pressures than with the rise of a warrior culture. As the personal relationships of samurai warriors to their lords replaced marriage alliances as a political strategy, the influence of women in political life was reduced, but this was an internal Japanese phenomenon, not a reflection of Chinese influence.

Japan's ability to borrow extensively from China while developing its own distinctive civilization perhaps provided a model for its encounter with the West in the nineteenth century. Then, as before, Japan borrowed selectively from a foreign culture without losing either its political independence or its cultural uniqueness.

Lady Murasaki Shikibu Lady Murasaki Shikibu drew on her experience as a lady-in-waiting at the imperial court to craft her famous novel, *The Tale of Genji*. She allegedly began to write the novel in 1004 at the Buddhist temple of Ishiyama-dera under the inspiration of a full moon, as depicted in this eighteenth-century woodblock print. (Pictures from History/ Bridgeman Images)

China and the Eurasian World Economy

Beyond China's central role in East Asia was its economic interaction with the wider world of Eurasia generally. On the one hand, China's remarkable economic growth, taking place during the Tang and Song dynasties, could hardly be contained within China's borders and clearly had a major impact throughout Eurasia. On the other hand, China was recipient as well as donor in the economic interactions of the third-wave era, and its own economic achievements owed something to the stimulus of contact with the larger world.

Spillovers: China's Impact on Eurasia

One of the outcomes of China's economic revolution was the diffusion of its many technological innovations to peoples and places far from East Asia. (See Snapshot, page 237, for a wider view of Chinese technological achievements.) Papermaking, known in China since the Han dynasty, spread to Korea and Vietnam by the fourth century c.e., to Japan and India by the seventh, to the Islamic world by the eighth, to Muslim Spain by 1150, to France and Germany in the 1300s, and to England in the 1490s. Printing, likewise a Chinese invention, rapidly reached Korea, where movable type became a highly developed technique, and Japan as well. Both technologies were heavily influenced by Buddhism, which accorded religious merit to the reproduction of sacred texts. The Islamic world, however, highly valued handwritten calligraphy and generally resisted printing as impious until the nineteenth century. The adoption of printing in Europe was likewise delayed because of the absence of paper until the twelfth century. Then movable type was reinvented by Johannes Gutenberg in the fifteenth century, although it is unclear whether he was aware of Chinese and Korean precedents. With implications for mass literacy, bureaucracy, scholarship, the spread of religion, and the exchange of information, papermaking and printing were Chinese innovations of revolutionary and global dimensions.

Chinese technologies were seldom simply transferred from one place to another. More often, a particular Chinese technique or product stimulated innovations in more distant lands in accordance with local needs.[17] For example, as the Chinese formula for gunpowder, invented in the ninth century, became available in Europe, together with some early and simple firearms, these innovations triggered the development of cannons in the early fourteenth century. Soon cannons appeared in the Islamic world, and by the 1350s they were commonly used in China itself, which first used cast iron rather than bronze in their construction. But the highly competitive European state system drove the "gunpowder revolution" much further and more rapidly than in China's imperial state. Chinese textile, metallurgical, and naval technologies such as the magnetic compass likewise stimulated imitation and innovation all across Eurasia.

SNAPSHOT   CHINESE TECHNOLOGICAL ACHIEVEMENTS

Before the technological explosion of the European Industrial Revolution during the eighteenth and nineteenth centuries, China had long been the major center of global technological innovation. Many of those inventions spread to other civilizations, where they stimulated imitation or modification. Since Europe was located at the opposite end of the Eurasian continent from China, it often took considerable time for those innovations to give rise to something similar in the West. That lag is also a measure of the relative technological development of the two civilizations in premodern times.

Innovation	First Used in China (approximate)	Adoption/Recognition in the West: Time Lag in Years (approximate)
Iron plow	6th–4th century B.C.E.	2,000+
Cast iron	4th century B.C.E.	1,000–1,200
Efficient horse collar	3rd–1st century B.C.E.	1,000
Paper	2nd century B.C.E.	1,000
Wheelbarrow	1st century B.C.E.	900–1,000
Rudder for steering ships	1st century C.E.	1,100
Iron chain suspension bridge	1st century C.E.	1,000–1,300
Porcelain	3rd century C.E.	1,500
Magnetic compass for navigation	9th–11th century C.E.	400
Gunpowder	9th century C.E.	400
Chain drive for transmission of power	976 C.E.	800
Movable type printing	1045 C.E.	400

Source: Joseph Needham, *Science and Civilization in China* (Cambridge: Cambridge University Press, 1965), 1:242; Robert Temple, *The Genius of China* (New York: Simon and Schuster, 1986).

In addition to its technological influence, China's prosperity during the Song dynasty greatly stimulated commercial life and market-based behavior all across the Afro-Eurasian trading world. China's products — silk, porcelain, lacquerware — found eager buyers from Japan to East Africa, and everywhere in between. The immense size and wealth of China's domestic economy also provided a ready market for hundreds of commodities from afar. For example, the lives of many thousands of people in the spice-producing islands of what is now Indonesia were transformed as they came to depend on Chinese consumers' demand for their products. "One hundred million [Chinese] people," wrote historian William McNeill, "increasingly caught up within a commercial network, buying and selling to supplement every day's livelihood, made a significant difference to the way other human beings made their livings throughout a large part of the civilized world."[18] Such was the ripple effect of China's economic revolution.

On the Receiving End: China as Economic Beneficiary

But Chinese interaction with the wider world was not a one-way street, for China too was changed by its engagement with other parts of Eurasia. During the third-wave era, for example, China had learned about the cultivation and processing of both cotton and sugar from India. From Vietnam, around 1000, China gained access to the new, fast-ripening, and drought-resistant strains of rice that made a highly productive rice-based agriculture possible in the drier and more rugged regions of southern China. This marked a major turning point in Chinese history, as the frontier region south of the Yangzi River grew rapidly in population, over-taking the traditional centers of Chinese civilization in the north. In the process, the many non-Chinese peoples of the area were painfully overwhelmed by Chinese military forces and by the migration of at least a million Han Chinese farmers by 1400.

Technologically as well, China's extraordinary burst of creativity owed something to the stimulus of cross-cultural contact. Awareness of Persian windmills, for example, spurred the development of a distinct but related device in China. Printing arose from China's growing involvement with the world of Buddhism, which put a spiritual premium on the reproduction of the Buddha's image and of short religious texts that were carried as charms. It was in Buddhist monasteries during the Tang dynasty that the long-established practice of printing with seals was elaborated by Chinese monks into woodblock printing. The first printed book, in 868 C.E., was a famous Buddhist text, the *Diamond Sutra*.

A further transforming impact of China's involvement with a wider world derived from its growing participation in Indian Ocean trade. By the Tang dynasty, thousands of ships annually visited the ports of southern China, and settled communities of foreign merchants — Arabs, Persians, Indians, Southeast Asians — turned some of these cities into cosmopolitan centers. Buddhist temples, Muslim mosques and cemeteries, and Hindu phallic sculptures graced the skyline of Quanzhou, a coastal city in southern China. Occasionally the tensions of cultural diversity erupted in violence, such as the massacre of tens of thousands of foreigners in Canton during the 870s when Chinese rebel forces sacked the city. Indian Ocean commerce also contributed much to the transformation of southern China from a subsistence economy to one more heavily based on producing for export. In the process, merchants achieved a degree of social acceptance not known before, including their frequent appointment to high-ranking bureaucratic positions. Finally, much-beloved stories of the monkey god, widely popular even in contemporary China, derived from Indian sources transmitted by Indian Ocean commerce.

China and Buddhism

By far the most important gift that China received from India was neither cotton nor sugar, but a religion, Buddhism. Until the adoption of Marxism in the twentieth century, Buddhism was the only large-scale cultural borrowing in Chinese history. It also made China into a launching pad for Buddhism's dispersion to Korea and from there to Japan as well (see Map 8.5).

Making Buddhism Chinese

Buddhism initially entered China via the Silk Road trading network during the first and second centuries C.E. The stability and prosperity of the Han dynasty, then at its height, ensured that the new "barbarian" religion held little appeal for native Chinese. Furthermore, the Indian culture from which Buddhism sprang was at odds with Chinese understandings of the world in many ways. Buddhism's commitment to a secluded and monastic life for monks and nuns seemed to dishonor Chinese family values, and its concern for individual salvation or enlightenment appeared selfish, contradicting the social orientation of Confucian thinking. Furthermore, the Buddhist concept of infinite eons of time, endlessly repeating themselves, was quite a stretch for the Chinese, who normally thought in terms of finite family generations or dynastic cycles. No wonder that for the first several centuries C.E., Buddhism was largely the preserve of foreign merchants and monks living in China.

In the half millennium between roughly 300 and 800 C.E., however, Buddhism took solid root in China within both elite and popular culture, becoming a permanent, though fluctuating, presence in Chinese life. It began, arguably, with the collapse of the Han dynasty around 200 C.E. The chaotic, violent, and politically fragmented centuries that followed seriously discredited Confucianism and opened the door to alternative understandings of the world. Nomadic rulers, now governing much of northern China, found Buddhism useful in part because it was foreign. "We were born out of the marches [beyond the realm of Chinese culture]," declared one of them, "and though we are unworthy, we have complied with our appointed destiny and govern the Chinese as their prince. . . . Buddha being a barbarian god is the very one we should worship."[19] Rulers and elite families provided patronage for Buddhist monasteries, temples, and works of art. In southern China, where many northern aristocrats had fled following the disastrous decline of the Han dynasty, Buddhism provided some comfort in the face of a collapsing society. Its emphasis on ritual, morality, and contemplation represented an intellectually and aesthetically satisfying response to times that were so clearly out of joint.

Meanwhile, Buddhist monasteries increasingly provided an array of services for ordinary people. In them, travelers found accommodation; those fleeing from China's many upheavals discovered a place of refuge; desperate people received charity;

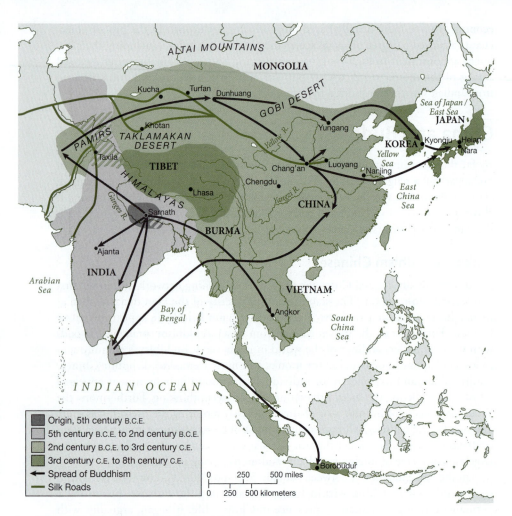

MAP 8.5   The World of Asian Buddhism
Originating in India, Buddhism later spread widely throughout much of Asia to provide a measure of cultural or religious commonality across this vast region.

farmers borrowed seed for the next planting; the sick were treated; and children learned to read. And for many, Buddhism was associated with access to magical powers as reports of miracles abounded. Battles were won, rain descended on drought-ridden areas, diseases were cured, and guilt was relieved—all through the magical ministrations of charismatic monks.

Accompanying all of this was a serious effort by monks, scholars, and translators to present this Indian religion in terms that Chinese could more readily grasp. Thus the Buddhist term *dharma*, referring to the Buddha's teaching, was translated as *dao*, or "the way," a notion long familiar in both Daoist and Confucian thinking. The Buddhist notion of "morality" was rendered with the Confucian term that referred to "filial submission and obedience." Some Indian concepts were modified in the process of translation. For example, the idea that "husband supports wife," which reflected a considerable respect for women and mothers in early Indian Buddhism, became in translation "husband controls wife."[20]

As Buddhism took hold in China, it was primarily in its broader Mahayana form — complete with numerous deities, the veneration of relics, many heavens and hells, and bodhisattvas to aid the faithful — rather than its more psychological and individualistic Theravada form (see "The Buddhist Challenge" in Chapter 4). One of the most popular expressions of Buddhism in China was the Pure Land School, in which faithfully repeating the name of an earlier Buddha, the Amitabha, was sufficient to ensure rebirth in a beautifully described heavenly realm, the Pure Land. In its emphasis on salvation by faith, without arduous study or intensive meditation, Pure Land Buddhism became a highly popular and authentically Chinese version of the Indian faith.

China's reunification under the Sui and early Tang dynasties witnessed growing state support for Buddhism. The Sui emperor Wendi (r. 581–604 C.E.) had monasteries constructed at the base of China's five sacred mountains, further identifying the imported religion with traditional Chinese culture. He even used Buddhism to justify his military campaigns. "With a hundred victories in a hundred battles," he declared, "we promote the practice of the ten Buddhist virtues."[21] By 600 C.E., some 4,000 monasteries had been established. With state support and growing popular acceptance, they became centers of great wealth. They were largely exempt from taxation and owned large estates; ran businesses such as oil presses, water mills, and pawn shops; collected gems, gold, and lavish works of art; and employed millions of enslaved people, serfs, and other unfree and dependent workers. But Buddhism never achieved the independence from state authorities that the Christian Church acquired in Europe. The examinations for becoming a monk were supervised by the state, and education in the monasteries included the required study of the Confucian classics. In the mid-ninth century, the state showed quite dramatically just how much control it could exercise over the Buddhist establishment.

Losing State Support: The Crisis of Chinese Buddhism

The impressive growth of **Chinese Buddhism** was accompanied by a persistent undercurrent of resistance and criticism. Some saw the Buddhist establishment, at least potentially, as a "state within a state" and a challenge to imperial authority. More important was a deepening resentment of its enormous wealth. One fifth-century critic, referring to monks, put the issue squarely: "Why is it that their ideals are noble and far-reaching and their activities still are base and common? [They] become merchants and engage in barter, wrangling with the masses for profit."[22] Nor did the environmental impact of Buddhist monasteries escape the notice of state officials. In 707 C.E., one such official wrote: "Extensive construction of monasteries are undertaken and large mansions are built. Even though for such works trees are felled to the point of stripping the mountains, it does not suffice. . . . Though earth is moved to the point of obstructing roads, it does not suffice."[23] When state treasuries were short of funds, government officials cast a covetous eye on these wealthy and tax-exempt monasteries. Furthermore, Buddhism was clearly of foreign origin and offensive for that reason to some Confucian and Daoist thinkers. The celibacy of the monks and their withdrawal from society, the critics argued, undermined the Confucian-based family system of Chinese tradition.

Such criticisms took on new meaning in the changed environment of China after about 800 C.E. Following centuries of considerable foreign influence in China, a growing resentment against foreign culture, particularly among the literate classes, increasingly took hold. The turning point may well have been the An Lushan rebellion (755–763), in which a general of foreign origin led a major revolt against the Tang dynasty. Whatever its origin, an increasingly xenophobic reaction set in among the upper classes, reflected in a desire to return to an imagined "purity" of earlier times. In this setting, the old criticisms of Buddhism became more sharply focused. In 819, Han Yu, a leading figure in the Confucian counterattack on Buddhism, wrote a scathing memorial to the emperor criticizing his willingness to honor a relic of the Buddha's finger.

> Now the Buddha was of barbarian origin. His language differed from Chinese speech; his clothes were of a different cut; his mouth did not pronounce the prescribed words of the Former Kings. . . . He did not recognize the relationship between prince and subject, nor the sentiments of father and son. . . . I pray that Your Majesty will turn this bone over to the officials that it may be cast into water or fire.[24]

Several decades later, the Chinese state took direct action against the Buddhist establishment as well as against other foreign religions. A series of imperial decrees between 841 and 845 ordered some 260,000 monks and nuns to return to normal life as tax-paying citizens. Thousands of monasteries, temples, and shrines were either destroyed or turned to public use, while the state confiscated the lands, money, metals, and serfs belonging to monasteries. Buddhists were now forbidden to use gold, silver, copper, iron, and gems in constructing their images. These actions dealt a serious blow to Chinese Buddhism. Its scholars and monks were scattered, its creativity was diminished, and its institutions came even more firmly under state control.

Despite this persecution, Buddhism did not vanish from China. At the level of elite culture, its philosophical ideas played a role in the reformulation of Confucian thinking that took place during the Song dynasty. At the village level, Buddhism became one element of Chinese popular religion, which also included the veneration of ancestors, the honoring of Confucius, and Daoist shrines and rituals. Temples frequently included statues of Confucius, Laozi, and the Buddha, with little sense of any incompatibility among them. "Every black-haired son of Han," the Chinese have long said, "wears a Confucian thinking cap, a Daoist robe, and Buddhist sandals." Unlike in Europe, where an immigrant religion triumphed over and excluded all other faiths, Buddhism in China became assimilated into Chinese culture alongside its other traditions.

Conclusions and Reflections: Pondering Change in China

"Change" is perhaps the central focus of all historical study — identifying it, explaining it, and sometimes evaluating it. Certainly there was change aplenty in China during the third-wave era. After centuries of political fragmentation, the empire reunited, though several dynasties collapsed and were replaced by new ones. China's population grew substantially, and many moved to its growing cities or migrated to the south. Its economy became much more commercialized amid considerable technological innovation. The lives of women surely changed as foot binding became more widespread and as men increasingly took over the weaving of textiles. Culturally, too, China changed as Buddhism took hold, though by the ninth century the state sharply restricted the activities of the Buddhist establishment.

Nor did China's interaction with its neighbors remain static. Relationships with northern pastoral peoples, "barbarians" to the Chinese, fluctuated between war and more peaceful encounters. On occasion those peoples invaded China and actually governed its northern regions. Furthermore, Chinese intervention in Korea prompted strong military resistance that forced Chinese withdrawal in 688 c.e. And after conquering and ruling parts of Vietnam for 1,000 years, China lost political control of the region in 939 c.e. In both cases, however, these neighboring states continued to participate in China's tribute system and to selectively embrace elements of Chinese culture.

Explaining why change occurred is often a more controversial matter than simply identifying what changed. Sometimes historians focus on sources of change operating within particular societies. China's technological achievements, its flourishing economy, its long-standing bureaucratic traditions, and its sophisticated network of canals and waterways help to explain the remarkable continuity of Chinese civilization and its extended periods of internal unity and stability. But the massive inequalities of Chinese society generated the peasant upheavals that periodically shattered that unity and led to new ruling dynasties.

World historians are often inclined to find the primary source of change in contact with strangers, in external connections and interactions, whether direct or indirect. For example, conceptions of China as the "middle kingdom," infinitely superior to all surrounding societies, grew out of centuries of involvement with its "barbarian" neighbors. The greater freedom of women in those societies had some influence on Chinese women, especially during the Tang dynasty. And Chinese power and prestige in East Asia became a source of important cultural changes in Vietnam, Korea, and Japan, though each of these states retained its separate identity.

China's engagement with the wider world also helps to explain its remarkable economic growth, especially during the Song dynasty. Chinese farmers adopted new strains of rice from Vietnam and learned about cultivating cotton and sugar from India, even as demand for Chinese products from both Indian Ocean and Silk Road commercial networks stimulated the Chinese economy. But repeated foreign invasions from the north, especially that of the Mongols in the thirteenth century, may well have contributed to stalling that period of economic and technological growth.

Even more controversial than explaining change is any attempt to evaluate it. Many scholars, for example, have judged the Tang and Song dynasties as a "golden age" of Chinese history, based largely on China's remarkable cultural achievements in arts and literature as well as its economic growth and technological creativity. But "golden" for whom? What about Chinese women subjected to foot binding or forbidden to remarry after the death of a husband? And how much of the prosperity of the "golden age" filtered down to the masses of rural peasants? The twelfth-century Song dynasty writer Fan Chengda offered a different evaluation: "I'm a hired man now, always hungry; I'll never be able to pay the rice tax this year! . . . I sold my clothes to pay the tax. . . . My second daughter got engaged this year, but I'll have to sell her too, for bushels and pecks."[25]

So should historians be in the business of evaluating the changes they identify and seek to explain? Is it even possible to avoid doing so? If evaluate we must, what standards should we use? Do the values of our own times provide appropriate criteria for making judgments about the distant past? These are among the questions that historians everywhere confront.

Revisiting Chapter 8

REVISITING SPECIFICS

Sui dynasty, 220
Tang dynasty, 220
Song dynasty, 220
China's economic revolution, 221
Hangzhou, 222
gunpowder, 223
foot binding, 224
tribute system, 225

Xiongnu Empire, 227
Silla kingdom, 229
hangul, 231
chu nom, 232
Shotoku Taishi, 233
bushido, 234
Chinese Buddhism, 241

REVISITING CORE IDEAS

1. **Making Judgments** Why are the centuries of the Tang and Song dynasties in China sometimes referred to as a golden age?

2. **Exploring Cross-Cultural Encounters** How did the Chinese and their nomadic neighbors to the north view and interact with each other?

3. **Comparing China's Influence** In what different ways did Korea, Vietnam, Japan, and northern nomads experience and respond to Chinese power and culture?

4. **Describing Connections** In what ways did China participate in the world of Eurasian commerce and exchange, and with what outcomes?

5. **Analyzing Buddhism's Reception** How might you explain both the appeal of Buddhism in China and opposition to it?

A WIDER VIEW

1. How did China influence the world of the third-wave era? How was China itself transformed by its encounters with the wider world?

2. How might China's position in the world during the Tang and Song dynasty era compare to its emerging role in global affairs in the twenty-first century?

3. Is the term "golden age" an appropriate description of China during the Tang and Song dynasties? Why or why not?

4. Looking Back In what ways did Tang and Song dynasty China resemble the earlier Han dynasty period, and in what ways had China changed?

CHRONOLOGY

200 B.C.E.–200 C.E.	• Xiongnu Empire
300–800 C.E.	• Buddhism takes root in China
581–618	• Sui dynasty: reunification of China
604	• Shotoku Taishi issues Seventeen Article Constitution in Japan
618–907	• Tang dynasty: more freedom for elite women
688	• Founding of Unified Silla Kingdom (Korea)
750s	• Uighurs assist Tang dynasty rulers in suppressing rebellion
794–1185	• Heian period in Japanese history: highly refined court life
841–845	• Suppression of Buddhism
868	• First printed book, in China
907–1234	• Khitan and Jurchen peoples rule parts of northern China
939	• Vietnam establishes independence from China
960–1279	• Song dynasty: China's "economic revolution"
1000	• *The Tale of Genji* published in Japan
1443	• Korea establishes phonetic alphabet, *hangul*

9

The Worlds of Islam
Afro-Eurasian Connections

600–1450

CONNECTING PAST AND PRESENT

"THERE ARE MORE THAN A BILLION variations of lived belief among people who define themselves as Muslim—one for each human being, just as there are among those who describe themselves as Christian, or Buddhist, or Hindu."[1] So wrote the Pakistani writer Mohsin Hamid in 2013 while seeking to dispel an all-too-common impression that Islam is a monolithic or singular tradition. To illustrate the point, he noted that "many millions of Muslims apparently believe that women should have no role in politics. But many millions more have had no qualms electing women prime ministers in Muslim-majority countries such as Pakistan and Bangladesh."

The vast diversity of the contemporary Islamic world—divided along lines of nationality, class, gender, education, and religious belief—echoes the earlier history of this newest of humankind's major civilizations. During the first Muslim millennium (600–1600 c.e.), the Islamic world found expression in many and varied forms—Sunni, Shia, Sufi, Arab, Persian, Turkic, West African—some displaying a broad acceptance of diversity and others engaged in serious and at times violent conflict with those of a different religious outlook. Men and women then, as now, experienced Islamic life quite differently, as did urban elites, widely traveled merchants, and ordinary farmers or herders.

And yet for many Muslims, both then and now, the world of Islam was an inclusive community that transcended the many divisions of human civilizations. In ancient and contemporary times alike, that sensibility found expression in the *hajj*, the pilgrimage to Mecca, which brought believers together from the far corners of the Islamic world in common remembrance of their faith. Unity and diversity—these are twin themes in the long history of the Islamic civilization.

The significance of a burgeoning Islamic world during the third-wave era was enormous. It thrust the previously marginal and largely nomadic Arabs into a central role in world history, for it was among them and in their language that the newest of the world's major religions was born. The sudden emergence and rapid spread of that religion in the seventh century c.e. were accompanied by the creation of a huge empire that stretched from Spain to India. Both within that empire and beyond it, a new and innovative civilization took shape, drawing on Arab, Persian, Turkic, Greco-Roman, South Asian, and African cultures. It was clearly the largest and most influential of the new third-wave civilizations. Finally, the broad reach of Islam generated many of the great cultural encounters of this era as Islamic civilization challenged and provoked Christendom, penetrated and was transformed by African cultures, and also took root in India, Central Asia, and Southeast Asia.

SEEKING THE MAIN POINT	In what ways did the civilization of Islam interact with other civilizations in the Afro-Eurasian world before 1450? And in what different ways was that civilization expressed and experienced?

The Birth of a New Religion

Most of the major religious or cultural traditions of the second-wave era had emerged from the core of established civilizations—Confucianism and Daoism from China, Hinduism and Buddhism from India, and Zoroastrianism from Persia. Christianity and Islam, by contrast, emerged more from the margins of Mediterranean and

Middle Eastern civilizations. Christianity appeared among a small Middle Eastern people, the Jews, in a remote province of the Roman Empire, while Islam took hold in the cities and deserts of the Arabian Peninsula.

The Homeland of Islam

The central region of the Arabian Peninsula had long been inhabited by various nomadic peoples, sometimes known as Bedouins, who herded their sheep and camels in seasonal migrations. With no clearly defined sense of an "Arab" political identity, these peoples had long lived in fiercely independent clans and tribes that often engaged in bitter blood feuds with one another. They recognized a variety of gods, ancestors, and nature spirits; valued personal bravery, group loyalty, and hospitality; and greatly treasured their highly expressive oral poetry. At the same time, some Arabians practiced sedentary village-based agriculture in scattered oases, the highlands of Yemen, and interior mountain communities, while in earlier times, the northern and southern regions of the Arabian peninsula possessed flourishing small kingdoms. Arabia also sat astride increasingly important trade routes that connected the Indian Ocean world with that of the Mediterranean Sea, a location that gave rise to cosmopolitan commercial cities whose values and practices were often in conflict with those of traditional nomadic tribes (see Map 9.1).

One of those cities, Mecca, came to occupy a distinctive role in Arabia, for it was the site of the Kaaba, the most prominent religious shrine in Arabia, which housed representations of some 360 deities and was the destination for many religious pilgrims. Mecca's dominant tribe, the Quraysh (koor-EYE'SH), controlled access to the Kaaba, and its leading families had grown wealthy by taxing the local trade that accompanied the annual pilgrimage season.

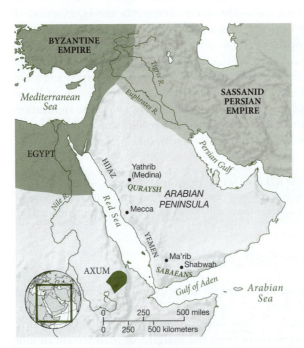

MAP 9.1 Arabia at the Time of Muhammad
Located adjacent to the Byzantine and Persian empires, the eastern coast of Arabia was the site of a major trade route between the Indian Ocean and the Mediterranean Sea.

Furthermore, Arabia was located on the periphery of two established and rival civilizations of that time—the Byzantine Empire, heir to the Roman world, and the Sassanid Empire, heir to the imperial traditions of Persia. Many Jews and Christians, as well as some Zoroastrians, lived in Arabia, and their monotheistic ideas became widely known. By the time of Muhammad, most of the settled peoples of Arabia had acknowledged the preeminent position of Allah, the supreme god, although they usually found the lesser gods, including the three daughters of Allah, far more accessible. Moreover, they increasingly identified Allah with Yahweh, the Jewish High God, and regarded themselves too as "children of Abraham." Some were beginning to explore the possibility that Allah/Yahweh was the only God and that the many others residing in the Kaaba and in shrines across the peninsula were nothing more than "helpless and harmless idols."[2]

To an outside observer around 600, it might well have seemed that the peoples of Arabia were moving toward Judaism religiously or that Christianity, the most rapidly growing religion in western Asia, would encompass Arabia as well. Any such expectations, however, were thoroughly confounded by the dramatic events of the seventh century.

The Messenger and the Message

The catalyst for those events and for the birth of this new religion was a single individual, **Muhammad** Ibn Abdullah (570–632 C.E.), who was born in Mecca to a Quraysh family. As a young boy, Muhammad lost his parents, came under the care of an uncle, and worked as a shepherd to pay his keep. Later he became a trader and traveled as far north as Syria. At the age of twenty-five, he married a wealthy widow, Khadija, herself a prosperous merchant, with whom he fathered six children. A highly reflective man deeply troubled by the religious corruption and social inequalities of Mecca, he often undertook periods of withdrawal and meditation in the arid mountains outside the city. There, like the Buddha and Jesus, Muhammad had a powerful, overwhelming religious experience that left him convinced, albeit reluctantly, that he was Allah's messenger to the Arabians, commissioned to bring to them a scripture in their own language.

According to Muslim tradition, the revelations began in 610 and continued periodically over the next twenty-two years. Those revelations, recorded in the **Quran**, became the sacred scriptures of Islam, which to this day most Muslims regard as the very words of God. Intended to be recited rather than simply read for information, the Quran, Muslims claim, when heard in its original Arabic, conveys nothing less than the very presence of the Divine. Its unmatched poetic beauty, miraculous to Arabic-speaking Muslims, convinced many that it was indeed a revelation from God. One of the earliest converts testified to its power: "When I heard the Quran, my heart was softened and I wept and Islam entered into me."[3]

In its Arabian setting, the Quran's message, delivered through Muhammad, was revolutionary. Religiously, it was radically monotheistic, presenting Allah as the only God, the all-powerful Creator, the "Lord sustainer of the worlds, the Compassionate, the Caring, master of the day of reckoning" and known to human beings "on the farthest horizon and within their own selves."[4] Here was an exalted conception of Deity that drew heavily on traditions of Jewish and Christian monotheism.

As "the Messenger of God," Muhammad presented himself in the line of earlier prophets—Abraham, Moses, Jesus, and many others. He was the last, "the seal of the prophets," bearing God's final revelation to humankind. It was not so much a call to a new faith as an invitation to return to the old and pure religion of Abraham from which Jews, Christians, and Arabian peoples alike had deviated. Jews had wrongly conceived of themselves as a uniquely "chosen people"; Christians had made their prophet into a god; and Arabian nomads had become wildly polytheistic. To all of this, the message of the Quran was a corrective.

Submission to Allah ("Muslim" means "one who submits") was the primary obligation of believers and the means of achieving a God-conscious life in this world and a place in Paradise after death. According to the Quran, however, submission was not merely an individual or a spiritual act, for it involved the creation of a whole new society. Over and again, the Quran denounced the prevailing social practices of an increasingly prosperous Mecca: the hoarding of wealth, the exploitation of the poor, the charging of high rates of interest on loans, corrupt business deals, the abuse of women, and the neglect of widows and orphans. Like the Jewish prophets of the Old Testament, the Quran demanded social justice and laid out a prescription for its implementation. It sought a return to the older values of nomadic tribal life—solidarity, equality, concern for the poor—which had been undermined, particularly in Mecca, by growing wealth and commercialism.

The message of the Quran challenged not only the ancient polytheism of Arabia and the social injustices of Mecca but also the entire tribal and clan structure of Arabian society, which was so prone to war, feuding, and violence. The just and moral society of Islam was the ***umma*** (OOM-mah), the community of all believers, replacing tribal, ethnic, or racial identities. In this community, women too had an honored and spiritually equal place. "The believers, men and women, are protectors

Islamic Scholars at Work
As the umma—the community of all believers—grew and developed, mosques and their libraries became a focus for the faithful's study of Islam. In this twelfth-century miniature, scholars are listening intently to the figure reading from a book, while numerous texts lie stacked on shelves in the background. With a written text as the core of their religion, Muslims were a "people of the book."
(De Agostini Picture Library/Bridgeman Images)

of one another," declared the Quran.[5] The umma, then, was to be a new and just community, bound by common belief rather than by territory, language, or tribe.

The core message of the Quran—the remembrance of God—was effectively summarized as a set of five requirements for believers known as the **Pillars of Islam**. The first pillar expressed the heart of the Islamic message: "There is no god but God, and Muhammad is the messenger of God." The second pillar was ritual prayer, performed five times a day. The third pillar, almsgiving, reflected the Quran's repeated demands for social justice by requiring believers to give generously to support the poor and needy of the community. The fourth pillar established a month of fasting during Ramadan, which meant abstaining from food, drink, and sexual relations from the first light of dawn to sundown. It provided an occasion for self-purification and a reminder of the needs of the hungry. The fifth pillar encouraged a pilgrimage to Mecca, known as the *hajj* (HAHJ), during which believers from all over the Islamic world assembled once a year and put on identical simple white clothing as they rehearsed key events in Islamic history. For at least the few days of the hajj, the many worlds of Islam must surely have seemed a single realm.

A further requirement for believers, sometimes called the sixth pillar, was "struggle," or *jihad* in Arabic. Its more general meaning, which Muhammad referred to as the "greater jihad," was an interior personal effort of each believer against greed and selfishness, a spiritual striving toward living a God-conscious life. In its "lesser" form, the "jihad of the sword," the Quran authorized armed struggle against the forces of unbelief and evil as a means of establishing Muslim rule and of defending the umma from the threats of aggressive "infidels" (adherents of another religion). The understanding and use of the jihad concept have varied widely over the many centuries of Islamic history and remain a matter of much controversy among Muslims in the twenty-first century.

The Transformation of Arabia

As the revelations granted to Muhammad became known in Mecca, they attracted a small following of some close relatives, a few prominent Meccan leaders, and an assortment of lower-class dependents, formerly enslaved individuals, and members of poorer clans. Those teachings also soon attracted the vociferous opposition of Mecca's elite families, particularly those of Muhammad's own tribe, the Quraysh. Muhammad's claim to be a "messenger of Allah," his unyielding monotheism, his call for social reform, his condemnation of Mecca's business practices, and his apparent disloyalty to his own tribe enraged the wealthy and ruling families of Mecca. So great had this opposition become that in 622 Muhammad and his small band of followers emigrated to the more welcoming town of Yathrib, soon to be called Medina, the city of the Prophet. This agricultural settlement of mixed Arab and Jewish population had invited Muhammad to serve as an arbitrator of their intractable conflicts. The migration to Yathrib, known in Arabic as the *hijra* (HIJJ-ruh) ("the journey"), was a momentous turning point in the early history of Islam and thereafter marked the beginning of a new Islamic calendar.

The new community, or umma, that took shape in Medina was a kind of "supertribe," but very different from the traditional nomadic tribes. Membership was a matter of belief rather than birth, allowing the community to expand rapidly. Furthermore, all authority, both political and religious, was concentrated in the hands of Muhammad, who proceeded to introduce radical changes. Charging interest on loans was outlawed as exploitative, tax-free marketplaces were established, and a mandatory payment to support the poor was imposed.

In Medina, Muhammad not only began to create a new society but also declared his movement's independence from its earlier affiliation with Judaism. In the early years, he had anticipated a warm response from Jews and Christians, based on a common monotheism and prophetic tradition, and had directed his followers to pray facing Jerusalem. But when some Jewish groups allied with his enemies, Muhammad acted harshly to suppress them, exiling some and enslaving or killing others. This was not, however, a general suppression of Jews, since others among them remained loyal to Muhammad's new state. But the Prophet now redirected his followers' prayer toward Mecca, essentially declaring Islam independent of its Jewish origins.

From its base in Medina, the Islamic community rapidly extended its reach throughout Arabia. Early military successes against Muhammad's Meccan opponents convinced other tribes that his followers and their God were on the rise, and they sought to negotiate alliances with the new power. The religious appeal of the new faith, the end of incessant warfare among feuding tribes, successful military actions skillfully led by Muhammad, and the Prophet's willingness to enter into marriage alliances with leading tribes — all of this contributed to the consolidation of Islamic control throughout Arabia. In 630, Muhammad triumphantly and peacefully entered Mecca itself, purging the Kaaba of its idols and declaring it a shrine to the one God, Allah. By the time Muhammad died in 632, most of Arabia had come under the control of this new Islamic state, and many had embraced the new faith.

Thus the birth of Islam differed sharply from that of Christianity. Early Christians found themselves periodically persecuted by Roman authorities for more than three centuries, requiring them to work out some means of dealing with an often hostile state. The answer lay in the development of a separate church hierarchy and the concept of two coexisting authorities, one religious and one political.

The young Islamic community, by contrast, constituted a state, and soon a huge empire, at the very beginning of its history. Muhammad was not only a religious figure but also, unlike Jesus or the Buddha, a political and military leader able to implement his vision of an ideal Islamic society. Nor did Islam give rise to a separate religious organization. No professional clergy mediating between God and humankind emerged within Islam. Teachers, religious scholars, prayer leaders, and judges within an Islamic legal system did not have the religious role that priests held in the Christian world. No distinction between religious law and civil law, so important within Christendom, existed within the realm of Islam. One law, known as the *sharia* (shah-REE-ah), regulated, at least in theory, political, economic, social, and religious life. The sharia (literally, "a path to water," the source of life) evolved over the several centuries following the birth of this new religion and found expression in a number of separate schools of Islamic legal practice.

In little more than twenty years (610–632), a profound transformation had occurred in the Arabian Peninsula. What would subsequently become a new religion had been born, though it had roots in earlier Jewish, Christian, and Zoroastrian traditions. A new and vigorous state had emerged, bringing peace to the warring tribes of Arabia. Within that state, a distinctive society had begun to take shape, one that served ever after as a model for Islamic communities everywhere. In his farewell sermon, Muhammad described the outlines of this community:

> All mankind is from Adam and Eve, an Arab has no superiority over a non-Arab nor a non-Arab has any superiority over an Arab; also a white has no superiority over a black nor a black has any superiority over a white—except by piety and good action. Learn that every Muslim is a brother to every Muslim and that the Muslims constitute one brotherhood.[6]

The Making of an Arab Muslim Empire

In the centuries that followed the Prophet's death, the energies born of those vast changes in Arabia profoundly transformed much of the Afro-Eurasian world. The new Islamic state became a huge empire, encompassing all or part of Egyptian, Roman/Byzantine, Persian, Mesopotamian, and Indian civilizations. In the process, some of the conquerors began to think of themselves as "Arabs," a new and more distinct ethnic and political identity that distinguished them from their subject peoples. But the Islamic faith spread widely within and outside that empire. So too did the culture and language of Arabia, as many Arabic speakers migrated far beyond their original homeland and many others found it advantageous to learn Arabic. From the mixing and blending of these many peoples emerged the new and distinctive third-wave civilization of Islam, bound by the ties of a common faith but divided by differences of culture, class, politics, gender, and religious understanding. These enormously consequential processes—the making of a new religion, a new political identity as Arabs, a new empire, and a new civilization—were central to world history during the third-wave era.

War, Conquest, and Tolerance

Within a few years of Muhammad's death in 632, armies originating among his followers in Arabia and led by adherents to his new faith engaged the Persian Sassanid and Byzantine empires, the great powers of the region. Those armies soon included conquered peoples who had become believers (Persians, Greeks, Egyptians, and North African Berbers). Within a century they had created an Arab-ruled Muslim empire stretching from Spain to India (see Map 9.2).

Already by 644, invading armies from Arabia had defeated a Persian Sassanid Empire that had been significantly weakened before their arrival by periodic bouts of plague and earlier wars with their Byzantine rivals. A similarly weakened Byzantium, the remaining eastern regions of the old Roman Empire, also soon lost the southern half of its territories to the invaders. Beyond these victories, forces operating on both land and sea swept westward across North Africa (642–698), conquered Spain in the early 700s, and attacked southern France. To the east, armies reached the Indus River and seized some of the major oasis towns of Central Asia. In 751, they inflicted a crushing defeat on Chinese forces in the Battle of Talas River, which checked the further expansion of China to the west and made possible the conversion to Islam of Central Asia's Turkic-speaking people. Most of the violence of conquest involved imperial armies, though on occasion civilians too were caught up in the fighting and suffered terribly.

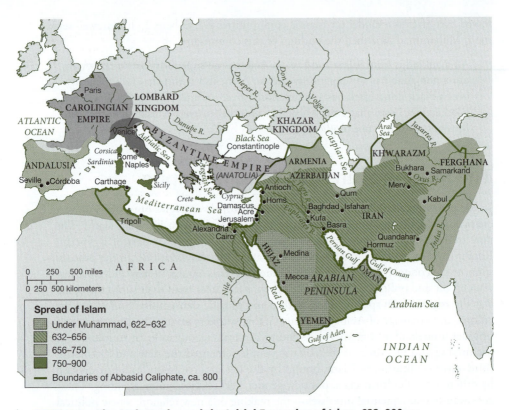

MAP 9.2   The Arab Empire and the Initial Expansion of Islam, 622–900 C.E.
Far more so than with Buddhism or Christianity, the initial spread of Islam was both rapid and extensive. And unlike the other two world religions, Islam quickly gave rise to a huge empire, ruled by Muslim Arabs, that encompassed many of the older civilizations of the region.

The motives driving the creation of this empire were broadly similar to those of other empires. The merchant leaders of the new Islamic community wanted to capture profitable trade routes and wealthy agricultural regions. Individuals found in military expansion a route to wealth and social promotion. The fragile unity of the umma threatened to come apart after Muhammad's death, and external expansion provided a common task for the community.

While many among the new conquerors viewed the mission of empire in terms of jihad, bringing righteous government to the peoples they conquered, this did not mean imposing a new religion. In fact, for the better part of a century after Muhammad's death, his followers usually referred to themselves as "believers," a term that appears in the Quran far more often than "Muslims" and one that included pious Jews and Christians as well as newly monotheistic Arabs.

Such a posture eased the acceptance of the new political order, for many people recently incorporated in the emerging empire were already monotheists and familiar with the core ideas and practices of the "believers' movement" — prayer, fasting, pilgrimage, revelation, and prophets. Furthermore, the new rulers were remarkably tolerant of established Jewish and Christian faiths. The first governor of Jerusalem after its conquest was a Jew. Many old Christian churches continued to operate, and new ones were constructed. A Christian patriarch in Iraq, writing to one of his bishops around 647 C.E., observed that the new rulers "not only do not fight Christianity, they even commend our religion, show honor to the priests and monasteries and saints of the Lord, and make gifts to the monasteries and churches."[7] Formal agreements or treaties recognized Jews, Christians, and Zoroastrians as "people of the book," that is, followers of true faiths based on the teachings of earlier prophets like Abraham, Moses, or Jesus, for whom Muhammad was the last great prophet or "seal of the prophecy." Muslim authorities granted people of the book the status of *dhimmis* (dihm-mees), protected but second-class subjects. Such people were permitted to freely practice their own religion as long as they paid a special tax known as the *jizya*. Many of them served in the highest offices within Muslim kingdoms and in their armies as well.

In other ways too, the Arab rulers of this expanding empire sought to limit the disruptive impact of conquest. To prevent indiscriminate destruction and exploitation of conquered peoples, occupying armies were restricted to garrison towns, segregated from the native population. Local elites and bureaucratic structures were incorporated into the new Arab Muslim Empire. Nonetheless, the empire worked many changes on its subjects, the most enduring of which was the mass conversion of Middle Eastern peoples to what became by the eighth century the new and separate religion of Islam.

Conversion

For some people, no doubt, converting to Islam was or subsequently became a matter of profound spiritual or psychological transformation, but far more often, at least initially, it was "social conversion," motivated more by convenience than conviction.[8] It happened at various rates and in different ways, but in the four centuries or so after the death of Muhammad, millions of individuals and many whole societies within the Arab Empire found their cultural identity bound up with a belief in Allah and the message of his Prophet. They had become Muslims.

In some ways, perhaps, the change was not so dramatic, as major elements of Islam — monotheism; ritual prayer and cleansing ceremonies; fasting; divine revelation; the ideas of Heaven, Hell, and final judgment — were quite familiar to Jews, Christians, and Zoroastrians. Furthermore, Islam was from the beginning associated with the sponsorship of a powerful state, quite unlike the experience of early Buddhism or Christianity. Conquest called into question the power of old gods, while the growing prestige of the Arab Empire attracted many to Islam. Although deliberately forced conversion was rare and explicitly forbidden in the Quran, living in an Islamic-governed state provided a variety of incentives for claiming Muslim identity. People aspiring to official positions in government found conversion to Islam an aid to social mobility. For merchants, Islamic law, which defined proper commercial relationships between believers, reduced the uncertainty of long-distance commerce. Converts also avoided the jizya, the tax imposed on non-Muslims.

Conversion was not an automatic or easy process. Vigorous resistance delayed conversion for centuries among the Berbers of North Africa; a small group of zealous Spanish Christians in the ninth century provoked their own martyrdom by publicly insulting the Prophet; and some Persian Zoroastrians fled to avoid Muslim rule. More generally, though, a remarkable and lasting religious transformation occurred throughout the Arab Empire.

In Persia, for example, between 750 and 900, about 80 percent of the population made the transition to a Muslim religious identity. But they did so in a manner quite distinct from the people of Iraq, Syria, Egypt, and North Africa. In these regions, converts to Islam gradually abandoned their native languages, adopted Arabic, and came to see themselves as Arabs. In Iran or Persia, by contrast, Arab conquest did not involve cultural Arabization, despite some initial efforts to impose the Arabic language. By the tenth century, the vast majority of Persians had become Muslims, but the Persian language (called Farsi in Iran) flourished, enriched now by a number of Arabic loan words and written in an Arabic script. Thus, in places where large-scale Arab migration had occurred, such as Egypt, North Africa, and Iraq, Arabic culture and language, as well as the religion of Islam, took hold. Such areas are today both Muslim and Arab, while the peoples of Iran, Turkey, Pakistan, Indonesia, and West Africa, for example, have "Islamized" without "Arabizing."

The preservation of Persian language and culture had enormous implications for the world of Islam. In Iran, Central Asia, India, and later in the Ottoman Empire, Islam was accompanied by pervasive Persian influences. Persian administrative and bureaucratic techniques; Persian court practices with their palaces, gardens, and splendid garments; Persian architecture, poetry, music, and painting—all of this decisively shaped the high culture of these eastern Islamic lands. One of the Abbasid caliphs, himself an Arab, observed: "The Persians ruled for a thousand years and did not need us Arabs even for a day. We have been ruling them for one or two centuries and cannot do without them for an hour."[9]

Divisions and Controversies

The ideal of a unified believers' community, so important to Muhammad, proved difficult to realize as conquest and conversion vastly enlarged the Islamic umma. A central problem involved leadership and authority in the absence of Muhammad's towering presence. Who should hold the role of caliph (KAY-lihf), the successor to Muhammad as the political leader of the umma, the protector and defender of the faith? That issue crystallized a variety of emerging conflicts within the Islamic world—between early and later converts, among various Arab tribes and factions, between Arabs and non-Arabs, and between privileged and wealthy rulers and their far less fortunate subjects. Many of these political and social conflicts found expression in religious terms as various understandings of the Quran and of Muhammad's life and teachings took shape within the growing Islamic community.

The first four caliphs, known among most Muslims as the Rightly Guided Caliphs (632–661), were close "companions of the Prophet," selected by the Muslim elders of Medina. Division surfaced almost immediately as a series of Arab tribal rebellions and new "prophets" persuaded the first caliph, Abu Bakr, to suppress them forcibly. The third and fourth caliphs, Uthman and Ali, were both assassinated, and from 656 to 661, less than twenty-five years after Muhammad's death, civil war pitted Muslim against Muslim. A second civil war (680–692) continued that bitter and often savage family feud among the leaders of the "Believers' Movement."

Out of that conflict emerged one of the deepest and most enduring rifts within the Islamic world. On one side were the Sunni (SOON-nee) Muslims, who held that the caliphs were rightful political and military leaders, selected by the Islamic community. On the other side of this sharp divide was the Shia (SHEE-ah) (an Arabic word meaning "party" or "faction") branch of Islam. Its adherents felt strongly that leadership in the Islamic world should derive from the line of Ali and his son Husayn, blood relatives of Muhammad, both of whom died at the hands of their political or religious enemies. If the caliph was the idealized communal leader for Sunnis, *imams* (leaders) served this purpose for most of the Shia Muslims. They were widely thought to have some special charisma based on descent from the Prophet, giving them a religious authority that the caliphs lacked and allowing them to infallibly interpret divine revelation and law.

Thus what began as a purely political conflict acquired over time a deeper significance. For much of early Islamic history, Shia Muslims saw themselves as the minority opposition within Islam. They felt that history had taken a wrong turn and that they were "the defenders of the oppressed, the critics and opponents of privilege and power," while the Sunnis were the advocates of the established order.[10] Various armed revolts by Shias over the centuries, most of which failed, led to a distinctive conception of martyrdom and to the expectation that their defeated leaders were merely in hiding and not really dead and that they would return in the fullness of time. Thus a messianic element entered Shia Islam. The Sunni/Shia schism became a lasting division in the Islamic world, reflected in conflicts among various Islamic states, and was exacerbated by further splits among the Shia. Those divisions echo still in the twenty-first century.

As the Arab Muslim Empire grew, its caliphs were transformed from modest Arab chiefs into absolute monarchs, "the shadow of God on earth," of the Byzantine or Persian variety, complete with elaborate court rituals, a complex bureaucracy, a standing army, and centralized systems of taxation and coinage. They were also subject to the dynastic rivalries and succession disputes common to other empires. The first dynasty, following the era of the Rightly Guided Caliphs, came from the Umayyad (oo-MEYE-ahd) family (r. 661–750). Under the leadership of the **Umayyad caliphate**, the Arab Empire expanded greatly, caliphs became hereditary rulers, and the capital moved from Medina to the cosmopolitan Roman/Byzantine city of Damascus in Syria. Its ruling class was an Arab military aristocracy, drawn from various tribes. But Umayyad rule provoked growing criticism and unrest. The emerging Shia faction viewed the Umayyad caliphs as illegitimate usurpers, and non-Arab Muslims resented their second-class citizenship in the empire. Many Arabs protested the luxurious living and impiety of their rulers. The Umayyads, they charged, "made God's servants slaves, God's property something to be taken by turns among the rich, and God's religion a cause of corruption."[11]

Such grievances lay behind the overthrow of the Umayyads in 750 and their replacement by a new Arab dynasty, the Abbasids. With a splendid new capital in Baghdad, the **Abbasid caliphate** presided over a flourishing and prosperous Islamic civilization in which non-Arabs, especially Persians, now played a prominent role. But the political unity of the Abbasid Empire did not last long. Beginning in the mid-ninth century, many local governors or military commanders effectively asserted the autonomy of their regions, while still giving formal allegiance to the caliph in

Baghdad. Long before Mongol conquest put an official end to the Abbasid Empire in 1258, the Islamic world had fractured politically into a series of "sultanates," many ruled by Persian or Turkish military dynasties.

A further tension within the world of Islam, though one that seldom produced violent conflict, lay in different answers to one central question: what does it mean to be a Muslim, to submit wholly to Allah? One answer lay in the development of the sharia, the body of Islamic law developed primarily in the eighth and ninth centuries by religious scholars, Sunni and Shia alike, who were known as the *ulama*. The emerging sharia addressed in great detail practically every aspect of life. It was a blueprint for an authentic Islamic society, providing meticulous guidance for prayer and ritual cleansing; marriage, divorce, and inheritance; business and commercial relationships; the treatment of enslaved people; political life; personal hygiene; dietary requirements; and much more. Debates among the ulama led to the creation of four schools of law among Sunni Muslims and still others in the lands of Shia Islam. To the ulama and their followers, living as a Muslim meant following the sharia and thus participating in the creation of an Islamic society.

A second and quite different understanding of the faith emerged between 800 and 1000 c.e. among those who saw the worldly success of Islamic civilization as a distraction and deviation from the purer spirituality of Muhammad's time. Known as Sufis (SOO-fees), they represented Islam's mystical dimension, in that they sought a direct and personal experience of the Divine. Through renunciation of the material world, meditation on the words of the Quran, the chanting of the names of God, the use of music and dance, and the veneration of Muhammad and various "saints," adherents of **Sufism** pursued an interior life, seeking to tame the ego and achieve spiritual union with Allah. To describe that inexpressible experience, they often resorted to metaphors of drunkenness or the embrace of lovers. "Stain your prayer rug with wine," urged the famous Sufi poet Hafiz, referring to the intoxication of the believer with the Divine Presence.

This mystical tendency in Islamic practice, which became widely popular by the ninth and tenth centuries, was at times sharply critical of the more scholarly and legalistic practitioners of the sharia. To Sufis, establishment teachings about the law and correct behavior, while useful for daily living, did little to bring the believer into the presence of God. Furthermore, Sufis felt that many of the ulama had been compromised by their association with worldly and corrupt governments. Sufis therefore often charted their own course to God, implicitly challenging the religious authority of the ulama. For these orthodox religious scholars, Sufi ideas and practice sometimes verged on heresy, as Sufis on occasion claimed unity with God, received new revelations, or incorporated novel religious practices from outside the Islamic world.

Despite their differences, adherents of the legalistic emphasis of the sharia and practitioners of Sufi spirituality coexisted, mostly peacefully, mixing and mingling, collaborating and disagreeing, in various combinations. For many centuries, roughly 1100 to 1800, Sufism was central to mainstream Islam, and many, perhaps most, Muslims affiliated with one or another Sufi organization, making use of its spiritual practices. Nonetheless, differences in emphasis about the essential meaning of Islam remained an element of tension and sometimes discord within the Muslim world.

Sufis and Worldly Power This early seventeenth-century painting from India illustrates the tension between Sufis and worldly authorities. Here the Muslim Mughal emperor Jahangir, seated on an hourglass throne, gives his attention to the white-bearded Sufi holy man rather than to the prominent men, including a European figure, shown in the bottom left. (Photo: Georg Niedermeiser/bpk Bildagentur/Museum für Islamische Kunst, Staatlisch Museen, Berlin, Germany/Art Resource, NY)

Women and Men in Early Islam

What did the rise of Islam and the making of the Arab Empire mean for the daily lives of women and their relationship with men? Virtually every aspect of this question has been and remains highly controversial. The debates begin with the Quran itself. Did its teachings release women from earlier restrictions, or did they impose new limitations? At the level of spiritual life, the Quran was quite clear and explicit: men and women were equal. Numerous passages in the Quran use gender-inclusive language, referring to "believers, both men and women."

But in social terms, and especially within marriage, the Quran, like the written texts of almost all civilizations, viewed women as inferior and subordinate: "Men have authority over women because Allah has made the one superior to the other, and because they spend their wealth to maintain them. Good women are obedient."[12] More specifically, the Quran provided a mix of rights, restrictions, and protections for women. Female infanticide, for example, widely practiced in many cultures as a means of gender selection, was now forbidden for Muslims. Women were given control over their own property, particularly their dowries, and were granted rights of inheritance, but at half the rate of their male counterparts. Marriage was considered a contract between consenting parties, thus making marriage by capture illegitimate. Divorce was possible for both parties, although it was far more readily available for men. The practice of taking multiple husbands, which operated in some pre-Islamic Arab tribes, was prohibited, while polygyny (the practice of having multiple wives) was permitted, though more clearly regulated than before. Men were limited to four wives and required to treat each of them equally. (The difficulty of doing so has been interpreted by some as virtually requiring monogamy.) Men were, however, permitted to have sexual relations with enslaved women, but any children born of those unions were free, as was the mother once her owner died. Furthermore, men were strongly encouraged to marry orphans, widows, and enslaved women.

Such Quranic prescriptions were but one factor shaping the lives of women and men. At least as important were the long-established practices of the societies into which Islam spread and the growing sophistication, prosperity, and urbanization of Islamic civilization. In early Islamic times, a number of women played visible public roles, particularly Muhammad's youngest wife, Aisha. Women prayed in the mosques, although separately, standing beside the men. Nor were women generally veiled or secluded.

However, as had been the case in Athens and China during their "golden ages," upper-class Muslim women experienced growing restrictions as Islamic civilization flourished culturally and economically. Now veiling and the seclusion of women became standard practice among the upper and ruling classes, removing them from public life. Separate quarters within the homes of the wealthy were the domain of women, from which they could emerge only completely veiled. Seclusion was less possible for lower-class women, who lacked the servants of the rich and had to leave the home for shopping or work.

Such practices derived far more from established traditions of Middle Eastern cultures than from the Quran itself, but they soon gained an Islamic rationale in the writings of Muslim thinkers. The famous philosopher and religious scholar al-Ghazali clearly saw a relationship between Muslim piety and the separation of the sexes:

> If [a man] knocks at the door, it is not proper for the woman to answer him softly and easily because men's hearts can be drawn to [women] for the most trifling [reason]. . . . However, if the woman has to answer the knock, she should stick her finger in her mouth so that her voice sounds like that of an old woman.[13]

Other signs of a tightening patriarchy — such as "honor killing" of women by their male relatives for violating sexual taboos and, in some places, clitoridectomy (female genital cutting) — likewise derived from local cultures, with no sanction in the Quran or Islamic law, though they often came to be seen as Islamic. Negative views of women, presenting them variously as weak, deficient, and a sexually charged threat to men and social stability, emerged in the *hadiths* (hah-DEETHS), traditions about the sayings or actions of Muhammad that became an important source of Islamic law.

Even as women faced growing restrictions in society generally, Islam, like Buddhism and Christianity, also offered new outlets for them in religious life. While Sunni Islam prohibited women from studying in *madrassas* (religious schools or colleges), it did allow them to become transmitters of the hadiths by studying with prominent scholars. Aisha, a fourteenth-century woman from Damascus, studied under some of the most renowned teachers of her generation, attracted students of her own, and later gained a reputation as her generation's most reliable transmitter of the hadith. Within the world of Shia Islam, women teachers of the faith were called mullahs, the same as their male counterparts. Visits to the tombs of major Islamic figures, as well as the ritual of the public bath, likewise provided some opportunity for women to interact with other women beyond their own family circle.

Sufi mystical practice allowed a greater role for women than did mainstream Islam, for the spiritual equality that the Quran accorded to male and female alike allowed women also to aspire to union with God. Among the earliest of well-known Sufi practitioners was Rabia, an eighth-century woman from Basra in southern Iraq who renounced numerous proposals of marriage and engaged, apparently successfully, in repeated religious debates with men. But for some male Sufi scholars, such as the twelfth-century mystical poet Attar, Rabia's spiritual attainments meant that "she is a man and one cannot any more call her a woman."[14]

Islam and Cultural Encounter: A Four-Way Comparison

In its earliest centuries, the rapid spread of Islam had been accompanied by the creation of an immense empire, very much in the tradition of earlier Mediterranean and Middle Eastern empires. By the tenth century, however, little political unity remained, and in 1258 even the powerless symbol of that earlier unity vanished as Mongol forces sacked Baghdad and killed the last Abbasid caliph. But even as the empire disintegrated, the civilization that was born within it grew and flourished. Perhaps the most significant sign of a flourishing Islamic civilization was the continued spread of the religion both within and beyond the boundaries of that vanishing empire (see Map 9.3). For example, Islam rode the waves of Indian Ocean commerce to penetrate both Southeast Asia and East Africa (see Chapter 7). The further examples of India, Anatolia, West Africa, and Spain illustrate the various ways that Islam penetrated these societies as well as the rather different outcomes of these epic cultural encounters.

The Case of India

In South Asia, Islam found a permanent place in a long-established civilization through a variety of avenues. Invasions by Turkic-speaking warrior groups from Central Asia, recently converted to Islam, brought the faith to northern India. Thus Turkic peoples became the third major carrier of Islam, after the Arabs and Persians, as their conquests initiated an enduring encounter between Islam and a Hindu-based Indian civilization. Beginning around 1000, those conquests gave rise to a series of Turkic and Muslim regimes that governed much of India into the nineteenth century. The early centuries of this encounter were violent indeed, as the invaders

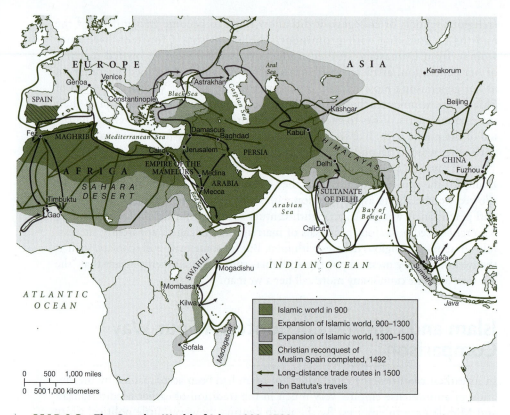

MAP 9.3   The Growing World of Islam, 900–1500
Islam as a religion, a civilization, and an arena of commerce continued to grow even as the Arab
Muslim Empire fragmented.

smashed Hindu and Buddhist temples and carried off vast quantities of Indian treasure. With the establishment of the Sultanate of Delhi in 1206 (see Map 9.4), Turkic
rule became more systematic, although the Turks' small numbers and internal conflicts allowed only a very modest penetration of Indian society.

In the centuries that followed, substantial Muslim communities emerged in
India, particularly in regions less tightly integrated into the dominant Hindu culture. Disillusioned Buddhists as well as low-caste Hindus and untouchables found
the more egalitarian Islam attractive. So did peoples just beginning to make the transition to settled agriculture. Others benefited from converting to Islam by avoiding
the tax imposed on non-Muslims. Sufis were particularly important in facilitating
conversion, for India had always valued "god-filled men" who were detached from
worldly affairs. Sufi holy men, willing to accommodate local gods and religious festivals, helped to develop a "popular Islam" that was not always so sharply distinguished
from the more devotional (*bhakti*) forms of Hinduism.

Further to the south, well beyond the boundaries of the Delhi sultanate and
its successors, several Hindu states flourished. Perhaps the most impressive was the

MAP 9.4   The Sultanate of Delhi

Between 1206 and 1526 a number of Muslim dynasties ruled northern India as the Delhi sultanate, while an explicitly Hindu kingdom of Vijayanagar arose in the south after 1340. It drew on north Indian Muslim architectural features, hosted Muslim merchant communities, and made use of Muslim mercenaries for its military forces.

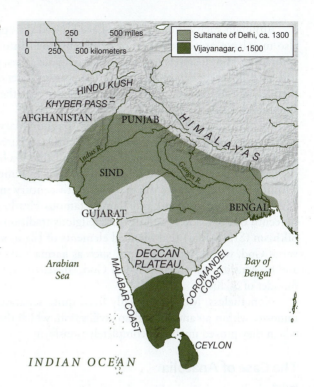

powerful Vijayanagar empire (1336–1646), which at its height controlled nearly all of southern India from a thriving capital city of perhaps half a million people that was described by one sixteenth-century European visitor as "the best provided city in the world . . . as large as Rome and very beautiful to the sight."[15] Formed in part to resist Muslim incursions from the north, the Vijayanagar empire was also a site of sustained and more peaceful Hindu-Muslim encounters. Muslim merchants were a prominent presence in many trading ports, and there was a vibrant Muslim district in the capital. As in northern India, the Hindu faith predominated, but a permanent Muslim presence in the south fostered an ongoing encounter between the two faiths and cultures.

Unlike the earlier experience of Islam in the Middle East, North Africa, and Persia, where it rapidly became the dominant faith, in India Islam was never able to claim more than 20 to 25 percent of the total population. Furthermore, Muslim communities were especially concentrated in the Punjab and Sind regions of northwestern India and in Bengal to the east. The core regions of Hindu culture in the northern Indian plain were not seriously challenged by the new faith, despite centuries of Muslim rule. One reason perhaps lay in the sharpness of the cultural divide between Islam and Hinduism. Islam was the most radically monotheistic of the world's religions, largely forbidding any representation of Allah, while Hinduism was surely among the most prolifically polytheistic, generating endless statues and images of the Divine in many forms. The Muslim notion of the equality of all believers also contrasted sharply with the hierarchical assumptions of the caste system. Believing in sexual modesty, Muslims were deeply offended by the open eroticism of some Hindu religious art.

Although such differences may have limited the appeal of Islam in India, they also may have prevented it from being absorbed into the tolerant and inclusive embrace of Hinduism, as so many other religious ideas, practices, and communities had been. The religious exclusivity of Islam, born of its firm monotheistic belief and the idea of a unique revelation, set a boundary that the great sponge of Hinduism could not completely absorb.

Certainly, not all was conflict across that boundary. Many prominent Hindus willingly served in the political and military structures of a Muslim-ruled India. Mystical seekers after the Divine blurred the distinction between Hindu and Muslim, suggesting that God was to be found "neither in temple nor in mosque." "Look within your heart," wrote the great fifteenth-century mystic poet Kabir, "for there you will find both [Allah] and Ram [a famous Hindu deity]."[16] During the early sixteenth century, a new and distinct religious tradition emerged in India known as **Sikhism** (SIHK-iz'm) that blended elements of Islam, such as devotion to one universal God, with Hindu concepts, such as karma and rebirth. "There is no Hindu and no Muslim. All are children of God," declared Guru Nanak (1469–1539), the founder of Sikhism.

Nonetheless, Muslims usually lived quite separately, remaining a distinctive minority within an ancient Indian civilization, which they now largely governed but which they proved unable to completely transform.

The Case of Anatolia

While India was being subjected to Turkic invasion, so too was Anatolia (now modern Turkey), where the largely Christian and Greek-speaking population was then governed by the Byzantine Empire (see Map 9.2 and Map 9.5). Here, as in India, the invaders initially wreaked havoc as Byzantine authority melted away beginning in the eleventh century. Sufi practitioners likewise played a major role in the process of conversion. The outcome, however, was a far more profound cultural transformation than in India. By 1500, the population was 90 percent Muslim and largely Turkic-speaking, and Anatolia was the heartland of the powerful Turkic Ottoman Empire that had overrun Christian Byzantium and captured Constantinople in 1453. Why did the Turkic intrusion into Anatolia generate a much more thorough Islamization than in India?

One factor clearly lies in a very different demographic balance. The population of Anatolia — perhaps 8 million — was far smaller than India's roughly 48 million people, but far more Turkic-speaking peoples settled in Anatolia, giving them a much greater cultural weight than the smaller colonizing force in India. Furthermore, the disruption of Anatolian society was much more extensive. Massacres, enslavement, famine, and flight led to a sharp drop in the native population. The Byzantine state had been fatally weakened. Church properties were confiscated, and monasteries were destroyed or deserted. Priests and bishops were sometimes unable to serve their congregations. Christians, though seldom forced to convert, suffered many discriminations. They had to wear special clothing and pay special taxes, and they were forbidden to ride saddled horses or carry swords. Not a few Christians came to believe that these disasters represented proof that Islam was the true religion. Thus Byzantine civilization in Anatolia, previously focused on the centralized institutions of church

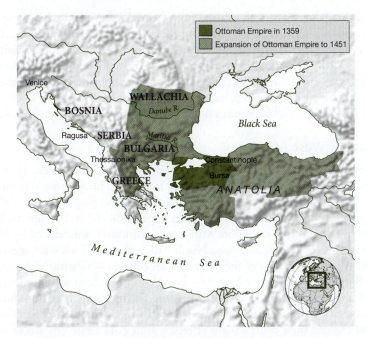

MAP 9.5　The Ottoman Empire by the Mid-Fifteenth Century
As Turkic-speaking migrants bearing the religion of Islam penetrated
Anatolia, the Ottoman Empire took shape, reaching into southeastern
Europe and finally displacing the Christian Byzantine Empire. Subsequently,
it came to control much of the Middle East and North Africa as well.

and state, was rendered leaderless and dispirited, whereas India's decentralized civilization, lacking a unified political or religious establishment, was better able to absorb the shock of external invasion while retaining its core values and identity.

The Turkic rulers of Anatolia built a new society that welcomed converts and granted them material rewards and opportunity for high office. Moreover, the cultural barriers to conversion were arguably less severe than in India. The common monotheism of Islam and Christianity, and Muslim respect for Jesus and the Christian scriptures, made conversion easier than crossing the great gulf between Islam and Hinduism. Such similarities lent support to the suggestion of some Sufi teachers that the two religions were but different versions of the same faith. Sufis also established schools, mills, orchards, hospices, and rest places for travelers and thus replaced the destroyed or decaying institutions of Christian Anatolia. All of this contributed to the thorough religious transformation of Anatolia and laid a foundation for the Ottoman Empire, which by 1500 had become the most impressive and powerful state within the Islamic world. It reached across Anatolia and the Black Sea, encompassed parts of Greece and southeastern Europe, and in the sixteenth century extended into the Arab lands of the Middle East and North Africa.

But the Islamization of Anatolia occurred within a distinctly Turkic context. A Turkic language, not Arabic, predominated. Some Sufi religious practices, such as ecstatic turning dances, actually derived from Central Asian Turkic shamanism. And Turkic tradition, common among pastoral peoples, offered a freer, more gender-equal life for women. This practice caught the attention of the Arab Moroccan visitor Ibn Battuta (1304–1368) during his travels among the Turks. He commented, "A remarkable thing that I saw . . . was the respect shown to women by the Turks, for they hold a more dignified position than the men. . . . The windows of the tent are open and her face is visible, for the Turkish women do not veil themselves."[17] He was not pleased.

The Case of West Africa

Still another pattern of Islamic expansion prevailed in West Africa. Here Islam accompanied Muslim traders across the Sahara rather than being brought by invading Arab or Turkic armies. Its gradual acceptance in the emerging civilization of West African states in the centuries after 1000 was largely peaceful and voluntary, lacking the incentives associated elsewhere with foreign conquest. Introduced by Muslim merchants from an already Islamized North Africa, the new faith was accepted primarily in the urban centers of the West African empires—Ghana, Mali, Songhay, Kanem-Bornu, and others (see Map 9.6). For African merchant communities, Islam provided an important link to Muslim trading partners, much as Buddhism and Hinduism had connected Southeast Asians to India-based commercial networks. For the monarchs and their courts, Islam offered a source of literate officials to assist in

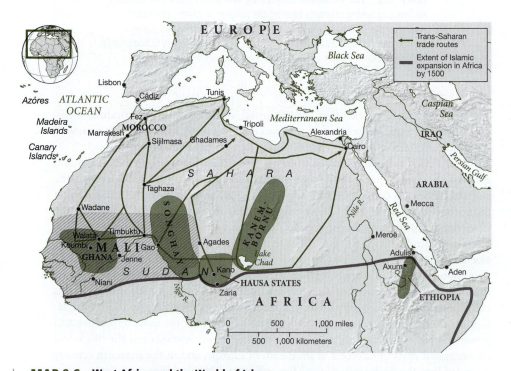

MAP 9.6   West Africa and the World of Islam
Both trans-Saharan commerce and Islam linked the civilization of West Africa to the larger Muslim world.

state administration as well as religious legitimacy, particularly for those who gained the prestige conferred by a pilgrimage to Mecca. The most prominent such pilgrim was Mansa Musa, the ruler of Mali, who in 1324 undertook the hajj accompanied by a huge entourage and enormous quantities of gold. As a world religion with a single universal Creator-God, Islam had a religious appeal for societies that were now participating in a wider world.

By the sixteenth century, a number of West African cities had become major centers of Islamic religious and intellectual life, attracting scholars from throughout the Muslim world. **Timbuktu** boasted more than 150 lower-level Quranic schools and several major centers of higher education, with thousands of students from all over West Africa and beyond. Libraries held tens of thousands of books and scholarly manuscripts. Monarchs subsidized the construction of mosques as West Africa became an integral part of a larger Islamic world. Arabic became an important language of religion, education, administration, and trade, but it did not become the dominant language of daily life. Nor did West Africa experience the massive migration of Arab peoples that had promoted the Arabization of North Africa and the Middle East.

Islam remained the culture of urban elites and spread little into the rural areas of West Africa until the nineteenth century. No thorough religious transformation occurred in West Africa as it had in Anatolia. Although many rulers adopted Islam, they governed people who steadfastly practiced African religions and whose

The Great Mosque at Jenne This mosque in the city of Jenne, initially constructed in the thirteenth century, illustrates the assimilation of Islam into West African civilization. (Antonello Lanzellotto/AGE Fotostock)

sensibilities they had to respect if social peace were to prevail. Thus they made few efforts to impose the new religion on their rural subjects or to govern in strict accordance with Islamic law. During his mid-fourteenth-century travels in West Africa, Arab visitor Ibn Battuta was appalled that practicing Muslims in Mali permitted their women to appear in public almost naked and to mingle freely with unrelated men. "The association of women with men is agreeable to us," he was told, "and a part of good conduct to which no suspicion attaches. They are not like the women of your country."[18] Sonni Ali, a fifteenth-century ruler of Songhay, observed Ramadan and built mosques, but he also consulted traditional diviners and performed customary sacrifices. In such ways, Islam became Africanized even as parts of West Africa became Islamized.

The Case of Spain

The chief site of Islamic encounter with Christian Europe occurred in Spain, called **al-Andalus** by Muslims, which was conquered by Muslim forces in the early eighth century during the first wave of Islamic expansion. By the tenth century, Muslim Spain was a vibrant civilization, often portrayed as a place of harmony and tolerance between its Muslim rulers and its Christian and Jewish subjects.

Certainly, Spain's agricultural economy was the most prosperous in Europe during this time, and its capital of Córdoba was among the largest and most splendid cities in the world. Muslims, Christians, and Jews alike contributed to a brilliant high culture in which astronomy, medicine, the arts, architecture, and literature flourished. Furthermore, social relationships among upper-class members of different faiths were easy and frequent. By 1000, perhaps 75 percent of the population had converted to Islam. Many of the remaining Christians learned Arabic, veiled their women, stopped eating pork, appreciated Arabic music and poetry, and sometimes married Muslims. One Christian bishop complained that Spanish Christians knew the rules of Arabic grammar better than those of Latin. During the reign of Abd al-Rahman III (r. 912–961), freedom of worship was declared as well as the opportunity for all to rise in the bureaucracy of the state.

But this so-called golden age of Muslim Spain was both limited and brief. Even assimilated or Arabized Christians remained religious infidels and second-class citizens in the eyes of their Muslim counterparts, and by the late tenth century toleration began to erode. The Córdoba-based regime fragmented into numerous rival states. Warfare with the remaining Christian kingdoms in northern Spain picked up in the tenth and eleventh centuries, and more puritanical and rigid forms of Islam entered Spain from North Africa. Tolerance turned to overt persecution against Christians and Jews. Social life also changed. Devout Muslims increasingly avoided contact with members of other faiths, and Arabized Christians were permitted to live only in particular places. Thus, writes one scholar, "the era of harmonious interaction between Muslim and Christian in Spain came to an end, replaced by intolerance, prejudice, and mutual suspicion."[19]

That intolerance intensified as the Christian reconquest of Spain gained ground after 1200. The end came in 1492, when Ferdinand and Isabella, the Catholic monarchs of a unified Spain, took Granada, the last Muslim stronghold on the Iberian Peninsula. Despite initial promises to maintain the freedom of Muslims to worship, in the opening decades of the sixteenth century the Spanish monarchy issued a series of edicts outlawing Islam in its various territories, forcing Muslims to choose between conversion or exile. Many Muslims were thus required to emigrate, often to North Africa or the Ottoman Empire, along with some 200,000 Jews expelled from Spain because they too refused to convert. In the early seventeenth century, even Muslim converts to Christianity were likewise banished from Spain. And yet cultural interchange persisted for a time. The translation of Arab texts into Latin continued under Christian rule, while Muslim palaces and mosques were often converted to Christian uses and new Christian buildings incorporated Islamic artistic and architectural features.

Thus Spain, unlike most other regions incorporated into the Islamic world, experienced a religious reversal as Christian rule was reestablished and Islam was painfully eradicated from the Iberian Peninsula. In world historical terms, perhaps the chief significance of Muslim Spain was its role in making the rich heritage of Islamic learning available to Christian Europe. As a cross-cultural encounter, it was largely a one-way street. European scholars wanted the secular knowledge—Greek as well as Arab—that had accumulated in the Islamic world, and they flocked to Spain to acquire it. That knowledge of philosophy, mathematics, medicine, optics, astronomy, botany, and more played a major role in the making of a new European civilization in the thirteenth century and beyond. Muslim Spain remained only as a memory.

The World of Islam as a New Civilization

As the religion spread and the Abbasid dynasty declined, the civilization of Islam, unlike that of China but similar to Western Christendom, operated without a dominant political center, bound more by a shared religious culture than by a shared state. Twice that civilization was threatened from outside. The most devastating intrusion came during the thirteenth century from the Mongols, who conquered Central Asia and Persia while incorporating many Muslims within the huge Mongol domains. Less serious but more well known, at least in the West, were the Christian Crusades (1095–1291), which seized Jerusalem and established several small and temporary outposts along the eastern Mediterranean (see "Europe Outward Bound" in Chapter 10).

Despite these external threats and its various internal conflicts, Islamic civilization flourished and often prospered, embracing at least parts of virtually every other civilization in the Afro-Eurasian hemisphere. It was in that sense "history's first truly global civilization," although the Americas, of course, were not involved.[20] What held this Islamic world together? What enabled many people to feel themselves part of a single civilization despite its political fragmentation, religious controversies, and cultural and regional diversity?

Networks of Faith

At the core of that vast civilization was a common commitment to Islam. No group was more important in the transmission of those beliefs and practices than the ulama. These learned scholars were not "priests" in the Christian sense, for in Islam, at least theoretically, no person could stand between the believer and Allah. Rather, they served as judges, interpreters, administrators, prayer leaders, and reciters of the Quran, but especially as preservers and teachers of the sharia. Supported mostly by their local communities, some also received the patronage of sultans, or rulers, and were therefore subject to criticism for corruption and undue submission to state authority. In their homes, mosques, shrines, and Quranic schools, the ulama passed on the core teachings of the faith. Beginning in the eleventh century, formal colleges called *madrassas* offered more advanced instruction in the Quran and the sayings of Muhammad; grammar and rhetoric; sometimes philosophy, theology, mathematics, and medicine; and, above all else, law. Teaching was informal and mostly oral, and it involved much memorization of texts. It was also largely conservative, seeking to preserve an established body of Islamic learning.

The ulama were an "international elite," and the system of education they created served to bind together an immense and diverse civilization. Common texts were shared widely across the world of Islam. Students and teachers alike traveled great distances in search of the most learned scholars. From Indonesia to West Africa, educated Muslims inhabited a "shared world of debate and reference."[21]

Paralleling the educational network of the ulama were the emerging religious orders of the Sufis. By the tenth century, particular Sufi *shaykhs* (shakes), or teachers, began to attract groups of disciples who were eager to learn their unique devotional practices and techniques of personal transformation. The disciples usually swore allegiance to their teacher and valued highly the chain of transmission by which those teachings and practices had come down from earlier masters. In the twelfth and thirteenth centuries, Sufis began to organize in a variety of larger associations, some limited to particular regions and others with chapters throughout the Islamic world.

Sufi orders were especially significant in the frontier regions of Islam because they followed conquering armies or traders into Central and Southeast Asia, India, Anatolia, parts of Africa, and elsewhere. Their devotional teachings, modest ways of living, and reputation for supernatural powers gained a hearing for the new faith. Their emphasis on personal experience of the Divine, rather than on the law, allowed the Sufis to accommodate elements of local belief and practice and encouraged the growth of a popular or blended Islam. The veneration of deceased Sufi "saints," or "friends of God," particularly at their tombs, created sacred spaces that enabled Islam to take root in many places despite its foreign origins. But that flexibility also often earned Sufi practitioners the enmity of the ulama, who were sharply critical of any deviations from the sharia.

Like the madrassas and the sharia, Sufi religious ideas and institutions spanned the Islamic world and were yet another thread in the cosmopolitan web of Islamic civilization. Particular devotional teachings and practices spread widely, as did the writings of such famous Sufi poets as Hafiz and Rumi. Devotees made pilgrimages to the distant tombs of famous teachers, who, they often believed, might intercede with God on their behalf. Wandering Sufis, in search of the wisdom of renowned shaykhs, found fellow seekers and welcome shelter in the compounds of Sufi religious orders.

In addition to the networks of the Sufis and the ulama, many thousands of people, from kings to peasants, made the grand pilgrimage to Mecca—the hajj—no doubt gaining some sense of the umma. There men and women together, hailing from all over the Islamic world, joined as one people to rehearse the central elements of their faith. The claims of local identities based on family, clan, tribe, ethnicity, or state never disappeared, but now overarching them all was the inclusive unity of the Muslim community.

Networks of Exchange

The world of Islamic civilization cohered not only as a network of faith but also as an immense arena of exchange in which goods, technologies, food products, and ideas circulated widely. By 1000, large areas of the Afro-Eurasian world operated within a single cultural realm, practicing Islam or speaking Arabic. This huge region rapidly became a vast trading zone of hemispheric dimensions. In part, this was due to its central location in the Afro-Eurasian world and the breaking down of earlier political barriers between the Byzantine and Persian empires. Furthermore, commerce was valued positively within Islamic teaching, and laws regulating it figured prominently in the sharia, creating a predictable framework for exchange across many cultures. The pilgrimage to Mecca, as well as the urbanization that accompanied the growth of Islamic civilization, likewise fostered commerce. Baghdad, established in 756 as the capital of the Abbasid Empire, soon grew into a magnificent city of half a million people. The appetite of urban elites for luxury goods stimulated both craft production and the desire for foreign products.

Thus Muslim merchants quickly became prominent and sometimes dominant players in all the major Afro-Eurasian trade routes of the third-wave era — in the Mediterranean Sea, along the revived Silk Roads, across the Sahara, and throughout the Indian Ocean basin. By the eighth century, Arab and Persian traders had established a commercial colony in Canton in southern China, thus linking the Islamic heartland with Asia's other giant and flourishing economy. Various forms of banking, partnerships, business contracts, and instruments for granting credit facilitated these long-distance economic relationships and generated a prosperous, sophisticated, and highly commercialized economy that spanned the Old World.

The vast expanse of Islamic civilization also contributed to ecological change as agricultural products and practices spread from one region to another, a process already under way in the earlier Roman and Persian empires. Among the food crops that circulated within and beyond the Islamic world were different varieties of sugarcane, rice, apricots, artichokes, eggplants, lemons, oranges, almonds, figs, and bananas. Equally significant were water-management practices, so important to the arid or semi-arid environments of many parts of the Islamic world. Persian-style reservoirs and irrigation technologies spread as far as Tunisia and Morocco, the northern fringes of the Sahara, Spain, and Yemen. All of this contributed to an "Islamic Green Revolution" of increased food production, as well as to population growth, urbanization, and industrial development across the Islamic world.

Technology too diffused widely within the realm of Islam. Muslim technicians made improvements on rockets, first developed in China, by developing one that carried a small warhead and another that was used to attack ships. Papermaking techniques entered the Abbasid Empire from China in the eighth century or earlier, with paper mills soon operating in Persia, Iraq, and Egypt. This revolutionary technology, which served to strengthen bureaucratic governments, passed from the Middle East into India and Europe over the following centuries. Everywhere it spurred the emergence of books and written culture at the expense of earlier orally based cultural expressions.

Ideas likewise circulated across the Islamic world. The religion itself drew heavily and quite openly on Jewish and Christian precedents. Persia also contributed much in the way of bureaucratic practice, court ritual, and poetry, with Persian becoming a major literary language in elite circles. Scientific, medical, and philosophical texts, especially from ancient Greece, the Hellenistic world, and India, were systematically translated into Arabic, providing an enormous boost to Islamic scholarship and science for several centuries. In 830, the Abbasid caliph al-Mamun, himself a poet and scholar with a passion for foreign learning, established the **House of Wisdom** in Baghdad as an academic center for this research and translation. Stimulated by Greek texts, a school of Islamic thinkers known as Mutazalites ("those who stand apart") argued that reason, rather than revelation, was the "surest way to truth."[22] In the long run, however, the philosophers' emphasis on logic, rationality, and the laws of nature was subject to increasing criticism by those who held that only the Quran, the sayings of the Prophet, or mystical experience represented a genuine path to God.

But the realm of Islam was much more than a museum of ancient achievements from the civilizations that it encompassed. Those traditions mixed and blended to generate a distinctive Islamic civilization with many new contributions to the world of learning. (See Snapshot: Key Achievements in Islamic Science and Scholarship, page 273.) Using Indian numerical notation, for example, Arab scholars developed algebra as a novel mathematical discipline. They also undertook much original work in astronomy and optics. They built on earlier Greek and Indian practice to create a remarkable tradition in medicine and pharmacology. Arab physicians such as al-Razi and Ibn Sina accurately diagnosed many diseases, such as hay fever, measles, smallpox, diphtheria, rabies, and diabetes. In addition, Arab doctors developed treatments such as a mercury ointment for scabies, cataract and hernia operations, and gold fillings

A Muslim Astronomical Observatory Drawing initially on Greek, Indian, and Persian astronomy, the Islamic world after 1000 developed its own distinctive tradition of astronomical observation and prediction, reflected in this Turkish observatory constructed in 1557. Muslim astronomy later exercised considerable influence in both China and Europe. (Bridgeman Images)

| SNAPSHOT | KEY ACHIEVEMENTS IN ISLAMIC SCIENCE AND SCHOLARSHIP |

Person/Dates	Achievement
al-Khwarazim (790–840)	Mathematician; spread use of Arabic numerals in Islamic world; wrote first book on algebra
al-Razi (865–925)	Discovered sulfuric acid; wrote a vast encyclopedia of medicine, drawing on Greek, Syrian, Indian, and Persian work and his own clinical observation
al-Biruni (973–1048)	Mathematician, astronomer, cartographer; calculated the radius of the earth with great accuracy; worked out numerous mathematical innovations; developed a technique for displaying a hemisphere on a plane
Ibn Sina (Avicenna) (980–1037)	Prolific writer in almost all fields of science and philosophy; especially known for *Canon of Medicine*, a fourteen-volume work that set standards for medical practice in Islamic and Christian worlds for centuries
Omar Khayyam (1048–1131)	Mathematician; critic of Euclid's geometry; measured the solar year with great accuracy; Sufi poet; author of *The Rubaiyat*
Ibn Rushd (Averroës) (1126–1198)	Translated and commented widely on Aristotle; rationalist philosopher; made major contributions in law, mathematics, and medicine
Nasir al-Din Tusi (1201–1274)	Founder of the famous Maragha observatory in Persia (data from Maragha probably influenced Copernicus); mapped the motion of stars and planets
Ibn Khaldun (1332–1406)	Greatest Arab historian; identified trends and structures in world history over long periods of time

for teeth. The first hospitals, traveling clinics, and examinations for physicians and pharmacologists were also developed within the Islamic world. In the eleventh and twelfth centuries, this enormous body of medical scholarship entered Europe via Spain, and it remained at the core of European medical practice for many centuries.

Conclusions and Reflections: The Islamic World and the Uses of History

Among the many benefits of history is the perspective it provides on the present. Given the obvious importance of the Islamic world in the international arena of the twenty-first century, how might some grasp of the early development of Islamic civilization assist us in understanding our present circumstances?

Certainly, that history reminds us of the central role that Islamic civilization played in the Afro-Eurasian world for a thousand years or more. From 600 to 1600 or later, it was a proud, cosmopolitan, often prosperous, and frequently powerful civilization that spanned Africa, Europe, the Middle East, and Asia. It embodied the world's newest religious tradition, which drew on Zoroastrian, Jewish, and Christian precedents. Everywhere, Muslims embraced the Quran, honored the Prophet Muhammad, and sought to practice the required ritual prayers, the month of fasting during Ramadan, and the pilgrimage (hajj) to Mecca. For several centuries a huge empire gave a measure of political unity to this emerging civilization. Even when that empire fragmented, Muslim merchants and religious teachers traveled across those vast domains. Muslims absorbed much from the Greco-Roman world, Persia, India, and China, while passing on their own cultural achievements in mathematics, medicine, technology, and the arts to other civilizations.

Over the past several centuries, Islamic civilization, like many others, has confronted a European or Western imperialism that many Muslims have found humiliating, even if some have been attracted by elements of modern Western culture. In their recent efforts to overcome those centuries of subordination and exploitation, Muslims have found encouragement and inspiration in their more distant and perhaps more glorious past. But they have not all chosen to emphasize the same past. Those labeled as "fundamentalists" have often viewed the early Islamic community associated with Medina, Mecca, and Muhammad as a model for Islamic renewal in the present and have sought to return to it, sometimes quite rigidly. Others, often known as Islamic modernizers, have looked to the somewhat later achievements of Islamic science and scholarship as a foundation for a more open engagement with the West and the modern world.

The history of Islam also reveals a world of great diversity and debate. Sharp religious differences between Sunni and Shia understandings of the faith; differences in emphasis between advocates of the sharia and of Sufi spirituality; political conflicts among various groups and regions within the larger Islamic world; different postures toward women—all of this and more divided the umma and divide it still.

Historical experiences also differed. Persians adopted Islam but retained their own language, while Egyptians assimilated both Islam and the Arabic language. Conversion to Islam in Anatolia encompassed the vast majority of people, but only a minority in South Asia. Islam spread slowly in West Africa, largely in urban areas and without the pressures of foreign conquest that many other areas had to endure. Spain was one of the few places in the Islamic world that experienced a religious reversal as the Christian reconquest unfolded. Recalling these elements of diversity is a useful reminder for any who would tag all Muslims with a single label.

A further dimension of that diversity lies in the many cultural encounters that the spread of Islam has spawned. Sometimes great conflict and violence have accompanied those encounters, as in the Crusades and in Turkic invasions of India and Anatolia. At other times and places, Muslims and non-Muslims have lived together in relative tranquility and tolerance—in Spain, in West Africa, in India, and in the Ottoman Empire. Some commentaries on the current interaction of Islam and the West seem to assume an eternal hostility or an inevitable clash of civilizations. The record of the past, however, shows considerable variation in the interaction of Muslims and others.

While the past certainly shapes and conditions what happens next, the future, as always, remains open. And so, within limits, Muslims and non-Muslims alike have been able to choose the history on which they seek to build. History, like many texts, can be mobilized for a wide variety of purposes.

Revisiting Chapter 9

REVISITING SPECIFICS

Muhammad, 249
Quran, 249
umma, 250
Pillars of Islam, 251
hijra, 251
sharia, 252
jizya, 255
Umayyad caliphate, 257

Abbasid caliphate, 257
ulama, 258
Sufism, 258
Sikhism, 264
Timbuktu, 267
al-Andalus, 268
madrassas, 270
House of Wisdom, 272

REVISITING CORE IDEAS

1. **Explaining the Origins of Islam** In what ways did the early history of Islam reflect its Arabian origins?
2. **Identifying Change** How was Arabia transformed by the rise of Islam?
3. **Explaining Success** How might you account for the immense religious and political/military success of Islam in its early centuries?
4. **Defining Conflicts** What divisions and controversies broke the unity of the early Islamic world?
5. **Making Comparisons** What similarities and differences can you identify in the spread of Islam to India, Anatolia, West Africa, and Spain?
6. **Defining the Islamic World** What makes it possible to speak of the Islamic world around 1450 as a distinct, coherent, and somewhat unified civilization?

A WIDER VIEW

1. In what ways might Islamic civilization around 1450 be described as cosmo-politan, international, or global?
2. "Islam was simultaneously a single world of shared meaning and interaction and a series of separate, distinct, and conflicting communities." What evidence could you provide to support both parts of this statement?
3. "Islam had a revolutionary impact on every society that it touched." What evidence might support this statement, and what might challenge it?
4. How did Islam as a religion interact with the political, military, economic, and cultural dimensions of the civilization in which it was located? Is it possible or useful to separate these elements of Islamic civilization?
5. **Looking Back** What distinguished the early centuries of Islamic history from a similar phase in the history of Christianity and Buddhism?

CHRONOLOGY

570–632	• Life of Muhammad
633–644	• Muslim conquest of Persian Sassanid Empire
642–698	• Arab conquest of North Africa
656–692	• Civil war in the Arab Empire; beginning of Sunni-Shia division
661–750	• Umayyad caliphate
711–718	• Muslim conquest of Spain
751	• Battle of Talas River
750–900	• Flourishing of Abbasid caliphate
800–1000	• Emergence of Sufism
ca. 900–1000	• Golden age of Muslim Spain
1000	• Beginning of Turkic Muslim conquests in India
1000–1300	• Penetration of Islam into West Africa
1095–1291	• Christian Crusades
1206	• Sultanate of Delhi established in India
1258	• Mongols end Abbasid caliphate
1324	• Mansa Musa's pilgrimage to Mecca
1352–1354	• Ibn Battuta's visit to West Africa
1359–1481	• Ottoman conquests in southeastern Europe
1453	• Ottoman conquest of Constantinople; end of Byzantine Empire
1464–1492	• Sonni Ali rules Songhay
1492	• Christian reconquest of Spain completed

The Worlds of Christendom
Contraction, Expansion, and Division

600–1450

CONNECTING PAST AND PRESENT

YAO HONG, A CHINESE WOMAN, WAS ABOUT twenty years of age around 1990 when, distraught at discovering that her husband was having an affair, she became a Christian. As a migrant from a rural village to the huge city of Shanghai, Yao Hong found support and a sense of family in a Christian community. Interviewed in 2010, she observed, "Whether they know you or not, they treat you as a brother or sister. . . . [T]hey help out with

277

money or material assistance or spiritual aid." Nor did she find the Christian faith alien to her Chinese culture. To the contrary, she felt conversion to Christianity as a patriotic act, even a way of becoming more fully modern. "God is rising here in China," she declared. "If you look at the United States or England, . . . [t]heir churches are rich, because God blesses them."[1]

Yao Hong is but one of many millions who have made Christianity a very rapidly growing faith in China over the past forty years or so. And not only in China. Neighboring South Korea now has more practicing Christians than Buddhists. Even more impressively, sub-Saharan Africa witnessed an explosive advance of Christianity during the past century, leading a recent report to conclude that "Christianity's future lies in Africa."[2] By 2019, some 67 percent of the world's Christians lived in the Global South of Asia, Africa, or Latin America, while just 33 percent found their home in the Global North of Europe and North America, which in 1910 had housed over 80 percent of those claiming the Christian faith.[3] In little more than a century, the distribution of the world's Christians had shifted dramatically—in a pattern that was broadly similar to the reach of Christianity in the sixth- and seventh-century world.

Christianity in the sixth and seventh centuries enjoyed an Afro-Eurasian reach with flourishing communities in Anatolia, Arabia, Egypt, North Africa, Ethiopia, Nubia, Syria, Armenia, Persia, India, and China, as well as Europe. But during the third-wave era, radical changes reshaped that Christian world. Its African and Asian outposts largely vanished, declined, or were marginalized as Christianity became primarily a European phenomenon for the next thousand years or more. Furthermore, this European Christian world became deeply divided. Its eastern half, known as the Byzantine Empire or Byzantium (bihz-ANN-tee-uhm), continued the traditions of the Greco-Roman world in the eastern Mediterranean basin until its conquest by the Muslim Ottoman Empire in 1453. Centered on the magnificent city of Constantinople, Byzantium gradually developed a particular form of Christianity known as Eastern Orthodoxy and a distinctive third-wave civilization.

In Western, or Latin, Christendom, encompassing what we now know as Western Europe, the setting was far different. There the Roman imperial order had largely vanished by 500 C.E., replaced by highly localized societies—fragmented, decentralized, and competitive—in sharp contrast to the unified state of Byzantium. In Western Europe, a Roman Catholic version of the faith gradually emerged, increasingly centered on the pope and with an independence from political authorities that the Eastern Orthodox Church did not possess. Moreover, the Western Church in particular and its society in general were far more rural than Byzantium and certainly had nothing to compare to the imperial splendor of Constantinople. However, slowly at first and then with increasing speed after 1000, Western Europe emerged as an especially dynamic, expansive, and innovative third-wave civilization, combining elements of its Greco-Roman-Christian past with the culture of Germanic and Celtic peoples to produce a distinctive hybrid, or blended, civilization.

Thus the story of global Christendom in the era of third-wave civilizations is one of contractions and expansions. As a religion, Christianity contracted sharply in Asia and Africa even as it expanded in Western Europe and Russia. As a civilization, Christian Byzantium flourished for a time, then gradually contracted and in 1453 finally disappeared. The trajectory of civilization in the West traced an opposite path, at first contracting as the Roman Empire collapsed and later expanding as a new and blended civilization took hold in Western Europe.

SEEKING THE MAIN POINT	In what different ways did the history of Christianity and Christian civilizations unfold in various parts of the Afro-Eurasian world during the third-wave era?

Christian Contraction in Asia and Africa

It was the wholly unforeseen birth of Islam, an expanding Arab Empire, and a sophisticated transcontinental Muslim civilization that led to the contraction of Christendom in Asia and Africa. As a result, European civilization emerged as the principal center of the Christian faith.[4]

Asian Christianity

In Arabia, the homeland of Islam, the decimation of earlier Christian communities occurred most completely and most quickly, for within a century or so of Muhammad's death in 632, only a few Christian groups remained. During the eighth century, triumphant Muslims marked the replacement of the old religion by using pillars of a demolished Christian cathedral to construct the Grand Mosque of Sana'a in southern Arabia.

Elsewhere in the Middle East, other Jewish and Christian communities soon felt the impact of Islam. Expanding Muslim forces took control of Jerusalem in 638 and subsequently constructed the Muslim shrine known as the Dome of the Rock (687–691). In doing so, Muslim authorities appropriated for Islam a city long sacred to both Jews and Christians. In Syria and Persia, with more concentrated populations of Christians, the new Muslim rulers generally accommodated the religion of their new Christian subjects. In both areas, however, the majority of people turned to Islam voluntarily, attracted perhaps by its aura of success.

Treatment of Christians varied with the attitudes of local Muslim rulers. On occasion, churches were destroyed, villages plundered, fields burned, and Christians forced to wear distinctive clothing. By contrast, a wave of church building took place in Syria under Muslim rule, and Christians were recruited into the administration, schools, translation services, and even the armed forces of the Arab Empire. Thus the Nestorian Christian communities of Syria, Iraq, and Persia, sometimes called the Church of the East, survived the assault of Islam, but they did so as shrinking communities of second-class subjects, regulated minorities forbidden from propagating their message to Muslims. They also abandoned their religious paintings and sculptures, fearing to offend Muslims, who generally objected to any artistic representation of the Divine.

Nestorian Christianity in China This wall painting from western China, dating to the seventh or eighth century C.E., shows Nestorian priests in a procession on Palm Sunday. It provides visual evidence of a meaningful Christian presence in Tang dynasty China. (Pictures from History/Bridgeman Images)

But farther east, a small and highly creative Nestorian Church, initiated in 635 by a Persian missionary monk, had taken root in China with the approval of the country's Tang dynasty rulers. Both its art and literature articulated the Christian message using Buddhist and Daoist concepts. The written texts themselves, known as the **Jesus Sutras**, refer to Christianity as the "Religion of Light from the West" or the "Luminous Religion." They describe God as the "Cool Wind," sin as "bad karma," and a good life as one of "no desire" and "no action." "People can live only by dwelling in the living breath of God," the Jesus Sutras declare. "All the Buddhas are moved by this wind, which blows everywhere in the world."[5] By the end of the Tang dynasty (907 C.E.), the Nestorian Church had substantially faded away. The contraction of this remarkable experiment owed little to Islam and more to the vagaries of Chinese politics. In the mid-ninth century, the Chinese state turned against all religions of foreign origin, Islam and Buddhism as well as Christianity (see "Losing State Support: The Crisis of Chinese Buddhism" in Chapter 8). Wholly dependent on the goodwill of Chinese authorities, this small outpost of Christianity withered.

African Christianity

The churches of Africa, like those of the Middle East and Asia, also found themselves on the defensive and declining in the face of an expanding Islam. Across coastal North Africa, widespread conversion to Islam over several centuries reduced to virtual extinction Christian communities that had earlier provided many of the martyrs and intellectuals of the early Church.

In Egypt, however, Christianity had become the religion of the majority by the time of the Muslim conquest around 640, and for the next 500 years or so, large numbers continued to speak Coptic and practice their religion as *dhimmis*, legally inferior but protected people paying a special tax, under relatively tolerant Muslim rulers. Many found Arab government less oppressive than that of their former Byzantine overlords, who considered Egyptian Christians heretics. By the thirteenth century, things changed dramatically as Christian Crusaders from Europe and Mongol invaders from the east threatened Egypt. In these circumstances, the country's Muslim rulers came to suspect the political loyalty of their Christian subjects. The mid-fourteenth century witnessed violent anti-Christian pogroms, destruction of churches, and the forced removal of Christians from the best land. Many felt like "exiles in their own country." As a result, most rural Egyptians converted to Islam and moved toward the use of Arabic rather than Coptic, which largely died out. But although Egypt was becoming an Arab and Muslim country, a substantial Christian minority persisted, especially among the literate in urban areas and in monasteries located in remote regions. In the early twenty-first century, Egyptian Christians still numbered about 10 percent of the population.

Even as Egyptian Christianity was contracting, a new center of African Christianity was taking shape during the fifth and sixth centuries in the several kingdoms of Nubia to the south of Egypt, where the faith had been introduced by Egyptian traders and missionaries. Parts of the Bible were translated into the Nubian language, while other writings appeared in Greek, Arabic, and the Ethiopian language of Ge'ez. A great cathedral in the Nubian city of Faras was decorated with magnificent murals, and the earlier practice of burying servants to provide for rulers in the afterlife stopped abruptly. At times, kings served as priests, and Christian bishops held state offices. By the mid-seventh century, both the ruling class and many commoners had become Christian. At the same time, Nubian armies twice defeated Arab incursions, and following these defeats an agreement with Muslim Egypt protected this outpost of Christianity for some 600 years. But pressures mounted in the thirteenth and fourteenth centuries as Egypt adopted a more hostile stance toward Christians, while Islamized peoples from the desert and Arab migrants pushed against Nubia. By 1500, **Nubian Christianity**, like its counterparts in coastal North Africa, had largely disappeared.

An important exception to these various contractions of Asian and African Christianity lay in Ethiopia. There the rulers of Axum had adopted Christianity in the fourth century, and it later took root among the general population as well. Over the centuries of Islamic expansion, Ethiopia became a Christian island in a Muslim sea, protected by its mountainous geography and its distance from major centers of Islamic power. Nonetheless, the spread of Islam largely cut Ethiopia off from other parts of Christendom and rendered its position in Northeast Africa precarious.

In its isolated location, **Ethiopian Christianity** developed some of its most distinctive features. One of these was a fascination with Judaism and Jerusalem, reflected in a much-told story about the visit of an Ethiopian Queen of Sheba to King Solomon. The story includes an episode in which Solomon seduces the queen, producing a child who becomes the founding monarch of the Ethiopian state. Since Solomon figures in the line of descent to Jesus, it meant that Ethiopia's Christian rulers could legitimate their position by tracing their ancestry to Jesus himself. Furthermore, Ethiopian monks long maintained a presence in Jerusalem's Church of the Holy Sepulcher, said to mark the site where Jesus was crucified and buried. Then, in the twelfth century, the rulers of a new Ethiopian dynasty constructed a remarkable cluster of about a dozen linked underground churches and buildings, apparently attempting to create a New Jerusalem on Christian Ethiopian soil, as the original city lay under Muslim control. Those churches are in use to this day in modern Ethiopia, where over 60 percent of the country's population retains an affiliation with this ancient Christian church.

Byzantine Christendom: Building on the Roman Past

The contraction of the Christian faith and Christian societies in Asia and Africa left the two civilizations of western Eurasia, the **Byzantine Empire** and Western Europe, largely by default, as the centers of Christendom. At the end of the third century, the Roman Empire was divided into eastern and western halves in an effort to provide more effective governance in the face of mounting political instability. This action launched a division of Christendom that has lasted into the twenty-first century.

Unlike most empires, Byzantium has no clear starting point. Its own leaders, as well as its neighbors and enemies, viewed it as simply a continuation of the Roman Empire, and it lasted for a thousand years after the collapse of Roman rule in the West. Housing the ancient civilizations of Egypt, Greece, Syria, and Anatolia, the eastern Roman Empire (Byzantium) was far wealthier, more urbanized, and more cosmopolitan than its western counterpart; it possessed a much more defensible capital in the heavily walled city of **Constantinople**; and it had a shorter frontier to guard. Byzantium also enjoyed access to the Black Sea and command of the eastern Mediterranean. With a stronger army, navy, and merchant marine as well as clever diplomacy, its leaders were able to deflect the Germanic and Hun invaders who had overwhelmed the western Roman Empire.

Much that was late Roman — its roads, taxation system, military structures, centralized administration, imperial court, laws, Christian Church — persisted in the East for many centuries. Like Tang dynasty China seeking to restore the glory of the Han era, Byzantium consciously sought to preserve the legacy of classical Greco-Roman civilization. Constantinople, established in 330 C.E., was to be a "New Rome," and people referred to themselves as "Romans." Fearing contamination by "barbarian" (non-Roman) customs, emperors forbade the residents of Constantinople to wear boots, trousers, clothing made from animal skins, and long hairstyles, all of which were associated with Germanic peoples, and insisted instead on Roman-style robes and sandals. But much changed as well over the centuries, marking the Byzantine Empire as the home of a distinctive civilization.

The Byzantine State

Perhaps the most obvious change was one of scale, as the Byzantine Empire never approximated the size of its Roman predecessor (see Map 10.1). The western Roman Empire was permanently lost to Byzantium, despite Emperor Justinian's (r. 527–565) impressive but short-lived attempt to reconquer the Mediterranean basin. The rapid Arab/Islamic expansion in the seventh century resulted in the loss of Syria/Palestine, Egypt, and North Africa. Nonetheless, until roughly 1200, a more compact Byzantine Empire remained a major force in the eastern Mediterranean, controlling Greece, much of the Balkans (southeastern Europe), and Anatolia. From that territorial base, the empire's naval and merchant vessels were active in both the Mediterranean and Black seas.

In its heyday, the Byzantine state was an impressive creation. Political authority remained tightly centralized in Constantinople, where the emperor claimed to govern

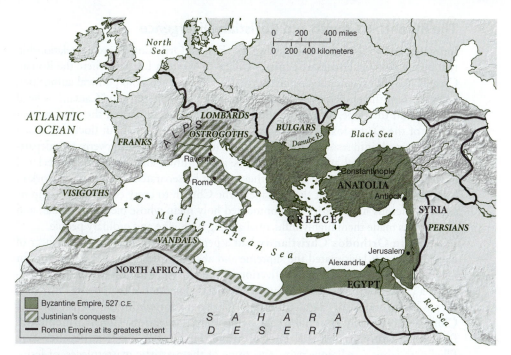

MAP 10.1   The Byzantine Empire
The Byzantine Empire reached its greatest extent under Emperor Justinian in the mid-sixth century C.E. It later lost considerable territory to various Christian European powers as well as to Muslim Arab and Turkic invaders.

all creation as God's worldly representative, styling himself the "peer of the Apostles" and the "sole ruler of the world." The imperial court tried to imitate the awesome grandeur of what it thought was God's heavenly court, but in fact it resembled ancient Persian imperial splendor. Aristocrats trained in Greek rhetoric and literature occupied high positions in the administration, participating in court ceremonies that maintained their elite status. But this centralized state touched only lightly on the lives of most people, as it focused primarily on collecting taxes, maintaining order, and suppressing revolts. The Byzantine central authorities proved quite adaptable in their efforts to give local elites the autonomy necessary to reduce tensions within the empire and to mount an effective defense of its borders.

Nonetheless, the ongoing inability of the empire to develop an orderly system for selecting new rulers sparked civil wars several times. Furthermore, periodic invasions by powerful neighbors — Huns, Persians, Arabs, Western Europeans, and Turks — weakened and diminished the empire even as it showed remarkable resilience and capacity for revival. After 1085 the empire entered a period of slow and ultimately terminal decline. Byzantine territory shrank, owing to incursions by aggressive Western European powers, by Catholic Crusaders, and by Turkic Muslim invaders. The end came in 1453 when the Turkic Ottoman Empire, then known as the "sword of Islam," finally took Constantinople.

The Byzantine Church and Christian Divergence

Intimately tied to the Byzantine state was the Eastern Orthodox Church, a relationship that became known as **caesaropapism**. Unlike in Western Europe, where the Roman Catholic Church maintained some degree of independence from political authorities, in Byzantium the emperor assumed something of the role of both "Caesar," as head of state, and the pope, as head of the Church. Thus he appointed the patriarch, or leader, of the Orthodox Church; sometimes made decisions about doctrine; called church councils into session; and generally treated the Church as a government department. "The [Empire] and the church have a great unity and community," declared a twelfth-century patriarch. "Indeed they cannot be separated."[6] A dense network of bishops and priests brought the message of the Church to every corner of the empire, while numerous monasteries accommodated holy men, whose piety, self-denial, and good works made them highly influential among both elite and ordinary people.

Eastern Orthodox Christianity had a pervasive influence on every aspect of Byzantine life. It legitimated the supreme and absolute authority of the emperor, for he was a God-anointed ruler, a reflection of the glory of God on earth. It also provided a cultural identity for the empire's subjects. Even more than being "Roman," they were orthodox, or "right-thinking," Christians for whom the empire and the Church were equally essential to achieving eternal salvation. Constantinople was filled with churches and the relics of numerous saints. And the churches were filled with icons—religious paintings, some of them artistic masterpieces, of Jesus, Mary, and numerous saints—that many believed conveyed the Divine Presence to the faithful. Complex theological issues about the Trinity and especially about the

St. Mark's Basilica Consecrated in 1094, this ornate cathedral, although located in Venice, Italy, is a classic example of Byzantine architecture. Such churches represented perhaps the greatest achievement of Byzantine art and were certainly the most monumental expressions of Byzantine culture. (Erich Lessing/Art Resource, NY)

relationship of God and Jesus engaged the attention of ordinary people. For example, partisans of competing chariot-racing teams, known as the Greens and the Blues, vigorously debated theological issues as well as the merits of their favorite drivers.

In its early centuries and beyond, the Christian movement was rent by theological controversy and political division. But the most lasting and deepest division within the Christian world occurred as Eastern Orthodoxy came to define itself against an emerging Latin Christianity centered on papal Rome. Both had derived, of course, from the growth of Christianity in the Roman Empire and therefore had much in common—the teachings of Jesus; the Bible; the sacraments; a church hierarchy of patriarchs, bishops, and priests; a missionary impulse; and intolerance toward other religions. Despite these shared features, any sense of a single widespread Christian community was increasingly replaced by an awareness of difference, competition, and outright hostility that even a common fear of Islam could not overcome. In part, this growing religious divergence reflected the political separation and rivalry between the Byzantine Empire and the emerging kingdoms of Western Europe. As the growth of Islam in the seventh century submerged earlier centers of Christianity in the Middle East and North Africa, Constantinople and Rome alone remained as alternative hubs of the Church. But they were now in different states that competed with each other for territory and for the right to claim the legacy of imperial Rome.

Beyond such political differences were those of language and culture. Although Latin remained the language of the Church and of elite communication in the West, it was abandoned in the Byzantine Empire in favor of Greek, which remained the basis for Byzantine education. More than in the West, Byzantine thinkers sought to formulate Christian doctrine in terms of Greek philosophical concepts.

Differences in theology and church practice likewise widened the gulf between Orthodoxy and Catholicism. Disagreements about the nature of the Trinity, the source of the Holy Spirit, original sin, and the relative importance of faith and reason gave rise to much controversy. So too, for a time, did the Byzantine efforts to prohibit the use of icons, popular paintings of saints and biblical scenes that were usually painted on small wooden panels. Other more modest differences also occasioned mutual misunderstanding and disdain. Priests in the West shaved and, after 1050 or so, were supposed to remain celibate, while those in Byzantium allowed their beards to grow long and were permitted to marry. Orthodox ritual called for using bread leavened with yeast in the Communion, but Catholics used unleavened bread. Far more significant was the question of authority. Eastern Orthodox leaders sharply rejected the growing claims of Roman popes to be the sole and final authority for all Christians everywhere.

This rift in the world of Christendom grew gradually from the seventh century on, punctuated by various efforts to bridge the mounting divide between the Western and Eastern branches of the Church. A sign of this continuing deterioration occurred in 1054 when representatives of both churches mutually excommunicated each other, declaring in effect that those in the opposing tradition were not genuine Christians. The **Crusades**, launched in 1095 by the Catholic pope against the forces of Islam, made things worse. Western Crusaders, passing through the Byzantine Empire on their way to the Middle East, engaged in frequent conflict with Eastern Orthodox Christians, whom they regarded as "blasphemous, even heretical." During the Fourth Crusade in 1204, Western forces seized and looted Constantinople, and they ruled Byzantium for the next half century. According to one Byzantine account, "They sacked the sacred places and trampled on divine things . . . they tore children from their mothers . . . and they defiled virgins in the holy chapels, fearing neither God's anger nor man's vengeance."[7] After this, the rupture in the world of Christendom proved irreparable.

Byzantium and the World

Beyond its tense relationship with Western Europe, the Byzantine Empire, located astride Europe and Asia, also interacted intensively with its other neighbors. On a political and military level, Byzantium continued the long-term Roman struggle with the Persian Empire. That persisting conflict weakened both of them and was one factor in the remarkable success of Arab armies as they marched out of Arabia in the seventh century. Although Persia quickly became part of the Islamic world, Byzantium held out, even as it lost considerable territory to the Arabs. A Byzantine military innovation known as "Greek fire"—a potent and flammable combination of oil, sulfur, and lime that was launched from bronze tubes—helped hold off the Arabs. It operated as something like a flamethrower and subsequently passed into Arab and Chinese arsenals as well. Byzantium's ability to defend its core regions delayed for many centuries the Islamic advance into southeastern Europe, which finally occurred at the hands of the Turkish Ottoman Empire in the fifteenth and sixteenth centuries.

Economically, the Byzantine Empire was a central player in the long-distance trade of Eurasia, with commercial links to Western Europe, Russia, Central Asia, the Islamic world, and China. Its gold coin, the bezant, was a widely used currency in the Mediterranean basin for more than 500 years, and wearing such coins as pendants was a high-status symbol in the less developed kingdoms of Western Europe. The luxurious products of Byzantine craftspeople—jewelry, gemstones, silver and gold work, linen and woolen textiles, purple dyes—were much in demand. Byzantium's silk industry, based on Chinese technology, supplied much of the Mediterranean basin with this precious fabric.

The cultural influence of Byzantium was likewise significant. Preserving much of ancient Greek learning, the Byzantine Empire transmitted this classical heritage to the Islamic world as well as to the Christian West. In both places, it had an immensely stimulating impact among scientists, philosophers, theologians, and other intellectuals. Some saw it as an aid to faith and to an understanding of the world, while others feared it as impious and distracting. Byzantine religious culture also spread widely among Slavic-speaking peoples in the Balkans and Russia. As lands to the south and the east were overtaken by Islam, Byzantium looked to the north. By the early eleventh century, steady military pressure had brought many of the Balkan Slavic peoples and the Turkic-speaking Bulgars under Byzantine control. Christianity and literacy accompanied this Byzantine offensive. Already in the ninth century, two Byzantine missionaries, Cyril and Methodius, had developed an alphabet, based on Greek letters, with which Slavic languages could be written. This Cyrillic script made it possible to translate the Bible and other religious literature into these languages and greatly aided the process of conversion.

The Conversion of Russia

The most significant expansion of Orthodox Christianity occurred among the Slavic peoples of what is now Ukraine and western Russia. In this culturally diverse region, which also included Finnic and Baltic peoples as well as Viking traders, a modest state known as **Kievan Rus** (KEE-yehv-ihn ROOS)—named after the most prominent city, Kiev—emerged in the ninth century. (See Map 10.3, page 292.) As in many of the new third-wave civilizations, the development of Rus was stimulated by trade, in this case along the Dnieper River, which linked Scandinavia and Byzantium. Loosely led by various princes, especially the prince of Kiev, Rus was a society of enslaved persons and freemen, privileged people and commoners, dominant men and subordinate women. This stratification marked it as a third-wave civilization in the making.

Religion reflected the region's cultural diversity, as ancestral spirits, household deities, and various gods related to the forces of nature were worshipped. Small numbers of Christians, Muslims, and Jews were likewise part of the mix. Then, in 988, a decisive turning point occurred. The growing interaction of Rus with the larger world prompted its prince, **Vladimir of Kiev**, to affiliate with the Eastern Orthodox faith of the Byzantine Empire. The prince was searching for a religion that would unify the diverse peoples of his region while linking Rus into wider networks of communication and exchange.

As elsewhere in Europe, the coming of Christianity to Rus was a top-down process in which ordinary people followed their rulers into the Church. It was also a slow process, and elements of traditional religious sensibility long lingered among those who defined themselves as Christian. Perun, the god of thunder, continued to speak to some, and "magicians" sometimes led people astray in the eyes of church authorities. But building churches on the site where images of Perun and other gods once stood helped to anchor the new faith in its new land.

It was a fateful choice with long-term implications for Russian history, for it brought this fledgling civilization firmly into the world of Orthodox Christianity, separating it from both the realm of Islam and the Roman Catholic West. Like many new civilizations, Rus borrowed extensively from its older and more sophisticated Byzantine neighbor. Among these borrowings were Byzantine architectural styles, the Cyrillic alphabet, the extensive use of icons, a monastic tradition stressing prayer and service, and political ideals of imperial control of the Church, all of which became part of a transformed Rus. Orthodoxy also provided a more unified identity for this emerging civilization and religious legitimacy for its rulers. Centuries later, when Byzantium had fallen to the Turks, a few Russian church leaders proclaimed the doctrine of a "third Rome." The original Rome had abandoned the true Orthodox faith for Roman Catholicism, and the second Rome, Constantinople, had succumbed to Muslim infidels. Moscow was now the third Rome, the final protector and defender of Orthodox Christianity. Though not widely proclaimed in Russia itself, such a notion reflected the "Russification" of Eastern Orthodoxy and its growing role as an element of Russian national identity. It was also a reminder of the enduring legacy of a thousand years of Byzantine history, long after the empire itself had vanished.

Western Christendom: Rebuilding in the Wake of Roman Collapse

The western half of the European Christian world followed a rather different path than that of the Byzantine Empire. For much of the third-wave era, **Western Christendom** was distinctly on the margins of world history, partly because of its geographic location at the far western end of the Eurasian landmass. Thus it was at a distance from the growing routes of world trade—by sea in the Indian Ocean and by land across the Silk Roads to China and the Sand Roads to West Africa. Internally, Europe's geography made political unity difficult, for population centers were divided by mountain ranges and dense forests as well as by five major peninsulas and two large islands (Britain and Ireland). However, Europe's extensive coastlines and interior river systems facilitated exchange, while a moderate climate, plentiful rainfall, and fertile soils enabled a productive agriculture that could support a growing population.

Political Life in Western Europe

In the early centuries of this era, history must have seemed more significant than geography, for the Roman Empire was gone. Much that had characterized Roman civilization also weakened, declined, or disappeared in the several centuries before and after 476, the traditional date marking the collapse of Roman rule in the West when German general Odoacer overthrew the last Roman emperor. Any semblance of large-scale centralized rule vanished. Disease and warfare reduced Western Europe's population by more than 25 percent. Land under cultivation contracted, while forests, marshland, and wasteland expanded. Urban life too diminished sharply, as Europe reverted to a largely rural existence. Rome at its height was a city of 1 million people, but by the tenth century it numbered perhaps 10,000. Public buildings crumbled from lack of care. Outside Italy, long-distance trade dried up as Roman roads deteriorated, and money exchange gave way to barter in many places. Literacy lost ground as well. Germanic peoples, whom the Romans had viewed as barbarians—Goths, Visigoths, Franks, Lombards, Angles, Saxons—now emerged as the dominant peoples of Western Europe. In the process, Europe's center of gravity moved away from the Mediterranean toward the north and west.

Yet much that was classical or Roman persisted, even as a new order emerged in Europe. On the political front, a series of regional kingdoms—led by Visigoths in Spain, Franks in France, Lombards in Italy, and Angles and Saxons in England—arose to replace Roman authority. As these Germanic peoples migrated into or invaded Roman lands, many were deeply influenced by Roman culture, especially if they had served in the Roman army. On the funeral monument of one such person was a telling inscription: "I am a Frank by nationality, but a Roman soldier under arms."[8]

The prestige of things Roman remained high, even after the empire itself had collapsed. Now as leaders of their own kingdoms, the Germanic rulers actively embraced written Roman law, using fines and penalties to provide order and justice in place of feuds and vendettas. One Visigoth ruler named Athaulf (r. 410–415), who had married a Roman noblewoman, gave voice to the continuing attraction of Roman culture and its empire:

> At first I wanted to erase the Roman name and convert all Roman territory into a Gothic empire. . . . But long experience has taught me that . . . without law a state is not a state. Therefore I have more prudently chosen the different glory of reviving the Roman name with Gothic vigour, and I hope to be acknowledged by posterity as the initiator of a Roman restoration.[9]

Several of the larger, though relatively short-lived, Germanic kingdoms also had aspirations to re-create something of the unity of the Roman Empire.

Charlemagne (SHAHR-leh-mane) (r. 768–814), ruler of the Carolingian Empire, occupying what is now France, Belgium, the Netherlands, and parts of Germany and Italy, erected an embryonic imperial bureaucracy, standardized weights and measures, and began to act like an imperial ruler. On Christmas Day of the year 800, he was crowned as a new Roman emperor by the pope, although his realm splintered shortly after his death (see Map 10.2). Later Otto I of Saxony (r. 936–973) gathered much of Germany under his control, saw himself as renewing Roman rule, and was likewise invested with the title of emperor by the pope. Otto's realm, later known as the **Holy Roman Empire**, was largely limited to Germany and soon proved little more than a collection of quarreling principalities. Though unsuccessful in reviving anything approaching Roman imperial authority, these efforts testify to the continuing appeal of the classical world, even as a new political system of rival kingdoms blended Roman and Germanic elements.

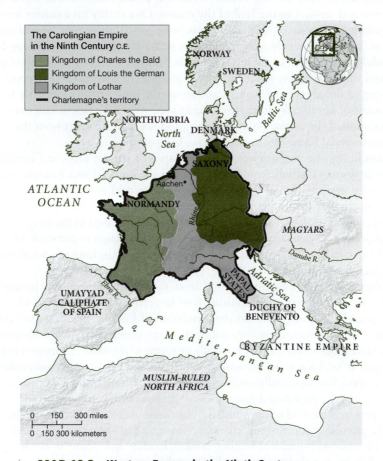

MAP 10.2   Western Europe in the Ninth Century
Charlemagne's Carolingian Empire brought a temporary political unity to parts of Western Europe, but it was subsequently divided among his three sons, who then waged war on one another.

Society and the Church

Within these new kingdoms, a highly fragmented and decentralized society emerged with great local variation. In a practice widely known as **feudalism**, lesser lords and knights swore allegiance to greater lords or kings and thus became their vassals, frequently receiving lands and plunder in return for military service. Meanwhile, on thousands of independent, self-sufficient, and largely isolated landed estates or manors, power — political, economic, and social — was exercised by landowning lords primarily drawn from the warrior elite, in a system known as **manorialism**.

Such reciprocal ties between superior and subordinate were also apparent at the bottom of the social hierarchy, as Roman-style slavery gradually gave way to serfdom. Unlike enslaved people, serfs were not the personal property of their masters, could not be arbitrarily thrown off their land, and were allowed to live in families. However, they were bound to their masters' estates as peasant laborers and owed various payments and services to the lord of the manor. One family on a manor near Paris in the ninth century owed four silver coins, wine, wood, three hens, and fifteen eggs per year. Women generally were required to weave cloth and make clothing for the lord, while men labored in the lord's fields. In return, the serf family received a small farm and such protection as the lord could provide. In a violent and insecure world adjusting to the absence of Roman authority, the only security available to many individuals or families lay in these communities, where the ties to kin, manor, and lord constituted the primary human loyalties. It was a world apart from the stability of life in imperial Rome or its continuation in Byzantium.

Also filling the vacuum left by the collapse of empire was the Church, later known as Roman Catholic, yet another link to the now-defunct Roman world. Its hierarchical organization of popes, bishops, priests, and monasteries was modeled on that of the Roman Empire and took over some of the empire's political, administrative, educational, and welfare functions. Latin continued as the language of the Church even as it gave way to various vernacular languages in common speech. In fact, literacy in the classical languages of Greek and Latin long remained the hallmark of educated people in the West.

Like the Buddhist establishment in China, the Church subsequently became quite wealthy, with reformers often accusing it of forgetting its central spiritual mission. It also provided a springboard for the conversion of Europe's many "pagan" peoples. Numerous missionaries, commissioned by the pope, monasteries, or already converted rulers, fanned out across Europe, generally pursuing a "top-down" strategy. Frequently it worked, as local kings and warlords found status and legitimacy in association with a literate and "civilized" religion that still bore something of the grandeur that was Rome. With "the wealth and protection of the powerful," ordinary people followed their rulers into the fold of the Church.[10] Christianity, like Buddhism in China, also bore the promise of superior supernatural powers, and its spread was frequently associated with reported miracles of healing, rainfall, fertility, and victory in battle.

But it was not always an easy sell. Outright coercion was sometimes part of the process. More often, however, softer methods prevailed. The Church proved willing to accommodate a considerable range of earlier cultural practices, absorbing them into an emerging Christian tradition. For example, amulets and charms to ward off evil became medals with the image of Jesus or the Virgin Mary; traditionally sacred wells and springs became the sites of churches; and festivals honoring ancient gods became Christian holy days. By 1100, most of Europe had embraced Christianity. Even so, for centuries priests and bishops had to warn their congregations against the worship of rivers, trees, and mountains, and for many people, ancient gods, monsters, trolls, and spirits still inhabited the land. The spreading Christian faith, like the new political framework of European civilization, was a blend of many elements.

Political elites and church authorities reinforced each other. Rulers and nobles provided protection for the papacy and strong encouragement for the faith. In return, the Church offered religious legitimacy for the powerful and the prosperous. "It is the will of the Creator," declared the teaching of the Church, "that the higher shall always rule over the lower. Each individual and class should stay in its place [and] perform its tasks."[11] But church and political authorities competed as well as cooperated, for they were rival centers of power in post-Roman Europe. Particularly controversial was the right to appoint bishops and the pope himself; this issue, known as the investiture conflict, was especially prominent in the eleventh and twelfth centuries. Was the right to make such appointments the responsibility of the Church alone, or did kings and emperors also have a role? In the compromise that ended the conflict, the Church won the right to appoint its own officials, while secular rulers retained an informal and symbolic role in the process.

Accelerating Change in the West

After various invaders — Huns, Magyars (Hungarians), and Vikings (see Map 10.3) — had been absorbed into settled society and in some cases had converted to Christianity, the pace of change in this emerging European civilization picked up considerably. In the several centuries after 1000, the greater security and stability that came with relative peace arguably opened the way to an accelerating tempo of change. The climate also seemed to cooperate. A generally warming trend after 750 reached its peak in the eleventh and twelfth centuries, enhancing agricultural production, especially in northern and highland regions.

During this new phase of European civilization, commonly called the High Middle Ages (1000–1300), the signs of expansion and growth were widely evident. The population of Europe grew from perhaps 35 million in 1000 to about 80 million in 1340. Many new lands were opened for cultivation in a process paralleling China's expansion to the south at the same time. Great lords, bishops, and religious orders organized new villages on what had recently been forest, marshes, or wasteland. Warmer weather during the summer months allowed farmers and pastoralists to herd their flocks into previously wild highland regions. Everywhere trees were felled at tremendous rates to clear agricultural land and to use as fuel or building material. By 1300, the forest cover of Europe had been reduced to about 20 percent of the land area. "I believe that the forest . . . covers the land to no purpose," declared a German abbot, "and hold this to be an unbearable harm."[12] These developments took a heavy toll on both the terrestrial and aquatic environments. Deforestation, overfishing, human waste, and the proliferation of new water mills and their associated ponds damaged freshwater ecosystems in many places. Lamenting the declining availability of fish, the French king Philip IV declared in 1289: "Today each and every river and waterside of our realm, large and small, yields nothing."[13]

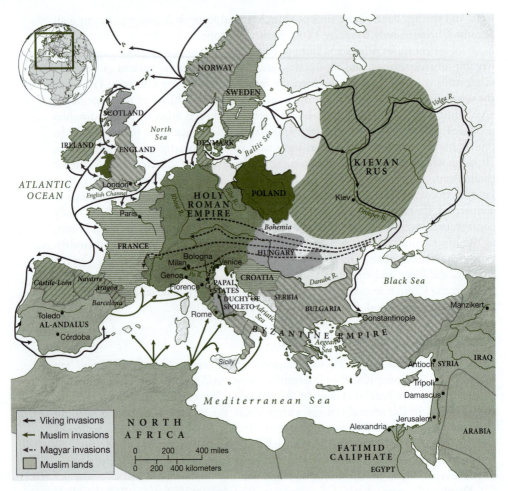

MAP 10.3   Europe in the Middle Ages

By the eleventh century, the national monarchies that would organize European political life—France, Spain, England, Poland, and Germany—had begun to take shape. The earlier external attacks on Europe from Vikings, Magyars, and Muslims had largely ceased, although it was clear that European civilization was developing in the shadow of the Islamic world.

The increased production associated with this agricultural expansion stimulated a considerable growth in long-distance trade, much of which had dried up in the aftermath of the Roman collapse. One center of commercial activity lay in Northern Europe from England to the Baltic coast. The other major trading network centered on northern Italian towns such as Florence, Genoa, and Venice. Their trading partners were the more established civilizations of Islam and Byzantium, and the primary objects of trade included silks, drugs, precious stones, and spices from Asia. At great trading fairs, particularly those in the Champagne area of France near Paris, merchants from Northern and Southern Europe met to exchange the products of their respective areas, such as northern woolens for Mediterranean spices. Thus the self-sufficient communities of earlier centuries increasingly forged commercial bonds among themselves and with more distant peoples.

The population of towns and cities likewise grew on the sites of older Roman towns, at trading crossroads and fortifications, and around cathedrals all over Europe. In the early 1300s, London had about 40,000 people, Paris had approximately 80,000, and Venice by the end of the fourteenth century could boast perhaps 150,000. To keep these figures in perspective, Constantinople housed some 400,000 people in 1000, Córdoba in Muslim Spain about 500,000, and the Song dynasty capital of Hangzhou more than 1 million in the thirteenth century. These towns gave rise to and attracted new groups of people, particularly merchants, bankers, artisans, and university-trained professionals such as lawyers, doctors, and scholars. Many of these groups, including university professors and students, organized themselves into guilds (associations of people pursuing the same line of work) to regulate their respective professions. Thus, from the rural social order of lord and peasant, a new more productive and complex division of labor was reshaping European society.

A further sign of accelerating change in the West lay in the growth of territorial states with more effective institutions of government commanding the loyalty, or at least the obedience, of their subjects. Since the disintegration of the Roman Empire, Europeans' loyalties had focused on the family, the manor, or the religious community, but seldom on the state. But in the eleventh through the thirteenth centuries, the nominal monarchs of Europe gradually and painfully began to consolidate their authority, and the outlines of French, English, Spanish, Scandinavian, and other states began to appear, each with its own distinct language and culture (see Map 10.3). Royal courts and fledgling bureaucracies were established, and groups of professional administrators appeared. In Italy, city-states flourished as urban areas grew wealthy and powerful, while the Germans remained divided among a large number of small principalities within the Holy Roman Empire.

These changes, which together represented the making of a new civilization, had implications for the lives of countless women and men. Economic growth and urbanization initially offered European women substantial new opportunities. Women were active in a number of urban professions, such as weaving, brewing, milling grain, midwifery, small-scale retailing, laundering, spinning, and prostitution. In twelfth-century Paris, for example, a list of 100 occupations identified 86 as involving women workers, of which 6 were exclusively female. However, much as economic and technological change in China had eroded female silk production, by the fifteenth century artisan opportunities were declining for European women as well. Most women's guilds were gone, and women were restricted or banned from many others. Even brothels were run by men. In England, guild regulations now outlawed women's participation in manufacturing particular fabrics and forbade their being trained on new and larger weaving machines. Women might still spin thread, but the more lucrative and skilled task of weaving fell increasingly to men. Technological progress may have been one reason for this change. Water- and animal-powered grain mills replaced the hand-grinding previously undertaken by women, and larger looms making heavier cloth replaced the lighter looms that women had worked. Men increasingly took over these professions and trained their sons as apprentices, making it more difficult for women to remain active in these fields.

The Church had long offered some women an alternative to home, marriage, family, and rural life. As in Buddhist lands, substantial numbers of women, particularly from aristocratic families, were attracted to the secluded monastic life of poverty, chastity, and obedience within a convent, in part for the relative freedom from male control that it offered. Here was one of the few places where women might exercise authority as abbesses of their orders and obtain a measure of education. The twelfth-century abbess Hildegard of Bingen, for example, won wide acclaim for her writings on theology, medicine, botany, and music.

But by 1300, much of the independence that such abbesses and their nuns had enjoyed was curtailed and male control tightened, even as veneration of the Virgin Mary swept across Western Christendom. Restrictions on women hearing confessions, preaching, and chanting the Gospel were now more strictly enforced. The educational activities of monastic centers, where men and women could both participate, now gave way to the new universities, where only ordained men could study and teach. Furthermore, older ideas of women's intellectual inferiority, the impurity of menstruation, and their role as sexual temptresses were mobilized to explain why women could never be priests and must operate under male control.

Thus tightening male control of women took place in Europe as it did in Song dynasty China at about the same time. Accompanying this change was a new understanding of masculinity, at least in the growing towns and cities. No longer able to function as warriors protecting their women, men increasingly defined themselves as "providers"; a man's role was to brave the new marketplaces "to win wealth for himself and his children." In one popular tale, a woman praised her husband: "He was a good provider; he knew how to rake in the money and how to save it." By 1450, the English word "husband" had become a verb meaning "to keep" or "to save."[14]

Europe Outward Bound: The Crusading Tradition

Accompanying the growth of a new European civilization after 1000 were efforts to engage more actively with both near and more distant neighbors. This "medieval expansion" of Western Christendom took place as the Byzantine world was contracting under pressure from the West, from Arab invasion, and later from Turkish conquest (see Map 10.1, page 283). The western half of Christendom was on the rise, while the eastern part was in decline. It was a sharp reversal of their earlier trajectories.

As Western Europe's population mounted, settlers cleared new land, much of it on the eastern fringes of Europe. The Vikings of Scandinavia, having raided much of Europe, set off on a maritime transatlantic venture around 1000 that briefly established a colony in Newfoundland in North America, and more durably in Greenland and Iceland. As Western economies grew, merchants, travelers, diplomats, and missionaries brought European society into more intensive contact with more distant peoples and with Eurasian commercial networks. By the thirteenth and fourteenth centuries, Europeans had direct, though limited, contact with India, China, and Mongolia. Europe clearly was outward bound.

Nothing more dramatically revealed European expansiveness and the religious passions that informed it than the Crusades, a series of "holy wars" that captured the imagination of Western Christendom for several centuries, beginning in 1095.

The Crusades This fourteenth-century painting depicts Crusaders using a catapult to batter a city's defenses, while Muslim defenders fire arrows and hurl projectiles at the attackers. During the First Crusade, Christian forces seized Jerusalem after a lengthy siege that was followed by a bloody massacre of its Muslim and Jewish inhabitants. (Bibliothèque Nationale, Paris, France/Bridgeman Images)

In European thinking and practice, the Crusades were wars undertaken at God's command and authorized by the pope as Christ's representative on earth. Crusaders were required to swear a vow and in return received an indulgence, which removed the penalties for any confessed sins, and were also granted various material benefits, such as immunity from lawsuits and a moratorium on the repayment of debts. Any number of political, economic, and social motives underlay the Crusades, but at their core they were religious wars. Within Europe, the amazing support for the Crusades reflected an understanding that they provided "security against mortal enemies threatening the spiritual health of all Christendom and all Christians."[15] Crusading drew on both Christian piety and the warrior values of the elite, with little sense of contradiction between these impulses.

The most famous Crusades were those aimed at wresting Jerusalem and the holy places associated with the life of Jesus from Islamic control and returning them to Christendom (see Map 10.4). Beginning in 1095, wave after wave of Crusaders from all walks of life and many countries flocked to the eastern Mediterranean, where they temporarily carved out four small Christian states, the last of which was recaptured by Muslim forces in 1291. Led or supported by an assortment of kings, popes, bishops, monks, lords, nobles, and merchants, the Crusades demonstrated a growing

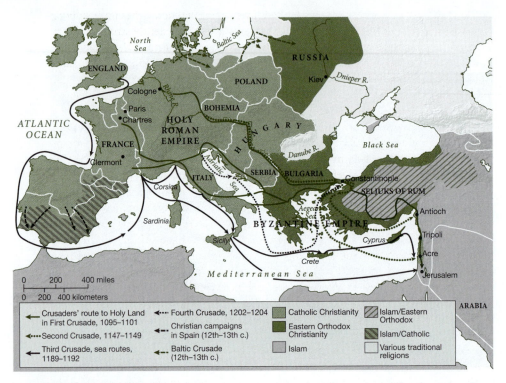

MAP 10.4   The Crusades

Western Europe's crusading tradition reflected the expansive energy and religious impulses of an emerging civilization. It was directed against Muslims in the Middle East, Sicily, and Spain as well as the Eastern Orthodox Christians of the Byzantine Empire and followers of traditional religions in Eastern Europe. The Crusades also involved attacks on Jewish communities, probably the first organized mass pogroms against Jews in Europe's history.

European capacity for organization, finance, transportation, and recruitment, made all the more impressive by the absence of any centralized direction for the project. They also demonstrated considerable cruelty. The seizure of Jerusalem in 1099 was accompanied by the slaughter of many Muslims and Jews as the Crusaders made their way to the tomb of Christ through streets littered with corpses and ankle deep in blood, according to no doubt exaggerated reports.

Crusading was not limited to targets in the Islamic Middle East, however. Those Christians who waged war for centuries to reclaim the Iberian Peninsula from Muslim hands were likewise declared "crusaders," with a similar set of spiritual and material benefits. So too were Scandinavian and German warriors who took part in wars to conquer, settle, and convert lands along the Baltic Sea. The Byzantine Empire and Russia, both of which followed Eastern Orthodox Christianity, were also on the receiving end of Western crusading, as were Christian heretics, Jews, and various enemies of the pope in Europe itself. Crusading, in short, was a pervasive feature of European expansion, which persisted as Europeans began their oceanic voyages in the fifteenth century and beyond.

Surprisingly perhaps, the Crusades had little lasting impact, either politically or religiously, in the Middle East. European power was not sufficiently strong or long-lasting to induce much conversion, and the small European footholds there had come under Muslim control by 1300. The penetration of Turkic-speaking peoples from Central Asia and the devastating Mongol invasions of the thirteenth century were far more significant in Islamic history than were the temporary incursions of European Christians. In Europe, however, crusading in general and interaction with the Islamic world in particular had very significant long-term consequences. Spain, Sicily, and the Baltic region were brought permanently into the world of Western Christendom, while a declining Byzantium was further weakened by the Crusader sacking of Constantinople in 1204 and left even more vulnerable to Muslim Turkish conquest. In Europe itself, popes strengthened their position, at least for a time, in their continuing struggles with secular authorities. Tens of thousands of Europeans came into personal contact with the Islamic world, from which they picked up a taste for the many luxury goods available there, stimulating a demand for Asian goods. They also learned techniques for producing sugar on large plantations using slave labor, a process that had incalculable consequences in later centuries as Europeans transferred the plantation system to the Americas. Muslim scholarship, together with the Greek learning that it incorporated, also flowed into Europe, largely through Spain and Sicily.

If cross-cultural contacts born of crusading opened channels of trade, technology transfer, and intellectual exchange, they also hardened cultural barriers between peoples. The rift between Eastern Orthodoxy and Roman Catholicism deepened further and remains to this day a fundamental divide in the Christian world. Christian anti-Semitism was both expressed and exacerbated as Crusaders on their way to Jerusalem found time to massacre Jews, regarded as "Christ-killers," in a number of European cities, particularly in Germany. Such pogroms, however, were not sanctioned by the Church. A leading figure in the Second Crusade, Bernard of Clairvaux, declared, "It is good that you march against the Muslims, but anyone who touches a Jew to take his life, is as touching Jesus himself."[16] The Crusades also had other long-term influences. European empire building, especially in the Americas, continued the crusading notion that "God wills it." And more recently, over the past two centuries, as the world of the Christian West and that of Islam have collided, both sides have found many occasions for which images of the Crusades, however distorted, have proved politically popular or ideologically useful.

The West in Comparative Perspective

At one level, the making of Western civilization was unremarkable. Civilizations had risen, fallen, renewed themselves, and evolved at many times and in many places. The European case has received extraordinary scrutiny, not so much because of its special significance at the time, but because of its later role as a globally dominant region. However we might explain Europe's subsequent rise to prominence on the world stage, its development in the several centuries after 1000 made only modest ripples beyond its own region. Europe was surely distinctive, as are all civilizations, but it was not yet a major player in the global arena. Comparisons, particularly with China and the Islamic world, help to place these European developments in a world history context.

Catching Up

As the civilization of the West evolved, it was clearly less developed in comparison to Byzantium, China, India, and the Islamic world. Europe's cities were smaller, its political authorities weaker, its economy less commercialized, and its technology inferior. Muslim observers who encountered Europeans saw them as barbarians. An Arab geographer of the tenth century commented: "Their bodies are large, their manners harsh, their understanding dull, and their tongues heavy. . . . Those of them who are farthest to the north are the most subject to stupidity, grossness and brutishness."[17] Muslim travelers over the next several centuries saw more to be praised in West African kingdoms, where Islam was practiced and gold was plentiful.

Furthermore, thoughtful Europeans who directly encountered other peoples often acknowledged their own comparative backwardness. "In our time," wrote a twelfth-century European scholar, "it is in Toledo [a Spanish city long under Muslim rule] that the teaching of the Arabs . . . is offered to the crowds. I hastened there to listen to the teaching of the wisest philosophers of this world."[18] The Italian traveler Marco Polo in the thirteenth century proclaimed Hangzhou in China "the finest and noblest [city] in the world." In the early sixteenth century, Spanish invaders of Mexico were stunned at the size and wealth of the Aztec capital, especially its huge market, claiming that they "had never seen such a thing before."[19]

Curious about the rest of the world, Europeans proved quite willing to engage with and borrow from the more advanced civilizations to the east. Growing European economies, especially in the northwest, reconnected with the Eurasian trading system, with which they had lost contact after the fall of Rome. Now European elites eagerly sought spices, silks, porcelain, and sugar from afar even as they assimilated various technological, intellectual, and cultural innovations, as the Snapshot on page 299 demonstrates. When the road to China opened in the thirteenth and fourteenth centuries, many Europeans, including the merchant-traveler Marco Polo, were more than willing to make the long and difficult journey, returning with amazing tales of splendor and abundance far beyond what was available in Europe. When Europeans took to the oceans in the fifteenth and sixteenth centuries, they were seeking out the sources of African and Asian wealth. Thus the accelerating growth of European civilization was accompanied by its reintegration into the larger Afro-Eurasian networks of exchange and communication.

In this willingness to borrow, Europe resembled several other third-wave civilizations of the time. Japan, for example, took much from China; West Africa drew heavily on Islamic civilization; and Russia actively imitated Byzantium. All of them were then developing civilizations, in a position analogous perhaps to the developing countries of recent times.

Technological borrowing required adaptation to the unique conditions of Europe and was accompanied by considerable independent invention as well. Together these processes generated a significant tradition of technological innovation that allowed Europe by 1500 to catch up with, and in some areas perhaps to surpass, China and the Islamic world. That achievement bears comparison with the economic revolution of Song dynasty China (960–1279), although Europe began at a lower level and depended more on borrowing than did its Chinese counterpart. But in the several centuries surrounding 1000, at both ends of Eurasia, major processes of technological innovation were under way.

SNAPSHOT	EUROPEAN BORROWING

Like people in other emerging civilizations of the third-wave era, Europeans borrowed extensively from their near and more distant counterparts. They adapted these imports, both technological and cultural, to their own circumstances and generated distinctive innovations as well.

Borrowing	Source	Significance
Horse collar	China / Central Asia via Tunisia	Enabled heavy plowing and contributed to European agricultural development
Stirrup	India/Afghanistan	Revolutionized warfare by enhancing cavalry forces
Gunpowder	China	Enhanced the destructiveness of warfare
Paper	China	Enabled bureaucracy; fostered literacy; prerequisite for printing
Spinning wheel	India	Sped up production of yarn, usually by women at home
Wheelbarrow	China	Laborsaving device for farm and construction work
Aristotle	Byzantium / Islamic Spain	Recovery of classical Greek thought
Medical knowledge / treatments	Islamic world	Enriched European medicine by contributing sedatives, antiseptics, surgical techniques, optics, and knowledge of contagious diseases
Christian mysticism	Muslim Spain	Mutual influence of Sufi, Jewish, and Christian mysticism
Music/poetry	Muslim Spain	Contributed to tradition of troubadour poetry about chivalry and courtly love
Mathematics	India / Islamic world	Foundation for European algebra
Chess	India/Persia	A game of prestige associated with European nobility

In Europe, technological breakthroughs first became apparent in agriculture as Europeans adapted to the very different environmental conditions north of the Alps in the several centuries following 500 C.E. They developed a heavy wheeled plow that could handle the dense soils of Northern Europe far better than the light, or "scratch," plow used in Mediterranean agriculture. To pull the plow, Europeans began to rely increasingly on horses rather than oxen and to use iron horseshoes and a more efficient collar, which probably originated in China or Central Asia and could support much heavier loads. In addition, Europeans developed a new three-field system of crop rotation that allowed considerably more land to be planted at any one time.

These were the technological foundations for a more productive agriculture that could support the growing population of European civilization, especially in its urban centers, far more securely than before.

Beyond agriculture, Europeans began to tap non-animal sources of energy in a major way, particularly after 1000. A new type of windmill, very different from an earlier Persian version, was widely used in Europe by the twelfth and thirteenth centuries. The water-driven mill was even more important. By the ninth century water mills were rapidly becoming more evident in Europe. In the early fourteenth century, a concentration of sixty-eight mills dotted a one-mile stretch of the Seine River near Paris. In addition to grinding grain, these mills provided power for sieving flour, tanning hides, making beer, sawing wood, manufacturing iron, and making paper. Devices such as cranks, flywheels, camshafts, and complex gearing mechanisms, when combined with water or wind power, enabled Europeans of the High Middle Ages to revolutionize production in a number of industries and to break with the ancient tradition of depending almost wholly on animal or human muscle as sources of energy. So intense was the interest of European artisans and engineers in tapping mechanical sources of energy that a number of them experimented with perpetual-motion machines, an idea borrowed from Indian philosophers.

Technological borrowing was also evident in the arts of war. Gunpowder was invented in China, but Europeans were probably the first to use it in cannons, in the early fourteenth century, and by 1500 they had the most advanced arsenals in the world. In 1517, one Chinese official, on first encountering European ships and weapons, remarked with surprise, "The westerners are extremely dangerous because of their artillery. No weapon ever made since memorable antiquity is superior to their cannon."[20] Advances in shipbuilding and navigational techniques — including the magnetic compass and sternpost rudder from China and adaptations of the Mediterranean or Arab lateen sail, which enabled vessels to sail against the wind — provided the foundation for European mastery of the seas.

Europe's passion for technology was reflected in its culture and ideas as well as in its machines. About 1260, the English scholar and Franciscan friar Roger Bacon wrote of the possibilities he foresaw, and in doing so, he expressed the confident spirit of the age:

> Machines of navigation can be constructed, without rowers . . . which are borne under the guidance of one man at a greater speed than if they were full of men. Also a chariot can be constructed, that will move with incalculable speed without any draught animal. . . . Also flying machines may be constructed so that a man may sit in the midst of the machine turning a certain instrument by means of which wings artificially constructed would beat the air after the manner of a bird flying . . . and there are countless other things that can be constructed.[21]

Pluralism in Politics

Unlike the large centralized states of Byzantium, the Islamic world, and China, this third-wave European civilization never regained the earlier unity it had under Roman rule. Rather, political life gradually crystallized into a system of competing states (France, Spain, England, Sweden, Prussia, the Netherlands, and Poland, among others) that has persisted into the twenty-first century and that the European

Union still confronts. Geographic barriers, ethnic and linguistic diversity, and the shifting balance of power among its many states prevented the emergence of a single European empire, despite periodic efforts to re-create something resembling the still-remembered unity of the Roman Empire.

This multicentered political system shaped the emerging civilization of the West in many ways. It gave rise to frequent wars, enhanced the role and status of military men, and drove the "gunpowder revolution." Thus European society and values were militarized far more than in China, which gave greater prominence to scholars and bureaucrats. Intense interstate rivalry, combined with a willingness to borrow, also stimulated European technological development. By 1500, Europeans had gone a long way toward catching up with their more advanced Asian counterparts in agriculture, industry, war, and sailing.

The states within this emerging European civilization also differed from those to the east. Their rulers generally were weaker and had to contend with competing sources of power. Unlike the Orthodox Church in Byzantium, with its practice of caesaropapism, the **Roman Catholic Church** in the West maintained a degree of independence from state authority that served to check the power of kings and lords. Moreover, European vassals had certain rights in return for loyalty to their lords and kings. By the thirteenth century, this meant that in many places high-ranking nobles, acting through formal councils, had the right to advise their rulers and to approve new taxes.

The inability of kings, warrior aristocrats, or church leaders to prevail over the others provided room for urban-based merchants in Europe to achieve an unusual independence from political authority. Many cities where wealthy merchants exercised local power won the right to make and enforce their own laws and appoint their own officials. Some of them — Venice, Genoa, Pisa, and Milan, for example — became almost completely independent city-states. Elsewhere, kings were often in search of allies and resources for their struggles with aristocrats and the Church. Thus they granted charters that allowed cities to have their own courts, laws, and governments, while paying their own kind of taxes to the king instead of feudal dues. After 1100 or so, powerful, independent cities were a distinctive feature of European life. By contrast, Chinese cities, which were far larger than those of Europe, were simply part of the empire and enjoyed few special privileges. Although commerce was far more extensive in China than in the emerging European civilization, the powerful Chinese state favored the landowners over merchants and monopolized the salt and iron industries. It also actively controlled and limited merchant activity far more than the new and weaker royal authorities of Europe were able to do.

The relative weakness of Europe's rulers allowed urban merchants more leeway and, according to some historians, opened the way to a more thorough development of capitalism in later centuries. It also led to the development of representative institutions or parliaments through which the views and interests of these contending forces could be expressed and accommodated. Intended to strengthen royal authority by consulting with major social groups, these embryonic parliaments did not represent the "people" or the "nation" but instead embodied the three great "estates of the realm" — the clergy (the first estate), the landowning nobility (the second estate), and urban merchants (the third estate).

Reason and Faith

A further feature of this emerging European civilization was a distinctive intellectual tension between the claims of human reason and those of faith. Christianity had developed in a world suffused with Greek rationalism. Some early Christian thinkers sought to maintain a clear separation between the new religion and the ideas of Plato and Aristotle. "What indeed has Athens to do with Jerusalem?" asked Tertullian (150–225 C.E.), an early church leader from North Africa. More common was the notion that Greek philosophy could serve as a "handmaiden" to faith, more fully disclosing the truths of Christianity. In the reduced circumstances of Western Europe after the collapse of the Roman Empire, however, the Church had little direct access to the writings of the Greeks, although some Latin translations and commentaries provided a continuing link to the world of classical thought.

But intellectual life in Europe changed dramatically in the several centuries after 1000, amid a rising population, a quickening commercial life, emerging towns and cities, and the Church's growing independence from royal or noble authorities. Moreover, the West was developing a legal system that provided a measure of independence for a variety of institutions — towns and cities, guilds, professional associations, and especially universities. An outgrowth of earlier cathedral schools, these European universities — in Paris, Bologna, Oxford, Cambridge, Salamanca — became "zones of intellectual autonomy" in which scholars could pursue their studies with some freedom from the dictates of religious or political authorities, although that freedom was never complete and was frequently contested.[22]

This was the setting in which a small group of literate churchmen began to emphasize, quite self-consciously, the ability of human reason to penetrate divine mysteries and to grasp the operation of the natural order. In the late eleventh century, students in a monastic school in France asked their teacher, Anselm, to provide a proof for the existence of God based solely on reason, without using the Bible or other sources of divine revelation.

The new interest in rational thought was applied first and foremost to theology, the "queen of the sciences" to European thinkers. Logic, philosophy, and rationality would operate in service to Christ. Of course, some opposed this new emphasis on human reason. Bernard of Clairvaux, a twelfth-century French abbot, declared, "Faith believes. It does not dispute."[23] His contemporary and intellectual opponent, the French scholar William of Conches, lashed out: "You poor fools. God can make a cow out of a tree, but has he ever done so? Therefore show some reason why a thing is so or cease to hold that it is so."[24]

European intellectuals also applied their newly discovered confidence in human reason to law, medicine, and the world of nature, exploring optics, magnetism, astronomy, and alchemy. Slowly and never completely, the scientific study of nature, known as "natural philosophy," began to separate itself from theology. This mounting enthusiasm for rational inquiry stimulated European scholars to seek out original Greek texts, particularly those of Aristotle. They found them in the Greek-speaking world of Byzantium and in the Islamic world, where they had long ago been translated into Arabic. In the twelfth and thirteenth centuries, an explosion of translations from Greek and Arabic into Latin, many of them undertaken in Spain, gave European scholars direct access to the works of ancient Greeks and to the remarkable results of

Arab scholarship in astronomy, optics, medicine, pharmacology, and more. One of these translators, Adelard of Bath (1080–1142), remarked that he had learned, "under the guidance of reason from Arabic teachers," not to trust established authority.[25]

It was the works of the prolific Aristotle, with his logical approach and "scientific temperament," that made the deepest impression. His writings became the basis for university education and largely dominated the thought of Western Europe in the five centuries after 1200. In the work of the thirteenth-century theologian Thomas Aquinas, Aristotle's ideas were thoroughly integrated into a logical and systematic presentation of Christian doctrine. In this growing emphasis on human rationality, which some considered to be at least partially separate from divine revelation, lay one of the foundations of the later Scientific Revolution and the secularization of European intellectual life.

Surprisingly, nothing comparable occurred in the Byzantine Empire, where knowledge of the Greek language was widespread and access to Greek texts was easy. Although Byzantine scholars kept the classical tradition alive, their primary interest lay in the humanities (literature, philosophy, history) and theology rather than in the natural sciences or medicine. Furthermore, both state and church had serious

European University Life in the Middle Ages This fourteenth-century manuscript painting shows a classroom scene from the University of Bologna in Italy. Note the sleeping and disruptive students. Some things apparently never change. (bpk Bildagentur/Kupferstichkabinett, Staatliche Museen, Berlin, Germany/Photo: Joerg P. Anders/Art Resource, NY)

reservations about Greek learning. In 529, the emperor Justinian closed Plato's Academy in Athens, claiming that it was an outpost of paganism. Its scholars dispersed into lands that soon became Islamic, carrying Greek learning into the Islamic world. Church authorities as well were suspicious of Greek thought, sometimes persecuting scholars who were too enamored with the ancients. Even those who did study the Greek writers did so in a conservative spirit, concerned with preserving and transmitting the classical heritage rather than with using it as a springboard for creating new knowledge. "The great men of the past," declared the fourteenth-century Byzantine scholar and statesman Theodore Metochites, "have said everything so perfectly that they have left nothing for us to say."[26]

In the Islamic world, Greek thought was embraced "with far more enthusiasm and creativity" than in Byzantium.[27] A massive translation project in the ninth and tenth centuries made Aristotle and many other Greek writers available in Arabic. That work contributed to a flowering of Arab scholarship, especially in the sciences and natural philosophy, between roughly 800 and 1200, but it also stimulated a debate about faith and reason among Muslim thinkers, many of whom greatly admired Greek philosophical, scientific, and medical texts. As in the Christian world, the issue was whether secular Greek thought was an aid or a threat to the faith. Western European church authorities after the thirteenth century had come to regard natural philosophy as a wholly legitimate enterprise and had thoroughly incorporated Aristotle into university education, but learned opinion in the Islamic world swung the other way. Though never completely disappearing from Islamic scholarship, the ideas of Plato and Aristotle receded after the thirteenth century in favor of teachings that drew more directly from the Quran or from mystical experience. Nor was natural philosophy a central concern of Islamic higher education, as it was in the West. The integration of political and religious life in the Islamic world, as in Byzantium, contrasted with their separation in the West, where there was more space for the independent pursuit of scientific subjects.

Conclusions and Reflections: Remembering and Forgetting

History is about actively remembering the past from our vantage point in the present. It seeks to counteract the natural fading of our collective memories. It links us to our ancestors and provides a larger, richer, and more meaningful context for our lives in the here and now. And so we recall that many of the characteristic features of Christendom that emerged during the era of third-wave civilizations have persisted well into the modern era.

The rift between Eastern Orthodoxy and Roman Catholicism, for example, remains one of the major divides in the Christian world, though without the deep hostility and violence of earlier times. In 1988, Russians celebrated 1,000 years of Christianity as they recalled the decision of Prince Vladimir to align the new state of Kievan Rus with the Orthodox faith. The subsequent revival of the Russian Orthodox Church, following many decades of communist oppression of the Church in the Soviet Union, is clearly a link between past and present that is deeply meaningful to many Russians.

The historical experience of Western Europe in the third-wave era likewise connects the past to more recent times. Consider these examples:

- The emergence of a new and innovative civilization after 1000 C.E. laid the foundation for something close to European global dominance in the nineteenth century.
- The endemic military conflicts of European states, unable to recover the unity of the Roman Empire, found terrible expression in the world wars of the twentieth century.
- The crusading element of European expansion echoes still in the early twenty-first century as Islamic radicals have viewed European and American action in the Middle East as a renewal of the Crusades.
- Europe's relative freedom for merchant activity and its eagerness to borrow foreign technology arguably contributed to the growth of capitalism and industrialization in later centuries.
- Modern universities and the separation of religious and political authority likewise originated during the Middle Ages in Europe.

Deliberately recalling a past that is beyond individual memory and linking it to our own times is among the great benefits of the study of history.

Yet that very strength of historical study can be misleading, particularly if it suggests a kind of inevitability, in which the past determines the present and future. Knowing the outcomes of the historical processes we explore can be a serious disadvantage, for it may blind us to the uncertainty and confusion that our ancestors surely experienced and to the surprising, even astonishing, outcomes of those processes. In 500 C.E., few people would have predicted that Europe would become the primary center of Christianity, while the African and Asian expressions of that faith withered away. No one then could foresee the sudden eruption of Islam. As late as 1000, the startling reversal of roles between the Eastern and Western wings of Christendom that the next several centuries witnessed was hardly on the horizon. At that time, the many small, rural, unsophisticated, and endlessly quarreling warrior-based societies of Western Europe would hardly have borne comparison with the powerful Byzantine Empire and its magnificent capital of Constantinople. Even in 1500, when Europe had begun to catch up with China and the Islamic world in various ways, there was little to predict its remarkable transformation over the next several centuries and the dramatic change in the global balance of power that this transformation produced. And in 1850 who could have imagined the vast expansion of Christianity in Africa and Asia and its erosion in Europe and North America that occurred in the twentieth century?

Usually students of history are asked to remember. But forgetting can also be an aid to historical understanding. To recapture the unexpectedness of the historical process and to allow ourselves to be surprised, it may be useful to forget—or at least set aside—what we know about what happened next and to see the world as contemporaries viewed it. All of us, both then and now, live with a vast ignorance about the future even as we seek to navigate uncertainly into that future. To avoid the arrogance of historical hindsight, we might do well to forget, at least on occasion, the eventual outcomes of certain historical developments, while also remembering that current developments can have long-term consequences.

Revisiting Chapter 10

REVISITING SPECIFICS

REVISITING CORE IDEAS

1. **Comparing Differences** What variations in the experience of African and Asian Christian communities can you identify?
2. **Identifying Connections** In what ways was the Byzantine Empire linked to a wider world?
3. **Defining Change** What replaced the Roman order in Western Europe?
4. **Exploring Change** In what ways was European civilization changing after 1000?
5. **Comparing the West and Byzantium** How did the historical development of the European West differ from that of Byzantium in the third-wave era?
6. **Analyzing Cultural Borrowing** In what ways did borrowing from abroad shape European civilization after 1000?
7. **Using Comparisons** How might comparisons with China and the Islamic world assist our understanding of European history during the third-wave era?

A WIDER VIEW

1. What accounts for the different historical trajectories of the Byzantine and West European expressions of Christendom?
2. What might an observer living in 500 or 1000 have found surprising about what happened in the centuries that followed?
3. In what respects was the civilization of Western European Christendom distinctive and unique, and in what ways was it broadly comparable to other third-wave civilizations?
4. **Looking Back** How does the evolution of the Christian world in the third-wave era compare with that of Tang and Song dynasty China and of the Islamic world?

CHRONOLOGY

ca. 300–400	• Christianity established in Axum and Armenia
330	• Constantinople established
ca. 400–600	• Christianity introduced into Nubia
ca. 635–835	• Nestorian Christianity flourishing in China
ca. 640	• Muslim conquest of Christian Egypt
800	• Charlemagne crowned as new Roman emperor
988	• Conversion of Kievan Rus to Orthodox Christianity
1000–1300	• High Middle Ages
1054	• Mutual excommunication of pope and patriarch
1095–1291	• Crusaders in Islamic Middle East
ca. 1100–1300	• Translations of Greek and Arab works become available in Europe
1200–1400	• Contraction of Egyptian and Nubian Christianity
1453	• Ottoman conquest of Constantinople
1492	• Completion of Christian conquest of Muslim Spain

11

Pastoral Peoples on the Global Stage

The Mongol Moment

1200–1450

CHAPTER OUTLINE

The Long History of Pastoral Peoples
- The World of Pastoral Societies
- Before the Mongols: Pastoralists in History

Breakout: The Mongol Empire
- From Temujin to Chinggis Khan: The Rise of the Mongol Empire
- Explaining the Mongol Moment

Encountering the Mongols in China, Persia, and Russia
- China and the Mongols
- Persia and the Mongols
- Russia and the Mongols

The Mongol Empire as a Eurasian Network
- Toward a World Economy
- Diplomacy on a Eurasian Scale
- Cultural Exchange in the Mongol Realm
- The Plague: An Afro-Eurasian Pandemic

Controversies: Debating Empire

Conclusions and Reflections: Historians, Bias, and the Mongols

---

CONNECTING PAST AND PRESENT

"HE [CHINGGIS KHAN] IS LIKE A GOD TO US," said Bat-Erdene Batbayar, a Mongolian historian and political figure, in the early twenty-first century. "He is the founder of our state, the root of our history. The communists very brutally cut us off from our traditions and history. . . . Now we are becoming Mongols again."[1] Such sentiments marked a distinct shift in Mongolian thinking about Chinggis Khan that has been under way since the 1990s. Under the country's earlier communist government, closely

308

aligned with the Soviet Union, the great Mongol leader had been regarded in very negative terms. After all, his forces had decimated Russia in the thirteenth century, and resentment lingered. But as communism faded in both Russia and Mongolia at the end of the twentieth century, the memory of Chinggis Khan made a remarkable comeback in the land of his birth.

In 2012, the 850th birthday of the country's epic hero was celebrated with great fanfare. Increasingly, his bloody conquests were played down, and he was portrayed as a unifier of the Mongolian peoples, the creator of an empire tolerant of various faiths, and a promoter of economic and cultural ties among distant peoples. Vodka, cigarettes, a chocolate bar, two brands of beer, the country's most prominent rock band, and the central square of the capital city all bore his name, while his picture appeared on Mongolia's stamps and money. Rural young people on horseback sang songs in his honor, and their counterparts in urban Internet cafés constructed websites to celebrate his achievements.

All of this is a reminder of the enormous and surprising role that the Mongols played in the Eurasian world of the thirteenth and fourteenth centuries and of the continuing echoes of that long-vanished empire. More generally, the story of the Mongols serves as a useful corrective to the almost exclusive focus that historians often devote to agricultural peoples and their civilizations, for the Mongols, and many other such peoples, were pastoralists who disdained farming while centering their economic lives around their herds of animals. Normally they did not construct elaborate cities, enduring empires, or monumental works of art, architecture, and written literature. Nonetheless, they left an indelible mark on the historical development of the entire Afro-Eurasian hemisphere, and particularly on the agricultural civilizations with which they so often interacted.

SEEKING THE MAIN POINT	What has been the role in world history of pastoral peoples in general and the Mongols in particular?

The Long History of Pastoral Peoples

On the arid margins of agricultural lands, where productive farming was difficult or impossible, an alternative kind of food-producing economy emerged around 4000 B.C.E., focused on the raising of livestock. Horses, camels, goats, sheep, cattle, yaks, and reindeer were the primary animals that separately, or in some combination, enabled the construction of herding or **pastoral societies**. Such societies took shape in the vast grasslands of inner Eurasia and sub-Saharan Africa, in the Arabian and Saharan deserts, in the subarctic regions of the Northern Hemisphere, and in the high plateau of Tibet. (See Snapshot: Varieties of Pastoral Societies, page 310.)

SNAPSHOT   VARIETIES OF PASTORAL SOCIETIES

Region and Peoples	Primary Animals	Features
Inner Eurasian steppes (Xiongnu, Yuezhi, Turks, Uighurs, Mongols, Huns, Kipchaks)	Horses; also sheep, goats, cattle, Bactrian (two-humped) camel	Domestication of horse by 4000 B.C.E.; horseback riding by 1000 B.C.E.; site of largest pastoral empires
Southwestern and Central Asia (Seljuks, Ghaznavids, Mongol il-khans, Uzbeks, Ottomans)	Sheep and goats; used horses, camels, and donkeys for transport	Close economic relationship with neighboring towns; pastoralists provided meat, wool, milk products, and hides in exchange for grain and manufactured goods
Arabian and Saharan deserts (Bedouin Arabs, Berbers, Tuareg)	Dromedary (one-humped) camel; sometimes sheep	Camel caravans made possible long-distance trade; camel-mounted warriors central to early Arab/Islamic expansion
Grasslands of sub-Saharan Africa (Fulbe, Nuer, Turkana, Masai)	Cattle; also sheep and goats	Cattle were a chief form of wealth and central to ritual life; little interaction with wider world until nineteenth century
Subarctic Scandinavia, Russia (Sami, Nenets)	Reindeer	Reindeer domesticated only since 1500 C.E.; many also fished
Tibetan plateau (Tibetans)	Yaks; also sheep, cashmere goats, some cattle	Tibetans supplied yaks as baggage animals for overland caravan trade; exchanged wool, skins, and milk with valley villagers and received barley in return
Andean Mountains	Llamas and alpacas	Andean pastoralists in a few places relied on their herds for a majority of their subsistence, supplemented with horticulture and hunting

Source: Thomas J. Barfield, "Pastoral Nomadic Societies," in *Berkshire Encyclopedia of World History* (Great Barrington, MA: Berkshire, 2005), 4:1432–37.

The World of Pastoral Societies

Despite their many differences, pastoral societies shared several important features that distinguished them from settled agricultural communities and civilizations. Their generally less productive economies and their need for large grazing areas meant that they supported far smaller populations than did agricultural societies. People generally lived in small and widely scattered encampments or seasonal settlements made up of related kinfolk rather than in the villages, towns, and cities characteristic of agrarian civilizations. Beyond the family unit, pastoral peoples organized themselves in kinship-based groups or clans that claimed a common ancestry, usually through the male line. Related clans might on occasion come together as a tribe, which could also absorb unrelated people into the community. Although their values stressed equality and individual achievement, in some pastoral societies clans were ranked as noble or commoner, and considerable differences emerged between wealthy aristocrats owning large flocks of animals and poor herders. Many pastoral societies included enslaved people as well.

Furthermore, pastoral peoples generally offered women a higher status, fewer restrictions, and a greater role in public life than their counterparts in agricultural civilizations. Everywhere pastoral women were involved in productive labor as well as having domestic responsibility for food and children. The care of smaller animals such as sheep and goats usually fell to women, although only rarely did women own or control their own livestock. Among the Mongols, the remarriage of a widow, often to a male relative of her husband, carried none of the negative connotations that it did among the Chinese, and women could initiate divorce. Mongol women frequently served as political advisers and were active in military affairs as well. A thirteenth-century European visitor, the Franciscan friar Giovanni DiPlano Carpini, recorded his impressions of Mongol women:

> Girls and women ride and gallop as skillfully as men. We even saw them carrying quivers and bows, and the women can ride horses for as long as the men; they have shorter stirrups, handle horses very well, and mind all the property. . . . They all wear trousers, and some of them shoot just like men.[2]

Certainly, literate observers from adjacent civilizations noticed and clearly disapproved of the freedom granted to pastoral women. Ancient Greek writers thought that the pastoralists with whom they were familiar were "women governed." To Han Kuan, a Chinese Confucian scholar in the first century B.C.E., China's northern pastoral neighbors "[made] no distinction between men and women."[3]

The most characteristic feature of pastoral societies was their mobility, as local environmental conditions largely dictated their patterns of movement. In some favorable regions, pastoralists maintained seasonal settlements, migrating, for instance, between highland pastures in the summer and less harsh lowland environments in the winter. Others lived more nomadic lives, moving their herds frequently in regular patterns to systematically follow the seasonal changes in vegetation and water supply. But even the most nomadic pastoralists were not homeless; they took their homes, often elaborate felt tents, with them. Whatever their patterns of movement, pastoralists shared a life based on turning grass, which people cannot eat, into usable food and energy through their animals.

Although pastoralists represented an alternative to the agricultural way of life that they disdained, they were almost always deeply connected to, and often dependent on, their farming neighbors. Few of these peoples could live solely from the products of their animals, and most of them actively sought access to the foodstuffs, manufactured goods, and luxury items available from nearby farming communities. Particularly among the pastoral peoples of inner Eurasia, this desire for the fruits of civilization periodically stimulated the creation of tribal confederations or states that could more effectively deal with the powerful agricultural societies on their borders.

Constructing a large state among pastoralists was no easy task. Such societies generally lacked the surplus wealth needed to pay for the professional armies and bureaucracies that everywhere sustained the states and empires of agricultural civilizations. And the fierce independence of widely dispersed pastoral clans and tribes as well as their internal rivalries made any enduring political unity difficult to achieve. Nonetheless, charismatic leaders, such as Chinggis Khan, were periodically able to weld together a series of tribal alliances that for a time became powerful states. Despite their limited populations, such states had certain military advantages in confronting larger and more densely populated civilizations. They could draw on the horseback-riding and hunting skills of virtually the entire male population and some women as well. But what sustained these states was their ability to extract wealth, through raiding, trading, or extortion, from agricultural civilizations such as China, Persia, and Byzantium.

Pastoralists interacted with their agricultural neighbors not only economically and militarily but also culturally, as they "became acquainted with and tried on for size all the world and universal religions."[4] At one time or another, Judaism, Buddhism, Islam, and several forms of Christianity all found a home somewhere among the pastoral peoples of inner Eurasia. So did Manichaeism, a religious tradition born in third-century Persia and combining elements of Zoroastrian, Christian, and Buddhist practice. Usually conversion was a top-down process as pastoral elites and rulers adopted a foreign religion for political purposes, sometimes changing religious allegiance as circumstances altered. Pastoral peoples, in short, did not inhabit a world totally apart from their agricultural and civilized neighbors.

The Scythians An ancient horse-riding pastoral people during the second-wave era, the Scythians occupied a region in present-day Kazakhstan and southern Russia. Their pastoral way of life is apparent in this detail from an exquisite gold necklace from the fourth century B.C.E. (Photo © Boltin Picture Library/Bridgeman Images)

The pastoral peoples of the Inner Asian steppes learned the art of horseback riding by roughly 1000 B.C.E., and their societies then changed dramatically. Now they could accumulate and tend larger herds of horses, sheep, and goats and move more rapidly over a much wider territory. As they invented or adapted new technologies that added to the mastery of their environment, they spread widely across the Eurasian steppes, creating something of a common culture in this vast region. These innovations included complex horse harnesses, saddles with iron stirrups, a small compound bow that could be fired from horseback, various forms of armor, and new kinds of swords. Agricultural peoples were amazed at the centrality of the horse in pastoral life. As a Roman historian noted about the Huns, "From their horses, by day and night every one of that nation buys and sells, eats and drinks, and bowed over the narrow neck of the animal relaxes in a sleep so deep as to be accompanied by many dreams."[5]

Before the Mongols: Pastoralists in History

What enabled pastoral peoples to make their most visible entry onto the stage of world history was the military potential of horseback riding, and of camel riding somewhat later. Their mastery of mounted warfare made possible a long but intermittent series of pastoral empires across the steppes of inner Eurasia and parts of Africa. For 2,000 years, those states played a major role in Afro-Eurasian history and represented a standing challenge to and influence upon the agrarian civilizations on their borders.

One early large-scale pastoral empire was associated with the people known as the Xiongnu, who lived in the Mongolian steppes north of China. Provoked by Chinese penetration of their territory, the Xiongnu in the third and second centuries B.C.E. created a huge military confederacy that stretched from Manchuria deep into Central Asia. "All the people who draw the bow have now become one family," declared **Modun** (r. 210–174 B.C.E.), the charismatic founder of the **Xiongnu Empire**. Tribute, exacted from other pastoral peoples and from China itself, sustained the Xiongnu Empire and forced the Han dynasty emperor Wen to acknowledge, unhappily, the equality of people he regarded as barbarians. "Our two great nations," he declared, "the Han and the Xiongnu, stand side by side."[6] Although it subsequently disintegrated under sustained Chinese counterattacks, the Xiongnu Empire provided a model and inspiration for later Turkic and Mongol empires.

It was during the era of third-wave civilizations that pastoral peoples made their most significant mark on the larger canvas of world history. Arabs, Berbers, Turks, and Mongols—all of them of pastoral origin—created the largest and most influential empires of that era. The most expansive religious tradition of that time, Islam, derived from a largely pastoral people, the Arabs, and was carried to new regions by another pastoral people, the Turks. Most of the great civilizations of outer Eurasia—Byzantium, Persia, India, and China—had come under the control of previously pastoral people, at least for a time. But as pastoralists entered and shaped the arena of world history, they too were transformed by the experience.

The first and most dramatic of these incursions came from Arabs. In the Arabian Peninsula, the development of a reliable camel saddle somewhere between 500 and 100 B.C.E. enabled pastoral Bedouin (desert-dwelling) Arabs to fight effectively from atop their enormous beasts. With this new military advantage, they came to control the rich trade routes in incense running through Arabia. Even more important, these camel pastoralists subsequently served as the shock troops of Islamic expansion, providing many of the new religion's earliest followers and much of the military force that initially carved out the Arab Empire. Although intellectual and political leadership came from urban merchants and settled farming communities, the Arab Empire was in some respects a pastoralist creation that later became the foundation of a new and distinctive civilization.

Even as the pastoral Arabs encroached on the world of Eurasian civilizations from the south, Turkic-speaking pastoralists were making inroads from the north. Never a single people, various Turkic-speaking clans and tribes migrated from their homeland in Mongolia and southern Siberia generally westward and entered the historical record as creators of a series of empires between 552 and 965 C.E., most of them lasting little more than a century. Like the Xiongnu Empire, they were fragile alliances of various tribes headed by a supreme ruler known as a *kaghan*, who was supported by a faithful corps of soldiers called "wolves," for the wolf was the mythical ancestor of **Turkic peoples**. From their base in the steppes, these Turkic states confronted the great civilizations to their south — China, Persia, Byzantium — alternately raiding them, allying with them against common enemies, trading with them, and extorting tribute payments from them. Turkic language and culture spread widely over much of Inner Asia, and elements of that culture entered the agrarian civilizations. In the courts of northern China, for example, yogurt thinned with water, a drink derived from the Turks, replaced for a time the traditional beverage of tea, and at least one Chinese poet wrote joyfully about the delights of snowy evenings in a felt tent.[7]

A major turning point in the history of the Turks occurred with their conversion to Islam between the tenth and fourteenth centuries. This extended process represented a major expansion of the faith and launched the Turks into a new role as the third major carrier of Islam, following the Arabs and the Persians. It also brought the Turks into an increasingly important position within the heartland of an established Islamic civilization as they migrated southward into the Middle East. There they served first as slave soldiers within the Abbasid caliphate, and then, as the caliphate declined, they increasingly took political and military power themselves. In the **Seljuk Turkic Empire** of the eleventh and twelfth centuries, centered in Persia and present-day Iraq, Turkic rulers began to claim the Muslim title of *sultan* (ruler) rather than the Turkic *kaghan*. Although the Abbasid caliph remained the formal ruler, real power was exercised by Turkic sultans.

Not only did Turkic peoples become Muslims themselves, but they carried Islam to new areas as well. Their invasions of northern India solidly planted Islam in that ancient civilization. In Anatolia, formerly ruled by Christian Byzantium, they brought both Islam and a massive infusion of Turkic culture, language, and people, even as they created the Ottoman Empire, which by 1500 became one of the great powers of Eurasia. In both places, Turkic dynasties governed and would continue to do so well into the modern era. Thus Turkic people, many of them at least, had transformed themselves from pastoralists to sedentary farmers, from creators of steppe empires to rulers of agrarian civilizations, and from polytheistic worshippers of their ancestors and various gods to followers and carriers of a monotheistic Islam.

Broadly similar patterns prevailed in Africa as well. All across northern Africa and the Sahara, the introduction of the camel, probably during the first millennium B.C.E., gave rise to pastoral societies. Much like the Turkic-speaking pastoralists of Central Asia, many of these peoples later adopted Islam, but at least initially had little formal instruction in the religion. In the eleventh century C.E., a reform movement arose among the Sanhaja Berber pastoralists living in the western Sahara; they had only recently converted to Islam and were practicing it rather superficially. The movement was sparked by a scholar, Ibn Yasin, who returned from a pilgrimage to Mecca around 1039 seeking to purify the practice of the faith among his own people in line with orthodox principles. That religious movement soon became an expansive state, the **Almoravid Empire**, that incorporated a large part of northwestern Africa and in 1086 crossed into southern Spain, where it offered vigorous opposition to Christian efforts to conquer the region.

For a time, the Almoravid state enjoyed considerable prosperity, based on its control of much of the West African gold trade and the grain-producing Atlantic plains of Morocco. The Almoravids also brought to Morocco the sophisticated Islamic culture of southern Spain, still visible in the splendid architecture of the city of Marrakesh, for a time the capital of the Almoravid Empire. By the mid-twelfth century, that empire had been overrun by its longtime enemies, Berber farming people from the Atlas Mountains. But for roughly a century, the Almoravid movement represented an African pastoral people who had converted to Islam, had come into conflict with their agricultural neighbors and built a short-lived empire, and had a considerable impact on neighboring civilizations in both North Africa and Europe.

Breakout: The Mongol Empire

Of all the pastoral peoples who took a turn on the stage of world history, the Mongols made the most stunning entry. Their thirteenth-century breakout from Mongolia gave rise to the largest land-based empire in all of human history, stretching from the Pacific coast of Asia to Eastern Europe (see Map 11.1). This empire joined the pastoral peoples of the inner Eurasian steppes with the settled agricultural civilizations of outer Eurasia more extensively and more intimately than ever before. It also brought the major civilizations of Eurasia—Europe, China, and the Islamic world—into far more direct contact than in earlier times. Both the enormous destructiveness of the process and the networks of exchange and communication that it spawned were the work of the Mongols, numbering only about 700,000 people. It was another of history's unlikely twists.

For all of its size and fearsome reputation, the Mongol Empire left a surprisingly modest cultural imprint on the world it had briefly governed. Unlike the Arabs, the Mongols bequeathed to the world no new language, religion, or civilization. Mongol religion centered on rituals invoking the ancestors that were performed around the family hearth. Rulers sometimes consulted religious specialists, known as shamans, who might predict the future, offer sacrifices, and communicate with the spirit world, particularly with Tengri, the supreme sky god of the Mongols. There was little in this tradition to attract outsiders, and in any event the Mongols proved uninterested in spreading their own faith among subject peoples.

Although people with skills were put to work in ways useful to Mongol authorities, Mongols offered the majority of their conquered people little more than the status

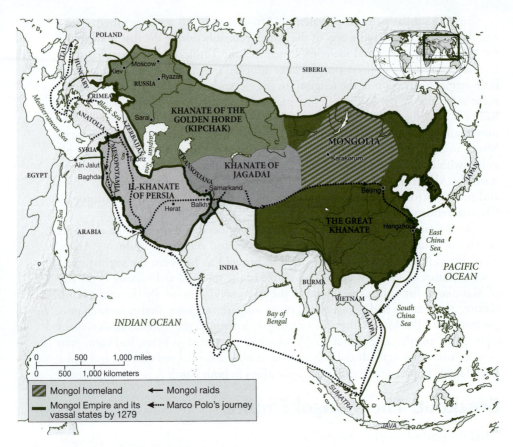

MAP 11.1   The Mongol Empire
Encompassing much of Eurasia, the Mongol Empire was divided into four khanates after the death of Chinggis Khan.

of defeated, subordinate, and exploited subjects. Unlike the Turks, whose languages and culture flourish today in many places far from the Turkic homeland in Central Asia, Mongol culture remains confined largely to Mongolia. The Mongol Empire proved to be "the last, spectacular bloom of pastoral power in Inner Eurasia."[8] After the decline and disintegration of the Mongol Empire, the tide turned against the pastoralists of inner Eurasia, who were increasingly swallowed up in the expanding Russian or Chinese empires. Nonetheless, while it lasted and for a few centuries thereafter, the Mongol Empire made an enormous impact throughout the entire Eurasian world.

From Temujin to Chinggis Khan: The Rise of the Mongol Empire

World historians are prone to focus attention on large-scale and long-term processes of change in explaining "what happened in history," but in understanding the rise of the Mongol Empire, most scholars have found themselves forced to look closely at the role of a single individual — **Temujin** (TEM-oo-chin) (1162–1227), later known as **Chinggis Khan** (universal ruler). The twelfth-century world into which he was born found the Mongols an unstable and fractious collection of tribes and clans, much reduced from a somewhat earlier and more powerful position in the shifting alliances in what is now Mongolia. "Everyone was feuding," declared a leading Mongol shaman. "Rather than sleep, they robbed each other of their possessions. . . . There was no respite, only battle. There was no affection, only mutual slaughter."[9]

The early life of Temujin showed few signs of a prominent future. The boy's father had been a minor chieftain of a noble clan, but he was murdered by tribal rivals before Temujin turned ten, and the family was soon deserted by other members of the clan. As social outcasts without livestock, Temujin's small family, headed by his resourceful mother, was forced to abandon pastoralism, living instead by hunting, fishing, and gathering wild foods. It was an enormous and humiliating drop in their social status. In these desperate circumstances, Temujin's remarkable character came into play. His personal magnetism and courage and his inclination to rely on trusted friends rather than ties of kinship allowed him to build up a small following and to ally with a more powerful tribal leader. This alliance received a boost from Chinese patrons, always eager to keep the pastoralists divided. Soon Temujin was recognized as a chief in his own right with a growing band of followers.

Temujin's rise to power within the complex tribal politics of Mongolia was a surprise to everyone, as it took place amid shifting alliances and betrayals. Temujin achieved a mounting string of military victories, aided by the indecisiveness of his enemies, a reputation as a leader generous to friends and ruthless to enemies, and the incorporation of warriors from defeated tribes into his own forces. In 1206, a Mongol tribal assembly recognized Temujin as Chinggis Khan, supreme leader of a now unified Great Mongol Nation. It was a remarkable achievement, but one little noticed beyond the highland steppes of Mongolia. That would soon change.

The unification of the Mongol tribes raised an obvious question: what was Chinggis Khan to do with the powerful army he had assembled? Without a common task, the new and fragile unity of the Mongols would surely dissolve into quarrels and chaos; and without external resources to reward his followers, Chinggis Khan would be hard-pressed to maintain his supreme position. Both considerations pointed in a single direction — expansion, particularly toward China, long a source of great wealth for pastoral peoples.

In 1209, the first major attack on the settled agricultural societies south of Mongolia set in motion half a century of a **Mongol world war**, a series of military campaigns, massive killing, and empire building without precedent in world history. In the process, Chinggis Khan, followed by his sons and grandsons (Ogodei, Mongke, and Khubilai), constructed an empire that contained China, Central Asia, Russia, much of the Islamic Middle East, and parts of Eastern Europe (see Map 11.1). "In a flash," wrote a recent scholar, "the Mongol warriors would defeat every army, capture every fort, and bring down the walls of every city they encountered. Christians, Muslims, Buddhists, and Hindus would soon kneel before the dusty boots of illiterate young Mongol horsemen."[10]

Various setbacks marked the outer limits of the Mongol Empire — the Mongols' withdrawal from Eastern Europe (1242), their defeat at Ain Jalut in Palestine at the hands of Egyptian forces (1260), the failure of their invasion of Japan owing to typhoons, and the difficulty of penetrating the tropical jungles of Southeast Asia.

But what an empire it was! How could a Mongol confederation, with a total population of less than 1 million people and few resources beyond their livestock, assemble an imperial structure of such staggering transcontinental dimensions?

Explaining the Mongol Moment

Like the Roman Empire but far more rapidly, the Mongol realm grew of its own momentum without any grand scheme or blueprint for world conquest. Each fresh victory brought new resources for making war and new threats or insecurities that seemed to require further expansion. As the empire took shape and certainly by the end of his life, Chinggis Khan had come to see his career in terms of a universal mission. "I have accomplished a great work," he declared, "uniting the whole world in one empire."[11] Thus the Mongol Empire acquired an ideology in the course of its construction.

What made this "great work" possible? The odds seemed overwhelming, for China alone outnumbered the Mongols 100 to 1 and possessed incomparably greater resources. Furthermore, the Mongols did not enjoy any technological superiority over their many adversaries. They did, however, enjoy the luck of good timing, for China was divided, with the Song dynasty having already lost control of its northern territory to the pastoral Jurchen people, while the decrepit Abbasid caliphate, once the center of the Islamic world, had shrunk to a fraction of its earlier size. But clearly, the key to the Mongols' success lay in their army. According to one scholar, "Mongol armies were simply better led, organized, and disciplined than those of their opponents."[12] In an effort to diminish a divisive tribalism, Chinggis Khan reorganized the entire social structure of the Mongols into military units of 10, 100, 1,000, and 10,000 warriors, an arrangement that allowed for effective command and control. Conquered tribes, especially, were broken up, and their members were scattered among these new units, which enrolled virtually all men and supplied the cavalry forces of Mongol armies. A highly prestigious imperial guard also recruited members across tribal lines.

An impressive discipline and loyalty to their leaders characterized Mongol military forces, and discipline was reinforced by the provision that should any members of a unit desert in battle, all were subject to the death penalty. More positively, loyalty was cemented by the leaders' willingness to share the hardships of their men. "I eat the same food and am dressed in the same rags as my humble herdsmen," declared Chinggis Khan. "I am always in the forefront, and in battle I am never at the rear."[13] Such discipline and loyalty made possible the elaborate tactics of encirclement, retreat, and deception that proved decisive in many a battle. Furthermore, the enormous flow of wealth from conquered civilizations benefited all Mongols, though not equally. Even ordinary Mongols could now dress in linens and silks rather than hides and felt, could own enslaved people derived from the many prisoners of war, and had far greater opportunities to improve their social position in a constantly expanding empire.

To compensate for their own small population, the Mongols incorporated huge numbers of conquered peoples into their military forces. "People who lived in felt tents" — mostly Mongol and Turkic pastoralists — were conscripted en masse into the cavalry units of the Mongol army, while settled agricultural peoples supplied the

Mongol Warriors
Horseback-riding skills, honed in herding animals and adapted to military purposes, were central to Mongol conquests, as illustrated in this fourteenth-century Persian manuscript image of Mongol mounted warriors fighting with bows and swords. (De Agostini Picture Library/M. Seemuller/Bridgeman Images)

infantry and artillery forces. As the Mongols penetrated major civilizations, with their walled cities and elaborate fortifications, they quickly acquired Chinese techniques and technology of siege warfare. Some 1,000 Chinese artillery crews, for example, took part in the Mongol invasion of distant Persia. Beyond military recruitment, Mongols demanded that their conquered people serve as laborers, building roads and bridges and ferrying supplies over long distances. Artisans, craftsmen, and skilled people generally were carefully identified, spared from massacre, and often sent to distant regions of the empire where their services were required. A French goldsmith captured and enslaved by Mongol forces in Hungary wound up in the Mongol capital of Karakorum (kah-rah-KOR-um), where he constructed an elaborate silver fountain that dispensed wine and other intoxicating drinks.

A further element in the military effectiveness of Mongol forces lay in a growing reputation for a ruthless brutality and utter destructiveness. City after city was utterly destroyed. Chinggis Khan's policy was clear: "Whoever submits shall be spared, but those who resist, they shall be destroyed with their wives, children and dependents . . . so that the others who hear and see should fear and not act the same."[14] One scholar explained such policies in this way: "Extremely conscious of their small numbers and fearful of rebellion, Chinggis often chose to annihilate a region's entire population, if it appeared too troublesome to govern."[15] These policies also served as a form of psychological warfare, a practical inducement to surrender for those who knew of the Mongol terror. Historians continue to debate the extent and uniqueness of the Mongols' brutality, but their reputation for unwavering harshness proved a military asset.

Underlying the purely military dimensions of the Mongols' success was an impressive ability to mobilize both the human and material resources of their growing empire. Elaborate census-taking allowed Mongol leaders to know what was available to them and made possible the systematic taxation of conquered people. An effective system of relay stations, about a day's ride apart, provided rapid communication across the empire and fostered trade as well. The beginnings of a centralized bureaucracy with various specialized offices took shape in the new capital of Karakorum. There scribes translated official decrees into the various languages of the empire, such as Persian, Uighur, Chinese, and Tibetan.

Other policies appealed to various groups among the conquered peoples of the empire. Interested in fostering commerce, Mongol rulers often offered merchants 10 percent or more above their asking price and allowed them the free use of the relay stations for transporting their goods. In administering the conquered regions, Mongols held the highest decision-making posts, but Chinese and Muslim officials held many advisory and lower-level positions in China and Persia, respectively. In religious matters, the Mongols welcomed and supported many religious traditions — Buddhist, Christian, Muslim, Daoist — as long as they did not become the focus of political opposition. This policy of religious toleration allowed Muslims to seek converts among Mongol troops and afforded Christians much greater freedom than they had enjoyed under Muslim rule. One of Chinggis Khan's successors, Mongke, arranged a debate among representatives of several religious faiths, after which he concluded: "Just as God gave different fingers to the hand, so has He given different ways to men."[16] Such economic, administrative, and religious policies provided some benefits and a place within the empire — albeit subordinate — for many of its conquered peoples.

Encountering the Mongols in China, Persia, and Russia

The Mongol moment in world history represented an enormous cultural encounter between pastoralists and the settled civilizations of Eurasia. The process of conquest, the length and nature of Mongol rule, the impact on local people, and the extent of Mongol assimilation into the cultures of the conquered — all this and more varied considerably across the Eurasian domains of the empire. The experiences of China, Persia, and Russia provide brief glimpses into several expressions of this massive encounter of cultures.

China and the Mongols

Long the primary target for pastoral steppe dwellers in search of agrarian wealth, China proved the most difficult and extended of the Mongols' many conquests, lasting some seventy years, from 1209 to 1279. The invasion began in northern China, which had been ruled for several centuries by various dynasties of pastoral origin, and was characterized by destruction and plunder on a massive scale. Southern China, under the control of the native Song dynasty, was a different story, for there the Mongols were far less violent and more concerned with accommodating the local population. Landowners, for example, were guaranteed their estates in exchange for their support or at least their neutrality. By whatever methods, the outcome was the unification of a divided China, a treasured ideal among educated Chinese.

This achievement persuaded some of them that the Mongols had indeed been granted the Mandate of Heaven and, despite their foreign origins, were legitimate rulers. One highly educated Chinese scholar wrote a short biography of a recently deceased Mongol official, praising him for curtailing the violence of Mongol soldiers, offering leniency to rebels, and providing tax relief and food during a famine. In short, he was behaving like a good Confucian Chinese official.

Having acquired China, what were the Mongols to do with it? One possibility, apparently considered by the Great Khan Ogodei (ERG-uh-day) in the 1230s, was to exterminate everyone in northern China and turn the country into pastureland for Mongol herds. That suggestion, fortunately, was rejected in favor of extracting as much wealth as possible from the country's advanced civilization. Doing so meant some accommodation to Chinese culture and ways of governing, for the Mongols had no experience with the operation of a complex agrarian society.

That accommodation took many forms. The Mongols made use of Chinese administrative practices and techniques of taxation as well as their postal system. They gave themselves a Chinese dynastic title, the Yuan, suggesting a new beginning in Chinese history. They transferred their capital from Karakorum in Mongolia to what is now Beijing, building a wholly new capital city there known as Khanbalik, the "city of the khan." Thus the Mongols were now rooting themselves solidly on the soil of a highly sophisticated civilization, well removed from their homeland on the steppes. **Khubilai Khan** (koo-buh-l'eye kahn), the grandson of Chinggis Khan and China's Mongol ruler from 1271 to 1294 who initiated the **Yuan dynasty**, ordered a set of Chinese-style ancestral tablets to honor his ancestors and posthumously awarded them Chinese names. Many of his policies evoked the values of a benevolent Confucian-inspired Chinese emperor, as he improved roads, built canals, lowered some taxes, patronized scholars and artists, limited the death penalty and torture, supported peasant agriculture, and prohibited Mongols from grazing their animals on peasants' farmland. Mongol khans also made use of traditional Confucian rituals, supported the building of some Daoist temples, and were particularly attracted to a Tibetan form of Buddhism, which returned the favor with strong political support for the invaders.

Despite these accommodations, Mongol rule was still harsh, exploitative, foreign, and resented. Marco Polo, who was in China at the time, reported that some Mongol officials or their Muslim intermediaries treated Chinese "just like slaves," demanding bribes for services, ordering arbitrary executions, and seizing women at will—all of which generated outrage and hostility. The Mongols did not become Chinese, nor did they accommodate every aspect of Chinese culture. Deep inside the new capital, the royal family and court could continue to experience something of steppe life as their animals roamed freely in large open areas, planted with steppe grass. Many of the Mongol elite much preferred to live, eat, sleep, and give birth in the traditional tents that sprouted everywhere. In administering the country, the Mongols largely ignored the traditional Chinese examination system and relied heavily on foreigners, particularly Muslims from Central Asia and the Middle East, to serve as officials, while keeping the top decision-making posts for themselves. Few Mongols learned Chinese, and Mongol law discriminated against the Chinese, reserving for them the most severe punishments. Furthermore, the Mongols honored and supported merchants and artisans far more than Confucian bureaucrats had been inclined to do.

In social life, the Mongols forbade intermarriage and prohibited Chinese scholars from learning the Mongol script. Mongol women never adopted foot binding and scandalized the Chinese by mixing freely with men at official gatherings and riding to the hunt with their husbands. The Mongol ruler Khubilai Khan retained the Mongol tradition of relying heavily on female advisers, the chief of which was his favorite wife, Chabi. Ironically, she urged him to accommodate his Chinese subjects, forcefully and successfully opposing an early plan to turn Chinese farmland into pastureland. Unlike many Mongols, biased as they were against farming, Chabi recognized the advantages of agriculture and its ability to generate tax revenue. With a vision of turning Mongol rule into a lasting dynasty that might rank with the splendor of the Tang, she urged her husband to emulate the best practices of that earlier era of Chinese history.

However one assesses Mongol rule in China, it was relatively brief, lasting little more than a century. By the mid-fourteenth century, intense factionalism among the Mongols, rapidly rising prices, furious epidemics of the plague, and growing peasant rebellions combined to force the Mongols out of China. By 1368, rebel forces had triumphed, and thousands of Mongols returned to their homeland in the steppes. For several centuries, they remained a periodic threat to China, but during the Ming dynasty that followed, the memory of their often brutal and alien rule stimulated a renewed commitment to Confucian values and restrictive gender practices and an effort to wipe out all traces of the Mongols' impact.

Persia and the Mongols

A second great civilization conquered by the Mongols was Islamic Persia. There the Mongol takeover was far more abrupt than the extended process of conquest in China. A first invasion (1219–1221), led by Chinggis Khan himself, was followed thirty years later by a second assault (1251–1258) under his grandson **Hulegu** (HE-luh-gee), who became the first il-khan (subordinate khan) of Persia. Although Persia had been repeatedly attacked, from the invasion of Alexander the Great to that of the Arabs and Turkic peoples, nothing prepared it for the Mongols. In the eyes of Persian Muslims, the Mongols were infidels, and their stunning victory was a profound shock to people accustomed to viewing history as the progressive expansion of Islamic rule. Furthermore, Mongol military victory brought in its wake a degree of ferocity and slaughter that had no parallel in Persian experience. The Persian historian Juvaini described it in fearful terms:

> Every town and every village has been several times subjected to pillage and massacre and has suffered this confusion for years so that even though there be generation and increase until the Resurrection [end of the world] the population will not attain to a tenth part of what it was before.[17]

The sacking of Baghdad in 1258, which put an end to the Abbasid caliphate, was accompanied by the massacre of more than 200,000 people, according to Hulegu himself.

Beyond this human catastrophe lay the damage to Persian and Iraqi agriculture and to those who tilled the soil. Heavy taxes, sometimes collected twenty or thirty times a year and often under torture or whipping, pushed large numbers of peasants off their land. Furthermore, the in-migration of pastoral Mongols, together with their immense herds of sheep and goats, turned much agricultural land into pasture and sometimes into desert. As a result, a fragile system of underground water channels that provided irrigation to the fields was neglected, and much good agricultural land was reduced to waste. Some sectors of the Persian economy gained, however. Wine production increased because the Mongols were fond of alcohol, and the Persian silk industry benefited from close contact with a Mongol-ruled China. In general, though, even more so than in China, Mongol rule in Persia represented "disaster on a grand and unparalleled scale."[18]

Nonetheless, the Mongols in Persia were themselves transformed far more than their counterparts in China. They made extensive use of the sophisticated Persian bureaucracy, leaving the greater part of government operations in Persian hands. During the reign of Ghazan (haz-ZAHN) (1295–1304), they made some efforts to repair the damage caused by earlier policies of ruthless exploitation by rebuilding damaged cities and repairing neglected irrigation works. Most important, the Mongols who conquered Persia became Muslims, following the lead of Ghazan, who converted to Islam in 1295. No such widespread conversion to the culture of the conquered occurred in China or in Christian Russia. Members of the court and Mongol elites learned at least some Persian, unlike most of their counterparts in China. A number of Mongols also turned to farming, abandoning their pastoral ways, while some married local people.

When the Mongol dynasty of Hulegu's descendants collapsed in the 1330s for lack of a suitable heir, the Mongols were not driven out of Persia as they had been from China. Rather, they and their Turkic allies simply disappeared, assimilated into Persian society. From a Persian point of view, the barbarians had been civilized, and Persians had successfully resisted cultural influence from their uncivilized conquerors. When the great Persian historian Rashid al-Din wrote his famous history of the Mongols, he apologized for providing information about women, generally unmentioned in Islamic writing, explaining that Mongols treated their women equally and included them in decisions of the court.[19] Now Persian rulers could return to their more patriarchal ways.

Russia and the Mongols

When the Mongol military machine rolled over Russia between 1237 and 1240, it encountered a relatively new third-wave civilization located on the far eastern fringe of Christendom. Whatever political unity this new civilization of Kievan Rus had earlier enjoyed was now gone, and various independent princes proved unable to unite even in the face of the Mongol onslaught. Although they had interacted extensively with pastoral people of the steppes north of the Black Sea, Mongol ferocity was stunning. City after city fell to Mongol forces, which were now armed with the catapults and battering rams adopted from Chinese or Muslim sources. What followed was described in horrific terms by Russian chroniclers, who reported mass slaughter of "men, women, and children, monks, nuns and priests" and the violation of "good women and girls in the presence of their mothers and sisters." From the survivors and the cities that surrendered early, laborers and skilled craftsmen were deported to other Mongol lands or sold into slavery. A number of Russian crafts were so depleted of their workers that they did not recover for a century or more.

If the violence of initial conquest bore similarities to the experiences of Persia, Russia's incorporation into the Mongol Empire was very different. To the Mongols, it was the Kipchak (KIP-chahk) Khanate, named after the Kipchak Turkic-speaking peoples north of the Caspian and Black seas, among whom the Mongols had settled. To the Russians, it was the "**Khanate of the Golden Horde**." By whatever name, the Mongols had conquered Russia, but they did not occupy it as they had China and Persia. Thus in Russia there were no garrisoned cities, permanently stationed administrators, or Mongol settlers. From the Mongol point of view, Russia had little to offer. Its economy was not nearly so sophisticated or productive as that of more established civilizations; nor was it located on major international trade routes. It was simply not worth the expense of occupying. Furthermore, the availability of extensive steppe lands north of the Black and Caspian seas for pasturing their flocks meant that the Mongols could maintain their preferred pastoral way of life, while remaining in easy reach of Russian cities when the need arose to send further military expeditions. They could dominate and exploit Russia from the steppes.

And exploit they certainly did. Russian princes received appointment from the khan and were required to send substantial tribute to the Mongol capital at Sarai, located on the lower Volga River. A variety of additional taxes created a heavy burden, especially on the peasantry, while continuing border raids sent tens of thousands of Russians into slavery. The Mongol impact was highly uneven, however. The Russian Orthodox Church flourished under the Mongol policy of religious toleration, for it received exemption from many taxes. Russian nobles who participated in Mongol raids earned a share of the loot. Some cities, such as Kiev, resisted the Mongols and

Mongol Russia This sixteenth-century painting depicts the Mongol burning of the Russian city of Ryazan in 1237. Similar destruction awaited many Russian towns that resisted the invaders. (akg-images/Universal Images Group /Sovfoto)

were devastated, while others surrendered and collaborated and were left undamaged. Moscow in particular emerged as the primary collector of tribute for the Mongols, with one of its rulers, Ivan I, earning the nickname Ivan the Moneybags because of the riches that flowed to him from this position. Moscow's princes parlayed this position into a leading role as the nucleus of a renewed Russian state when Mongol domination receded in the fifteenth century.

The absence of direct Mongol rule had implications for the Mongols themselves, for they were far less influenced by or assimilated within Russian cultures than their counterparts in China and Persia had been. The Mongols in China had turned themselves into a Chinese dynasty, with the khan as a Chinese emperor. Some learned calligraphy, and a few came to appreciate Chinese poetry. In Persia, the Mongols had converted to Islam, with some becoming farmers. Not so in Russia. There "the Mongols of the Golden Horde were still spending their days in the saddle and their nights in tents."[20] They could dominate Russia from the adjacent steppes without in any way adopting Russian culture. Even though they remained culturally separate from Christian Russians, eventually the Mongols assimilated to the culture and the Islamic faith of the Kipchak people of the steppes, and in the process they lost their distinct identity and became Kipchaks.

Despite this domination from a distance, "the impact of the Mongols on Russia was, if anything, greater than on China and Iran [Persia]," according to a leading scholar.[21] Russian princes, who were more or less left alone if they paid the required tribute and taxes, found it useful to adopt the Mongols' weapons, diplomatic rituals, court practices, taxation system, and military draft. Mongol policies facilitated, although not intentionally, the rise of Moscow as the core of a new Russian state, and that state made good use of the famous Mongol mounted courier service. Mongol policies also strengthened the hold of the Russian Orthodox Church and enabled it to penetrate the rural areas more fully than before. Some Russians, seeking to explain their country's economic backwardness and political autocracy in modern times, have held the Mongols responsible for both conditions, though most historians consider such views vastly exaggerated.

Divisions among the Mongols, the disruptive influence of plague, and the growing strength of the Russian state—centered now on the city of Moscow—enabled the Russians to break the Mongols' hold by the end of the fifteenth century. With the earlier demise of Mongol rule in China and Persia, and now in Russia, the Mongols had retreated from their brief but spectacular incursion into the civilizations of outer Eurasia. Nonetheless, they continued to periodically threaten these civilizations for several centuries, until their homelands were absorbed into the expanding Russian and Chinese empires. But the Mongol moment in world history was over.

The Mongol Empire as a Eurasian Network

During the third-wave era, Chinese culture and Buddhism provided a measure of integration among the peoples of East Asia; Christianity did the same for Europe, while the realm of Islam connected most of the lands in between. But it was the Mongol Empire, during the thirteenth and fourteenth centuries, that brought all of these regions into a single interacting network, enabling the circulation of goods, information, disease, and styles of warfare all across Eurasia and parts of Africa.

Toward a World Economy

The Mongols themselves did not produce much of value for distant markets, nor were they active traders. Nonetheless, they consistently promoted international commerce, largely so that they could tax it and thus extract wealth from more developed civilizations. The Great Khan Ogodei, for example, often paid well over the asking price to attract merchants to his capital of Karakorum. The Mongols also provided financial backing for caravans, introduced standardized weights and measures, and gave tax breaks to merchants.

In providing a relatively secure environment for merchants making the long and arduous journey across Central Asia between Europe and China, the Mongol Empire brought the two ends of the Eurasian world into closer contact than ever before and launched a new phase in the history of the Silk Roads. Marco Polo was only the most famous of many European merchants, mostly from Italian cities, who made their way to China through the Mongol Empire. So many traders attempted the journey that guidebooks circulated with much useful advice about the trip. Merchants returned with tales of rich lands and prosperous commercial opportunities, but what they described were long-established trading networks of which Europeans had been largely ignorant.

The Mongol trading circuit was a central element in an even larger commercial network that linked much of the Afro-Eurasian world in the thirteenth century (see Map 11.2). Mongol-ruled China was the fulcrum of this vast system, connecting the overland route through the Mongol Empire with the oceanic routes through the South China Sea and Indian Ocean.

Diplomacy on a Eurasian Scale

Not only did the Mongol Empire facilitate long-distance commerce, but it also prompted diplomatic relationships from one end of Eurasia to the other. As their invasion of Russia spilled over into Eastern Europe, Mongol armies destroyed Polish, German, and Hungarian forces in 1241–1242 and seemed poised to march on Central and Western Europe. But the death of the Great Khan Ogodei required Mongol leaders to return to Mongolia, and Western Europe lacked adequate pasture for Mongol herds. Thus Western Europe was spared the trauma of conquest, but fearing the possible return of the Mongols, both the pope and European rulers dispatched delegations to the Mongol capital, mostly led by Franciscan friars. They hoped to learn something about Mongol intentions, to secure Mongol aid in the Christian crusade against Islam, and, if possible, to convert Mongols to Christianity. These efforts were largely in vain, for no alliance or widespread conversion occurred. In fact, one of these missions came back with a letter for the pope from the Great Khan Guyuk, demanding that Europeans submit to him.

Perhaps the most important outcome of these diplomatic probings was the useful information about lands to the east that European missions brought back. Those reports contributed to a dawning European awareness of a wider world, and they have certainly provided later historians with much useful information about the Mongols. Somewhat later, in 1287, the il-khanate of Persia sought an alliance with European powers to take Jerusalem and crush the forces of Islam, but the Persian Mongols' conversion to Islam soon put an end to any such anti-Muslim coalition.

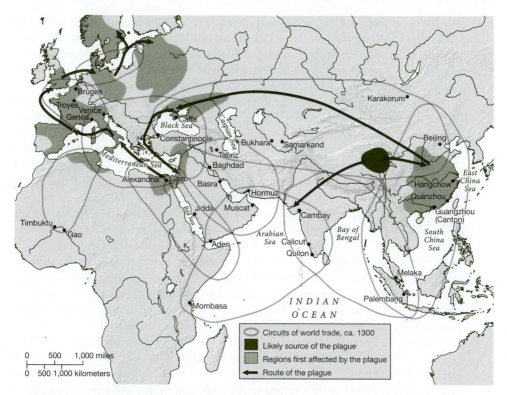

MAP 11.2 Trade and Disease in the Fourteenth Century
The Mongol Empire played a major role in the commercial integration of the Eurasian world as well as in the spread of the plague across this vast area.

Within the Mongol Empire itself, close relationships developed between the courts of Persia and China. They regularly exchanged ambassadors, shared intelligence information, fostered trade between their regions, and sent skilled workers back and forth. Thus political authorities all across Eurasia engaged in diplomatic relationships with one another more than ever before.

Cultural Exchange in the Mongol Realm

Accompanying these transcontinental economic and political relationships was a substantial exchange of peoples and cultures. Mongol policy forcibly transferred many thousands of skilled craftsmen and educated people from their homelands to distant parts of the empire, while the Mongols' religious tolerance and support of merchants drew missionaries and traders from afar. The Mongol capital at Karakorum was a cosmopolitan city with places of worship for Buddhists, Daoists, Muslims, and Christians. Chinggis Khan and several other Mongol rulers married Christian women. This relatively open Mongol outlook facilitated the exchange and blending of religious ideas. In Persia, for example, images of the Prophet Muhammad appeared, drawing on Chinese painting techniques and using Buddhist and Christian traditions as models. One such painting even portrayed the birth of the Prophet in a distinctly Christian nativity scene. Actors and musicians from China, wrestlers from Persia, and a jester from Byzantium provided entertainment for the Mongol court. Persian and Arab doctors and administrators were sent to China, while Chinese physicians and engineers found their skills in demand in the Islamic world.

This movement of people facilitated the exchange of ideas and techniques, a process actively encouraged by Mongol authorities. A great deal of Chinese technology and artistic conventions—such as painting, printing, gunpowder weapons, compass navigation, high-temperature furnaces, and medical techniques—flowed westward. But cultural sensibilities shaped the reception of foreign ideas and practices. Acupuncture, for example, was poorly received in the Middle East because it required too much bodily contact for Muslim taste, even as Chinese techniques for diagnosing illness by taking the pulse of patients proved quite popular, as they involved minimal body contact. Muslim astronomers brought their skills and knowledge to China because Mongol authorities wanted "second opinions on the reading of heavenly signs and portents" and assistance in constructing the accurate calendars needed for ritual purposes.[22] Plants and crops likewise circulated within the Mongol domain. Lemons and carrots from the Middle East found a welcome reception in China, while the Persian il-khan Ghazan sent envoys to India, China, and elsewhere to seek "seeds of things which are unique in that land."[23]

Europeans arguably gained more than most from these exchanges, for they had long been cut off from the fruitful interchange with Asia, and in comparison to the Islamic and Chinese worlds, they were less technologically developed. Now they could reap the benefits of new technology, new crops, and new knowledge of a wider world. And almost alone among the peoples of Eurasia, they could do so without having suffered the devastating consequences of Mongol conquest. In these circumstances, some historians have argued, lay the roots of Europe's remarkable rise to global prominence in the centuries that followed. (See "Controversies: Debating Empire" for a look at how historians think about empires.)

The Plague: An Afro-Eurasian Pandemic

Any benefits derived from participation in Mongol networks of communication and exchange must be measured alongside the hemispheric catastrophe known as the "plague" or the "pestilence" and later called the **Black Death**. Originating most likely in China, the bacteria responsible for the disease, known as *Yersinia pestis*, spread across the trade routes of the vast Mongol Empire in the early fourteenth century (see Map 11.2). Carried by rodents and transmitted by fleas to humans, the plague erupted initially in 1331 in modern northeastern China and had reached the Middle East and Western Europe by 1347. Some genetic evidence suggests that it penetrated sub-Saharan Africa as well.

The disease itself was associated with swelling of the lymph nodes, terrible headaches, high fever, and internal bleeding just below the skin. Infected people generally died within a few days. In the densely populated civilizations of China, the Islamic world, and Europe as well as in the steppe lands of the pastoralists, the plague claimed enormous numbers of human victims, causing a sharp contraction in Eurasian population for a century or more. Chroniclers reported rates of death that ranged from 50 to 90 percent of the affected population, depending on the time and place. Recent scholarship suggests that about half of Europe's people perished during the initial outbreak of 1348–1350.[24] A fifteenth-century Egyptian historian wrote that within a month of the plague's arrival in 1349, "Cairo had become an abandoned desert. . . . Everywhere one heard lamentations and one could not pass by any house without being overwhelmed by the howling."[25] The Middle East generally had lost perhaps one-third of its population by the early fifteenth century.[26] The intense first wave of the plague was followed by periodic visitations over the next several centuries. However, other regions of the Eastern Hemisphere, especially India and sub-Saharan Africa, were much less affected.

In those places where it struck hardest, the plague left thoughtful people grasping for language with which to describe a horror of such unprecedented dimensions. One Italian man, who had buried all five of his children with his own hands, wrote in 1348 that "so many have died that everyone believes it is the end of the world."[27] Another Italian, the Renaissance scholar Francesco Petrarch, was equally stunned by the impact of the Black Death; he wrote to a friend in 1349:

> When at any time has such a thing been seen or spoken of? Has what happened in these years ever been read about: empty houses, derelict cities, ruined estates, fields strewn with cadavers, a horrible and vast solitude encompassing the whole world? Consult historians, they are silent; ask physicians, they are stupefied; seek the answers from philosophers, they shrug their shoulders, furrow their brows, and with fingers pressed against their lips, bid you be silent. Will posterity believe these things, when we who have seen it can scarcely believe it?[28]

In the Islamic world, the famous historian Ibn Khaldun, who had lost both of his parents to the plague, also wrote about it in apocalyptic terms:

> Civilization in both the East and the West was visited by a destructive plague which devastated nations and caused populations to vanish. It swallowed up many of the good things of civilization and wiped them out. . . . It was as if the voice of existence had called out for oblivion and restriction, and the world responded to its call.[29]

Beyond its immediate devastation, the Black Death worked longer-term social changes in Europe, the region where the plague's impact has been most thoroughly studied. Labor shortages following the initial outburst provoked sharp conflict between scarce workers, who sought higher wages or better conditions, and the rich, who resisted those demands. A series of revolts by peasants and urban workers in the fourteenth century reflected this tension, which also undermined the practice of serfdom. That labor shortage created, at least for a time, more employment opportunities for women. It may also have fostered greater interest in technological innovation, especially in labor-enhancing devices, from ships that replaced oarsmen with sails, to water mills that harnessed mechanical instead of muscle power, to improved armor to protect soldiers, to reading glasses to extend the working life of scribes. The revival of the slave trade that had nearly disappeared in Europe in the centuries before the plague was also spurred by the growing value of labor. Thus a resilient European civilization survived a cataclysm that had the power to destroy it. In a strange way, that catastrophe may have actually fostered its future growth.

Whatever its impact in particular places, the plague also had larger consequences. Ironically, that human disaster, born of the Mongol network, was a primary reason for the demise of that network in the fourteenth and fifteenth centuries. Population contracted, cities declined, and the volume of trade diminished all across the Mongol

The Plague Produced just a few years after the event, this image from a medical text depicts the townspeople of Tournai in modern Belgium burying their dead during an outbreak of the plague in 1349. Cities often resorted to mass graves as the numbers of dead mounted. (Bibliothèque Royale de Belgique, Brussels, Belgium/Bridgeman Images)

world. By 1350, the Mongol Empire itself was in disarray, and within a century the Mongols had lost control of Chinese, Persian, and Russian civilizations. The Central Asian trade route, so critical to the entire Afro-Eurasian world economy, largely closed.

This disruption of the Mongol-based land routes to the East, coupled with a desire to avoid Muslim intermediaries, provided incentives for Europeans to take to the sea in their continuing efforts to reach the riches of Asia. Their naval technology gave them military advantages on the seas, much as the Mongols' skill with the bow and their mobility on horseback gave these pastoralists a decisive edge in land battles. As Europeans penetrated Asian and Atlantic waters in the sixteenth century, they took on, in some ways, the role of the Mongols in organizing and fostering world trade and in creating a network of communication and exchange over an even larger area. Like the Mongols, Europeans were people on the periphery of the major established civilizations; they too were economically less developed in comparison to Chinese and Islamic civilizations. Both Mongols and Europeans were apt to forcibly plunder the wealthier civilizations they encountered, and European empire building in the Americas, like that of the Mongols in Eurasia, brought devastating disease and catastrophic population decline in its wake.[30] Europeans, of course, brought far more of their own culture and many more of their own people to the societies they conquered, as Christianity, European languages, settler societies, and Western science and technology took root within their empires. Although their imperial presence lasted far longer and operated on a much larger scale, European actions at the beginning of their global expansion bore some resemblance to those of their Mongol predecessors. Perhaps they were, as one historian put it, "the Mongols of the seas."[31]

Controversies: Debating Empire

The empires of the third-wave era—Chinese, Byzantine, Arab, and Mongol—have attracted considerable attention from historians, as have both earlier and later empires. And no wonder. Over the past 2,500 years, more people have lived in empires, where multiple distinct ethnic communities were ruled and often exploited by a dominant group, than in any other type of state or society.

Historians have long been intrigued by the various ways in which empires were born. The early Chinese and Egyptian empires, for example, took root in the heartland of already settled agricultural regions. The Persian, Greek, and Roman empires, by contrast, expanded from the edges of established agriculture civilizations, while the pastoralist empires of the Arabs, Mongols, and Turks found their origins in regions without much settled agriculture. More recently, European powers conquered and colonized regions thousands of miles from their home countries, creating the first overseas empires. But some civilizations developed for centuries without generating empires, such as those in ancient Sumer, in post-Roman Europe, and among the cities of the Maya and the Niger River valley. Was it because the rivalry of many small states or cities confounded efforts to develop larger imperial systems?

Other variations on the imperial theme have likewise surfaced in the work of historians. Empires were most frequently constructed through violence and conquest, but with important exceptions. The Athenian empire, for instance, started as a voluntary league. The European domains of the Habsburg Empire were largely brought together through family marriage strategies and inheritance. Some empires were constructed deliberately, like those of the Greek ruler Alexander the Great, the first Chinese emperor Qin Shihuangdi, and the Mongol leader Chinggis Khan. Others, like the Roman and Arab empires, grew more slowly in reaction to frontier insecurity or internal pressures. Autocrats frequently ruled over imperial enterprises, but democracies and republics have also created empires, including two of the largest, the ancient Roman and nineteenth-century British empires. Scholars have emphasized the durability of empires like that of Byzantium, which persisted for over a millennium, or its Ottoman successor, which survived for six centuries. But abortive or short-lived imperial adventures are also common, including that of the Mauryan dynasty in India, Axum in Northeast Africa, and Japan's East Asian empire in the early twentieth century. Explaining these variations provides grist for the mill of historical controversy.

So too does the collapse of empires. Historians have discovered that few imperial regimes have been toppled by internal rebellions of the oppressed. Even the largest rebellions, like the Yellow Turban in Han China or Spartacus's slave revolt in ancient Rome, were ultimately crushed. More commonly, empires fell or fragmented due to external invasion, as happened to the Aztec and Inca empires, or when the ruling elite split, as was the case following the deaths of Alexander the Great, Charlemagne, and Chinggis Khan. The end of the western Roman Empire has fostered endless controversy, with scholars emphasizing various factors: economic decline owing to war, corruption, and overreliance on slavery; penetration of the empire and its military forces by Germanic peoples; frequent turnover of emperors, often by murder; the invasion of the Huns; the coming of Christianity and the erosion of traditional values; environmental degradation; and many others. Scholars even disagree about when or if the empire ended. Was it in 476 C.E. when Emperor Romulus was overthrown by a German warlord? Or had the empire ceased to function as a state decades before Romulus was deposed? Still others date its demise to the fall of Constantinople nearly 1,000 years later in 1453, arguing that the Roman Empire lived on in Byzantium.

Historians have also differed in their assessments of empire, in part reflecting the cultural attitudes of the times in which they wrote. The rapid expansion of European imperial enterprises in Africa and parts of Asia in the late nineteenth century coincided with the emergence of university history departments and professional historians in Europe and the United States. In this context, many Western historians produced studies of the remarkable accomplishments of empires through history, focusing on their military and administrative successes and exploring how imperial projects brought "civilization" to "traditional" societies. Historians identified the freer spread of ideas, goods, and people; the standardization of laws and currency; and the building of infrastructure and establishment of peace as advances for humankind as a whole—or, as Lord Curzon, a prominent imperial official and writer about empire, put it in 1894: "the British Empire is under Providence the greatest instrument for good that the world has seen."[32]

However, an increasingly negative assessment of empire gained influence among historians as the twentieth century progressed. Already in the nineteenth century some historians had emphasized the exploitative and oppressive aspects of modern European empires, which were built to feed the capitalist world's insatiable appetite for raw materials and markets. But the global spread of anticolonial ideologies and the breakup of European empires in the aftermath of World War II sparked a reassessment of imperial rule by historians and the emergence of the new fields of colonial and postcolonial studies in which the experiences of colonized peoples found voice. These historians put new emphasis on the massive bloodshed and oppression—enslavement, impoverishment, forced tribute and taxes, deportation—that frequently accompanied imperial conquest and rule. They also questioned the alleged "civilizing" missions of empires, instead highlighting the repression or destruction of the cultures and societies of conquered peoples. Commenting on this more negative assessment of empire, one scholar has recently noted that "in our time 'imperialist' ranks second only to 'fascist' in the lexicon of political swear words."[33]

Over the past century, empires have been largely replaced by nation-states organized around the very different idea that sovereign countries should be composed of a single people or ethnic group. This transformation of the political landscape has sparked some nostalgic reflections on empires, perhaps none so influential or controversial as that of Niall Ferguson, a historian of the British Empire who recently argued that European empires were often better for their subjects than the local regimes they replaced. "It's hard to make the case . . . ," he declared, "that somehow the world would have been better off if the Europeans had stayed home. . . . Imperial guilt can lead to self-flagellation . . . [and] very simplistic judgements."[34] Other scholars, when comparing empires to modern nation-states, have found advantages to empires, especially their tolerance toward ethnic minorities within their boundaries.

The theme of empire resonates still among historians and the general public in the early twenty-first century. Is contemporary Russia seeking to re-create the old Russian Empire? Does Turkey want to replicate something of the Ottoman Empire?

Does the global reach of the United States represent a new kind of empire, even if a declining one? The debates continue.

Conclusions and Reflections: Historians, Bias, and the Mongols

Are historians biased in favor of civilizations? Certainly they seem to give much greater prominence to these urban- and city-based societies than to bands of gathering and hunting peoples, to agricultural village communities, and to pastoral peoples. In this chapter, we seek to redress this imbalance by highlighting the significance of herding or pastoral peoples in world history. Their adaptation to arid environments represented a creative alternative to agriculturally based economies. The greater freedom of their women contrasts sharply with that of patriarchal civilizations. And their empires — Xiongnu, Arab, Turkic, Almoravid, and Mongol — challenged adjacent agricultural civilizations all across the Afro-Eurasian world.

The Mongol Empire was the largest, the most explosive, and almost the last of these pastoral incursions into the world of civilizations. It conquered and united a previously divided China and acquired a measure of acceptance as the Yuan dynasty. While the Mongols devastated the ancient civilization of Persia, they were themselves converted to Islam and assimilated into Persian society. In Russia, however, the Mongols remained quite separate from local culture, while dominating Russia politically and exploiting it economically. More broadly, the Mongols brought much of Eurasia into an interacting network of exchange that facilitated the movement of people, technologies, cultures, and perhaps most critically, the bacteria that spread the Black Death across the Eastern Hemisphere.

Until recently, pastoralists generally and the Mongols in particular received bad press in history books. Normally they entered the story only when they were threatening or destroying established civilizations. This negative image of pastoral peoples reflected the long-held attitudes of literate elites in the civilizations of Eurasia. Fearing and usually despising such peoples, educated observers in China, the Middle East, and Europe often described them as bloodthirsty savages or barbarians, bringing only chaos and destruction in their wake. To the European Christian Saint Jerome (340–420 C.E.), the Huns "filled the whole earth with slaughter and panic alike as they flitted hither and thither on their swift horses."[35] Almost a thousand years later, the famous Arab historian Ibn Khaldun described pastoralists in a very similar fashion: "It is their nature to plunder whatever other people possess."[36]

Because pastoral peoples generally did not have written languages, the sources available to historians came from less-than-unbiased observers in adjacent agricultural civilizations. Furthermore, in the long-running conflict across the farming/pastoral frontier, agricultural civilizations ultimately triumphed. By the early twentieth century, and in most places much earlier, pastoral peoples everywhere had lost their former independence and had often shed their pastoral life as well. Since "winners" usually write history, the negative views of pastoralists held by agrarian civilizations normally prevailed.

In recent decades, however, historians have sought to present a more balanced picture of pastoralists' role in world history, emphasizing what they created as well as what they destroyed. These historians have highlighted the achievements of herding peoples, such as their adaptation to inhospitable environments; their technological innovations; their development of horse-, camel-, or cattle-based cultures; their role in fostering cross-cultural exchange; and their state-building efforts.

A less judgmental posture toward the Mongols perhaps derives from the "total wars" and genocides of the twentieth century, in which mass slaughter was common. During the cold war, the United States and the Soviet Union were prepared, apparently, to obliterate each other's entire population with nuclear weapons in response to an attack. In light of this recent history, Mongol massacres may appear a little less unique. Historians living in the glass houses of contemporary societies are perhaps more reluctant to cast stones at the Mongols. In understanding the Mongols, as in so much else, historians are shaped by the times and circumstances of their own lives as much as by "what really happened" in the past.

Revisiting Chapter 11

REVISITING SPECIFICS

REVISITING CORE IDEAS

1. **Assessing Significance** In what ways did the Xiongnu, Arabs, Turks, and Berbers make an impact on world history?

2. **Explaining Success** What accounts for the political and military success of the Mongols?

3. **Comparing Conquests** In what different ways did Mongol conquest shape the history of China, Persia, and Russia?

4. **Describing Connections** What kinds of cross-cultural interactions did the Mongol Empire generate?

5. **Analyzing Cause and Effect** How did the plague change the societies it touched?

A WIDER VIEW

1. How might you summarize the understanding that people in agricultural civilizations and those in pastoral societies had of each other?

2. In brief, what was the significance of the Mongols in world history?

3. What do you make of the statement at the end of the chapter that Europeans were "the Mongols of the sea"? Does that comparison represent a criticism, a celebration, or a neutral judgment of the Europeans?

4. Why did the Mongol Empire last only a relatively short time?

5. Looking Back In what ways did the Mongol Empire resemble previous empires (Arab, Roman, Chinese, or the Greek empire of Alexander, for example), and in what ways did it differ from them?

CHRONOLOGY

ca. 500–1000 c.e.	• Succession of Turkic empires
ca. 600–1000	• Arab Empire
ca. 900–1400	• Conversion of Turkic peoples to Islam
ca. 1000–1147	• Almoravid Empire
1162–1227	• Life of Chinggis Khan
1209–1368	• Mongol rule in China
1219–ca. 1335	• Mongol rule in Persia
1237–1480	• Mongol rule in Russia
1241–1242	• Mongol attacks in Eastern Europe
1258	• Mongol seizure of Baghdad
1271–1295	• Marco Polo in Mongol Empire
1295	• Mongol ruler of Persia converts to Islam
1300–1500	• Establishment of Turkic Ottoman Empire
1348–1350	• High point of Black Death in Europe

12

The Worlds of the Fifteenth Century

| CONNECTING PAST AND PRESENT | **"FOR MANY PEOPLE IN OUR COMMUNITY,** the statue [of Christopher Columbus] represents patriarchy, oppression and divisiveness," |

declared Andrew Ginther, mayor of Columbus, Ohio, in June of 2020. "We will no longer live in the shadow of our ugly past. . . . Now is the right time to replace this statue with artwork that demonstrates our enduring fight to end racism and celebrate the themes of diversity and inclusion."[1] One of many such removals all across the country in the summer of 2020, the city council's action occurred in the context of a nationwide eruption of protest against police killings of African Americans under the slogan "Black Lives Matter."

The statue, which had stood in a prominent place in front of city hall since 1955, was a gift from Genoa, Italy, Columbus's sister city and birthplace of the famous explorer. According to its dedication plaque, it was intended to celebrate his "values and virtues" and the connection between these two distant cities that embraced him. But by 2020 it had become a local focus of a wider and growing debate about the significance and legacy of Columbus. Was he, as one prominent activist for indigenous rights put it, "a perpetrator of genocide . . . , a slave trader, a thief, a pirate, and most certainly not a hero"?[2] Or should Americans celebrate Columbus because he was, as one public commentator claimed, "a man ahead of his time whose vision and discovery changed the course of world history by connecting the peoples of the world for the first time"?[3]

This sharp debate about Columbus reminds us that the past is endlessly contested and that it continues to resonate in the present. But it also reflects a broad agreement that the voyages of Columbus marked a decisive turning point, for better or worse, in world history and represent arguably the most important event of the fifteenth century.

It was not, however, the only globally significant development of that century. If Columbus launched a European empire-building process in the Americas, other empires were also in the making during the fifteenth century. In 1383, a Central Asian Turkic warrior named Timur launched the last major pastoral invasion of adjacent civilizations. In 1405, an enormous Chinese fleet set out across the entire Indian Ocean basin, only to voluntarily withdraw twenty-eight years later, thus forgoing an empire in Asia. Four new empires gave the Islamic world a distinct political and cultural shape. One of them, the Ottoman Empire, put a final end to Christian Byzantium with the conquest of Constantinople in 1453, even as Spanish Christians completed the "reconquest" of the Iberian Peninsula from the Muslims in 1492. And in the Americas, the Aztec and Inca empires gave a final and spectacular expression to Mesoamerican and Andean civilizations before they were both swallowed up in the burst of European imperialism that followed the arrival of Columbus.

Because the fifteenth century was an era of transition on many fronts, it provides an occasion for a bird's-eye view of the world through an imaginary global tour. This excursion around the world will briefly review the human saga thus far and establish a baseline from which the enormous transformations of the centuries that followed might be measured. How, then, might we describe the world, and the worlds, of the fifteenth century?

SEEKING THE MAIN POINT	What elements of fifteenth-century world history represented a continuation of earlier patterns, and what elements signaled a break with the past?

Societies and Cultures of the Fifteenth Century

One way to describe the world of the fifteenth century is to identify the various types of human communities that it contained. Bands of gatherers and hunters, villages of agricultural peoples, newly emerging chiefdoms or small states, pastoral communities, established civilizations and empires — all of these social or political forms would have been apparent to a widely traveled visitor in the fifteenth century. Representing alternative ways of organizing human life, all of them were long established by the fifteenth century, but the balance among them in 1500 was quite different than it had been a thousand years earlier.

Paleolithic Persistence: Australia and North America

Despite millennia of agricultural advance, substantial areas of the world still hosted gathering and hunting societies, known to historians as Paleolithic (Old Stone Age) peoples. All of Australia, much of Siberia, the arctic coastlands, and parts of Africa and the Americas fell into this category. These peoples were not simply relics of a bygone age, for they too had a history and a sizable presence in the world during the fifteenth century, although most history books largely ignore them after the age of agriculture arrived.

Consider, for example, Australia. That continent's many separate groups, some 250 of them, still practiced a gathering and hunting way of life in the fifteenth century, a pattern that continued well after Europeans arrived in the late eighteenth century. Over many thousands of years, these people had assimilated various material items or cultural practices from outsiders—outrigger canoes, fishhooks, complex netting techniques, artistic styles, rituals, and mythological ideas—but despite the presence of farmers in nearby New Guinea, no agricultural practices penetrated the Australian mainland. Was it because large areas of Australia were unsuited for the kind of agriculture practiced in New Guinea? Or did the peoples of Australia, enjoying an environment of sufficient resources, simply see no need to change their way of life?

Despite the absence of agriculture, Australia's peoples had mastered and manipulated their environment, in part through "firestick farming," the practice of deliberately setting fires, which they described as "cleaning up the country." These controlled burns cleared the underbrush, thus making hunting easier and encouraging the growth of certain plant and animal species. In addition, native Australians exchanged goods among themselves over distances of hundreds of miles, created elaborate mythologies and ritual practices, and developed sophisticated traditions of sculpture and rock painting. They accomplished all of this with an economy and technology rooted in the distant Paleolithic past.

A very different kind of gathering and hunting society flourished in the fifteenth century along the northwest coast of North America among the Chinookan, Tulalip, Skagit, and other peoples. With some 300 edible animal species and an abundance of salmon and other fish, this extraordinarily bounteous environment provided the foundation for what scholars sometimes call "complex" or "affluent" gathering and hunting cultures. What distinguished the northwest coast peoples from those of Australia were permanent village settlements with large and sturdy houses, considerable economic specialization, ranked societies that sometimes included slavery, chiefdoms dominated by powerful clan leaders or "big men," and extensive storage of food.

Although these and other gathering and hunting peoples persisted in the fifteenth century, both their numbers (an estimated 1 percent of the world's population by 1500) and the area they inhabited had contracted greatly as the Agricultural Revolution unfolded across the planet. That relentless advance of the farming frontier continued in the centuries ahead as the Russian, Chinese, and European empires encompassed the lands of the remaining Paleolithic peoples.

Agricultural Village Societies: The Igbo and the Iroquois

Far more numerous than gatherers and hunters but still a small percentage of the total world population were those many peoples who, though fully agricultural, had avoided incorporation into larger empires or civilizations and had not developed their own city- or state-based societies. Living usually in small village-based communities and organized in terms of kinship relations, such people predominated during the fifteenth century in much of North America; in most of the tropical lowlands of South America and the Caribbean; in parts of the Amazon River basin, Southeast Asia, and Africa south of the equator; and throughout Pacific Oceania. Historians have often treated them as marginal to the cities, states, and large-scale civilizations that predominate in most accounts of the global past. Viewed from within their own circles, though, these societies were at the center of things, each with its own history of migration, cultural transformation, social conflict, incorporation of new people, political rise and fall, and interaction with strangers.

East of the Niger River in the heavily forested region of West Africa lay the lands of the **Igbo** (EE-boh) peoples. By the fifteenth century, their neighbors, the Yoruba and Bini, had begun to develop small states and urban centers. But the Igbo, whose dense population and extensive trading networks might well have given rise to states, declined to follow suit. The deliberate Igbo preference was to reject the kingship and state-building efforts of their neighbors. They boasted on occasion that "the Igbo have no kings." Instead, they relied on other institutions to maintain social cohesion beyond the level of the village: title societies in which wealthy men received a series of prestigious ranks, women's associations, hereditary ritual experts serving as mediators, and a balance of power among kinship groups. It was a "stateless society," famously described in Chinua Achebe's *Things Fall Apart*, the most widely read novel to emerge from twentieth-century Africa.

But the Igbo peoples and their neighbors did not live in isolated, self-contained societies. They traded actively among themselves and with more distant peoples, such as the large African kingdom of Songhay (sahn-GEYE) far to the north. Cotton cloth, fish, copper and iron goods, decorative objects, and more drew neighboring peoples into networks of exchange. Common artistic traditions reflected a measure of cultural unity in a politically fragmented region, and all of these peoples seem to have changed from a matrilineal to a patrilineal system of tracing their descent. Little of this registered in the larger civilizations of the Afro-Eurasian world, but to the peoples of the West African forest during the fifteenth century, these processes were central to their history and their daily lives. Soon, however, all of them would be caught up in the transatlantic slave trade and would be changed substantially in the process.

Across the Atlantic in what is now central New York State, other agricultural village societies were also undergoing major change during the several centuries preceding their incorporation into European trading networks and empires. The Iroquois-speaking peoples of that region had only recently become fully agricultural, adopting maize- and bean-farming techniques that had originated centuries earlier in Mesoamerica. As this productive agriculture took hold by 1300 or so, the population grew, the size of settlements increased, and distinct peoples emerged. Frequent warfare also erupted among them. Some scholars have speculated that as agriculture,

Iroquois Women This seventeenth-century French engraving depicts two Iroquois women preparing a meal. Among the Iroquois, women controlled both agriculture and property and had a significant voice in public affairs. (De Agostini Picture Library/M. Seemuller/ Bridgeman Images)

largely seen as women's work, became the primary economic activity, "warfare replaced successful food getting as the avenue to male prestige."[4]

Whatever caused it, this increased level of conflict among **Iroquois** peoples triggered a remarkable political innovation around the fifteenth century: a loose alliance or confederation among five Iroquois-speaking peoples — the Mohawk, Oneida, Onondaga, Cayuga, and Seneca (see Map 12.5, page 354). Based on an agreement known as the Great Law of Peace, the Five Nations, as they called themselves, agreed to settle their differences peacefully through a confederation council of clan leaders, some fifty of them altogether, who had the authority to adjudicate disputes and set reparation payments. Operating by consensus, the Iroquois League of Five Nations effectively suppressed the blood feuds and tribal conflicts that had only recently been so widespread. It also coordinated its peoples' relationship with outsiders, including the Europeans, who arrived in growing numbers in the centuries after 1500.

The Iroquois League gave expression to values of limited government, social equality, and personal freedom, concepts that some European colonists found highly attractive. One British colonial administrator declared in 1749 that the Iroquois had "such absolute Notions of Liberty that they allow no Kind of Superiority of one over another, and banish all Servitude from their Territories."[5] Such equality extended to gender relationships, for among the Iroquois, descent was matrilineal (reckoned through the woman's line), married couples lived with the wife's family, and women controlled agriculture and property. While men were hunters, warriors, and the primary political officeholders, women selected and could depose those leaders.

Wherever they lived in 1500, over the next several centuries independent agricultural peoples such as the Iroquois and Igbo, like many other such peoples before them, were increasingly encompassed by expanding economic networks and conquest empires based in Western Europe, Russia, China, or India.

Pastoral Peoples: Central Asia and West Africa

Pastoral peoples had long impinged more directly and dramatically on civilizations than did gathering and hunting or agricultural village societies. The Mongol incursion, along with the enormous empire to which it gave rise, was one in a long series of challenges from the steppes, but it was not quite the last. As the Mongol Empire disintegrated, a brief attempt to restore it occurred in the late fourteenth and early fifteenth centuries under the leadership of a Turkic warrior named **Timur**, born in what is now Uzbekistan and known in the West as Tamerlane (see Map 12.1, page 342).

With a ferocity that matched or exceeded that of his model, Chinggis Khan, Timur's army of pastoralists brought immense devastation yet again to Russia and Persia, and also to India. Timur himself died in 1405, while preparing for an invasion of China. Conflicts among his successors prevented any lasting empire, although his descendants retained control of the area between Persia and Afghanistan for the rest of the fifteenth century. That state hosted a sophisticated elite culture combining Turkic and Persian elements, particularly at its splendid capital of Samarkand, as its rulers patronized artists, poets, traders, and craftsmen. Timur's conquest proved to be the last great military success of pastoral peoples from Central Asia. In the centuries that followed, their homelands were swallowed up in the expanding Russian and Chinese empires, as the balance of power between steppe pastoralists of inner Eurasia and the civilizations of outer Eurasia turned decisively in favor of the latter.

In Africa, pastoral peoples stayed independent of established empires several centuries longer than those of Inner Asia, for not until the late nineteenth century were they incorporated into European colonial states. The experience of the **Fulbe** (fulb), West Africa's largest pastoral society, provides an example of an African herding people with a highly significant role in the fifteenth century and beyond. From their homeland in the western fringe of the Sahara along the upper Senegal River, the Fulbe had migrated gradually eastward in the centuries after 1000 C.E. (see Map 12.3, page 347). Unlike the pastoral peoples of Inner Asia, they generally lived in small communities among agricultural peoples and paid various grazing fees and taxes for the privilege of pasturing their cattle. Relations with their farming hosts often were tense because the Fulbe resented their subordination to agricultural peoples, whose way of life they despised. That sense of cultural superiority became even more pronounced as the Fulbe, in the course of their eastward movement, slowly adopted Islam. Some of them in fact dropped out of a pastoral life and settled in towns, where they became highly respected religious leaders. In the eighteenth and nineteenth centuries, the Fulbe were at the center of a wave of religiously based uprisings, or jihads, that greatly expanded the practice of Islam and gave rise to a series of new states ruled by the Fulbe themselves.

Civilizations of the Fifteenth Century: Comparing China and Europe

Beyond the foraging, farming, and pastoral societies of the fifteenth-century world were its civilizations, those city-centered and state-based societies that were far larger and more densely populated, more powerful and innovative, and much more unequal in terms of class and gender than other forms of human community. Since the First Civilizations had emerged between 3500 and 1000 B.C.E., both the geographic space they encompassed and the number of people they embraced had grown substantially. By the fifteenth century, about 30 percent of the world's land was controlled by states and a considerable majority of the world's population lived within one or another of these civilizations. But most of these people, no doubt, identified more with local communities than with a larger civilization. What might an imaginary global traveler notice about the world's major civilizations in the fifteenth century?

Ming Dynasty China

Such a traveler might well begin his or her journey in China. That civilization had been greatly disrupted by a century of Mongol rule, and its population had been sharply reduced by the plague. During the **Ming dynasty** (1368–1644), however, China recovered (see Map 12.1). In the early decades of that dynasty, the Chinese

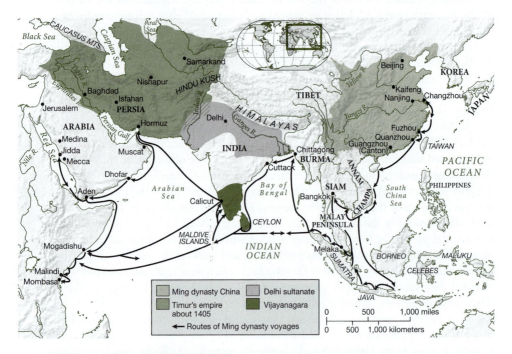

MAP 12.1 Asia in the Fifteenth Century
The fifteenth century in Asia witnessed the massive Ming dynasty voyages into the Indian Ocean, the last major eruption of pastoral power in Timur's empire, and the flourishing of the maritime city of Melaka.

attempted to eliminate all signs of foreign rule, discouraging the use of Mongol names and dress while promoting Confucian learning and orthodox gender roles based on earlier models from the Han, Tang, and Song dynasties. Emperor Yongle (YAHNG-leh) (r. 1402–1424) sponsored an enormous *Encyclopedia* of some 11,000 volumes. With contributions from more than 2,000 scholars, this work sought to summarize or compile all previous writing on history, geography, philosophy, ethics, government, and more. Yongle also relocated the capital to Beijing, ordered the building of a magnificent imperial residence known as the Forbidden City, and constructed the Temple of Heaven, where subsequent rulers performed Confucian-based rituals to ensure the well-being of Chinese society. Two empresses wrote instructions for female behavior, emphasizing traditional expectations after the disruptions of the previous century. Culturally speaking, China was looking to its past.

Politically, the Ming dynasty reestablished the civil service examination system that had been neglected under Mongol rule and went on to create a highly centralized government. Power was concentrated in the hands of the emperor himself, while a cadre of eunuchs (castrated men) personally loyal to the emperor exercised great authority, much to the dismay of the official bureaucrats. The state acted vigorously to repair the damage of the Mongol years by restoring millions of acres to cultivation; rebuilding canals, reservoirs, and irrigation works; and planting, according to some estimates, a billion trees in an effort to reforest China. As a result, the economy rebounded, both international and domestic trade flourished, and the population grew. During the fifteenth century, China had recovered and was perhaps the best governed and most prosperous of the world's major civilizations.

China also undertook the largest and most impressive maritime expeditions the world had ever seen. Since the eleventh century, Chinese sailors and traders had been a major presence in the South China Sea and in Southeast Asian port cities, with much of this activity in private hands. But now, after decades of preparation, an enormous fleet, commissioned by Emperor Yongle himself, was launched in 1405, followed over the next twenty-eight years by six more such expeditions. On board more than 300 ships of the first voyage was a crew of some 27,000, including 180 physicians, hundreds of government officials, 5 astrologers, 7 high-ranking or grand eunuchs, carpenters, tailors, accountants, merchants, translators, cooks, and thousands of soldiers and sailors. Visiting many ports in Southeast Asia, Indonesia, India, Arabia, and East Africa, these fleets, captained by the Muslim eunuch **Zheng He** (JUHNG-huh), sought to enroll distant peoples and states in the Chinese tribute system (see Map 12.1). Dozens of rulers accompanied the fleets back to China, where they presented tribute, performed the required rituals of submission, and received in return abundant gifts, titles, and trading opportunities. Officially described as "bringing order to the world," Zheng He's expeditions served to establish Chinese power and prestige in the Indian Ocean and to exert Chinese control over foreign trade in the region. The Chinese, however, did not seek to conquer new territories, establish Chinese settlements, or spread their culture, though they did intervene in a number of local disputes.

The most surprising feature of these voyages was how abruptly and deliberately they were ended. After 1433, Chinese authorities simply stopped such expeditions and allowed this enormous and expensive fleet to deteriorate in port. "In less than a hundred years," wrote a recent historian of these voyages, "the greatest navy the world had ever known had ordered itself into extinction."[6] Part of the reason involved the death of the emperor Yongle, who had been the chief patron of the enterprise. Many high-ranking officials had long seen the expeditions as a waste of resources because China, they believed, was the self-sufficient "middle kingdom," the center of the civilized world, requiring little from beyond its borders. In their eyes, the real danger to China came from the north, where barbarians constantly threatened. Finally, they viewed the voyages as the project of the court eunuchs, whom these officials despised. Even as these voices of Chinese officialdom prevailed, private Chinese merchants and craftsmen continued to settle and trade in Japan, the Philippines, Taiwan, and Southeast Asia, but they did so without the support of their government. The Chinese state quite deliberately turned its back on what was surely within its reach — a large-scale maritime empire in the Indian Ocean basin.

European Comparisons: State Building and Cultural Renewal

At the other end of the Eurasian continent, similar processes of demographic recovery, political consolidation, cultural flowering, and overseas expansion were under way. Western Europe, having escaped Mongol conquest but devastated by the plague, began to regrow its population during the second half of the fifteenth century. As in China, the infrastructure of civilization proved a durable foundation for demographic and economic revival.

Politically too, Europe joined China in continuing earlier patterns of state building. In China, however, this meant a unitary and centralized government that encompassed almost the whole of its civilization, while in Europe a decidedly fragmented system of many separate, independent, and highly competitive states made for a sharply divided Western civilization (see Map 12.2). Many of these states — Spain, Portugal, France, England, the city-states of Italy (Milan, Venice, and Florence), various German principalities — learned to tax their citizens more efficiently, to create more effective administrative structures, and to raise standing armies. A small Russian state centered on the city of Moscow also emerged in the fifteenth century as Mongol rule faded away. Much of this state building was driven by the needs of war, a frequent occurrence in such a fragmented and competitive political environment. England and France, for example, fought intermittently for more than a century in the Hundred Years' War (1337–1453) over rival claims to territory in France. Nothing remotely similar disturbed the internal life of Ming dynasty China.

A renewed cultural blossoming, the **European Renaissance**, likewise paralleled the revival of all things Confucian in Ming dynasty China. In Europe, however, that blossoming celebrated and reclaimed a classical Greco-Roman tradition that earlier had been lost or obscured. Beginning in the vibrant commercial cities of Italy between roughly 1350 and 1500, the Renaissance reflected the belief of the wealthy male elite that they were living in a wholly new era, far removed from the confined religious world of feudal Europe. Educated citizens of these cities sought inspiration in the art and literature of ancient Greece and Rome; they were "returning to the sources," as they put it. Their purpose was not so much to reconcile these works with the ideas of Christianity, as the twelfth- and thirteenth-century university scholars had done, but to use them as a cultural standard to imitate and then to surpass. The elite patronized great Renaissance artists such as Leonardo da Vinci, Michelangelo, and Raphael, whose paintings and sculptures were far more naturalistic, particularly in portraying

MAP 12.2   Europe in 1500

By the end of the fifteenth century, Christian Europe had assumed its early modern political shape as a system of competing states threatened by an expanding Muslim Ottoman Empire.

the human body, than those of their medieval counterparts. Some of these artists looked to the Islamic world for standards of excellence, sophistication, and abundance.

Although religious themes remained prominent, Renaissance artists now included portraits and busts of well-known contemporary figures and scenes from ancient mythology. In the work of those scholars known as humanists, reflections on secular topics such as grammar, history, politics, poetry, rhetoric, and ethics complemented more religious matters. For example, Niccolò Machiavelli's (1469–1527) famous work *The Prince* was a prescription for political success based on the way politics actually operated in a highly competitive Italy of rival city-states rather than on idealistic and religiously based principles. His slim volume was filled with ruthless advice, including the observation that "the ends justify the means" when ruling a state and that it was safer for a sovereign to be feared than loved by his subjects. But the teachings in *The Prince* were controversial, with many critics at the time rejecting its amoral analysis of political life and its assertion that rulers should — indeed must — set aside moral concerns to rule effectively.

While the great majority of Renaissance writers and artists were men, among the remarkable exceptions to that rule was Christine de Pizan (1363–1430), the daughter of a Venetian official who lived mostly in Paris. Her writings pushed against the misogyny of many European thinkers of the time. In her *City of Ladies*, she mobilized numerous women from history, Christian and pagan alike, to demonstrate that women too could be active members of society and deserved an education equal to that of men. "No matter which way I looked at it," she wrote, "I could find no evidence from my own experience to bear out such a negative view of female nature and habits. Even so . . . I could scarcely find a moral work by any author which didn't devote some chapter or paragraph to attacking the female sex."[7]

Heavily influenced by classical models, Renaissance figures were more interested in capturing the unique qualities of particular individuals and in describing the world as it was than in portraying or exploring eternal religious truths. In its focus on the affairs of this world, Renaissance culture reflected the urban bustle and commercial preoccupations of Italian cities. Its secular elements challenged the otherworldliness of Christian culture, and its individualism signaled the dawning of a more capitalist economy of private entrepreneurs. A new Europe was in the making, one more different from its own recent past than Ming dynasty China was from its pre-Mongol glory.

European Comparisons: Maritime Voyaging

A global traveler during the fifteenth century might be surprised to find that Europeans, like the Chinese, were also launching outward-bound maritime expeditions. Initiated in 1415 by the small country of Portugal, those voyages sailed ever farther down the west coast of Africa, supported by the state and blessed by the pope (see Map 12.3). As the century ended, two expeditions marked major breakthroughs, although few suspected it at the time. In 1492, Christopher Columbus, funded by Spain, Portugal's neighbor and rival, made his way west across the Atlantic hoping to arrive in the East and, in one of history's most consequential mistakes, ran into the Americas. Five years later, in 1497, Vasco da Gama launched a voyage that took him around the tip of South Africa, along the East African coast, and, with the help of a Muslim pilot, across the Indian Ocean to Calicut in southern India.

The differences between the Chinese and European oceangoing ventures were striking, most notably perhaps in terms of size. Columbus captained three ships and a crew of about 90, while da Gama had four ships, manned by perhaps 170 sailors. These were minuscule fleets compared to Zheng He's hundreds of ships and a crew in the many thousands. "All the ships of Columbus and da Gama combined," according to a recent account, "could have been stored on a single deck of a single vessel in the fleet that set sail under Zheng He."[8]

Motivation as well as size differentiated the two ventures. Europeans were seeking the wealth of Africa and Asia—gold, spices, silk, and more. They also were in search of Christian converts and of possible Christian allies with whom to continue their long crusading struggle against threatening Muslim powers. China, by contrast, faced no similar threat in the Indian Ocean basin, needed no military allies, and required little that these regions produced. Nor did China possess an impulse to convert foreigners to its culture or religion, as the Europeans surely did. Furthermore, the confident and overwhelmingly powerful Chinese fleet sought neither conquests

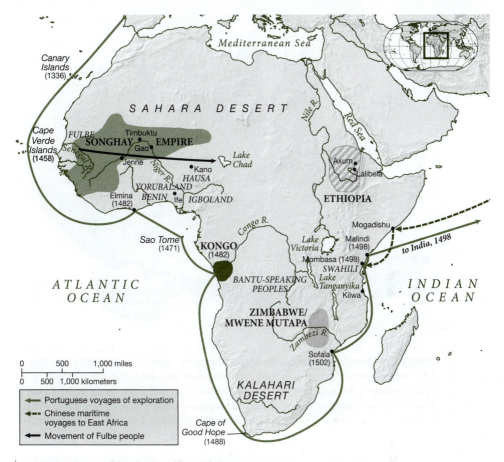

MAP 12.3   Africa in the Fifteenth Century
By the fifteenth century, Africa was a panorama of political and cultural diversity, encompassing large empires, such as Songhay; smaller kingdoms, such as Kongo; city-states among the Yoruba, Hausa, and Swahili peoples; village-based societies without states at all, as among the Igbo; and pastoral peoples, such as the Fulbe. Both European and Chinese maritime expeditions touched on Africa during that century, even as Islam continued to find acceptance in the northern half of the continent.

nor colonies, while the Europeans soon tried to monopolize by force the commerce of the Indian Ocean and violently carved out huge empires in the Americas.

The most striking difference in these two cases lay in the sharp contrast between China's decisive ending of its voyages and the continuing, indeed escalating, European effort, which soon brought the world's oceans and growing numbers of the world's people under its control. This is why Zheng He's voyages were so long neglected in China's historical memory. They led nowhere, whereas the initial European expeditions, so much smaller and less promising, were but the first steps on a journey to world power. But why did the Europeans continue a process that the Chinese had deliberately abandoned?

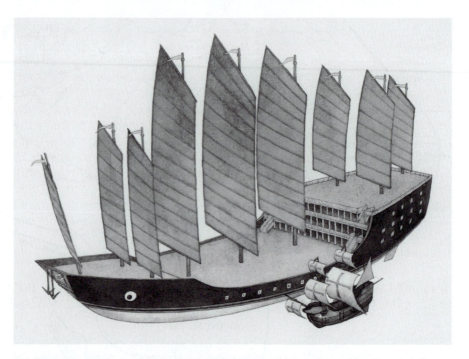

Comparing Chinese and European Ships Among the largest vessels in Zheng He's fleet were "treasure ships" such as this vessel, measuring more than 400 feet long and carrying a crew of perhaps 1,000 men. The much smaller European ship next to it is similar to the *Santa Maria* on which Christopher Columbus made his voyage to the Americas. Chinese treasure ships were the largest vessels of the period, with four decks, nine masts, watertight compartments, and sophisticated rudders. (Gregory A. Harlin/National Geographic Image Collection/Bridgeman Images)

In the first place, Europe had no unified political authority with the power to order an end to its maritime outreach. Its system of competing states, so unlike China's single state, ensured that once begun, rivalry alone would drive the Europeans to the ends of the earth. Beyond this, much of Europe's elite had an interest in overseas expansion. Its budding merchant communities saw opportunity for profit; its competing monarchs eyed the revenue from taxing overseas trade or from seizing overseas resources; the Church foresaw the possibility of widespread conversion; and impoverished nobles might imagine fame and fortune abroad. In China, by contrast, support for Zheng He's voyages was very shallow in official circles, and when the emperor Yongle passed from the scene, those opposed to the voyages prevailed within the politics of the court.

Finally, the Chinese were very much aware of their own antiquity, believed strongly in the absolute superiority of their culture, and felt with good reason that, should they desire something from abroad, others would bring it to them. Europeans too believed themselves unique, particularly in religious terms as the possessors of Christianity, the "one true religion." In material terms, though, they were seeking out the greater riches of the East, and they were highly conscious that Muslim power blocked easy access to these treasures and posed a military and religious threat to

Europe itself. All of this propelled continuing European expansion in the centuries that followed.

The Chinese withdrawal from the Indian Ocean facilitated the European entry. It cleared the way for the Portuguese to penetrate the region, where they faced only the eventual naval power of the Ottomans. Had Vasco da Gama encountered Zheng He's massive fleet as his four small ships sailed into Asian waters in 1498, world history may well have taken quite a different turn. As it was, however, China's abandonment of oceanic voyaging and Europe's embrace of the seas marked different responses to a common problem that both civilizations shared—growing populations and land shortage. In the centuries that followed, China's rice-based agriculture was able to expand production internally by more intensive use of the land, while the country's territorial expansion was inland toward Central Asia. By contrast, Europe's agriculture, based on wheat and livestock, expanded primarily by acquiring new lands in overseas possessions, which were gained as a consequence of a commitment to oceanic expansion.

Civilizations of the Fifteenth Century: The Islamic World

Beyond the domains of Chinese and European civilization, our fifteenth-century global traveler would surely have been impressed with the transformations of the Islamic world. Stretching across much of Afro-Eurasia, the enormous realm of Islam experienced a set of remarkable changes during the fifteenth and early sixteenth centuries, as well as the continuation of earlier patterns. The most notable change lay in the political realm, for an Islamic civilization that had been severely fragmented since at least 900 now crystallized into four major states or empires (see Map 12.4). At the same time, a long-term process of conversion to Islam continued the cultural transformation of Afro-Eurasian societies both within and beyond these new states.

In the Islamic Heartland: The Ottoman and Safavid Empires

The most impressive and enduring of the new Islamic states was the **Ottoman Empire**, which lasted in one form or another from the fourteenth to the early twentieth century. It was the creation of one of the many Turkic warrior groups that had migrated into Anatolia, slowly and sporadically, in the several centuries following 1000 C.E. By the mid-fifteenth century, these Ottoman Turks had already carved out a state that encompassed much of the Anatolian peninsula and had pushed deep into southeastern Europe (the Balkans), acquiring in the process a substantial Christian population. During the sixteenth century, the Ottoman Empire extended its control to much of the Middle East, coastal North Africa, the lands surrounding the Black Sea, and even farther into Eastern Europe.

The Ottoman Empire was a state of enormous significance in the world of the fifteenth century and beyond. In its huge territory, long duration, incorporation of many diverse peoples, and economic and cultural sophistication, it was one of the great empires of world history. In the fifteenth century, only Ming dynasty China and the Incas matched it in terms of wealth, power, and splendor. The empire represented the emergence of the Turks as the dominant people of the Islamic world,

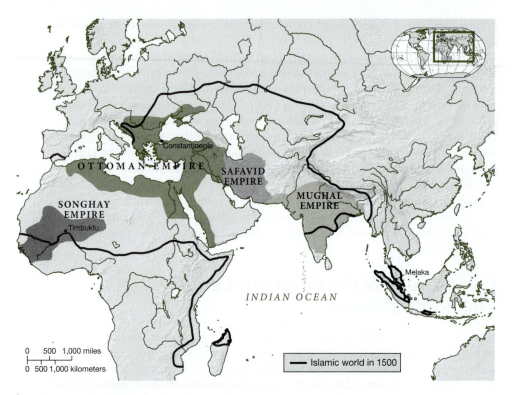

MAP 12.4 Empires of the Islamic World
The most prominent political features of the vast Islamic world in the fifteenth and sixteenth centuries were four large states: the Songhay, Ottoman, Safavid, and Mughal empires.

ruling now over many Arabs, who had initiated this new faith more than 800 years before. In adding "caliph" (successor to the Prophet) to their other titles, Ottoman sultans claimed the legacy of the earlier Abbasid Empire. They sought to bring a renewed unity to the Islamic world, while also serving as protector of the faith, the "strong sword of Islam."

The Ottoman Empire also represented a new phase in the long encounter between Christendom and the world of Islam. In the Crusades, Europeans had taken the aggressive initiative in that encounter, but the rise of the Ottoman Empire reversed their roles. The **Ottoman seizure of Constantinople** in 1453 marked the final demise of Christian Byzantium and allowed Ottoman rulers to see themselves as successors to the Roman Empire. It also opened the way to further expansion, and in 1529 a rapidly expanding Ottoman Empire laid siege to Vienna in the heart of Central Europe. The political and military expansion of Islam, at the expense of Christendom, seemed clearly under way. Many Europeans spoke fearfully of the "terror of the Turk."

In the neighboring Persian lands to the east of the Ottoman Empire, another Islamic state was also taking shape in the late fifteenth and early sixteenth centuries—the Safavid (SAH-fah-vihd) Empire. Its leadership was also Turkic, but in this case it had emerged from a Sufi religious order founded several centuries earlier by Safi al-Din (1252–1334). The long-term significance of the **Safavid Empire**, which was established in the decade following 1500, was its decision to forcibly impose a Shia version of Islam as the official religion of the state. Over time, this form of Islam gained popular support and came to define the unique identity of Persian (Iranian) culture.

This Shia empire also introduced a sharp divide into the political and religious life of heartland Islam, for almost all of Persia's neighbors practiced a Sunni form of the faith. For a century (1534–1639), periodic military conflict erupted between the Ottoman and Safavid empires, reflecting both territorial rivalry and sharp religious differences. In 1514, the Ottoman sultan wrote to the Safavid ruler in the most bitter of terms:

> You have denied the sanctity of divine law . . . you have deserted the path of salvation and the sacred commandments . . . you have opened to Muslims the gates of tyranny and oppression . . . you have raised the standard of irreligion and heresy. . . . [Therefore] the *ulama* and our doctors have pronounced a sentence of death against you, perjurer and blasphemer.[9]

This Sunni/Shia hostility has continued to divide the Islamic world into the twenty-first century.

On the Frontiers of Islam: The Songhay and Mughal Empires

While the Ottoman and Safavid empires brought both a new political unity and a sharp division to the heartland of Islam, two other states performed a similar role on the expanding African and Asian frontiers of the faith. In the West African savannas, the **Songhay Empire** rose in the second half of the fifteenth century. It was the most recent and the largest in a series of impressive states that operated at a crucial intersection of the trans-Saharan trade routes and that derived much of their revenue from taxing that commerce. Islam was a growing faith in Songhay but was limited largely to urban elites. This cultural divide within Songhay largely accounts for the religious behavior of its fifteenth-century monarch Sonni Ali (r. 1464?–1492), who gave alms and fasted during Ramadan in proper Islamic style but also enjoyed a reputation as a magician and possessed a charm thought to render his soldiers invisible to their enemies. Nonetheless, Songhay had become a major center of Islamic learning and commerce by the early sixteenth century. A North African traveler known as Leo Africanus remarked on the city of **Timbuktu**:

> Here are great numbers of [Muslim] religious teachers, judges, scholars, and other learned persons who are bountifully maintained at the king's expense. Here too are brought various manuscripts or written books from Barbary [North Africa] which are sold for more money than any other merchandise. . . . It is a wonder to see the quality of merchandise that is daily brought here and how costly and sumptuous everything is.[10]

The Mughal (MOO-guhl) Empire in India bore similarities to Songhay, for both governed largely non-Muslim populations. Much as the Ottoman Empire initiated a new phase in the interaction of Islam and Christendom, so too did the **Mughal Empire** continue an ongoing encounter between Islamic and Hindu civilizations.

Established in the early sixteenth century, the Mughal Empire was the creation of yet another Islamized Turkic group that invaded India in 1526. Over the next century, the Mughals (a Persian term for Mongols) established unified control over most of the Indian peninsula, giving it a rare period of political unity. During its first 150 years, the Mughal Empire, a land of great wealth and imperial splendor, undertook a remarkable effort to blend many Hindu groups and a variety of Muslims into an effective partnership. The inclusive policies of the early Mughal emperors showed that Muslim rulers could accommodate their overwhelmingly Hindu subjects.

Together these four Muslim empires — Ottoman, Safavid, Songhay, and Mughal — brought to the Islamic world a greater measure of political coherence, military power, economic prosperity, and cultural brilliance than it had known since the early centuries of Islam. This new energy, sometimes called a "second flowering of Islam," impelled the continuing spread of the faith to yet new regions.

The most prominent of these was oceanic Southeast Asia, which for centuries had been intimately bound up in the world of Indian Ocean commerce, while borrowing elements of both Hindu and Buddhist traditions. By the fifteenth century, that trading network was largely in Muslim hands, and the demand for Southeast Asian spices was mounting as the Eurasian world recovered from the devastation of Mongol conquest and the plague. Growing numbers of Muslim traders settled along

Ottoman Janissaries Originating in the fourteenth century, the Janissaries became the elite infantry force of the Ottoman Empire. Complete with uniforms, cash salaries, and marching music, they were the first standing army in the region since the days of the Roman Empire. When gunpowder technology became available, Janissary forces soon were armed with muskets, grenades, and handheld cannons. This Turkish miniature painting dates from the sixteenth century. (Topkapi Palace Museum, Istanbul, Turkey/Album/Art Resource, NY)

the Malay Peninsula and in Java and Sumatra, bringing their faith with them. Eager to attract those traders to their port cities, some rulers in the region converted to Islam, transforming themselves into Muslim sultans and imposing Islamic law. Thus, unlike in the Middle East and India, where Islam was established in the wake of Arab or Turkic conquest, in Southeast Asia, as in West Africa, it was introduced by traveling merchants and solidified through the activities of Sufi holy men.

The rise of **Melaka**, strategically located on the waterway between Sumatra and Malaya, was a sign of the times (see Map 12.1). During the fifteenth century, it was transformed from a small fishing village to a major Muslim port city (see "Sea Roads as a Catalyst for Change: Southeast Asia" in Chapter 7). A Portuguese visitor in 1512 observed that Melaka had "no equal in the world. . . . Commerce between different nations for a thousand leagues on every hand must come to Malacca."[11] The city also became a springboard for the spread of Islam throughout the region. In the eclectic style of Southeast Asian religious history, the Islam of Melaka demonstrated much blending with local and Hindu/Buddhist traditions, while the city itself, like many port towns, had a reputation for "rough behavior." An Arab Muslim pilot in the 1480s commented critically: "They have no culture at all. . . . You do not know whether they are Muslim or not."[12] Nonetheless, Melaka, like Timbuktu on the West African frontier of an expanding Islamic world, became a center for Islamic learning, attracting students from elsewhere in Southeast Asia in the fifteenth century. As the core regions of Islam were consolidating politically, the frontier of the faith continued to move steadily outward.

Civilizations of the Fifteenth Century: The Americas

Across the Atlantic, centers of civilization had long flourished in Mesoamerica and in the Andes. The fifteenth century witnessed new, larger, and more politically unified expressions of those civilizations, embodied in the Aztec and Inca empires. Both were the work of previously marginal peoples who had forcibly taken over and absorbed older cultures, giving them new energy, and both were decimated in the sixteenth century at the hands of Spanish conquistadores and their diseases (see Map 12.5).

The Aztec Empire

The state known to history as the **Aztec Empire** was largely the work of the Mexica (meh-SHEEH-kah) people, a semi-nomadic group from northern Mexico who had migrated southward and by 1325 had established themselves on a small island in Lake Texcoco. Over the next century, the Mexica developed their military capacity, served as mercenaries for more powerful people, negotiated elite marriage alliances with those people, and built up their own capital city of Tenochtitlán (te-nawch-tee-tlahn). In 1428, a Triple Alliance between the Mexica and two nearby city-states launched a highly aggressive program of military conquest that in less than 100 years brought more of Mesoamerica within a single political framework than ever before. Aztec authorities, eager to shed their rather undistinguished past, now claimed descent from earlier Mesoamerican peoples such as the Toltecs and Teotihuacán.

MAP 12.5   The Americas in the Fifteenth Century
The Americas before Columbus represented a world almost completely separate from Afro-Eurasia. The Americas featured societies similar to those found in the Eastern Hemisphere, though with a different balance among them and with pastoral peoples nearly absent.

With a core population recently estimated at 5 to 6 million people, the Aztec Empire was a loosely structured and unstable conquest state that witnessed frequent rebellions by its subject peoples. Conquered peoples and cities were required to provide labor for Aztec projects and to regularly deliver to their Aztec rulers impressive quantities of textiles and clothing, military supplies, jewelry and other luxuries, various foodstuffs, animal products, building materials, rubber balls, paper, and more. The process was overseen by local imperial tribute collectors, who sent the required goods on to Tenochtitlán, a metropolis of 150,000 to 200,000 people, where they were meticulously recorded.

That city featured numerous canals, dikes, causeways, and bridges. A central walled area of palaces and temples included a pyramid almost 200 feet high. Surrounding the city were "floating gardens," artificial islands created from swamplands that supported a highly productive agriculture. Vast marketplaces reflected the commercialization of the economy. A young Spanish soldier who beheld the city in 1519 declared, "Gazing on such wonderful sights, we did not know what to say, or whether what appeared before us was real."[13]

Beyond tribute from conquered peoples, ordinary trade, both local and long-distance, permeated Aztec domains. The extent of empire and rapid population growth stimulated the development of markets and the production of craft goods, particularly in the fifteenth century. Virtually every settlement, from the capital city to the smallest village, had a marketplace that hummed with activity during weekly market days. The largest was that of Tlatelolco, near the capital city, which stunned the Spanish with its huge size, its good order, and the immense range of goods available. Hernán Cortés, the Spanish conquistador who defeated the Aztecs, wrote that "every kind of merchandise such as can be met with in every land is for sale there, whether of food and victuals, or ornaments of gold and silver, or lead, brass, copper, tin, precious stones, bones, shells, snails and feathers."[14] Professional merchants, known as *pochteca*, were legally commoners, but their wealth, often exceeding that of the nobility, allowed them to rise in society and become "magnates of the land."

Among the "goods" that the pochteca obtained were enslaved people, many of whom were destined for sacrifice in the bloody rituals so central to Aztec religious life. Long a part of Mesoamerican and many other world cultures, human sacrifice assumed an unusually prominent role in Aztec public life and thought during the fifteenth century. Tlacaelel (1398–1480), who was for more than half a century a prominent official of the Aztec Empire, is often credited with crystallizing the ideology of state that gave human sacrifice such great importance.

In this cyclical understanding of the world, the sun, central to all life and identified with the Aztec patron deity Huitzilopochtli (wee-tsee-loh-pockt-lee), tended to lose its energy in a constant battle against encroaching darkness. Thus the Aztec world hovered always on the edge of catastrophe. To replenish its energy and thus postpone the descent into endless darkness, the sun required the life-giving force found in human blood. Because the gods had shed their blood ages ago in creating humankind, it was wholly proper for people to offer their own blood to nourish the gods in the present. The high calling of the Aztec state was to supply this blood, largely through its wars of expansion and from prisoners of war, who were destined for sacrifice. The victims were "those who have died for the god." The growth of the Aztec Empire therefore became the means for maintaining cosmic order and avoiding utter catastrophe. This ideology also shaped the techniques of Aztec warfare, which put a premium on capturing prisoners rather than on killing the enemy. As the empire grew, priests and rulers became mutually dependent, and "human sacrifices were carried out in the service of politics."[15] Massive sacrificial rituals, together with a display of great wealth, served to impress enemies, allies, and subjects alike with the immense power of the Aztecs and their gods.

Alongside these sacrificial rituals was a philosophical and poetic tradition of great beauty, much of which mused on the fragility and brevity of human life. Such an outlook characterized the work of Nezahualcoyotl (1402–1472), a poet and king of the city-state of Texcoco, which was part of the Aztec Empire:

> Truly do we live on Earth?
> Not forever on earth; only a little while here.
> Although it be jade, it will be broken.
> Although it be gold, it is crushed.
> Although it be a quetzal feather, it is torn asunder.
> Not forever on earth; only a little while here.[16]

The Inca Empire

While the Mexica were constructing an empire in Mesoamerica, a relatively small community of Quechua-speaking people, known to us as the Incas, was building the Western Hemisphere's largest imperial state along the entire spine of the Andes Mountains. Much as the Aztecs drew on the traditions of the Toltecs and Teotihuacán, the Incas incorporated the lands and cultures of earlier Andean civilizations: Chavín, Moche, Wari, and Tiwanaku. The **Inca Empire**, however, was

Machu Picchu   Machu Picchu, high in the Andes Mountains, was constructed by the Incas in the fifteenth century on a spot long held sacred by local people. Its 200 buildings stand at some 8,000 feet above sea level, making it a "city in the sky." It was probably a royal retreat or religious center, rather than a location serving administrative, commercial, or military purposes. The outside world became aware of Machu Picchu only in 1911, when it was popularized by a Yale University archeologist. (fStop/Superstock)

much larger than the Aztec state; it stretched some 2,500 miles along the Andes and contained perhaps 10 million subjects. Whereas the Aztec Empire controlled only part of the Mesoamerican cultural region, the Inca state encompassed practically the whole of Andean civilization during its short life in the fifteenth and early sixteenth centuries. In the speed of its creation and the extent of its territory, the Inca Empire bears some similarity to that of the Mongols.

Both the Aztec and Inca empires represent rags-to-riches stories in which quite modest and remotely located people very quickly created by military conquest the largest states ever witnessed in their respective regions, but the empires themselves were quite different. In the Aztec realm, the Mexica rulers largely left their conquered people alone, if the required tribute was forthcoming. No elaborate administrative system arose to integrate the conquered territories or to assimilate their people to Aztec culture.

The Incas, on the other hand, erected a rather more bureaucratic empire. At the top reigned the emperor, an absolute ruler regarded as divine, a descendant of the creator god Viracocha and the son of the sun god Inti. Each of the some eighty provinces in the empire had an Inca governor. In theory, the state owned all land and resources, though in practice state lands, known as "lands of the sun," existed along-side properties owned by temples, elites, and traditional communities. At least in the central regions of the empire, subjects were grouped into hierarchical units of 10, 50, 100, 500, 1,000, 5,000, and 10,000 people, each headed by local officials, who were appointed and supervised by an Inca governor or the emperor. A separate set of "inspectors" provided the imperial center with an independent check on provincial officials.

Births, deaths, marriages, and other population data were carefully recorded on *quipus*, the knotted cords that served as an accounting device. A resettlement program moved one-quarter or more of the population to new locations, in part to disperse conquered and no doubt resentful people and sometimes to reward loyal followers with promising opportunities. Efforts at cultural integration required the leaders of conquered peoples to learn Quechua (keh-choo-wah). Their sons were removed to the capital of Cuzco for instruction in Inca culture and language. Even now, millions of people from Ecuador to Chile still speak Quechua, and it is the official second language of Peru after Spanish.

But the sheer human variety of the Incas' enormous empire required great flexibility. In some places Inca rulers encountered bitter resistance; in others local elites were willing to accommodate Incas and thus benefit from their inclusion in the empire. Where centralized political systems already existed, Inca overlords could delegate control to native authorities. Elsewhere they had to construct an administrative system from scratch. Everywhere they sought to incorporate local people into the lower levels of the administrative hierarchy. While the Incas required their subject peoples to acknowledge major Inca deities, these peoples were then largely free to carry on their own religious traditions. The Inca Empire was a fluid system that varied greatly from place to place and over time. It depended as much on the posture of conquered peoples as on the demands and desires of Inca authorities.

Like the Aztec Empire, the Inca state represented an especially dense and extended network of economic relationships within the "American web," but these relationships took shape in quite a different fashion. Inca demands on their conquered people were expressed, not so much in terms of tribute, but as labor service, known as *mita*, which was required periodically of every household. What people produced at home usually stayed at home, but almost everyone also had to work for the state. Some labored on large state farms or on "sun farms," which supported temples and religious institutions; others herded, mined, served in the military, or toiled on state-directed construction projects.

Those with particular skills were put to work manufacturing textiles, metal goods, ceramics, and stonework. The most well known of these specialists were the "chosen women," who were removed from their homes as young girls, trained in Inca ideology, and set to producing corn beer and cloth at state centers. Later they were given as wives to men of distinction or sent to serve as priestesses in various temples, where they were known as "wives of the Sun." In return for such labor services, Inca ideology, expressed in terms of family relationships, required the state to arrange elaborate feasts at which large quantities of food and drink were consumed and to provide food and other necessities when disaster struck. Thus the authority of the state penetrated and directed Inca society and economy far more than did that of the Aztecs.

If the Inca and Aztec civilizations differed sharply in their political and economic arrangements, they resembled each other more closely in their gender systems. Both societies practiced what scholars call "gender parallelism," in which "women and men operate in two separate but equivalent spheres, each gender enjoying autonomy in its own sphere."[17] In both Mesoamerican and Andean societies, such systems had emerged long before their incorporation into the Aztec and Inca empires. In the Andes, men reckoned their descent from their fathers and women from their mothers, while Mesoamericans had long viewed children as belonging equally to their mothers and fathers. Parallel religious cults for women and men likewise flourished in both societies. Inca men venerated the sun, while women worshipped the moon, with matching religious officials. In Aztec temples, both male and female priests presided over rituals dedicated to deities of both sexes. Particularly among the Incas, parallel hierarchies of male and female political officials governed the empire, while in Aztec society, women officials exercised local authority under a title that meant "female person in charge of people." Social roles were clearly defined and different for men and women, but the domestic concerns of women—childbirth, cooking, weaving, cleaning—were not regarded as inferior to the activities of men. Among the Aztecs, for example, sweeping was a powerful and sacred act with symbolic significance as "an act of purification and a preventative against evil elements penetrating the center of the Aztec universe, the home."[18] In the Andes, men broke the ground, women sowed, and both took part in the harvest.

This was gender complementarity, not gender equality. Men occupied the top positions in both political and religious life, and male infidelity was treated more lightly than women's unfaithfulness. As the Inca and Aztec empires expanded, military life, limited to men, grew in prestige, perhaps skewing an earlier gender parallelism. The Incas in particular imposed a more rigidly patriarchal order on their subject peoples. In other ways, the new Aztec and Inca rulers adapted to the gender systems of the people they had conquered. Among the Aztecs, the tools of women's work, the broom and the weaving spindle, were ritualized as weapons; sweeping the home was believed to assist men at war; and childbirth was regarded by women as "our kind of war."[19] Inca rulers replicated the gender parallelism of their subjects at a higher level, as the *sapay Inca* (the Inca ruler) and the *coya* (his female consort) governed jointly, claiming descent respectively from the sun and the moon.

Webs of Connection

Few people in the fifteenth century lived in entirely separate and self-contained communities. Almost all were caught up, to one degree or another, in various and overlapping webs of influence, communication, and exchange.[20] Perhaps most obvious were the webs of empire, large-scale political systems that brought together a variety of culturally different people. Christians and Muslims encountered each other directly in the Ottoman Empire, as did Hindus and Muslims in the Mughal Empire. And no empire tried more diligently to integrate its diverse peoples than the fifteenth-century Incas.

Religion too linked far-flung peoples, and divided them as well. Christianity provided a common religious culture for peoples from England to Russia, although the great divide between Roman Catholicism and Eastern Orthodoxy endured, and in the sixteenth century the Protestant Reformation would shatter permanently the Christian unity of the Latin West. Although Buddhism had largely vanished from its South Asian homeland, it remained a link among China, Korea, Tibet, Japan, and parts of Southeast Asia, even as it splintered into a variety of sects and practices. More than either of these, Islam actively brought together its many peoples. In the hajj, the pilgrimage to Mecca, Africans, Arabs, Persians, Turks, Indians, and many others joined as one people as they rehearsed together the events that gave birth to their common faith. And yet divisions and conflicts persisted within the vast realm of Islam, as the violent hostility between the Sunni Ottoman Empire and the Shia Safavid Empire so vividly illustrates.

Long-established patterns of trade among peoples occupying different environments and producing different goods were certainly much in evidence during the fifteenth century, as they had been for millennia. Hunting societies of Siberia funneled furs and other products of the forest into the Silk Road trading network traversing the civilizations of Eurasia. In the fifteenth century, some of the agricultural peoples in southern Nigeria were receiving horses brought overland from the drier regions of Africa to the north, where those animals flourished better. The Mississippi River in North America and the Orinoco and Amazon rivers in South America facilitated a canoe-borne commerce along those waterways. Coastal shipping in large seagoing canoes operated in the Caribbean and along the Pacific coast between Mexico and Peru. In Pacific Polynesia, the great voyaging networks across vast oceanic distances that had flourished especially since 1000 were in decline by 1500 or earlier, leading to the abandonment of a number of islands.

The great long-distance trading patterns of the Afro-Eurasian world, in operation for a thousand years or more, continued in the fifteenth century, although the balance among them was changing (see Map 12.6). The Silk Road overland network, which had flourished under Mongol control in the thirteenth and fourteenth centuries, contracted in the fifteenth century as the Mongol Empire broke up and the devastation of the plague reduced demand for its products. The rise of the Ottoman Empire also blocked direct commercial contact between Europe and China, but oceanic trade from Japan, Korea, and China through the islands of Southeast Asia and

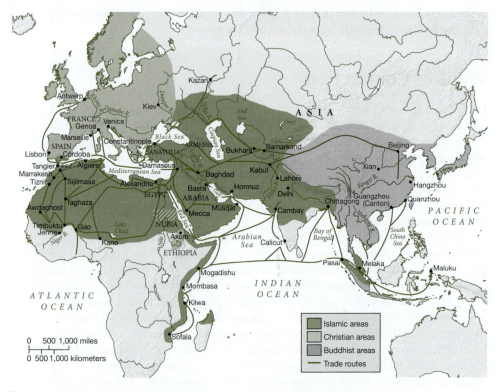

MAP 12.6 Religion and Commerce in the Afro-Eurasian World
By the fifteenth century, the many distinct peoples and societies of the Eastern Hemisphere were linked
to one another by ties of religion and commerce. Of course, most people were not directly involved in
long-distance trade, and many people in areas shown as Buddhist or Islamic on the map practiced other
religions. While much of India, for example, was ruled by Muslims, the majority of its people followed
some form of Hinduism. And although Islam had spread to West Africa, that religion had not penetrated
much beyond the urban centers of the region.

across the Indian Ocean picked up considerably. Larger ships made it possible to
trade in bulk goods such as grain as well as luxury products, while more sophisticated
partnerships and credit mechanisms greased the wheels of commerce. A common
Islamic culture over much of this vast region likewise smoothed the passage of goods
among very different peoples, as it also did for the trans-Saharan trade.

After 1500: Looking Ahead to the Modern Era

While ties of empire, culture, commerce, and disease surely linked many of the peoples in the world of the fifteenth century, none of those connections operated on a
genuinely global scale. Although the densest webs of connection had been woven
within the Afro-Eurasian zone of interaction, this huge region had no enduring ties
with the Americas, and neither of them had sustained contact with the peoples of
Pacific Oceania. That situation was about to change as Europeans in the sixteenth

century and beyond forged a set of genuinely global relationships that generated sustained interaction among all of these regions. That huge process and the many outcomes that flowed from it marked the beginning of what world historians commonly call the modern age—the more than five centuries that followed the voyages of Columbus starting in 1492.

Over those five centuries, the previously separate worlds of Afro-Eurasia, the Americas, and Pacific Oceania became inextricably linked, with enormous consequences for everyone involved. Global empires, a global economy, global cultural exchanges, global migrations, global disease, global wars, and global environmental changes have made the past 500 years a unique phase in the human journey. Those webs of communication and exchange—the first defining feature of the modern era—have progressively deepened, so much so that by the end of the twentieth century few if any people lived beyond the cultural influences, economic ties, or political relationships of a globalized world.

Several centuries after the Columbian voyages, and clearly connected to them, a second distinctive feature of the modern era took shape: the emergence of a radically new kind of human society, first in Europe during the nineteenth century and then in various forms elsewhere in the world. The core feature of such societies was industrialization. That revolutionary economic process was accompanied by a host of other transformations: accelerating technological innovation; the massive consumption of energy and raw materials; a scientific outlook on the world; an unprecedented increase in human population (see the Snapshot); rapid urbanization; widespread commercialization; more powerful and intrusive states; the growing prominence and dominance of Europeans on the world stage; and a very different balance of global power.

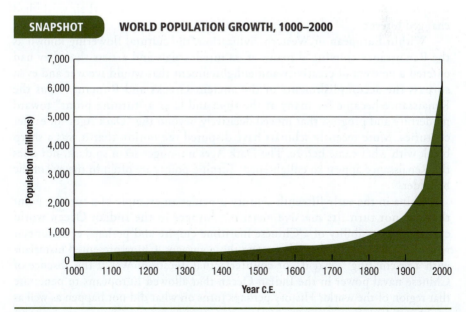

SNAPSHOT   **WORLD POPULATION GROWTH, 1000–2000**

Source: Data from David Christian, *Map of Time* (Berkeley: University of California Press, 2004), 343; https://www.worldometers.info/world-population/world-population-by-year/.

This was the revolution of modernity, comparable in its pervasive consequences only to the Agricultural Revolution of some 10,000 years ago. It usually meant a self-conscious and often uneasy awareness of living and thinking in new ways that deliberately departed from tradition. Sorting out what was gained and what was lost during the modern transformation has been a persistent and highly controversial thread of human thought over the past several centuries. And it is a central concern of historians who trace the contours of the human journey in the centuries after 1500.

Conclusions and Reflections: Perspectives on Turning Points

In our endless efforts to discover meaning in our lives, we are inclined to find "turning points," times when something seems to shift, when new directions or possibilities arise. In personal life, birthdays, graduations, marriages, divorces, and losing or gaining a job are among the events that mark turning points for individuals. Historians too seek to identify turning points, both globally and for particular civilizations, cultures, and peoples. In this chapter, such turning points abound.

For many historians, the fifteenth century in general marks the beginning of a modern era of global entanglement, symbolized by "1492" and the voyages of Columbus and to a lesser extent by "1498," when the Portuguese explorer Vasco da Gama arrived in India. At the time, of course, few people understood that they had experienced a major turning point and were now living in a new era. In just a few decades, however, Spanish conquest and rampant disease made it crystal clear to the people of the Aztec and Inca empires that their world had changed forever.

Within European or Western civilization, the cultural flowering known as the Renaissance convinced many of its intellectuals and artists that they had entered a new era of creativity and enlightenment that would recover and even surpass the accomplishments of the ancient Greeks and Romans. Thus the Renaissance became for many at the time and later a "turning point" toward modernity and progress that moved decisively beyond the "Dark Ages" of earlier centuries. More recently scholars have disputed the notion that it was a sharp break with what came before. The Dark Ages no longer seem so dark, nor does the Renaissance appear so enlightened. Turning points are often in the eye of the beholder.

China in the early fifteenth century provides an example of a turning point that did not turn. Its massive maritime voyages in the Indian Ocean world created the possibility of a Chinese maritime empire and perhaps even contact with the Americas. In abruptly ending those voyages, China presented historians with a fascinating "what if" or counterfactual question. Was it the absence of Chinese naval power in the Indian Ocean that allowed Europeans to penetrate that region of the world? History perhaps turns on what did not happen as well as on what did.

The fifteenth century also represented a turning point in the Islamic world as four major Muslim empires took shape, thus ending, or at least diminishing, a long period of intense political fragmentation. The most important of those new states was the Ottoman Empire. Its conquest of Constantinople in 1453 marked a decisive turning point that was instantly recognizable to all. The Christian Byzantine Empire was dead; the world of European Christendom faced a formidable threat both militarily and religiously; and the Ottoman Empire was one of the great powers of the Mediterranean world. In the long relationship between the Christian and Islamic worlds, things had changed.

In the Americas as well the emergence of new empires represented a turning point in the history of the region, for the Aztec and Inca empires were the largest and most powerful states ever to take shape in the Western Hemisphere. And yet they also represented a continuation of earlier traditions of civilization in both Mesoamerica and the Andes. So while turning points imply a break with the past, they can also call attention to striking continuities with it.

Globally too, "turning points" and continuities intersect. The world of the fifteenth century was increasingly dominated by civilizations and empires, but other kinds of human societies persisted from the more distant past. All of Australia and parts of North America continued to support Paleolithic peoples practicing a gathering and hunting way of life. And the Igbo of West Africa and the Iroquois of North America represent the persistence of agricultural village societies operating without the cities, states, and empires characteristic of civilizations.

The notion of "turning points" can be useful for highlighting important changes in the lives of individuals and in human history. But the complexity or messiness of personal life and of the historical process, as well as the constant interplay of persistence and change, suggest that we treat this notion with caution. Neither individual lives nor historical processes can be adequately captured by any list of "turning points."

Revisiting Chapter 12

REVISITING SPECIFICS

REVISITING CORE IDEAS

1. **Identifying Alternatives to Civilizations** What alternatives to the cities, states, and empires of established civilizations persisted in the world of the fifteenth century?

2. **Comparing China and Europe** What major differences stand out in the histories of fifteenth-century China and Western Europe? What similarities are apparent?

3. **Noticing Change** What new departures can you identify in the Islamic world of the fifteenth and sixteenth centuries?

4. **Comparing Civilizations** In what ways did the civilizations of China, Europe, and the Islamic world seem to be moving in the same direction, and in what respects were they diverging from one another?

5. **Comparing Empires** What distinguished the Aztec and Inca empires from each other?

6. **Describing Connections** In what different ways did the peoples of the fifteenth century interact with one another?

A WIDER VIEW

1. Assume for the moment that the Chinese had not ended their maritime voyages in 1433. How might the subsequent development of world history have been different? What value is there in asking this kind of "what if" or counterfactual question?

2. How does this chapter distinguish among the various kinds of societies contained in the world of the fifteenth century? What other ways of categorizing the world's peoples might work as well or better?

3. What common patterns might you notice across the world of the fifteenth century? And what variations in the historical trajectories of various regions can you identify?

4. **Looking Back** What would surprise a knowledgeable observer from 500 or 1000 C.E., were he or she to make a global tour in the fifteenth century? What features of that earlier world might still be recognizable?

CHRONOLOGY

1337–1453	• Hundred Years' War
ca. 1350–1500	• European Renaissance
1368–1644	• Ming dynasty
ca. 1400–1450	• Iroquois League established

1402–1424	• Emperor Yongle relocates capital to Beijing; Forbidden City constructed
1405–1433	• Chinese maritime voyages
1415–1497	• Portuguese exploration of West African coast
1428–1528	• Aztec Empire
1438–1533	• Inca Empire
1453	• Ottoman seizure of Constantinople
ca. 1464	• Founding of Songhay Empire in West Africa
1492–1498	• Columbus's voyage to the Americas; da Gama's voyage to India
1492	• Christian reconquest of Muslim Spain completed
1501	• Founding of Safavid Empire in Persia
1526	• Founding of Mughal Empire in India

Notes

Prologue

1. See David Christian, *Maps of Time: An Introduction to Big History* (Berkeley: University of California Press, 2004).

2. Voltaire, *Treatise on Toleration*, chap. 22.

3. See David Christian, "World History in Context," *Journal of World History* 14, no. 4 (December 2003): 437–58.

Chapter 1

1. Richard Rainsford, "What Chance, the Survival Prospects of East Africa's Last Hunting and Gathering Tribe the Hadzabe, in a Gameless Environment?" March 1997, http://www.ntz.info/gen/b00473.html.

2. What follows comes from Sally McBrearty and Alison S. Brooks, "The Revolution That Wasn't: A New Interpretation of the Origin of Modern Human Behavior," *Journal of Human Evolution* 39 (2000): 453–563.

3. Fred Spier, *Big History and the Future of Humanity* (West Sussex: Wiley-Blackwell, 2011), 132; Christian, *Maps of Time*, 143.

4. Richard B. Lee, *The Dobe Ju/'hoansi*, 4th ed. (Belmont, CA: Wadsworth, 2013), 99.

5. J. C. Beaglehole, *The Journals of Captain James Cook* (Cambridge: Hakluyt Society, 1968), 1:399.

6. Inga Clendinnen, *Dancing with Strangers* (Cambridge: Cambridge University Press, 2005), 159–67.

7. Steven Pinker, *The Better Angels of Our Nature* (New York: Viking, 2011), 47–52.

8. Marshall Sahlins, *Stone Age Economics* (London: Tavistock, 1972), 1–39.

9. Christopher Ehret, *The Civilizations of Africa* (Charlottesville: University of Virginia Press, 2002), chap. 2.

10. Marija Gimbutas, *The Language of the Goddess* (San Francisco: HarperCollins, 1989), 316–18.

11. Neil Roberts, *The Holocene: An Environmental History* (Oxford: Blackwell, 1998), 116.

12. Nina V. Federoff, "Prehistoric GM Corn," *Science* 302 (November 2003): 1158.

13. Andrew Sherrat, "The Secondary Exploitation of Animals in the Old World," *World Archeology* 15, no. 1 (1983): 90–104.

14. Yuval Noah Harari, *Sapiens: A Brief History of Humankind* (New York: HarperCollins, 2015), chap. 5.

15. Anatoly M. Khazanov, *Nomads and the Outside World* (Madison: University of Wisconsin Press, 1994), 15.

16. Ian Hodder, "Women and Men at Catalhoyuk," *Scientific American* 15, no. 1 (2005): 83.

17. Gimbutas, *Language of the Goddess*, xix.

18. Charles V. Langlois and Charles Seignobos, *Introduction to the Study of History*, translated by G. G. Berry (New York: Holt, 1898), 17.

19. David Christian, Cynthia Stokes Brown, and Craig Benjamin, *Big History: Between Nothing and Everything* (New York: McGraw-Hill, 2014), 2.

20. William H. McNeill, "History and the Scientific Worldview," *History and Theory* 37, no. 1 (1998): 12.

21. Christian et al., *Big History*, 4.

22. David Christian, *Maps of Time: An Introduction to Big History* (Berkeley: University of California Press, 2004), 1–5.

23. Thomas Hobbes, *Leviathan* (Cambridge: Cambridge University Press, 1996), 89.

Chapter 2

1. Bryan Nelson, "Becoming One with Nature," Mother Nature Network, http://www.mnn.com/earth-matters/wilderness-resources/photos/7-people-who-gave-up-on-civilization-to-live-in-the-wild-0.

2. Charles C. Mann, *1491: New Revelations of the Americas before Columbus* (New York: Alfred A. Knopf, 2005), 174–91.

3. Jonathan Mark Kenoyer, *Ancient Cities of the Indus Valley Civilization* (Oxford: Oxford University Press, 1998), 83–84.

4. David Christian, *A History of Russia, Central Asia and Mongolia* (Oxford: Blackwell, 1998), 114.

5. Robert Carneiro, "A Theory of the Origin of the State," *Science* 169 (1970): 733–38.

6. Susan Pollock, *Ancient Mesopotamia* (Cambridge: Cambridge University Press, 1999), 48.

7. *The Epic of Gilgamesh*, translated and edited by Benjamin R. Foster (New York: W. W. Norton, 2001), 10, tablet 1: 232.

8. James Legge, trans., *The Chinese Classics* (London: Henry Frowde, 1893), 4:171–72.

9. Margaret Ehrenberg, *Women in Prehistory* (London: British Museum, 1989), 107.

10. Sherry Ortner, "Is Female to Male as Nature Is to Culture?" in *Women, Culture, and Society*, edited by Michelle Rosaldo and Louise Lamphere (Stanford, CA: Stanford University Press, 1974), 67–88.

11. Gerda Lerner, *The Creation of Patriarchy* (New York: Oxford University Press, 1986), 70.

12. I Samuel 8: 11–17.

13. Steven Pinker, *The Better Angels of Our Nature* (New York: Viking, 2011), chaps. 2, 3.

14. Hammurabi, *The Code of Hammurabi King of Babylon,* edited by Robert Francis Harper (Chicago: University of Chicago Press, 1904), http://oll.libertyfund.org/titles/1276#Harper_0762_26.

15. Adolf Erman, *The Literature of the Ancient Egyptians*, translated by Aylward M. Blackman (London: Methuen, 1927), 137.

16. Henri Frankfort et al., *Before Philosophy: The Intellectual Adventure of Ancient Man* (Baltimore: Penguin Books, 1963), 39, 138.

17. Quoted in Peter Stearns et al., *World Civilizations* (New York: Longman, 1996), 1:30.

18. See Clive Ponting, *A Green History of the World* (New York: St. Martin's Press, 1991), chap. 5.

19. K. J. W. Oosthoek, "The Role of Wood in World History," Environmental History Resources, 1998, http://www.eh-resources.org/wood.html#_ednref1.

20. James B. Pritchard, ed., *Ancient Near Eastern Texts Relating to the Old Testament* (Princeton, NJ: Princeton University Press, 1969), 647–48.

21. Miriam Lichtheim, *Ancient Egyptian Literature* (Berkeley: University of California Press, 1975), 1:25–27.

22. M. J. Rowlands et al., eds., *Center and Periphery in the Ancient World* (Cambridge: Cambridge University Press, 1987), 59.

23. Marvin Harris, ed., *Cannibals and Kings* (New York: Vintage, 1978), 102.

Part 2

1. Martin Jones, "Into a Warming World," in *The Oxford Illustrated History of the World*, edited by Felipe Fernández-Armesto (Oxford: Oxford University Press, 2019), 140.

2. Colin Ronan and Joseph Needham, *The Shorter Science and Civilization in China* (Cambridge: Cambridge University Press, 1978), 58.

Chapter 3

1. Tom Holland, "America Is Not Rome. It Just Thinks It Is," *New York Review of Books*, August 6, 2019.

2. J. M. Cook, *The Persian Empire* (London: J. M. Dent, 1983), 76.

3. George Rawlinson, trans., *The Histories of Herodotus* (London: Dent, 1910), 1:131–40.

4. Erich F. Schmidt, *Persepolis I: Structures, Reliefs, Inscriptions*, Oriental Institute Publications 68 (Chicago: University of Chicago Press, 1953), 63.

5. Quoted in Anthony N. Penna, *The Human Footprint* (Oxford: Wiley-Blackwell, 2010), 151.

6. Quoted in Thomas R. Martin, *Ancient Greece from Prehistoric to Hellenistic Times* (New Haven, CT: Yale University Press, 1996), 86.

7. Christian Meier, *Athens* (New York: Metropolitan Books, 1993), 93.

8. Arrian, *The Campaigns of Alexander*, translated by Aubrey de Selincourt, revised by J. R. Hamilton (London: Penguin, 1971), 395–96.

9. Stanley Burstein, *The Hellenistic Period in World History* (Washington, DC: American Historical Association, 1996), 12.

10. Norman F. Cantor, *Antiquity* (New York: HarperCollins, 2003), 25.

11. Paul Halsall, "Early Western Civilization under the Sign of Gender," in *A Companion to Gender History*, edited by Teresa A. Meade and Merry E. Wiesner-Hanks (London: Blackwell, 2004), 293–94.

12. Roger Boesche, *The First Great Political Realist: Kautilya and His Arthashastra* (Lanham, MD: Lexington Books, 2002), 17.

13. Stanley Wolpert, *A New History of India* (New York: Oxford University Press, 1993), 90.

14. Zhengyuan Fu, *Autocratic Tradition and Chinese Politics* (New York: Cambridge University Press, 1993), 188.

Chapter 4

1. "Birthday of Confucius celebrated with grand ceremony . . . ," Embassy of the People's Republic of China in Australia, September 29, 2009, http://au.china-embassy.org/eng/xw/t608286.htm.

2. Quoted in Arthur Waley, *Three Ways of Thought in Ancient China* (Garden City, NY: Doubleday, 1956), 159–60.

3. Nancy Lee Swann, trans., *Pan Chao: Foremost Woman Scholar of China* (New York: Century, 1932), 111–14.

4. Kam Louie and Morris Low, *Asian Masculinities* (London: Routledge, 2003), 3–6.

5. Quoted in Huston Smith, *The Illustrated World's Religions* (San Francisco: HarperCollins, 1994), 123.

6. Robert Marks, *China: Its Environment and History* (Lanham, MD: Rowman and Littlefield, 2012), 94–95.

7. Lao-tzu, *Tao Te Ching,* translated by James Legge, in *Sacred Books of the East* (Oxford: The Clarendon Press, 1891), 39:122.

8. Catherine Clay et al., *Envisioning Women in World History* (New York: McGraw-Hill, 2009), 1:67–77.

9. Quoted in Karen Andrews, "Women in Theravada Buddhism," Institute of Buddhist Studies, accessed November 21, 2017, http://www.bhikkhuni.net/women-in-theravada-buddhism/.

10. A. L. Basham, *The Wonder That Was India* (London: Sidgwick and Jackson, 1967), 309.

11. Isaiah 1:11–17.

12. Plato, *Apologia*, translated by Benjamin Jowett (1891).

13. Hippocrates, *On the Sacred Disease*, translated by Francis Adams, Internet Classics Archive, accessed February 2, 2012, http://classics.mit.edu/Hippocrates/sacred.html.

14. Galatians 3:28.

15. Ephesians 5:22–23; 1 Corinthians 14:35.

16. Robert Sider, "Early Christians in North Africa," *Coptic Church Review* 19, no. 3 (1998): 2.

17. Quoted in Mary Ann Rossi, "Priesthood, Precedent, and Prejudice: On Recovering the Women Priests of Early Christianity," *Journal of Feminist Studies* 7, no. 1 (1991): 73–94.

18. Chai-Shin Yu, *Early Buddhism and Christianity* (Delhi: Motilal Banarsidass, 1981), 211.

19. Karl Jaspers, *The Origin and Goal of History* (New Haven, CT: Yale University Press, 1953).

20. See, for example, Robert N. Bellah, "What Is Axial about the Axial Age?" *European Journal of Sociology* 46, no. 1 (2005): 69–89.

21. Jaspers, *Origin and Goal of History,* 6.

22. See Iain Provan, *Convenient Myths* (Waco, TX: Baylor University Press, 2013), 2–3, 41.

Chapter 5

1. Quoted in Lydia Polgreen, "Business Class Rises in Ashes of Caste System," *New York Times*, September 10, 2010.

2. Po Chu-I, "After Passing the Examination," in *More Translations from the Chinese*, edited by Arthur Waley (New York: Alfred A. Knopf, 1919), 37.

3. Quoted in Michael Lowe, *Everyday Life in Early Imperial China* (New York: Dorset, 1968), 38.

4. Li Shen, "Old Style," Selected Poems from T'ang Dynasty, accessed May 25, 2017, http://www.shigeku.org/xlib/lingshidao/hanshi/tang1.htm.

5. Confucius, *The Analects of Confucius*, translated by Burton Watson (New York: Columbia University Press, 2007), 4.16.

6. Orlando Patterson, *Slavery and Social Death* (Cambridge, MA: Harvard University Press, 1982).

7. A. L. Basham, *The Wonder That Was India* (London: Sidgwick and Jackson, 1967), 152.

8. Sarah Pomeroy et al., *Ancient Greece* (New York: Oxford University Press, 1999), 63, 239.

9. R. Zelnick-Abramovitz, *Not Wholly Free* (Leiden: Brill, 2005), 337, 343.

10. I Peter 2:18.

11. Milton Meltzer, *Slavery: A World History* (New York: Da Capo Press, 1993), 189.

12. Judith Bennett, *History Matters: Patriarchy and the Challenge of Feminism* (Philadelphia: University of Pennsylvania Press, 2006), chap. 4.

13. Quoted in Bret Hinsch, *Women in Early Imperial China* (Oxford: Rowman and Littlefield, 2002), 155.

14. Nancy Lee Swann, trans., *Pan Chao: Foremost Woman Scholar of China* (New York: Century, 1932), 111–14.

15. Quoted in Valerie Hansen, *The Open Empire* (New York: W. W. Norton, 2000), 183–84; see also Thomas Barfield, *The Perilous Frontier* (Cambridge: Blackwell, 1989), 140.

16. Aristotle, *Politica*, translated by H. Rackham, Loeb Classical Library, no. 264 (Cambridge, MA: Harvard University Press, 1932), 1254b10–14.

17. Sarah B. Pomeroy, *Spartan Women* (Oxford: Oxford University Press, 2002), 63.

18. Anton Powell, "Dining Groups, Marriage, Homosexuality," in *Sparta*, edited by Michael Whitby (New York: Routledge, 2002), 93.

Chapter 6

1. "Morales Becomes Head of a Pluri-national State Blessed by Aymara Gods," *MercoPress*, January 22, 2010, http://en.mercopress.com/2010/01/22/morales-becomes-head-of-a-pluri-national-state-blessed-by-aymara-gods.

2. Roderick J. McIntosh, *Ancient Middle Niger* (Cambridge: Cambridge University Press, 2005), 10.

3. Roderick J. McIntosh, *The Peoples of the Middle Niger* (Oxford: Blackwell, 1998), 177.

4. Quotation from Richard E. W. Adams, *Ancient Civilizations of the New World* (Boulder, CO: Westview Press, 1997), 56. See also T. Patrick Culbert, "The New Maya," *Archeology* 51, no. 5 (1998): 47–51.

5. George L. Cowgill, "The Central Mexican Highlands . . . ," in *The Cambridge History of the Native Peoples of the Americas*, vol. 2, pt. 1, "Mesoamerica," edited by Richard E. W. Adams and Murdo J. MacLeod (Cambridge: Cambridge University Press, 2000), 289.

6. Gordon F. McEwan, *The Inca: New Perspectives* (New York: W. W. Norton, 2008), 39–41.

7. Christopher Ehret, *The Civilizations of Africa* (Charlottesville: University of Virginia Press, 2002), 175.

8. David Schoenbrun, "Gendered Themes in Early African History," in *A Companion to Gender History*, edited by Teresa Meade and Merry Wiesner-Hanks (Oxford: Blackwell, 2004), 253–56.

9. See Jan Vansina, *Paths in the Rainforest* (Madison: University of Wisconsin Press, 1990), 95–99.

10. David Hurst Thomas, *Exploring Ancient Native America* (New York: Routledge, 1999), 137–42.

11. Brian M. Fagan, *Ancient North America* (London: Thames and Hudson, 2005), 475.

12. Quoted in Lynda Norene Shaffer, *Native Americans before 1492* (Armonk, NY: M. E. Sharpe, 1992), 70.

13. Steven R. Fischer, *A History of the Pacific Islands* (New York: Palgrave Macmillan, 2013), 37. This section draws heavily on Fischer, chaps. 1, 2; Ian Campbell, *Worlds Apart* (Cambridge: Cambridge University Press, 2011), chaps. 1, 2; and Matt K. Matsuda, *Pacific Worlds* (Cambridge: Cambridge University Press, 2012), chaps. 1, 2.

14. Campbell, *Worlds Apart*, 48.

15. Terry L. Hunt, "Rethinking the Fall of Easter Island," *American Scientist* 94, no. 5 (September/October 2006), 412–19.

Chapter 7

1. Nayan Chanda, *Bound Together* (New Haven, CT: Yale University Press, 2007), 35–36.

2. Quoted in Patricia Buckley Ebrey, *The Inner Quarters* (Berkeley: University of California Press, 1993), 150.

3. Seneca the Elder, *Declamations* (Cambridge, MA: Harvard University Press, 1999), 1:374–75.

4. Kenneth McPherson, *The Indian Ocean* (Oxford: Oxford University Press, 1993), 15.

5. Janet L. Abu-Lughod, *Before European Hegemony* (Oxford: Oxford University Press, 1989), 269.

6. McPherson, *Indian Ocean*, 97.

7. This section draws heavily from Craig A. Lockard, *Southeast Asia in World History* (Oxford: Oxford University Press, 2009), chaps. 2, 3. See also Victor Lieberman, *Strange Parallels* (Cambridge: Cambridge University Press, 2009), chaps. 1, 7.

8. Kenneth R. Hall, *Maritime Trade and State Development in Early Southeast Asia* (Honolulu: University of Hawaii Press, 1985), 101.

9. Excerpts from Zhou Daguan's *A Record of Cambodia: The Land and Its People*, https://www.virtualangkor.com/tradediplomacy.

10. M. C. Horton and T. R. Burton, "Indian Metalwork in East Africa: The Bronze Lion Statuette from Shanga," *Antiquities* 62 (1988): 22.

11. Ross Dunn, *The Adventures of Ibn Battuta* (Berkeley: University of California Press, 1986), 124.

12. Christopher Ehret, *The Civilizations of Africa* (Charlottesville: University of Virginia Press, 2002), 255.

13. Nehemia Levtzion and Jay Spaulding, eds., *Medieval West Africa: Views from Arab Scholars and Merchants* (Princeton, NJ: Marcus Wiener, 2003), 5.

14. David Schoenbrun, "Gendered Themes in Early African History," in *A Companion to Gender History*, edited by Teresa Meade and Merry Wiesner-Hanks (Oxford: Blackwell, 2004), 263.

15. Quoted in John Iliffe, *Africans: The History of a Continent* (Cambridge: Cambridge University Press, 1995), 75–76.

16. J. R. McNeill and William McNeill, *The Human Web* (New York: W. W. Norton, 2003), 160.

17. William H. McNeill, "The Changing Shape of World History," *History and Theory* 34, no. 2 (1995): 18.

Chapter 8

1. Tom Phillips, "China's Xi Jinping Says Paris Climate Deal Must Not Be Allowed to Fail," *The Guardian*, January 18, 2017.

2. Quoted in Mark Elvin, *The Retreat of the Elephants* (New Haven, CT: Yale University Press, 2004), 19.

3. Mark Elvin, *The Pattern of the Chinese Past* (London: Eyre Methuen, 1973), 55.

4. Samuel Adshead, *Tang China: The Rise of the East in World History* (New York: Palgrave, 2004), 30.

5. William McNeill, *The Pursuit of Power* (Chicago: University of Chicago Press, 1984), 50.

6. See "The Attractions of the Capital," in *Chinese Civilization: A Sourcebook*, edited by Patricia Buckley Ebrey (New York: Free Press, 1993), 178–85.

7. Marco Polo, *The Travels of Marco Polo*, translated by Henry Yule (Toronto: General, 1993), 2:185.

8. J. R. McNeill and William H. McNeill, *The Human Web* (New York: W. W. Norton, 2003), 123.

9. Quoted in Francesca Bray, *Technology and Gender: Fabrics of Power in Late Imperial China* (Berkeley: University of California Press, 1997), 116.

10. Quoted in Patricia Buckley Ebrey, *The Inner Quarters* (Berkeley: University of California Press, 1993), 207.

11. Ebrey, *Inner Quarters*, 37–43.

12. Ebrey, *Inner Quarters*, 6.

13. Burton Watson, trans., *Records of the Grand Historian of China*, rev. ed. (New York: Columbia University Press, 1993), 2:144–45, as quoted in Thomas J. Barfield, "Steppe Empires, China, and the Silk Route," in *Nomads in the Sedentary World*, edited by Anatoly M. Khazanov and Andre Wink (New York: Routledge, 2001), 237.

14. Susan Mann, "Women in East Asia," in *Women's History in Global Perspective*, edited by Bonnie G. Smith (Urbana: University of Illinois Press, 2005), 2:53–56.

15. Quoted in McNeill, *Pursuit of Power*, 40.

16. John K. Fairbank et al., *East Asia: Tradition and Transformation* (Boston: Houghton Mifflin, 1978), 353.

17. Arnold Pacey, *Technology in World Civilization* (Cambridge, MA: MIT Press, 1991), 50–53.

18. McNeill, *Pursuit of Power*, 24–25.

19. Quoted in Arthur F. Wright, *Studies in Chinese Buddhism* (New Haven, CT: Yale University Press, 1990), 16.

20. Arthur F. Wright, *Buddhism in Chinese History* (Stanford, CA: Stanford University Press, 1959), 36–39.

21. Quoted in Wright, *Buddhism in Chinese History*, 67.

22. Quoted in Eric Zurcher, *The Buddhist Conquest of China* (Leiden: E. J. Brill, 1959), 1:262.

23. Quoted in Robert Marks, *China: Its Environment and History* (Lanham, MD: Rowman and Littlefield, 2012), 139–40.

24. Edwin O. Reischauer, *Ennin's Travels in Tang China* (New York: Ronald Press, 1955), 221–24.

25. Jonathan Chaves, trans., *Heaven My Blanket, Earth My Pillow* (Buffalo, NY: White Pine Press, 2004), 25.

Chapter 9

1. Mohsin Hamid, "Islam Is Not a Monolith," *The Guardian*, May 19, 2013, https://www.theguardian.com/global/2013/may/19/mohsin-hamid-islam-not-monolith.

2. Reza Aslan, *No God but God* (New York: Random House, 2005), 14.

3. Quoted in Karen Armstrong, *A History of God* (New York: Ballantine Books, 1993), 146.

4. Quran 1:5 and 41:53.

5. Quran 9:71.

6. "Prophet Muhammad's Farewell Sermon," IslamiCity, accessed November 28, 2014, http://www.islamicity.com/articles/Articles.asp?ref=ic0107-322.

7. Quoted in Fred M. Donner, *Muhammad and the Believers* (Cambridge, MA: Harvard University Press, 2010), 114. The preceding section draws on chapter 3.

8. Richard Bulliet, *Conversion to Islam in the Medieval Period* (Cambridge, MA: Harvard University Press, 1979), 33.

9. Quoted in Bertold Spuler, *The Muslim World*, vol. 1, *The Age of the Caliph* (Leiden: E. J. Brill, 1960), 29.

10. Bernard Lewis, *Islam and the West* (New York: Oxford University Press, 1993), 157.

11. Quoted in Patricia Crone, "The Rise of Islam in the World," in *Cambridge Illustrated History of the Islamic World*, edited by Francis Robinson (Cambridge: Cambridge University Press, 1996), 14.

12. Quran 4:34.

13. Quoted in Judith Tucker, "Gender and Islamic History," in *Islamic and European Expansion*, edited by Michael Adas (Philadelphia: Temple University Press, 1993), 46.

14. Ria Kloppenborg and Wouter Hanegraaf, eds., *Female Stereotypes in Religious Traditions* (Leiden: E. J. Brill, 1995), 111.

15. Domingos Paes, "Narrative of Domingos Paes of Things Which I Saw and Contrived to Learn Concerning the Kingdom of Narasimga," in *A Forgotten Empire (Vijayangar), a Contribution to the History of India*, edited by Robert Sewell, 2nd Indian ed. (New Delhi: National Book Trust, 1970), 247–48.

16. Quoted in William T. de Bary, ed., *Sources of Indian Tradition* (New York: Columbia University Press, 1958), 2:355–57.

17. Quoted in Nikki R. Keddie, "Women in the Middle East since the Rise of Islam," in *Women's History in Global Perspective*, edited by Bonnie G. Smith (Urbana: University of Illinois Press, 2005), 81.

18. Ross Dunn, *The Adventures of Ibn Battuta* (Berkeley: University of California Press, 1986), 300.

19. Jane I. Smith, "Islam and Christendom," in *The Oxford History of Islam*, edited by John L. Esposito (Oxford: Oxford University Press, 1999), 317–21.

20. Richard Eaton, "Islamic History as Global History," in *Islamic and European Expansion*, edited by Michael Adas (Philadelphia: Temple University Press, 1993), 12.

21. Francis Robinson, "Knowledge, Its Transmission and the Making of Muslim Societies," in *Cambridge Illustrated History of the Islamic World*, edited by Francis Robinson (Cambridge: Cambridge University Press, 1996), 230.

22. Robinson, "Knowledge," 215.

Chapter 10

1. Louisa Lim, "In the Land of Mao, a Rising Tide of Christianity," *All Things Considered*, NPR, July 19, 2010, http://www.npr.org/templates /story/story.php?storyId=128546334.

2. Adam R. Taylor, "Christianity's Future Lies in Africa," *Sojourners*, April 12, 2019, https://sojo .net/articles/christianitys-future-lies-africa.

3. Todd M. Johnson, "The 100 Year Shift of Christianity to the South," Gordon Conwell Theological Seminary, October 9, 2019, https://www.gordonconwell.edu/blog/the -100-year-shift-of-christianity-to-the-south/.

4. This section relies heavily on Diarmaid MacCulloch, *Christianity: The First Three Thousand Years* (New York: Viking, 2010), chap. 8.

5. Quoted in Ray Riegert and Thomas Moore, eds., *The Lost Sutras of Jesus* (Berkeley, CA: Ulysses Press, 2006), 103.

6. Quoted in Deno John Geanakoplos, *Byzantium: Church, Society, and Civilization Seen through Contemporary Eyes* (Chicago: University of Chicago Press, 1984), 143.

7. Quoted in Geanakoplos, *Byzantium*, 369.

8. Quoted in Patrick J. Geary, *Before France and Germany* (New York: Oxford University Press, 1988), 79.

9. Quoted in Stephen Williams, *Diocletian and the Roman Recovery* (London: Routledge, 1996), 218.

10. Peter Brown, *The Rise of Western Christendom* (London: Blackwell, 1996), 305.

11. Quoted in John M. Hobson, *The Eastern Origins of Western Civilization* (New York: Cambridge University Press, 2004), 113.

12. Quoted in Clive Ponting, *A Green History of the World* (New York: St. Martin's, 1991), 121–23.

13. Quoted in Richard C. Hoffman, "Economic Development and Aquatic Ecosystems in Medieval Europe," *American Historical Review* 101, no. 3 (1996): 648.

14. Bonnie Anderson and Judith Zinsser, *A History of Their Own* (Oxford: Oxford University Press, 2000), 1:393–94.

15. Christopher Tyerman, *Fighting for Christendom: Holy Wars and the Crusades* (Oxford: Oxford University Press, 2004), 16.

16. Quoted in Elizabeth Hallam, *Chronicles of the Crusades* (New York: Welcome Rain, 2000), 127.

17. Quoted in Peter Watson, *Ideas* (New York: Harper, 2006), 319.

18. Quoted in Jean Gimple, *The Medieval Machine* (New York: Holt, 1976), 178.

19. Quoted in Stuart B. Schwartz, ed., *Victors and Vanquished* (Boston: Bedford/St. Martin's, 2000), 147.

20. Quoted in Carlo Cipolla, *Before the Industrial Revolution* (New York: Norton, 1976), 207.

21. Quoted in S. Lilley, *Men, Machines, and History* (New York: International, 1965), 62.

22. See Toby Huff, *The Rise of Early Modern Science* (Cambridge: Cambridge University Press, 1993).

23. Quoted in Edward Grant, *Science and Religion from Aristotle to Copernicus* (Westport, CT: Greenwood Press, 2004), 158.

24. Quoted in L. Thorndike, *A History of Magic and Experimental Science* (New York: Columbia University Press, 1923), 2:58.

25. Quoted in Edward Grant, *God and Reason in the Middle Ages* (Cambridge: Cambridge University Press, 2001), 70.

26. Quoted in Grant, *Science and Religion*, 228–29.

27. Marcia L. Colish, *Medieval Foundations of the Western Intellectual Tradition* (New Haven, CT: Yale University Press, 1997), 128.

Chapter 11

1. Jehangir S. Pocha, "Mongolia Sees Genghis Khan's Good Side," *New York Times,* May 10, 2005.

2. Giovanni Carpini, *The Story of the Mongols*, translated by Erik Hildinger (Boston: Braden, 1996), 54.

3. Quoted in Peter B. Golden, "Nomads and Sedentary Societies in Eurasia," in *Agricultural and Pastoral Societies in Ancient and Classical History*, edited by Michael Adas (Philadelphia: Temple University Press, 2001), 73.

4. Anatoly Khazanov, "The Spread of World Religions in Medieval Nomadic Societies of the Eurasian Steppes," in *Nomadic Diplomacy, Destruction and Religion from the Pacific to the Adriatic*, edited by Michael Gervers and Wayne Schlepp (Toronto: Joint Center for Asia Pacific Studies, 1994), 11.

5. Quoted in J. Otto Maenchen-Helfer, *The World of the Huns* (Berkeley: University of California Press, 1973), 14.

6. Quoted in Christopher Kaplonski, *The History of Mongolia* (Leiden: Brill, 2010), vol. 1, 54.

7. Carter Finley, *The Turks in World History* (Oxford: Oxford University Press, 2005), 40.

8. David Christian, *A History of Russia, Central Asia, and Mongolia* (London: Blackwell, 1998), 1:385.

9. Quoted in Christian, *History of Russia*, 389.

10. Jack Weatherford, *Genghis Khan and the Making of the Modern World* (New York: Crown, 2004), 86.

11. Chinggis Khan, "Letter to Changchun," in *Mediaeval Researches from Eastern Asiatic Sources*, edited by E. Bretschneider (London: Kegan, Paul, Trench, Trübner, 1875), 1:37–39.

12. Thomas T. Allsen, *Mongol Imperialism* (Berkeley: University of California Press, 1987), 6.

13. Chinggis Khan, "Letter to Changchun," 38.

14. Quoted in Weatherford, *Genghis Khan*, 111.

15. Thomas J. Barfield, *The Nomadic Alternative* (Englewood Cliffs, NJ: Prentice Hall, 1993), 166.

16. Quoted in Christian, *History of Russia*, 1:425.

17. Quoted in David Morgan, *Medieval Persia* (London: Longman, 1988), 79.

18. Morgan, *Medieval Persia*, 82.

19. Guity Nashat, "Women in the Middle East," in *A Companion to Gender History*, edited by Teresa A. Meade and Merry E. Wiesner-Hanks (London: Blackwell, 2004), 243.

20. Charles J. Halperin, *Russia and the Golden Horde* (Bloomington: Indiana University Press, 1985), 126.

21. Charles H. Halperin, "Russia in the Mongol Empire in Comparative Perspective," *Harvard Journal of Asiatic Studies* 43, no. 1 (1983): 261.

22. Thomas Allsen, *Culture and Conquest in Mongol Eurasia* (Cambridge: Cambridge University Press, 2001), 211.

23. Quoted in Allsen, *Culture and Conquest*, 121.

24. James Belich, "The Black Death and the Spread of Europe," in *The Prospect of Global History*, edited by James Belich, John Darwin, Margret Frenz, and Chris Wickham (Oxford: Oxford University Press, 2016), 93–96.

25. Quoted in John Aberth, *The Black Death: The Great Mortality of 1348–1350* (Boston: Bedford/St. Martin's, 2005), 84–85.

26. Michael Dols, *The Black Death in the Middle East* (Princeton, NJ: Princeton University Press, 1977), 212, 223.

27. Quoted in John Aberth, *A Knight at the Movies: Medieval History on Film* (New York: Routledge, 2003), 225.

28. Quoted in Aberth, *Black Death*, 72.

29. Quoted in Dols, *Black Death in the Middle East*, 67.

30. Andre Gunder Frank, *ReOrient: Global Economy in the Asian Age* (Berkeley: University of California Press, 1998), 256.

31. Arnold Pacey, *Technology in World Civilization* (Cambridge, MA: MIT Press, 1990), 62.

32. George Nathaniel Curzon, *Problems of the Far East* (London: Longmans, Green, 1894), vi.

33. Yuval Noah Harari, *Sapiens: A Brief History of Humankind* (New York: HarperCollins, 2015), 191.

34. William Skidelsky, "Niall Ferguson: 'Westerners Don't Understand How Vulnerable Freedom Is,'" *The Observer*, February 19, 2011, accessed May 22, 2017, https://www.theguardian.com/books/2011/feb/20/niall-ferguson-interview-civilization.

35. Quoted in Gregory Guzman, "Were the Barbarians a Negative or Positive Factor in Ancient and Medieval History?" *Historian* 50 (August 1988): 558–72.

36. Quoted in Barfield, *Nomadic Alternative*, 3.

Chapter 12

1. Columbus to Remove Christopher Columbus Statue at City Hall," *IdeaStream,* June 18, 2020, https://www.ideastream.org/news/columbus -to-remove-christopher-columbus-statue-at -city-hall.

2. Winona LaDuke, "We Are Still Here: The 500 Year Celebration," *Sojourners*, October 1991.

3. "The Truth about Columbus," http://www .truthaboutcolumbus.com/.

4. Brian Fagan, *Ancient North America* (London: Thames and Hudson, 2005), 503.

5. Quoted in Charles C. Mann, *1491: New Revelations of the Americas before Columbus* (New York: Alfred A. Knopf, 2005), 334.

6. Louise Levanthes, *When China Ruled the Seas* (New York: Simon and Schuster, 1994), 175.

7. Christine de Pisan, *The Book of the City of Ladies*, translated by Rosalind Brown-Grant (New York: Penguin Books, 1999), pt. 1, p. 1.

8. Frank Viviano, "China's Great Armada," *National Geographic*, July 2005, 34.

9. Quoted in John J. Saunders, ed., *The Muslim World on the Eve of Europe's Expansion* (Englewood Cliffs, NJ: Prentice Hall, 1966), 41–43.

10. Leo Africanus, *History and Description of Africa* (London: Hakluyt Society, 1896), 824–25.

11. Quoted in Craig A. Lockhard, *Southeast Asia in World History* (Oxford: Oxford University Press, 2009), 67.

12. Quoted in Patricia Risso, *Merchants and Faith* (Boulder, CO: Westview Press, 1995), 49.

13. Quoted in Stuart B. Schwartz, ed., *Victors and Vanquished* (Boston: Bedford/St. Martin's, 2000), 8.

14. Quoted in Michael E. Smith, *The Aztecs* (London: Blackwell, 2003), 108.

15. Smith, *The Aztecs*, 220.

16. Quoted in Miguel Leon-Portilla, *Aztec Thought and Culture*, translated from the Spanish by Jack Emory Davis (Norman: University of Oklahoma Press, 1963), 7.

17. For a summary of this practice among the Aztecs and Incas, see Karen Vieira Powers, *Women in the Crucible of Conquest* (Albuquerque: University of New Mexico Press, 2005), chap. 1.

18. Powers, *Women in the Crucible of Conquest*, 25.

19. Louise Burkhart, "Mexica Women on the Home Front," in *Indian Women of Early Mexico*, edited by Susan Schroeder et al. (Norman: University of Oklahoma Press, 1997), 25–54.

20. The "web" metaphor is derived from J. R. McNeill and William H. McNeill, *The Human Web* (New York: W. W. Norton, 2003).

Acknowledgments

Excerpt beginning "In those Days" from James B. Pritchard, editor, *Ancient Near Eastern Texts Relating to the Old Testament*, by James Bennett Pritchard. Reproduced with permission of Books on Demand in the format Book via Copyright Clearance Center, Inc.

Excerpt beginning "Truly do we live on Earth?" from *Aztec Thought and Culture: A Study of the Ancient Nahuatl Mind*, by Miguel Leon Portilla. © 1963 University of Oklahoma Press. Republished with permission of University of Oklahoma Press. Permission conveyed through Copyright Clearance Center, Inc.

Glossary

Abbasid caliphate An Arab dynasty of caliphs (successors to the Prophet) who governed much of the Islamic world from its capital in Baghdad beginning in 750 C.E. After 900 C.E. that empire increasingly fragmented until its overthrow by the Mongols in 1258. (Ch. 9)

Agricultural/Neolithic Revolution The "new stone age," referring to the introduction of agriculture between roughly 4,000 and 12,000 years ago in societies that had long survived with a gathering and hunting economy. (Ch. 1)

Alexander the Great A ruler of Macedonia who unified the Greek city-states and during a ten-year military expedition (334–323 B.C.E.) conquered Egypt, the Persian Empire, and part of northwest India, creating a vast Greek empire. (Ch. 3)

Alexandria A cosmopolitan Egyptian city established by Hellenistic rulers, with a population of half a million people; a major avenue for the spread of Greek culture and learning. (Ch. 3)

Almoravid Empire Emerging out of an Islamic reform movement among the Sanhaja Berber pastoralists in the eleventh century, the Almoravid Empire incorporated a large part of northwestern Africa and southern Spain. The empire collapsed by the mid-twelfth century. (Ch. 11)

American web A term used to describe the network of trade that linked parts of the pre-Columbian Americas; although less densely woven than the Afro-Eurasian trade networks, this web nonetheless provided a means of exchange for luxury goods and ideas over large areas. (Ch. 7)

al-Andalus Arabic name for Spain, most of which was conquered by Arab and Berber forces between 711 and 718 C.E. Muslim Spain represented a point of encounter between the Islamic world and Christian Europe. (Ch. 9)

Angkor Wat The largest religious structure in the premodern world, this temple was built by the powerful Angkor kingdom (located in modern Cambodia) in the twelfth century C.E. to express a Hindu understanding of the cosmos centered on a mythical Mount Meru, the home of the gods in Hindu tradition. It was later used by Buddhists as well. (Ch. 7)

Arabian camel Introduced to North Africa and the Sahara in the early centuries of the Common Era, this animal made trans-Saharan commerce possible by 300 to 400 C.E. (Ch. 7)

Aristotle A Greek philosopher (384–322 B.C.E.); student of Plato and teacher of Alexander the Great. (Ch. 4)

Ashoka The most famous ruler of India's Mauryan Empire (r. 268–232 B.C.E.), who converted to Buddhism and tried to rule peacefully and with tolerance. (Ch. 3)

Aspasia A foreign resident in Athens (ca. 470–400 B.C.E.) who was famed for her learning and wit. She was the partner of the statesman Pericles. (Ch. 5)

Athenian democracy A radical form of direct democracy in which most of the free males of Athens were able to vote in the Assembly and officeholders were chosen by lot. (Ch. 3)

Augustus A title that implied divine status for Octavian (r. 27 B.C.E.–14 C.E.), who emerged as sole ruler of the Roman state at the end of an extended period of civil war. (Ch. 3)

Austronesian migrations The last phase of the great human migration that established a human presence in every habitable region of the earth. Austronesian-speaking people settled the Pacific islands and Madagascar in a series of seaborne migrations that began around 3,500 years ago. (Ch. 1)

Axum Second-wave era kingdom of East Africa in present-day Eritrea and northern Ethiopia with a highly productive plow-based farming system; an early adopter of Christianity. (pron. AX-uhm) (Ch. 6)

Aztec Empire Major state that developed in what is now Mexico in the fourteenth and fifteenth centuries; dominated by the semi-nomadic Mexica, who had migrated into the region from northern Mexico. (Ch. 12)

Banpo An early agricultural village in northern China dating to around 6,000 years ago. It consisted of approximately forty-five thatched buildings that housed an estimated 500 people. Archeological evidence suggests that millet, pigs, and dogs had been domesticated, and diets were supplemented with wild plants, animals, and fish. (Ch. 1)

Bantu migrations Gradual movements of Bantu-speaking peoples, beginning in ca. 3000 B.C.E., from their homeland in what is now southern Nigeria and the Cameroons into most of eastern and southern Africa by ca. 400 C.E. The agricultural techniques and iron-working technology of Bantu-speaking farmers gave them an advantage over the gathering and hunting peoples they encountered. (Chs. 1, 6)

Ban Zhao A major female Confucian author of China (45–116 C.E.) whose works explore the implications of Confucian thinking for women. (pron. bahn jow) (Ch. 4)

Bhagavad Gita A great Hindu epic text that conveyed the message that ordinary people could find spiritual fulfillment by selflessly performing the ordinary duties of their lives. (pron. BUH-guh-vahd GEE-tuh) (Ch. 4)

***bhakti* movement** Meaning "worship," this Hindu movement began in south India and moved northward between 600 and 1000 C.E.; it involved the intense adoration of and identification with a particular deity through songs, prayers, and rituals. (pron. BAHK-tee) (Ch. 4)

Black Death A massive pandemic that swept through Eurasia in the early fourteenth century, spreading along the trade routes within and beyond the Mongol Empire and reaching the Middle East and Western Europe by 1347. Associated with a massive loss of life. (Ch. 11)

bushido The "way of the warrior," referring to the martial values of the Japanese samurai, including bravery, loyalty, and an emphasis on death over surrender. (pron. boo-shee-doh) (Ch. 8)

Byzantine Empire One of the main centers of Christendom during the medieval centuries, the Byzantine Empire was a continuation of the eastern portion of the Roman Empire. It lasted for a thousand years after the collapse of Roman rule in the West, until its conquest by Muslim forces in 1453. (Ch. 10)

caesaropapism A political-religious system in which the secular ruler is also head of the religious establishment, as in the Byzantine Empire. (Ch. 10)

Cahokia The dominant center of an important Mississippi valley mound-building culture located near present-day St. Louis, Missouri; flourished from about 900 to 1250 C.E. (Ch. 6)

Caral The largest of some twenty-five urban centers that emerged in the Norte Chico region along the central coast of Peru from 3000 B.C.E. to 1800 B.C.E. (Ch. 2)

Çatalhüyük An early agricultural village and archeological site in what is now Turkey; flourished between 7400 and 6000 B.C.E. With a settled population of several thousand people, the village displayed few signs of class or gender inequality. (pron. cha-TAHL-hoo-YOOK) (Ch. 1)

Central Asian / Oxus civilization A major First Civilization that emerged around 2100 B.C.E. in Central Asia in the Oxus or Amu Darya River valley in what is now northern

Afghanistan and southern Turkmenistan. An important focal point for a Eurasian-wide system of intellectual and cultural exchange, it faded away by about 1700 B.C.E. (Ch. 2)

Chaco Phenomenon Name given to a major process of settlement and societal organization that occurred in the period 860–1130 C.E. among the peoples of Chaco Canyon, in what is now northwestern New Mexico; the society formed is notable for its settlement in large pueblos and for the building of hundreds of miles of roads, the purpose of which is not known. (Ch. 6)

Charlemagne Ruler of the Carolingian Empire (r. 768–814) who staged an imperial revival in Western Europe. (pron. SHAHR-leh-mane) (Ch. 10)

Chavín An Andean town strategically located between the western coast and eastern rain forests that was the center of a large Peruvian religious movement from around 900 to 200 B.C.E. (pron. cha-BEEN) (Ch. 6)

chiefdom A societal grouping governed by a chief who typically relies on generosity, ritual status, or charisma rather than force to win obedience from the people. (Ch. 1)

China's economic revolution A major rise in prosperity that took place in China under the Song dynasty (960–1279); was marked by rapid population growth, urbanization, economic specialization, the development of an immense network of internal waterways, and a great increase in industrial production and technological innovation. (Ch. 8)

China's scholar-gentry class A term used to describe members of China's landowning families, reflecting their wealth from the land and the privileges that they derived as government officials. (Ch. 5)

Chinese Buddhism Buddhism was China's only large-scale cultural borrowing before the twentieth century; it entered China from India in the first and second centuries C.E. but only became popular in 300 to 800 C.E. through a series of cultural accommodations. At first supported by the state, Buddhism suffered persecution during the ninth century but continued to play a role in Chinese society alongside Confucianism and Daoism. (Ch. 8)

chu nom A variation of Chinese writing developed in Vietnam that became the basis for an independent national literature; "southern script." (Ch. 8)

Church of the East An early theologically and organizationally distinct Christian church based in Syria and Persia but with followers in southern India and Central Asia. (Ch. 4)

Clovis culture The earliest widespread and distinctive culture of North America, dating to about 13,000 years ago; named for a particular kind of projectile point, initially found near the city of Clovis, New Mexico. (Ch. 1)

Code of Hammurabi A series of laws publicized at the order of King Hammurabi of Babylon that reveals much about the social order of Mesopotamian civilization. (pron. hahm-moo-RAH-bee) (Ch. 2)

Confucianism The Chinese philosophy first enunciated by Confucius, advocating the moral example of superiors as the key element of social order. (Ch. 4)

Constantinople New capital for the eastern half of the Roman Empire; Constantinople's highly defensible and economically important site helped ensure the city's cultural and strategic importance for many centuries. (Ch. 10)

Crusades A term used to describe the "holy wars" waged by Western Christendom, especially against the forces of Islam in the eastern Mediterranean from 1095 to 1291 and on the Iberian Peninsula into the fifteenth century. Further Crusades were also conducted in non-Christian regions of Eastern Europe from about 1150 on. Crusades could be declared only by the pope; participants swore a vow and received in return an indulgence removing the penalty for confessed sins. (Ch. 10)

Daoism A Chinese philosophy / popular religion that advocates a simple and unpretentious way of living and alignment with the natural world, founded by the legendary figure Laozi. (pron. dow-ism) (Ch. 4)

Dreamtime A complex worldview of Australia's Aboriginal people that held that living humans exist in a vibration or echo of ancestral happenings. (Ch. 1)

Eastern Orthodox Christianity Branch of Christianity that developed in the eastern part of the Roman Empire and gradually separated, mostly on matters of practice, from the branch of Christianity dominant in Western Europe; noted for the subordination of the Church to political authorities, a married clergy, the use of leavened bread in the Eucharist, and a sharp rejection of the authority of Roman popes. (Ch. 10)

Egypt One of the earliest civilizations in world history, with a three-thousand-year history as an intact state ruled by pharaohs. It became part of an international political system that included Babylon and Mesopotamia. (Ch. 2)

Empress Wu China's only female ruler (r. 690–705 C.E.), who patronized scholarship and worked to elevate the position of women. (Ch. 5)

Epic of Gilgamesh Mesopotamia's ancient epic poem dating from around 2000 B.C.E. (Ch. 2)

Ethiopian Christianity Emerging in the fourth century with the conversion of the rulers of Axum, this Christian church proved more resilient than other early churches in Africa. Located in the mountainous highlands of modern Ethiopia, it was largely cut off from other parts of Christendom and developed traditions that made it distinctive from other Christian churches. (Ch. 10)

European Renaissance A "rebirth" of classical learning that is most often associated with the cultural blossoming of Italy in the period 1350–1500 and that included not just a rediscovery of Greek and Roman learning but also major developments in art, as well as growing secularism in society. It spread to Northern Europe after 1400. (Ch. 12)

Fertile Crescent Region sometimes known as Southwest Asia that includes the modern states of Iraq, Syria, Israel/Palestine, Jordan, and southern Turkey; the earliest home of agriculture and some of the First Civilizations. (Ch. 1)

feudalism A highly fragmented and decentralized society in which power was held by the landowning warrior elite. In this highly competitive system, lesser lords and knights swore allegiance to greater lords or kings and thus became their vassals, frequently receiving lands and plunder in return for military service. (Ch. 10)

foot binding The Chinese practice of tightly wrapping girls' feet to keep them small, prevalent in the Song dynasty and later; an emphasis on small size and delicacy was central to views of female beauty. (Ch. 8)

Fulbe West Africa's largest pastoral society, whose members gradually adopted Islam and took on a religious leadership role that led to the creation of a number of new states by the nineteenth century. (pron. fulb) (Ch. 12)

Ghana An early and prominent state within West African civilization. With a reputation for great riches, Ghana flourished between 750 and 1076 and was later absorbed into the larger Kingdom of Mali. (Ch. 7)

Göbekli Tepe A ceremonial site in southeastern Turkey comprising twenty circles made up of large carved limestone pillars. The site, which dates to almost 12,000 years ago, was built by gatherers and hunters who lived at least part of the year in settled villages. (pron. goh-BEHK-lee TEH-peh) (Ch. 1)

Great Zimbabwe A powerful state in the southern African interior that apparently emerged from the growing trade in gold to the East African coast; flourished between 1250 and 1350 C.E. (Ch. 7)

Greco-Persian Wars A half century of intermittent conflict (499–449 B.C.E.) between the Greek city-states and the Persian Empire. During two major Persian invasions of Greece, in 490 B.C.E. and 480 B.C.E., the Persians were defeated on both land and sea. (Ch. 3)

Greco-Roman slavery In the Greek and Roman world, most enslaved people were captives from war, raiding, and piracy (and their descendants); manumission was common. Among the Greeks, household service was the most common form of slavery, but slavery was entrenched in all areas of Roman society except the military. (Ch. 5)

Greek rationalism A secularizing system of scientific and philosophic thought that developed in classical Greece in the period 600 to 300 B.C.E.; it emphasized using human reason to understand the world in nonreligious terms. (Ch. 4)

gunpowder A Chinese invention that came about during the ninth century. A mix of saltpeter, sulfur, and charcoal, it was originally created by Daoist alchemists seeking to discover an elixir of immortality. Ultimately, though, it revolutionized global military affairs. (Ch. 8)

Gupta Empire An era of Indian civilization from 320 to 550 C.E. that witnessed considerable political unity, cultural flourishing, and thriving trade. (Ch. 3)

Han dynasty The Chinese dynasty (206 B.C.E.–220 C.E.) that emerged after the Qin dynasty collapsed, establishing political and cultural patterns that lasted into the twentieth century. (Ch. 3)

hangul A phonetic alphabet developed in Korea in the fifteenth century in a move toward greater cultural independence from China. (pron. HAHN-gool) (Ch. 8)

Hangzhou China's capital during the Song dynasty, with a population at its height of more than a million people. (Ch. 8)

Hellenistic era The period from 323 to 30 B.C.E. in which Greek culture spread widely in the Middle East and parts of India in the cities and kingdoms ruled by Alexander's political successors. (Ch. 3)

helots The dependent, semi-enslaved class of ancient Sparta whose social discontent prompted the militarization of Spartan society. (Ch. 5)

hijra The "journey" of Muhammad and his original followers from Mecca to Yathrib (later Medina) in 622 C.E.; the journey marks the starting point of the Islamic calendar. (pron. HIJJ-ruh) (Ch. 9)

Holy Roman Empire A loose confederation of regional states, centered on what is now Germany but stretching from Denmark to Rome and the borders of France to Poland. From its beginning in the early ninth century, it was headed by an emperor, but in practice regional states proved effective in limiting his power. (Ch. 10)

Hopewell culture A common name for the Mississippi valley mound-building culture, after an archeological site in Ohio. Significant for the wide variety of artifacts found in elaborate burial mounds. (Ch. 6)

House of Wisdom An academic center for research and translation of foreign texts that was established in Baghdad in 830 C.E. by the Abbasid caliph al-Mamun. (Ch. 9)

Hulegu Grandson of Chinggis Khan who became the first il-khan (subordinate khan) of Persia. (pron. HE-luh-gee) (Ch. 11)

Igbo People whose lands were east of the Niger River in what is now southern Nigeria in West Africa. They built a complex society that rejected kingship and centralized statehood, while relying on other institutions to provide social coherence. (pron. EE-boh) (Ch. 12)

Inca Empire The Western Hemisphere's largest imperial state in the fifteenth and early sixteenth centuries. Built by a relatively small community of Quechua-speaking people (the Incas), the empire stretched some 2,500 miles along the Andes Mountains, which run nearly the entire length of the west coast of South America, and contained perhaps 10 million subjects. (Ch. 12)

Indus Valley civilization A major civilization that emerged in what is now Pakistan during the third millennium B.C.E., in the valleys of the Indus and Saraswati rivers, noted for the uniformity of its elaborately planned cities over a large territory. (Ch. 2)

Iroquois Iroquois-speaking peoples in what is now New York State; around the fifteenth century they formed a loose alliance based on the Great Law of Peace, an agreement to settle disputes peacefully through a council of clan leaders. (Ch. 12)

jatis The thousands of occupationally based social groups, each associated with a *varna*, that became the primary cells of social life in the Indian caste system. (Ch. 5)

Jesus of Nazareth A peasant/artisan "wisdom teacher" and Jewish mystic (ca. 4 B.C.E.– 29 C.E.) whose life, teachings, death, and alleged resurrection gave rise to the new religion of Christianity. (Ch. 4)

Jesus Sutras The written product of Nestorian Christians living in China, these texts articulate the Christian message using Buddhist and Daoist concepts. (Ch. 10)

jizya Special tax paid by *dhimmis* (protected but second-class subjects) in Muslim-ruled territory in return for freedom to practice their own religion. (Ch. 9)

Judaism The monotheistic religion developed in the Middle East by the Hebrews, emphasizing a sole personal god (Yahweh) with concerns for social justice. (Ch. 4)

Khanate of the Golden Horde The Russian name for the incorporation of Russia into the Mongol Empire in the mid-thirteenth century; known to Mongols as the Kipchak Khanate. (Ch. 11)

Khubilai Khan Grandson of Chinggis Khan who ruled China from 1271 to 1294. (pron. koo-buh-l'eye kahn) (Ch. 11)

Kievan Rus A culturally diverse civilization that emerged around the city of Kiev in the ninth century C.E. and adopted Christianity in the tenth, thus linking this emerging Russian state to the world of Eastern Orthodoxy. (Ch. 10)

Legalism A Chinese philosophy distinguished by an adherence to clear laws with vigorous punishments. (Ch. 4)

madrassas Formal colleges for higher instruction in the teachings of Islam as well as in secular subjects like law, established throughout the Islamic world beginning in the eleventh century. (Ch. 9)

Mahayana Buddhism "Great Vehicle," the popular development of Buddhism in the early centuries of the Common Era, which gives a much greater role to supernatural beings and to compassion and proved to be more popular than original (Theravada) Buddhism. (Ch. 4)

maize An ancient version of corn, first domesticated in southern Mexico by 4000 to 3000 B.C.E. This ancestor of corn was a mountain grass that looks nothing like today's corn or maize. Selective adaptation of this plant over thousands of years allowed for the development of sustainable agriculture in Mesoamerica and elsewhere. (Ch. 1)

Mali A prominent state within West African civilization; it was established in 1235 C.E. and flourished for several centuries. Mali monopolized the import of horses and metals as part of the trans-Saharan trade; it was a large-scale producer of gold; and its most famous ruler, Mansa Musa, led a large group of Muslims on the pilgrimage to Mecca in 1324–1325. (Ch. 7)

mana and tapu Religious concepts in Oceania; people or objects became sacred through a spiritual energy or power (mana) that was kept pure with ritual restrictions (tapu), which came into English as "taboo." (Ch. 6)

manorialism A socioeconomic system prominent in medieval Europe, through which a lord exercised political, economic, and social power over peasants on largely independent and self-sufficient manors. (Ch. 10)

Mauryan Empire The first and largest of India's short experiments with a large-scale political system (321–184 B.C.E.), it encompassed all but the southern tip of the Indian subcontinent. (pron. MORE-yuhn) (Ch. 3)

Maya civilization A major civilization of Mesoamerica known for the most elaborate writing system in the Americas and other intellectual and artistic achievements; flourished from 250 to 900 C.E. (Ch. 6)

megafaunal extinction The dying out of a number of large animal species, often associated with the arrival of humans. Examples include the mammoth and several species of horses and camels in North America and the Moa bird in New Zealand. Historians debate the relative importance of excessive hunting and changes in the climate. (Ch. 1)

Melaka Muslim port city that came to prominence on the waterway between Sumatra and Malaya in the fifteenth century C.E.; it was the springboard for the spread of a syncretic form of Islam throughout the region. (Chs. 7, 12)

Meroë City in southern Nubia that was the center of Nubian civilization between 300 B.C.E. and 100 C.E.; had a reputation for great riches and was culturally distinct from Egypt. (pron. MER-oh-ee) (Ch. 6)

Ming dynasty Chinese dynasty (1368–1644) that succeeded the Yuan dynasty of the Mongols; noted for its return to traditional Chinese ways and restoration of the land after the destructiveness of the Mongols. (Ch. 12)

Moche An important regional civilization of northern Peru, governed by warrior-priests; flourished from around 100 to 800 C.E. (pron. MOH-chee) (Ch. 6)

Modun Great ruler of the Xiongnu Empire (r. 210–174 B.C.E.) who exacted tribute from other Central Asian pastoral peoples as well as China itself, forcing Han dynasty emperor Wen to acknowledge the Xiongnu Empire as an equal. (Ch. 11)

Mohenjo Daro / Harappa Major cities of the Indus Valley civilization, both of which flourished around 2000 B.C.E. (pron. moe-hen-joe DAHR-oh) / (pron. hah-RAHP-uh) (Ch. 2)

Mongol world war Term used to describe half a century of military campaigns, massive killing, and empire building pursued by Chinggis Khan and his successors in Eurasia after 1209. (Ch. 11)

Mound Builders Members of a number of cultures that developed east of the Mississippi River in what is now the United States and that are distinguished by their large earthen mounds; most widespread between 200 B.C.E. and 1250 C.E. (Ch. 6)

Mughal Empire A successful state founded by Muslim Turkic-speaking peoples who invaded India and provided a rare period of relative political unity (1526–1707); their rule was noted for efforts to create partnerships between Hindus and Muslims. (pron. MOO-guhl) (Ch. 12)

Muhammad (570–632 C.E.) The Prophet and founder of Islam whose religious revelations became the Quran, bringing a radically monotheistic religion to Arabia and the world. (Ch. 9)

Neolithic Revolution *See* **Agricultural/Neolithic Revolution**. (Ch. 1)

Niger Valley civilization Distinctive city-based civilization that flourished from about 300 B.C.E. to about 900 C.E. in the floodplain of the middle Niger and that included major cities like Jenne-jeno; the Niger Valley civilization is particularly noteworthy for its apparent lack of centralized state structures, having been organized instead in clusters of economically specialized settlements. (Ch. 6)

Norte Chico A region along the central coast of Peru, home to an early civilization that developed from 3000 B.C.E. to 1800 B.C.E. (Ch. 2)

Nubia A region to the south of Egypt in the Nile Valley, noted for its development of a separate civilization with an alphabetic writing system and a major ironworking industry by 500 B.C.E. (Ch. 2)

Nubian Christianity Emerging in the fifth and sixth centuries in the several kingdoms of Nubia to the south of Egypt, this Christian church thrived for six hundred years but had largely disappeared by 1500 C.E., by which time most of the region's population practiced Islam. (Ch. 10)

Olmec civilization An early civilization that developed along the coast of the Gulf of Mexico around 1200 B.C.E. and possibly created the first written language in the Americas. (Ch. 2)

"the original affluent society" Term coined to describe Paleolithic societies, which are regarded as affluent not because they had so much but because they wanted or needed so little. (Ch. 1)

Ottoman Empire Major Islamic state centered on Anatolia that came to include the Balkans, parts of the Middle East, and much of North Africa; lasted in one form or another from the fourteenth to the early twentieth century. (Ch. 12)

Ottoman seizure of Constantinople The city of Constantinople, the capital and almost the only outpost left of the Byzantine Empire, fell to the army of the Ottoman sultan Mehmed II "the Conqueror" in 1453, an event that marked the end of Christian Byzantium. (Ch. 12)

Paleolithic era The long period during which human societies sustained themselves through gathering, hunting, and fishing without the practice of agriculture. Such ways of living persisted well after the advent of agriculture in many places. (Ch. 1)

Paleolithic settling down The process by which some Paleolithic peoples moved toward permanent settlement in the wake of the last Ice Age. Settlement was marked by increasing storage of food and accumulation of goods, as well as growing inequalities in society. (Ch. 1)

pastoral societies Based on an alternative kind of food-producing economy focused on the raising of livestock, pastoral societies emerged in the Afro-Eurasian world where settled agriculture was difficult or impossible. Pastoral peoples often led their animals to seasonal grazing grounds rather than settling permanently in a single location. (Chs. 1, 11)

patriarchy A social system in which women have been made subordinate to men in the family and in society; often linked to the development of plow-based agriculture, intensive warfare, and private property. (Ch. 2)

Paul, Saint An early convert and missionary (ca. 6–67 C.E.) and the first great popularizer of Christianity, especially to Gentile (non-Jewish) communities. (Ch. 4)

pax Romana The "Roman peace," a term typically used to denote the stability and prosperity of the early Roman Empire, especially in the first and second centuries C.E. (Ch. 3)

Peloponnesian War The Greek civil war (431–404 B.C.E.) that followed the Greco-Persian Wars, with Sparta defending city-state independence against Athenian dominance; the war left the Greeks in a state of distrust and disunity. (Ch. 3)

Perpetua Christian martyr (181–203 C.E.) from an upper-class Roman family in Carthage. Her refusal to renounce her faith made her an inspiration for other early Christians. (Ch. 4)

Persian Empire A major empire of the second-wave era that expanded from the Iranian plateau to incorporate the Middle East from Egypt to India; flourished from around 553 to 330 B.C.E. (Ch. 3)

Pillars of Islam The five core requirements of the Quran: the belief in one God, regular prayer, charitable giving, fasting during Ramadan, and a pilgrimage to Mecca (if financially and physically possible). (Ch. 9)

Plato A Greek philosopher (429–348 B.C.E.) who famously sketched out a design for a good society in *The Republic*. (Ch. 4)

pochteca Professional merchants among the Aztecs who undertook large-scale trading expeditions in the fifteenth century C.E. (pron. pohch-TEH-cah) (Ch. 7)

Pohnpei Micronesian island dubbed the "Venice of the Pacific" where a complex urban construction made of coral and stone served as the ceremonial, administrative, and burial center. (Ch. 6)

Qin Shihuangdi Literally "first emperor from the Qin"; Shihuangdi (r. 221–210 B.C.E.) forcibly reunited China and established a strong state that governed, often brutally, according to a Legalist philosophy. (pron. chin shee-HUANG-dee) (Ch. 3)

Quran Also transliterated as Qur'án and Koran, this is the most holy text of Islam, which records the words of God through revelations given to the Prophet Muhammad. (Ch. 9)

ritual purity and pollution The idea that members of higher Indian castes must adhere to strict regulations limiting or forbidding their contact with "polluted" objects and members of lower castes to preserve their own caste standing and personal purity. (Ch. 5)

Roman Catholic Church Western European branch of Christianity that gradually defined itself as separate from Eastern Orthodoxy, with a major break occurring in 1054 C.E. that still has not been overcome. By the eleventh century, Western Christendom was centered on the pope as the ultimate authority in matters of doctrine. The Church struggled to remain independent of established political authorities. (Ch. 10)

Safavid Empire Major Turkic empire established in Persia in the early sixteenth century and notable for its efforts to convert its people to Shia Islam. (pron. SAH-fah-vid) (Ch. 12)

Sand Roads A term used to describe the routes of the trans-Saharan trade, which linked interior West Africa to the Mediterranean and North African world. (Ch. 7)

Sea Roads The world's largest sea-based system of communication and exchange before 1500 C.E. Centered on India, it stretched from southern China to eastern Africa. (Ch. 7)

secondary products revolution The series of technological changes that began ca. 4000 B.C.E. as people in the Eastern Hemisphere began to use their domesticated animals in new ways, such as for their milk, wool, and manure. Also involved learning to ride horses and camels and using animals to pull carts, plows, and chariots. (Ch. 1)

Seljuk Turkic Empire An empire of the eleventh and twelfth centuries, centered in Persia and present-day Iraq. Seljuk rulers adopted the Muslim title of *sultan* (ruler) as part of their conversion to Islam. (Ch. 11)

shamans Persons believed to be especially skilled at dealing with the spirit world, often through trances induced by psychoactive drugs. (Ch. 1) *sharia* Islamic law, dealing with political, economic, social, and religious life. It literally translates as "a path to water," which is considered the source of all life. (pron. shah-REE-ah) (Ch. 9)

Shotoku Taishi Japanese statesman (572–622) who launched the drive to make Japan into a centralized bureaucratic state modeled on China; he is best known for issuing the Seventeen Article Constitution in 604 C.E., which lays out the principles of this reform. (Ch. 8)

Siddhartha Gautama (the Buddha) The Indian prince whose exposure to human suffering led him to develop a path to Enlightenment that became the basis for the emerging religious tradition of Buddhism; lived ca. 566–ca. 486 B.C.E. (pron. sidd-ARTH-uh gow-TAHM-uh) (Ch. 4)

Sikhism Religious tradition of northern India founded by Guru Nanak (1469–1539); combines elements of Hinduism and Islam and proclaims the brotherhood of all humans and the equality of men and women. (Ch. 9)

Silk Roads Land-based trade routes that linked many regions of Eurasia. They were named after the most famous product traded along these routes. (Ch. 7)

Silla kingdom The first ruling dynasty to bring a measure of political unity to the Korean peninsula (688–900). (pron. SHEE-lah) (Ch. 8)

Socrates Influential Greek philosopher (469–399 B.C.E.), whose constant questioning of conventional thinking led to his death sentence from an Athenian jury. (Ch. 4)

Song dynasty The Chinese dynasty (960–1279) that rose to power after the Tang dynasty. During the Song dynasty, an explosion of scholarship gave rise to Neo-Confucianism, and a revolution in agricultural and industrial production made China the richest and most populated country on the planet. (Ch. 8)

Songhay Empire Major Islamic state of West Africa that formed in the second half of the fifteenth century. (pron. song-GAH-ee) (Ch. 12)

Spartacus A Roman gladiator who led the most serious slave revolt in Roman history in 73 B.C.E. (Ch. 5)

Srivijaya A Malay kingdom that dominated the critical choke point in Indian Ocean trade at the Strait of Melaka between 670 and 1025 C.E. Like other places in Southeast Asia, Srivijaya absorbed various cultural influences from India. (pron. SREE-vih-juh-yuh) (Ch. 7)

Sufism An understanding of the Islamic faith that saw the worldly success of Islamic civilization as a distraction and deviation from the purer spirituality of Muhammad's time. By renouncing the material world, meditating on the words of the Quran, chanting the names of God, using music and dance, and venerating Muhammad and various "saints," Sufis pursued an interior life, seeking to tame the ego and achieve spiritual union with Allah. (Ch. 9)

Sui dynasty Ruling dynasty of China (581–618) that effectively reunited the country after several centuries of political fragmentation. This unity was solidified through the extension of canals economically linking northern and southern China, but harsh leadership and futile efforts to conquer Korea eventually prompted the overthrow of the dynasty. (Ch. 8)

Sumer The region in the southern reaches of Mesopotamia between the Tigris and Euphrates rivers, mostly in present-day Iraq. Home to an early civilization that arose around 3500 B.C.E. to 3000 B.C.E., this area likely gave rise to the world's earliest written language. (Ch. 2)

Swahili civilization An East African civilization that emerged in the eighth century C.E. as a set of commercial city-states linked into the Indian Ocean trading network. Combining African Bantu and Islamic cultural patterns, these competing city-states accumulated goods from the interior and exchanged them for the products of distant civilizations. (Ch. 7)

Tang dynasty Ruling dynasty of China (618–907) noted for its openness to foreign cultural influences. Together with its successor, the Song dynasty, it represented a golden age of arts and literature and established patterns of Chinese life that endured into the twentieth century. (Ch. 8)

Temujin (Chinggis Khan) Birth name of the Mongol leader better known as Chinggis Khan (1162–1227), or "universal ruler," a name he acquired after unifying the Mongols. (pron. TEM-oo-chin) (Ch. 11)

Teotihuacán The largest city of pre-Columbian America, with a population between 125,000 and 150,000; seemingly built to a plan in the Valley of Mexico, Teotihuacán flourished between 300 and 600 c.e., during which time it governed or influenced much of the surrounding region. The name Teotihuacán is an Aztec term meaning "city of the gods." (pron. tay-uh-tee-wah-KAHN) (Ch. 6)

Theravada Buddhism "Teaching of the Elders," the early form of Buddhism according to which the Buddha was a wise teacher but not divine; emphasizes practices rather than beliefs. (pron. THAIR-ah-VAH-dah) (Ch. 4)

"three obediences" In Chinese Confucian thought, the notion that a woman is permanently subordinate to male control: first to her father, then to her husband, and finally to her son. (Ch. 5)

Timbuktu A major commercial city of West African civilization and a noted center of Islamic scholarship and education by the sixteenth century. (Chs. 9, 12)

Timur Turkic warrior, also known as Tamerlane, whose efforts to restore the Mongol Empire in the late fourteenth and early fifteenth centuries devastated parts of Persia, Russia, and India. His successors created a vibrant elite culture drawing on both Turkic and Persian elements, especially in the city of Samarkand. Timur's conquests represent the last major military success of Central Asian pastoral peoples. (Ch. 12)

Tonga Islands Polynesian state (ca. 1000 c.e.) with a central royal court, specialized craftsmen, and widespread military and commercial influence in the central Pacific. (Ch. 6)

trans-Saharan slave trade A fairly small-scale commerce in enslaved people that flourished especially from 1100 to 1400, exporting enslaved West Africans across the Sahara for sale in Islamic North Africa. (Ch. 7)

tribute system A set of practices that required a show of subordination from all non-Chinese authorities and the payment of tribute — products of value from their countries — to the Chinese emperor. In return, China would grant trading rights to foreigners and offer gifts even more valuable than the tribute itself. (Ch. 8)

Turkic peoples Turkic speakers from Central Asia, originally nomads, who spread westward, creating a series of nomadic empires between 552 and 965 c.e. Having converted to Islam between the tenth and fourteenth centuries, Turkic peoples carried that faith into new lands, most notably the Christian Byzantine Empire, and became a politically powerful presence in the Islamic world. (Ch. 11)

ulama Islamic religious scholars, both Sunni and Shia, who shaped and transmitted the core teachings of Islamic civilization. (Ch. 9)

Umayyad caliphate Family of caliphs who ruled the Islamic world from 661 to 750 c.e., expanding the Arab Empire and creating a ruling class of Arab military aristocrats. (pron. oo-MEYE-ahd) (Ch. 9)

umma The community of all believers in Islam, bound by common belief rather than territory, language, or tribe. (pron. OOM-mah) (Ch. 9)

Upanishads Indian mystical and philosophical works written between 800 and 400 b.c.e. (pron. oo-PAHN-ee-shahds) (Ch. 4)

Uruk The largest city of ancient Mesopotamia, with a population around 50,000 in the third millennium B.C.E. (pron. OOH-rook) (Ch. 2)

varnas The four inherited, ranked social classes of the Indian caste system. (Ch. 5)

Vedas The earliest religious texts of India, a collection of ancient poems, hymns, and rituals that were transmitted orally before being written down ca. 600 B.C.E. (pron. VAY-duhs) (Ch. 4)

Venus figurines Paleolithic carvings of the female form, often with exaggerated breasts, buttocks, hips, and stomachs. (Ch. 1)

vertical integration Control of a variety of ecological zones (and thus a variety of crops and animals) in areas with diverse climates and competing cities, chiefdoms, and states; common in Mesoamerican and Andean civilizations. (Ch. 6)

Vladimir of Kiev Grand prince of Kiev whose conversion to Orthodox Christianity in 988 C.E. led to the incorporation of an emerging Russian state into the sphere of Eastern Orthodoxy. (Ch. 10)

Wang Mang A Han court official who usurped the throne and ruled from 8 C.E. to 23 C.E.; noted for his Confucian-inspired reform movement that included the breakup of large estates. (Ch. 5)

Wari and Tiwanaku Two states that flourished between 400 and 1000 C.E. in the interior highlands of the Andean region. At their height, they possessed urban capitals with populations in the tens of thousands and productive agricultural systems. (pron. wah-ree) (Ch. 6)

West African civilization A series of important states that developed in the region stretching from the Atlantic coast to Lake Chad in the period 500 to 1600 C.E. Developed in response to the economic opportunities of trans-Saharan trade (especially control of gold production), it included the states of Ghana, Mali, Songhay, and Kanem-Bornu, as well as numerous towns and cities. (Ch. 7)

Western Christendom Western European branch of Christianity, also known as Roman Catholicism, that gradually defined itself as separate from Eastern Orthodoxy, with a major break occurring in 1054 C.E.; characterized by its relative independence from the state and its recognition of the authority of the pope. (Ch. 10)

Xiongnu Empire An imperial creation of nomadic steppe peoples who inhabited lands north of China. In the third and second centuries B.C.E., this empire stretched from Manchuria to Central Asia, establishing a model for later Turkic and Mongol empires. (Chs. 8, 11)

Yap An island in western Micronesia that developed ceremonial tributary relationships with surrounding islands based in part on fear of Yapese sorcery. (Ch. 6)

Yellow Turban Rebellion A massive Chinese peasant uprising around 184 C.E. that was inspired by Daoist teachings; it aimed to establish a new golden age of equality, harmony, and common ownership of property. (Ch. 5)

Yuan dynasty Mongol dynasty initiated by Khubilai Khan that ruled China from 1271 to 1368. (Ch. 11)

Zheng He Great Chinese admiral who commanded a huge fleet of ships in a series of voyages in the Indian Ocean that began in 1405. Intended to enroll distant peoples and states in the Chinese tribute system, those voyages ended abruptly in 1433 and led to no lasting Chinese imperial presence in the region. (pron. JUHNG-huh) (Ch. 12)

Zoroastrianism Persian monotheistic religion founded by the prophet Zarathustra and emphasizing free will and the choice between good and evil. (pron. zohr-oh-ASS-tree-ahn-i'zm) (Ch. 4)

Index

A Note about the Index: Names of individuals are in **boldface**. Letters in parentheses following pages refer to the following: *(i)* illustrations, including photographs and artifacts; *(m)* maps; *(f)* figures, including charts and graphs; *(t)* tables.

About the Authors

Jerry Burke

Robert W. Strayer (Ph.D., University of Wisconsin) brings wide experience in world history to the writing of *Ways of the World.* His teaching career began in Ethiopia, where he taught high school world history for two years as part of the Peace Corps. At the university level, he taught African, Soviet, and world history for many years at the College at Brockport: State University of New York, where he received the Chancellor's Awards for Excellence in Teaching and Excellence in Scholarship. In 1998 he was visiting professor of world and Soviet history at the University of Canterbury in Christchurch, New Zealand. Since moving to California in 2002, he has taught world history at the University of California, Santa Cruz; California State University, Monterey Bay; and Cabrillo College. He is a longtime member of the World History Association and served on its Executive Committee. He has also participated in various AP World History gatherings, including two years as a reader. His publications include *Kenya: Focus on Nationalism, The Making of Mission Communities in East Africa, The Making of the Modern World, Why Did the Soviet Union Collapse?,* and *The Communist Experiment.*

Jesse Scheve/Missouri State University

Eric W. Nelson (D.Phil., Oxford University) is a professor of history at Missouri State University. He is an experienced teacher who has won a number of awards, including the Missouri Governor's Award for Teaching Excellence in 2011 and the CASE and Carnegie Foundation for the Advancement of Teaching Professor of the Year Award for Missouri in 2012. His publications include *Layered Landscapes: Early Modern Religious Space across Faiths and Cultures, The Legacy of Iconoclasm: Religious War and the Relic Landscape of Tours, Blois and Vendôme,* and *The Jesuits and the Monarchy: Catholic Reform and Political Authority in France.*